MW01618180

TO COUNT OUR DAYS

TO COUNT OUR DAYS

A History of
Columbia Theological Seminary

ERSKINE CLARKE

Published by the University of South Carolina Press
Columbia, South Carolina 29208

www.sc.edu/uscpress

Manufactured in the United States of America

28 27 26 25 24 23 22 21 20 19
10 9 8 7 6 5 4 3 2 1

Library of Congress Cataloging-in-Publication Data
can be found at http://catalog.loc.gov/.

ISBN 978-1-61117-996-5 (hardback)
ISBN 978-1-61117-997-2 (ebook)

To
Loryn, Colleen,
Samuel, and Lucas

“So teach us to count our days
that we may gain a wise heart.”

Psalm 90:12

CONTENTS

PART IV

New Horizons

PREFACE

Institutional histories can invite a yawn. They are important for specialists and for those with a personal interest in a specific institution, but as a category of historical writing they do not evoke an imagine of a page-turning narrative. Yet institutions have cultures with their own rituals and character, and they reflect in their own internal life larger historical developments. And institutions, perhaps especially smaller institutions, have within them individual players with their own histories and commitments, quirks and oddities, and those individuals not only help to shape the institution's life but also bring the complexities and mysteries of the human personality to the story of an institution's history. Moreover when an institution exists over many generations, its history is an unfolding story of tension between continuities and change, between remembered ways and practices and the demands of new social and cultural contexts. At least all this has been true for Columbia Theological Seminary.

For the author this has meant that as I studied the seminary's history I became increasingly fascinated by it—by Columbia's distinctive and peculiar character, by the personalities of the major players and their eccentricities, and by the ways its history tells a larger story of the American South and of religion in the United States. To be sure, I have a personal interest in Columbia as a graduate and as a longtime member of its faculty. But I hope that others without such personal connections will find in the history of Columbia a story that intrigues and that helps to inform their understanding of southern history with all its ironies and of the religious life of the American people with all its complex intermingling of peoples and traditions, of light and deep shadows.

The story of the seminary emerges from the antebellum world of the American South and begins to unfold in an antebellum mansion in Columbia, South Carolina, across the street from the home of Wade Hampton, the South's largest slave owner. In and around this particular place a brilliant and conflicted cluster of white Presbyterian intellectuals gathered, and from that place they exerted an extraordinary influence on the culture and religious thought of the white South. They included theologians and educators, political leaders and scientists, reformers (the kind white southerners could tolerate) and lovers of a southern home and homeland. With them were wives who were helping to shape in their own ways the male-dominated culture of Columbia and who were quickly becoming a part of dense networks of closely connected families. There among them as well in that particular place were black men and women, enslaved "servants," who cleaned houses, cooked meals, and stood beside dinner tables listening to the conversations of white Presbyterian professors and students as they discussed religion and politics and related the latest news of personal interest. Meanwhile on distant plantations black men and women, people with names and distinct personalities and histories, were providing in their labors and in their very bodies the wealth that made the seminary possible.

To this place came students from all over the country and from the nation's most prestigious colleges. Most who graduated after three years of Greek and Hebrew, of Latin texts and of dense histories by German scholars, went out to a southern world intent on building what they called "our southern Zion" not only on the established eastern seaboard but also in what they regarded as the howling wildernesses of south Georgia, Alabama, and Mississippi. They were to be "gentlemen theologians," Presbyterian bearers of civility and a paternalistic tradition and of a "Carolina culture" by which they meant the ways and social institutions of the South Carolina and Georgia lowcountry, of Charleston and Savannah and their hinterlands of rice and sea island cotton plantations. They sought to be prudent and moderate men—those who avoided the dangers of extremes as they navigated between rationalists and revivalists and between proslavery radicals and abolitionists. But when they discovered in 1860 that they had to make a choice between slavery and freedom, they abandoned their much-vaulted moderation and with unrestrained wrath cast their lot with slavery and their southern homeland.

When Sherman's army left Columbia a burned and smoldering city, the seminary campus—which had escaped the fires—became a refuge for city residents and for frightened survivors of a ravaged countryside. During the coming years the seminary was to be a refuge for white southerners in other ways as well. From the campus and its professors came attempts to explain the ways of God in allowing such massive destruction and death and to explain how God could allow a corrupt and oppressive North to be victorious in its fight against a righteous South defending its independence and "property rights." The seminary was also to become a refuge, a Presbyterian bastion, against the assaults of the modern world and a rising industrial capitalism with its radical individualism. An ideological wall—composed largely of the "phraseology of the past," the language and remembered history of the white South and Presbyterian orthodoxy—was constructed to keep out the infidelity and chaos of modernity and to protect a "southern way of life."[1]

When an apparent threat to orthodoxy and a white South appeared within the seminary in the guise of Darwinism, a fierce internal war ensued. Forty years before the famous Scopes monkey trial in Dayton, Tennessee, an intellectually rigorous debate broke out on the Columbia campus in the 1880s over evolution and over the concept of development not only in biology but also in human culture—including religion. While the conclusions were ambiguous, the debate left the seminary with its horizons narrowed and its world constricted. A comfortable and genteel mediocrity settled over the seminary as it became as intellectually impoverished as it was financially poor. In this it reflected the realities of its constituency in the Southeast and the social and intellectual climate in the little city of Columbia and at its University of South Carolina.

Remarkably seminary graduates from this period included not only those who were serious and faithful pastors but also some of genuine distinction including Rhodes Scholars and those who played important roles in defense of human rights in distant lands.

Nevertheless a comfortable and tightly knit mediocrity marked the seminary during the last years of the nineteenth and the early years of the twentieth centuries. And closely tied to that intellectual mediocrity was ideological support for a white South where blacks were kept "in their place." That "place" on the Columbia campus and in faculty homes was largely behind the scenes where food was cooked and rooms were cleaned. And from such a place in the shadows, black men and women, even as they went about their work and their lives, observed and listened to preoccupied white Presbyterians.

In 1927 the seminary moved from Columbia, South Carolina, to the Atlanta suburb of Decatur, Georgia. It was in many ways a move out of the Old South toward the New South, which embodied a vision and social reality most forcefully experienced in the rushing traffic and rumbling streetcars of Atlanta. Of course much of the Old South lingered in the New—especially its racism and insistence on keeping the South white. Still the New South was new in many ways with its urban businessmen, its quest for efficiency, and its desire to be rid of the burdens of southern history. The poverty of the South, white southerners' preoccupation with a mythic past, and the provincialism of the region were all to be overcome by the adoption of modern business practices and the values of the marketplace. Columbia Seminary moved slowly into this new world even as it settled on a campus of rolling hills and hardwood forests seven miles from the heart of Atlanta. Atlanta churches and businessmen largely funded the initial construction of the new campus. And for a brief moment the seminary flourished, but then the Great Depression rolled over it and threatened its very life. Two men were largely responsible for Columbia's survival—J. McDowell Richard, Rhodes Scholar, Columbia graduate, and the seminary's young president; and John Bulow Campbell, Presbyterian elder and wealthy Atlanta businessman and philanthropist. Together they were primarily responsible for keeping the seminary afloat during the Depression and Second World War and for laying the foundation for the seminary's rapid expansion during the twenty-five years that followed the war. When Richards retired in 1970, the seminary had a large campus with handsome collegiate Gothic buildings and a young faculty well-positioned to move Columbia beyond the vestiges of old orthodoxies that taught a propositional understanding of the faith and that was closely aligned with efforts to keep blacks "in their place."

The last years of the Richards presidency had been buffeted by the social and cultural turbulence of the 1960s. The early years of the 1970s were consequently lean years for Columbia as the Vietnam War encouraged the plunging of enrollment, as some congregations began leaving the denomination over the ordination of women and the church's stand on various social issues, and as an economic recession undercut Columbia's financial vitality. But a new curriculum, new administrative structures, and new faculty prepared the way for the remarkable growth of the seminary during the next thirty-five years. The faculty gained unprecedented strength, with some members gaining national recognition for the depth of their scholarship and engagement with the U.S. culture. International scholars and church leaders began spending significant periods of time on the campus, entering the life of the seminary and greatly broadening its understanding of the global church and issues of faith and life in the late twentieth and early twenty-first centuries. The endowment soared, making Columbia one of the wealthiest theological institutions in the country. Student enrollments reached all-time highs, and new advanced degrees brought a greatly expanded racial, ethnic, and denominational diversity to the campus. By the early years of the new century, Columbia had a national reputation as a theological seminary known for its scholarship, for its deep ties to the Presbyterian Church, and for its commitments to nurturing Christian faith and life in a variety of denominational and international settings.

Beneath the growing strength of the seminary were two powerful currents of social change that were having an increasing impact on Columbia, on its self-understanding, and on its relationship to its traditional Presbyterian constituency that had thought of Columbia as "our seminary." First, a new egalitarian and inclusive spirit was rejecting hierarchies and old authorities. That spirit not only called for greater racial, ethnic, and gender diversity at the seminary but also called into question Columbia's Presbyterian character and its relationship to a Presbyterian constituency that had owned and supported the seminary for generations. Second, the emergence of free-market economics as the means of solving political and social problems was leaving behind confidence in the government's ability to solve the great issues before the nation and confidence in any institution, including the church. A new hyperindividualism emphasized unlimited choice and unfretted desire that could be serviced by the marketplace. Such market values were lodging themselves in the institutional structures of the seminary and the culture of the campus as multiple programs began to be developed and tested to see what the market could bear. When the stock market plunged in 2008, not only did the seminary's endowment and budget plunge but also its enrollments—especially students from its traditional Presbyterian constituencies and from beyond the immediate Atlanta area—and Columbia lost much of its former ability to attract participants to multiple programs. By 2016 the endowment had recovered, but the budget continued under stress as the recovery of old loyalties was slow and programs struggled to regain old vitalities. But encouraging signs were beginning to appear as more students from beyond Atlanta began once again to enroll as they were attracted by the strength of younger faculty and by a campus of uncommon beauty.

In such a context fundamental questions are being asked both within the seminary and within its constituency about the character of Columbia Theological Seminary and about its direction as it moves deeper into the new century. As in the past the life of the seminary in the twentieth-first century reflects the social and cultural realities in which it lives and breathes. Yet the seminary has understood itself to be called to that very world, so deeply divided in so many ways. Columbia today continues to understand its mission to be one of announcing a Word and demonstrating a life that tells of God's good purposes for all creation. With such a self-understanding and such an animating spirit, the seminary rich with history looks to the future and trusts that the God who has sustained it in the past will be with it in the present and will guide it into the waiting years.

ACKNOWLEDGMENTS

More than an ordinary number of people have contributed to this study. As might be expected, those who have been a part of the seminary community during the last decades have played a particularly important role in helping me gather materials and interpret Columbia's history. Among these none has been more important than my colleague Lee Carroll. He helped conceive and frame the structure of the study, he gathered and put into an orderly format summaries of catalogs and seminary bulletins, he analyzed curriculum changes, and he utilized considerable skill in unraveling the deep genealogical mysteries of white southern families who gave their children names that duplicated, overlapped, and crossed and recrossed with other families. He also read and critiqued each chapter and gave me his informed judgments. While he is not responsible for the results, this history of Columbia could not have been written without his careful attention to many details and his wise counsel. I am deeply grateful not only for all his help on this project, but also for his friendship over many years.

Other faculty colleagues have made contributions in less direct ways. Catherine and Justo González and Walter Brueggemann have been conversation partners for many years, shaping in innumerable ways my understanding of large issues of culture and society and of Christian faith and life. One of the great privileges of my life has been to call them friends and colleagues. William Yoo gave early and helpful advice about the relationship of Columbia to U.S. religious history. Beth Johnson, George Stroup, Cam Murchison, Phil Gehman, Christine Yoder, Charles Raynal, Mark Douglas, David Bartlett, Kim Clayton, and Kim Long all provided important reflections on specifics of Columbia's history and on the history of their academic disciplines. Marcia Riggs once again helped me to see more clearly issues of race, gender, and ethnicity in the seminary's life. Bill Brown gave details of Columbia's new program on science and religion sponsored by the American Association for the Advancement of Science.

Jennifer Carlier and Lucy Trumbull Baum served as exceptionally able research assistants. They gathered and copied documents, checked names, looked up statistical reports, and in innumerable ways contributed to the work of this project. I am especially grateful for their cheerful and prompt work. Elizabeth Jones provided invaluable help in preparing the manuscript for the press.

Staff members, who constitute much of the heart of Columbia, were enormously helpful. Ann Clay Adams provided—in response to my incessant appeals!—important statistical summaries and analyses as did Monica Wedlock Kilpatrick and Kim LeVert.

Michael Thompson and Jeff Vaughan went out of their way to be helpful in the securing of photographs. Barbara Poe, Jane Gleim, and MaryLynn Darden provided public documents not readily available. Several board members reflected with me on Columbia's history and their experience of Columbia. Particularly important have been conversations with Phil Noble, Joe Harvard, Florida Ellis, Charles Heyward, Joanna Adams, Jim Lowry, Bill Scheu, Buzz Wilcoxon, and Richard DuBose. Many graduates have shared their experiences as students. Joe Conyers provided not only class notes and letters from his time at Columbia but also those of his father's from the early twentieth century. Bill Arnold reflected on the history of his alma mater from the perspective of his years as academic dean at Union Seminary, Virginia. Some graduates—including Phil Noble, Mack Hart, John Ellington, and Eade Anderson—shared their stories of civil rights struggles and local congregations in the 1950s and 1960s. Bert Carmichael and Ed Loring provided innumerable stories from the 1960s while Murphy Davis told of the struggles of women students in the 1970s.

Spouses of retired faculty and staff have been particularly helpful in their descriptions of campus life, of faculty and staff relationships, and of the hosting responsibilities expected of spouses. Betty Cousar, Kay Philips, Vivian Guthrie, Nan Clarke, Shirley Hussel, Pat Hix, Betty Carroll, Kay Gehman, and Kaye Carmichael have been especially emphatic in describing the expected role of wives and how those expectations were handled. Children of faculty have added their voices to the story of campus life. Mary Amos and Sally Richardson told of their experiences when their father, Richard Gillespie, was attacked by fundamentalist students in the 1950s. Muriel Gear Hart remembered life on the campus during the long years her father, Felix Gear, was dean and reminisced about relationships between faculty families. Important too were the stories told by Kemie Richards Nix about life in the president's home and the threats against her father, J. McDowell Richards, for his stand on racial justice. Legare Clarke Hartbarger and Elizabeth Clarke Rogers reflected on their experience of living close to the seminary village and having as friends the children of students. They told as well of living in a home where international students and scholars brought to their dinner table lively discussions and stories of distant places.

Library staff, of course, played a critical role in the gathering of archival materials and secondary sources. Former archivist Chris Patton demonstrated not only a high level of professional competence but also an eagerness to cooperate in every possible way. Mary Martha Riviere and Griselda Lartey provided encouragement and much help in the securing of books and articles. More recently Erica Dunham and Caitlin Reeves have been a great help with photographs and research questions. Sara Myers, as director of the library, gave much personal support and encouragement to the project in its early stages, and her successor Kelly Campbell provided orderly and efficient procedures as the project drew to its conclusion.

Not surprisingly senior administrators have been central supporters for the writing of this history. Steve Hayner, Deborah Mullen, Doug Taylor, and Marty Sadler originally endorsed the writing of the history and gave it their enthusiastic support. Laura Mendenhall, Cam Murchison, and Richard DuBose generously gave their time and insights in discussing their years of leadership. Doug Oldenburg came to my home in Montreat to discuss the "Oldenburg years," and Claudia Oldenburg provided a wonderful journal and scrapbook of their time at Columbia. Jim Hudnut-Beumler, writing from the perspective of his long years as dean of Vanderbilt Divinity School, provided insights into developments at Columbia during his tenure as dean of faculty in the 1990s. Doug Hix was his usual erudite self in his analysis of Columbia during the Philips and early years of the Oldenburg administration. Leanne Van Dyk and Stephen Miller, following their recent arrival at Columbia, have given generous encouragement to this project, which they inherited.

A number of scholars from outside the Columbia community were important conversation partners during the writing of the history. David Molke-Hansen helped me see Columbia's history in light of the complex history of the American South and the recent scholarship on that history. Peter Wood listened to my descriptions of the project and added insights from his long study of African American history. Rod Hunter provided particularly revealing interpretations of the therapeutic culture and the history of pastoral care and counseling. Fielding Freed, director of Historic House Museums for Historic Columbia, spent time with me exploring the old campus and the Woodrow Wilson home in Columbia, South Carolina. Milton Winter brought to my aid his deep knowledge of Mississippi history and of the Presbyterians in that state. Ron Vinson of the Presbyterian Heritage Center in Montreat, North Carolina, helped me in the early stages of the project reflect on Columbia's relationship to the larger Presbyterian story, and he later provided helpful resources for the work. Alex Moore and Linda Fogle of the University of South Carolina Press gave much appreciated support and guidance for its publication.

Nan Clarke was, as always, a wonderful support during the writing of this history even as she went about her own busy life. During thirty-five years as a faculty spouse she had hosted innumerable evenings with faculty and students and regular dinner parties for visiting international scholars and students. While teaching and preparing lesson plans for her students of German, she had found time to take internationals to the farmers market, to help students with sick children, and to enjoy greatly her many friends associated with Columbia. She, like so many other faculty spouses, was an integral part of Columbia's story, and to many in the community she was a gift of extraordinary vitality and delight. The book is dedicated to our grandchildren—Loryn, Colleen, Samuel, and Lucas—in the hope that one day they will discover in these pages a world where for a season their mothers and their Clarke grandparents were privileged to dwell.

PART I

An Antebellum World

1

Beginnings

In 1822 the Reverend Thomas Goulding announced to his Georgia congregation of white planters and black slaves that he was moving. He hoped, he said, that a change of location would help him recover his health. Repeated bouts of malaria—country fever he called it—had wracked his body and had left him largely debilitated. Goulding resigned as pastor of the White Bluff Presbyterian Church, near Savannah, and reported that he had bought a small farm in Oglethorpe County in northeast Georgia. There among rolling hills and hardwood forests he hoped to escape recurrent bouts of the fever and regain his health and strength.[1]

When Goulding left White Bluff for his newly purchased farm, he took with him his wife, Ann Holbrook of Connecticut, four children, and six slaves. On the arduous journey inland, Goulding also carried with him an experience of theological education as it had been practiced by Presbyterian pastors in colonial America and in the young republic. What he did not know was that ahead of him was not only a farm but also an important role in the establishment of something new that was beginning to emerge in American religious life—a southern theological seminary.[2]

Thomas Goulding had been born in 1786 on his father's plantation in Liberty County, Georgia, where black rivers flowed slowly out of cypress swamps into St. Catherine Sound. This landscape and the social arrangements of white owners and black slaves shaped and informed young Goulding's earliest memories and the deep assumptions and dispositions that he would carry for the rest of his life. When he was eighteen he left his plantation home and made his way to New Haven, Connecticut, to enter Yale College. On his arrival in New Haven, however, he found a system of hazing had recently been established by older students. Unwilling to be a servant to anyone, he refused to join his class. Instead he began to study law with a local judge while still enjoying some of the privileges of the college. In 1806 he married Ann Holbrook and shortly thereafter returned to Georgia, where he taught the sons and daughters of Georgia planters at two academies, both of which looked out over marshes to the distant Sea Islands and their plantations.[3]

While Goulding was busy with his teaching responsibilities, a religious awakening was spreading across the young republic, and in time it began to penetrate the plantation communities of the Georgia coast. Goulding began to struggle with his own religious feelings, hoping that the Spirit of the Lord would touch his heart and awaken him to God's grace and love in his own life. He had, he later reported, a strange conversion experience—it happened while he slept. Wearied, he said, with his burden of sin and his fruitless search to find a savior, he sank despairingly into a profound slumber and awoke praising God for his great salvation. Shortly thereafter he began to prepare for the ministry in the way earlier generations of American Presbyterian ministers had been prepared—he began an intense course of study under the direction of other ministers. In 1811 Harmony Presbytery took him under its care as a candidate for the ministry to guide him in his preparation. After two years of study, he was licensed by the presbytery and began a trial period as stated supply of the White Bluff congregation. After another three years, he was finally ordained and installed as pastor of the congregation. During this time he proved himself to be a serious scholar, and in a few years the University of North Carolina honored him with the degree of doctor of divinity.[4]

When Goulding arrived in Oglethorpe County in 1822 with his family and slaves, he found a young community that was growing rapidly. A new cotton kingdom was pushing westward, bringing with it not only whites eager for land and profits but also massive numbers of slaves being uprooted from seaboard areas and carried to rich new lands in the interior. Within three decades of Goulding's arrival on his farm, over seventy-eight hundred slaves would be chopping and picking cotton in the county.[5]

Among the newcomers to the county were farmers from the upcountry of South Carolina. They were largely descendants of Scotch Irish immigrants who had arrived in Philadelphia during the colonial period and had traveled south on the Great Philadelphia Wagon Road that ran from Pennsylvania through the Shenandoah Valley into the Catawba River valley and on to Augusta, Georgia. In South Carolina they spread over the upcountry, where they cut small farms out of the wilderness, organized Presbyterian churches after the pattern of the Church of Scotland, and slowly began to establish schools. When upcountry settlers moved into Oglethorpe County, they, together with settlers from the lowcountry of South Carolina and Georgia, began to create cotton plantations, some of which soon became large and prosperous. Two years after his arrival in the county, Goulding left his small farm and moved into the little village of Lexington, where he became pastor of the newly organized Presbyterian church and a teacher in an academy for the children of planters in the region. He soon became a leader in an effort to establish a "Literary and Theological Seminary for the South."[6]

Presbyterian leaders—clergy and lay—were eager to establish an institution that would serve the educational needs of the church and society in the Lower South with its expanding frontier. A board of directors was organized to pursue this objective, and Goulding was elected a member. At first they hoped for a college with a theological seminary attached. They purchased land near Pendleton, South Carolina, and began a vigorous fund-raising effort. But soon questions began to be raised. Did Presbyterians need to establish a college in the upcountry? They already largely controlled Franklin

College in Athens (later to be the University of Georgia), and while the South Carolina College in Columbia was suspect because of the supposed infidel leanings of some of its faculty, it was a prestigious institution with an impressive library. After long debates in the Synod of South Carolina and Georgia, and many committee meetings, the synod decided to drop the idea of a college and to establish a freestanding theological seminary. Both Athens and Columbia were proposed as the site of the new seminary. The synod selected Columbia.[7]

Beneath the synod's desire for a theological seminary were revival fires that had been sweeping over the country since the beginning of the nineteenth century. Goulding's conversion had been part of a general religious awakening—a Second Great Awakening, which followed a First Great Awakening during the colonial period. The awakening had been not only warming individual hearts but also spawning a rapidly increasing number of churches and benevolent societies. The demand for ministers was consequently intensifying, especially to meet the challenge of an expanding frontier and the rising call of foreign missions. More was needed than the kind of preparation Goulding had received when he went to live with mentoring pastors in "household schools." At the same time, an increasing secularization of collegiate education was turning many colleges away from an older classics curriculum—which had been largely designed for the education of ministers—toward a new emphasis on the sciences and legal subjects. Church leaders, left uneasy by such shifts, began to search for alternatives. Congregationalists in Massachusetts led the way when they established Andover Theological Seminary in 1808.[8]

Andover's founders wanted an institution of the church for the professional education of ministers. Moreover they believed that a theological seminary would be the means of nurturing and transmitting a theological tradition, of responding to theological controversies, and of advancing sectional and ideological interests. Columbia's founders had the same hopes for their southern Presbyterian theological seminary.[9]

Andover set the institutional character of the seminaries that would soon be established across the country—a graduate professional institution with a full-time faculty, capital funds and a campus, a library, a resident student body, a three-year curriculum, and a board of directors. The requirement of a bachelor of arts degree, although not always maintained, was intended to ensure that theological students had both the philosophical and linguistic background provided by a collegiate education and—not incidentally—the general culture and manners taught in the colleges.[10]

Not all denominations, however, welcomed the arrival of theological seminaries. The Second Great Awakening had a powerful egalitarian thrust and released a democratic spirit that invited the pious, even the most unlearned, to preach. The Baptists were calling "farmer preachers," godly men known to congregations, to plow their farms during the week and sow the Word on the Sabbath. In this way Baptist congregations were spreading rapidly, especially across a southern frontier that was already reaching into Alabama and Mississippi, Tennessee and Arkansas, Louisiana and Texas. But Methodists were the most prominent of a host of opponents to seminaries or "priest factories." For the Methodists a seminary education threatened to "dry up the sparks of the Holy Spirit" and separate the clergy from the laity in an elitist fashion. Perhaps ironically the Methodists would in time become the primary sponsors of university-related divinity schools where secular and religious leaders would be educated in single institutions.[11]

In December 1828 the synod elected Goulding professor of theology and gave him permission to remain in Lexington as plans were developed for the establishment of the seminary in Columbia. Five students came to Lexington and, after the old pattern, began their study for the ministry in the Lexington manse. While their work was preparatory for a full course of theological education, their arrival in Lexington in 1829 marked the founding moment for the seminary. In January 1830 Goulding with his family and slaves, together with his little clutch of students, moved to Columbia and occupied the former manse of the Presbyterian church in the city. Plans were already underway for an impressive new campus.[12]

Colonel Abraham Blanding, a prominent Presbyterian, had raised the handsome sum of $8,000 from members of several denominations in Columbia. He had then proceeded, with an additional mortgage of $6,000, to purchase the magnificent Ainsley Hall mansion and to offer it with the mortgage to the synod.

Ainsley Hall, an immigrant from the north of England, had made a fortune with his cotton and general merchandise business as the little town of Columbia expanded following its establishment in the late 1780s. By 1810 Hall was also raising cotton on several plantations scattered across the central portion of the state. In 1818 Hall moved his family into a new mansion he had built on a four-acre town lot. Six years later Wade Hampton I, already one of the wealthiest men in the nation, rode in from his country estate and asked Hall to name his price for the house. Hampton wanted immediate occupancy, and when Hall named the princely sum of $37,000, Hampton bought the house, complete with its elegant furniture. Hampton could easily afford the price. He owned plantations not only in South Carolina but also in Mississippi and in Louisiana, where his plantations made him the largest sugar producer in the state. At the time of his purchase of the Hall mansion, Hampton owned almost one thousand slaves.[13]

Hall then purchased a four-acre track immediately across the street from his former home and hired the architect Robert Mills to design a handsome new mansion. Mills, a member of the Presbyterian church in the city, had already established a reputation as one of the nation's leading architects. He had worked with his mentor James Hoban on the construction of the White House and he would himself design many of Washington's most famous buildings. When he began work on the new Ainsley Hall mansion, he was already responsible for helping to set a classical style for many of the nation's public buildings. Later he would be best known as the architect of the Washington Monument.[14]

Mills designed a classical brick mansion for Ainsley Hall. Every aspect of the building said to passersby and visitors, "Look, here is the home of wealth and influence!" Two stories rose high over an elevated, first-level basement. A front gate acted as a threshold and entrance into an expansive landscape, and a walk led a visitor to wide and imposing steps that climbed to the second level of the house. There a brick arcade provided a porch for the main entrance, and on the arcade stood four massive columns that made of the porch an Ionic-temple portico. The front door, handsome in its detail, faced north and looked competitively across the street to the Hampton mansion. Going through the door, a visitor entered a large rectangular hall and the world of the mansion.[15]

It was this handsome mansion that Colonel Blanding purchased for the new theological seminary. But the mansion was not the only building on the lot. An unpretentious house—a story and a half—had been built for domestic slaves who were to do the cooking and washing and cleaning for the white owner. And on the other side of the lot was another unpretentious house built for the family of a slave gardener who was to spread sand on the walks, tend the flower beds, and plant azaleas, camellias, and sweet-smelling tea olives. The elegant design of the Ainsley Hall mansion, together with its slave quarters and its location across the street from the Hampton mansion, pointed not only to the physical character and social location of the new seminary, but also to important elements in the seminary's character and purpose. Blanding, in a letter to the board of directors, said that those who had contributed to the purchase of the mansion and its outbuildings had as their object the establishment of "a Southern theological seminary." And the synod itself had noted earlier the distinctive habits and feelings of southerners on many subjects and "other circumstances that need not now be particularly detailed." The synod meant, of course, the distinctive habits and feelings of white southerners. Those habits and feelings, the synod declared, made the establishment of the seminary "of vital importance to the Southern Church." The seminary was to be an institution serving "Our Southern Zion." In this way the Ainsley Hall mansion represented an embodiment of the theological commitments and ideological interests of South Carolina and Georgia Presbyterians. Columbia was to be an elite institution of higher education to prepare ministers for a rapidly growing church. It was to be a center for the most serious theological reflection advocating and defending a Calvinist tradition. And it was to provide an ideological undergirding to a southern way of life—it was to help hide the harsh realities of slavery and to help legitimize the power and wealth of slave owners and the social order that kept them powerful and wealthy.[16]

The selection of such a building for the new seminary echoed the world of its board of directors. Benjamin Morgan Palmer Sr., president of the board, was the pastor of the Circular Congregational Church in Charleston, whose magnificent sanctuary had also been designed by Robert Mills. During the first decade of the seminary's history, the congregation included among many distinguished Charlestonians U.S. senator Robert Young Hayne, Congressman Henry Laurens Pinckney, and U.S. attorney general Hugh Swinton Legaré. Other ministers on the board included those from affluent country congregations made up of white planter families and many slaves—Elipha White from Johns Island, south of Charleston; John Cousar and Robert James from the Sumter District of South Carolina, where cotton was turning farmers into wealthy planters; and Horace Pratt from the little village of St. Mary's in the midst of Georgia's great rice and Sea Island cotton plantations.[17]

The Presbyterian minister Moses Waddell brought to the board a long career as an educator. He had recently retired as president of Franklin College (University of Georgia) and had earlier been the far-famed educator at his Willington Academy in the upcountry of South Carolina. He had taught a generation of southern leaders—most famously John

C. Calhoun. By the end of the antebellum period, his former students would include two U.S. vice presidents, three secretaries of state, three secretaries of war, one U.S. attorney general, ministers to France, Spain and Russia, one U.S. Supreme Court justice, eleven governors, seven U.S. senators, and thirty-two members of the U.S. House of Representatives—to enumerate only the political leaders! Waddell emphasized a strict classic education, and his students were expected to recite Horace, Livy, and Cicero in Latin, and Homer, Herodotus, and Thucydides in Greek.[18]

The vice president of the board for the first years of seminary's life was John Taylor, former U.S. congressman, senator, and South Carolina governor. A strong supporter of state's rights, he was very much a part of the state's social and political elite. Joseph Lumpkin was a future chief justice of the Georgia Supreme Court and one of the founders of the law school at the University of Georgia. Wealthy planters were also well represented on the board. Thomas Legaré with his many slaves grew Sea Island cotton on Johns Island. He would serve a term as president of the seminary's board. Barrington King's South Hampton plantation was one of the great rice-producing plantations on the Georgia coast. In 1837 King would sell his planting interests to his brother Roswell King Jr. and invest in textile mills in the newly established village of Roswell, Georgia. William Seabrook raised Sea Island cotton on Edisto Island, where his plantation home was one of the most handsome in the South. Seabrook invested his earnings not only in slaves and acre upon acre of numerous plantations but also in such industrial ventures as the Saluda Manufacturing Company and the steamboat William Seabrook.[19]

So the Ainsley Hall mansion with its outbuildings and its location across the street from the Wade Hampton mansion seemed to the board of directors a well-suited place for the education of southern ministers. In the years ahead when theological faculty and students walked up the mansion's high front steps and through its front door, they entered a carefully constructed world for teaching and learning where the walls themselves helped to shape and contain what was taught and learned within them. And in the future when faculty and students walked out the front door and stood on the high front porch beneath massive Ionic columns, they saw across the street the Wade Hampton mansion. From such a vantage point and with such a view, they saw a powerful symbol of a particular southern world and a particular southern way of life.[20]

In this way the Ainsley Hall mansion's architecture and its physical location provided a place to nurture a distinct tone and character among its students and faculty. Here in this mansion, a style of life, a moral and aesthetic spirit, and a way of understanding human life all came together to help create and reflect a southern Presbyterian world. That world did not suddenly drop from the sky with the creation of the seminary, but the seminary was to play for generations a major role in shaping the particular contours of that world and in seeking to maintain its social cohesion and its distinctive character.[21]

In January 1831 the Theological Seminary of the Synod of South Carolina and Georgia finally held its first formal classes. Only seven students gathered on the new campus that January, but they were joined by others in a few months. Since work was being done on the Ainsley Hall mansion, the students moved into the two frame houses on the grounds. Thomas Goulding and his family and slaves also moved in as did George Howe, a young

New Englander hired for a term as an instructor of biblical languages. No one realized it at the time, but Howe was beginning fifty-one years as a professor at the seminary and was soon to become the "Head and Father and Soul" of the seminary, the embodiment of its piety and its ethos, the guiding spirit during years of great prosperity and years of great loss and desperate struggle.[22]

Howe had been born in Massachusetts in 1802 into a Yankee family that reached back to the earliest settlers of the Massachusetts Bay colony. He had graduated at age twenty from Middlebury College, Vermont, first in his class, and had immediately entered Andover Theological Seminary. At his graduation in 1825, he was appointed Abbott Scholar, a position that allowed him to plunge even more deeply into his study of Bible and theology at a time when German scholarship was beginning to have a profound impact on these disciplines. Two years later, Dartmouth College called him to be the Phillips Professor of Sacred Theology. He was popular and showed great promise as a scholar, but the threat of consumption made his doctor recommend he spend the winter in the South. So in November 1830, he boarded a packet in Boston harbor and arrived in Charleston in early December 1830. Those who met him in Charleston were greatly impressed by his piety and his learning, and when the synod met a few weeks later it elected him, on the recommendation of Moses Waddell, for a term as an instructor in the biblical languages. The little group of students who gathered on the campus that January immediately liked Howe and soon respected him greatly, and the board thought they had been sent a great gift in the young New Englander. After he had spent less than a year in Columbia, the synod elected him professor of sacred literature and biblical criticism.[23]

Howe found a small but impressive group of students during his first year at the seminary. Francis Goulding was following his father, Thomas, into the ministry. After graduating from Franklin College in Athens, where he had studied under the rigorous discipline of Moses Waddell, he had begun his theological studies with his father in the Lexington manse. He later became famous as the author of *Robert and Harold; or, The Young Marooners on the Florida Coast* (1852), which would go through many editions, be translated into a number of European languages, and become a classic children's book.[24]

James Merrick, a graduate of Amherst, was from Massachusetts and brought to the campus an intense interest in the emerging Protestant mission movement. After his graduation from Columbia, he became a missionary in Persia, where the Shan granted him permission to open a school in Tabriz. He wrote and translated several books on Islam including *The Life and Religion of Mohammed: As Contained in the Sheeah Traditions of the Hyat Ul Kuloobsoon.* On his return to the United States in 1852, he was a professor of oriental literature at Amherst College for a few years before his death.[25]

John Leighton Wilson, a graduate of Union College in New York, had grown up on a plantation in the rich cotton country of South Carolina. He became after his graduation the most famous and influential American missionary in West Africa. In both Liberia and Gabon, he was a vigorous opponent of the international slave trade, an advocate for the richness of West African cultures and civilizations, and an ardent foe of French and American imperialism. Through his ministry, a number of Grebo and Mpongwe were converted and with their families helped prepare the way for the great expansion of Christianity in

Africa. In 1856 Harper Brothers published Wilson's *Western Africa: Its History, Condition, and Prospects,* which became an important resource for future anthropologists and historians of West Africa.[26]

Other students whom Howe soon encountered were I. S. K. Axson from Charleston, whose granddaughter would marry Woodrow Wilson in 1885; William Dana, whose father had been president of Dartmouth College; I. S. K. Legaré, whose father was the wealthy planter Thomas from Johns Island; Richard Hooker, a graduate of Yale and direct descendant of the founder of Connecticut and son of a distinguished Massachusetts judge; John Winn, graduate of Amherst and a member of a large and influential family in Liberty County, Georgia; and Theodore Dwight, graduate of Yale, descendant of Jonathan Edwards and from a family that furnished several presidents of Yale.[27]

When the work on the Ainsley Hall mansion was complete and the professors had found homes near the campus, the students moved into the mansion, taking rooms on the top floor and on the ground level. There was more than enough room in the mansion for everyone during these early years, but there was no easy way for them to get their meals—the idea of their doing their own cooking seemed beyond them. They struggled through the early months of 1831 eating here and there, but when more students joined them they decided to band together and form an eating club. Leighton Wilson wrote his father and asked if they could hire for their cook Jacob, an elderly slave who managed the Wilson's plantation kitchen. And the seminarian added in a note to his sister Martha, "and we need some other servants immediately." Wilson's father was unwilling to hire out his old cook, so Jacob stayed on the plantation, and the seminarians found help in Columbia to do their cooking and washing and cleaning. Later, as the student body grew, the gardener's house was enlarged for a refectory and dining room.[28]

The little group of students and faculty who gathered daily in the Ainsley Hall mansion for lectures and worship were not, of course, isolated from turbulent events taking place around them. A nullification crisis had been brewing since 1828 when the U.S. Congress passed a federal tariff. Following the lead of John C. Calhoun, lowcountry planters were insisting that the state had the right to nullify tariffs passed by the Congress that the nullifiers regarded as antislavery acts. Unionists in the state, primarily from the nonplantation upcountry, were horrified and condemned the nullifiers as unpatriotic. The seminarians began to fear the state was in danger of plunging into a civil war between the two parties and that such a war could lead to a slave uprising and a national civil war. Compromises, however, were finally reached, and the crisis passed, but nullification was a clear signal of dangers to come. South Carolina radicals had shown themselves willing to act in reckless ways to split the nation and protect slavery.[29]

And if nullification did not seem enough to worry about, some seminarians were deeply troubled by what was happening to the Cherokees and to the missionaries who were working among them in Georgia. The state, in its bloody aggression against the Cherokees, had arrested and thrown in prison the missionaries who stood with the native people. Leighton Wilson wrote to his fiancée and wondered if Andrew Jackson would send federal troops into the state to liberate the missionaries and to protect the Cherokees from white aggression. The situation in Georgia was particularly troubling because the seminary had been established, it was said, to help meet the challenge of an expanding southern frontier. The seminary was to "light up another sun which shall throw still farther west the light of the gospel, to shine upon the pathway of the benighted, and those who have long groped in the dim twilight of unenlightened reason." Indeed during the coming years, many graduates would be founding pastors of churches in the former territories of the Cherokee and Creek, in Florida, and in the new states of Alabama, Mississippi, Tennessee, and Arkansas.[30]

In late 1833 the synod elected Aaron Whitney Leland professor of theology. He was, like George Howe, a New Englander by background, but by 1833 he was deeply acculturated to the peculiar ways of South Carolina. He had grown up in Massachusetts, the son of an old Yankee family, and had graduated from Williams College in 1808. Immediately after his graduation, however, he had moved to South Carolina, where he taught school for a year in the little village of Mount Pleasant across the Cooper River from Charleston. There he had met and married Eliza Hibben, the daughter of the Honorable James Hibben, a wealthy and influential planter. Like Thomas Goulding, Leland had had a powerful religious experience as the revival fires of the Second Great Awakening swept across the country. And like Goulding he followed the old pattern of studying theology under mentoring pastors. In 1813 Charleston's First (Scots) Presbyterian Church called him to be their minister. He served this large and affluent congregation for eight years before moving across the Ashley River to James Island, where he served as pastor to planter families and a growing number of Africa Americans who joined the church under his ministry. So when he came to the new seminary in Columbia, he brought with him a southern wife, a deep knowledge of southern ways, and a houseful of children born in the lowcountry. He also brought fourteen slaves.[31]

Leland was a tall and handsome man, somewhat vain and aloof, but a splendid preacher who was widely admired. He received an honorary degree from Brown University in 1814 and from the South Carolina College in 1815. George Howe said of him that he was a "commanding person" with "high native endowments." A former student and graduate of Princeton College wrote years later of his "manly beauty, dignity, and grace." In the lavish style of a Victorian obituary, he said that Leland possessed a "majestic form, courtly manners, a voice which was harmony itself, and a style cultivated and fervid." It all, the former student said, "made an impression on those who heard him not soon to be forgotten." Still Leland never had the close relationship with students that Howe had, and some later colleagues found him annoying and not a little pompous.[32]

More serious tensions, however, developed almost immediately between Goulding and Howe. Goulding had been the leader of the seminary until Howe arrived, and Howe had quickly come to dominate the life and thought of the seminary. Leland wrote his friend and board member Thomas Smyth in Charleston: "The state of the seminary is bad: we talk of peace but there is no kinship or cordiality. The efforts of Dr. G. . . . against Dr. H. are secret but untiring. The accusation now is heresy." The ostensible problem was Howe's use of Leonard Woods's *Theological Lectures* as a textbook for his classes. Howe had studied under Woods at Andover and believed him to be an orthodox Calvinist.

But others disagreed, pointing to a New England theology that had emerged during the closing years of the eighteenth century and the early years of the nineteenth. Governmental metaphors had begun to be used to understand the character of the atonement. Conservative Presbyterians—they were beginning to be called "Old School"—had become alarmed by what they regarded as an unorthodox Calvinism among scholars and pastors associated with Andover and Yale. While many theological issues swirled in the growing debate, the question of human freedom was central.[33]

Charles Jones was a member of Columbia's board at the time tensions were heating up between Goulding and Howe. Several years earlier, having transferred as a student from Andover to Princeton Seminary, he had explained to his fiancée the differences between the Andover theology and the Old School theology being taught at Princeton. The Princeton people, he said, insisted that repentance is a pure gift of God, that the "sinner cannot repent; that he has no power at all to repent. He must do what he can and wait God's time." But the Andover theology insisted that the inability of a sinner to repent consists in "*disinclination,* and disinclination only. . . . The sinner has all the natural power to repent; he is able to repent. The reason why he does not, is because he *will* not."[34]

So the Andover theology, represented by Woods's textbook, was said to make repentance and belief largely a matter of the *will,* of volition. One simply had to *decide,* to make up one's mind, to accept Christ as one's personal savior and to change the direction of one's life. The New Englanders were insisting moreover, that a converted Christian would have a disposition they called "disinterested benevolence." For them the essence of sin was selfishness and self-love. A Christian conversion, however, made possible in a person a disposition for the good of others that did not take one's own interest into account. This New England theology had already become a mighty engine for the creation of social reformers, and its followers had been among the first to denounce slavery as immoral. If Columbia seminary were teaching such a theology, it would put the seminary in the camp with revivalists and social reformers and with the broad cultural optimism of nineteenth-century America that celebrated the freedom and power of the human will. And such a theology had the potential of making the new southern seminary a place that nurtured antislavery sentiment.[35]

Most pressing during the coming years for those who taught at Columbia and for those who slept, studied, and worshipped in the Ainsley Hall mansion and who looked across the street to the Wade Hampton mansion was their own freedom of will. Did they have the freedom to turn from self-love and self-interest to a concern for the good of others? Most specifically did they have the freedom to reject the slavery of sin, the self-love and the self-interest of privileged whites, and attack the harsh physical slavery of the South's "peculiar institution?" Did the contingencies of their own lives—the fact that many had been born into slave-owning families, that many had been loved and nurtured by slave owners, and that all of them were a part of a long cultural history that justified human slavery—were these contingencies simply "disinclinations" to be overcome with an act of the will?[36]

Goulding resigned his professorship in 1835 and accepted a call to the Presbyterian church in Columbus, Georgia, in the midst of the former Creek territory where white settlers were beginning to develop cotton plantations. His concerns about Howe's orthodoxy, however, had apparently slipped out of the confines of the Columbia campus and were causing alarm among certain pastors and congregations. Soon charges against the seminary were made in local newspapers. To make matters worse, tensions were building in the Presbyterian Church between an Old School party and a New School party that had been deeply influenced by New England theology. The board, feeling it must act to safeguard the reputation of the young seminary, conducted extensive interviews with both Howe and Leland. They found that "our Professors are sound in the faith," that they received the church's standards (the Westminster Confession and Catechisms) "in their plan and obvious import," and that in their teaching, the professors would conscientiously adhere to the standards. It would not be the last time Columbia professors would have to account for their orthodoxy, but in 1837, when the church split between an Old School Presbyterian Church and a New School Presbyterian Church, Columbia would be solidly in the Old School.[37]

At the same meeting of the board in which Howe and Leland were cleared of any charges of heresy, the board learned that Charles C. Jones had agreed to accept the synod's election of him as professor of ecclesiastical history and polity. Jones, like Goulding, who preceded him in the position, was from Liberty County, Georgia, and through inheritance and the inheritance of his wife was the owner in 1836 of almost a hundred slaves and two plantations. While still a student at Princeton, he had struggled with the question of slavery and in particular his responsibility toward those whose labors provided him so many privileges and comforts. He had written his fiancée, "I am, moreover, undecided whether I ought to continue to *hold slaves.* As to the *principle* of slavery, it is *wrong!* It is unjust, contrary to nature and religion to hold men enslaved. But the question is, in my present circumstances, with evil on my hands entailed from my father, would the general interests of the slaves and community at large, with reference to the slaves, be promoted best, by emancipation?"[38]

He had considered freeing his slaves and helping them go to the new colony for freed slaves in Liberia, West Africa. (Georgia law in the 1830s would not allow newly freed slaves to remain in the state.) He had decided, however, to return home and to become both a missionary among the slaves of Liberty County and an advocate for more humane treatment of slaves throughout the American South. He thought his efforts could help prepare black men and women for freedom when, in the providence of God, the time arrived and they were emancipated.[39]

Already by 1836 whites were beginning to call Jones the "Apostle to the Negro Slave." He had published in 1834 a widely used *Catechism for Colored Persons* through which he sought to teach slaves the lessons of the Bible and how to be obedient to their masters. And he sought as well in his catechism to teach masters how they were to be just in their dealings with their slaves. There is one Master of all in heaven, Jones taught, who does not show favor to earthly masters for they will have to "render an account for the manner in which they treat their slaves." Jones had already become in 1837 the best-known advocate for the reform of slavery and for the humane treatment of slaves—owners, he was insisting, should provide their slaves good housing, adequate food, time off on Saturdays to tend their gardens, Sabbath rest, and protection for their marriage and family life. Even Harriett Beecher Stowe would later praise his efforts. "The Rev. Charles C. Jones" is, she would write, "a man of the finest feelings of humanity, and for many years an assiduous laborer for the benefit of the slave." She called him an "earnest and indefatigable laborer for the good of the slave," and she thought his writings manifested "a spirit of sincere and earnest benevolence, and of devotedness to the cause he has undertaken, which cannot be too highly appreciated." Yet for Mrs. Stowe, Jones's sincerity and benevolent spirit made his work as a reformer of slavery—rather than an advocate for the abolition of the system—all the more deplorable. After declaring that he possessed a "sublime spirit" and a "mind capable of the very highest impulses," she was to lament: "And yet, if we look over his whole writings, we shall see painfully how the moral sense of the finest mind may be perverted by constant familiarity with such a system."[40]

Jones hoped that by becoming a professor at Columbia, he could stir in young seminarians a similar paternalistic vision of their responsibilities for the "religious instruction of slaves." Through their efforts as southern ministers, he hoped growing numbers of slaves would become Christian and growing numbers of masters and mistresses would assume their Christian responsibility to treat their slaves with justice and Christian charity.[41]

Jones's election revealed a central conviction that marked Columbia in its earliest days and that was to mark it for generations to come—that wisdom was found in moderation and prudence, that extremes led to trouble and heresy, and that a middle way was the way of Christian faithfulness and discipleship. To be sure, few institutions would define themselves as extreme, and other schools of theology frequently were to defend themselves by insisting, when under attack, that they were following a moderate or mediating path. But Columbia's quest for moderation, its love for the middle, was to be particularly intense. And in the years to come, many would find its middle way not only stogy but also an ideological cover for a deep commitment to the status quo and to the social arrangements and oppression that made the Ainsley Hall and Hampton mansions possible. Nevertheless until the firing of the guns on Fort Sumter, Columbia seminary would embody a quest for a middle way: a middle way in regard to knowledge, between rationalists and romantics; a middle way in regard to ethics—asking not what does my conscience demand in regard to slavery, but what is my present allotted sphere and task; and a middle way in politics, between those on one extreme or the other who would divide the union.

2

Slaves

In the Shadows of Columbia

Hidden in the shadows of the seminary's history, waiting to tell their stories, were black men and women whose labors, sorrows, and dark bodies provided the financial foundations for Columbia Seminary and its development. Slavery as a system, as a way of organizing human society, engulfed the seminary's life so that even as slavery fed the seminary's existence it also consumed much of the seminary's energy and shaped its style of life and the ways it saw the world.

In all this the seminary was reflecting a larger story of higher education in America. The nation's leading colleges and universities—from Harvard, Yale, and Princeton to Rutgers, Williams, and the University of North Carolina—were rooted in slavery and a slave economy. To a large extent, money from slave trading and slave labors built the campuses of schools, North and South, filled their libraries, and provided for their endowments. College presidents and trustees, North and South, owned slaves. Faculty and students, North and South, had slaves wait on them. "The academy," wrote historian Craig Steven Wilder, "never stood apart from American slavery—in fact, it stood beside church and state as the third pillar of a civilization built on bondage."[1]

Perhaps most revealing for Columbia Seminary's history was the deep engagement in slavery of the Reverend John Witherspoon, president of the College of New Jersey (Princeton) and signer of the Declaration of Independence. A Scotsman by birth and background and an acknowledged national leader of Presbyterians, Witherspoon eagerly sought and secured for Princeton the financial support of southern and Caribbean planters whose wealth was extracted from the labor and bodies of slaves. He had, moreover, begun buying slaves himself shortly after his arrival in New Jersey. Slaves cooked his meals, waited on his table, cleaned and prepared his clothes, and carried out his chamber pots. And when neighboring Princeton Theological Seminary was established in 1812, faculty members owned slaves and continued to own slaves for a generation. Some of its graduates were large slave owners, and many would spend their ministries in the midst of slavery and in support of slavery.[2]

If Columbia Seminary was consequently an example of the many ways higher education in America was intertwined with slavery, it was, nevertheless, a particularly potent example. Located in South Carolina and strongly supported by affluent whites in the lowcountry of South Carolina and Georgia, it was near the demographic center and ideological heart of U.S. slavery. Charleston had been by far the leading port for the importation of slaves into the United States until the abolition of the international slave trade in 1808. Perhaps half of all Africans brought to the United States had been "unloaded" at Sullivan's Island for a short quarantine before being sold in Charleston. Lowcountry counties had many more slaves than whites, and by 1830 many interior counties of South Carolina and Georgia were rapidly gaining black majorities. Moreover by the time the seminary was established in Columbia, large numbers of slaves were being carried to rich cotton lands of Alabama and Mississippi, Tennessee and Arkansas. Many whites would regard these new states an extension of a "Carolina culture" as they adopted laws, manners, and habits first consolidated in South Carolina. Indeed every time seminary professors or students walked out of the front door of the Ainsley Hall mansion and looked across the street to the home of Wade Hampton with his many plantations and slaves in Mississippi and Louisiana, they could see a vivid reminder of the expansion of slavery into the Old Southwest. And the seminary itself had as one of its founding purposes the mission to throw the light of the Gospel onto this southern frontier and soon was deeply linked to these slave states. "It had always been the design of this institution," wrote trustee Benjamin Morgan Palmer, to extend its influence over this southern frontier, "which seemed to be the territory from which its patronage should largely be drawn." By the end of the antebellum period, Presbyterians in these states were supporting Columbia with gifts flowing from cotton plantations. So it is not surprising that while some colleges and seminaries in the north had begun to be centers of antislavery agitation by the time Columbia was founded, Columbia never made that move.[3]

The seminary's deep enmeshment in the system of slavery involved not only figures on financial records or numbers on census reports or the ways a culture of slave owning penetrated the life and thought of Columbia. It also involved particular people—particular white people and particular black people. Both the white people and the black people have their stories to tell. And the stories of both overlap and intertwine even as the stories show the great distances between whites and blacks, between those who owned and those who were owned. The stories of the enslaved, however, have been largely repressed by the power of the whites so that the voices of black slaves have been hard to hear, and the intertwining of black lives with white lives in the history of the seminary has been hard to see. Nevertheless the stories of particular blacks are a critical part of Columbia's story, and the details and contours of their lives reveal much about the character of the seminary.

In January 1834 Major Andrew Maybank died at his plantation on Colonel's Island, Liberty County, Georgia, and was buried in the cemetery of the Midway Congregational Church. There, beneath the outstretched limbs of ancient oaks, a tombstone was placed over his grave. "His Christian life," declared the inscription, "was active and exemplary, and at his death he bequeathed a large portion of his estate to charitable purposes." As is often the case in such circumstances, Maybank's will was more complex than what was conveyed on his tombstone.[4]

In the first item of his will, Maybank left a bequest of cash and stock to the American Tract Society and the American Board of Commissioners for Foreign Missions. Both were benevolent societies closely associated with Andover Theological Seminary, with Lyman Beecher and other evangelical reformers. In the second item he bequeathed to his young relatives Laura and Edward Maxwell twelve slaves and "their issue to them and their heirs forever." Laura later inherited Edward's slaves, and in 1856 she married a young Columbia Seminary graduate who was to serve for years as pastor of the Presbyterian church in Marietta, Georgia.

In the third item Maybank gave and bequeathed to the Reverend Charles C. Jones and his wife and children, "the following property: viz. All my lands on Colonel's Island. . . . Also the following Negroes: Fanny & Prince, and their children Agrippa, Titus, Phillis, and Niger; also driver Andrew and his wife Mary Ann, and their children, viz. Charles, Sylvia, Gilbert, Dinah, George and Delia; also to them and their heirs forever, with their issue. Also my carpenter Sandy to them and their heirs."

In other items eight slaves were given to Maybank's pastor the Reverend Robert Quarterman, and eight were divided among several relatives and friends. The young woman Cora and her three children Maybank gave to Charles Jones "to dispose of as he thinks proper." The rest of his property—lands, slaves, farm animals, farm tools, boats, household items—were to be sold, and the proceeds were to be given to the new Presbyterian Theological Seminary in Columbia. Charles Jones was made executor, with responsibility to see that the instructions of the will were carried out.[5]

So in this way the Reverend Charles Jones, a member of Columbia's board and soon to be a faculty member, found himself not only the owner of a second plantation and fifteen more slaves but also responsible for the sale of eighteen men, women, and children. While a student at Andover, before his transfer to Princeton, he had written his fiancée that the more he looked at slavery, "the more enormous does it appear." Slavery, he had said, is a "violation of all the laws of God and man at once. A complete annihilation of justice. An inhuman abuse of power, and an assumption of the responsibility of fixing the life and destiny of immortal beings, fearful in extreme." Now as the executor of Andrew Maybank's will, he had, as he had never before had, "the responsibility of fixing the life and destiny of immortal beings." He did not appear to find it "fearful in extreme," but he did make arrangements that seemed to him the most humane way to proceed.[6]

Jones talked to Cora, whom, along with her three children, he was to dispose of as he thought proper. She wanted to be sold to John B. Bacon in order "to be with her husband in Savannah." Charles negotiated with Bacon, made the sale for $1,000, and set the funds aside for Columbia Seminary. At the same time, he had an ad for an "Executor's Sale" circulated, and on March 5, 1834, fourteen slaves were brought from their home on Colonel's Island to the courthouse in the little village of Riceboro to stand in a sandy yard shaded by live oaks. There they experienced the humiliation and terror of a slave sale. The oldest was Clarissa—she was in her sixties and was already referred to as Old Clarissa. She had belonged to Jones's grandparents and had through the marriage of Jones's aunt become a part of the Maybank estate. Standing with Old Clarissa before the courthouse was her daughter Rachael. Rachael's son Andrew had been willed to a cousin of Jones's, and Rachael's daughters Sally and Sue had gone to Jones's father-in-law, Joseph Jones, as had Sally's son Jack and Sue's son Aaron. So Old Clarissa knew, as she stood beneath the long, grieving wisps of Spanish moss in Riceboro, that her family on Colonel's Island, her grandson and granddaughters and great-grandsons, had already been divided.[7]

Planters had gathered from around the county for the auction, but most were neighbors from the island or from nearby on the mainland. There was much to be auctioned—everything from land and slaves to a fine new boat to silverware to a wharf in Riceboro. The slaves were put up in the first lot. They were all to be sold together except for Old Clarissa and Old Tom, who, in the appraisal of the estate, had been declared of no monetary value because of their age. When the bidding began, it became immediately clear that a gentleman's agreement had already been reached between Charles Jones and his father-in-law, Joseph. Joseph Jones bid the appraised value for the lot, and they were sold to him for $2,603.25. Then came Old Clarissa and Old Tom. Charles Jones bought them together with ten cows, ten calves, twenty-seven hogs, fourteen geese, and four beehives. The two old slaves were returned to their home on the island, and Clarissa was to be able to stay with her daughter and grandchildren at the nearby Joseph Jones plantation whenever she wished and could get a ride there. (No one at the sale could have imagined that the old woman would live another twenty years!) The rest of the estate was quickly sold to neighbors, and all the proceeds of the auction—together with the $1,000 for Cora and her family—were used to establish the Maybank Endowment at Columbia Theological Seminary.

As the executor of the Maybank estate and member of Columbia's board of directors, Charles Jones was made administrator of the Maybank Endowment. He deposited the funds at 8 percent with William King, a cotton factor and commission merchant in Savannah. King's business involved buying and selling cotton, making loans to planters, and providing planters with the supplies they needed. He was the brother of Barrington King, a member of Columbia's board, and Charles Jones and his wife had lived with the William King family in Savannah for a year and a half when Jones had been a pastor in Savannah. It was not unusual for planters, wishing to buy slaves, to seek loans from factors and merchants such as King. In 1837 Jones transferred the Maybank funds to the board and the management of the funds to the seminary's investment committee. In this way the funds from the sale of Cora and her children, of Clarissa and her family, and all the others sold to Joseph Jones became a part of the permanent endowment of the seminary.[8]

The seminary board invested the school's endowment in a variety of ways. Sometime it placed funds in a bank. Sometime it bought state or city bonds. In the 1840s it began investing in railroad stock as tracks were rapidly stretching from Charleston and Savannah into the Old Southwest. But the seminary also made loans to planters. The seminary's investment committee loaned $2,500, at 8 percent interest, to Dr. Charles West and took as a mortgage 485 acres of his North Hampton plantation that lay close by the Charles Jones plantation of Montevideo in Liberty County. In 1842 the loan was satisfied by a new mortgage at the same rate, only this time the mortgage was not for land but for fifteen slaves. Five years later the mortgage was paid and the seminary did not have to foreclose on the slaves. But when crops failed or prices fell or a planter experienced some other financial difficulty, the seminary did find on occasion that it had to foreclose on some mortgage. At the time West paid off his mortgage, the seminary foreclosed on the mortgage of another Georgia planter and became the owner of valuable rice land in McIntosh County. So when the directors made loans to planters and held slaves as mortgage, they knew there was the risk that the seminary could become the owner of slaves. But such risks were part of an economic system that seemed as ordinary as what later generations would find when they invested in textiles or coal mines or in corporations that manufactured tanks or napalm.[9]

Such financial entanglements of the seminary with slavery were not incidental but fundamental to the seminary's life. The Telfair Scholarship was a gift from a family whose firm had, in one decade alone, "handled and disposed of fifteen cargoes" of slaves. The Seabrook Endowment came from board member William Seabrook, owner of many plantations and many slaves. In 1845 an auction of eight slaves in Mississippi added to the seminary's endowment. These and other financial entanglements involved people—black people like Cora and Old Clarissa and their families—who were bought and sold and whose labors in rice and cotton fields produced funds for the establishment and maintenance of the seminary. But other black men and women were directly connected with Columbia's faculty and students. They provided not only financial resources for them but also personal service as domestic slaves and as drivers who largely oversaw the planting interests of those who taught and studied in the Ainsley Hall mansion.[10]

In December 1836 George Howe wrote to the board of directors of Union Theological Seminary in New York declining his election as Union's professor of sacred literature. "I must say," he wrote, "that it appears still my duty to cast in my lot and earthly destiny with the people of the South, among whom I have made my home. When I accepted the Professorship I hold, it was with the hope that I might be the means of building up the wastes, and extending the borders, of our Southern Zion. This motive still holds me here. Though our institution must be a small one through the present generation, and yours will be large, it is important, it is necessary, whatever be the fate of our beloved country, that this Seminary should live. If I leave it at the present juncture, its continuance is exceedingly doubtful. If I remain, though the field of my effort must be small, and must live on in obscurity, we may yet transmit to the men of the next generation an institution which will bless them and the world."[11]

Howe's letter reflected the modest and gentle spirit that made him loved by so many. He obviously had a deep commitment to the seminary's mission to the South. He saw a great need for well-educated ministers to bring not only Christian piety but also learning and order to the howling wildernesses and new plantations of a southern frontier. In this he was like other church leaders in the East who looked with no little anxiety to the developing regions of the West and worried if chaos and infidelity would flourish beyond the more ordered and civilized portions of the country. And Howe, writing from Columbia, was obviously alert to the dangers that threatened "our beloved country." In such a moment, he felt that it was his "duty to cast in my lot and earthly destiny with the people of the South," and he tellingly noted, "among whom I have made my home."[12]

Two weeks after writing the letter to the Union board, Howe married the thirty-three-year-old widow Sarah Ann Walthour McConnell. The wedding took place in her home in the little village of Walthourville, Liberty County. The Reverend Robert Quarterman, the same who had been willed eight slaves by Andrew Maybank, performed the service. Not far from Walthourville, on the road to Riceboro, was the bride's plantation with its slave settlement of some sixty black men, women, and children. Her brother, George Washington Walthour, had been successfully managing the plantation for her and was himself the wealthiest planter in the county and one of the largest slave owners in the South.[13]

When Howe responded to the marriage vows with "I do," he became the owner of his wife's property including her slaves and her plantation Halifax. In this way the professor from New England made his home in the South and cast his lot and earthly destiny with the whites of the South. A few weeks later, Howe took his young wife to the seminary in Columbia. They brought with them her daughter Augusta and six slaves, including Caroline, who was Augusta's personal servant. Both mistress and maid were fourteen years old. Shortly thereafter the Howes bought a large, comfortable home close to the seminary. In back of the house, in a kind of compound, two frame houses provided quarters for Caroline and the other five slaves.[14]

The management of a plantation from a distance was no easy task, and George Walthour apparently continued to look after the now Howe plantation and to direct its overall operations. But the day-to-day running of the plantation was done by Caesar, the slave driver. His position as driver required a kind of tightrope performance—he had to convince his master that the work of the plantation was proceeding smoothly and efficiently, and he had to demonstrate to the other slaves on the plantation that he was a buffer between them and the master. He used many strategies to walk this narrow line. No strategy, however, was more important than his cultivation within Howe of a sense of dependence, for Howe knew that without a skilled driver, his plantation would be both unprofitable and also difficult to manage. Howe knew almost nothing about running a plantation and soon became known as a very poor manager of slaves, so his dependence on Caesar steadily grew.[15]

Caesar assigned daily tasks to Sue, Betsy, and Rose, to Jim and Phillis, to Rosanna, Bob, and Jacob, to Prime and Bella and all those whose names call out from plantation records and reveal the deep anonymity of slaves. Caesar assigned some to plow, some to go down in muddy rice fields to plant or weed, and some to put up fences. He had the children carry water or clean up the yards around slave cabins or work at some other light tasks. When they became a little older, when the children grew into half-hands and then full-hands, Caesar gave them tasks for the heavy work of a rice plantation. And Caesar had the elderly women look after the youngest children and the elderly men do what they could to help around barns or to repair harnesses or to chop wood.[16]

Tony was the carpenter on the Howe plantation, and he had responsibility for maintaining the slave cabins and building a barn when necessary and for making the trunks and gates that regulated the flow of water into rice fields. He was also rented out to neighboring planters when they needed a carpenter and were willing to pay for his work. Most of Tony's wages were sent to Columbia to support the Howe household. But because of their importance to the operations of the plantation, Howe allowed Caesar and Tony to begin to accumulate some property of their own—chickens, pigs, cows and even horses. In time Caesar would own his own buggy and a wagon and would be considered wealthy by the standards of lowcountry slaves. But like most of Tony's wages, the profits of the plantation flowed from Liberty County to Columbia. Caesar's work and the work of all those who did their daily tasks on a lowcountry plantation went to support the Howe household in Columbia and to supplement Howe's salary from the seminary.[17]

A few weeks before Howe's marriage, Charles C. Jones reported to the seminary board that, after an initial refusal, he had accepted the synod's election of him to be professor of ecclesiastical history and polity. Jones felt ill prepared for such a teaching post, but more significantly he was reluctant to leave his missionary labors among the slaves of Liberty County. After an initial period of mentoring by the slave preacher Sharper, he was beginning to have some success among those who lived in the slave settlements of the county. But the synod had continued to press the call of the seminary on him, so he had finally accepted. He moved his family to Columbia, and they eventually settled into a rented house. They had with them Jack, the family butler and manager of the house, and his wife, Marcia, who was the cook. Jack and Marcia's granddaughter Clarissa was brought from the settlement at the Jones's Montevideo plantation to help with the cleaning of the Columbia house. Her cousin Patience was there as well. She worked in the kitchen with Marcia and was well on her way to becoming a famous lowcountry cook. And young Lucy had been brought to Columbia to help with the Jones children. Her mother, Rosetta, had been Charles Jones's nurse when he was a child, and now Lucy was being carefully trained to be a personal servant to Mary Jones. These black men and women and young adults had all lived in Liberty County, in slave settlements on the two Jones plantations, dense networks of family and friends who were chopping cotton and harvesting rice. Eight years earlier Charles Jones had written Mary Jones about how his slaves were "employed to furnish me with those conveniences of life of which they are in consequence deprived."[18]

Charles Jones had immediately taken up his teaching duties at the seminary, but he also organized a "colored school" for religious instruction of slaves and a black congregation for worship that met near the Saluda River. He took with him seminary students and sought to encourage in them a commitment to teach and preach the Gospel among the slaves of the South. And he organized a debate among students under the title question "Can the Religious Instruction of the Negroes Be Carried On Better by Missionaries Than by Pastors?" And he delivered a series of lectures for the seminary and for the white community in Columbia entitled "The Religious Instruction of the Blacks." When the Methodists held their annual conference in Columbia, he spoke to them on the same theme and encouraged them in their work among plantation slaves of the lowcountry. But he wondered if Columbia was the right place for him. "It is indeed a question," he wondered, "if I am doing as much for the Religious Instruction of the Negroes here as I was doing at home. If the seminary was larger, I might do more: but small as it is, and is likely to be, it is a question." So after two years of teaching at the seminary he resigned and returned to Montevideo and Maybank plantations and his work among the slaves of Liberty County. The synod quickly elected him once again to be on the seminary's board.[19]

Ten years later Jones was once again elected to his old position, and he once again returned to Columbia to teach ecclesiastical history and polity. He rented a large, if old, house not far from the seminary and brought to it his family and five slaves. Jack the butler was to oversee the Joneses' Columbia home to make sure that all was done as his master and mistress expected. His wife, Marcia, was once again to do the cooking for the family and the many guests—especially seminary students who would come to a hospitable seminary professor's home. With Jack and Marcia was their eighteen-year-old grandson John and their ten-year-old granddaughter Jane. They were being trained to be domestic servants, and their grandfather Jack was not only to look after them but also to provide them with training that would help it was hoped to offset some of the bad influences of their parents, Phoebe and Cassius. The parents had become known as troublesome slaves and had been suspended from communion by the Midway Congregational Church. With John and Jane was nineteen-year-old Phillis. She had already become an accomplished maid who knew the routines and expectations of Charles and Mary Jones and their family.[20]

Jack with his good manners and cheerful spirit had become a polished and elegant servant whose dignified ways added to the comfort of the Jones family and reinforced the family's image of itself. For years Jack had stood beside the Joneses' dinner table and had served those who sat around it. Now he stood beside the table in Columbia and served while the Jones family entertained seminary professors and students and faculty friends from the South Carolina College and guests from far and wide. George Howe and his wife, Sarah Ann, were frequent dinner guests as was the brilliant James Henley Thornwell and his wife, Nancy Witherspoon. And Benjamin Morgan Palmer, the younger, and his wife, Augusta McConnell, who was George Howe's stepdaughter, sat often at the Joneses' dinner table as did many students who were warmly welcomed. And while serving them, Jack had listened to the conversations of these whites who talked as if he were not there. He knew what whites thought of black people and how blind whites were to what really went on in the slave settlements and how deaf they were to what blacks said among themselves outside the hearing of whites. To be sure, Jack knew the kindness of Charles and Mary Jones and their concern for the welfare of the slave and how exceptional they were among whites. But Jack was not deceived by the kindness of his owners. He was well-known for the folk stories he told, and in them he revealed that he was savvy to the ways of whites, perhaps especially to well-meaning white seminary professors and students. He told about the trickster Buh Rabbit who knew how to outfox the stronger and supposedly wiser Buh Fox. And in his folk stories blacks could hear how careful they had to be around whites and how they could adopt strategies for resisting the harsh oppression of whites.[21]

Because Jack had probed the character of white culture, he had come to understand the assumptions of those who sat around the dinner table in Columbia and how they saw the world. They were, he knew, dependent on his good sense and on the work of Marcia in the kitchen and all the others who labored for them. So in a strange and ironic reversal of roles, he had a sympathetic, one could almost say paternalistic, attitude toward these needy white seminary professors and students who could not get along without him or without all those who chopped cotton or planted rice on southern plantations. He was consequently more than a "good and faithful servant"—Charles and Mary Jones regarded him as a friend and as an integral part of their household. And he was well known on the seminary campus and was called "a gentleman of the old school."[22]

Among the students who enjoyed the hospitality of the Jones home during his two tenures on the Columbia faculty were those students who had little experience with slaves. Most obviously were those from the North—Samuel Brown and W. W. Eells, for example, both from Connecticut and graduates of Yale; and Washington Peace from Pennsylvania and a graduate of Princeton. But there were also those from the upcountry of South Carolina and from other areas of small farms and few slaves—Robert McLees and John McLees grew up on a small farm in Anderson County, South Carolina, and James McCarter came from a little farm in Franklin County, Georgia. They were among those who made their way out of very limited circumstances to college and seminary.[23]

But a number of students came from slaveholding families, and some came from families that had many slaves and large plantations—I. S. K. Legaré and Thomas Legaré from Charleston and Johns Island; John E. DuBose from Miller's Bluff, Camden County, Georgia; and Samuel Chandler from Sumter County, South Carolina. While students from such backgrounds came from many areas, the single most concentrated area was Liberty County, Georgia, with its remarkable Midway Congregational Church. During the sixty years before the Civil War, some forty Presbyterian ministers came out of this one congregation, twenty-eight of whom studied at Columbia Seminary. All twenty-eight came from slave-owning families, and most of them large slave owners. William LeConte's grandfather owned the famous Woodmanston plantation with its beautiful botanical gardens, and his father, a Savannah lawyer, owned another Liberty County plantation and some forty-five slaves. The father of James Bullock Dunwody owned the two-thousand-acre Acadia plantation with its rich rice and cotton lands. The father sold the plantation and most of his slaves in the 1840s, having moved to Roswell, Georgia, where he invested in the Roswell Manufactory Company and built the handsome Mimosa Hall mansion. Joseph Quarterman's father, the Reverend Robert Quarterman, owned a family plantation and seventy-eight slaves he had inherited from his family and from parishioners such as Andrew Maybank. David Buttolph married, four years after he graduated from Columbia, Laura Maxwell of Liberty County and with the marriage became the owner of Lambert plantation and seventy-eight slaves.[24]

Two sons of the Midway congregation, who had long and important connections to the seminary, stand out as important examples of students who came from large slave-owning families. John Jones grew up on the great Retreat plantation in whose settlement over two hundred slaves lived. Shortly after he graduated from Columbia Seminary in 1839, he received from his father thirty-six slaves as his share of his mother's estate. He immediately sold twenty-three back to his father, Joseph, and they remained at the Retreat. But that same month he married Jane Dunwody, and in the marriage agreement thirty-four slaves became a joint possession of the young couple. Jones was perplexed about how to manage the slaves from a distant parish, and on his father's advice he bought Bonaventure plantation in Liberty County and hired a white neighbor to oversee its management. He selected the slave Augustus to be the driver at Bonaventure and, like other slave drivers, to run the daily operations of the plantation. John Jones also purchased, apparently from some family friends, several slaves to work as domestic servants under the supervision of Sylvia, who had been his nurse as a child. She became his family cook and moved with the family as John Jones accepted calls over the coming years to different churches. He called her "my old Mama" or simply "Momma," but she was far from a Mammy figure with her strong personality and independence. Wise like Jack to the ways of whites, she knew how to insist and how to complain and how far she could go in her insistence and her complaining and when she should be cautious and discrete. From within such a world, John Jones served for years as a member of the seminary board of directors and made decisions about its life and mission.[25]

Robert Quarterman Mallard graduated from Columbia in the class of 1855. He had grown up not far from the Midway Congregational Church on the Mallard Place plantation, where his father, Thomas, owned some eighty slaves. Thirty slave houses were on the place when Mallard was a student in Columbia, and in them lived the driver Pompey and the slave carpenter Harry Stevens. Stevens was well known as a healer and was called by both blacks and whites "Dr. Harry." Drawing on West African traditions of healing and an evolving lowcountry folk medicine, he knew that chewing sweet-gum leaves or drinking a tea of marsh rosemary could cure diarrhea; that an infusion of dogwood bark helped cool a fever; that the juice of Jerusalem oak could clean hookworms and tapeworms out of a child; and that boiling the roots of devil's walking stick and drinking its tea could give a man courage and sexual prowess. He was also a kind of slave engineer who helped planters design dams and canals for rice production. The year Mallard graduated from seminary, Stevens through his own extraordinary efforts and the help of admiring whites was able to buy his freedom and the freedom of his family and to emigrate to the colony of freed people in Liberia.[26]

Major was another prominent figure in the Mallard slave settlement. He was a Watchman, a kind of deacon for the blacks of the Midway congregation and a greatly respected figure in the slave community. During Robert Mallard's childhood and youth, Charles Jones had come frequently in the evening to preach among and teach those who lived in the settlement, and they had, in significant numbers, joined the Midway congregation. There they sat in the balcony and listened to the long, logical, and passionate sermons of Robert Quarterman and nurtured their own Christian faith and community of Christian slaves.

In 1857 Mallard married Charles and Mary Jones's daughter Mary Sharpe Jones, and with her came—as a marriage gift—sixteen slaves who were to be their domestic servants. Among them were a son and a granddaughter of Andrew, the driver on the Jones's Maybank plantation. Andrew had been left to Charles and Mary Jones when Cora and her family and other Maybank slaves had been sold and the proceeds sent to the seminary in Columbia. When Robert Mallard accepted a call to Atlanta's Central Presbyterian Church, he and his wife, Mary Sharpe, brought to Atlanta six of their slaves from Liberty County, including Andrew's son and granddaughter.[27]

Years later when he was a pastor in New Orleans, Robert Mallard wrote *Plantation Life before Emancipation* and told what he remembered about Pompey, Dr. Harry, Major, and others who lived in the slave settlements of Liberty County. They no doubt had a different memory and different stories to tell about life on Liberty County plantations, but clearly the lives of blacks and whites overlapped on the contested ground of the Mallard Place plantation. And it was that ground that nurtured and shaped the future Columbia student, board member, and moderator of the Southern Presbyterian General Assembly—Robert Quarterman Mallard.[28]

One notable Columbia graduate responded in a different way to slavery. John Leighton Wilson was a member of the first graduating class in 1833. Raised on a plantation near the Black River in Sumter County, South Carolina, he was part of a dense network of Presbyterian families descended from Scotch Irish settlers who had arrived in South Carolina in the 1730s. When he graduated from seminary, he owned two slaves inherited from his mother, and when he married Jane Bayard in 1834 he became with his wife the owner of another thirty-six slaves. Together husband and wife agreed, as they prepared to leave as missionaries to West Africa, to emancipate their slaves. They provided the funds and made arrangements for them to go either to a free state in the North or to the young colony of freed blacks at Cape Palmas, Liberia. Yet even this act with all its good intentions revealed the oppressive power of slavery. Both Georgia and South Carolina had enacted in the 1820s draconian laws that left it impossible for newly emancipated slaves to remain in the state. This meant that some of the Wilson slaves had to decide if they wished to claim a new freedom for themselves by leaving behind families owned by other whites. Most of the Wilson slaves chose to go to Liberia, leaving behind either husbands or wives and children. But two young men refused to leave families. They remained in South Carolina, where they lived in a kind of twilight zone between slavery and freedom—they lived in the old Wilson slave settlement but received pay for the work that they did. Years later, after Sherman's army had shaken the land, one of them would help to bring relief supplies to a devastated Columbia and seminary.[29]

So Columbia Seminary was not only created in the midst of a slave society; it was also an integral part of that society. Wherever one looked, behind every feature of the seminary's life, slavery was there not as something extraneous, not simply as the context within which the seminary existed, but rather as a fundamental part of the seminary's life. The theology taught at the seminary and the ways its graduates understood the character and tasks of ministry were not autonomous cultural phenomena but were inescapably part of a slave society.[30]

But Columbia Seminary was not simply a reflection of a slave society. Its Calvinism, its understanding of God and human life, its piety that taught a love of Jesus and neighbor, all provided powerful ways of interpreting the world of which it was so intimately a part. The theological traditions taught at Columbia offered students and their parishioners explanations of the incongruent and contradictory character of life in a slave society and provided ethical standards for living in such a world. The antebellum South was not a bare, uninterpreted reality but was always understood within an interpretative framework. What was taught and what was learned at Columbia helped to interpret what students saw when they looked across the street to the Hampton mansion; it helped to interpret what students saw when they walked through a slave settlement or looked up into a slave balcony into the faces of black parishioners; and it helped to interpret and shape what they came to believe was their Christian duty and their calling as ministers of the Gospel.[31]

The life and character of Columbia Seminary was consequently complex and dynamic. At its heart was a two-way street—a reciprocal interaction between a slave society and a theological tradition. The influences moved both ways, intertwining with one another to make a coherent whole that was known as Columbia Theological Seminary. What emerged from the intertwining was an understanding of ministry that valued prudence and moderation and that sought to provide paternalistic care not only to black slaves but also to whites in piney woods and sand hills and on an expanding southern frontier.

3

Gentlemen Theologians in a Slave Society

What kind of ministers did Presbyterians look for and want in the antebellum South? To be sure, like Presbyterians in other times and places, they wanted ministers who possessed both substantial learning and a genuine Christian piety. But what kind of learning did antebellum southern Presbyterians regard as substantial and what kind of Christian piety did they regard as genuine?[1]

Southern Presbyterians certainly gloried in and claimed a rich tradition of learning and piety that could be found in Scotland and among English Puritans, French Huguenots, and other European Calvinists. They thought of themselves as standing in this tradition and being a contemporary part of it along with many in the North, especially Old School Presbyterians most closely associated with Princeton Theological Seminary. But antebellum southern Presbyterians also knew that they lived in a particular place—the American South—and that they lived in a particular time when the South's "peculiar institution" of slavery was under increasing pressure and the foundations of southern society were being challenged by powerful political, economic, and ideological forces. So while they thought of themselves as standing within a broad Calvinist or Reformed tradition, southern Presbyterians began to recognize that the received traditions of learning and piety were taking on a distinctive southern character marked by life in a slave society. Indeed, in time antebellum southern Presbyterians—and their descendants—became convinced that they were true preservers and defenders of the larger Reformed tradition. They came to believe that the Reformed tradition as it found expression in southern society among white southern Presbyterians was not some aberration, some peculiar development within the tradition, but the tradition's most faithful and trustworthy contemporary expression in the United States.[2]

The constitution of the seminary, adopted by the Synod of South Carolina and Georgia in 1828, began by asserting "the superior claims of the present age to an enlightened ministry," and the synod resolved to establish "an institution of sacred learning." Over the next decade and a half the synod and the seminary board occasionally addressed questions about the character of theological education, but it was only in the early 1840s that George Howe made explicit and wrote in great detail about the expectations the church had for "enlightened" ministers and what a theological seminary needed to do and be in order to nurture such ministers.[3]

Charleston Presbytery, of which Howe was a member, requested that he write an essay on theological education. Howe's essay was to be one of several the presbytery intended to share with congregations on the bicentenary of the Westminster Assembly that had in the 1640s composed the confession and catechisms of the Presbyterian Church. So Howe began to work on his essay and soon found it growing and growing until the essay had become a book of 243 pages. In it he laid out not only the long history of theological education in the life of the church across the ages but also basic assumptions, commitments, and details that marked the young seminary in Columbia.[4]

Howe began by insisting that within the Reformed tradition the advantages of education had long been honored and that learning had been regarded as "the handmaid of religion." Men of influence within the tradition, in all ages, had been those who "united ardour of piety with discipline of mind and extent of knowledge." There were, he insisted, biblical roots for such a union of piety and learning. In an introductory chapter he reviewed the Old Testament stories of patriarchs and priests, prophets and kings, and then he told of scribes and rabbis and the piety and deep learning that they possessed. Since the Christian churches were formed on the model of the synagogue, and mostly among persons who had been educated as Jews, what other view, Howe asked, could early Christians have of the Christian ministry than that it should be a learned ministry. To confirm this conclusion, Howe spent a chapter on the theological education of the apostles and early church leaders, refuting the claim that because the disciples were poor fishermen then ministers should be simple, unlearned folk. Jesus, Howe wrote, had gathered his disciples into his own school of theology, and they had spent three intense years listening and watching as Jesus taught them. And Paul, the apostle to the gentiles, had spent years at the feet of the great Jewish teacher Gamaliel before his encounter with the Risen Jesus—and who could deny that Paul was a theologian of the deepest learning? A chapter followed that began with the church fathers—Polycarp and Origen, Jerome and Ambrose—with special attention to the great school at Alexandria under Origen. Then came a discussion of the medieval cathedral schools and praise for the Irish monk St. Columba and the monastery on the island of Iona off the coast of Scotland. They all pointed to a learned and pious ministry. But in spite of places and periods of learning, the church, Howe wrote, had entered deeper and deeper into darkness, ignorance, and superstition until the Reformation had emerged as a burst of new learning and renewed piety. The Reformation, Howe declared, was "almost wholly effected by men of learning, and men who occupied posts of responsibility in schools of theology and halls of science." Howe insisted that the study of the Hebrew and Greek scriptures was the single most important factor in reforming the church according to the Word of God and should consequently be the fundamental foundation for a ministry that was both deeply learned and genuinely pious. In all this Howe demonstrated his own learning—his ease in the use of Hebrew, Greek, and Latin, and his familiarity with a broad literature in English, German, and French. And he also placed Columbia Theological Seminary within this Protestant interpretation of church history and this narrative of theological education.[5]

After reviewing more contemporary forms of theological education associated with the universities of Britain and continental Europe, Howe turned to the distinctive form of theological education as it had developed in the United States—the theological seminary after the Andover model. He pointed out that this model required a student to obtain a college degree before entering seminary in preparation for ministry. Because he believed theology was the "comprehension of all knowledge and makes every department of human thought tributary to it," all areas of college study were important preparation for seminary. Each area, he said, helped to discipline the mind and to convey valuable and useful knowledge for the student of theology. All the sciences were necessary if the student was to be prepared to grapple with natural theology and the design and plan of the Author of Nature. How could a student read and critique, for example, William Paley's *Natural Theology or Evidences of the Existence and Attributes of the Deity* if a student knew nothing of geology, botany, and zoology? Or how could a student profitably read *Astronomical Discourses* by the great Scottish churchman Thomas Chalmers without some knowledge of astronomy? And history was, of course, important "in a thousand ways" as "illustrating the dealings of God with nations as well as individuals." And moral philosophy that dealt with the laws of nations and political economy, Howe said, was also critical for the minister who was in some ways a conservator of the public morals and, like the Old Testament prophets, "a watchman over the whole nation."[6]

But Howe insisted that of all the subjects needed in preparation for a seminary education the most indispensable were metaphysics and the classical languages of Greece and Rome. Metaphysics was necessary to prepare the student to probe the character of humanity and to introduce the student into "the secrets of the human heart." How could one be a theologian, a pastor, and a preacher of the Gospel without some understanding of human nature? And as for the classical languages—so dear to Howe's own heart—they were sine qua non preparation for any student entering a theological seminary.[7]

The study of Latin and Greek had long been at the core of college curriculums. Yale, in a famous report in 1828, had reaffirmed the necessity of the classical languages for a liberal education. The study of Greek and Latin, it was said in the report, not only "lays the foundations for a correct taste, and furnishes the student with those elementary ideas that are found in the literature of modern times," but the study of the classical languages also "forms the most effectual discipline of the mental faculties." Howe echoed the conclusions and sentiments of the Yale report, insisting that "the beautiful and chaste models of classic Greece, and the noble majesty of the Roman orators and bards, are necessary to chasten the style, to furnish a mould in which all the composures of the mind, and all the performances of the orators are to be cast." A mastery of Latin was, moreover, essential for the theological student since for ages it had been the language of learned men and many theological works were only available in Latin. As for Greek a theological student obviously needed to know not only the vocabulary and grammar of the language of the

New Testament but also something of the manners and customs of the people who played such a large role in the early church.[8]

The expectation that Columbia seminary students come with a solid background in Latin and Greek was consequently part of broad assumptions about the character of a liberal education and what was necessary in preparation for professional theological studies. But a distinct southern environment and culture also played its part at Columbia. At least among many educated white southerners there was a kind of distant love affair with the classical world of Greece and Rome. These ancient civilizations provided an aesthetic spirit and standards of beauty that southerners sought to replicate most vividly in Greek Revival plantation and city houses with their white columns and careful symmetry. Indeed the Ainsley Hall mansion and its neighbor the Hampton mansion embodied classical ideals as they were being interpreted in the nineteenth-century South. Of course such an architectural style was not limited to the American South, but it found in the South a white culture that celebrated the civilizations built on slavery and patriarchy. It was not by chance that white slave owners frequently gave Greek and Roman names to black slaves. George Howe's driver was Caesar. The driver on Charles Jones's Montevideo plantation was Cato, and his brother was Cassius. On the Mallard plantation Pompey was the driver, and on John Jones's Bonaventure plantation the driver was Augustus. And there were others—Agrippa and Titus, Markus and Brutus, Dorcas and Phoebe—all slaves of those who taught or studied at the Ainsley Hall mansion.[9]

Students who had spent years reading Caesar's *Commentarii de Bello Gallico,* Cicero's eloquent *De Officiis* with its discussion of what is honorable, and Tacitus's *Annales* had entered into the great traditions of Roman oratory and Stoic philosophy. And those students who had sailed with Homer's Odysseus on wine-dark seas had had their imaginations stretched and enlivened, while those who had marched in the Greek texts with Herodotus's hoplites against Persian armies had learned how free citizens had to defend their freedom against foreign tyrannies, even neighboring states. The student formed by the study of such classical texts, it was hoped, would be able to speak and write with great eloquence and power.

But perhaps what had entered most deeply into the hearts and minds of students so educated and so prepared for their theological studies was a type of Stoicism, a kind of stiff upper lip and preoccupation with virtue. Indeed Stoicism was the great competitor for the hearts and minds of white southern Presbyterians with their Reformed tradition and evangelical experiences. There is, wrote Howe's colleague James Henley Thornwell, "more affinity with the Gospel in Cicero than in the whole tribe of [modern] utilitarians." Generations later a great Presbyterian elder and historian of the South would write that educated white southerners had "tried to use Stoicism to bridge the gap between its social culture and its individualistic religion." This mingling of Stoicism with Christian faith was most evident in times of great distress. When a young kinsman of Thornwell's lost his wife and his grief spilled over into public displays of anguish, Thornwell wrote frankly about his concern for him. While expressing concern for "his sore and terrible affliction," Thornwell said his lack of fortitude was "inconsistent alike with the dignity which becomes a man, and the submission which belongs to a Christian. To bear with firmness what cannot be avoided, is the dictate of philosophy; to bear with resignation what God appoints, is the dictate of religion." Students who spent years reading not only the Bible but also Greek and Latin writers would generally make ministers who would give such counsel.[10]

A broad liberal education was thus critical preparation for a student before he entered seminary. While the faculty and board tried to maintain this standard, approximately 20 percent of Columbia's students during its first decade did not have a college degree. Those who did not had apparently studied at some academy where they had at least taken up a Latin grammar and had plunged into some of the less demanding Latin writers so that they could pass an entrance exam given by the faculty. Still Howe and his colleagues lamented the poor preparation of such students and how hard it was to have them in the same class with students who had been well prepared at Yale or under the demanding Moses Waddell at Georgia. "The teacher of theology," wrote Howe, "is often pained at seeing with what a small degree of knowledge and mental disciple, young men sometimes think themselves competent to enter upon the study of theology." They sometimes present themselves "for admission to our seminaries who are as yet too little advanced to make use of the labours of those mighty minds which have gone before them, too little to have any proper conception of the method of critical investigation which the theologian must adopt, or to understand a lengthened argument, much less to conduct one himself with success." Howe was but the first in a long line of Columbia Seminary faculty members who would lament the admission of unprepared students.[11]

A disciplined and well-informed mind, however, was not the only requirement for admission to Columbia Seminary. A student needed to demonstrate as well what Howe called an "ardour of piety." The piety that was expected had deep roots—it reached back through a British Reformed tradition to Calvin, and from Calvin it went back to Augustine, and from Augustine it was said to reach back to the New Testament, especially to Paul, to his conversion on the road to Damascus and his letters to the early churches around the Mediterranean. Thornwell before his conversion wrote: "My understanding assents [to the doctrines of Christianity], but my feelings are dead. My religion seems to be all in the head. Would to God it were otherwise." And Thomas Smyth declared: "It is not enough to believe aright so far as mere words and doctrines can delineate the truth as it is in Jesus." Such a belief would be the faith of only a part of a person, "and that the least active, powerful, and controlling." What was needed was the Spirit of Christ to breathe on the dry bones of orthodoxy. The revivals and awakenings in the United States had strengthened the experiential emphasis in this tradition of piety, but Presbyterian piety also had deep roots in the Old Testament and expressed itself in a pervasive love for the Psalms and a deep concern for law and discipline.[12]

At the heart of this piety was an emphasis on the sovereignty of God, the Holy One of Israel, whose ways, Presbyterians were fond of saying, are not our ways and whose thoughts are not our thoughts. This One, who inhabits eternity, who is the Maker of the heavens and the earth, is the One they insisted whom we are to worship and adore. Before this God there is no room for sentimentality or for the trivial. This God, all seeing and all knowing, cannot be manipulated, nor can this God's eternal purposes be finally thwarted by the vain and evil ways of humanity.[13]

Presbyterian piety felt at a deep level the estrangement of the heart from this High and Holy One, the God of all creation. As Presbyterians read the scriptures, as they looked around them at the world and human history, and as they peered into the recesses of their own hearts, they confessed that all are sinners and that every human being is altogether sinful—there is no one who is not a sinner and altogether sinful. Such a cool-eyed view of human nature made them realists in regard to politics and human affairs, but it also often left them somber and too easily judgmental. This meant that other white antebellum southerners often regarded the faculty and students at Columbia with mixed feelings. They respected them for their disciplined lives and sometime feared their intellectual prowess. But especially among those white southerners who gave themselves to a wholehearted devotion to amusement—to horse racing or cock fighting, to the theater and balls and other "worldly entertainment"—these Presbyterian sometimes seemed too morose and best avoided and were sometimes mocked.[14]

What, however, made Presbyterian piety appealing to many was the confession that the sovereign God who is high and lifted up reveals Himself in Jesus Christ. And what Christ reveals is not only God's majesty and sovereignty but a majesty and sovereignty that have at their heart mercy and forgiveness, gracious humility and compassion. God's mercy and forgiveness is received by grace alone—grace is a pure gift; it comes from above to the sinner whose righteousness is "but a filthy rag." It is "Amazing grace that saved a wretched like me!" the sinner could sing. "I once was lost, but now am found, was blind but now I see."[15]

Thomas Smyth, longtime seminary board member, drew together these themes in a series of sermons in the early 1840s. In appealing to the troubled soul, he pointed to the power of the sovereign God to rescue sinners: "In all of the Scriptures . . . there is not one hard word against a poor sinner, stripped of all self-righteousness, and who cast himself for life, light, and peace, on the Lord Jesus Christ." If you cannot make yourself believe, Smyth told his Charleston congregation, "you can remember that Christ 'is the author of faith.'" To you, he said, who feel no sense of pardon, "remember that Christ 'gives remission of sins,' and secures the favor the Father." "Are you," he asked, "full of infirmities?" Christ "is not a high-priest who cannot be touched with them, but one who was at all points tried as we are." This same Christ "works in the heart to will and to do." "By grace, then," Smyth declared, you "are saved through faith and that not of yourself, it is the gift of God."[16]

This was no altar call demanding that the sinner make a decision for Christ, but a call to trust in the mercy of the sovereign God. Yet everyone who was saved by God's elective grace must have had an experience of regeneration—of being born again for eternity. That some experienced such grace while others did not was a part of the great mystery of God's providence. But one thing seemed sure. Those who had an experience of grace had their lives changed. If a person is "really the servant of Christ," Thornwell told his Columbia students, "it must be his supreme desire to glorify his Father in heaven by a well-ordered life and godly conversation." One who is truly converted will strive, pray, and labor "that the body of sin may be mortified in him, and that he may day by day become more conformed to the image of Christ."[17]

So when Columbia Seminary expected entering students to have not only substantial learning but also a lively piety, the faculty expected students to confess that they had experienced such saving grace in their lives. The faculty looked for two indications of grace in a student's life.

First, a prospective student needed to be able to give a personal testimony to an inward experience of grace. A person could experience saving grace in different ways and under different circumstances—Thomas Goulding had even experienced it while asleep! But what all needed to confess was an inward experience. A prospective student needed to be able to say, "The Lord has touched my heart, and I know that Jesus is my savior! I put all my trust, not in my own works, but in my precious savior." Such a confession often came after a crisis of faith. Leighton Wilson, in the first graduating class at Columbia, had grown up in a loving Christian family that said morning and evening prayers together, that sang together in church and listened together to the preaching of faithful pastors. Yet shortly after he had graduated from Union College in New York and was teaching in Charleston, he began to feel the absence of God in his life despite his churchgoing and his daily Bible reading and prayer. "God," he wrote his sister, "has hidden his face from me and if I really ever had a hope, for the present it is absent." The absence of God and a sense of absolute loneliness and abandonment left him deeply shaken. During a church service, he suddenly had a vision of being utterly alone and abandoned, cut off from those whom he loved and from those who loved him, cut off in profound isolation from love itself. He saw himself standing before the judgment seat of God before whom all pretenses were swept away and all was made clear. In that moment, he wrote his sister in great despair, he saw "the deceitfulness and obstinacy of my heart of which I had no previous conception and the depth and nature of that deceitfulness!!" His conversion followed several weeks later. With overwhelming emotion he experienced the "perfect love of God which casts out all fear." Christ, the love of God incarnate, had not abandoned him, Wilson confessed, but had come after him and was his Redeemer and Friend, the Lamb of God who takes away the sin of the world, who, in the final day, would stand in his place before the judgment seat of God. This conversion experience was the turning point of Wilson's remarkable life. And his testimony about his conversion prepared the way for his entrance into Columbia seminary.[18]

Second, a student needed an outward demonstration of the inward experience of grace. If a student's heart had been touched, if one had genuine piety and love of God, then the student was living a disciplined and morally upright life—a life that would not bring scandal on the church or to the name of minister. A student's character and reputation were consequently important. And the primary judges of character and reputation were the student's home congregation and presbytery—the student was expected to be a member of a local congregation and if a Presbyterian to have the endorsement of his presbytery. Those in the church who were closest to the student, who had known him for the longest time, were to give their approbation to his sense of call to the ministry, and they were to testify to the student's good character. And when the student entered seminary, he was to acknowledge that he was "deeply impressed with a sense of the importance of improving in knowledge, prudence, and piety preparatory to the

Gospel ministry." And he was to promise to yield to "all the wholesome admonitions of the professors and directors."[19]

Daily routines at the seminary were intended to nurture the student's Christian faith and life. Students and faculty went together to morning and evening worship, where they sang together, read scripture together, and heard brief meditations together. Students set aside time each day for private prayer and scripture reading and often met together in their rooms for prayer. "This evening," wrote one student in his journal, "several of the brethren met in my room for prayer. We confessed our faults one to another, and prayed for one another. Our hearts flowed together: the Holy Spirit seemed present to bless." Once each week a student was required to meet with a faculty member to talk about questions of faith and to be guided about "practical duties of the ministry." During such sessions professors frequently counseled students struggling with inner conflicts, with questions about motivation, intentions, and vocation and what they regarded as the deceptions of their own hearts. But professors also advised students how to improve not only in knowledge and piety but also in prudence. Professors encouraged students to remember Proverbs 8:12: "I wisdom dwell with prudence." Prudence, discretion, and good sense were to guide a southern Presbyterian minister, for a lack of such virtues led to discord in the church and much trouble for the minister. One area for prudence regarded money and how a student spent money. Appearances mattered so a student could not keep a horse. "A horse cannot be kept," the board declared, "but at an expense which students of theology should not be willing to incur simply for their own comfort." Such an ethic of frugality was also extended to wealthy students—they were not allowed to keep a carriage which would also involve having a driver.[20]

An important part of this informal curriculum took place when students visited in faculty homes and ate with faculty families. Charles Jones, for example, wrote in 1849 that they had two students who took their meals with them and that "almost any evening some of the students drop in and take a cup of tea with us." In such a setting, faculty wives played an important role in the preparation of students for ministry. Sara Ann Howe, in particular, was greatly loved by students, who sometimes referred to her as "Mother Howe," and she possessed a fierce loyalty to what she called "our seminary." Most students who came to her table or who took afternoon tea with the family knew which fork to use, and they knew the tea-drinking etiquette of long established custom. Being a gentleman, as was often said, meant knowing how to act without being told how to act. Few would need to be reminded—as Professor Samuel Miller of Princeton reminded prospective ministers—that they were not to spit on floors and carpets, or cut their nails, or comb their hair, or pick their teeth in public. A college education, after all, had as one of its primary purposes the making of gentlemen and the internalization of a certain gentility.[21]

But "Mother Howe" and other faculty wives not only reinforced or taught such etiquette; they also counseled and gave advice about prudent behavior for ministers and on occasion, no doubt, about matters of the heart. The board forbade students connected with the seminary to "enter a marriage contract" and affectionately and solemnly cautioned them while in the seminary to "avoid becoming involved in matrimonial engagements." Still nothing prevented students from socializing with the young women in Columbia, which some did—if their diaries can be trusted—with regularity. And when graduation approached, the securing of a wife became a subject of intense interest. Francis Goulding fell madly in love, rules or no rules, with Mary Howard of Savannah. A classmate discretely wrote that Goulding thought her "not only the best girl in Savannah but in the world." They married immediately after his graduation. Some students even had the courage to court, no doubt with prudence, the daughters of their professors. Moultrie Reid married Thomas Goulding's daughter Margaret a few months after graduation. And Benjamin Morgan Palmer, the younger, married Howe's step-daughter Augusta, whom he had boldly courted while a student. Howe had tried to keep them apart, had told them not to see each other, but the strong-willed couple had simply found ways to ignore his admonitions and the seminary rules. They all perhaps felt what a young James Henley Thornwell confessed in his journal shortly after his marriage. Writing about his "inordinate affection," he admitted: "I have made resolution after resolution on this subject—but my strength is perfect weakness. My soul is chained down to sensual gratification."[22]

Whatever they might have felt, students and faculty were forming tight networks of interlocking white southern families that would shape the character of the seminary for generations. Sons and daughters, parents and grandparents, aunts and uncles, endless cousins and in-laws swirled around the seminary supporting it with their affection and financial contributions and thinking of it as "our seminary." Benjamin Morgan Palmer was only one among many such examples. Not only did he become Howe's son-in-law; he was also the nephew of Benjamin Morgan Palmer, the elder, who was a leader in Columbia's founding and president of its board. And the younger Palmer had four double first cousins who were students at Columbia during its first two decades, and each of them was related in complex ways with other Columbia faculty and students. These dense family networks were to become over time increasingly intricate and bewildering, and family dynamics were sometimes to play important roles in debates and divisions that occasionally struck the seminary. But such networks reinforced and made tighter a Columbia community of remarkable cohesion. Columbia faculty and graduates and their extended families shared a religious tradition and a social identity that asserted with confidence their place in American religious life and their prominent role in what they called "Our Southern Zion."[23]

The daily routines of seminary life consequently provided an informal curriculum for the preparation of students for ministry. But, of course, within those daily routines were classes and recitations, books to read, and exams to take. The board set the formal curriculum, and the faculty structured the classes, assigned the reading, and gave the lectures. During three years students were to study "Biblical literature, Christian theology, church history and polity, pastoral duties and sacred rhetoric." Such a course of study had first been developed at Andover and had been largely adopted by other seminaries as they were established in the years immediately preceding the founding of Columbia.[24]

The first year was devoted to the study of biblical literature. Because most students entered seminary with no knowledge of Hebrew, they immediately plunged into its grammar and vocabulary. Howe was the stern taskmaster in this, warning students that they must not force on "the truly oriental structure of the language" the "rules of occidental tongues," which students had been studying. He recommended a variety of Hebrew grammars but expected students to have and utilize a translation of the German scholar Heinrich Gesenius's grammar. Students, of course, were to own a Hebrew Bible and lexicon and were to work hard on pronouncing Hebrew distinctly by reading out loud to one another. After advancing in the language, students began translating portions of the Greek New Testament into Hebrew as a useful exercise in mastering Hebrew. This also allowed a student to review Greek grammar and to deepen his knowledge of the "whole syntactical construction of the language."[25]

While thus engaged in language studies, students began to enter the demanding world of interpretation. Here the primary text was August Ernesti's *Principles of New Testament Interpretation,* which had been translated from the German by Howe's old professor at Andover Moses Stuart. Ernesti emphasized that each biblical author must be understood according to an author's particular style and choice of literary genre. Theological assumptions were not to be imposed on a text—a scholar's task was to establish a text's grammatical meaning. Words of the same class or subject were to be compared, and the student was to seek the meaning of words at the time they were written. By studying the science of interpretation, first-year students prepared to begin exegesis—the careful interpretation of particular texts. Howe had students begin Old Testament exegesis with the "most striking and important parts of the Pentateuch." But he had students, toward the end of their first year, take up the Psalms in order to become acquainted with the poetry of the Hebrews. For those students who knew many of the Psalms by heart, the translation of say Psalm 1 or Psalm 23 must have come as a relief after translating less well known passages from Genesis or Deuteronomy.[26]

For New Testament exegesis, the first-year student was required to begin work in the Gospels using a harmony before turning to one of the epistles. In each of these areas of study, the student was expected to consult commentaries and a wide array of secondary sources. Howe noted in reviewing the first year curriculum that "the student has much to do. *Vita brevis est, ars longa.*"[27]

The second year was devoted primarily to systematic theology. Aaron Leland began by plunging students into the doctrine of the trinity, then the doctrine of eternal election, and on to subject after subject including the decrees of God, freedom of the will, the origin of moral evil, the atonement, regeneration, and the nature of holiness. Francis Turretin's *Institutio Theologiae Elencticae* was the text and it was a demanding one in Latin. Students had to follow Turretin's long, complex Latin sentences as he spelled out in scholastic fashion the rationality of faith and the ways reason could prove the truths of Christian doctrines. Students composed essays in Latin on theological topics and had long recitations in class. After Thornwell became professor of theology in 1856, Turretin was dropped and Calvin was adopted. And Thornwell's pedagogy was much more dynamic and even more demanding. Using a Socratic method, he pressed students with questions until a student "was driven back through all the steps of a rigorous analysis." Thornwell, wrote Palmer in admiration, wanted students to "think in the light of other men's thoughts," to "take the suggestions, and work them over in the laboratory of their own minds, to reproduce them again with the stamp of their own coinage, and to systematize them into form by a logic of their own."[28]

During their second year students also began their study of church history. While they utilized Johann L. Mosheim's monumental *Institutes of Ecclesiastical History* and later had to study Johann August Neander's *History of the Planting and Training of the Christian Church by the Apostles* and Merle D'Aubigne's *History of the Reformation of the Sixteenth Century,* church history played a rather minor part in their theological education. Theological students, Howe noted, did not have time to read much church history. It was assumed their collegiate study of "the history of nations, literature, and philosophy" was necessary preparation for theological education, but surprisingly there was at Columbia a resistance—that would last for generations—to the study of history in a serious way. Charles C. Jones served for a few years as professor of church history, but he was poorly prepared for the task—he confessed that it was only by the utmost exertion that he kept ahead of the students in their study. To be sure Howe wrote a *History of the Presbyterian Church in South Carolina* that ran to two fat volumes. But it was more a chronicle than a history, more a register of events without any attempt to provide an interpretation of the events. Perhaps this reluctance to engage history seriously was related to a fear of the Roman Catholic insistence that doctrine was shaped by tradition and not simply by biblical authority. And perhaps such a widespread Calvinist fear was intensified for southern Presbyterians by the possibility that key doctrines for white southern Presbyterians—especially the doctrine of the spirituality of the church—might be seen to be unduly shaped by a Southern context of slavery and racism.[29]

Third year students continued studies from the previous years. For Old Testament exegesis, they began to explore the world and message of Isaiah or Zechariah or one of the other prophets giving special attention to "messianic prophecies." For New Testament exegesis, they turned to the Apocalypse of John or to the Acts of the Apostles. They read the short Pastoral Epistles to Timothy and Titus "with a special regard to the various points of pastoral and practical Theology." And they took up topics in systematic theology that they had not studied during their second year. But the primary focus of the third year was pastoral theology. In this area the student was to apply what he had learned in previous years to the practices of ministry. While such practices could only be refined in the actual doing of ministry, certain theoretical principles and the experiences of others were to provide necessary foundations. Leland, as an experienced pastor, carried much of the responsibility for this area, although he was sometimes assisted by visiting pastors. Homiletics, or the theory and art of preaching, was a great concern, and students had to prepare sermons, preach them, and have them evaluated by the faculty. Public prayers, hymnology, and catechetics all demanded the attention of future ministers. And of course polity and practices of pastoral care—the care of souls it was called—were critical areas of study as graduation approached. Students read Richard Baxter's *Reformed Pastor* and George Herbert's *Country Parson* and sought to prepare themselves to comfort the sick and dying, to counsel and encourage the perplexed, and to admonish the wayward.[30]

To support the students in their studies and to provide resources for the faculty's scholarship, significant attention was given to the seminary's library. A small collection of just over a thousand volumes was gathered when the seminary moved to Columbia. By 1850 that had grown to 4,754 volumes, approximately the size as the library at the College of William and Mary and about five hundred volumes larger than Union Seminary in Virginia, but far behind Union in New York, which had seventeen thousand. But in 1856 Columbia purchased 11,520 volumes from Thomas Smyth, pastor of Second Presbyterian in Charleston. Smyth, who had both inherited wealth and married into the immensely wealthy Adger family of Charleston, had collected over twenty thousand volumes, which he housed on the third floor of his handsome Meeting Street mansion in Charleston. His was by far the largest private library in the South and was larger than the library of the College of New Jersey, Princeton.[31]

The Smyth library was particularly rich in books by English Puritans and about English Puritanism—there were forty works by members of the Westminster Assembly alone in addition to ten quarto volumes of their discourse. But there were others. The classics were of course well represented: Homer and Pindar, Sophocles and Euripides, Solon and Democritus, as well as the expected Plato and Aristotle, Plutarch and Cicero, Horace and Tacitus. The multivolume *Patrologia Latina* stood next to shelves of *Opera:* Augustini, Origenis, Chrysostomi, Tertulliani and other works of church fathers. For law there was Montesquieu and Blackstone; for science a host from Newton to Linnaeus to Lyell to Agassiz; for literature there was Dante, Shakespeare and Milton, Pope and Addison, Wordsworth, Coleridge, and Byron, Irving and Hawthorne. Among the historians were Mosheim and Neander, Carlyle and Macaulay, Bossuet and von Ranke. The philosophers included Locke and Hobbes and Hume, Pascal and Rousseau, and the Scots who advocated common sense—Thomas Reid, Dugald Stewart, and William Hamilton. On and on they went, thousands and thousands of volumes, and the result was that Columbia Seminary had in 1856 one of the finest theological libraries in the nation. With the impressive library at the South Carolina College and the large State Library, it made the city of Columbia "the richest place in the South" for books.[32]

Throughout the three years of seminary education faculty gave exams and read student essays. And when the seminary board met on the campus, time was set aside for the board to give oral exams, to hear from students what they were learning and how they were "improving in knowledge, prudence, and piety preparatory to the Gospel ministry." The student's presbytery, however, gave the final exam and made the final determination if the student was ready to be ordained for the Gospel ministry.[33]

In 1851 twelve students graduated from Columbia. All had entered with college degrees—one from the University of Glasgow, two from Princeton, three from Davidson, and two from Oglethorpe, and one each from the College of Charleston, South Carolina College, Oakland in Mississippi, and Jefferson (Washington and Jefferson) in Pennsylvania. Because Columbia was located within Charleston Presbytery, the presbytery examined several of the graduates as candidates for the ministry.[34]

Before they traveled to Charleston for the presbytery meeting, the candidates had to exegete and write a paper on an Old Testament Hebrew text and on a New Testament

Greek text. An essay in Latin on the theme "*An scriptura sit verbum Dei?*" was also required as was a theological paper on "the nature and necessity of repentance." These four papers were turned over to the presbytery when the candidates arrived in Charleston. When the presbytery gathered at the Second Presbyterian Church, it assigned responsibilities for the examination to its clergy members. The moderator began the examination by questioning the candidates regarding their "personal piety and reasons for seeking the ministry." Then Howe and Benjamin Morgan Palmer (now pastor of the church in Columbia) tested them to determine if they had sufficiently mastered the "Ancient Languages, including Hebrew." James Bulloch Dunwody, graduate of Yale and Columbia Seminary—and pastor of the affluent Stoney Creek Presbyterian Church in plantation country—probed their knowledge of "Natural Sciences, including Mathematics," astronomy, geography, and botany. Thornwell and John L. Girardeau, future professors of theology at Columbia, examined their competence in "Moral Sciences," which covered philosophy, rhetoric, and logic. Leland, Palmer, and John Adger asked about "Evidences of Christianity," while Leland and Thornwell tested them in "Christian Theology," and Smyth and Howe examined them on "The Sacraments." For "Church Government, History, and Pastoral Care," they had to face Thornwell, Smyth, and Palmer. Because the presbytery meeting lasted three days, there was ample time for the papers to be read and the examinations given.[35]

This ordination examination at the stately Second Presbyterian Church Charleston—and other examinations like it—was a carefully enacted ritual for entrance into the Presbyterian ministry. It revealed a disciplined elite guarding with great vigilance the gate into its membership. Those who passed through the gate entered a community of interest and tradition, a southern Presbyterian world that was declaring its self-understanding and that was asserting its legitimacy. These cultured young men revealed the kind of antebellum ministers Columbia Seminary was expected to send out into the church. They were to be a learned clergy—ministers who were representatives of an established order, who possessed a broadly based education, who had achieved a thorough grounding in the traditional disciples of theology, and who displayed an evangelical piety and moral rectitude. And they were also to be men who were bearers of civility and tradition, men who had internalized at some deep level dispositions marked by prudence and discretion. Obviously all Columbia graduates did not meet these expectations. Some were great disappointments to the church and sometimes sources of strife and scandal in the church. Some were great disappointments to themselves. Yet to a remarkable degree the graduates were the kind of men and ministers whom the founders and supporters of the seminary had envisioned for the Presbyterian Church in the antebellum South. Of all the southern clergy, wrote historians Elizabeth Fox-Genovese and Eugene D. Genovese, Presbyterian ministers "held pride of place as the best educated and most intellectually impressive of the denominational leaders. Their power and influence spread well beyond the number of their constituents in a society in which Presbyterians were heavily outnumbered by Methodists and Baptists." And among these Presbyterian ministers, none did more to shape the life and thought of southern society than those associated with Columbia Theological Seminary. During the generation preceding the Civil War, wrote Ernest Trice Thompson, the historian of southern Presbyterianism, those connected with Columbia were without question the most influential leader of southern Presbyterianism. As such they served a powerful ideological function—they supported an established order and a southern world where blacks were owned and whites were owners.[36]

4

"A golden era"

In the spring of 1850, Charles Colcock Jones was back on the Columbia faculty teaching ecclesiastical history and polity. He had returned to his old position in 1848, and he and his wife, Mary, had brought with them from their Georgia home their three children and four domestic slaves—Jack the butler, his wife Marcia the cook, and their two grandchildren: John who was seventeen and Jane who was ten. Jones had rented a large and comfortable home near the seminary. In the backyard there was a kitchen and a house for Jack and Marcia and their grandchildren.[1]

Jones found on his return to the seminary that the little city was "much improved." Columbia was bustling with cotton pouring in from the upcountry—trains were constantly coming and going on the newly constructed railroads, and those who studied on the seminary campus could hear the distant rumblings of engines and cars. In the midst of such economic activity, Jones also found a military culture permeating the city. He wrote a Georgia planter that South Carolina "is as military a state as any in the Union," and he noted that "the Mexican war and the gallant conduct of their Palmetto Regiment has made them more so." Parades and reviews were a regular part of Columbia's social life.[2]

The neatly laid-out city with its fine homes was inviting and seductive, especially in the spring, when color and fragrance blended and cast their spell of sensory delight. The trees planted along the streets years earlier had grown much since the Jones family had been at the seminary in the 1830s, and he thought they improved the appearance of the streets wonderfully. Many of the homes surrounding the seminary had beautiful gardens with azaleas and dogwoods, camellias and tea olives and a host of other flowers, both indigenous and imported. Particularly impressive were the gardens of the Hampton mansion, now the home of Hampton relatives, the Preston family. The Prestons invited their seminary neighbors to enjoy the gardens, which had welcomed, among other visitors, Daniel Webster, and would soon welcome Presidents Millard Fillmore and Franklin Pierce.[3]

Such was the context as the seminary entered the 1850s—a decade in which the seminary achieved strength and influence that would not be matched again for over a hundred years. But first there would be a crisis and no little despair among those who loved Columbia and called it "our seminary."

In the spring of 1850 two of the Jones children became sick with pneumonia. The oldest son soon recovered, but the pneumonia lingered with daughter Mary Sharpe. Then Jack and Marcia became ill with the disease. The doctor came and bled them, and they appeared to be improving, but they suddenly took a turn for the worse. Jones stayed day and night by the bedside of his old butler. "Almost every dose of medicine he took," Jones wrote his sister, "and every spoonful of nourishment he took from my hands." Mary Jones cared for Marcia with equal attention. When Jack's death seemed certain, they asked him the familiar questions addressed to the dying—"Is Christ precious to you?" "Do you put all your trust in him for salvation?" He responded that he was "in God's sight but a filthy rag," but "his hope was in Jesus" and that "his Saviour was shedding unnumbered mercies all around him." All the Jones family gathered around his bed together with Jack's grandchildren to say their farewells. "He took them one by one by the hand and charged them in the Lord and commended them to God." And to Mary Jones he said, knowing how she depended on him, "I am so sorry to leave you; I know how you will miss me." In this way Jack died. He had served the Jones family as their butler for forty years. And during part of that time, he had gotten to know Columbia Theological Seminary from the perspective of a slave, of one who had stood by the Jones dining-room table while seminary faculty and students talked about Christian faith and Christian duty and discussed what was happening in South Carolina and in the nation. And Charles Jones wrote his sister in Georgia that Jack's death was "the loss not only of one of the most faithful and excellent, long-tried servants, but of a devoted, long-tried and affectionate friend—to us and to all our family. Jack was one of the family." Such was the perspective and memory of one of the seminary's best known and most respected faculty members.[4]

On the evening of Jack's death, the Jones family sat in their parlor around the fireplace. They had secured someone to sit up with Marcia during the night, and plans had been made for Jack's funeral the next day. He lay in the house in the backyard wearing in death "that smile of life" that was "so natural and constant with him." The family stayed up late talking and grieving together. They banked the fire and all went to bed. About half past one in the morning there was a cry, "Fire! Fire!" The house was full of smoke, and the family barely managed to escape. Some young men rushed to the servants' quarters where Jack lay in his coffin and "bore him out of the servants' house and carried him across the street and laid him down on the sidewalk." Others took up the dying Marcia and put her, cot and all, through the window farthest from the fire; and she was covered with blankets and carried over to a neighbor's house. The fire did its work, and the house was soon nothing but smoldering ashes. All of Jones's papers and lectures were destroyed. Rats had evidently loosened the mortar around the chimney in the parlor providing the source of the fire.[5]

A few days later Marcia died, and they buried her beside Jack in Columbia's "Negro Cemetery." In contrast to the deep anonymity of most slave graves, Charles Jones wanted Jack and Marcia remembered in stone. He had a tombstone cut and engraved and placed over their final resting place:

John Anderson Jones
A Servant of God
A. 60
And Marcia his Wife
A. 55
Of Liberty County, Ga.
Died
April 17th and 20th 1850
Our Kind and Faithful
Friends
John 6:39–40[6]

The destruction of the Jones home and the death of Jack and Marcia in such a dramatic fashion became one of those long-remembered events in the seminary's life. But it also helped to precipitate a crisis for the seminary. Charles Jones was distraught by the loss of his lectures and especially by the loss of many of the papers related to his years of work among the slaves of the Georgia coast. And Jack and Marcia had been such central figures in the Jones home, managing in many ways the daily routines of life, that their deaths seemed a great shaking of the foundations for the Jones family. So three weeks later when Jones received a letter saying he had been elected the executive of the Presbyterian Board of Domestic Missions in Philadelphia, he accepted.[7]

With Jones's departure the seminary was left with only Howe and Leland as professors. After some negotiations the synods called in 1851 Alexander T. McGill to take Jones's place as professor of ecclesiastical history and polity. McGill, a Pennsylvanian, found Columbia a delightful place, but he stayed for only a year before returning to Pennsylvania and accepting two years later a position at Princeton Seminary. To make matters worse, students and supporters of the seminary were increasingly unhappy with Leland as professor of theology. He was sixty-five when McGill left Columbia, and while Leland remained a powerful preacher and a disciplined scholar, his scholarship lacked the depth and breadth needed for the seminary to thrive. Thornwell later described the situation of the seminary in 1853: "Things had reached a crisis, and something vigorous was to be done, or the Seminary virtually abandoned. It was ascertained that, if things remained another year as they were, the next session would, in all likelihood, open with the merest handful of students, not more than six or eight." In this context supporters of the seminary began an intense effort to strength the faculty, increase the endowment, and enlarge the campus.[8]

After much arm twisting, Benjamin Morgan Palmer was persuaded to leave the pulpit of the Presbyterian church in Columbia and take Jones's old position on the faculty. Palmer had grown up in Walterboro, South Carolina, a lowcountry village originally established for planters to escape the miasmas that arose from fetid rice fields in summer and early fall. Palmer's father, Edward, served as pastor of the Presbyterian church in Walterboro and on alternating Sundays he rode out into the country to the Stoney Creek church, where rich planters gathered with large numbers of slaves to worship. Young Benjamin, as he was growing up, had seen black slaves all around him—they constituted three-quarters of the county population. He saw whites giving orders to blacks, and he absorbed at some deep level of his being white assumptions about the inferiority of blacks. And no doubt on occasion he saw, even in his little village, the sale of black men, women, and children before the county courthouse. His father Edward gave special attention to the "religious instruction of slaves." In 1845 he reported that he had two meeting places where slaves gathered "which together," he wrote, "place under my spiritual charge some 600." Such a village, surrounded by large rice and cotton plantations, shaped the earliest contours of young Benjamin's life and horizons. Here amid such a physical and social landscape, place and personality mingled, and his dispositions and long-lasting commitments began to emerge.[9]

But a larger world also had its part to play in shaping the character of the future seminary professor. He had spent two years as a young boy in Andover, Massachusetts, while his father was in seminary there. And there had been trips to Charleston, where Edward Palmer's brother, Benjamin Morgan Palmer, the elder, was pastor of the Circular Congregational Church and was the most influential minister in the city. He apparently had a strong influence on his nephew and namesake.

When the younger Benjamin was fourteen, he left his village home, traveled alone to Charleston, took a ship to New York, and then went overland to the scenic Pioneer Valley of Western Massachusetts. There he entered Amherst College and soon became friends with a number of New Englanders, including Henry Ward Beecher. He was said to be at the top of his class when, during his second year, he was expelled for refusing to divulge the secrets of a literary society. The faculty had quickly regretted its decision and tried to get him to remain, but the young Palmer felt deeply offended, rejected the faculty's entreaties, and returned to South Carolina. He graduated with first honors from the University of Georgia in 1838 and entered Columbia seminary. When he married Howe's stepdaughter, Augusta McConnell, he became with her the owner of two slaves who were her personal servants—eighteen-year-old Caroline and fifteen-year-old Maria. After two years as pastor of Savannah's First Presbyterian Church, Palmer accepted a call to Columbia's First Presbyterian Church, a position he kept until his call to the seminary in 1854.[10]

When the synods of South Carolina and Georgia called Palmer to teach church history and polity, they also called James Henley Thornwell to teach theology—he was clearly the lynchpin in the ambitious plan to strengthen the seminary. For years Thornwell had been closely associated with the seminary, but he had refused to leave his position as president of the South Carolina College and join the faculty unless the church history position was filled with a strong person. So when Palmer accepted the church history position, Thornwell said "yes" to the synods' call and prepared to move down the street from the college to the seminary. In the meantime Leland had agreed to move from theology to the position of sacred rhetoric and pastoral theology, where he would teach homiletics and pastoral care. So in this way Thornwell became the new professor of didactic and polemical theology. The title of his new position fit perfectly his disposition and commitments.[11]

Thornwell had been born in 1812 in the Marlboro District of South Carolina, a region whose loamy soil was beginning to produce—through the labor of slaves—great wealth for white planters. Thornwell's father was a plantation overseer, and when he died in 1820 the family found itself in great distress. By then, however, young Thornwell's fame as a prodigy was already beginning to be known in the district, and two neighbors became his sponsors and assumed financial responsibility for his education. After attending a local academy, he entered South Carolina College as a junior. A brilliant student he quickly demonstrated an amazing capacity and consuming passion for study. He loved the late-night hours and often stayed up until dawn as he explored the world of Greek and Roman classics, or as he probed throughout the night the logic of a Scottish philosopher who was insisting on a commonsense way of knowing, or as he wrestled with a German heavyweight—Kant or Schelling or Hegel—who was leading him night by night through the labyrinth of German idealism. Graduating at the top of his class in 1831, he was ready to take on the world if he could only discover what he was going to do with his life.[12] One thing, however, seemed sure: whatever vocational path beckoned, it would not do so because of some commanding appearance. The young scholar was far from some southern Adonis—very far! He was a short and very thin young man, and his dark black hair fell around his head while thick sideburns ran down to his jaw and framed freckles on a pale face. Yet he made friends easily—despite his seriousness and his long hours of intense study—and he had a contagious sense of humor that he could readily turn against himself. The year after he graduated from college, when he had taken a temporary teaching position in the village of Sumter, he wrote a friend: "I find myself most sadly puzzled about selecting a profession; and if I can get along without one, I will never study one. If I had anything of an ordinary human shape and size, I might marry into wealth enough to support me; but as it is, if I should happen to have a son, it would be a hard matter to distinguish the sire from his issue. Fancy to yourself what a figure I would cut with a wife, especially if she were fat and portly."[13]

Whatever figure Thornwell might cut with a wife of any size or shape, both his vocational decision and his religious conversion apparently mingled, in the complexity of the human heart, with his quest for a wife—at least that was what his good friend J. Marion Sims thought. (Sims was later famous as the "father of modern gynecology.") In a letter in 1832, Thornwell admitted, "We enter into matrimony, not for the good of society—not to perform those high and sacred duties which we owe to our God, but for the sensual gratification which we hope to receive from roseate virginity." Sims recalled in later years that Thornwell fell in love with a friend's beautiful sister who was "a rigid member of the Presbyterian Church." She told him that if he studied the Westminster Confession of Faith, he would find truth in its pages. With such charming encouragement, he eagerly turned to the confession and to his own surprise was converted. "My own [conversion] experience," he later confessed, "was the most mysterious thing I know of." And while sometime in the future he doubted if Christ was his personal savior, he said he never again doubted the truth that "God is in Christ, reconciling the world unto Himself."[14]

The conversion, however, did not win the young woman's heart for as a wry commentator later noted, "He had disadvantages as a suitor. He was, to be sure, brilliant and obliging, but also scrawny and poor, so she turned him down, despite his holding the Westminster Confession in hand." Whatever the reasons for his reading of the confession, his conversion had a profound impact on his life. He now had the faith of a convert. He never had "ease or smiling Episcopalian comfort, but rather was drawn to what marked Calvinism, anxiety and the iron will. Mind had to be satisfied, before faith could be licensed." At least that is what many later commentators have thought they saw when they have looked at Thornwell's life. But perhaps Thornwell's memory of his love of a young woman lingered and helped to shape some surprising aspects of the later man. Perhaps—only perhaps—his reading of the confession while in love with her shaped a theology that was not as cold and logical as has often been portrayed. He later wrote that religion is "a state of heart which holds *knowledge* and *affection* in solution, not successively, but in unity. If you take away affection, you have only *dogmatism;* if you take away knowledge, you have a mere *spiritualism,* a mere fancy, an *idolatry.*" And he wrote that "the form of Christian knowledge is love; it is a higher energy than bare speculation; it blends into indissoluble unity, intelligence, and emotion; knows by loving, and loves by knowing. The mind sees not only the reality of truth, but its beauty and glory."[15]

Thornwell's conversion led to his vocational decision—he would become a Presbyterian minister. He entered Andover Theological Seminary in the summer of 1834 with the expectation of studying "Syriac, Chaldee, and Arabic" but found on his arrival in Massachusetts that the professor who taught those subjects had left Andover. He transferred to Harvard and took up German and Hebrew while living among Unitarian students in the divinity school. But New England weather, manners, and theology did not appeal to him. "The peculiarity of their belief," he said of his Unitarian classmates, "consists in *not believing.* . . . Ask them to tell you what they *do* believe, and they will begin to recount certain doctrines of the Orthodox, and tell you very politely that they do *not* believe these." So when his physician told him he could not survive a New England winter, he packed his bags and returned to South Carolina.[16]

Shortly after his return home, Thornwell presented himself for ordination. Despite his not having a seminary education, the presbytery was deeply impressed by his learning and piety. Thomas Goulding, who was then on the Columbia faculty, declared: "Brethren, I feel like sitting at this young man's feet, as a learner." A call soon followed—it was not what he had hoped for, but rather a call to a new congregation in the little village of Lancaster. He had hoped for something grander, some pulpit where his learning could be more fully displayed and appreciated. He struggled with his ambition, recognized it as a great temptation, accepted the call, and with no little anxiety entered the work of a pastor. Because of his learning, people feared his preaching would be dry as dust, but he surprised them by preaching with power and conviction and with deep empathy with the people, and soon the church was overflowing.[17]

One of his parishioners, Nancy Witherspoon, caught his special attention. The daughter of Colonel James H. Witherspoon, she was tall with a large frame, attractive but better known for the strength of her character and her kind and loving ways. Her family was deeply entwined with some of the wealthiest families in the state and was related to the Reverend John Witherspoon, early president of Princeton and signer of the Declaration of Independence. Thornwell had been a college classmate of two of her brothers, and the family knew his reputation for brilliance. Colonel Witherspoon, who had served as the state's lieutenant governor, was a prudent man, and consequently he was at first less than enthusiastic about the romantic relationship that was beginning to develop between his daughter and their young minister with his pale complexion, skinny frame, and $600 a year salary. But his prudence may also have led him to realize that Nancy was twenty-eight and that the twenty-three-year-old Thornwell was her best chance for a respectable husband. Whatever ruminations passed through the colonel's head and heart as he thought about his daughter's future, he soon came to believe Thornwell a remarkable young man. He was, the colonel declared, the intellectual equal of John C. Calhoun—the highest encomium he could bestow on Thornwell. So the father gave his permission for his daughter to marry the young minister, and he provided a dowry that included eight slaves and a fine upcountry farm, and he made arrangements in his will for other slaves to go to his daughter and her husband on his death. When the census was taken in 1860, Thornwell was the owner of thirty-two slaves ages one to seventy-five. They had been inherited by Nancy or were the natural increase of those inherited. They lived at Dryburg Abbey, the former farm that had become an upcountry plantation.[18]

In 1837 Thornwell was elected professor of belle letters and logic at the South Carolina College. Thornwell and belle letters, however, did not sit easily together. Logic was one thing, aesthetics something else. The young scholar had little interest in theories of taste or the fine arts, so after two years he resigned to accept a call to the First Presbyterian Church in Columbia. But a year later, when Stephen Elliott resigned as chaplain of the college and professor of sacred literature and the evidences of Christianity to become the first Episcopal bishop of Georgia, Thornwell returned to the college and took his friend's old position. During the next ten years, he became hugely popular among students as his fame grew as a scholar and churchman. He resigned in 1850 to take a church in Charleston, but the next year he was back as president. He introduced written examinations—replacing oral ones in use since the college's founding—and fought successfully to maintain a classical curriculum when some were calling for a more utilitarian approach. While others, he wrote, "are veering to the popular pressure and introducing changes and innovations which are destructive of the very nature of liberal education—let it be our glory to abide by the old landmarks—improving where improvement is desirable—but substituting nothing. Let it be our aim to make Scholars and not sappers or miners—apothecaries—doctors or farmers." He raised entrance requirements to the highest level during the antebellum period and oversaw major improvements in the campus, and perhaps most important he wrote a long and celebrated letter to Governor Manning in defense of public education. After he resigned to join the faculty at the seminary, he served on the college's board of trustees. The historian of the college and later university wrote that from Thornwell's appointment in 1837 until his death in 1862 he was "perhaps the most important person connected with the institution."[19]

Thornwell was also making his mark as a church leader. In 1847, when he was only thirty-five, he was elected moderator of the Old School General Assembly, the youngest man to ever hold such a position in American Presbyterianism. He engaged Charles Hodge and his colleagues at Princeton Seminary in a heated battle over church government, especially over the question of General Assembly boards. The Princetonians said that since the scriptures did not expressly forbid boards, the church was free to employ them. Thornwell insisted that the boards must be "*sanctioned, positively sanctioned*" by the scriptures or "they are null and void." It was a position, Eugene Genovese has pointed out, not unlike Calhoun's assertion that the government may not take action unless expressly directed to do so by the Constitution. Political theory and ecclesiology were clearly intertwined in Thornwell's thought. For Thornwell the boards also represented a centralization of power in the hands of the few, when church courts themselves needed to be their own agencies. Fearing concentrations of power, he also insisted on parity between presbyters. He argued that lay elders had to be present for any meeting of a church court while Hodge and his northern supporters said church courts could meet with only the clergy present. In all this Thornwell reflected a deep southern hostility to distant, centralized, bureaucracies. And ironically he also demonstrated a kind of southern egalitarianism among white men of a certain class. Lay elders, "ruling elders," were to have equal power with the clergy in church courts. It was consequently no wonder that Thornwell came to be known as "the Calhoun of the Church." Certainly by the end of the twentieth century, no one associated with Columbia—except for Woodrow Wilson—had matched Thornwell's influence within America culture.[20]

When Thornwell accepted the call to the seminary, the trustees of the college insisted he stay until the end of his term. During the interim Palmer accepted a call to the First Presbyterian Church in New Orleans. He was the most deeply read and one of the most brilliant of Columbia graduates, but he hated teaching. After two years on the faculty, he wrote his friend John Adger: "Academic life does not suit me, as I have neither the taste nor the learning for it, and as a professor I am only a wretched sham." He was convinced of the importance of teaching church history, but he said "I am too old to begin at the beginning of an Encyclopedic Department, and go through all the drudgery of microscopic investigation, to be fit for an office which I must vacate by death as soon as the qualifications for it have been attained." And so when he received a call in 1856 to become the pastor of the First Presbyterian Church of New Orleans, he accepted. But before he left, he helped convince his friend John Adger to accept the church history position at Columbia rather than a call to be president of Davidson College in North Carolina.[21]

John Adger had been born in Charleston in 1810, the son of James and Sarah Elizabeth Adger. In 1818 his father had become the Charleston agent for the Baltimore banking and mercantile house of Brown Brothers, who were in the process of capturing a significant share of the global cotton trade. Through this connection and his own enterprise, James Adger had gained great wealth and was ranked at one time the fourth-richest man in the United States. John Adger had graduated from Union College in New York in 1828 and from Princeton Theological Seminary in 1833. From 1834 to 1847 he and his wife, Elizabeth, had been missionaries in Constantinople and Smyrna among the Armenians.[22]

After intensive language study with several Armenian scholars, his work had focused on translation: "I was," he later wrote, "very confined to my desk, revising the work of my translators, and reading proof sheets, as they came from the printing office." Working with Armenian colleagues, he translated the New Testament into modern Armenian (an ancient translation, done in a.d. 410–31, was largely unreadable for modern Armenians). He also translated the Psalms, the Westminster Shorter Catechism, and interestingly Charles Colcock Jones's catechism for the religious instruction of slaves, including—for the slave-holding world of Turkey—questions and answers about the duties of masters and slaves.[23]

Adger's years in Turkey were not easy ones for him and Elizabeth. Three of their children died as did Elizabeth's sister visiting from Charleston. And Elizabeth and John were themselves deathly ill on several occasions—he barely survived a terrible ordeal with small pox. But they came to have genuine affection for the people among whom they lived, and they grew to love the countryside around Smyrna.[24]

In the spring of 1844, the Adgers went with four other Americans to Jerusalem. They sailed to Beirut and from there traveled several weeks by horseback across a landscape and through villages they had known only in their imaginations—Bethsaida and Capernaum, Tiberius and Cana of Galilee, Nazareth and Samaria. In Jerusalem they visited the Valley of Kidron and the Mount of Olives and watched Catholics and Orthodox fighting at holy places until broken up by the whips of Turkish guards. They hired Turkish soldiers to accompany them to the Dead Sea and the barren lands around it, and they went to Jericho, where the walls had once come tumbling down. They found it all deeply moving despite what they regarded as the superstition and idolatry surrounding shrines with their relics. And while they dismissed the veneration of sacred places such as "the so-called tomb of Christ," they knew they were seeing the land where patriarchs and judges, kings and prophets had once lived and where the "Saviour walked." They returned to Beirut by horseback, this time camping out along the way and enjoying the beauty of spring in places made familiar by years of daily Bible reading.[25]

This trip to Jerusalem, along with their travels in Turkey and in Europe—to Marseilles and Avignon, to Lyon and Paris, London and Liverpool, Dublin and Belfast—all left a deep impression on the future seminary professor. Despite deep memories of a South Carolina boyhood that shaped much of his character, Adger's wide travel and serious engagement with another culture left him with a more cosmopolitan outlook than many of his later colleagues at the seminary—especially younger more provincial colleagues who joined the faculty after the Civil War.

While they were in Turkey, the Adgers learned that Elizabeth had inherited eight slaves. John owned no slaves himself—although he had grown up in a slave-owning family—but with his wife's inheritance he suddenly found himself a slave owner. He immediately wrote to Elizabeth's family in Charleston saying that he and Elizabeth renounced "all right or title to any property in these slaves." But on their return to Charleston after having been away for many years, they found that the mission board that had sponsored them—the American Board of Commissioners for Foreign Mission located in Boston—was being greatly troubled by the slavery issue. At the same time, Adger saw a great need in Charleston for mission work among the large slave population of the city. He therefore resigned from the board and proposed a new work as a missionary pastor among the blacks of the city. Adger labored for five years as a missionary in Charleston until ill health forced him to give up the work. He bought Woodburn, Charles Cotseworth Pinckney's fine upcountry estate near the village of Pendleton. There among rolling hills and hardwood forests, Adger oversaw the expansion of the house and farm, slowly regained his health, and was ready to accept the call to Columbia in 1856. He quickly became a much-loved professor. Thornwell called him "one of the truest men I know; a man after God's own heart" and said of him that he was "a noble Roman, or rather an Israelite in whom there is no guile."[26]

Before Palmer left for New Orleans, he and Adger set out to raise $40,000 for the seminary's endowment—the amount needed to provide for Thornwell's salary. They went first to Georgia—to Augusta, Savannah, and Athens—and raised $4,672. They went to Alabama, where Palmer talked to leading citizens in Montgomery and Adger visited planters and merchants in Selma. They raised $5,264 from these and other Alabama Presbyterians. They headed for New Orleans, and there they raised $2,865. Finally they returned to South Carolina and raised $5,448 in the upcountry, $17,783 in Charleston, and $4,000 from wealthy planters on Johns Island and Edisto Island. They took two months to make the trip, but they returned to Columbia with the needed funds. Such success encouraged others to give, and in 1860 the endowment reached $260,000—enough, it seemed, to ensure the future prosperity of the seminary.[27]

The largest single gift to come to the seminary during the 1850s—and it would be the largest for several generations—was $50,000 given in 1859 by Judge John Perkins of Mississippi. Two years earlier the judge had given his son his vast Louisiana holdings that he had consolidated into the Hapaka and Somerset plantations valued at over $600,000. Given at the same time were 250 slaves to work the rich lands bordering the Mississippi River. The judge then purchased the Oaks plantation near Columbus, Mississippi, and there he became a friend of the Reverend James A. Lyon. With Lyon's encouragement the judge gave the seminary $40,000 for the Perkins Professor of Natural Science in Connection with Revelation. And he gave another $10,000 to the seminary to support "disabled ministers of the gospel and their widows and children." These large gifts came the same year Charles Darwin published his *On the Origin of Species by Means of Natural Selection.* Thornwell, Adger, Palmer, and Smyth all thought the new professorship a wonderful position for a theological seminary. Others were not so sure—especially Robert Lewis Dabney at Union Seminary in Virginia. But twenty difficult years would pass before the most serious battle in Columbia's history would begin to be waged over the Perkins Professorship.[28]

While the supporters of the seminary were making these moves to strengthen its faculty and raise its endowment, they were also busy making sure that the seminary had an adequate campus to meet their vision of its mission. Two handsome brick dormitories were erected, one on each side of the Ainsley Hall mansion. The first, Simons Hall, was named for Mrs. Eliza Lucilla Simons of Charleston, who had left a substantial bequest to the seminary. The second, Law Hall, was named for William Law and his wife, Agnes. He had served for many years as a member of the board and as the seminary's treasurer. On his death she made a generous contribution that allowed the construction of the dormitory that bore their name. About the same time, a wealthy planter in the upcountry, John Bull of the Abbeville District, left a bequest to the seminary. Part of it went into the endowment, and part went to convert the carriage house on the property into a chapel. And the house that had originally been built by Ainsley Hall for domestic slaves was then enlarged and made into a steward's hall or refectory. In this way space was available on the upper floor of the mansion for the newly acquired Smyth library with all its valuable volumes.[29]

As the faculty and endowment grew in strength, as new buildings were added to the campus and the library expanded, the student enrollment grew—in 1860 it stood at sixty-nine. The great majority of them, as expected, were southerners, but they had as classmates four students from Pennsylvania, two from Massachusetts, two from Missouri, and two from New York in addition to one from Connecticut and one from Ireland. They were graduates of southern colleges and universities and from Princeton, Yale, and Harvard; from Union College in New York; from Hanover in Indiana; from Jefferson and Washington Colleges in Pennsylvania; and Westminster College in Missouri. During the previous thirty years, 350 graduates had entered the ministry. Except for a few Baptists and Congregationalists, all were Presbyterians.[30]

The two most influential graduates of the seminary were Palmer and John Leighton Wilson. By the mid-1850s their reputations added significantly to Columbia's growing strength. Palmer was an acknowledged "prince of the pulpit," but he was much more than a famous and eloquent preacher. He was a serious pastor theologian who, along with his mentor Thornwell, was engaging the deep currents of nineteenth-century theology. He lamented what he saw as a "deeply seated prejudice" in many parts of the church "against the systematic exposition of the doctrines of the Bible." In the face of popular evangelicalism that emphasized experience and a nineteenth-century Romanticism that sought truth in instinct and imagination, Palmer insisted on the importance of doctrine. He believed that doctrines were behind experience and that ideas were beneath instinct and imagination. A person first had, for example, some understanding, some doctrine of God and of sin, before he or she had a conversion experience. Such doctrines and ideas, Palmer insisted, needed to be acknowledged and systematized, and it was the pastor's duty to teach orthodox doctrines to congregants so that their experiences and imaginations would flow from a correct understanding of God's grace and purposes for a lost and wayward humanity. Perhaps ironically, however, during the coming years Palmer's fame would rest more on his advocacy of southern nationalism in state and church despite his advocacy of the doctrine of the spirituality of the church.[31]

John Leighton Wilson and his wife, Jane Bayard Wilson, were the most influential American missionaries to West Africa during the antebellum years. Their affluent—and for her aristocratic—backgrounds added to their fame as did their freeing of their slaves in the 1830s. At Cape Palmas in Liberia and later in Gabon, Jane Wilson established flourishing schools among first the Grebo and then the Mpongwe. In reports published in both U.S. and British papers, the Wilsons told of bright African students who were as fully capable of mastering languages and other subjects as students anywhere in the world. In this and other ways they challenged demeaning white stereotypes of Africans especially in the face of a rising scientific racism. Leighton Wilson was himself a brilliant linguist. He produced the first dictionary and grammar of both the Grebo and Mpongwe languages, translated portions of the Bible into each language, and played an important role in the identification of a great language family—Bantu—that stretches across southern Africa.

The Wilsons fought the international slave trade with widely published articles and tracts, resisted the imperialism of both the Americans and the French in West Africa, and brought to the United States an astonishing skeleton of a huge ape never before known in the West—the gorilla. In 1856 Leighton Wilson's *Western Africa* was published to much acclaim. In it he demonstrated the great diversity of African peoples and the richness of many African cultures. It remains in the twenty-first century an important resource for historians and anthropologists of West Africa. Because of ill health the Wilsons returned to the United States in 1852 after seventeen years in West Africa, and in 1856 they were living in New York, where he was secretary for the Presbyterian board of foreign missions.[32]

The growing influence of the seminary was also greatly enhanced by the *Southern Presbyterian Review*, published by an "association of ministers" who were part of a tight circle of ministers closely connected to the seminary—Howe and Leland, Adger and Smyth, Palmer and Thornwell. During the 1850s the journal became the most high-powered religious journal in the Old South and one of the most influential in the nation. Because the editors believed theology was the "comprehension of all knowledge and makes every department of human thought tributary to it," the journal carried a wide range of articles on many subjects. The future Confederate lieutenant general D. H. Hill and brother-in-law of Stonewall Jackson wrote under the title "Religion and Mathematics"; James McFadden Gaston, surgeon and physician, wrote "Action and Reaction of Mind and Body, as Affecting Insanity," and "The Influence of Stimulants on Manifestation of Mind"; and Professor Daniel Kirkwood of Indiana University wrote "The Telluric Portion of the Cosmos." Joseph LeConte, the famous geologist and a future founder with John Muir of the Sierra Club and a member of Columbia's board, wrote numerous articles for the journal—"Morphology, and Its Connection with Fine Art," "The Relation of Organic Science to Sociology," "The School, the College, and the University, in Relation to One Another and to Active Life," and "Female Education."[33]

Contemporary political issues also had their place in the journal's pages. Adger and Wilson each blasted proposals before the South Carolina legislature to reopen the international slave trade. Adger showed the insanity of a proposal that would allow slave ships to once again arrive in Charleston Harbor after having been illegal since 1808, while Wilson insisted that the "South cannot countenance the revival of this traffic without dishonoring herself, and inflicting renewed and incalculable misery and wretchedness upon the inhabitants of Africa." Howe wrote an ominous piece titled "The Raid of John Brown and the Progress of Abolition," and in the April 1861 issue Palmer wrote "A Vindication of Secession and the South."[34]

Such articles seemed to the editors of the review to be just the kind of articles needed for serious theologians and pastors and for a well-informed Christian laity. But, of course, theology itself was the central subject for the journal, and around this "Queen of the Sciences" the journal focused its attention during the 1850s. From Iowa came an article by Samuel Baird titled "Edwards and the Theology of New England." From Maine came "Objections to the German Transcendental Philosophy," by Enoch Pond, professor of theology at Bangor Theological Seminary. Palmer wrote "Baconianism and the Bible"; Smyth wrote "Testimony of the Early Fathers to the Doctrine of the Trinity" and "The

Province of Reason, Especially in Matters of Religion." But Thornwell was the star that shone brightest in the journal's pages.[35]

Thornwell's erudition astonished his contemporaries. George Bancroft, the Harvard historian, called Thornwell "the most learned of the learned." Thornwell's many articles in the *Southern Presbyterian Review* revealed the depth and breadth of his learning. He wrote, for example, two long essays on John Morell's *Historical and Critical View of the Speculative Philosophy of Europe in the Nineteenth Century* in which he demonstrated the range of his reading in contemporary German philosophy and theology and his own strongly argued refusal to make a distinction between reason and understanding. Indeed a review of the indexes of the four volumes of his *Collected Writing,* which includes many articles from the journal, reveals an impressive range of thinkers whom he engaged in his writing—Victor Cousin and Descartes, William Hamilton and Kant, Locke and J. S. Mill, William Paley and Dugald Steward, and then Fichte, Schelling, and Schleiermacher.[36]

With its distinguished faculty, its expanding campus, its growing endowment and student body, and its high-powered journal, the seminary reached during the 1850s a position of strength that would seem to later generation a golden era. Yet beneath its strength and its spreading influence, intertwined in every aspect of the seminary's life, were the harsh realities of slavery. These seemingly intractable national and international realities increasingly consumed the seminary's strength, and the faculty with increasing urgency poured out its strength in support of an impossible cause. The tone of that support and its ideological thrust can be best seen in the work of Adger and Thornwell in the years immediately before they joined the faculty.

When John Adger returned to Charleston from Turkey, he became convinced that there was a need for some special work among the slaves and free blacks in the city. With the promise of financial support from his brothers and his father, he envisioned the establishment of a separate congregation specifically for the city's large black population. He would be their pastor, a missionary among them, and a small group of whites from Second Presbyterian would belong as elders. While this seemed to him eminently reasonable, it was a radical proposal for Charleston—since the attempted slave revolt by Denmark Vesey in 1822, no separate black church had been allowed in the city. Blacks did belong in large numbers to the white-dominated churches in the city, but Adger insisted that more needed to be done and that blacks needed a church whose primary focus was their spiritual needs. In May 1847 Adger presented his plan to the congregation of Second Church. Francis H. Elmore, soon to take John C. Calhoun's seat in the U.S. Senate, presided. Adger preached on the text "The poor have the gospel preached unto them." And who, he asked, are the poor of Charleston? They are easily distinguishable he answered:

> They are a class separated from ourselves by their color, their position in society, their relation to our families, their national origin, and their moral, intellectual, and physical condition. Nowhere are the poor so closely and intimately connected with the higher classes as are our poor with us. They belong to us. We also belong to them. They are divided out among us and mingled up with us, and we with them, in

a thousand ways. They live with us, eating from the same storehouse, drinking from the same fountains, dwelling in the same enclosures, forming parts of the same families. Our mothers confide us, when infants, to their arms, and sometimes to the very milk of their breasts. Their children are, to some extent, unavoidably the playmates of our childhood—grow up with us under the same roof—sometimes pass through all the changes of life with us, and then, either they stand weeping by our bedsides, or else we drop a tributary tear by theirs, when death comes to close the long connection and to separate the good master and his good servant.

Such, my friends, are those whom we consider the poor of this city. There they are—behold them. See them all around you, in these streets, in all these dwellings; a race distinct from us, yet closely united to us, brought in God's mysterious providence from a foreign land, and placed under our care, and made members of our households. They fill the humblest places of our state of society; they serve us; they give us their strength, yet they are not more truly ours than we are truly theirs. They are our poor—our poor brethren; children of our God and Father; dear to our Savior; to the like of whom he preached; for the like of whom he died, and to the least of whom every act of Christian compassion and kindness which we show he will consider as shown also to himself.[37]

While Adger's sermon was preached before he joined the Columbia faculty, the sermon revealed in its clarity and eloquence a paternalistic ideal that embraced the seminary's social and cultural imagination—a paternalistic ideal that was to shape with amazing tenacity the deep contours of Columbia's life for generations to come. The sermon painted in memorable phrases and broad strokes a picture of the world as envisioned by whites associated with the seminary, and it revealed with great transparency their understanding of themselves and their relationship to the black people of the South. What Adger was proposing was a middle way as a path to the future. On the one hand, no question was raised about the system of slavery: it was accepted as a given, as a legitimate way of ordering human life and human relationships. On the other hand, whites had a special responsibility to "our poor brethren," the blacks of the South, to whom they were to show the compassion and kindness they owed their Lord.[38]

Not all whites in Charleston, however, were happy about such paternalism and such a middle way as Adger proposed. An angry mob threatened the construction of a church building, and later the activities of the church would provoke angry cries that it be closed. It took a committee of "influential citizens, jealous for the honor of their city," to ease the tension and to allow the construction of the Anson Street Presbyterian Church and Calvary Episcopal Church too, a similar effort by the Episcopal minister Paul Trapier.[39]

Alongside fears that a "black church" would be a seedbed for black resistance was a rising scientific racism that was insisting that blacks were less than fully human and were unable to appropriate Christian faith or Western civilization except in a kind of rude imitation of whites. In 1847 Louis Agassiz, the distinguished Swiss naturalist and professor at Harvard, had delivered an address before the Charleston Literary and Philosophic Society in which he argued for the dual origin of the races. Because the black and white races were so different, said the Harvard professor, they must have had separate origins since in nature one type always remains the same. Agassiz's position was enthusiastically endorsed by many—it seemed to verify scientifically the claim that the Negro was naturally inferior to the Caucasian. Not only the history of the African race but also the composition of the African's body, so the argument went, explained the reason for the inferior status of blacks as slaves. Such an extreme racism, with all its bitter consequences, presented a profound challenge to the Christian confession that all people have a common origin in the First Adam and all people are called to trust as their savior Jesus Christ, the Second Adam.[40]

Those associated with Columbia responded vigorously to the claims of a dual origin of the races and to what they regarded as its extremism. Leighton Wilson spent years challenging the view that preaching the Gospel to Africans was a waste of time because Africans were said to be incapable of understanding and receiving the Christian Gospel. In letters from West Africa, in scholarly articles, and in political pamphlets he spoke repeatedly of the brilliance and linguistic abilities of some of his African students, of the richness of past African civilizations, and of the deep spirituality he encountered among many African people. George Howe, in a lengthy review of a book by a southern advocate of the dual origins, spoke of his "painful astonishment" about such views and insisted they contradicted "every declaration of the Scriptures." He regarded the scientific "hypothesis" as radical and compared it to the radical "perversions of Abolitionists" that also rejected the Bible's authority. Thomas Smyth, however, provided the most impressive response from the circle of Columbia leaders. In his book *The Unity of the Human Races* he focused on the history of African civilizations and cultures and on the testimony of the Bible. In three chapters in the section "Former Civilization of Black Races of Men," Smyth drew from a wide range of historical and anthropological evidence to show that "dark or black races, with more or less of the Negro physiognomy, were in the earliest period of their known history cultivated and intelligent, having kingdoms, arts, and manufacturers." Columbia leaders would have nothing to do with what they regarded as extremes—abolitionists, on the one hand, or radical proslavery people, on the other, who were trying to utilize scientific evidence to dehumanize Africans and provide a scientific prop for the enslavement of Africans and African Americans.[41]

In 1850, when the new building for the Anson Street Church was completed, Adger asked Thornwell to preach the opening sermon "Duties of Masters." He took as his text "Masters, give unto your servants that which is just and equal; knowing that you also have a master in heaven." If Adger's earlier sermon had set the paternalistic tone that would long mark Columbia Seminary, Thornwell's sermon provided the theological and ideological foundations for that paternalism and for the quest for a middle way that it embodied. His vision was of a hierarchical and paternalistic society, stable and orderly, where each person has certain rights and certain corresponding duties.

Speaking before a large Charleston congregation of whites only, Thornwell challenged the assumption of abolitionists that the heart of slavery was the ownership of another person's body, soul, and will. Rather Thornwell made a stunning definition of slavery—that the right of the master was only to the labor of the slave. That was, he said, all that a Christian could concede about the rights of masters. The right of the slave, on the other hand, involved "all the essential rights of humanity" and included such temporal rights as the right to acquire knowledge—which though legally denied "is practically admitted" by southerners—the right of the family, and the right to personal safety. Such rights were sacred, and the state had a responsibility to protect them for the slave, to have the rights "defined by law and enforced by penalties." In another amazing sentence Thornwell insisted that "it is no part of the essence of Slavery" that the "rights of the slave should be left to the caprice or to the interest of the master." In this Thornwell was challenging the fundamental assumption of the slaveholding South—that masters, and masters alone, had full dominion over the whole body and soul and will of the slave; that masters and masters alone had the right to decide if a slave was to be sold and a family divided; and that masters and masters alone had the right to decide if their slaves could attend religious services. Thornwell's sermon made clear that he was attacking the basic assumptions of both abolitionists and also the white slaveholding South. His was fundamentally a reformist position that both abolitionists and white southerners dismissed. Yet he hoped that the opening of the Anson Street Church was an indication that reforms could be initiated that would lead to a stable, prosperous, and harmonious society for whites and blacks. "If God shall enable us to maintain the moderation and dignity which become us," he told his Charleston congregation, "and to set an example of faithfulness and diligence in the discharge of the duties which spring from the relation of master and servant, it will be an omen of good."[42]

Once again what Thornwell was seeking to present was a utopian vision of a proper social order. In the face of all the disintegrative forces of modern life, of an emerging industrial society, Thornwell sought to envision his paternalistic, class-stratified society. He set his vision within the broad context of the economic and political turmoil shaking the Western world. A student of the economists David Ricardo and Thomas Malthus, Thornwell believed that an industrializing economy was not leading to the amelioration of the conditions of labor but to a growing immiseration. He had been greatly shocked on a visit to Europe by the wretched conditions of the laboring classes and of the homeless wandering the streets in London, Manchester, and Liverpool. Anticipating the great clashes between labor and capital that he saw on the horizon of Western civilization, he insisted that the world was "now the theatre of an extraordinary conflict of great principles. . . . The foundations of society are about to be explored to their depths, and the sources of social and political prosperity laid bare." The great question, he told his white audience, "is not the narrow question of Abolitionism or Slavery—not simply whether we shall emancipate our Negroes or not; the question is the relations of man to society, of states to the individual, and of the individual to States—a question as broad as the interests of the human race."[43]

Thornwell was convinced that the answer to this great question and the answer to the turmoil of the time was his proposed humane, well-ordered, class-stratified society. Only such a social system could provide an order capable of withstanding the increasing anarchy of the modern world. What Thornwell was constantly searching for was some middle way between extremes, a middle way between radical proslavery southerners and radical abolitionists. Thornwell told the white Charlestonians that slavery was a natural evil resulting from the Fall, part of "the curse which sin has introduced into the world, and stands in the same general relation to Christianity as poverty, sickness, disease or death. It springs not from the nature of man as man, nor from the nature of society as such, but from the nature of man as sinful and the nature of society as disordered." In such a sinful and disordered world, white southerners should not declare slavery a blessing as some radical proslavery whites were doing. But the enemies of slavery, especially radical abolitionists, should not forget that the "Gospel does not propose to make our present state a perfect one—to make our earth a heaven." The friends and enemies of slavery, he argued, "are equally tempted to run into extravagance and excess; the one party denying the inestimable value of freedom, the other exaggerating the nature and extent of human rights, and both overlooking the real scope and purpose of the Gospel, in its relation to the present interests of man." What was needed was a course indicated by "the stern necessity" of a fallen, disorder world. At the heart of that course was a quest for what Thornwell called "regulated freedom" or "regulated liberty." In contrast to the abolitionists, who thought freedom was necessary for order, Thornwell insisted order was necessary for freedom. Without order freedom was an illusion and anarchy the result.[44]

What seemed clear to Thornwell and the well-meaning whites in his audience was that such a middle way and such regulated liberty led to a social order where whites both were in charge and also had, as Adger had said, a special responsibility to "our poor brethren," the blacks of the South, to whom they were to show the compassion and kindness they owed their Lord. They would learn later what blacks—including those whose labors supported Columbia Seminary—thought about their middle way and their well-meaning paternalism.

Beyond the immediate questions regarding slavery and a response to it by paternalistic whites, Thornwell's sermon pointed to deep tensions that exists within the Reformed tradition and that were to continue to churn through the coming generations of Columbia's history. On the one hand, in the face of the disorders of the world and various threats of social chaos, there is in the tradition a quest for order, harmony, and balance. Reason and fixed principles are utilized to put up boundaries, to provide intelligibility and certainty to guard against disorders and uncertainty, and to establish social hierarchies. This side of the tradition famously wants to do things "decently and in order" and reflects a scholastic impulse. On the other hand, there is a fear not of chaos but of boundaries being too tightly drawn, of people and positions being boxed in by rigid systems. This side of the tradition recognizes the powerlessness of human beings to control life and build perfect systems and to construct impenetrable boundaries. It sees mystery in the universe and acknowledges the ambiguities and paradoxes of human life. This is the evangelical side of the tradition—it is more concerned with persuasion and conversion than with neat systems of theology or polity. It insists that the heart is as important as the mind, that piety is more essential than learning, and that the glorious liberty of the children of God breaks through boundaries and dismantles social hierarchies.[45]

At Columbia these competing impulses were held together in the antebellum years, and were to continue to be held together in the years to come, by the metaphor of a middle way—a middle way that bridges the experiential and intellectual rift in the seminary's life. Thornwell in his Anson Street sermon spoke again and again of the dangers of extremes, of "Scylla on the one side and Charybdis on the other." To be sure, the competing impulses were never—and were never to be—evenly balance. Throughout most of its history the conservative, hierarchical, orderly impulse was to be the stronger of the two, especially in the classroom. But during periods when the intellectual life of the seminary was weak and piety was more prized, or when a therapeutic culture emphasized the importance of experience, or when a growing diversity in the seminary community called for boundaries to be breached, then the impulse for freedom and openness was to dominate. Nevertheless the quest for a middle way was to persist and was to mark the most fundamental character of the seminary's life. Indeed it would be strange for such a quest not to mark a seminary with its constituency of prudent Presbyterians who believe that extremes get you into trouble and that the middle is the place where duty leads and truth most likely resides. The quest has consequently served ideological purposes at Columbia—not only for Thornwell and Adger and Howe but also for those who were to follow them. It has legitimized present social arrangements in the society, including white Presbyterians' place in that society, and it has hidden harsh realities in American life. But the quest has also provided a means of integration and social identity for the seminary and its constituency. Thornwell and his contemporaries said this is who we are—Christians who avoid extremes and follow a wise middle way. We honor order and freedom, intellect and piety, moderation and prudence. Look where we live, at the campus we construct, and the curriculum that we follow. They are an embodiment of who we are; they speak of "our kind of people." And the generations who followed these antebellum leaders at Columbia were to echo these identity claims as they sought to build up the church and serve "our poor brethren" to whom its faculty and graduates were to show the compassion and kindness they owed their Lord.[46]

Adger's and Thornwell's quest for some middle way during the 1850s was finally confronted in 1860 with the necessity of choice—to take a stand for the Union or for home and for a home place with all its deep attachments. Were they to cast their lot for the forces of freedom that could be seen in the election of Lincoln or for a new Confederacy built within the harsh boundaries of human slavery. The strength of the seminary that had been achieved during the 1850s had been made possible by the labors and sorrows of black men, women, and children. Now with the necessity of a choice, that strength was to be poured out in defense of the Confederacy, and the seminary's internal vigor was to be consumed by its support of the very system, human slavery, that had undergirded its strength.

Ainsley Hall mansion, central building of the old campus.

Wade Hampton's home across the street from the seminary. He was the largest slave owner in the South at the time the seminary was established.

Simons Hall dormitory, built in the 1850s, with chapel in background.

Midway Congregational Church, the most influential congregation in the seminary's antebellum life.

George Howe, widely regarded as the father of the seminary.

Charles C. Jones, board member and professor known among whites as "the Apostle to the Negro Slave."

James H. Thornwell, board member, professor, and leading theologian of a slaveholding South.

John Adger, professor, former missionary, member of the wealthy Adger family of Charleston.

J. Leighton Wilson and Jane Wilson, early missionaries to West Africa and strong opponents of the international slave trade.

Benjamin Morgan Palmer, graduate, professor, board member, and strong defender of slavery and the South.

Thomas Smyth, prolific author, owner of one of the largest libraries in the nation, and closely connected to seminary faculty.

Joseph LeConte, distinguished scientist, seminary board member, and friend of seminary faculty.

5

Moderates Enraged

Throughout the antebellum period those most closely associated with Columbia Seminary were ardent supporters of the federal union. They were Unionists during the early years of the seminary when the nullification controversy broke over South Carolina. And they expressed an ardent love for the Union and its Constitution during the 1850s as the rumblings for secession grew louder and stronger. Their commitments to moderation, their wide travel, their close ties with northern conservatives (especially at Princeton), their relationship to southern business and commercial interests, and their vision of a great destiny for the nation—all nurtured in them a strong sense of national identity and a deep loyalty to the American republic.[1]

The controversies that swirled around the Compromise of 1850, however, sent tremors through the Unionists associated with the seminary. The vast new territories of the Far West, taken by military power from Mexico in 1848, had created a crisis. Were the recently conquered territories to be open to slavery, or were they to be free from slavery and open for white pioneers of modest means? The Compromise of 1850 had finally seemed to settle the question, promising stability for the nation. California had been allowed to enter the Union as a free state. In other territories the slavery question was to be decided by popular sovereignty. The slave trade was abolished in Washington, D.C., and a harsh new fugitive slave law was established. But many, North and South, felt the compromise was a betrayal of fundamental principles.[2]

In the midst of the debate that preceded the Compromise of 1850 and in the controversies that followed, the Unionists associated with Columbia sought to hold back the rush toward civil war. Thornwell wrote a friend in 1850: "I can well and heartily sympathize with you in your despondency in regard to the condition of the country. The times are indeed portentous. The prospect of disunion is one which I cannot contemplate without absolute horror. A peaceful dissolution is utterly impossible." A few months later, having recently left Columbia and moved to Philadelphia, Charles Colcock Jones wrote Columbia graduate John Jones, pastor in Marietta, Georgia: "South Carolina has gone beyond reason. I was going to say *politically mad:* she will pitch Georgia into the sea if we break her hopes a second time. We did so in nullification days. She remembers it." He believed that "*the people* of the United States—North, East, South, and West—are true to the Union. It is the *ultras,* the factionists—few in comparison to the masses—that create excitements by their noise and impudence. I am still of the opinion all will come right."[3]

In January 1851 Thornwell articulated a Unionist's vision of the United States as a redeemer nation. "The finger of God," he said, could be traced "in every stage of its history. We have looked upon it as destined to be a blessing to mankind." The geography of the United States—between Europe and Asia, "in the very center of the earth"—pointed toward the nation's central role in human history. The United States seemed to be commissioned from the skies as "the apostle of civilization, liberty, and Christianity to all the races of man." Thornwell was convinced that "we cannot relinquish the idea of this mission: We Have Been Called to it; and if in our folly and wickedness we refuse to walk worthily of it, we may righteously expect, in addition to the ordinary disasters of revolution, the extraordinary retributions of God." He clearly shared the bold claims made by zealous patriots North and South that the United States had a special manifest destiny.[4]

But Thornwell was deeply concerned by what he saw happening all around him. In late March 1851, he wrote to a Presbyterian colleague in Kentucky. South Carolina, he said, seemed bent on secession. "The excitement is prodigious. Men, from whom one would have expected better things, are fanning the flame, and urging the people on to the most desperate measures. From the beginning I have opposed, according as I had opportunity, all revolutionary measures. But I am sorry to say that many of our clergy are as rash and violent as the rashest of their hearers." He took comfort, however, in the fact that the Old School Presbyterian Church had not split. Unlike the Methodists and Baptists, who had split in the 1840s along North–South lines, conservative Old School Presbyterians had managed to stay together by insisting on the spirituality of the church, by saying that slavery was a question for the state and not the church, and by rigorously excluding from church courts any debate about the South's peculiar institution. Such a course seemed both theologically correct and also a prudent and moderate course for the church in the midst of extremes on both sides. But following such a course was increasingly difficult as the bonds that held the nation together were increasingly fractured and the forces of disunion gained in strength. The difficulty was made clear—perhaps ironically—in attempts to have widely circulated through the American Tract Society none other than Thornwell's sermon "Duties of Masters," which he had preached at the opening of the Anson Street Church in Charleston.[5]

The American Tract Society was one of the great interdenominational benevolent societies of antebellum America, a tool for the evangelization of the nation. The constitution of the society sought to make it ecumenical by making it dead center. It was to remain neutral on controversial issues and not publish anything that might unduly ruffle denominational or regional sensitivities. The strategy worked until 1856 when the Congregational Association of New York asked the society to begin issuing antislavery tracts. The society, seeking to maintain its neutrality, agreed to publish tracts on "duties and evils" associated with slavery if evangelical Christians in both the North and the South agreed that a particular tract could be published. Such a decision seemed a prudent, reasonable compromise, but it almost wrecked the society. The problem was that evangelical Christians could not agree about the duties and evils connected with slavery.[6]

Shortly after this decision, the society was asked to publish Thornwell's sermon. Immediately there were objections from anxious southerners who could not tolerate Thornwell's attempt to find a middle way on the slavery question. And many in the North found the sermon acceptable only if it were the first of a series that would ultimately condemn slavery. Religious papers North and South were filled with the controversy, so the society decided not to publish the sermon. But this only added fuel to the fire. To try and still the controversy a special committee was appointed that included some of the most influential Protestant leaders in the country, among whom were a number of college presidents: Theodore Frelinghuysen of Rutgers, Martin Anderson of Colgate, Mark Hopkins of Williams, and Francis Wayland of Brown.[7]

As the committee was beginning its investigation, Wayland surprised them all by publishing an attack on the society's attempt to remain neutral. He insisted that as tracts on "dancing, theatrical amusements, intemperance, lying and perjury" did not receive the approbation of those who sinned in such matters, so tracts on the evils of slavery were not tolerated by slaveholders, but they were to be published nevertheless. And, he added, if southerners did not like such publications, they should form their own society "for the teachings of which we are not responsible." That as it turned out was exactly what some South Carolinians were already contemplating. The Episcopalian C. C. Pinckney, head of the South Carolina Tract Society, wrote that the South Carolinians would withdraw from the national organization if any tracts on slavery were published.[8]

At this point Thomas Smyth came to the defense of Thornwell's sermon and the tract society. As a member of Columbia's board and a director of the American Tract Society, he was eager for the whole matter to be settled and for the neutrality of the American Tract Society to be maintained. He wrote a series of articles entitled "Why Do I Love the American Tract Society" in which he expressed his love for the society because it was an American society, not simply a northern or southern institution, and because it united Christians throughout the nation in the work of evangelism. Seeking to establish a basis for cooperation between antislavery evangelicals and southern evangelicals, he attempted to rebut Wayland's argument that the society needed to publish the "whole will of God." Smyth argued that as far as the American Tract Society was concern, the "whole will of God" was a matter of dispute among evangelicals. They held, for example, different views on baptism, communion, and church government, and consequently the society would not publish tracts on these subjects. In like manner Smyth thought that slavery did not require the society to decide either for it or against it. Like baptism slavery was a debatable subject on which reasonable people could reach a compromise and agree to disagree. Smyth's position, his hopes for prudent compromises and a middle way between extremes, embodied the ethos and worldview of the Unionists at Columbia Seminary and their hopes for maintaining the unity of the nation and the bonds of peace.[9]

Despite their hopes that moderation and prudence could hold together people of good will, the Columbia Unionists watched with growing frustration and then mounting anger the fracturing of the nation and the church. They had great difficulty grasping the growing chasm between what they regarded as extremes, and they did not adequately comprehend that their middle way could not bridge the distance between those extremes. Their metaphor of a middle way assumed a common language and worldview shared by North and South. The earlier successes of such a middle way had confirmed, they thought, a shared national culture and language. But what they saw and experienced as the nation moved toward war was each side beginning to speak in ways the other did not understand. Each side, as it were, was beginning to excommunicate the other, to use a language the other did not speak, and to see the world in ways different than the other. The differences in languages, the different symbolic systems through which they looked at the world and one another, were most clearly seen in the word *liberty*.[10]

When Thornwell spoke of "regulated liberty" in his sermon "Duties of Masters," he meant a liberty located between the extremes of tyranny and anarchy. "Regulated liberty" had everything to do with one's allotted sphere and duty, with one providential place in society. In the South whites had one place in society, and blacks had another place, and both were to stay in their own place. The kind of liberty each enjoyed was shaped and regulated by their different, distinctive, and providential places. Such an understanding of *regulated liberty* allowed the Unionists at Columbia to think of themselves as "the friends of liberty and human rights."[11]

For increasing numbers in the North, Thornwell's "regulated liberty" was nothing other than what William Lloyd Garrison called an "unmoral rhetoric." Twelve years after Thornwell's Anson Street sermon, Lincoln spelled out in the midst of war the reality of the two languages and the differences between the conceptual worlds of the North and of the South. "The world has never had a good definition of the word liberty, and the American people, just now, are much in want of one," he said. "We all declare for liberty; but in using the same *word* we do not all mean the same *thing*. With some the word liberty may mean for each man to do as he pleases with himself, and the product of his labor; while with others the same may mean for some men to do as they please with other men, and the product of other men's labor." Here, declared Lincoln, "are two, not only different, but incompatible things, called by the same name—liberty." It was this profound difference, this incompatibility, that was becoming increasingly clear as the nation moved in the 1850s toward war. A chasm was opening between the North and the South—a chasm that moderates could not bridge with their calls for moderation and a middle way between extremes.[12]

The Columbia Unionists, nevertheless, had continued throughout the 1850s to try to build their moderate bridge across the growing divide. What they struggled to avoid was the realization that their metaphor of a middle way could not draw within its circle of conversation and interpretations the incompatible and conflicting meanings of *liberty* that Lincoln would soon name. Thornwell, Smyth, Adger, Jones, Palmer, Howe, and their colleagues wanted compromises; they wanted to agree to disagree about slavery. But what they increasingly found was that their reasonable agreements were impossible when North and South seemed to be talking past one another, that even their conservative friends in the North were beginning to use a different language. Columbia moderates were finding that their moderation was a distinctly southern moderation that did not seem so moderate to those on the other side of the Mason-Dixon Line. In 1861 Thornwell would finally acknowledge the depth of the chasm and the incompatible and conflicting meanings of *liberty.* He concluded that "two Governments upon this continent may work out the problem of human liberty more successfully than one."[13]

Two events in the late 1850s were particularly important harbingers of what was to come. The first was the proposal in 1857 by Governor James H. Adams of South Carolina that the international slave trade be reopened and that once again ships be allowed to arrive in Charleston Harbor loaded with cargoes of African slaves. Writing in the *Southern Presbyterian Review,* John Adger described the disastrous consequences of such a course. He said if one looked only at the practical aspects of such a proposal, it was clear that the importation of new Africans would undermine the South's economic and political stability. But what was more important, if such a policy were followed it would destroy any claims by white southerners to a high moral ground. Adger defended domestic slavery as it had developed in the South, but he said, "Let it never be forgotten for a moment," that although the debate over slavery "may terminate in an appeal to force, this has been from the first and still is a *moral* conflict. We lose strength whenever we abandon the ground of justice and of truth. The South cannot afford in such a struggle as this, to lose the approbation of the King of nations and the support of His Word against all her foes." If the South Carolina legislature tried to reopen the international slave trade, with all the horrors of the middle passage, it would confirm the abolitionist charge of an immoral South. The state and the South, Adger warned, had a "higher and nobler and more valuable interest to preserve" than any imagined financial or political interests promoted by the trade—"namely, her interest in honor and duty and truth."[14]

Leighton Wilson responded even more vehemently to the proposal before the South Carolina legislature. He had seen with his own eyes the huge loss of life and the devastations caused in West Africa by the ongoing slave trade to Brazil and Cuba. Such a trade, he insisted, never had been, and could not be, carried on except by fraud, by violence, and by perpetual warfare and bloodshed. "Is the South," he asked, "prepared for this? Will she forego her honor, her sense of justice, and her religion, so far as to associate herself with the vilest men that have ever disgraced the annals of humanity, and once more apply the torch of discord and war for the purpose of obtaining slaves?" It seemed inconceivable to him that the South he knew could be so blind as to accept such a course, or that South Carolinians could be so full of insane arrogance, so devoid of Christian compassion, and so confined to their little world that its leaders would propose such a course.[15]

If the proposals to reopen the international slave trade seemed to Columbia Unionists an expression of southern extremism, John Brown's raid on Harpers Ferry was the most dramatic and deeply alarming indication that moderation and the status quo were being fiercely assaulted by radical abolitionists. Those in the North who believed in a different liberty than Thornwell's "regulated liberty" now appeared ready to resort to violence to end what they saw as the deep violence of slavery. In October 1859 the abolitionist John Brown led a small raiding party that captured the U.S. Amory at Harpers Ferry, Virginia. Quickly overcome by U.S. marines under Robert E. Lee, Brown was captured and after a short trial hanged in early December. On the morning of his execution, Brown wrote "I

John Brown, am now quite *certain* that the crimes of this *guilty land* will never be purged way, but with Blood." By then he had already become for many in the North a martyr for freedom. Ralph Waldo Emerson called Brown the saint who "will make the gallows glorious like the Cross." And Henry David Thoreau declared that "no man in America has ever stood up so persistently for the dignity of human nature."[16]

The white South reacted with rage. Writing in the *Southern Presbyterian Review* an article titled "The Raid of John Brown and the Progress of Abolitionism," George Howe reviewed the role of slavery in the Bible, traced the long history of slavery and the Atlantic slave trade, and turned to the rise of abolitionism in Great Britain and the United States. The normally irenic Howe recounted in detail the horrors of the Haitian revolution—the torture and massacre of white men, the rape and murder of white women, and the slaughter of white children—and with mounting fury described the reaction of northern abolitionists to John Brown's raid. He asked northern abolitionists if they wanted the savagery of Haiti to be repeated throughout the South. He reviewed Brown's history of cold-blooded murder of whites in Kansas. And with undisguised revulsion and disgust, he told how abolitionists had celebrated the barbarous intentions of "the *pious* John Brown," the "martyr" who as "a traitor and murderer was hung under the laws of Virginia." Fortunately Brown was unsuccessful, Howe concluded, because he failed to understand southern blacks—he was "unable to poison their minds against their owners, whom they are accustomed to look up to with affection, reverence, and submission." Perhaps Howe was reflecting his image of his own slaves, of the eighty-five men, women, and children on Howe's Liberty County, Georgia, plantation—of Caesar the driver or Isaac the plowman or maybe Caroline who served tea in the Howe home to Columbia Seminary faculty and students.[17]

His rage spent Howe pulled back in his article as if recognizing how far he had himself echoed the extremism he denounced. He noted with gratification that "some of the noblest men of the North have come forth, at this critical juncture, and lifted their voice in favor of the union of these States, at this moment so greatly imperiled." He wondered if the Union could survive and noted that the "conviction here is becoming more and more fixed, that it is better to separate and meet the worst, than to live in perpetual broils." Yet, he said, there was a need to remember that beneath the surface turmoil of an ocean storm the ocean depths slumber in peace. His hope was that the slumbering depths of the nation, the great mass of the people North and South who desired peace and union, would rise to the occasion, calm the gathering fury, and bring a new unity and prosperity to the nation.[18]

Thornwell spent the summer of 1860 traveling in Europe. Traveling with him were a Columbia student, and three Columbia graduates and their wives—one of whom was Thornwell's daughter. It was a grand tour that began in England, took in Ireland and Scotland, then the cities of Germany and Switzerland, and finally Paris. Along the way they were hosted by American ambassadors, distinguished academics, and leading churchmen, and the travelers had ample opportunity to discuss with them unfolding events in the United States. They visited the expected sites, enjoyed the beauty of the English countryside, walked paths in the Black Forest, and felt the sublimity of the Swiss Alps. Thornwell's young traveling companions, with their energy and enthusiasms, helped him avoid the homesickness and melancholy that had marked his earlier travels in Europe. Still he could not forget home and its troubles. In a long letter to his wife, he noted that one of the benefits of travel "is to make us prize our own country. After all, there is no land like our own. In all that makes a people great and powerful, we are decidedly in advance of Europe." He thought that there was no such population on the global "as our own; and if we can have the grace to deal justly and honourably with one another, and to hold together as a people, the time is at hand when the distinction of being an American citizen will be as proud and glorious as it ever was to be a citizen of Rome." Everywhere he went he found that people treated them with respect and admiration because of the character of American institutions. We are felt, he wrote, to be a model people. What a shame, then, "it will be to be to forfeit, by our follies and our sins, the noble inheritance to which Providence has called us!"[19]

Thornwell returned to South Carolina in September 1860. He had, he told Palmer, made up his mind while in Europe to move, immediately upon his return, "for the gradual emancipation of the negro, as the only measure that would give peace to the country, by taking away, at least, the external cause of irritation." But he said when "I got home, I found it was too late; the die was cast." Lincoln was elected in November, and South Carolina quickly seceded. Palmer did not record what Thornwell meant by "gradual emancipation," but surely Thornwell thought it would begin with the reforms he and others associated with Columbia had advocated—especially the right of slaves to learn to read and write, and the right of slave families to remain together. A distinguished historian later wondered: "How could the Reverend James Henley Thornwell, the slavocracy's most important proslavery clergyman and one of South Carolina's most prestigious Unionists, have considered gradually abolishing masters' absolute power, and at the moment of disunion no less?!" Thornwell, like others at Columbia, thought that the end of slavery would come only in God's good and providential time, that like sin and war it would persist until the millennium. But perhaps while he was in Europe, away from his much-beloved home, he had concluded that the crisis of the Union could only be averted by a God who demanded the radical repentance of a people, even a repentance that demanded a shaking of the foundations of Thornwell's home and the gradual emancipation of black slaves. If he came to such a conclusion, he did not act on it when he returned to his duties at the seminary.[20]

Shortly before Thornwell left for his European tour, the Democratic National Convention was held in Charleston. It was a terrible location for such an event—not enough hotel rooms, even with five or six to a room, and few places to eat since for white Charlestonians eating out meant having dinner in a friend's home. The convention was raucous, even tumultuous, and it soon became clear that southerners were going to insist on a radical proslavery platform and that northerners would not accept such. Ballot after ballot was cast producing only frustration and heightened tempers. One the morning of the fifth day, in the midst of the balloting, Smyth was asked by Caleb Cushing, president of the convention, to have the opening prayer. He had only a short time to prepare himself, but he knew what he wanted to say. He prayed to the "God of order, from whom preceded all wise counsels and all prudent and effective measures." He thanked God for the United States and for God's fostering care that had allowed the nation to advance "to its present height of prosperity and progress." He prayed for unity in the convention and for the "spirit of discretion, moderation, and forbearance." And he prayed for triumphant success in the coming campaign in this crisis of the Republic.[21]

The prayer was widely quoted in newspapers North and South. Opposition papers denounced it as a political party prayer. But others applauded it. The New York *Journal of Commerce* said it had a most "happy effect" on the convention and declared that if it found a lodgment in every heart "we might entertain increased hope for the continued success of our government." But the prayer worked no miracle. Three days later W. L. Yancy of Alabama insisted that the Democratic Party declare flatly that slavery was right. "Gentlemen of the South," replied Senator Pugh of Ohio, "you mistake us—you mistake us—we will not do it." Nor did they, and with that refusal the delegations of eight cotton states withdrew. In November Lincoln was elected. He received a minority of the popular vote, but he took the electoral vote easily.[22]

Lincoln's election was a black day for Columbia Unionists. The South Carolina governor called for a day of fasting, humiliation, and prayer, "a time to implore the direction and blessing of Almighty God in this hour of difficulty, and to give us *one heart and one mind,* to oppose, by all just and proper means, every encroachment upon our rights." The Columbia Unionists responded with Fast Day sermons.[23]

In Charleston Smyth preached a sermon titled "The Sin and the Curse." "God's curse is poured out upon us," he cried. He mourned for his country and said that the U.S. Constitution was "an embodiment of wisdom, patriotism, sagacity and prudential foresight and moderation" and that the Union was the hope of all peoples. But God's curse was on the nation. Tossing to the wind his cherished moderation and prudence, Smyth laid the cause of the curse on "atheists, infidels, communists, free-lovers, rationalists, bible haters, anti-Christian levelers, and anarchists." But there were others as well—God-fearing and Christ-loving, conscientious people, who had perverted "the great doctrines of personal responsibility, liberty of conscience, liberty of thought, liberty of opinion and liberty of action," by making their own conscience, rather than the Bible, the infallible standard of right and wrong.[24]

In New Orleans Palmer preached his "Thanksgiving Sermon" in response to the Louisiana governor's call for a day of prayer and fasting. The former Unionist now insisted that the white South was composed of a distinct people, with a distinct history and identity, and with peculiar duties associated with their distinctiveness. White southerners, he said, have a "providential trust" committed to them as a people. And what, he asked, is their providential trust at this moment in history? "I answer," he said, "that it is *to conserve and to perpetuate the institution of domestic slavery as now existing.*" He told his congregation that it was not necessary at this point "to inquire whether this is precisely the best relation in which the hewer of wood and drawer of water can stand to his employer; although this proposition may perhaps be successfully sustained by those who chose to defend it. Still less are we required, dogmatically, to affirm that it will subsist through all time. . . . All that we claim for them [generations to come], for ourselves, is liberty to work out this problem, guided by nature and God, without obtrusive interference from abroad." Palmer insisted the white South was called in the present crisis to "defend the cause of God and religion." In that trust, he said, "we are resisting the power which wars against constitutions and laws and compacts, against Sabbaths and sanctuaries, against the family, the State, and the Church; which blasphemously invades the prerogatives of God, and rebukes the Most High for the errors of his administration; which, if it cannot snatch the reign of empire from his grasp, will lay the universe in ruins at his feet." Is it possible, he asked, "that we shall decline the onset?" So Palmer also abandoned moderation, and his sermon was printed and widely distributed throughout the South as a major piece of propaganda for southern nationalism.[25]

In Columbia Thornwell preached his Fast Day sermon entitled "National Sins." Of all the Columbia Unionists who preached Fast Day sermons, Thornwell was best able to maintain a spirit of moderation, although it was clear he spoke as a white South Carolinian. He introduced his sermon by rejecting what he called "the narrow and exclusive spirit" that claims "we alone, of all the people of the earth, are possessed of the true religion." Such arrogance and bigotry, he said, were utterly inconsistent with the penitential confessions required by a Fast Day. He told the white Carolinians that he did not intend in the sermon to debate political issues, "to plead the cause of States' rights or Federal authority," but to bring his hearers as penitents before the Supreme Judge of all nations. He therefore began by arguing that the state as well as the individual stood before the judgment seat of God. The foundations of the state were laid by God, and to God they owed whatever was "valuable in our laws, healthful in our customs, or precious in our history." This meant that the state, as a moral institution responsible to God, was capable of sin and of rebellion against God. Sin, said Thornwell, had been the ruin of every empire that ever flourished and fell. So states, like individuals, must repent or perish. Given the present crisis, Thornwell declared that God clearly had a controversy with the United States. South Carolina was part of the nation, and therefore Carolinians participated in the national sins and must repent of the national sins and seek God's mercy. It was consequently necessary to inquire, with all solemnity, into the cause of God's fierce anger against the nation. By naming the sins of the nation, the people might repent, turn from their rebellious ways, and receive mercy and not judgment.[26]

Thornwell's confession of sin began with what one might expect from an old Unionist: the penitential lament that the Union was on the verge of dissolution. "A name once dear to our hearts has become intolerable to entire States. Once admired, loved, almost adored, as the citadel and safeguard of freedom, it has become, in many minds, synonymous with oppression, with treachery, with falsehood, and with violence." Americans had had a great destiny to spread freedom, civilization and religion across a great continent. They had been a city upon on a hill whose light was intended to shine on every people and on every land. The nation's abandonment of this destiny was "an enormity of treason equaled only by the treachery of a Judas, who betrayed his Master with a kiss."[27]

Slavery, said Thornwell, was at the heart of the present crisis and the looming division of the nation. Beneath states' rights lay the question of slavery. Slavery was, said

Thornwell, the "institution which has produced the present convulsions of the country, and brought us to the verge of ruin." So once again Thornwell turned to the themes of his Anson Street sermon. He insisted that in the final analysis slavery was nothing but an organization of labor, an organization in which labor and capital coincided. Under such a system, the laborer is never without employment, and the wealth of the country feeds and cares for the laborer. And once again Thornwell warned about the capitalist system developing in the North. Where labor and capital were divided, he said, agrarian revolutions and great distress were sure to follow. Capital will accumulate, he predicted, and capitalists would look only to their own interests and not to the interests of labor. Wages would fall, and large numbers would be left unemployed. "While the capitalist is accumulating his hoards, rolling in affluence and splendor, thousands that would work if they had the opportunity are doomed to perish of hunger." Thornwell already could see the "most astonishing contrasts of poverty and riches" constantly increasing. Under such circumstances, the only way to avoid a revolution of the masses was for the government to provide the masses the necessities of life. But, asked Thornwell, shall it support them in idleness? Will the working poor consent to see others, as stout and able as themselves, clothed like the lilies of the field that toil not and spin not? Will this not, he asked like some modern critic of social welfare, give a premium to idleness? The only way that future revolution and disaster could be avoided was for the North to adopt a system where the employer has a right of property in the labor employed, "in other words, Slavery." If the North failed to adopt such a system, Thornwell predicted that the industrialized world was sure to suffer the most violent and disastrous insurrections against the system which creates and perpetuates the misery of the workers. Such a consequence seemed to Thornwell as certain as "the tendencies in the laws of capital and population to produce extremes of poverty and wealth."[28]

Thornwell then turned to the sins of the South and asked if white southerners had discharged their duty to their slaves. Had not the white South invited the attacks of abolitionists when white southerners made the slave a different kind of being from white owners? Thornwell attacked the rising scientific racism that insisted the differences between whites and blacks were so great that there must have been a dual origin of the races. "Those who defend Slavery," he warned, "upon the pleas that the African is not of the same stock with ourselves are aiming a fatal blow at the institution, by bringing it into conflict with the dearest doctrines of the Gospel." To arm the religious sentiment against slavery, he said, is to destroy slavery. But there were other charges that also could be brought against white southerners. "Are our laws such that we can heartily approve them in the presence of God? Have we sufficiently protected the person of the slave? Are our provisions adequate for giving him a fair and impartial trial when prosecuted for offences? Do we guard as we should his family relations? And, above all, have we furnished him with proper means of religious instruction?" Thornwell told his South Carolina congregation that they must answer these questions with the utmost solemnity and truth, for they had come before the Lord as penitents. He clearly thought the answer to all his questions was "No!" Our slaves, he declared, are a solemn trust, and "while we have a right to use and direct their labor, we are bound to feed, clothe and protect them, to give them the comforts of this life, and to introduce them to the hopes of a blessed immortality."[29]

Given the sins of the nation and of the white South, what should be the prayers of Carolinians on a day of fasting and penitential lament? First, said Thornwell, white Carolinians needed to pray for "the grace of magnanimity, that our moderation may be known unto all men." Next, they needed to pray that God would raise up patriotic statesmen, men of counsel and understanding, to lead the people in ways pleasing to God. Finally, they needed to pray for courage equal to the present emergency. He told the gathered congregation that even if they followed a just course to victory, it may be through a baptism of blood. Then out of the depths of his heart as a South Carolinian, Thornwell warned that his beloved state may suffer. "She may suffer grievously; she may suffer long: Be it so: we shall love her the more tenderly and the more intensely, the more bitterly she suffers." Peering into the future, he wondered if the destiny of the state and of a southern cause was defeat. Even then, he said, it will not follow that her course was wrong or her suffering in vain. They should look to the example of the ancient Greeks whom white southerners so admired. "Thermopylae was lost," cried the seminary professor, "but the moral power of Thermopylae will continue as long as valor and freedom have a friend, and reverence for law be one of the noblest sentiments of the human soul."[30]

The Fast Day sermons by Smyth, Palmer, and Thornwell were preached in late November 1860. On December 20 a South Carolina state convention meeting in Charleston voted unanimously to secede from the federal Union. Throughout the city church bells rang, bonfires were lit, and jubilant whites joined in spontaneous parades to celebrate the end of the Union. On the seminary campus in Columbia, students and faculty heard the booming of a cannon in the distance announcing the independence of South Carolina.[31]

While the leadership associated with the seminary had been strongly Unionists, many in its constituency were not. The state convention meeting in Charleston had Presbyterian members from all over the state—a Seabrook from Edisto Island, a Jenkins from Wilton, a Frampton and a Hudson from Stoney Creek, Isaac Hayne and Andrew Magrath, the soon to be governor, from Charleston, and a DeSaussure from Columbia. And they came from the Black River settlements of Scotch Irish, from Thornwell's old home region near the Pee Dee River, and from the upcountry, where Scotch Irish had been for several generations turning farms into plantations. And among those gathered in convention in Charleston were two longtime board members—the Reverend Thomas Reese English from Sumter, who gave the opening prayer on the day the convention voted for secession, and the Honorable Thomas C. Perrin, president of the seminary board and president of the Greenville and Columbia Railroad, who was the first to come forward and to sign his name under the Ordinance of Secession.[32]

Still the impulse for moderation lingered, and the quest for some middle way continued among the Columbia Unionists. Adger successfully blocked a move in the Synod of South Carolina to withdraw immediately from the Old School General Assembly and form a new Southern Presbyterian Church. Smyth wrote a series of articles for the New York *Journal of Commerce* in which he pled for compromises as he tried to "sober men down to calm reason." And he wrote long letters to ministerial colleagues in the North expressing his grief over the nation's division and his hope for some miracle that would turn the nation away from war. To one he wrote: "Though no longer united in the Union, we are united out of it; and will still be joined in heart, in hope, may we hope, in church; and is it, O God, beyond hope, in the Union purified and perfected!"

The personal grief felt by some of the Columbia Unionists could be heard perhaps most clearly in John Leighton Wilson's response to secession. The Wilsons were living in New York, where he was a secretary of the Presbyterian Board of Foreign Missions. In an exchange of anguished letters with Charles Hodge of Princeton, Wilson spoke as a South Carolinian who had been living away from his southern home for many years, first in West Africa and then for seven years in New York. Hodge, who was a cousin of Wilson's wife and a close friend of Wilson's, sent him a copy of an article Hodge was about to publish entitled "The State of the Country." Hodge condemned what he regarded as the extremism of the abolitionists and the way they were treading on the South's liberty; the South, he said, should be able to work out its own answer to slavery. But in even stronger language he condemned the "absurdities, abnormities and evils which flow from secession," likening those who would support it to Benedict Arnold. Wilson responded by saying that the North was the aggressor seeking to impose its will on the South. If the North would concede what is just and what the South imperatively needs, Wilson said the Union may still be saved. Otherwise, he said, "we go to pieces."[33]

Hodge replied: "My dear, precious friend. Your letter fills me with despair. That a man so wise, so gentle, so good as you are, one whom I unfeignedly regard as one of the best men I ever knew, should evidently approve of what I consider great crimes and disapprove of what I understand the plainest principles of truth and justice, shakes all confidence in human convictions. I never felt so deeply before that opinions are not thoughts, but feelings." We are, Hodge wrote, "almost as far apart as though we did not believe in the same God and Saviour or recognize the same moral law." If we, wrote Hodge, "who love each other and who sincerely desire that truth and justice should prevail, thus differ, what must be the case of those who are not thus united, or who are animated by feelings of mutual enmity!"[34]

Wilson wrote back: "My dear friend and brother. If the differences of views between you and myself on the general state of the country is the cause of despondency on the one side, it is of real heartfelt grief on the other." He reiterated and expanded once again his belief that the South was the aggrieved party, that it had been abandoned by the conservative men in the North who had stood with it against the attacks of the abolitionists, and that, with the election of Lincoln, the North was acting in an imperialistic and aggressive manner toward the South. He concluded: "I do not expect to pursue this correspondence further. I am afraid that the time for argument is gone by, but whatever may happen, I trust I shall always regard yourself as one of the dearest friends I have had. God save us all from terrible times and scenes."[35]

Those terrible times and scenes were soon to follow. Early on the morning of April 12, 1861, as the sky in the east began to pale, sand-duned batteries around Charleston Harbor began to fire on Fort Sumter. From the third-floor study of his handsome Charleston mansion, Smyth could see the red-hot shells streaking up and out over the marsh and wide channel. When the guns fell silent, he joined the crowd on the Battery at the end of Charleston peninsula. With him was George Howe, who had come down from Columbia. Cheering broke out—the blue palmetto flag of South Carolina now flew where the American flag had been flying. Beside it was the flag of the new Confederacy.[36]

In Columbia students had gathered at the Adger home, together with many young ladies, to await the news from Charleston. The telegraph office was nearby, and the life of the city seemed to have been bound up in suspense. Board member John A. Crawford had supplied the seminarians with Colt repeaters in late January, and they had been target practicing for several months and had volunteered to act as part of a home guard. "Toward two o'clock," one student wrote in his journal, "our hearts were gladdened by hearing that a white flag was raised over Sumter. And soon it was our privilege to shout that she was surrendered. Many a joyous heart bounded with glee as we heard of this first victory of our Confederate flag, and that too *without the loss of a single life on our side.* Surely the 'Lord of hosts is with us!'"[37]

The Old School General Assembly met in Philadelphia in May. Leighton Wilson was one of the few southerners in attendance. Gardiner Spring, pastor of New York's Brick Presbyterian Church and longtime friend of the Columbia Unionists and of the South, introduced a resolution calling on the church to "promote and perpetuate, so far as in us lies, the integrity of these United States, and to strengthen, uphold, and encourage, the Federal Government in the exercise of all its functions under our noble Constitution: and to this Constitution in all its provisions, requirements, and principles, we profess our unabated loyalty." Hodge protested and argued the resolution would be a novel introduction of political questions into the church and would mean its sure division. Spring did not think his resolution novel. Southern ministers had been busy addressing political issues and supporting secession: Palmer and Thornwell, Leland, Adger, and Smyth, "men of distinguished abilities," men who could sway the popular will, had not only justified and counseled the rebellion but had "instigated and urged it with all the enthusiasm and vehemence of the pulpit, and all the weight of their personal and official character." And in answer to Hodge's protests, the assembly asked: would those who supported Hodge's position "have us recognize, as good Presbyterians, men whom our own government, with the approval of Christendom, may soon execute as traitors? . . . What, when 'a crime, the heinousness of which can be only imperfectly estimate' . . . when armed rebellion joins issue with armed authority on battlefields, where tens of thousands must perish; . . . is it uncalled for, unnecessary, for this Christian Assembly to renew . . . respect for the majesty of law, and a sense of the obligation of loyalty?" Leighton Wilson resigned his position with the Board of Foreign Missions and headed home, back to South Carolina, where he met in Columbia his old friends at the seminary and with them began plans for a southern church.[38]

In December 1861 twelve months after South Carolina had seceded, southern Presbyterian leaders gathered in Augusta, Georgia, and organized a southern church. Those associated with Columbia clearly dominated the new church. Thornwell, Palmer, Howe, Leland,

Jones, Adger, and Wilson were all in attendance as was James Woodrow, the newly elected Perkins Professor of Natural Science in Connection with Revelation. With them were board members Thomas Perrin and Chancellor Job Johnston of the South Carolina Supreme Court. Palmer was elected moderator, and Thornwell moved and Leland seconded that the "new-born church" be named the Presbyterian Church in the Confederate States of America. Wilson was elected to head the foreign mission efforts of the denomination and reported on his recent trip to the Indian nations in Arkansas and Oklahoma. Jones was made head of domestic mission and wrote the "Letter on the Religious Instruction of the Colored People," which the church quickly issued. And Adger played a key role in shaping the church's polity along lines long advocated by Columbia faculty. Columbia graduate McNeill Turner was elected temporary clerk and future Columbia faculty member; Joseph R. Wilson was elected permanent clerk. Thornwell, however, was clearly the guiding star of the assembly. He was given responsibility for writing "An Address to All the Churches of Jesus Christ throughout the Earth." This address, perhaps the most important single document in the history of the white southern Presbyterian Church, announced to the churches of the world the formation of a new and independent church. A separate and distinct identity was articulated both for a southern church and for southern society.[39]

Thornwell gave two reasons for the creation of the new church. First, the General Assembly of the old, still united, church had abandoned its long-held doctrine of the "spirituality of the church." The Gardiner Spring resolution, wrote Thornwell, "conclusively shows that if we should remain together, the political questions which divide us as citizens will be obtruded on our Church Courts, and be discussed . . . with all the acrimony, bitterness and rancor with which such questions are usually discussed by men of the world." Thornwell then proceeded to develop in the most careful and logical manner the doctrine of the spirituality of the church: that the "provinces of Church and State are perfectly distinct, and the one has no right to usurp the jurisdiction of other." The state, he wrote, is "designed to realize the idea of justice. It is the society of rights." The church, on the other hand, is "designed to realize the idea of grace. It is the society of the redeemed." Church and state "are as planets moving in different orbits, and unless each is confined to its own track, the consequences may be as disastrous in the moral world, as the collision of different spheres in the world of matter."[40]

This understanding of the church and its relationship to the state had been carefully developed throughout the antebellum period by Old School Presbyterians, North and South. For Thornwell and his Columbia colleagues, the doctrine was fundamental for church polity and shaped their response to a wide range of issues, from boards and agencies for the church to slavery. But they all agreed that the spirituality of the church was a different matter from Christianity's influence in society. In 1861 the Columbia leaders saw Christianity at the heart of southern *culture.* If they thought church and state as institutions had distinct spheres, whose overlap would bring chaos, that did not mean for them that religion was not at the heart of a culture shaping its values, its shared meanings, and its identity. It was this distinction between the church on the one hand and the cultural role of religion on the other that would allow—for generations to come—the white southern Presbyterian Church to remain largely silent on social issues, especially race, while at the same time promoting a vision for a distinct southern society. Indeed the doctrine of the spirituality of the church and the loud silence of a "spiritual church" on social questions ironically functioned and was to function as a political agenda and an ideological prop for a "southern way of life."[41]

Thornwell identified national distinctions as the second reason for a new church. Protestant churches, he said, organize along national lines. He pointed to familiar examples of national churches, emphasized the benefits that flow from such arrangements, and insisted that it was altogether proper to organize a church within the bounds of the new Confederate nation. It was not that Presbyterians in the South no longer loved the former united church that had nurtured them over the generations. Nor was it that the Presbyterian Church in the Confederate States of America abjured the principles that had marked the united church. Rather the new church was seeking to "give these same principles a richer, freer, fuller development among ourselves than they possibly could receive under *foreign culture.*" In subjection to "*a foreign power,* we could no more accomplish [this development] than the Church in the United States could have been developed in dependence upon the Presbyterian Church of Scotland." The difficulty was not so much geographical distance but cultural distance: "the difference in the manners, habits, customs and ways of thinking, the social, civil and political institutions of the people." These same cultural distances "exist in relation to the Confederate and United States, and render it eminently proper that the Church in each should be a separate and independent as the Governments."[42]

Fifteen months earlier Thornwell had written his wife from Europe about his love for the United States. "After all," he had said, "there is no land like our own." Now in Georgia in December 1861, he insisted that the Confederate States had a separate culture from that of the northern states. Despite his Unionist sentiments and years of struggling to follow what he regarded as a reasonable middle way, Thornwell together, with his colleagues, asserted that the South possessed a separate culture—that southerners had their own manners, habits, customs, and ways of thinking; that the South possessed its own social, civil, and political institutions. Here Thornwell and his colleagues finally acknowledged, as battles raged between warring armies, that their middle way lacked what it most needed: a common culture, a shared language and set of assumptions, across which a middle way could traverse. Most clearly the North and South heard different meanings and envisioned different worlds when the word *liberty* was spoken. So seeing the cultural chasm and acknowledging the incompatible and conflicting meanings of *liberty,* Thornwell had concluded that "two Governments upon this continent may work out the problem of human liberty more successfully than one."[43]

Thornwell did not hesitate to push ahead with his argument and to name slavery as that which "so radically and fundamentally distinguishes" the North and the South. What followed was a brilliant summary of a proslavery argument that he and his colleagues at Columbia had developed throughout the antebellum years. So under Thornwell's leadership, the newly formed Presbyterian Church in the Confederates States of America asserted that the South was a distinct culture, one based on a hierarchical understanding of society and on pervasive racial assumptions. This South was the homeland they were defending, a South where whites had their place and where blacks had theirs.[44]

If Thornwell and the other Columbia Unionists turned their former Unionist position on its head in 1861, arguing for a separate southern culture, they knew that the war that raged was a civil war. The two armies that were fighting bloody battles, and the two governments that organized those warring armies, and the two peoples who supported those armies with patriotic frenzy shared not only much history but also many values and common commitments. This history and these shared values and commitments had been, after all, the strength of a middle way despite its profound flaws. As future developments would show, the Civil War that was only beginning in 1861 was more a war between subcultures than a war between completely alien cultures. To be sure, the blood that was being poured out in fierce fighting indicated the intensity of the struggle within American society about competing visions. And the coming victory of northern armies was going to mean that the northern vision, so powerfully articulated by Lincoln, was going to be perceived as the mainstream of American life.

It would not be, however, the only stream, for another with origins deep in southern history would continue to flow. This southern stream, shed of the burden of slavery but carrying with it hierarchical and pervasive racial assumptions, was to reemerge with surprising strength. Flowing far beyond the states of the Confederacy, joining similar streams from other sections of the country, this expanded southern stream would slowly merge with the mainstream of American life and become a powerful current within it. Flowing within this conservative current would be reminders here and there of the religious and cultural perspectives articulated by Thornwell and his Unionists colleagues in defense of their home and their homeland.[45]

PART II
A Southern Horizon

6

Civil War

Long before the first shots had been fired on Fort Sumter, Columbia Seminary leaders believed that a civil war would be long and bloody. During the 1850s they worked and pled for moderation and compromise—in part at least—because they imagined the dead and the wounded scattered across fields of battle and because they saw a looming vision of war's wasteland. By early 1862 that vision had emerged as a reality that was dreadful and personal and compelling. Columbia leaders plunged into the midst of this conflict hoping to do their part in defense of their homeland.[1]

Hurrying home from the General Assembly meeting in Augusta, Thornwell immediately began writing a propaganda tract to encourage southerners in their fight against an aggressive northern assault on the newly established Confederate States of America. The tract, "Our Danger and Duty," was quickly published and widely distributed not only throughout the Confederate armies but also among civilians. Thornwell's purpose, Palmer later wrote, was "to animate the people to maintain the struggle in which they were embarked."[2]

What might southerners expect, Thornwell asked, if northern armies prevailed? He answered that our homes will be pillaged; our cities will be sacked and destroyed; our property will be confiscated; our patriots will be hanged; and this beautiful country will "pass out of our hands." A northern victory would mean disaster for the slave as well who "will slowly pass away, as the red man did before him, under the protection of Northern philanthropy; and the whole country, now like the garden of Eden in beauty and fertility, will first be a blackened and smoking desert, and then the minister of Northern cupidity and avarice." If this night of thick darkness settled across the South, Thornwell foresaw that even sympathy, the last solace of the afflicted, would be denied to white southerners. "The civilized world will look coldly upon us," Thornwell warned, "or even jeer us with the taunt that we have deservedly lost our own freedom in seeking to perpetuate the slavery of others." The theology professor declared that such reproach and unjust accusations, propagated by arrogant and self-righteous Yankees, would be the most bitter of many burdens that white southerners would have to bear if northern armies conquered the South.[3]

But Thornwell also saw disaster awaiting the North if its armies were victorious. No longer would there be a federal republic, "the common agent of sovereign and independent States." Rather a central despotism would rule the land. Such a despotism would derive its powers from the will and would shape its policies, according to the wishes of a numerical majority of the people—"in other words, a supreme, irresponsible democracy." This democratic absolutism was sure to arrest the progress of that regulated liberty that Thornwell so loved. The result would be anarchy that would lead to a military dictatorship committed to preserving order by the sacrifice of the last vestiges of liberty.[4]

Thornwell called on white southerners to resist such a future with a fierce determination and an unflagging energy. He reminded them that they had a noble inheritance and were fighting to preserve the liberty won by the blood of patriots during the Revolution. They were not revolutionaries but were resisting the revolution being fostered by Lincoln and Yankee idealists. White southerners, he insisted, were upholding the true doctrines of the federal Constitution and were fighting for all that had been considered established in the past. And he solemnly warned—they must not fail! "The word failure must not be pronounced among us. It is not a thing to be dreamed of. We must settle it that we *must* succeed. We must not sit down to count chances. There is too much at stake to think of discussing probabilities. We must make success a certainty; and that, by the blessing of God, we can do."[5]

What was necessary for success, said Thornwell, was for white southerners to do their duty. And good Calvinist that he was, he had no difficulty spelling out that duty in great detail—white southerners were to shake off any apathy and realize the seriousness of the crisis before them; they must sacrifice private interests to the public good; they must reject any spirit of faction that would divide them; they must all work without ceasing and abandon any pursuit of leisure; they must put behind them "all fastidious notions of military etiquette" and expel "the enemy by any and every means that God has put in our power"; and finally they must guard against a presumptuous confidence. The cause is not ours, he told southerners, but God's. Not surprisingly the theologian insisted southern patriotism and courage must have beneath it the inspiration of religion. White southerners not only must have a righteous cause but must also be a righteous people. "We must abandon all of our sins and put ourselves heartily and in earnest on the side of Providence."[6]

Thornwell concluded his call for southern resistance with a ringing peroration that drew together his Christian faith with the history of his beloved "immortal" Greeks.

> Let our spirit be loftier than that of the pagan Greek, and we can succeed in making every pass a Thermopylae, every strait a Salamis, and every plain a Marathon. We can conquer, and we *must.* We must not suffer any other thought to enter our minds. If we are overrun, we can at least die; and if our enemies get possession of our land, we can leave it a howling desert. But under God, we shall not fail. If we are true to Him, and true to ourselves, a glorious future is before us. We occupy a sublime position. The eyes of the world are upon us; we are a spectacle to God, to angels, and to men. Can our hearts grow faint, or our hands feeble, in a cause like this? The spirits of

> our fathers call to us from their graves. The heroes of other ages and other countries are beckoning us on to glory. Let us seize the opportunity, and make to ourselves an immortal name, while we redeem a land from bondage and a continent from ruin.[7]

In this way and with letters to the press, Thornwell, the professor of theology at Columbia Theological Seminary, sought to make his contribution to the war effort and to the establishment of the Confederate States of America. He was joined in this effort by his Columbia colleagues, who threw themselves to the cause of rousing southern whites to the defense of their homeland by assuring them that their cause was God's cause.

In Charleston Thomas Smyth preached and then published as a tract "The Victory of Manassas Plain." Beneath this great southern victory, he explained, one could see the very hand of God. In 1863 he wrote "The War of the South Vindicated," and he published another tract titled "The Character and Conditions of Liberty" in which he reiterated once again that any true liberty must be a regulated liberty. And he wrote "The Soldier's Prayer Book" to give comfort, guidance, and encouragement to those who were facing the boredom and anxieties of army camps, and to those who were being called to charge across battlefields into a waiting hell at Antietam, Chancellorsville, and Gettysburg, and for those who found themselves suffering the filth and vermin and terror of the siege of Vicksburg and in the trenches before Petersburg.[8]

Benjamin Morgan Palmer also threw himself into the cause of rousing southern morale, and he quickly became the most famous and influential Columbia supporter of the Confederacy. In April 1862 he left New Orleans and visited the army of General Albert Sidney Johnston. Sitting astride a horse, Palmer delivered "a thrilling address" to a portion of Johnston's army immediately before they marched into the Battle of Shiloh. Shortly after the battle, the governor of Mississippi recruited Palmer to stump the state to encourage white Mississippians in their struggle against Yankee invaders. In Jackson he addressed a huge crowd. Reporting on his speech, the local paper called Palmer the "distinguished orator, philosopher and divine, whose services in the cause of civil and religious liberty have excited the admiration and gratitude of the whole Southern Confederacy." His address, said the paper, was a "most profound, philosophical and exhaustive exposition of the grounds of our defense in the great struggle in progress before the bar of God and in the forum of nations." Palmer was said to "cover the whole ground" on which "we rest our cause." He would later spend much time in Tennessee preaching to the troops, and he would address large public gatherings in Georgia and South Carolina trying to give encouragement and hope as battles raged. In an address before the Georgia legislature, he spoke of the "Rainbow Round the Throne" and asked if the present suffering of the South was a sign of penal judgment or paternal discipline. He wondered if amid the sorrow and blood of war, white southerners could discover the sign of the rainbow, the emblem of mercy and hope. He found the rainbow over the Confederacy and insisted that "we make our appeal to Him who ruled beneath the rainbow, on the ground that, touching this controversy between us and our foes, we are blameless." Our cause, he assured the Georgia legislators, "is preeminently the cause of God himself, and every blow struck by us is in defense of his supremacy." But Palmer already knew that the rainbow was hard to discern. In April 1862 the federal navy had taken New Orleans, and Palmer had had to wait anxiously for his family fleeing the city. They made their way to Columbia, where they moved in with his wife's mother and her stepfather, George Howe, and Palmer was soon once again on the Columbia faculty.[9]

But these and other Columbia colleagues were to make other contributions to the cause—contributions that would be more costly and more bitter than their propaganda tracts or their sermons and speeches. They gave their parental blessings to their sons who were offering themselves to the cause of a nation ruled by southern whites. Gillespie Thornwell, his father's pride, joined Wade Hampton's legion. Gillespie was only a boy of sixteen, but he was a fine horseman, and he had a fine mare, and he was eager to join the fight. So his father gave his permission, and young Gillespie became a proud member of Hampton's cavalry, and the sixteen-year-old was soon drilling on horseback with a drawn sword. Smyth's two sons, Augustine and Adger, were quickly engaged in the fighting that swirled around Charleston even as their father began the sad task of burying young men from his congregation. Augustine, a member of the Signal Corps, was to spend much of the war perched in the steeple of Charleston's St. Michael's Church watching the movement of the federal fleet. Since the steeple was the highest in Charleston, it was a primary target for federal gunners when they were shelling the city. But from the steeple young Augustine could watch his grandfather's ship—the *James Adger*—a side-wheel steamer seized in New York at the beginning of the war. She was a key player in the blockade of Charleston and served as the flagship of Rear Admiral DuPont during the powerful monitor attack on the city.[10]

Charles Jones's sons, who had spent such formative years in Columbia, became Confederate officers—Charlie was made a lieutenant colonel in charge of artillery for the military district of Georgia, and Joe, a physician, was made major and was given responsibility for investigating the wretched conditions of Confederate hospitals and prisoner-of-war camps, including the infamous Andersonville prison in south Georgia. Howe's nineteen-year-old son, Willie, enlisted in the Columbia Grays, an infantry unit, and was soon fighting bravely at First Manassas. After the battle he was promoted to an orderly sergeant to work among the wounded and dying. And so it went as sons went off to battle.[11]

The parents waited uneasily, eagerly looking for letters while anxiously watching the reports from battlefields. Board member John Jones followed his son Dunwody to Virginia and was working as a chaplain when news arrived of the costly victory at First Manassas. Dunwody had been in the midst of the battle. The father wrote his family of the cries of the wounded, of the dreadful stench from the battlefield, and of his own desperate search for Dunwody among the dead and the wounded and "in a wilderness of camps and tents and soldiers" until finally "I found our boy and ran and threw my arms around his neck and kissed him as one lost and dead suddenly found again." Willie Howe, while working among the wounded in the foul conditions of a Civil War hospital, contracted typhoid fever. It was known and feared as a "killer disease" with its ferocious fever, delirium, and intestinal hemorrhaging. George Howe rushed from Columbia to his son's aid. He arrived on a Thursday and found him on a narrow cot in his tent but so emaciated that Howe did not recognize him. Willie seemed to be recovering, but on Saturday evening he was taken with a hemorrhage of the bowels and began to sink rapidly. He died on Sunday evening with his grieving father by his side. Howe took his son's remains to Columbia, where his mother gazed with great anguish on the body of her son. "It is a terrible affliction," a friend wrote, "and oh, how many such there are and will be as long as this horrid war lasts!" And Mary Jones wrote from her Liberty County plantation "Such are the priceless treasures this vile enemy demands and receives from our hearts and homes."[12]

Three months after Willie Howe's death in February 1862, Gillespie Thornwell was involved in a cavalry skirmish as a part of the Battle of Williamsburg. A federal cavalryman thrust his sword into the now seventeen-year-old Gillespie. His parents received word that the wound was slight, but it later appeared to have been "within a hair's breadth of being fatal." His parents hurried to Virginia and found him able to make the trip home to Columbia. His father wrote a friend that Gillespie was "represented as having acted very bravely. That I knew he would do; he is all pluck. His heart is in the cause. . . . Though under age, he has enlisted for the war, with my full consent."[13]

As the war progressed and the number of wounded mounted, women associated with the seminary began to take leadership in efforts around the state to provide food and clothing for the South's fighting men and to care for the sick arriving from army camps and the wounded arriving from battle fronts. In Charleston Thomas Smyth's wife, Margaret Adger Smyth, was chair of the Executive Committee of the Relief Association and worked tirelessly organizing and shipping to army camps boxes of shirts, pants, drawers, and pillows as well as bags of rice and carefully packed bacon and smoked meat. In Liberty County Mary Jones worked with other plantation mistresses in weaving blankets and making quilts and tearing up old sheets and clothes for bandages. Leighton Wilson's wife, Jane, joined other church women from the Scotch Irish settlements along South Carolina's Black River in the Association for Relief. They made blankets, quilts, and uniforms; washed and boiled old clothes and cut them into strips for bandages; and gathered food from gardens, barns, and smokehouses to be sent to hospitals and to loved ones in muddy trenches. No one, however, worked harder and with more passion than Sarah Ann Howe. She was the primary organizer and served as president of the Ladies Hospital in Columbia. With contributions from around the state, she and a few other women purchased cots and sheets, blankets, buckets, and other materials needed for a Civil War hospital, which they established at the fairgrounds. As the wounded and sick were brought in, this daughter of one of the largest slave owners in the South helped them undress—she would kneel down and take off their shoes and socks and do all that she could to help them be comfortable. She organized and was president of the Wayside, a facility at the train station where soldiers arrived exhausted and hungry, sick and wounded. There they were fed and cared for for a few days before being sent on their way or carried to a hospital. In four years some seventy-five thousand troops were estimated to have passed through the Wayside. At the Ladies Hospital—which was soon known as "Mrs. Howe's Hospital"—she worked without hesitation among those with pneumonia, typhoid, and erysipelas. She contracted erysipelas herself and suffered dreadfully from the wretched skin disease that caused her to have high fevers, chills, and nausea and to have a painful rash and blisters on her face and arms. But as soon as she recovered she was back at work among the wounded, sick, and dying. No doubt the thoughts of her poor Willie dying of typhoid in a distant camp gave her energy and courage and a tender compassion.[14]

Not far from the Ladies Hospital at the fairgrounds, James Woodrow worked long hours in the Confederate medical laboratory making medicines for the war effort. As the seminary's new Perkins Professor of Natural Science in Connection with Revelation, Woodrow was well prepared for the task. He had received his scientific training and Ph.D. summa cum laude from the University of Heidelberg in Germany and was an expert in analytical and synthetic chemistry. With seminary board member Joseph LeConte, Woodrow helped manufacture such medicines as silver nitrate to be used as an antiseptic, and sulfuric ether and nitric ether so important for army surgeons to anesthetize their wounded patients. Woodrow, who needed little sleep, had a remarkable capacity for work and set up a laboratory in the seminary chapel, where he worked far into the night making silver nitrate.[15]

While Woodrow worked in the chapel with his chemicals, test tubes, retorts, and pans, refugees from the lowcountry began crowding into the seminary's Simons and Law dormitories. The dormitories were new, handsome brick buildings, and their rooms provided shelter for those who had been driven from their plantation homes on the Sea Islands. They came from Johns, James, and Edisto Islands—all places where generous planters had once provided funds for the seminary's endowment. Now Johns Island and James Island were places of fierce combat, and Edisto was held by federal troops while the adjoining mainland was subject to Yankee raids so that weeds now grew in its cotton fields and once great rice fields were abandoned to the mercy of high tides. Columbia faculty homes also welcomed the refugees. The Elias Vanderhorst family stayed with the Howes. The family of Robert W. Barnwell fled their elegant plantation home on the coast and moved in with the Thornwells for several months until they could find their own accommodations. Barnwell, a former U.S. senator, was a close friend of Thornwell's, and he was to serve in the Confederate Senate throughout the war.[16]

At the beginning of the war, the General Assembly appointed Leighton Wilson to organize and oversee the work of all Presbyterian chaplains. A skilled administrator Wilson frequently made the fifty-mile trip from his plantation home on the Black River to Columbia to consult with colleagues at the seminary. He worked out a system that led to more than a quarter of the Presbyterian pastors in the South spending some time as chaplains. They worked in hospitals among the wounded, wrote letters home for the dying, and preached to and counseled troops who knew they were facing death or terrible wounds. Wilson went to Virginia to work for months at a time as a chaplain. He talked and counseled and read scripture and served the Lord's Supper. He visited in hospitals and tried to comfort those who were suffering the traumas of wounds. And he sat by the beds of those who were afflicted by the scourges of the battlefield trenches and army camps—pneumonia or dysentery or typhoid or a rotting gangrene or some terrible combination of them. He met with Robert E. Lee, and together they spoke about the "spiritual wants of the army" and the need for chaplains among the troops.[17]

Wilson recruited many young Columbia graduates to become chaplains. William Boggs graduated from Columbia in 1860 and served as chaplain of the Sixth South

Carolina Regiment until it was surrendered by Lee at Appomattox in April 1865. George Petrie graduated in 1862 and served as chaplain to the Twenty-Second Alabama Regiment throughout the remainder of the war. Edward Green married the Howes' daughter Emily immediately after his graduation in June 1863 and was soon on his way to Virginia as a chaplain. Wilson's nephew, Charlton Wilson, class of 1855, served in Virginia as a chaplain to the cavalry of Holcombe's legion and died of typhoid fever in 1864. But the best known of many Columbia chaplains was John Lafayette Girardeau, who resigned as pastor of Charleston's Zion Church and became chaplain of the Twenty-Third Regiment of the South Carolina Volunteers. He was with the troops through bloody battle after bloody battle in Virginia, preached before large gatherings in which Lee and his staff were often present, and crouched in the muddy trenches before Petersburg trying to tell the good news of the Gospel and offering troops the body and blood of Christ. On Lee's retreat to Appomattox, Girardeau was captured by Union troops and spent the next three months on Johnson's Island, a prisoner-of-war camp for Confederate officers, located on the Ohio shore of Lake Erie. Such experiences lingered for a lifetime in the minds and imaginations of Columbia graduates and future faculty.[18]

During the summer of 1862, while his son Gillespie was recuperating in Columbia from his saber wound, Thornwell was struggling with his own health. He had never been a strong person, and his habit of staying up all night reading, drinking a little brandy, and smoking cigars had left him subject to various ailments. Over the years he had gone to Virginia springs that were famous for their healing properties, and he had sailed to Europe on three occasions in the hope that ocean air and a more relaxed schedule would allow his body some deep rest and healing. But each time when he returned to Columbia he quickly returned to his old ways. Family and friends warned him about his smoking, but he loved his cigars—he liked to smoke only the best—and he believed they did wonders for what ailed him. His closest friend, John Adger, remonstrated with him, but even though Thornwell called Adger "a friend who has no rival in my heart," he ignored his pleas. And he teased Adger's beautiful wife, Elizabeth, and encouraged her to take up "that most delectable of all weeds" to help with her neuralgia. "Let me advise you," he wrote, "as you prize your comfort, to provide yourself with a clean pipe and a short stem, and set to work upon the goodly process of inhaling the exquisite fragrance." And with no little amusement, he told the proud mistress of Woodburn plantation that "there is no sight more truly venerable than that of a mother in Israel, in the chimney corner, with her children about her refreshing their senses with gales of incense as sweet and cheering as the tones which proceed from her mouth." But however much he might tease and joke about tobacco, it, together with his work habits, had slowly undermined his health. His lungs were bad, and he seemed constantly threatened with consumption.[19]

By the summer of 1862 chronic dysentery had left him very weak. He went to stay with his daughter and her family in the western part of North Carolina. A mineral spring was nearby, and he hoped that by drinking its waters and bathing in one of its pools he would have some relief and that a good rest away from Columbia's heat would help him regain his strength. But he missed his wife, Nancy, terribly. "I think about you all the time," he wrote her. "I have long known that I have the best wife in the world, and it is a great grief for me that that I cannot do more to free her from care, anxiety, and sorrow." I want, he said, "to see you happy." When Gillespie headed back to Richmond and the battlefields of Virginia, Thornwell went to Charlotte to see him.[20]

The father and son had a day together in the little city, and Nancy Thornwell was there as well. But when Gillespie left on the train the next day, Thornwell collapsed, his energy exhausted. He sensed that death was near. He told a friend: "You have just come in time to see me die." When asked if he wished anything done when he was gone, he replied "The Judge of all the earth will do right." He began to move in and out of consciousness. At one point he raised his hand as if addressing a class of seminarians: "Well," he said, "you have stated your position, now prove it." John Adger rushed to be with him as death approached. Adger arrived at the last hour and found his friend lying quietly with smiles playing over his countenance. Then suddenly Thornwell cried out: "Wonderful! Beautiful! Nothing but Space! Expanse! Expanse! Expanse!" And he was gone.[21]

The next spring, in a skirmish near Warrenton, Virginia, Gillespie was shot through the abdomen. He was taken to a Union hospital in excruciating pain. He told those who attended him that he was not afraid to die, but the eighteen-year-old felt the deep loneliness of approaching death and called out to see his mother and family at home once more. He died the next morning. General Wade Hampton wrote Nancy Thornwell that Gillespie "was a noble and gallant soldier," and that while the mother "could not but mourn, as only a parent can mourn for a child," she could draw consolation from the knowledge that Gillespie had "fallen whilst sustaining nobly the sacred cause for which his father plead, and which he had dedicated himself." After the war Gillespie's body was brought home to Columbia and buried not far from his father's grave.[22]

Gillespie Thornwell's death was one among the appalling number of young men slaughtered on the battlefields of the war. After the Battle of Shiloh, where twenty-three thousand men were killed, the Union general Ulysses Grant wrote: "I saw an open field . . . so covered with dead that it would have been possible to walk across the clearing, in any direction, stepping only on dead bodies without a foot touching the ground." The same would be said after the horrors of Antietam, where in a single day twenty-two thousand were killed and wounded, and on other corpse-covered battlefields. "A battle is indescribable," a chaplain wrote after Fredericksburg, "but once seen it haunts a man till the day of his death." The death of family members, of friends and comrades, the stench, the uncovered bodies often left rotting for days in the fields—all left their mark on the nation's life and would haunt those associated with Columbia Seminary for several generations, shaping in profound ways the little world of the seminary.[23]

White southerners were not the only southerners to bear the grief and burdens of the war. Black slaves were made to labor in defense of the Confederacy even as they heard in distance battles the sounds of their approaching freedom. John Adger was required to send two men from his Woodburn plantation to help with the fortifications around Charleston. He sent Ben, a young man, and Daniel, an older man who went with only great reluctance. They worked first in the harbor on Fort Sumter—it had been badly damaged by the guns of the Union navy. The work was hard, sometimes exciting, and always dangerous. Later Ben was sent to Fort Johnson on James Island. There he was struck on the arm by a fragment of shell, and the arm had to be amputated by a Confederate surgeon. Ben spent the rest of his life known as "One Arm Ben."[24]

In Liberty County Charles Colcock Jones was required to send seven able-bodied men to do the wretched work of building earthen defenses on the muddy banks of the Savannah. Among those chosen were young men whose families had been working on the Maybank plantation that had been so important for the establishment of the Georgia Endowment for Columbia Seminary. The consequences of their labors on the banks of the Savannah were disastrous. Within weeks they were all back in Liberty County and were dangerously ill. River cholera had struck with its cramps, vomiting, and violent diarrhea. Three of them quickly died. But to make matters worse, they had apparently brought back with them a deadly form of measles. Before the epidemic was over, the measles had killed nine on the Jones's plantations. One was the daughter of the cook Patience who had labored as a young woman in the Jones kitchen in Columbia, where she had helped to serve seminary faculty and students. And the measles spread as well to the nearby Howe plantation, where many died and the old driver Caesar had to work hard to provide for the needs of the sick and the dying.[25]

The presence of Union gunboats on the coastal waters of South Carolina and Georgia meant that many slaves were removed from their homes and moved to inland plantations. Planters who had been among the strongest supporters of the seminary removed, as they were able, slaves from Johns, James, and Edisto Islands. Seminary graduate and board member John Jones moved his slaves from his Bonaventure plantation south of Savannah to a newly purchased plantation, Refuge, in southwest Georgia, which was far from any fighting. Most revealing was Charles Jones's decision to move most of his slaves from the coast to Indianola, a plantation in middle Georgia. For decades Jones and his wife, Mary, had been the embodiment of the paternalism advocated by Columbia leaders. When Jones was a member of the seminary faculty, he had taught Columbia students that slaves were a part of the owner's household and should be treated with a disciplined kindness and provided with adequate housing, nourishing food, and time they could call their own. When he was serving as president of Columbia's board during the 1840s, he had begun to be known among whites as "The Apostle to the Negro Slaves." He and Mary Jones expected their slaves to respond with loyalty, with a sense of belonging to the Jones household, and with some level of affection for master and mistress. But when federal gunboats began roaming the coastal waterways and rivers of Liberty County, Charles and Mary Jones acknowledged by the removal of their slaves that slavery was built on force and not affection. Master and mistress had become alarmed by slaves on neighboring plantations escaping to the enemy. Most alarming was the escape of some of the most highly trusted slaves in the county.[26]

Before he had removed his slaves from Bonaventure, John Jones had had five slaves make a successful break for freedom. And David Buttolph, the pastor of the Midway Congregational Church, which had sent so many of its white sons to Columbia Seminary, had his butler slip away to freedom. Buttolph, who had graduated from Columbia in 1852, had married Laura Maxwell, the niece of Charles Jones. She had inherited some of the slaves when the Maybank estate had been settled and funds secured for the seminary endowment. David Buttolph expressed the dismay that many paternalistic whites felt when they discovered that their slaves preferred freedom over the kindness of white owners. "Joe," Buttolph wrote John Jones, "has really gone, taking with him Isaac, his brother at Lambert, the most trusty fellow on the plantation. Joe's leaving was the hardest blow which could be given. I do not remember that I ever gave him a crossword. Indeed, I never had any occasion to do it, for he was a most faithful and willing servant. If he wanted anything, he had only to ask for it. I have felt deeply hurt and mortified at Joe's leaving, more so than if the whole plantation had left."[27]

Shortly after Joe's escape, General William T. Sherman began his Atlanta campaign. What followed brought destruction, terror, and lasting bitterness to those who were so closely associated with Columbia Seminary.

Robert Quarterman Mallard had grown up on the Mallard Place plantation not far from the Midway Congregational Church, had graduated from Columbia in 1855, and was married to Charles and Mary Jones's daughter Mary Sharpe. In 1864 he was serving as pastor of Atlanta's Central Presbyterian Church. With him in Atlanta were not only his wife and two children but also six slaves who had been a part of a wedding gift of slaves given by Charles and Mary Jones to their daughter and new son-in-law. As battles raged closer and closer to Atlanta, Mallard worked night and day among the wounded being brought into the city. In early July 1864, as both sides maneuvered for the Battle of Atlanta, the Mallards prepared to leave the city. They hastily packed all their belongings for shipment to Augusta and rushed to the depot in a little cart. This time when the train whistle blew, the white family was riding with their slaves in a boxcar. They all eventually made their way back to Liberty County, where they awaited the outcome of the battle and its consequences.[28]

In early September Atlanta fell, and with its fall there soon came fire and great destruction—the train depots and sheds, the rolling mills and machine shops, and the foundries and the arsenals were all put to the torch, and with them going up in the flames were hotels, churches, and businesses, as well as somewhere between four thousand and five thousand homes. In the middle of November, Sherman plunged into middle Georgia on a brilliant and daring march to the sea. Cutting his supply lines and all communications with the North, he moved his great army toward Savannah, declaring that the army would live off the land. Foragers were organized to plunder a large swath of Georgia, and to bring corn, peas, and bacon; cows, pigs, and chickens; horses and mules to the rumbling army. Behind them the foragers left burning barns and the ruins of smoldering homes, and following them came newly liberated black men, women, and children.[29]

When the army reached Savannah, it paused on the outskirts of the city like some great storm stalled after landfall. Foragers were sent out in every direction to bring back provisions for the army. They were soon in Liberty County. Over a thousand camped at the Mallard Place plantation, turning it into a wasteland. Robert Mallard was captured and carried to a prisoner-of-war camp outside of Savannah. Mary Jones and Mary Sharpe

Mallard huddled at Montevideo plantation as raiding party after raiding party arrived to carry away all that they could find.

On December 21 Sherman telegraphed Lincoln, presenting "as a Christmas gift the city of Savannah, with one hundred and fifty heavy guns and plenty of ammunition, also about twenty-five thousand bales of cotton." As the troops marched into the city, they brought with them freedom for the black slaves of Savannah, who greeted them wildly as the conquering agents of Almighty God. For the liberated slaves, the marching Yankees appeared as nothing less than a miracle, as a mighty act of a liberating God. "I'd always thought about this, and wanted this day to come, and prayed for it and knew God meant it should be here sometime," an enslaved woman declared as she looked around at the troops and shook her head in disbelief. "But I didn't believe I should ever see it and it is so great and good a thing, I cannot believe it has come now; and I don't believe I ever shall realize it, but I know it has though, and I bless the Lord for it."[30]

But the fall of Savannah did not mean an end to the raiders in Liberty County. On January 4, 1865, Mary Sharpe Mallard went into a long and painful labor while just outside her bedroom door Yankees continued to ransack the Joneses' plantation home. Only after a doctor from a neighboring plantation arrived to help with the delivery was a little girl safely born. A Jones slave had led the doctor along secret paths through the surrounding woods and swamps. In the meantime George Howe had visited his Liberty County plantation and had left instruction for his old driver Caesar to be prepared for the arrival of hungry Yankees. And shortly after the Yankees had come pouring into the county, Columbia board member Joseph LeConte had made his way from Columbia to Augusta and around the enemy lines and was hiding in the swamp waiting to get his sister and his daughter away from his sister's ravaged Liberty County plantation. It would be weeks before these whites, so intimately associated with the seminary, would make their way through dense swamps and the swollen waters of the Altamaha River to safety in southwest Georgia.[31]

On all these plantations, the food and property of black slaves was also taken by the raiders. On the Mallard plantation the driver Pompey at first welcomed the Yankee raiders, for he knew they were his liberators. The slave settlement and the barns on the plantation were full from an abundant harvest. Pompey's brother said, "it seemed to us as if the Lord has blessed the earth on purpose to help our deliverer." But the foragers soon showed themselves to be ravenous. "The soldiers did not say anything," Pompey later reported, "only that they were in need of the property & would have it." They took his bed sheets and his wife's underclothes and made them into sacks and stuffed them with corn. They took Pompey's horse and his wagon and shot his pigs and carried them away. On the Howe plantation, the driver Caesar and his wife had managed to accumulate substantial livestock over many years of labor. After the war his wife, Linda Roberts, reported to the federal authorities that the soldiers had taken their horse and buggy, twenty cows, thirty hogs, forty bee hives, eighteen ducks, fifty chickens, twenty bushels of corn, and one hundred bushels of rice as well as a saddle and bridle. So old Caesar, who had looked after George Howe's plantations for almost thirty years, who had directed the tasks of Howe's many slaves and had watched the profits from their labors go to support the seminary professor and his family, he now watched his liberators confiscate his property and leave the old man and his family desperately poor in the middle of a Georgia winter.[32]

In late January the union army began its move across the Savannah River into the Palmetto State. Before leaving the city, Sherman told a South Carolinian who was seeking to return home, "You will be going out from the frying pan into the fire." He did not believe he could control his troops as they entered the proud little state that was believed to have started all the death and destruction of the war. "You have heard of the horrors of war," Sherman warned. "Wait until my army gets into South Carolina and you will see the reality." And he told a Union officer that the time had come to punish the people of South Carolina. In a surprise move, Sherman marched toward Columbia and not Charleston. Town after town went up in flames, as did any barn or plantation house that lay in the path of the army. Soon it would be Columbia's turn.[33]

When it became clear that Sherman's army was heading toward Columbia, those associated with the seminary prepared for what seemed to be certain devastation. John Adger sold his handsome three story brick home for thirty thousand Confederate dollars and invested the money in Confederate bonds. He moved a large part of his library and some furniture to the home of his aunt Agnes Law, who had a decade earlier provided the funds for the building of Law dormitory on the seminary campus. The rest of his library and furniture he managed to get shipped to his home near Pendleton in the upcountry. There with his family he waited the arrival of federal raiders.[34]

Palmer, because of his well-known support of the Confederacy, fled the city, leaving his family under the care of George Howe. He found refuge in the village of York, south of Charlotte. Howe, having returned from his plantation before devastations rolled across Liberty County, stayed in Columbia to try and protect his family and also the seminary property. Aaron Leland also stayed. His wife had died several years earlier, and on a trip to England he had brought back a wife, Clara Blight, forty-five years his junior. Shortly after this he had had a stroke. So Leland, who was now unable to speak, and his young English wife waited together in their home as the union army drew near to the city. James Woodrow remained in Columbia, continuing to work in his medical laboratory. Andrew Crawford, a local elder and member of the board, was the seminary treasurer. He took the bonds and securities of the seminary to the little village of Chester between Columbia and Charlotte and gave them to Columbia graduate and longtime member of the seminary's board John A. Douglas, who buried the documents in a corn field. Joseph LeConte gathered his scientific papers and family silver and set out with a party trying to reach safety in an obscure part of the upcountry. But once again, as in Liberty County, he soon found himself hiding in the woods and using all the skills of an outdoorsman to avoid the enemy, which found his wagon, took the silver and other objects of value, and burned his papers and books.[35]

General Wade Hampton had been dispatched with two small divisions from Lee's army to help defend his native state. When Sherman threatened to encircle him, Hampton abandoned Columbia, and the mayor surrendered the city on February 17, 1865. Shortly after the arrival of federal troops in the city, Major General John A. Logan occupied the

Hampton-Preston mansion across the street from the seminary. Orders had been given to destroy public buildings, railroads, and manufacturing shops but to "spare libraries, asylums and private dwellings." A large supply of liquor that had been stored in the city was soon discovered, and many troops and Columbians became drunk and disorderly. A soldier accosted Howe and tried to take his gold watch, and the old man had to fight him off. Soldiers rushed into the Leland home looking for plunder. When a soldier attempted to take a glass decanter, Clara Leland fought him for it until an officer entered, stopped the struggle, and had the soldier arrested. Later when asked what she said to the soldier, she replied: "I will not tell you. I did not know I knew such words."[36]

A strong wind was blowing, and a fire, started amid chaos and confusion, was soon raging across the city. Palmer's family fled their home carrying with them what they could to the Howe's home close to the seminary, but they found it also threatened by fire, and all spent the night in the street. Not far away Agnes Law secured two soldiers to guard her beautiful house and gardens. But the guards became drunk, and soon her house was in flames, and the old woman was forced to find refuge in a neighboring home full of other women together with children huddled in terror. Two days later she was found roaming in her garden and was taken to Law dormitory on the seminary campus, and there she spent the rest of her life in the building whose construction she had financed.[37]

The fire consumed a third of the city. A Union chaplain wrote that the next day "when riding through the ruins of the city," he had found "all was quiet and still as death; broken furniture and charred fragments covered the streets, and burnt walls stood black, shattered and lonely." Palmer's home was among those burned and with it all his books, private papers, and household furniture. Woodrow lost his home as well. The seminary campus escaped the flames—perhaps because General Logan's headquarters were across the street—and miraculously the Thornwell, Howe, and Leland homes escaped as well. All were crowded with refugees as were the seminary buildings. When Sherman's troops left the city and headed toward the final battles of the war, John Leighton Wilson gathered provisions from the plantations along the Black River that had been out of the path of Sherman's main army. Wilson secured two four-horse wagons and with a former slave whom Wilson had freed decades earlier the white man and the black man made their way together over the fifty miles to city. There they found the seminary crowded with many hungry refugees. After unloading on the seminary campus what they had brought and after visiting among the dazed and distraught faculty families, the two men returned with their empty wagons to their Black River homes.[38]

When the way appeared safe, Benjamin Palmer began a sixty-mile walk back to the city. He and two traveling companions had to be on constant watch for Yankee marauders, and they had only some corn bread and a little wine, but with the aid of some frightened families along the rail track they were following, they eventually made their way to Columbia. Finding his family and friends in great distress, Palmer secured a wagon and went into the countryside, where he gathered provisions that had escaped the ravages of the army.[39]

John Adger spent the closing days of the war at his upcountry plantation. Union raiders came through and ransacked his home, but there was little destruction of property. A large part of his library had been burned when Agnes Law's house had been burned and his former home in Columbia had burned in the fire that swept over much of the city. And of course the money he had received for the sale of the house was lost because he had invested it all in Confederate bonds. Years later he could not even remember what had happened to the bonds.[40]

When Richmond fell Confederate president Jefferson Davis fled south with his cabinet. Some southerners hoped that organized guerrilla warfare might continue to resist Yankee domination and keep blacks in a subservient place. Passing through South Carolina, the Davis party stopped for the night at the Abbeville home of Thomas Perrin, who had been serving as president of the seminary's board. He had been the first to sign his name to the Ordinance of Secession that had led to the war and to so much death and destruction. And while he was presiding over the Columbia board meeting in May 1863 he had learned of the death of his son and his brother in the terrible Battle of Chancellorsville. Now in 1865 he was the host of a fleeing Confederate government. Later Perrin reported to John Adger that the last cabinet meeting of the Confederacy was held that night in his home as the members agreed that the next morning they would go their separate ways when they left Abbeville. The Confederate States of America had come to an end.[41]

Thornwell and Palmer and Adger, Howe and Leland, Smyth, Jones, and Woodrow, Perrin and LeConte, and a host of others associated with seminary—they all poured out their hearts and minds, their wealth and even, for some, their children in support of a homeland built on slavery. They were the most brilliant and influential generation in the seminary's history. But they were to bear, as Thornwell feared they would have to bear, the reproach of the world. They were to be accused, as Thornwell foresaw, of seeking their own freedom by perpetuating the slavery of black men, women, and children. This reproach, these accusations, and this burden of their history would be their most enduring legacy. And that legacy was to mark for generations to come both Columbia Seminary and the Southern Presbyterian Church it sought to serve.

7

"A just but lost cause"

When Joseph LeConte finally made his way back to Columbia after hiding in the woods and dodging Yankees for days, he found the city in smoldering ruins. Entering from the extreme northern end of the city and going down Main Street, he found not a house remaining, but only "the tall chimneys standing gaunt and spectral, and empty brick walls with vacant windows like death-heads with eyeless sockets." Back to his left, in a once fashionable neighborhood, stood the seminary campus: the Ainsley Hall mansion, Simons and Law dormitories, a carriage house that had been converted into a chapel, and a few other outbuildings. All were crowded with impoverished and hungry refugees, as were the faculty homes that had escaped the flames. The seminary, which had a few years earlier reflected its location in the wealthiest region of the United States, now stood in the midst of deep poverty, widespread destruction, and only remembered glory.[1]

Charleston was also in ruins. Federal forces had been bombarding the city for most of the war, and Confederate defenders had done their own damage—they had built great mounds of earthwork defenses before the elegant homes that lined the battery and had dug deep holes for artillery so that Meeting Street in front of Thomas Smyth's mansion looked pox marked. And when the end was near, retreating Confederates had ignited ammunition dumps, whose explosions had burned large areas of the Upper Peninsula. Most devastating of all, however, had been the great fire of 1861. Starting in a kitchen, it had roared across the peninsula until it died on the banks of the Cooper River. Among the many building burned was the great Circular Congregational Church, which had provided the seminary with the first president of its board and with students and with funds for the endowment. A *New York Times* correspondent wrote in 1865 that the city was "an indescribable scene of desolation and ruin . . . silent to all sounds of business, and voiceless only to the woe-begone, poverty-stricken, haggard people, who wander up and down amid the ruins, looking to a jubilant past, and disappointed present, and a hopeless future."[2]

Other cities and towns were also in ruins. Atlanta was only beginning to stir in 1865 and to find the strength to begin its rise from its ashes. Savannah was not burned, but it was a deeply impoverished and conquered city under military rule. And the small towns had suffered as well—Darien in Georgia had been looted and burned, and Sherman's troops had ransacked and burned portions of Winnsboro, Camden, Chester, and Cheraw in South Carolina. The destruction in the countryside matched and in some places surpassed that in urban areas. The Sea Islands—Johns, James, and Edisto—whose white planters had been generous supporters of the seminary, had been either the scene of intense fighting or largely under federal control throughout the war. When the war ended and the planters returned, they returned to a poverty made more visible by their formerly elegant but now plundered plantation homes. In Liberty County, Georgia, plantations lay stripped of livestock, wagons, and provisions, and many plantation houses were in ashes. Among those that had been burned was Maybank, from whose settlement slaves had been sold to establish the Georgia endowment for the seminary. In Mississippi Judge John Perkins saw the emancipation of his two hundred and fifty slaves from whose labors had come the wealth that endowed the Perkins Professorship at Columbia Seminary. The judge's son had fled to Mexico.[3]

Many of the wealthy country churches had been damaged or destroyed and their members widely scattered. The Midway Congregational Church, which had sent twenty-eight of its sons to study at Columbia Seminary, never recovered from the dislocations of the war and the devastations wrought by Sherman's hungry troops. With the collapse of the old rice economy that had made the congregation wealthy and with its members no longer living close to the old church, the congregation closed its doors. The church building housed for a while a congregation of former slave members, but soon the handsome meetinghouse and its cemetery with its moss-draped oaks became simply a place of shadows and of memories preserved by poor but proud descendants. Among those who left Liberty County, after struggling to reestablish old ways under new conditions, was Mary Jones. With her husband Charles buried beneath the oaks in the Midway cemetery, she felt the anguish of the war and of her forced departure from a much-loved home and homeland. "The enemy," she wrote in her journal shortly before her departure, "has destroyed every living thing; even the plainest food is made scanty. His robberies and oppressions force me from my beloved home, where it is no longer safe or prudent to remain. And I must leave it in my advancing years, knowing not where the gray hairs which sorrow and time have thickly gathered will find a shelter, or the fainting heart and weary body a resting place, or any spot that I may ever again on earth call home."[4]

More devastating than the wasteland left by Union armies had been the loss of life. Church after church mourned the death of husbands and fathers and sons who had been much-loved members of congregations. The Wappetaw congregation, with less than fifty white members, lost Gabriel Jervey, over sixty years old, and John Whilden, boy-major who fell at the First Battle of Manassas. And there were others from the little congregation: Colonel Thomas Wagner died at Fort Moultrie in 1861; William Jervey at Petersburg, and John Jervey at Seven Pines; Lieutenant James Anderson and Colonel Robert Jeffords at Cold Harbor; and Captain L. A. Whilden at Drewrys Bluff; young Bacheldor Anderson died of disease contracted in a wretched army camp. In Charleston Thomas Smyth had been busy burying the dead in the cemetery of Second Presbyterian—twenty-two fell in battle, many of them young men, the joy and bright hope of their families. They all died, declared the defiant but revealing memorial erected by the congregation at the entrance to the sanctuary: "For Their Country, While in The Service of the Confederate States. 1860–1865." And so it went in the cities, towns, and countryside, in all the areas that had been at the heart of the seminary's constituency and among the proud people who thought of Columbia as "our seminary."[5]

Hanging over the seminary and its supporters in 1865 were not only the smell of charred buildings and the grief of lost loved ones, but profoundly troubling questions for those who had provided such powerful ideological and theological support for the Confederacy. As they stood amid the ruins of a southern homeland, remembered their past, and contemplated their future, they inescapably asked how it was possible that the white South had lost the war. How had the Yankees beaten the brave and surely invincible people of the South? Their cause had been just, yet Union armies had been victorious. How, in a morally coherent universe, was it possible for Sherman to march through Georgia and South Carolina and leave behind death and destruction, and how could the disreputable Grant force the noble Lee to surrender at Appomattox? How could such evil come to a people who were so sure they were following God's way and will? Had God abandoned the Confederacy, or was God simply asleep and indifferent? Had God acted in infidelity and unrighteousness toward the white South? Or had the South—and the church, in particular—been terribly wrong about slavery? Had a white southern heart been hardened, like Pharaoh's toward the Israelite slaves, and had white southern ears been simply deaf to the cries of black men, women, and children?[6]

Emma LeConte, seventeen-year-old daughter of Joseph, had listened to Benjamin Palmer preach in Columbia during the war years, and Palmer had assured the gathered Presbyterians that God was on the side of the South. Even as Sherman neared Columbia, Palmer had insisted that they should not despair, for "even if we should be overthrown—not conquered—the next generation would see the South *free* and independent." So when the Confederacy fell she wrote in her journal that it was "impossible not to feel rebellious and bitter. It is impossible not to feel that it is unjust and cruel." And the presbytery of South Carolina confessed shortly after the end of the war that "the faith of many a Christian is shaken by the mysterious and unlooked-for course of divine Providence." But John Jones thought hard truth must be faced. Surrounded by white refugees in southwest Georgia, the Columbia graduate and board member confessed, "However we may be able to prove the wickedness of our enemies, we must acknowledge that the providence of God has decided against us in the tremendous struggle we have just made for property rights and country. The hand of the Lord is upon us!" And he prayed "for grace to be humble and behave aright before *Him* until these calamities be overpassed!"[7]

John Adger responded vigorously to this crisis of faith and expressed the seminary faculty's interpretation of the South's defeat and humiliation. Writing in the *Southern Presbyterian Review* in early 1866, Adger confessed that God was at work in the victory of Union armies and in the defeat of the southern nation. The South's cause had been just, but southerners were mistaken in thinking "that God must surely bless the right." They forgot how God, in God's infinite wisdom, allows the "righteous to be overthrown." Many southerners—he obviously meant white southerners—had consequently been tempted to doubt the doctrine of divine providence.

It was true, Adger acknowledged, that the Yankees had larger armies and much greater material resources, but these were only the instruments of the Almighty. The deeper meaning of the South's defeat could be found only in the mysterious but gracious providence of God. God, Adger wrote, chastened those whom God loved. Because God loved the South, God was disciplining the South for God's own good and wise purposes. But Adger warned the North that it should tremble if all the slaughter and destruction "has taught her only pride and self-confidence, censoriousness and severity towards brethren." He insisted that even if the South's defeat was the work of God, the South was not ashamed of the war, or penitent for her noble, but unavailing, defense of constitutional liberty. And he refused to acknowledge that white Christians in the South had been wrong in regard to slavery. "We retain," Adger wrote, "all of our former opinions respecting slavery," as he defiantly asserted slavery "was a kindly relation on both sides." Nevertheless emancipation had come and was an accomplished fact. Southern Christians, he said, had been preoccupied with the slavery question for decades and had conscientiously studied its duties and had sought to solve the problem of its future. But "our Northern brethren" claimed "a commission from the Almighty to solve the great problem, and they accordingly have abolished the institution. We cannot dispute their claim, nor are we so disposed." Now, said Adger, the burden of the emancipated slaves fell on those who had freed them. The North had assumed a great new responsibility for the freedpeople. On its part the white South could pray for the success of the emancipators—*if* the North worked for what was in the *true* interest of the former slaves and not some northern agenda. And, Adger added, white southerners "still love the negro."[8]

Adger not only addressed the crisis of faith precipitated by defeat, but he also defended the Presbyterian Church in the Confederate States against the attacks of Northern Presbyterians, in particular his old professor and former friend Charles Hodge. The southern General Assembly had affirmed in 1864 "that it is the peculiar mission of the Southern Church to conserve the institution of slavery, and to make it a blessing both to master and to slave. We could not, if we would, yield up these four millions of immortal beings to the dictates of fanaticism, and to the menaces of military power. We distinctly recognize the inscrutable providence which brought this benighted people into our midst, and we shall feel that we have not discharged our solemn trust until we have used every effort to bring them under the saving influences of the gospel of Christ."

Adger asked, "Was there anything very bad in all this?" The southern church had a missionary obligation to preach the Gospel to black slaves, which made the institution have "moral and religious aspects of the most conspicuous and manifest importance." But Hodge, in spite of his former willingness to support slavery in the deliberations of the still united Presbyterian Church, was now denouncing Southern Presbyterians for their support of slavery. He was now solemnly declaring that "since the death of Christ, no such dogma stains the record of any ecclesiastical body" as that of the southern assembly. Hodge's reversal of opinion and his denunciation of his former allies in the South was too much for Adger and his Columbia colleagues. Adger responded: "Dr. Hodge is somewhat given to this kind of *dicta*. He loves to speak for the whole Church in all ages, and by broad and sweeping assertions of this sort to crowd down opposition to his views; although it is not often that he has allowed himself to be quite so extravagant." He then went on to name pronouncements of church bodies that had horrified Protestants for generations—including councils "which decreed the extirpation of heretics with fire and sword"—and asked if none of these had stained the record of the church more than the southern church's proclamation on slavery and its commitment to the evangelization of the slaves under its providential care. In this way Adger helped lay the groundwork for Southern Presbyterian resistance to what they regarded as the efforts of Northern Presbyterians to take over the southern church now that southern armies had been defeated.[9]

Palmer took up this cause and quickly became the leading voice in the church against any reunion with Northern Presbyterians. The northern assembly had been denouncing Southern Presbyterians for their support of "the great rebellion" and had declared that the assembly "regards the civil rebellion for the perpetuation of negro slavery as a great crime, both against our national government and against God." The assembly had insisted that the creation of the southern church was "unwarranted, schismatical and unconstitutional" and had pledged to endeavor to establish its authority over the Presbyterian churches and church courts of the South. The Board of Domestic Mission was instructed to appoint missionaries, who "give satisfactory evidence to their loyalty to the National Government," to go into the South in order "to restore and build up the Presbyterian congregations in the Southern States of this Union."[10]

All these northern maneuvers Palmer denounced as an unlawful complicity of the church with the state. As the federal government, he said, had pinned with the bayonet the southern states to the Union, so the northern church was attempting to coerce southern presbyteries back into their old ecclesiastical relations and had become a religious arm of the federal government. Palmer and his colleagues regarded the actions of the northern assembly as nothing less than an ecclesiastical imperialism riding on the coattails of Sherman and Grant. Even after the northern assembly adopted a conciliatory stance toward the South, these defiant defenders of a Lost Cause would be convinced that Northern Presbyterians wanted to take over the southern church and its property and impose on it alien ideas and an alien culture of a northern industrial society with its centralization of power in distant places. In the coming years Palmer and his contemporaries and many of their successors at Columbia would do all that they could to prevent the reunion of the two churches—a reunion that they regarded as a fundamental threat to their much loved Southern Zion.[11]

The person who developed the most sophisticated strategy for this southern resistance was John Lafayette Girardeau. He had grown up on James Island across the Ashley River from Charleston, surrounded by a few closely connected white families and large numbers of Gullah slaves. He came from a modest background—more a child of a farm than one of the large plantations of the lowcountry. His father owned in 1840 six slaves, three of whom were under ten and only one of whom was engaged in agriculture. Girardeau thus stood in some social distinction from George Howe and Charles Jones with their Georgia plantations and many slaves, and from Leighton Wilson with his plantation background and aristocratic wife, and from the Smyths and Adgers with their urban-based wealth. Moreover unlike the other leaders associated with Columbia, he had little personal experience of a wider world. He had not studied in the North like Jones, Howe, Palmer, Smyth, and Wilson. Nor had he traveled widely throughout the nation and in Europe as had Thornwell, Smyth, and Leland. And certainly he never had the experience of sailing along the coast of West Africa and traveling up West African rivers as had Wilson. Nor did he have the experience of Adger, who had lived in the Ottoman Empire and rode horseback across the mountains of Lebanon and the plains of Palestine. Girardeau's world was rather a world with a South Carolina horizon. His heart and mind reflected the contours of his lowcountry home with its wide marshes and tidal creeks, its great spreading oaks and thick stands of palmettos and yucca. As a boy on his father's farm he had entered through all his senses a world of island isolation, of cotton fields that yielded their crops in season and slave cabins that leaned against long sandy roads. Girardeau knew and loved this island world, and he would later describe it with a transparent love. The physical environment of his youth—with its social arrangement of farms and plantations, of masters and slaves—had shaped his basic assumptions and his most fundamental dispositions. His love for this particular place, for this lowcountry home, was not, however, that of some lowcountry grandee or of some member of Charleston's urban elite. Rather his love for home was the love of a brilliant country boy who grew up in modest circumstances and who felt at some deep level of affection and self-understanding the mingling of place and personality. Out of this mingling and out of Girardeau's love for his particular lowcountry home there emerged his fierce response to Yankee armies, Northern Presbyterians, and the modern, alien world they were seeking to impose.[12]

During the 1850s Girardeau had been the most important reformer associated with Columbia and had followed John Adger as a missionary to the black slaves in Charleston. Under his leadership the Zion Presbyterian Church had been developed as an important experiment in paternalism. The largest church building in the city was constructed, where whites had to sit in the balcony and over two thousand slaves came weekly to sit and stand around the edges of the main floor of the sanctuary. Girardeau had led in the radical step of acknowledging slave family names. He had advocated teaching slaves to read, and he had called for keeping slave families together. In this and other ways, Girardeau had tried to make a profoundly oppressive system more humane even as he never raised his voice to oppose the system itself. And during the war, he had served as a chaplain and knelt beside young soldiers in the trenches before Petersburg and had prayed with the dying and the wounded and had written letters to families who had lost sons or fathers or brothers.[13]

When Girardeau had returned to Charleston at end of the war, he found that the Zion Church had become the meeting place and rallying point for the freed people of the city and for their northern liberators. Mass meetings had been celebrating the death of slavery and the end of the Confederacy. How bitter must have been the news for Girardeau when he learned that William Lloyd Garrison, the great abolitionist, had preached in Girardeau's old pulpit and had declared that as long as God gave him strength, he would demand for blacks everything claimed "for the whitest of the white in this country." And Henry Ward Beecher—brother of Harriet Beecher Stowe and provider of rifles ("Beecher's Bibles") that helped Kansas bleed before the war—had also been preaching at Zion. By the time that Girardeau returned to Charleston, Beecher had declared to the American Home Missionary Society: "The great trees of rebellion have been cut down by the sword of war. The stumps of treason still remain rooted in the hearts of the people. And these must be taken away before we shall obtain the fruits of a permanent peace." A new battle, Beecher warned, was about to begin: a "battle of thoughts, ideas, of truth against falsehood, of civilization against barbarism. Lee has capitulated; but the devil has not." The old thoughts and ideas, he said, that led to the rebellion have powerful champions: "There will be Lees, and Johnstons, and Jacksons, in the Southern pulpits. And we must send there Grants and Shermans, and Sheridans to wield our sword of God's truth. For the Southern clergy are neither conquered nor converted. . . . The work of the army is over. The work of the churches just begins. . . . The nation has conquered. The churches must redeem." Girardeau, who was soon to become professor of didactic and polemic theology at Columbia, was ready to take up the challenge and present a vigorous strategy for southern resistance.[14]

When some of the Confederate dead from Gettysburg where brought to Charleston to be reinterred at Magnolia Cemetery, Girardeau was asked to speak on Confederate Memorial Day before a huge crowd of whites who had gathered for the occasion. He began by asking if those who had died had died in vain. There are two senses, he said, "in which it must be admitted that they lost their cause—they failed to establish a Confederacy as an independent country, and they failed to preserve the relation of slavery."[15]

But Girardeau with his deep memories and struggling hopes could not admit that the white sons of the South had died in vain, that the suffering, terror, and blood had been for a lost cause. There were, he insisted, "fundamental principles of government, of social order, of civil and religious liberty, which underlay and pervaded," he said, "that complex whole which we denominate our Cause. And the question whether those who fell in its support died in vain, *as to those principles,* must depend for its answer upon the course which will be pursued by the [white] people of the South." Only one reply, he insisted, "deserves to be returned to these inquiries—our brethren will not have died in vain, if we cherish in our hearts, and, as far as in us lies, practically maintain, the principles for which they gave their lives." The great challenge before the South was now a social and cultural challenge. Thaddeus Stevens and other radical Republicans were insisting that Reconstruction must "revolutionize Southern institutions, habits, and manners. . . . The foundations of their institutions . . . must be broken up and relaid, or all our blood and treasure have been spent in vain."[16]

Girardeau and others on the Columbia faculty believed that what the white South had been fighting against, and against which it must now contend, was "radicalism" and all the disintegrating forces of the modern world. They were fighting for Thornwell's "regulated liberty" and against what Girardeau called a "ruthless, leveling Spirit," a kind of radical individualism where everyone worshipped the devises and desires of their own conscience. This leveling spirit was part of a new, unchecked capitalism and its radical individualism that was waging war against an organic understanding of society—against the family, the state, and the church. It threatened social anarchy, warned Girardeau, which would send people for refuge to an autocratic despotism. Old virtues, he said, must be maintained in the face of the growing luxuries, excesses, and enticements of what would come to be called the Gilded Age. Girardeau and others associated with Columbia were attempting to look back to republican and Christian traditions to resist the ravages of the radical capitalism that was already impoverishing both southern farmers and northern industrial workers in the 1870s. Their conservative, backward-looking assertion of traditional republican and Christian traditions stood in contrast to Marxists and socialists, who, in their critique of capitalism, focused on the future. The bitter irony for the southern conservatives, of course, was that their searing critic of a radical capitalist order had little moral authority because it was intertwined with deep racist assumptions.[17]

To meet the challenge of this modern radicalism, Girardeau called on the white South to remember its past and to retain its cultural independence—to resist being overwhelmed by the individualism and anarchic forces of an imperialistic North and a modern capitalist order. "We must cling to our identity as a people!" he cried. He warned the gathered whites that they were in danger of losing the identity they had fought so hard to maintain against invading Yankee armies.[18]

So when the white South—and also of course Columbia Seminary—was in danger of losing its identity, what needed to be done to meet the danger? Girardeau called white southerners to refuse to participate in the Reconstruction government; to establish "peculiar customs and organizations" to celebrate the South's past; and to collect and publish "materials for our own history." Then in a brilliant move, Girardeau insisted that the white South defend its identity by maintaining the heart of a culture—what he called "the inalienable, indestructible powers of thought and language—the faculty by which we form our opinions, and that by which we express them." The preservation of a southern culture could be accomplished, he said, by "scrupulously adhering to the phraseology of the past—for making it the vehicle for transmitting to our posterity ideas which once true are true forever. . . . We may do it by the education we impart to the young; by making our nurseries, schools and colleges channels for conveying from generation to generation our own type of thought, sentiment and opinion, by instamping on the minds of our children principles hallowed by the blood of patriots."[19]

In the face of military defeat and an aggressive attempt to remake the South in the image of the North, the "phraseology of the past" could thus be used to continue the southern struggle—only using different means. Language could become the bearer of an ideology that could integrate and consolidate the culture and identity of the white South. The "phraseology of the past," as a coherent body of shared images and ideas, could provide a unity to the white South not only in space, as a distinct geographical region—the South—but also in time, linking the South's past to the present critical moment and to the shape of the region's future. The white South would be a language community whose children's identity would be shaped by their initiation into its language. So the children would grow up saying, for example, simply "the South" when they meant "the white

South." In this language family to be a southerner was to be white, even though blacks outnumbered whites in many parts of the South and had deeper ancestry in the South than many whites. Consequently when Girardeau spoke of ideas that were once true and are true forever, he meant ideas that had to do above all with keeping the South white and with keeping blacks in their place.[20]

So memories of the past shaped the way Girardeau and others at the seminary interpreted the immediate crisis in church, state, and society. The past was present and intruded into their today and into their imagined future, for the vision they had of the future was rooted in the past, and memory shaped their hopes as much as it shaped their interpretations of the present crisis. Girardeau consequently wrote that black southerners, in order to save themselves from catastrophe, should place themselves in the position of a laboring class, abandon political aspirations, and "avoid that competition with and attrition against the white race, which must ultimately wipe them out."[21]

But paradoxically this white memory soon reflected a deep amnesia. It quickly forgot Palmer's insistence that white southerners had a "providential trust" committed to them as a people "*to conserve and to perpetuate the institution of domestic slavery as now existing.*" And this white memory quickly forgot the General Assembly's insistence that "it is the peculiar mission of the Southern Church to conserve the institution of slavery, and to make it a blessing both to master and to slave." Girardeau himself would help transform the phraseology of the past into a mythology of the Lost Cause, a mythology that claimed the Confederacy was not about conserving and perpetuating slavery. The propagation of such a mythology was a way of maintaining order and consolidating white power. Yet within that mythology was the story of the "faithful slave" who stayed with the white family and who had been happy and contented in the slave quarters and settlements of the South. So out of white southern amnesia there had flowed a contradictory conviction that the war had not been about slavery but somehow slavery was at the center of the white South's story and memory.[22]

Not incidentally, whites' "phraseology of the past" and its transformation into the mythology of the Lost Cause was sustained by bloody violence. The language of white southerners—its words, expressions, and phrases—was not ethereal. The "phraseology of the past" did not hang suspended in the air above a southern landscape but was a language that emerged from and then reinforced and interpreted the violence and brutality that was already being directed to the freedpeople of the South. Almost as soon as Lee surrendered, vigilante groups—the Ku Klux Klan would become the most prominent—began to organize in order to terrorize black southerners. And Wade Hampton III announced shortly after Girardeau's speech that it was time for white southerners to "dedicate themselves to the redemption of the South"—a call that would lead through violence and political maneuvering to the end of Reconstruction in 1876 and the re-establishment throughout the South of white control. To be sure, white faculty at Columbia and its graduates on occasion protested during the next several generations the shooting, emasculation, hanging, dismemberment, and burning alive of "troublesome blacks" often before large crowds of white spectators. Their protests were sincere and genteel. But their protests, like the earlier reform efforts of Girardeau and the Zion

Church in Charleston, were expressions of a paternalism that marked almost every aspect of the seminary's life, a paternalism that assumed a commanding place for whites and a dependent place for blacks.[23]

Of course there were other southerners who had different memories of the past. Black southerners remembered something radically different from what Girardeau and others at Columbia Seminary remembered. They remembered generations of deep oppression, and they remembered the liberation that came with Sherman's troops and that could be seen in the flames that consumed Atlanta, Charleston, and Columbia.

Those blacks who had been most closely associated with the seminary as slaves of faculty, students, and board members had to discover, like other freedpeople across the South, the meaning of their emancipation and the place they would call home. They had to learn the limitations now being placed on whites, and they had to find the boundaries of their new freedom—to decide where they were they going to live, now that they could move around, and how they were going to make a living, now that they no longer had to plow and cook for "master and missus." But they also had to face questions about how to respond to whites like Girardeau who were determined to keep them in their place of subordination. How were they, whose ancestors largely lay in unmarked graves, to challenge the memory of southern whites who were soon erecting on courthouse squares monuments to the Confederate dead and would soon name streets and parks and buildings after white southern heroes?[24]

When the war ended, John Adger had about thirty slaves. Most of these were slaves his wife had inherited, but when Adger had bought Woodburn, his upcountry plantation, he had purchased additional slaves to work the plantation. All these slaves, including those who had been domestic servants for the Adgers in Columbia, were told by Adger that they were free and that he could "no longer employ them." Charles Morris, the driver, Adger's "head man," protested that the government had treated them badly by setting them free without giving them what he called "a start." Morris was expressing the hope of many freedpeople across the South that they would receive some land in compensation for their years of slave labor, perhaps even forty acres and a mule. But such hopes had quickly faded, and they were left with questions about what they were to do without any land to farm or any place to lay their heads at night. Morris's children left for Memphis, where they heard jobs were plentiful, and Morris, with some help from Adger, set himself up in Columbia as a teamster with a wagon and a mule. And there he no doubt saw on occasion "One Arm Ben," whom Adger had sent in 1861 to help with the fortifications around Charleston and who had lost his arm to federal shrapnel. He had taken "Collins" as his family name, married, and made a living by selling vegetables from a little handcart he pushed around the city. The others, who had once been called Adger slaves, scattered, and Adger, who had once been a missionary to the slaves of Charleston, lost sight of them all.[25]

Caesar, George Howe's driver on his Halifax plantation, died shortly after the end of the war, and his wife, Linda, moved to another plantation where she worked as a cook. Pompey, the driver on the nearby Mallard Place plantation (where Robert Quarterman

Mallard had grown up), took the name Bacon and established himself as a small farmer near the old Midway Church. Cato—who had been Charles Colcock Jones's trusted driver, largely managing Montevideo plantation when Jones was teaching at the seminary—casts aside the rituals of subordination that had marked his life and asserted his independence from whites. He took the surname of "Holmes" and moved with his wife to Savannah. Mary Jones complained that "Cato has been to me a most insolent, indolent, and dishonest man," and she said, "I have not a shadow of confidence in him." Even more difficult for Mary Jones was her personal servant Patience and her decision to leave her former mistress. Patience had worked as a cook in the Joneses' home in Columbia and had watched seminary professors and students come and go from the Joneses' home and dining-room table. When freedom came she decided that she would cook for her own family, and she and her husband, Porter, rented and then bought a small farm across the road from a new school established by New England Congregationalists for the freedpeople of the Georgia coast. But some of the former slaves of Columbia faculty, board members, and students remained in the old quarters and settlements where they had lived all their lives. Now supervised by the Federal Freedmen's Bureau, they signed contracts with former owners and sought to build a new life on familiar ground even as they struggled with the harsh realities of those whom whites said had "stayed in their place."[26]

Most of the churches in Columbia's supporting synods had black members—some had only a few, others had many. Among the questions that came with emancipation was the question of a church home, a question about place and belonging for Presbyterians who were freedpeople. Were they to remain a part of the congregations where they had been baptized, where they had sung hymns and received the Lord's Supper, where they had listened to the long, logical sermons of white preachers, and where they had heard, in spite of white oppression, the liberating good news of the Gospel? If they remained, were they to remain as members who now had all the privileges of membership that whites possessed? Or were they to leave, go out as congregations from within white-dominated congregations, and established churches that would be more fully a church home than the old arrangements had ever been for them? Initially there had been a continuation of white and black Presbyterians worshipping together. But as the realities of emancipation began to be felt and as it became clear that whites were going to insist that the old order be maintained, black Presbyterians began to move out of the old congregations and go down nearby roads and establish their own congregations. On Johns Island, where there had been over six hundred black members in the Presbyterian church, five black congregations went out and formed themselves as African American Presbyterian churches. On neighboring James Island, the St. James congregation established itself as independent from the old James Island church and was soon the largest Presbyterian church in South Carolina. At Midway, in Georgia, the Midway Presbyterian Church was established a mile from the old Midway Congregational Church that had been the mother to so many Columbia Seminary students. And so it went across Columbia's constituency wherever there had been significant black membership in Presbyterian churches.[27]

The Columbia faculty and those on its board strongly opposed this development. Girardeau's call for maintaining the values and practices of the antebellum South meant the continuation of blacks and whites worshiping together and a paternalistic white control of black members of Presbyterian churches. While Girardeau was a vigorous advocate for the old order, board member John Leighton Wilson addressed the issue most directly with Northern Presbyterians who were supporting the formation of new black congregations in the South.

As black Presbyterians began to form their own congregations, Wilson received a letter from S. C. Logan, the secretary of the northern church's Committee on Freedmen, had been a great admirer of Wilson before the war, and he had taken up his work for the freedmen because of one of Wilson's missionary addresses. Now he wrote Wilson, who was serving as secretary for both the foreign and domestic missions for the southern church. He asked about possible cooperation between northern and Southern Presbyterians in the building of churches and schools for the freedpeople. He asked for Wilson's views about such cooperation and for any suggestions he might have about ways that the two churches could work together. Logan's letter provided Wilson with an opportunity to express in a candid manner just what he thought.[28]

Blacks, Wilson wrote, had been a happy part of congregations with white southerners until the southern country had been "deluged with Northern agents of every hue and stripe, the great mass of whom seemed to regard themselves as heaven-commissioned to fill the minds of the negroes with hatred and animosity toward their former owners." He insisted it "was utterly untrue to say there was any marked bitterness between the whites and blacks of the South, either before or subsequent to the war, save what was called into existence" by these northern agents.[29]

Wilson looked aghast at black Presbyterians leaving their old white-controlled congregations. He claimed black members were leaving because they believed that Northern Presbyterians would give them more financial support than impoverished southern whites could provide. Blacks would quickly become, Wilson claimed, dependent on this northern largess and expect the North to continue these favors indefinitely. Providence, Wilson insisted, had appointed the southern church to do the important work of evangelizing and lifting up the newly freed people of the South. White southerners, after all, had lived all their lives among blacks and knew not only their names and their families but also their ways. Northerners, however, had nothing but a theoretical knowledge of the freed people and of their character. They saw them only from a great distance, and that distance distorted what they saw and how they understood their needs.

Logan responded in a respectful but forceful manner. The alienation Wilson described between southern whites and blacks was not the result of northern inference, he said, but rather flowed from the "grand idea of *liberty*." Liberty and the "assertion of their manhood" had led blacks out of the balconies of white-controlled churches and had given them courage to establish their own churches. The freedpeople, Logan said, had not been seduced by northern promises; nor were they relying on northern charity. Rather they had left on their own and had made great sacrifices in the effort to build their own churches. As for white southerners knowing blacks better than northerners, Logan reminded the former missionary to West Africa that the church had been sending missionaries with great success beyond their home ground into other regions of the world.

Furthermore, he said, Wilson was simply misreading providence. It was true the southern church once had responsibility for the nurture and care of blacks in the church. "But that time has passed, and circumstances have changed; this people have changed also." And then Logan made his most telling point—"while you have been studying them, they have been as busily engaged in studying you." Logan was respectfully but clearly making his point—blacks had been watching white southerners for a long time. And because of their watching and what they had learned about white assumptions, intentions, and actions, they had gone out from the white-controlled congregations to form their own congregations, to worship in the ways the Spirit moved them, to call their own leaders, and to organize in freedom their own congregational life.[30]

Black Presbyterians were soon organizing not only their own congregations but also their own presbyteries that drew black Presbyterians together in tight networks of families and friends. Through their presbyteries, they became a part of the northern assembly and began to participate in it in ways that linked them to a national church and a broader world than the American South. But Columbia Seminary ignored these Presbyterians who lived in the heart of their constituency and refused to acknowledge their presence and soon largely forgot that they existed. As Girardeau's vision made "the South" mean "the white South," so his vision also made "Southern Presbyterian" mean "white Southern Presbyterian." In this way the "[white] Southern Presbyterian Church" came into existence, and the board and faculty at Columbia resolutely gave the seminary the task of nurturing and promoting this white church in a white South.[31]

But black Presbyterians were there among these white Presbyterians, however invisible they seemed to Columbia's leadership. They were in Charleston and Augusta, in Columbia and at Midway, in Atlanta and Macon, in Alabama and in Mississippi. And from among these black Presbyterians there emerged their own vision for the future, an alternative vision that challenged Girardeau's vision of a South that was white. At its heart their vision claimed that the history of the South could not be told without telling their history of oppression and struggle. Their vision called for an acknowledgement that the South was also their home, and that the future of the South must bring justice to those who had plunged into the mire of rice fields and who had chopped long rows of cotton and who had seen the fruit of their labors consumed by whites such as those who had taught and studied at Columbia Seminary. With deep roots both in the African American experience and in Presbyterian traditions, they envisioned a long and difficult road to a broader freedom and more secure and prosperous future for their children. To travel that road they insisted that their children needed not only the best education that could be secured but also a deep memory of the traditions of their people that had carried them through the deep waters of slavery.[32]

The alternative vision for the future that was emerging from black Presbyterians included a remarkable effort to establish an extensive school system for the newly freed people. Most were day schools established next to a black Presbyterian church or perhaps in the church building itself. By 1920 there were forty-seven such schools in South Carolina alone. Most ran only through the elementary level, but there were also academies and institutes where students boarded and went through the higher levels and received preparation for college. On Edisto Island, for example, the Hope (later Larimer) School was established by the Presbyterian minister Ishmael Moultrie. He had been born a slave on the island, and during the war he had been taken by his owner to the interior of the state. Seizing an opportunity to escape, he had led a band of slaves on a 150-mile trek back to his island home, which federal forces had captured early in the war. For the next several years he received private instructions in theology, and in this way he was able to pass the ordination exams. The school he established had two hundred students in 1870 and became "the community center for all progressive activities on the island." The brightest students, whose families could scrape together enough cash or goods to barter, were able to go on to one of the Presbyterian boarding schools—to Immanuel Institute in Aiken or to Brainer Institute in Chester, or to one of two jewels in the crown of Presbyterian academies: Coulter Memorial in Cheraw or Harbinson in Irmo. From among the graduates of these schools, a few were able to go to Charlotte and Biddle Memorial Institute (renamed Johnson C. Smith University in 1923) and from there some would later go to Johnson C. Smith Seminary, which was established in 1931.[33]

Biddle and then Johnson C. Smith University and Seminary came to embody a different memory and an alternative vision from the memory and vision articulated by Girardeau and his colleagues—a white memory and vision embodied by Columbia Seminary. Perhaps ironically one of the two white ministers responsible for the establishment of Biddle in 1867 was Samuel Carothers Alexander, a native of Pennsylvania who had graduated from Columbia in 1861. Alexander had served throughout the war as pastor of the second largest Presbyterian church in North Carolina—the Steele Creek Church in Charlotte. While he was at Columbia the seminary had nurtured within him a commitment to the religious instruction of the blacks of the South, and after the war he gave himself to work among the newly freed people of the South. In this way the two institutions and the two memories and the two visions would live close to one another even as they were very far apart. And the space between the two memories and the two visions would be contested ground for generations.[34]

8

An Impoverished World

The year the first shots were fired on Fort Sumter there had been sixty-one students at the seminary. For the students the shots rising high over Charleston Harbor had been a signal of what was to come, and so they had begun to give up their theological studies and move out of their secure world on the Columbia campus. Most northern students left quickly for home, and most southern students left for duty in the army as soldiers or chaplains. By September 1862 the number of students had dropped to eleven and was still dropping when the seminary closed its doors in 1863. Yet out of the desolations of the war there had emerged a determination to make Columbia once again a strong institution of the church, a seminary that could provide desperately needed pastors for a defeated but proud people.[1]

Six months after Sherman's troops left the ash-strewn capital of South Carolina, the seminary reopened with five students. Howe, the steady presence and much-loved professor, was eager to start the rebuilding of the seminary to which he had devoted his life. He had come to Columbia in January 1831, when there had been only seven students, so he had a memory of the work that small beginnings demanded. But his home across the street from the campus, crowded as it now was with refugees, was a reminder that the seminary was reopening to an impoverished South and not to the South of 1831 with its then wealthy antebellum planters and merchants.[2]

John Adger came down from his upcountry plantation to resume his place on the faculty. He did not return to his handsome three-story brick home on Main Street—it was now in ashes—but moved with his family into Law dormitory, where his aunt, the now homeless Agnes Law, was living in the confusion and distress caused by the burning of her home. James Woodrow and his family were also living in the same dormitory. They had rented a home when he joined the faculty in 1861, and it too had been consumed by fire. Aaron Leland's home had been preserved, but a paralytic stroke in 1863 had left him unable to fulfill the duties of his professorship, and he had been elected professor emeritus. By the time the seminary reopened, Benjamin Morgan Palmer had left for New Orleans and his old pastorate in the Crescent City.[3]

Palmer's departure was an indication that the leadership of the seminary was in transition. Thornwell was gone, Leland was incapacitated, and Charles Jones was dead. Howe remained, but he was in poor health and lacked the vitality of his prewar years. Because Woodrow had joined the faculty as war broke over the land and because he had been preoccupied during most of the war by his work for the Confederate medical laboratory, his engagement with the seminary's life had been limited by the time the seminary reopened in September 1865. Moreover during the midst of the war the synods had transferred ownership of Columbia to the General Assembly. This meant that the General Assembly, rather than the synods, would have oversight of the seminary, electing board members and faculty, receiving reports from the board, and approving or disapproving the actions of the board.[4]

Still there were important continuities as Columbia entered a new period in its life. Adger represented deep ties with the antebellum seminary. He had been Thornwell's closest friend and colleague, and Adger's brother-in-law Thomas Smyth had served the seminary in innumerable ways since the 1830s. The board of directors included those who had been associated with the seminary in its days of prosperity. Thomas Perrin remained president of the board, and John Leighton Wilson and Joseph LeConte continued to add the prestige of their names to the Columbia board. Wilson was widely regarded as the most respected leader of the Southern Presbyterian Church, and LeConte was one of the most influential scientists in the nation. Unfortunately for the seminary, LeConte would leave South Carolina in a few years and become one of the founding professors of the University of California. His leaving meant that his influential voice would be largely absent from the fierce debates that were to shake the seminary to its foundations in the 1870s and 1880s.[5]

Adger, Perrin, Wilson, and LeConte represented the widely traveled and cosmopolitan world of Columbia's antebellum leadership. That world continued to be represented in Columbia's life during the coming years. Confederate general James Gilliam joined the board, as did Colonel F. W. McMaster—he would become known as the "father of modern public education in Columbia" and would serve the city as a progressive mayor. The Honorable James Hemphill, a member of the South Carolina legislature and then the U.S. Congress, was to represent this cosmopolitan tradition during a long period of service as a board member and as chair of the board. But other leaders were soon to emerge out of a much more constricted world. Their horizons were limited by the bitterness of defeat, by an engulfing poverty, by a deep nostalgia for a lost world, and by Girardeau's "phraseology of the past." The lines in Columbia's life between the more cosmopolitan world and the more provincial world were often to overlap and seem blurred during the coming years, but they were going to be visible in the fissures that were soon to occur in the seminary community and in the white Southern Presbyterian Church.[6]

The library also linked the postwar seminary to its antebellum history. With the addition of the Smyth collection in the 1850s, the library had become one of the largest theological libraries in the country. In the years immediately after the war the most surprising and important gift to the library was the library of the early antislavery and African colonization leader Ralph R. Gurley. His widow made the gift as "a testimony of her regard for the Southern Church." With this and a few other substantial gifts of books the library retained its distinction for a few years until, with the new poverty of the seminary's constituencies, it began a long slow descent into mediocrity. Perhaps, however, the most important continuity in the seminary's life was the remarkable loyalty and even affection that many ministers and laity had for Columbia. Throughout its former supporting synods, but especially in South Carolina and Georgia, Columbia Seminary was regarded as "our seminary," the institution that embodied most fully the tone and character, the style of life and moral spirit of white Southern Presbyterians. The important role the seminary had played in shaping a white Southern Presbyterian identity and in defending a white South against the assaults of Yankees was remembered and honored. So it would be a matter of great consequent when, during coming controversies, this sense of loyalty and ownership began to erode. When those who had loved the seminary and its mission began to wonder if Columbia was trustworthy, and when they began to ask themselves "is Columbia still 'our seminary,'" then Columbia faced a challenge more threatening to its life than Sherman's troops.[7]

When the seminary reopened, the board had two immediate tasks to address. It had to fill the position left vacant by Thornwell's death (and Palmer's departure for New Orleans), and it had to find a replacement for Leland. To fill Thornwell's position they called the sixty-five-year-old William S. Plumer. A native of Pennsylvania, Plumer had served in the 1830s and 1840s as the influential pastor of the First Presbyterian Church, Richmond, where he had been a strong supporter of Charles C. Jones's efforts for the religious instruction of slaves and for more humane treatment of the South's black population. In 1838 Plumer had presided over the General Assembly at the time of the Old School–New School division. In 1854 he had joined the faculty of Western Theological Seminary in Allegheny, Pennsylvania (later Pittsburg Theological Seminary), as professor of theology. When war began Plumer had declared his love for the Union and his belief that secession was not legal, but he had refused to pray for God's blessings on the northern armies. He said he could not "pray for the success of our arms, nor give thanks for our victories, because arms and victories produce alienations rather than fraternal feelings; men cannot be coerced to love, swords and bayonets can never piece together these states in a happy and enduring Union." He had consequently been forced to resign his professorship.[8]

Plumer had been a handsome young man—tall with dark eyes, heavy eyebrows, and hair falling backward in great masses—and when he arrived on the Columbia campus as an old man he retained a graceful carriage and what was called a "noble countenance." But what was now most conspicuous about his appearance was his snowy white beard that exceeded in length even George Howe's rather scraggly beard. It was not, however, his striking appearance that attracted the admiration of Columbia's board but Plumer's writings, his leadership in the antebellum Presbyterian Church, and his conduct during the Civil War.[9]

Plumer had been and was to continue to be as a Columbia professor a prolific author. His *Grace of Christ; or, Sinners Saved by Unmerited Kindness* (1853) ran for over 450 pages and was to go through three editions, while his *Vital Godliness* (1864) was over six-hundred pages and was so popular that it ran through five editions. The year he arrived on the Columbia campus, his twelve-hundred-page *Studies in the Book of Psalms* (1866) was published by Lippincott, and the massive tome was to go through three editions. Three years later came his 658-page *Commentary on Paul's Epistle to the Romans* (four editions); in 1872 his 559-page *Commentary on the Epistle to the Hebrews* (two editions) appeared; and in 1874 Harpers published his *Hints and Helps in Pastoral Theology* (three editions), a volume long utilized by ministers around the country. Colleges and universities, North and South, including Princeton University, conferred on him the title of doctor of divinity. A century would pass before another Columbia professor would match and exceed Plumer's literary output and his wide influence on the American church.[10]

Because the war had wiped out a substantial part of the seminary's endowment, Columbia's board was not able to fill until 1870 the chair of pastoral theology left vacant by Leland's retirement. In the spring of that year the board called Joseph Ruggles Wilson, pastor of the First Presbyterian Church in Augusta and brother-in-law of James Woodrow, to teach homiletics and pastoral theology. A native of Ohio, Wilson had left a pastorate in Pennsylvania in early 1851 to become professor of chemistry and natural science at Hampden-Sydney College in Virginia. Later in the decade he was for a short time pastor in Stanton, Virginia, where his son Woodrow was born. He moved to Augusta in time to host the first meeting of the General Assembly of the Presbyterian Church in the Confederate States of America and to begin his long service as the assembly's stated clerk.

Wilson was no scholar after the model of Thornwell or Woodrow. But he was a fine preacher who believed in the power and the importance of preaching. Students thought him a splendid teacher—at least until they disagreed with him—and he apparently delighted in teaching the art of preaching. Years later Woodrow Wilson described his father as "steadfast, brilliant, devoted, loving and beloved. A master of serious eloquence, a thinker of singular power and penetration, a thoughtful student of life and God's purpose, a lover and servant of his fellow men, a man of God."[11]

In 1872, two years after Wilson moved his family into a home close by the seminary, his daughter Marion married Columbia graduate and Confederate veteran Anderson Ross Kennedy. The next year Wilson's daughter Annie married Howe's son, George Jr., a local physician. Annie's brother, Woodrow, was seventeen at the time. The future president of the United States consequently had deep connections with Columbia Seminary—his father, his uncle, and his sister's father-in-law were all members of the Columbia faculty, and a brother-in-law was a Columbia graduate. A few years later, Woodrow Wilson married Ellen Axson, the daughter, granddaughter, and niece of Columbia graduates. Clearly an ever-thickening network of personal and family relationships was surrounding and shaping the character of the seminary.[12]

In this way the faculty grew by 1870 to include Howe, Adger, Woodrow, Plumer, and Joseph Wilson. At the same time, the student body was showing an encouraging and steady growth—from five students in 1865 to thirty-five in 1870 to fifty-seven in 1874. Unlike the antebellum period, however, when there had been a substantial number of students from the North, the students were now overwhelmingly from the South—except for a Pennsylvanian and a lone Canadian, both of whom seemed to have landed on the Columbia campus like lost and exotic migrants. The southern students were overwhelmingly graduates of southern colleges and state universities, especially Davidson, Oglethorpe, South Carolina College, and the University of Mississippi. Among them were some who carried familiar names from Columbia's past—John Leighton Wilson, William LeConte, James H. Thornwell Jr., and Robert Smyth. And there were some who were to be future leaders in the church, in higher education, and in the mission movement. Between 1865 and 1874 six future moderators of the church would graduate from Columbia, as would a future chancellor of the University of Georgia, a founder of the Louisville Theological Seminary, a president of Davidson College, and a leader in the fight to end the opium trade in China.[13]

An antebellum vision of theological education continued to dominate Columbia during the two decades that followed Lee's surrender. That vision insisted that candidates for the Presbyterian ministry should possess both substantial learning and genuine Christian piety. Substantial learning continued to mean a broad liberal education with grounding in the classics and a familiarity with the natural sciences. Genuine Christian piety meant, as it had during antebellum days, that a prospective student could give a personal testimony to an inward experience of grace. And any student applying for admission was expected to receive the endorsement of his presbytery—an endorsement that declared the prospective student exhibited a disciplined and morally upright life, one that flowed from a sense of gratitude for God's amazing grace.[14]

With a grasp of Latin and at least an introductory knowledge of Greek, students began their formal theological education at postbellum Columbia by plunging into an intense study of Hebrew under Howe's direction. As a part of their work they had to translate from the Greek Apocrypha into Hebrew. They also took up their Greek New Testaments and with Howe as their guide began their exegesis using a harmony of the Gospels and some of Paul's epistles. They had one class a week with Plumer in an introduction to theology. They read Paley's *Evidences of Christianity* and focused on miracles and inspiration of the scriptures, and "Internal Evidences of Christianity." Toward the end of the year Plumer turned to "Mental and Moral Science," which was intended to ensure that students did not misunderstand the meaning of Plumer's vocabulary when he used philosophical and theological terms. Adger introduced them, during two class periods a week, to the early history of the church. "Since the church began," Adger explained, "at the very fall of man, its history should also begin there." They utilized Johann Heinrich Kurtz's *Lehrbuch der heiligen Geschichte,* translated as *Manual of Sacred History.* In one class a week Joseph Wilson led them in a study of "experimental and practical religion, sometimes called by the old divines *Theologia activa"* or a theology of an active life of service.[15]

During their second year, students continued their New Testament exegesis and added Old Testament exegesis in their newly acquired Hebrew. They had three classes a week with Plumer. In two they studied didactic theology, in which they focused on doctrines, and in one class they took up polemic theology, where they plunged into the arguments involved in major theological controversies. Adger taught church history two days a week, rushing from the apostles in the first century to the Enlightenment of the eighteenth century. He had students read the Irish historian W. D. Killen's *The Ancient Church: Its History, Doctrine, Worship, and Constitution Traced for the First Three Hundred Years* and Kurtz's volumes on the history of the church up to the contemporary period. Wilson introduced them to rhetoric—the art of persuasion—as preparation for their preaching and had them study the pastoral epistles as the foundation and guide for their pastoral ministries.[16]

Seniors continued their exegetical work in both the Old and New Testaments, and in theology they gave special attention to the covenant of grace, the divine purpose of salvation, and the doctrine of the last things. Adger turned from church history to polity and the sacraments for third-year students. In a significant move, he took them into the rich depths of Calvin's *Institutes,* a change from reading in Latin the scholastic theology of Francis Turretin's *Institutio Theologiae*—a change Thornwell had made in his theology courses and that Adger followed in his course on polity and the sacraments. This move, especially in regard to the sacraments, was to challenge the scholastic orthodoxy embodied by Turretin—with its severe tone and emphasis on "right belief"—that was to reemerge later at Columbia under Girardeau's influence.[17]

Wilson, for his part, had third-year students focus on the pastoral office and work. They also preached regularly in daily chapel services and had their sermons evaluated by the faculty and classmates. Like first- and second-year students, each senior met weekly with a faculty member for a conference on "personal piety, the best plan and method for study, and kindred topics."[18]

There was thus much continuity between what antebellum students had studied at Columbia and what postbellum students studied during the first two decades after the war. Two important continuities with the late antebellum curriculum, however, were of special note because their eventual rejection would come to mark the character of Columbia for several generations.

The first notable continuity was Adger's use of Calvin's *Institutes* as the text for his lectures on the sacraments. Adger had discovered in his reading of Calvin a sacramental theology that put him and Columbia over against what was being taught at Union by Robert Lewis Dabney. In 1846 John Williamson Nevin of Mercersburg Seminary in Pennsylvania had published *Mystical Presence: A Vindication of the Reformed or Calvinistic Doctrine of the Holy Eucharist.* Nevin, following Calvin, had argued for the real spiritual presence of Christ in the Lord's Supper. Dabney, however, following the scholasticism of Turretin, taught his students at Union that Calvin's position was an "impossible theory" that not only misread scripture but also violated "intuitive reason." Charles Hodge at Princeton took a similar position and dismissed Nevin's claim that in the Lord's Supper a communicant experienced the real spiritual presence of Christ. For Hodge to "take communion," to eat and drink of Christ, was simply a matter of having faith in Christ—a view that Calvin had explicitly rejected.[19]

Adger's reading of Calvin convinced him that Calvin and Nevin held the correct view of the sacrament and that Dabney and Hodge were reflecting a Protestant scholasticism that lacked the power to touch the human heart and unite the believer with Christ. In this Adger was standing with Thornwell, who "agreed with Calvin's doctrine." But it was not to survive the disruptions and turmoil that were to come to the seminary, and in their wake Calvin's and Adger's sacramental theology would be largely forgotten at Columbia, and the scholasticism of Dabney and Hodge would be represented by Girardeau and his followers. Indeed the sacraments and the Lord's Supper specifically were to be of so little interest to Girardeau that the index to his collected *Discussions of Theological Questions* contained no reference to them. And Girardeau, rather than require Calvin's *Institutes* as a text, required students to read Hodge's three-volume *Systematic Theology*.[20]

This shift from Adger's sacramental theology to Girardeau's late nineteenth-century scholasticism was not some obscure theological debate, but a shift that was to penetrate the tone, character, and aesthetic spirit of Columbia Seminary for several generations. Sacramental theology had room for mystery—for the mystical presence of Christ in the Lord's Supper and for the mystical union of Christ with the believer who receives as a gift the real spiritual presence of Christ in the bread and wine. With room for mystery there was also room on the campus for a spirit of free inquiry. The purpose of a theological seminary, Adger insisted, is not dogmatic. Its genius was "that of inquiry into all truth." Girardeau's scholasticism, on the other hand, had little room for mystery. It manifested, in the disappointed view of a former student, a "spirit of hostility to free inquiry." It sought certainty, order, and lessons to be taught. It was imbued with a dogmatic and didactic spirit that was, to be sure, tempered by an evangelical piety and the good manners of Southern Presbyterians who were intent on being genteel. But the theological shift to Girardeau's scholasticism represented a narrowing of the spirit that animated the seminary and that shaped the tone of what was taught and learned on the campus. That spirit and tone resonated deeply with an intensifying parochialism in the seminary's life that was to assert itself when Girardeau became in the 1880s the dominant member of the Columbia faculty.[21]

A second notable continuity between the antebellum and the early postbellum seminary curriculum was a focus on natural science and its relationship to revelation. George Howe, in the early days of the seminary, had insisted that some knowledge of all the sciences was necessary if a student was to grapple with natural theology and the design and plan of the Author of Nature. The establishment in 1859 of the Perkins Professor of Natural Science in Connection with Revelation had been an institutionalization of this commitment to engage the natural sciences in seminary classrooms. James Woodrow, as the Perkins Professor, had little time before the onslaught of war to develop his courses in the curriculum. But once the war ended and the seminary reopened Woodrow led students in their study of the natural sciences. He was particularly committed to having his students engage the new geology introduced by Charles Lyell—a geology that demonstrated the earth's vast timescale and deep history. Woodrow's lectures on geology easily led to the fascinating world of archaeology and fossil records and the strange appearance and disappearance of groups of plants and animals. Woodrow believed that theology students needed to know as well something of astronomy, for "the heavens declare the glory of God" (Psalm 19); and they had to be familiar with the debates on "the unity of the human races" that had been raging for decades. Students studied Harvard professor Louis

Agassiz's claim for a dual origin of the races because, he asserted, the Caucasian and the Negro had fundamental physical differences. And students studied the vigorous denial of such claims by Columbia faculty in the 1850s, and they learned of Thomas Smyth's *The Unity of the Human Races,* in which Smyth affirmed from historical and anthropological evidence the high achievements and full humanity of Africans.[22]

When Woodrow had begun his teaching at Columbia at the beginning of the war, he had declared that he would carry on the duties of his professorship with an "untrammeled freedom of inquiry." His commitment to freedom of inquiry on the seminary campus meant that he envisioned Columbia as a place where there was room for exploration and serious questions. The purpose of a theological seminary for Woodrow was not indoctrination but inquiry into truth. So Woodrow, like Adger, envisioned a different spirit and tone for theological education, a different ethos and culture for the Columbia campus than what Girardeau envisioned. Girardeau wanted Columbia to be a place where faculty and students scrupulously adhered "to the phraseology of the past" in order to make that phraseology the "vehicle for transmitting to our posterity ideas which once true are true forever." Girardeau regarded as dangerous Woodrow's insistence on an "untrammeled freedom of inquiry." Such freedom invited disorder and confusion not only regarding theological questions but also, as we shall see, in regard to white southern identity and the maintenance of a "southern way of life."[23]

Central to the rebuilding of the seminary was the effort to raise the seminary's endowment, at least to its antebellum level. The task, however, was formidable as the South struggled not only to rebuild but also to overcome sharp drops in cotton prices and periods of severe drought. Added to these economic woes was the political volatility and violence of Reconstruction present throughout the South but especially prominent in the states of the seminary's constituencies, particularly South Carolina. The passage by Congress of the Reconstruction Acts in 1867 mandated the voter registration of all adult males in the South and the holding of constitutional elections. In South Carolina the constitutional convention, composed largely of blacks, framed a constitution that followed northern states in regard to women's rights and public education but went beyond them in extending voters rights to all men, with no limitations imposed by education or a poll tax. Whites responded with intense guerrilla warfare and a bloody terrorism often led by the Ku Klux Klan. The federal government under President Grant attempted to suppress the rebellion with military force, but by the end of 1876 a unified and well-armed white South, with its hardened Confederate veterans, had overthrown the state governments created by the Reconstruction Acts. In South Carolina Wade Hampton III was elected governor, and control of the state returned to the old white elites, primarily from the lowcountry.[24]

Raising funds for the seminary amid such economic and political turmoil and violence was obviously no easy task. Plumer raised some money from northern friends, and small amounts were sent by churches and individuals in the South. These endowment funds were used as in the past to make loans to individuals, with the seminary holding mortgages on personal property—only now there was no slave property to mortgage, only real estate. By the 1870s the seminary trustees had begun a slow move away from such loans to other kinds of investments. City bonds became the largest category of invested funds followed by railroads, banks, and textiles. But the income remained meager, and the faculty agreed to salary cuts—from $3,000 a year to $2,500—and students struggled to meet the costs of tuition, room, and board. Small loans, administered by the faculty, were provided for students in need, and the students organized and ran the dining hall on the campus where they took all their meals. The seminary's buildings left behind their prosperous antebellum appearance and took on a shabby look as maintenance and repairs were delayed except for essentials.[25]

Critical to the seminary's financial survival was the continuing wealth of the Adger and Smyth families. Foreseeing the disastrous consequences of the approaching Civil War, Robert Adger—Thomas Smyth's brother-in-law—had converted much of the family's fortune into British pounds and had deposited them in England with the longtime business partners of the Adgers-Brown, Shipley and Company. There the funds remained until the end of the war, when the Smyths and Adgers utilized them to expand rapidly into new business opportunities. The Adgers developed, as principal owners, the Coosaw Mining Company, which mined the rich phosphate beds in lowcountry rivers and quickly became the "most prosperous example of Charleston's postwar enterprise." Thomas Smyth's son Ellison established textile mills in the upcountry. The mills were soon by far the most prosperous in the state. John Adger's son John Jr. would join his cousins as a leader in the state's textile industry. In this way the Adgers and the Smyths were well situated to play important roles in the efforts to reestablish the seminary's financial stability. Thomas Smyth left in his will funds to endow the maintenance and expansion of his library at the seminary and funds to endow a "Presbyterian Lectureship" that would eventually come to be known as the "Smyth Lectures." Other members of the family contributed to endowment funds. Socially they represented a cosmopolitan tradition at the seminary that would resist the seminary's increasing provincialism.[26]

James Woodrow played an important role in the efforts to secure some economic stability for the seminary. A man of enormous energy—he slept only a few hours each night—he was soon engaged in a variety of business enterprises. With a loan from a brother in Ohio, he purchased a large press, and he immediately set about establishing a prosperous printing business. During the coming years, he would serve as president of the Central National Bank of Columbia, the Carolina Loan and Investment Company, and the South Carolina Home Insurance Company. He was vice president of the Columbia Lumber and Furniture Company and the Columbia Land and Improvement Company and was a director of two railroads. He also accepted, with the encouragement of his colleagues and members of his presbytery, a position as professor of chemistry at the South Carolina College during a period when the college was experiencing the disruptions of Reconstruction. When accused of engaging in secular work to the neglect of his ministerial and professorial responsibilities, Woodrow responded that his secular work was largely done when other men were enjoying a social life or resting from their labors at night. No one ever accused him of sloth! Because of his frugality and his business income, he was able to go without his seminary salary for several critical years in Columbia's life and to contribute directly to its endowment fund. Perhaps of greater help to the seminary's finances was his purchase and publication of the weekly *Southern Presbyterian* and of the seminary's scholarly journal *Southern Presbyterian Review.* Through his financial underwriting of both publications he was able to promote the seminary's financial interests. And through the *Review* he was able to demonstrate for another generation Columbia Seminary's continuing role as an intellectual center in the religious life of the South.[27]

Because of Woodrow's business acumen, the General Assembly made him treasurer of its Executive Committee on Foreign Missions and Domestic Missions and the assembly's Executive Committee on Sustentation. Leighton Wilson was the secretary of the committees and as such was responsible for their day-to-day operations. Both committees were composed primarily of those associated with Columbia and included—in addition to Woodrow and Wilson—Adger, Howe, and Girardeau. Moreover Columbia dominated the trustees of the General Assembly with Perrin as chairman, Palmer as secretary, and with Howe, Robert Adger, and longtime Columbia supporter John A. Crawford as members. Of special importance for the rebuilding of Columbia's place in the life of the church was the Committee on Sustentation. Under Leighton Wilson's leadership, the General Assembly had established a "sustentation fund" to help congregations devastated by the war. Churches with some resources contributed to the fund, and Wilson traveled monthly to Columbia to meet with the committee charged with allocating funds to those churches and pastors most in need. To encourage support of the fund, Wilson began to travel widely—especially to Baltimore, Louisville, St. Louis, and New Orleans—where the devastations of the war had not been as severe and where there were large and affluent Southern Presbyterian congregations. Through the careful management of the collected funds, and the direction of the committee that met on the seminary campus, churches began to be rebuilt, pastors were sustained in their ministries, and new churches were established. Unfortunately for Woodrow and Leighton Wilson, this concentration of church leadership around Columbia was a cause for growing resentment in parts of the church and would be the source of charges against them.[28]

In the 1871 General Assembly reference was made to "putting so much money and office power into the hands of a few men." The statement obviously referred to the influence of Columbia leaders, but it also alluded to criticisms being leveled against the Committee on Foreign and Domestic Missions. Articles had been appearing in the *Christian Observer,* a Presbyterian paper published in Kentucky, that charged the committee with centralizing power and mishandling funds. Both Woodrow's and Leighton Wilson's integrity was called into question. Both men requested a full investigation by the assembly. An investigative committee, led by Governor Patton of Alabama, reviewed the charges, issued a ringing endorsement of Woodrow and Wilson, and condemned the insinuations made against them. Woodrow was given the floor of the assembly, and he delivered an impassioned speech in which he revealed the sources of the charges. A member of the Converse family, which owned the *Christian Observer,* was a missionary in China who had overdrawn his account with the Foreign Mission Committee. When reprimanded by the committee, he had circulated charges against Woodrow, which the *Observer* published. Woodrow also revealed that other articles in the *Observer,* which had questioned Woodrow's integrity, had been written by Edwin Cater using various initials as pseudonyms. Woodrow told an astonished assembly that Cater had applied for the same position at the South Carolina College that Woodrow had been selected to fill. A former student of Woodrow's noted that the effects of his speech were profound. "At its close many of the Commissioners were in tears, and the whole audience, filling the large auditorium was deeply moved, and indignation ran high." Leighton Wilson followed and told the assembly that on two occasions Woodrow had come to the rescue of the church's foreign mission effort—once in a crisis he had given over $4,000 to cover the expenses of missionaries, and once he had even mortgaged his own home to pay a debt owed by the Committee on Foreign Missions. It was a moment of great vindication for Woodrow, but enemies had been made, especially at the *Christian Observer,* who would not forget the deep embarrassment that followed Woodrow's speech.[29]

Woodrow's incessant labors and the personal attacks on him by Cater and members of the Converse family left him badly in need of a long vacation to recover his health. He was granted a leave of absence without pay in 1872, and he left almost immediately for an extended stay in Europe, where he was invited to join and participate in a number of leading scientific societies. While he was away, a controversy erupted at the seminary that plunged the institution into a crisis and ended Columbia's slow movement toward a renewed strength and prosperity.[30]

In September 1873 students requested the faculty to hold Sabbath morning services in the chapel for the exclusive use of students and others who were on the campus. When the faculty met in early October, a tie vote left undecided the student request. Two weeks later the faculty met, and Adger moved and Joseph R. Wilson seconded that since the faculty was divided, the services be allowed for all who wished to take part. Howe and Plumer vote against it, so the motion failed. The student request reflected not only their dissatisfaction with the First Presbyterian Church but also personal animosities that were building between Wilson and Plumer. The two men had strong personalities and had begun to irritate one another in the tight little world of the seminary community. Moreover Wilson had been serving as interim pastor at First Church, and Plumer, a great preacher, had supplied the pulpit from time to time. When Wilson resigned his interim position to clear the way for the church to call a new minister, he did so apparently with some resentment about the way he had been treated by the congregation and perhaps with the conviction that Plumer had encouraged the congregational action.[31]

When James Woodrow returned to the campus in January 1874, the student request for Sunday morning chapel was once again taken up. With Woodrow now voting with Adger and Wilson, the faculty responded positively to the student proposal of the previous September. But the students were themselves now divided. Some wanted the chapel services; others did not. So they requested that their attendance be optional as originally proposed by Adger and Wilson in October. In late January the faculty voted, without exception, to request that the students withdraw their petition. The students did so, but some were incensed at the requirement to attend the Sunday service in the chapel. The issue for them was their right to worship when and where they wished. The issue for

Wilson, Adger, and Woodrow was the question of discipline as a responsibility of the faculty under the seminary's constitution. On this point Howe joined them, leaving Plumer alone in insisting on the rights of the students. Despite an emphasis on freedom of inquiry, student life on the campus was in fact tightly controlled by the faculty—students had to ask permission to leave the campus for any period of time, stack wood for the stoves in the dormitory, preach at nearby churches, conduct Sunday schools, and do a myriad of other things. The restrictions were perhaps too much for college graduates and especially for those who were Confederate veterans.[32]

In early March a senior, Samuel Preston, asked to be dismissed from the seminary in good standing. The dismissal was granted, but when Preston learned that the faculty had not realized his request was because of his refusal to attend Sunday chapel, he wrote and explained his position and asked that his dismissal be considered again in light of his opposition to the faculty decisions. He asserted his freedom to attend worship not as a matter of obligation but as a matter of choice. "The faculty has the right to interpret the constitution of the seminary and so do I," he insisted. He quoted the Westminster Confession on liberty of conscience "which the Lord hath left free from the doctrines and commandments of man in matters of faith and worship." The faculty again gave him a dismissal in good standing but admonished him for his position and said he was "laboring under the misfortune of having, on these points, a conscience not duly enlightened." Plumer dissented. Twelve other students, indignant over what they considered the faculty's patronizing admonition to Preston, quickly followed Preston in requesting dismissal, a number of them to other seminaries.[33]

When the board met in early May, it approved the action of the faculty. But when the board's report reached the General Assembly meeting in late May, it precipitated three days of hot debate. Finally the assembly—after expressing its entire confidence in the faculty—voted sixty to fifty-three that attendance at chapel should be voluntary. Wilson and Adger immediately resigned from the faculty, and Girardeau, who was serving as moderator of the assembly, resigned from the board. In his letter of resignation, Wilson said he could not meet the responsibilities of a professor without "a power of discipline that can no longer be hoped for." And he added: "I am so divided, both in policy and principle, from at least one member of the existing faculty, as to render official co-operation with him impossible; and thus the prospect of my usefulness in your Seminary is wholly forbidden."[34]

Leaving the assembly Plumer quoted to a friend a version of a psalm:

He digged a pit, he digged it well,
He digged it for his brudder,
Into that selfsame pit he fell,
Himself and not anudder.[35]

The result of allowing the conflict to escalate and of turning these personal animosities into Great Principles of student freedom and professorial authority was disastrous for the seminary. The resignation of Adger and Wilson not only decimated the faculty; it also meant that the two would not be able to add their considerable authority to the coming debate within the seminary about evolution and freedom of inquiry—a serious loss for Woodrow, who would be at the center of the controversy. The student body dropped from fifty-seven in September 1873 to twenty-five in September 1875. The financial situation of the seminary grew increasingly desperate as giving dropped and a national recession restricted income. The board could not find replacements for Adger and Wilson. Plumer, now in his eighties, was pressured into moving from theology to pastoral theology, and Girardeau was finally convinced in 1876 that he should take up Thornwell's old position in theology to help save the seminary. But Girardeau abruptly resigned in 1880, giving no reason except that he wanted to go to a small country church and engage in scholarly work. With two of its important chairs vacant—theology and church history—the board found it necessary to close the seminary in 1880. Plumer was made professor emeritus, to his great indignation, and Woodrow, who did not need his seminary salary, was temporarily relieved of all responsibilities. Howe was left in charge of buildings, grounds, and the library. This was the context out of which a tumultuous controversy over evolution emerged and played itself out in the life of Columbia Seminary and the Southern Presbyterian Church.[36]

9

Evolution and "the phraseology of the past"

When John Lafayette Girardeau stood in 1871 before the graves of Confederate soldiers in Magnolia Cemetery and called for the preservation of the "phraseology of the past," he proposed a way for white southerners to preserve their cultural identity and social cohesion. If the white sons and daughters of the South maintained a coherent language of shared images and ideas, Girardeau promised they would be able to resist the social and cultural imperialism of the North and keep at bay the alien ways that Yankees were seeking to impose on a defeated Dixie. Girardeau was suggesting that white southerners could speak to each other in the accents of the white South and intuitively grasp the nuances and the far-rumbling assumptions carried by their words—"ya'll," "Yankee," "Negro," "white," "freedom," "home," "southerner," "Bible," and a dictionary full of other words. These words, together with a deep grammar that related them to one another, provided white southerners a "tongue," a native language, which had emerged out of their history to shape their memory and interpretation of their history. Even if Lee had surrendered, the language of Dixie could now stand defiantly before Yankee imperialism. For Girardeau this familiar language of the past could keep out of the South the erosive ideas of Yankee modernity—ideas that would undermine not only the social structures of the white South but also the very culture of the white South with its traditional morals, values, and religious life.

Girardeau was consequently alarmed when he discovered in the late 1870s that Charles Darwin's "scientific hypothesis of evolution"—or some variation of it—was being taught at Columbia Seminary. Here, at Columbia Seminary of all places, an insidious idea was lurking, an idea that interpreted the world using the new language of evolutionary development. This new and dangerous idea threatened to breach the language barrier constructed around the white South. And most alarming the threat was coming not from Yankees but from the inside the South by a Columbia Seminary faculty member.[1]

For Girardeau evolution and its language of development seemed to be emerging out of some anarchic mire to threaten not only the doctrinal commitments of Southern

Presbyterians but also the social and cultural foundations of Dixie. Girardeau saw clearly the revolutionary power of this scientific theory and of the ideas and interpretations of the world it was spawning. For Girardeau the broad theory of evolution in all its subtle variations was not simply a challenge to the traditional Christian understanding of the origin of human life and its relationship to the natural world. It was also a challenge to the traditional Christian claim about the purpose and destiny of human history—the claim that human history has a goal and is moving toward the promised Kingdom of God guided by God's providence. Against this Christian claim, evolution was presenting a powerful counterclaim—human history, it declared, is the story of natural selection. According to this story there is no waiting goal, no providential destiny, pulling history toward a future consummation. In the story of evolution there is no divine providence and design but rather complex contingencies that govern human life and shape the course of human history. Girardeau could clearly see that this new language and its deep assumptions were already seeping out of interpretations of the natural world into interpretations of human societies and cultural life. Even the Bible—the infallible word of God, the repository of the most fundamental phraseology of the past—was being interpreted as a series of evolutionary developments from the primitive religion of the early Hebrews to the exalted religion of Jesus.[2]

In the face of such a threat, Girardeau was convinced that the teaching of evolution in any form—except as a straw man to be shredded—must be banished from the seminary and that James Woodrow, the offending faculty member, must be dismissed from his chair as the Perkins Professor of Natural Science in Connection with Revelation. Girardeau consequently flung himself into the fight to eliminate the language of evolution from seminary classrooms and from the assumptions of seminary faculty and students. The battle, however, was to be no easy one—it was to lead to the greatest controversy in the Southern Presbyterian Church until the 1970s, and it was to leave Columbia Seminary battered and intellectually crimped for generations to come. And not incidentally the battle was also to be "the first large scale evolution controversy in American history"—some forty years before the famous "Scopes monkey trial."[3]

When the Perkins Professorship of Natural Science in Connection with Revelation was established in 1859, some had greeted its establishment with great enthusiasm, others with no little suspicion. Thornwell, Smyth, Adger, and Leighton Wilson were among those who were enthusiastic. They believed that reason and revelation were compatible and that the one corroborated the other. Because natural science was the most powerful expression of reason in the nineteenth-century, ministers, they believed, needed to be well informed about the latest scientific developments and well prepared to defend the reasonableness of revelation. Such well-prepared ministers could help repulse the assaults being launched against the Word of God by rationalists who were trying to use natural science to undermine Christianity.[4]

But other Southern Presbyterians were deeply suspicious of the Perkins Chair. Robert Lewis Dabney of Union Seminary in Virginia worried that the instructions of such a chair must have a "tendency toward naturalistic and anti-Christian opinions." And he soon began a systematic attack on the natural sciences that was to last until his death. In 1873 Woodrow finally responded to Dabney in a searing rebuttal published in the *Southern Presbyterian Review.* He pointed out that Dabney had been keeping up "an unremitting warfare against Physical Science as the mortal enemy of all the Christian holds dear," and he said such attacks, if not answered, would lead many to unbelief. Woodrow insisted science was neither religious nor irreligious—there is, he pointed out, no Christian law of gravity. But Woodrow also showed what a formidable controversialist he could be. Dabney, he essentially said, was an ignoramus when it came to scientific teaching and what scientists were actually trying to do. Dabney would not forget the sharpness of Woodrow's remarks, and later he would be a strong supporter of Girardeau in his efforts to banish Woodrow from Columbia Seminary.[5]

In his 1861 inaugural address as the new Perkins Professor, Woodrow had set the trajectory for the path he would follow at Columbia. He had noted that there was not "a single similar chair in any theological school either in America or Europe, to serve as a model." He had consequently set his own course by identifying supposed antagonisms between science and revelation. These included the age of the earth; the length of time humans had been on the earth; and an understanding of death—was there death before human sin? Troubling questions, he also said, swirled around Noah's flood—did its waters cover the whole earth? And there was the continuing issue that Smyth, Howe, and others associated with Columbia had addressed so vigorously in the 1850s—the unity of the human race. Are all the various races of humanity descended from the single pair, Adam and Eve? Woodrow had obviously been responding in 1861 primarily to questions raised by the new geology introduced by Charles Lyell, but just as obviously he had not mentioned evolution and the recent work of Charles Darwin that was just beginning its conquest of modern thought.[6]

What Woodrow had concluded in his inaugural was that nothing would be found in natural science that was inconsistent with the Bible. God's work (creation) and God's word (the Bible) could not contradict each other. But while Woodrow had acknowledged that the conclusions of science are always only probably true, he had also raised questions about language, about God's word, and he had noted that many interpretations of the Bible are not absolute. Every part of the Bible is absolutely true, but Woodrow had insisted that this was so only "in the sense in which it was the desire of its real Author, the Holy Spirit, that it should be understood." The central elements of Christianity could be clearly discerned in the Bible and understood by faith, but there was great diversity of views on many other matters in the Bible, and this diversity of interpretation indicated the difficulty of reaching the exact meaning of many passages, especially those that dealt with "material objects" and were related to natural science. In light of this diversity of interpretation and the difficulty of language to convey an exact meaning for many passages, Woodrow had declared that he would carry on the duties of his professorship with an "untrammeled freedom of inquiry." Woodrow had thus begun his time at Columbia by (1) staking out a position of "non-contradiction" between science and the Bible, (2) calling attention to the limitations of language to interpret parts of the Bible in the sense that the Holy Spirit desired them to be understood, and (3) insisting on freedom of inquiry.[7]

All three positions were going to be, with Girardeau leading the charge, vigorously protested and rejected. But because of the distractions of the war, little immediate attention had been paid to Woodrow's inaugural and its conclusions except for Dabney's rather generic attacks. That attention was to come with a vengeance as the seminary entered the crisis of the late 1870s and the early 1880s.

Following its decision to temporarily close the seminary in 1879, the board began vigorous efforts to secure new funds for the endowment and to find and call new faculty members. James Hemphill, a member of the South Carolina legislature and soon to be a U.S. congressman, was elected president of the board. Other board members included T. B. Fraser, a circuit court judge and member of a prominent lowcountry family; Thomas Law, class of 1862 and Adger's son-in-law; William Boggs, also of the class of 1862 and pastor of Atlanta's Central Church; and J. B. Mack, class of 1861, who had served as Girardeau's associate pastor in Charleston. They were all to be deeply involved in the controversy soon to sweep over Columbia. The board asked for and secured the transfer of the seminary from the control of the General Assembly back to the synods of South Carolina, George, and Alabama. J. B. Mack was made the agent for the seminary and instructed to give his full time to raising funds. The board persuaded Girardeau to return to the faculty (he had resigned in early 1880) and to join Mack in fund raising while the seminary remained closed. Charles R. Hemphill, class of 1874, was called to be professor of biblical literature when the seminary reopened. He had recently completed graduate study at Johns Hopkins and was, not incidentally, the son of the board president. Board member William Boggs accepted the call to fill Adger's long vacant position in church history and polity. Born in India of missionary parents, Boggs would become in a few years chancellor of the University of Georgia.[8]

With a full faculty now finally in place, the board announced the seminary was reopening in September 1882. In making the announcement, the board approved a report to the synods written by Mack that said the faculty at Columbia was "too honest secretly to impugn the verbal inspiration of any part of the original Scriptures or to covertly teach evolution and other insidious errors that undermine the foundations of our precious faith." In light of this statement, Woodrow thought it proper to report at the next board meeting the methodology he used in his classes on the relationship of the natural sciences to the Bible. He compared, he said, "scripture with scripture to discover the principles by which Biblical references to matters connected with Natural Science or Natural History are to be interpreted," and then he applied these principles "to various cases of real or supposed inconsistencies between the teaching of the Bible and Natural Science." What was found in every case, Woodrow reported, was that there "are no real inconsistencies." He went on to add, however, that "the Bible does not teach that the earth had not been in existence more than a week before man was created." And he said that "except in the case of man the Bible teaches nothing as to God's *method* of creation and therefore it is not teaching anything contradicting God's word to say that He may have formed the highest beings from the lower by successive differentiations." The next day Mack moved that since Columbia was the only seminary that had a chair such as the Perkins Chair, that since the question of evolution was examined by students in Woodrow's class, and that since skeptics were using natural science to impugn the Word of God, Woodrow be requested to give his full views on evolution and publish them in the *Southern Presbyterian Review.* The board passed the motion, but many did not realize that it flowed from Mack's suspicion about what Woodrow was teaching. Later prominent board members felt they had been betrayed by Mack, who was increasingly regarded as the front man for Girardeau. Board member Thomas Law, John Adger's son-in-law, went so far as to believe that Mack had a "sinister purpose" in proposing that Woodrow give his full views on evolution.[9]

Woodrow presented his views before the seminary alumni and board in May 1884, and the address was published in the July issue of the *Southern Presbyterian Review.* He began by asserting that the relationship between science and the Bible was not one of harmony, of reconciliation of the one to the other. One does not seek harmony between zoology and astronomy or between physics and metaphysics. In the same way, one should not seek harmony between the Bible and science. "Their contents are so entirely different that it is vain and misleading to be searching for harmonies." The Bible, he said, "does not teach science and to take its language in a scientific sense is grossly to pervert its meaning." What is rather needed is an attempt to see if there are contradictions between what the Bible says and what science claims. He then asserted that while he had found some things that he did not understand, he had found "nothing in my study of the Holy Bible and of natural science that shakes my firm belief in the divine inspiration of every word of that Bible, and in the consequent absolute truth, the absolute inerrancy, of every expression which it contains, from beginning to end."[10]

Woodrow then turned to the question of evolution, which he defined as "derivation" or in the case of organic beings, as "descent." He asked if the Bible taught anything about the *mode* "in which the world and its inhabitants were brought into their present state." The language of scripture, he said, speaks only of the *fact* of God's creation and says nothing of the *mode* by which God created the heavens and the earth, the sea and the dry land. Woodrow acknowledged that his views on evolution and the mode of creation had changed. For years he had taught that evolution was probably not true, but now after much study he thought it probably true. And among the things he thought probably true was that Adam's body had been created by the process of evolution and that his soul was immediately created by God. Such conclusions and his study of evolution, he said, had led him to deeper reverence for the "Lord God Almighty."[11]

Swift and severe criticism followed the address. The *Christian Observer,* long antagonistic toward Woodrow, led the charge in church newspapers, but it was not alone. The *Central Presbyterian,* the *North Carolina Presbyterian,* the *Southwestern Presbyterian,* and the *Texas Presbyterian* all carried editorials and letters critical of Woodrow. "'The Lord formed man of the dust of the ground.' Man was born of an ape by ordinary generation. If these are not logical contraries," declared the *Texas Presbyterian,* "it would, in ordinary circumstances, be accounted a very strange use of language." The paper agreed that Woodrow could not be convicted of heresy for saying evolution was a mere possible or probable theory of the mode of creation, so long as the first and all subsequent steps were due to the creative power of God. But having a professor fill the heads of seminary students with such ideas was, said the paper, an altogether different matter.[12]

For Mack, who was out trying to raise money for the seminary, Woodrow's very presence on the faculty was increasingly an obstacle blocking the way to Columbia's revitalization. Writing to Boggs, who had just joined the faculty, Mack said: "My view is clear and my path is plain. Either Dr. Woodrow must leave or else our Seminary must suffer for years, and perhaps almost die. . . . In private and in public, in the Board and in our Church courts everywhere and at all times, I will not hesitate to say that the issue is between the welfare of the Seminary and the retention of Dr. Woodrow."[13]

When the board met the following September, 1884, Mack and two other board members tried to get a resolution passed that condemned the idea that Adam was in anyway descended from lower animals and that forbade Woodrow's teaching such a theory. The resolution was voted down eight to three. Another resolution was then offered. It said that in Woodrow's address "the relations subsisting between the teachings of Scripture and the teachings of Natural Science are plainly, correctly and satisfactorily set forth in said address." It then declared that while "the board is not prepared to concur in the view expressed by Dr. Woodrow as to the probable creation of Adam's body, yet in the judgment of this board there is nothing in the doctrine of Evolution, as defined and limited by him, which is inconsistent with perfect soundness in the faith." This resolution was passed eight to three. The three who opposed it entered an immediate protest to be carried to the synods. The protest did not say that Woodrow's position was actually contrary to the scriptures or to the Westminster Confession of Faith, but that his teaching was contrary to the southern church's *traditional interpretation* of scripture and the confession. The critical issue was—could a seminary professor introduce a challenge to the church's traditional interpretations?[14]

What made Woodrow's position so threatening was that it called into question the way Southern Presbyterians had long identified themselves as defenders of the plain sense of the scriptures. Their self-understanding as white Southern Presbyterians was at stake. So too was what they understood to be the character of the South, of southern culture and society. At the time of Lincoln's election, Thomas Smyth had declared in Charleston that God in His providence had given to the South "the high and holy keeping, above all other conservators, of the Bible." That same week Benjamin Morgan Palmer had declared in New Orleans: "To the South the high position is assigned of defending, before all nations, the cause of all religion and of all truth." Both men had declared abolitionists were making their own conscience, rather than the Bible, the infallible standard of right and wrong. Indeed throughout the antebellum period, Thornwell and Palmer, Smyth and Howe, Adger and other white Southern Presbyterians had used a strict interpretation of the Bible as a key defense of the South against the attack of abolitionists who, they said, were Bible haters. Now in the years after the war, the Bible, as the inerrant Word of God, contained the most fundamental and precise "phraseology of the past" to be used as a defense of the postwar South, its way of life, and its special place in the providence of God. The foundation stone for the wall around the South, protecting it from the onslaught of Yankee cultural imperialism and the degenerating acids of modernity, was an inerrant Bible *as it had been interpreted by the white southern church.*[15]

The debate moved to the synods that controlled the seminary, including now the Synod of South Georgia and Florida. The most extended and influential debate took place in the Synod of South Carolina. The committee that reviewed the report of the board and the protest lodged with the synod brought in a majority report, signed by three members, and a minority report, signed by two members. J. S. Cozby, pastor of the First Presbyterian Church, Sumter, chaired the committee and spoke on behalf of the majority report. He had grown up in Liberty County on a plantation adjoining the Charles Colcock Jones plantation and was a person with deep ties to the old lowcountry elites. With him on the majority side was G. R. Brackett, pastor of Smyth's old church, Second Presbyterian, Charleston. He was closely associated with the Adger and Smyth families. Silas Johnston, the third member of the majority, was a lawyer and the son of Job Johnston, a distinguished jurist who had served on the Columbia board during the antebellum period. The father had been a part of the tight circle of Columbia leaders that included Thornwell, Adger, Smyth, and Howe. The author of the minority report was R. A. Webb, Girardeau's son-in-law and the pastor of a country church in the upstate. With him was a lay elder.[16]

The majority report sustained the action of the board and declared that evolution was a "purely scientific and extra-Scriptural hypothesis," and as such the church was "not called upon to make any deliverance concerning its truth or falsity." Cozby, Brackett, and Johnston appealed to the "spirituality of the church"—the very doctrine that Thornwell had so carefully developed to keep the church from addressing social questions, especially slavery! The minority report insisted that the issue was not whether Woodrow's views "contradict the Bible in its highest and absolute sense," but if they "contradict the interpretations of the Bible" by the Southern Presbyterian Church. The minority report asked the synod to prohibit at Columbia "the inculcation and defense" of evolution, even as a probable hypothesis. Evolution was said to be "contrary to the interpretation of the Scriptures by our Church and to her prevailing and recognized views."[17]

Woodrow was given the floor to respond in his own defense. In an impassioned five-hour speech, he spelled out in great detail two major themes. First, science and faith represent different spheres, and the boundaries between the two are clear. The Bible, he said once again, does "not teach science." Furthermore the church has no more authority to make pronouncements about scientific matters than it has authority to make pronouncements about political matters. Second, he dismissed the claim that he had violated "the interpretation of the Scriptures by our Church . . . and her prevailing and recognized views." Such a claim, he said, was nothing less than an acknowledgement "that the highest and absolute sense of the Sacred Scriptures is different from that which you pledge yourselves to teach as ministers." "I am under no more obligation," he told the synod, "to teach received interpretations than you are." The only standard by which he was to be judged was the Westminster Confession and its catechisms, not "received" interpretations of Westminster, of which there were many.[18]

Girardeau finally emerged from the shadows and responded as Woodrow's most formidable opponent. He showed himself to be a serious student of logic, and he demonstrated his ability to analyze and challenge Woodrow's assumptions about the character of "non-contradiction." He asked if it were possible for two statements to be "non-contradictory without being to some degree harmonious." He spoke at length on the law "of the excluded middle," and he explained to the synod that the law was one of the fundamental laws of thought that bear on and regulate all the processes of the thinking faculty.[19]

But this lecture was only an erudite introduction to what Girardeau regarded as the fundamental question before the synod—"the relation between Dr. Woodrow's hypothesis and the Bible as our church interprets it: between the scientific view and our Bible—the Bible as it is to us." Woodrow, Girardeau declared, was not being charged with heresy but with departing from the established traditions of the southern church. What made this such a critical issue was that Woodrow was a professor at a theological seminary that was designed to teach what the church holds and believes. "The church," said Girardeau, "has the right to require, is solemnly bound to require, that her doctrines be taught, and that what is contrary to her doctrines be not taught." The great end of a theological seminary, he said, "is to teach the church's interpretation of the Word of God." But Columbia seminary was not designed simply to teach the scriptures—every seminary of evangelical denominations was designed to teach the scriptures. What made Columbia distinct? Our seminary, he said, "was designed to teach the Scriptures as interpreted by the Presbyterian Church; and is now maintained for the purpose of teaching them as interpreted by the Southern Presbyterian Church." What is taught in the seminary cannot be left, he said, to any professor or even to the board of directors. The controlling synods "are ultimately to determine what is or is not to be taught at the Seminary." Girardeau ended by warning that Columbia faced the greatest danger in its history. The seminary, he said, "is on the edge of deadly peril. . . . Let the hypothesis of evolution be inculcated in the theological school at Columbia . . . and the majority of the people of God will withdraw from it their sympathy and their support."[20]

The supporters of Woodrow rallied to his side. James L. Martin, a physician and member of the class of 1870, declared that the synod had just as much right to discuss how Woodrow would vote in the next election as to discuss his views on evolution. "It might be argued that as the members of the Southern Presbyterian Church are Democratic to the core, and the Seminary is supported by Democrats, Dr. Woodrow's statement that he would probably vote for Blaine [a Republican] would be taken as likely to injure the institution, and he could have been investigated by the board, and brought before Synod to answer for his extra-scriptural politics." Woodrow's new colleague on the faculty C. R. Hemphill dismissed the issue of accepted "interpretations of the Bible" by Southern Presbyterians. There was, he said, no "accepted interpretations" by Southern Presbyterians except the Westminster Standards. Woodrow, he said, was being accused of contradicting certain interpretations of the Bible—"not those interpretations in the Confession which constitute the system of doctrine to which we are all pledged, but outside the Confession, somewhere or other; we are not told where." John Adger spoke against his old friend Girardeau, from whom he was increasingly alienated. He said that the aim of the opposition was now clear—to abolish or fundamentally alter the Perkins Professorship. But he said that would only encourage infidelity by ignoring science. Moreover, said Adger, the purpose of a theological seminary is not dogmatic: "its genius is that of inquiry into all truth." It will not do, he said, to teach seminary students to "fear and shun any truth." Mack responded by saying that he was "amazed and amused" by Adger's position. William Plumer Jacobs wrote in his journal that Girardeau and Mack had "lifted the black flag. It is a sad pity to have such men in the church of Jesus with the spirit of hate they manifest." And so it went for five days of debate.[21]

In the end both the majority report and the minority report from the board were rejected by an identical vote of fifty-two to forty-four. A compromise resolution was then adopted fifty to forty-five: "That in the judgment of this Synod the teaching of Evolution in the Theological Seminary at Columbia, except in a purely expository manner, without intention of inculcating its truth is hereby disapproved." The synod then adopted with a unanimous vote a resolution that declared the synod's "affection for Dr. Woodrow's person, its appreciation of the purity of his Christian character, its admiration of his distinguished talents and scholarly attainments both in Theology and Science, and its high estimate of his past activities."[22]

The Synod of Georgia met a few weeks later. Led by G. B. Strickler of Atlanta's Central Presbyterian Church, a ferocious attacked was launched against Woodrow. Strickler moved that the board of directors' action affirming Woodrow be "disapprove" and that the board be directed to take whatever steps necessary to prevent the teaching of evolution as expounded by Woodrow. Woodrow's friends made arguments similar to those that had been made before the South Carolina synod by supporters of the beleaguered professor. When Woodrow spoke he was clearly outraged by what had been said about him. False charges, he said, had been constantly reiterated, but none had been put in due form so that he could demand proof. "I charge," declared Woodrow, "that from this time forth, if any presbyter throughout the church shall bring such accusation in other than the due form, he must stand convicted as a slanderer. I demand a trial. You may go on and try me and condemn me by indirection if you will but I appeal to God against such an injustice." His call for a trial and the arguments of his friends did no good. Strickler's motion passed sixty to twenty. The synod then asked A. W. Clisby, a member of the board and strong supporter of Woodrow, to resign. Clisby, pastor of the First Presbyterian Church in Macon, refused. The synod then removed him and replaced him with William Adams, pastor of First Presbyterian in Augusta. At the same time they elected W. C. Sibley, a prominent businessman in Adams's congregation. They were both strongly anti-Woodrow.[23]

When the Synod of Alabama met it instructed, by a vote of forty-one to nineteen, the seminary board to do what was necessary in order to prevent the teaching of evolution at Columbia. Two board members who had supported Woodrow were not reelected to the board but were replaced. One of those not reelected was the highly esteemed Charles Stillman, founder of the Presbyterian school for African Americans that eventually became Stillman College. He had grown up in Thomas Smyth's Charleston congregation and had close personal ties with other supporters of Woodrow, especially John Adger. The Synod of South Georgia and Florida apparently felt some uncertainty about the issues and about the best course to follow. It adopted a report that said evolution "seems to be in conflict with the received interpretation of Scripture" and that it "would seem to affect some of the fundamental doctrines of the Bible." But the synod seemed sure that the teaching of evolution at the seminary would endanger Columbia's future, so it instructed its directors to "take whatever steps might be necessary for the carrying out of the will of the four controlling synods."[24]

The seminary board met in December 1884 after the four synods had acted. The preceding September eight members had voted to sustain Woodrow. The terms of five had expired, and only one, John Adger's son-in-law Thomas Law, had been reelected. Another member, A. W. Clisby, had been removed. The newly constituted board called for Woodrow to resign because he had publicly announced that he would continue to teach "as probably true the hypothesis of evolution." When called on and asked to resign, Woodrow refused, saying that he could not be dismissed, according to the seminary's constitution, without a judicial investigation and trial. The board then voted to remove him from his chair. W. E. Boggs promptly resigned as professor of church history, and Charles Hemphill resigned as professor of biblical literature. This left only Girardeau on the faculty. Woodrow later explained to the Synod of South Carolina that the board had not asked him or given any indication that it wanted to know if he would continue to teach evolution as probably true.[25]

The controversy now became increasingly bitter, tearing the tight web of relationships that had given such social cohesion to the world of Southern Presbyterians. John Adger, now seventy-five years old and a greatly respected leader in the church, declared that Columbia's board no longer had the confidence of many in the church. And he publicly charged Mack with being the primary manipulator of the attacks on Woodrow. He would later say to Girardeau that he and Mack together bore responsibility for the controversy that had so badly damaged the seminary and the church. "It is the opinion of many," Adger wrote in a church paper, "that personal animosity in more than one party has been at work in all this business."[26]

Woodrow appealed his dismissal to the four synods. The Synod of South Carolina supported Woodrow's appeal, and Mack and another director resigned. In an act that must have left Mack and Girardeau grinding their teeth, the synod elected to fill Mack's place on the board James Adger Smyth—Thomas's son, strong supporter of Woodrow, and soon to be mayor of Charleston. The other position on the board was filled by S. L. Morris, a supporter of Woodrow and a close associate of John Adger's. Girardeau resigned, once again, from the faculty. He told board that his resignation was impelled "by a sentiment of honor" occasioned by his "conscientious opposition to the inculcation in the Seminary" of Woodrow's views on evolution. Mack resigned as the financial agent for the seminary. The Synod of South Georgia and Florida also disapproved the action of the board in dismissing Woodrow. The Synods of Georgia and Alabama supported the actions of the board.[27]

When the board met in December 1885, it declared that because a majority of the synods did not support the board's action in dismissing Woodrow, he was still legally the Perkins Professor. Woodrow said in compliance with the directions of the synod he would not teach about the subject of evolution in his classes. Those who opposed him still sought his dismissal.[28]

Woodrow finally received the formal judicial review and trial that he had long demanded. After a complex process, he was acquitted of the charge of heresy. But it was clear from actions of the General Assembly and the synods that the great majority in the church wanted Woodrow to resign or be removed from the Perkins Chair. Student enrollment had dropped to twenty-two, the faculty had been decimated, and contributions to the seminary had been greatly reduced. The seminary had consequently been closed in September 1886. Recognizing the strength of the opposition in the actions of the synods and the General Assembly, the board, meeting in December 1886, asked Woodrow to resign. When he refused he was unanimously dismissed. The pro-Woodrow members had in the meantime attempted, against the vigorous protests of their opponents, to call a new professor to fill Girardeau's vacant position. They apparently hoped to block Girardeau's return to the faculty. They failed, however, to secure a new professor, and when Woodrow was dismissed, the way was clear for Girardeau to be elected once again to his old position. He quickly accepted. And Mack was called to take up again his position as the financial agent for the seminary. He too quickly accepted. Adger wrote an open letter to Girardeau that Woodrow published in the *Southern Presbyterian.* "Dr. Mack and yourself have been the chief actors on one side of the controversy. . . . Very much more than any other individual he and you are responsible for all that has been, and is yet to be, done. His reappointment and your re-election are a declaration that one party in the four Synods intend to keep control of the Institution to the exclusion of many of its oldest friends and supporters. United we can, with difficulty, sustain it; divided, it may not be found practicable."[29]

Girardeau and his side had won the battle, but they were not yet ready to end the war. The board assembled a new faculty. It called James Tadlock from the presidency of King College in Tennessee to the chair of church history, which he held until his death in 1898. Francis Beattie, a Canadian, was called to take the carefully renamed Perkins Chair Professorship of Natural Science in Connection with Revelation and Christian Apologetics. The new name emphasized his work was to be largely Christian apologetics—the task of defending the faith against any antagonistic system of thought. He remained for only a few years before moving to Louisville to become professor of theology and apologetics at the new Presbyterian seminary there. William Marcellus McPheeters arrived in 1888 and remained on the faculty as professor of Old Testament until his retirement in 1933. As much as anyone in the coming years, he was to carry in spirit and theological perspective Girardeau's legacy.[30]

While Woodrow remained in good standing as a minister and member of Augusta Presbytery, the attacks against him continued. They reflected both a vindictive animosity toward Woodrow and also a desire by Girardeau and his supporters to control all public discourse in the seminary and in the church. "The phraseology of the past," a language barrier, a protective wall around the church and Dixie, had to be maintained at all cost. William Flinn wrote in the *Southern Presbyterian Review* that not only had a "cruel wrong" been done to Woodrow, but "a Spirit of unreasonable jealousy and fear toward scientific inquiry and speculation" had been shown; "ill considered and ill informed criticism" had been indulged; "rash and harsh judgments" had been expressed; and a "spirit of hostility to free inquiry" had been manifest. The degree to which Girardeau and his new colleagues on the Columbia faculty would go in order to control public discourse and limit free inquiry was soon apparent.[31]

Charleston Presbytery, which included the city of Columbia and the reconstituted seminary faculty, under the leadership of Girardeau voted to forbid "the public contending against the decision of the Assembly" in regard to the Woodrow case. Outrage was expressed by many at this boldfaced attempt to squash public discourse. When the Synod of South Carolina met in October 1888, Thornton Whaling—a strong Woodrow supporter—was appointed chair of the committee to review the records of the presbyteries. The committee reported and the synod adopted a resolution that condemned the action of Charleston Presbytery as "unconstitutional, and irregular." It declared that the action of the Presbytery "is a trespass upon the sacred and inalienable right of private judgment, which belongs to every court and all the officers and members of the church of Christ." The action of the Presbytery, the committee said, "imposes a restraint upon the right of freedom in the expression of opinion, which is unwarranted by the law" and "assumes the infallibility of the General Assembly in deliverance of judicial decisions, which is a doctrine foreign to the Constitution and spirit of Presbyterianism." The synod then directed the presbytery to "convene as soon as practicable and review and correct these proceedings, which the Synod has now condemned." The General Assembly, however, "disapproved" the action of the synod because it appeared that the "action of Charleston Presbytery was not intended to limit either liberty or private judgment or the constitutional right of proper discussion." But Charleston Presbytery had already acted and had declared that it had "already obeyed Synod's order to 'review and correct it[s] proceeding,'" which Synod had condemned. The synod, in response to the assembly's action, accordingly declared that it was unnecessary for the synod to do more than "to reaffirm the doctrine that every minister, ruling elder, deacon and private member has the constitutional right to contend publicly, through the press or otherwise, against the decisions of all our courts from the lowest to the highest." All were apparently thoroughly exhausted by the ongoing controversy.[32]

But the controversy was still not over. The synod had to deal with another attempt by Girardeau and his new colleagues to tightly control the exposure of students to threatening ideas. A student, W. W. Elwang, requested in 1888 permission from the faculty to take courses under Woodrow at the University of South Carolina, where Woodrow was now a full-time faculty member. The Columbia faculty voted—and the board sustained its decision—that "in view of the late action of a majority of the synods controlling this Seminary, and of what it conceives to be its consequent duty, Mr. Elwang should abstain from attending the lectures of Professor Woodrow." The synod disapproved of the action, but the Synod of Georgia approved the action. The other two synods did not act, so the case seemed to be in limbo. Two years later a graduate of the university who had taken a number of courses with Woodrow entered the junior class of the seminary. On entering he requested to take a course in mineralogy with Woodrow. The faculty voted unanimously that he could take any classes at the university except those taught by Woodrow, a Presbyterian minister in good standing who had recently been elected moderator of his presbytery! Woodrow denounced the action of the faculty as cowardly, tyrannical, and infamous. This time the uproar was so intense that the board announced that a student's presbytery should make decisions about what a student should or should not take outside the confines of the seminary. Joseph Ruggles Wilson wrote his son Woodrow Wilson, "What asses Presbyterians are capable of becoming—whose ears extend to all the earth!"[33]

The Woodrow controversy obviously did not take place in an ecclesiastical vacuum. The debate over evolution and over Woodrow's remaining on the Columbia faculty came at a time of severe economic hardship in Columbia's primary constituencies and in the midst of political upheavals in much of the South. Rice production in the South Carolina and Georgia lowcountry continued its freefall as Asian rice began to pass through the newly opened Suez Canal and as economies of scale shifted much rice production from the lowcountry to Louisiana, Texas, and Arkansas. From 1881 to 1886 falling prices, army worms, and droughts devastated cotton farmers across much of the South, who were trying desperately to raise more cotton on increasingly abused and eroded land. In South Carolina alone, almost a million acres of land were foreclosed in 1886—the year of Woodrow's trial before his presbytery—because farmers could not pay their taxes. In 1860s the per capita wealth of South Carolinians—counting not only white South Carolinians but also impoverished African American slaves—was far above the national average. By the time of Woodrow's dismissal from the seminary, the state's per capita wealth had dropped to only a third of the national average. Similar economic conditions existed in the other states of the controlling synods.[34]

Out of such economic distress a white grassroots revolt was beginning to emerge that would overthrow in the 1880s and 1890s the old political domination of antebellum elites and that would be a part of a wider populist movement composed in the South largely of small farmers and textile workers. Tom Watson in Georgia and "Pitchfork" Ben Tillman in South Carolina were to become the best-know leaders of the revolt as they denounced the evils of northern capitalism, ridiculed Henry Grady's call for a New South, replaced the old paternalistic claims in regard to race with new laws that created a segregated Jim Crow South, and launched a barbarous attack on African Americans that intensified an already virulent racism in American society. Lynching became an increasingly common event in the 1890s as mutilated black bodies hung from trees across the South or burned before crowds of cheering whites.[35]

No neat lines can be drawn between these social and cultural developments and the Woodrow controversy and its major participants. The controversy was not simply a reflection of economic and social forces but also involved serious and distinct theological issues. Religious commitments shaped how Woodrow and Girardeau, Adger and Mack and their colleagues interpreted and responded to the challenge of evolution and the challenges of modernity even as their social context obviously helped to shape their religious commitments. But once this complex interaction between religious commitments and a particular historical context is acknowledged, certain connections between economic and political developments of the late nineteenth-century South and the Woodrow controversy can be emphasized. What stands out most clearly is the way the leading defenders of Woodrow were rooted in the old lowcountry elites. The Adgers and Smyths, John Leighton Wilson and James Smith Cozby, Thomas Law and William Flinn, Judge T. B. Fraser and Congressman James Hemphill are only the most obvious examples. Some of them were to come under fierce attack by populists. Hemphill, the longtime chair of the seminary board and supporter of Woodrow, was to lose his congressional seat to the Tillman forces in South Carolina. And the Adgers and Smyths were to come under attack by the rising populists. They were to fight Tillman on a number of fronts, but especially over his attempt while governor to gain more state control and income from the Coosaw Mining Company. On the other hand, Girardeau, Mack, and their supporters were more likely to be associated with the rising populists and their rejection of the old lowcountry leadership. Girardeau, while from the lowcountry, came not from the old lowcountry elite but from a modest farming background, and there was a deep resonance between the populists and the anxieties and fears expressed by Girardeau. To be sure, Palmer and Dabney were more closely associated with the old elites. But with their more populist colleagues, they shared a common fear of modernity with its urban and cosmopolitan culture and the threat it posed to a "southern way of life." Of course such links between the Woodrow controversy and economic and political developments in the South should not be exaggerated, but they need to be noted as a part of a dynamic context within which the controversy played out.[36]

Woodrow and his supporters were certainly more broadly traveled and cosmopolitan in outlook than Girardeau and Mack and the great host of their supporters. The Adgers and Smyths continued to spend time in New England, Canada, and Europe; and Leighton Wilson had behind him not only his years of experiencing and engaging various West African societies but also time spent in Brazil shortly before the Woodrow controversy broke into the open. Boggs had grown up in India. Flinn, after his graduation from Columbia in 1875, studied at the University of Edinburgh and traveled through parts of western Europe. And Woodrow not only had received his Ph.D. from the University of Heidelberg; he had also traveled widely in Europe while on leave during 1872–74. There he met many leading scientists, participated in the meetings of scientific societies, and visited with leading Protestant clergy. He was a member of the German Scientific Association, the Swiss Scientific Association, the Victoria Institute of London, the American Association for the Advancement of Science, and the International Congress of Geologists. In contrast Girardeau and Mack and most of their supporters were intensely parochial. They reflected the shrinking world of many white Southern Presbyterians leaders. Their experience of the world was bound by much loved southern horizons, and their response to modernity was marked by deep anxiety and by a determination to protect their church and their southern homeland from modernity's corrosive effects.[37]

The Woodrow controversy revealed once again the deep tension in the seminary's life between order and freedom. Girardeau's son-in-law and ardent admirer George Blackburn wrote that Girardeau "loved order. He feared disorder." In order to maintain order, Girardeau had called the white South to adhere scrupulously "to the phraseology of the past," to make it "the vehicle for transmitting to our posterity ideas which once true are true forever." Girardeau thought the strict control of language and its deep assumptions were a means of preserving order in church and southern society. For this reason Girardeau had insisted in his debate with Woodrow that "the great end of a theological seminary is to teach the church's interpretation of the Word of God." To maintain order and keep at bay disorder and alien ideas he had led the fight to have Woodrow dismissed; he had led the faculty to reject student requests to take classes from Woodrow at the university; and he had led his presbytery in the attempt to squash public debate about decisions of the General Assembly. In all this he was trying to build a protective language barrier around the church by carefully controlling what could be taught, or studied, or debated in public. He hoped to maintain order by erecting a wall composed of the received interpretations of the church's standard and, not incidentally, by using a traditional interpretation of the Bible he hoped to sustain a key defense of a "southern way of life."[38]

In contrast Woodrow insisted in his augural address as the Perkins Professor that he would carry on the duties of his professorship with an "untrammeled freedom of inquiry." This would be, over and over again, a theme in his speeches and in the articles he wrote in his defense. John Adger, in the debate before the Synod of South Carolina, declared that the genius of a theological seminary was "that of inquiry into all truth." C. R. Hemphill said before the same meeting of the synod that the charges against Woodrow had been "hush, I am afraid of evolution . . . silence! silence! 'Keep silence, O earth!' If the earth would keep silence and obey the Synod, very well. But the earth will not keep silence." And William Flinn declared we "are made free men by the truth" and that "we must claim and allow freedom of research."[39]

The church and Columbia Seminary sought to mediate between Girardeau's quest for order and Woodrow's insistence on freedom of inquiry. Woodrow was dismissed from his chair at Columbia, but shortly afterward he was elected moderator of his presbytery, and on a number of occasions the presbytery sent him as a commissioner to the General Assembly. He was elected president of the University of South Carolina in 1891, and in 1901 the Synod of South Carolina elected him moderator. When he died in 1907, he was lauded as a highly respected leader who had made important contributions to the life of Presbyterian Church. In 1911 Thornton Whaling, one of the strongest supporters of Woodrow, was elected not only the seminary's first president but also professor of didactic and polemic theology, Girardeau's old position. Whaling was invited to give in 1928 the prestigious McNair Lecture at the University of North Carolina. The "Scopes monkey trial" had captured the nation's attention only three years earlier, and Whaling delivered an address titled "Science and Religion Today." He dedicated the lecture to James Woodrow, "that peerless scholar and saint . . . who was above all a masterly expounder of the right relations between science and religion." Whaling concluded his lecture with an affirmation of Woodrow's old position: "The time has come to recognize that true science and real religion must be forever marked by the 'harmony of non-contradiction.'" And the memory of Woodrow was honored by others. In 1961 Clement Eaton, in his presidential address before the Southern Historical Society, reviewed the Woodrow controversy. He ended his address: "In the attainment of the large measure of freedom of teaching which we enjoy, the subject of my paper, James Woodrow, played a significant and triumphant role." Eaton saluted Woodrow's memory, and, thinking no doubt of the controversies and pressures swirling around the civil rights movement, he hoped that any professor in those tumultuous times who faced a similar crisis of academic freedom would display Woodrow's "great moral courage."[40]

Future admirers of Girardeau and the spirit of his world did not disappear with the arrival of the twentieth century. On the contrary they persisted and dominated the seminary—in spite of Whaling and a few others—for several generations. Forty years after the Woodrow controversy, the General Assembly of the white Southern Presbyterian Church declared that "Adam's body was directly fashioned by Almighty God without any natural animal parentage . . . and that any doctrine at any variance therewith is a dangerous error . . . and . . . will lead to the denial of doctrines fundamental to the faith." Furthermore the followers of Girardeau would see in him the embodiment of what they would come to call "Old Columbia"—a seminary fierce in its defense of orthodoxy and "a southern way of life" and eager to limit the seminary's teaching and public discourse to the "phraseology of the past." In many ways they would rightly see Girardeau as standing in the "Thornwellian tradition," carrying on the work of Thornwell as his faithful disciple. Yet Girardeau lacked the breath of Thornwell's scholarship and Thornwell's deep engagements with contemporary thought and the contemporary issues of his world. And Girardeau and his colleagues and his successors lacked the broad contacts and wide travels of their predecessors. Even Girardeau's most serious theological work—his *The Will in Its Theological Relations*—had about it the air of old debates and a commitment to the philosophical school of Scottish Common Sense Realism at a time when that school had largely lost most of its influence in American intellectual life. The seminary that Girardeau came to dominate and to bequeath to later generations was consequently not so much "Old Columbia" as it was "Girardeau's Columbia." After the Woodrow controversy "Girardeau's Columbia," in contrast to its predecessor, was deeply fearful of modern scholarship and had little engagement with the great intellectual issues of its day—with the thought of Darwin, Marx, or Freud, with the challenges of urban culture, immigration, industrialization, and the rise of great totalitarian regimes. This was, of course, partly a reflection of an impoverished South, where whites were trying to make their way to some new prosperity while keeping blacks in "their place." But it was also part of a defensive and impoverished intellectual world that had found a home on the campus of "Girardeau's Columbia."[41]

Columbia Seminary as "Girardeau's Columbia" lost its role as the intellectual center of white Southern Presbyterians and as a powerful voice in American religious life. Not only did Union Theological Seminary in Virginia take Columbia's place as the white Southern Presbyterian Church's most influential seminary, but the newly established Presbyterian seminaries in Louisville and Austin were stronger than Columbia. Columbia became the poorest and the weakest of the four seminaries. Only twenty students were enrolled in 1889—two seniors, twelve middlers, three juniors, and three special students. To be sure, many of Columbia's constituents continued to have a deep love for the seminary and to think of it as "our seminary," but Columbia and the church paid a significant price in the seminary's loss of intellectual vitality. Rather than vitality and intellectual rigor marking the seminary, a mediocrity settled over Columbia as it came to a comfortable ease in its Southern Zion. Indeed white Southern Presbyterians in general paid a heavy price for the way synods and the General Assembly dealt with James Woodrow and the controversy over evolution. Girardeau was not the only theology professor to oppose Woodrow. Robert Lewis Dabney and G. B. Strickler of Union, R. A. Webb of Louisville, and R. K. Smoot of Austin were all outspoken opponents of Woodrow. E. T. Thompson, the historian of Presbyterians in the South, summarized the consequences of the Woodrow controversy for white Southern Presbyterians: "theological writing, for all practical purposes, came to an end in the [white southern] Presbyterian Church for two generations and more. . . . There were doubtless many reasons for this fact. But creative writing could not be expected when the scholars of the church were not free to depart from traditional patterns. Perhaps it was here that the condemnation and expulsion of James Woodrow proved most costly to the church."[42]

10

Poor but Genteel

On the first Sunday of April 1883, as George Howe was returning from church he suddenly lost control of his carriage and was thrown violently to the ground. Friends carried him to his home. His physician son George hurried to his side. He found that his father's lame leg, which for years had required him to use a crutch, had been fractured. At first the injury did not seem life threatening, and for two weeks the old professor appeared to be recovering. But then a chill seized him, and he began hemorrhaging from the lungs. During a time when he was alert, he asked his wife, Sarah, to bring their Bible and sit beside him. The old couple had been married in 1836 in Liberty County, not far from Sarah's Halifax plantation, and over the years they had read the Bible daily to one other. Now he asked her to read to him the last two chapters of Romans. So she began: "We then that are strong ought to bear the infirmities of the weak, and not to please ourselves." When she finished the chapters, he took the Bible and read in his weakness the passages to her: "Now the God of hope fill you with all joy and peace in believing, that ye may abound in hope, through the power of the Holy Ghost." He closed the Bible, and, clasping his hands on his chest, he began to pray. He prayed for her and his loved one. And then he prayed for "the dear Seminary," caught up as it was in the fierce struggle over evolution. A little later Woodrow and Girardeau came and knelt together beside his bed. They were joined by their young colleagues Charles Hemphill and William Boggs. All but Woodrow had been his students. Gathered on their knees around his bed they prayed together and "commended him to the tender mercies of his God and Savior." One asked him the familiar question asked to the dying: "My dear brother, do you trust in Jesus?" And he replied: "Yes, what would I do, did I not trust in him?" He died shortly afterward and was buried in the Presbyterian church cemetery not far from his son Willie, who had died a painful death in a Confederate hospital in Virginia.[1]

Two years later John Leighton Wilson died at his Pine Tree plantation near the headwaters of South Carolina's Black River. He was buried beside his wife, his much loved and intrepid Jane, in the sandy soil of a country churchyard. They had once lived together in a cottage above the pounding surf of Cape Palmas in West Africa and on a hillside above the Gabon estuary. There they had fought the international slave trade and had sought to build up an indigenous ministry for an African church. A decade after Wilson's death, Girardeau retired from the seminary, and shortly thereafter a stroke left him partially paralyzed. Three years later he died quietly in his home surrounded by his family. He was buried in Columbia's Elmwood Cemetery "near where the dust of his beloved teacher, James Henley Thornwell, lies." John Adger died the next year at his upcountry plantation and was buried in the family plot at Second Presbyterian, Charleston, near Thomas Smyth. He and his beautiful wife, Elizabeth, had, like the Wilsons, see distant lands, and they had traveled boldly by horseback and caravan across deserts, mountains, and fertile valleys of the Ottoman Empire. Benjamin Morgan Palmer died in 1902 after being struck by a street car in New Orleans. Tributes poured in from across the South and parts of the North. He "realized in his activities," said the president of Tulane University, "the noblest conceptions of virtue, justice, tenderness, goodness and truth." In 1906 James Woodrow died—the last of these old colleagues and sometimes antagonists. Eulogies for Woodrow came from around the country, from the faculty of the University of South Carolina, and from many former seminary students. "Life to him was large," one wrote, "because its field was the world God upheld and ruled."[2]

For those who followed them, these nineteenth-century seminary leaders seemed to have been men who were larger than life—godly men who had once attracted the attention and admiration of those far beyond the little world of the seminary and its southern horizons. The new leaders for Columbia wanted to emulate those who had gone before them. They wanted to follow in their footsteps even as they knew both the narrowness of their own world and the forces of change that were beginning to erupt all around them.[3]

Two congregations in the seminary's constituency reflected the changes sweeping over the South and over white Southern Presbyterians as the nineteenth century gave way to the twentieth. One congregation—Charleston's Second Presbyterian—had played a large role in shaping the character of the seminary in the nineteenth century. The other congregation—Atlanta's Central Presbyterian—was to play an equally important role in the twentieth century. Both congregations responded vigorously to new social and cultural realities that were creating new forms of church life among white Southern Presbyterians.[4]

Members of Charleston's Second Presbyterian were the most generous and consistent contributors to the seminary's finances during the last three decades of the nineteenth century and the first two decades of the twentieth. During this period a clear if subtle transformation began to take place in how it understood itself as a congregation. In previous generations church membership had been for those who could testify publicly to an experience of regeneration—of being born again for eternity, of being touched by God's Spirit in a clear and forceful way and being assured of God's love in Jesus Christ. But by the end of the nineteenth century church membership had slowly become open to all who were respectable members of the community: to "Christian gentlemen" of good reputation and "Christian ladies" of good character who were carefully guided in their behavior by the requirements of proper Victorian manners. Those who had been only pew holders in earlier generations—and not able to take communion—were now able to leave behind any reservations about their place in the household of God and to become full communicant members. In this way the old practice of renting pews—with its assumptions that many would be attending church who were not communing members—was given up, and the new practice of stewardship was adopted following the most modern principles and methods.[5]

The congregation's buildings embodied many of the changes taking place in the church's life. Early in the nineteenth century the congregation had both its large and handsome sanctuary and also—like many other urban churches—a "lecture room." Second Presbyterian's lecture room was "a beautiful and creditable edifice" on Black Bird's Alley where Thomas Smyth had delivered lectures such as "Apostolic Succession" and the "Unity of the Human Races" and other on weighty matters. By the late 1880s, however, such erudite lectures seemed beyond the capacity of most ministers and the interests of audiences. A need was felt for a more modern approach to Christian education. As a result the congregation built a large and convenient Sunday school building next to the sanctuary in order that the "whole strength of the church" could be concentrated on Sunday school work. The new building quickly became a center of social activity and not only a place for education and informal worship. Women came to its comfortable parlor for their meetings, young people assembled in its rooms for their youth league, and the whole congregation gathered in its hall for concerts. Augustine Thomas Smythe (he added the *e* that had long been dropped from his family's name) was the leader in this effort. Smythe, a prominent lawyer and state senator, brought his practical wisdom and administrative ability to the development and management of the school. In a short time, the new building was teaming with children and adults.[6]

Atlanta's Central Presbyterian followed many of these same developments in the midst of the South's booming metropolis. Particularly noteworthy was the development of its Sunday school, which soon became the largest in the denomination and one of the largest in Georgia. Most revealing of the changes in church life, however, were two highly visible developments at Central. From the earliest establishment of Presbyterian churches in the British North American colonies, sessions had been primarily concerned with church discipline as a way of protecting the Lord's Supper from profanation. While such disciple could lead to legalism and to a stern self-righteousness, it was rooted in a sense of the holy and in reverence for the sacrament as the meeting of Christ and his people. Central's session like other sessions had been disciplining members for public drunkenness and for other behavior that brought scandal on the church. When in the 1880s several church members were disciplined for holding and attending a ball and another was disciplined for failure to pay a debt, protests began to gather that eventuated in the end of church discipline. At Central, where discipline had sought to draw a line between the worldly and the redeemed, discipline quickly faded into the gentle light of respectability. Now the person troubled with some sin of the flesh or some straying from the straight and narrow was quietly invited into the pastor's study for counseling or was referred to a growing host of trained professionals schooled in the new sciences of psychology and sociology.[7]

While discipline faded committees multiplied. Central began to be more highly organized. A quest for efficiency, for careful planning and control, sought to focus the energies of the congregation in various ministries in the city. Programs, led by prominent businessman John J. Eagan, were established to serve the urban poor, to aid young girls recently come to the city for work, and for the development of new congregations in various parts of the city. The values of a rising bureaucratically minded middle class, committed to being socially responsible, were clearly becoming visible at Central and among other white Southern Presbyterians.[8]

Women were not to be left behind in this quest for efficiency in service to the Master's Kingdom. Thomas Smyth's granddaughter, Louisa Smyth Stoney, traced in the 1920s the evolution of "women's work." She noted the changing place of women in southern society since the Civil War and the ways in which "women's work" had become increasingly organized to meet the demands of the modern world. Central to this effort had been the creation, in the early years of the twentieth century, of a denomination-wide women's auxiliary. "Women have learned," wrote Myrta Hutson of Second Church, "that efficiency and concentrated effort, marshalling the combined force for *all* the women for *all* the causes of the church, can be most successfully employed through the agency of this *one* twentieth century society."[9]

As these new values and new ways began to assert themselves here and there in the life of the white Southern Presbyterian Church, the seminary began to experience a difficult transition. Its revered nineteenth-century leaders—especially Thornwell, Palmer, and Girardeau—had warned of a looming disaster: an emerging modern society that would bring with it powerful disintegrative forces. Thornwell had sought to envision a paternalistic, class-stratified society as an alternative to modernity, and Girardeau had called for the maintenance of the "phraseology of the past" as a way to defend a remembered South worth living for and dying for. To be sure, there was much in the seminary's Reformed tradition that was not alien to the emerging world seen at Charleston's Second Church and Atlanta's Central. The new emphasis on efficiency, planning, and control resonated deeply with the old Reformed impulse that sought order and feared chaos. The rationalism of the tradition, especially of Girardeau's theology, had certainly encouraged a highly structured, tightly controlled, and orderly way of looking at the world. Moreover the highly interdependent economic and social order that some were calling the New South did not seem so far removed from the older emphasis on an organic society. Such similarities simply help to explain why many white Southern Presbyterians would be leaders in the creation of a New South. And among these leaders would be increasing numbers of businessmen, who would play critical roles in shaping the tone and character of Columbia as a twentieth-century seminary. They were to help provide the community's picture of "the way things really are" and help to mold the seminary's understanding of itself and of a changing world.[10]

Nevertheless the shifts taking place in the culture and in the churches were real shifts, and they were producing great challenges for the seminary. The older understanding of an organic society had been based on the conviction that every person has a God-given place in society, a place revealed most clearly by race. But the interdependence of the new social system was based not on such organic metaphors but on the demands of efficiency. While Augustine Smythe was organizing the many programs of Second Presbyterian's Sunday school, his brother Ellison Smyth was developing highly organized textile mills across the upcountry of South Carolina. His ideal of the perfect textile worker was a workman who possessed "a high toned moral life, loyalty to his friends and to his employer, honesty in fulfilling his contracts and in giving full return for value received." Here the emphasis was not on an organic social order—although racism of course continued to exert its oppressive power—but on the demands of efficiency with its calls for standardization, cooperation, and concentrated effort. Ellison Smyth's quest for order in his mill towns might serve the same purpose as Girardeau's obsession with order—social control and stability, the keeping at bay of chaos and anarchy. But the order that was sought in 1900 was rooted in efficiency and not in natural law or a vision of an organic, God-given, hierarchical structure. Increasingly in churches across the seminary's constituency, values of good management, of know-how and administrative skills, would replace the older values of theological acumen and the older ideals of an organic society. Moreover the ideological function of theology was being replaced by a market ideology. No longer was there a pressing need for a Thornwell to articulate a theology with a powerful ideological function. For Ellison Smyth and a growing host of white Southern Presbyterians, a secular market provided its own legitimation of power. And the market also provided its own utopian vision—not Thornwell's class-stratified and paternalistic commonwealth, but a society marked by unlimited growth and consumption.[11]

In such a context, new questions and new expectations were beginning to emerge for Columbia and for Protestant theological education in general throughout the United States. What kind of minister was needed in a church that had exchanged its lecture hall for a Sunday school building? What kind of theological education was required of ministers when pastoral counseling replaced church discipline—especially a pastoral counseling that was beginning its fervent embrace of twentieth-century psychology in its various and often competing schools? How was the seminary to prepare a student for ministry when the vitality of a congregation was increasingly measured by the number of its committees and programs and by the efficiency with which they were administered? These challenging questions were intensified for Columbia by its weakness as it entered the twentieth century and by its location in a city where the traditions of the past loomed large.[12]

Girardeau had resigned in the spring of 1895. The next fall five professors and one tutor were responsible for the theological education of twenty-seven students. James D. Tadlock, professor of ecclesiastical history and church polity, was the senior member of the faculty and consequently was serving as faculty chairman. William McPheeters was professor of Old Testament literature and exegesis, and Daniel Brimm was professor of New Testament literature and exegesis. Samuel Spahr Laws was serving in Woodrow's old chair, which had become essentially a position in apologetics. The sixty-one-year-old Law had joined the faculty in 1893 shortly after having retired as president of the University of Missouri. William T. Hall had been elected in the spring of 1895 to follow Girardeau as professor of didactic and polemical theology. Hall had graduated from Columbia in

1858, and for thirty-seven years he had served churches in South Carolina, Mississippi, and Virginia. A colleague later described him as a "considerate, unselfish, high-toned Christian gentleman." He certainly did not posses Girardeau's didactic and polemical disposition, but neither did he posses Girardeau's intellectual rigor. In his teaching he was said to give to his students "the best service of which he was capable."[13]

When classes began in the fall of 1905, only McPheeters and Hall remained from the faculty of 1895. They had as faculty colleagues Richard Clark Reed and Henry Alexander White. Both Reed and White were graduates of Union Seminary in Virginia, and both stood firmly in the conservative traditions of the church. Reed, a Tennessean, had been a pastor of churches for twenty-one years when he joined the faculty in 1898 as professor of ecclesiastical history and church polity. White, a Virginian, had been a professor of history at Washington and Lee for twelve years when he became professor of New Testament literature and exegesis at Columbia in 1902. The position in pastoral theology, sacred rhetoric (homiletics), and English Bible was vacant, a great concern to the board as the importance of the position was being increasingly emphasized.[14]

The Perkins Professorship was also vacant and was never to be filled again. To be sure, the board continued for some years to be concerned about the seminary's legal and moral responsibility to follow Judge Perkins's instructions on how to utilize his gift as the Perkins Endowment was maintained as a distinct and separate endowment within the seminary's larger endowment. With no one in the chair, the accumulating funds were growing steadily so that by 1910 the Perkins Endowment had overcome its losses during the Civil War and had grown to its original size. But the purpose of the endowment—a serious engagement with modern science—seemed not only too controversial but also beyond the capacity of Columbia seminary. Moreover the older understanding of the minister as a public intellectual, deeply informed by Western traditions and intellectual life, was being transformed by an understanding of the minister as an administrator and pastoral therapist. These new areas were where progressive voices were beginning to say the seminary needed to concentrate new energies. So the Perkins Endowment continued to grow year by year until memories began to fade, older legal and moral concerns began to be replaced by pressing new challenges, and the Perkins fund became simply a part of the general endowment to meet the routine expenses of the seminary. In this way the bold vision of Judge Perkins, which had been killed by Girardeau and his supporters, was finally given a quiet burial in the financial records of the seminary.[15]

Only sixteen students were enrolled in the fall 1905—two seniors, two middlers, seven juniors, and five special students. The students and professors thus made up a little community of twenty. The students lived in Law Hall, where they kept coal fires going in their rooms during the winter months. Electric lights, the only ones in the dormitory, illuminated the bathrooms. Several more years would past before student rooms had such a luxury. Students ate their meals in a mess hall that had been built on the campus in 1902. A matron, Mrs. Maggie Sanderson Ferguson, was a widow who supervised a black cook. The cook, like many African Americans, lived and worked among whites but seemed to whites so marginal that she remained unnamed in records. Mrs. Ferguson was advised by a student committee that managed kitchen finances and no doubt made many suggestions about menus. A telephone—the first on the campus—had been installed in the mess hall in 1903 to help her order groceries. For her work during the nine-month school year, Mrs. Ferguson received her meals, a two-room suit in Simons Hall, fuel, and an annual salary of $200.[16]

The students, who paid no tuition or room fees, paid fifteen dollars a month for their board. To help with this expense and the cost of books and the coal that they purchased and carried to their rooms, most students received financial aid up to $100 a year. A black janitor was responsible for the general upkeep of the grounds, for the sweeping of the dormitory halls, and the emptying of slop vessels. The matron was his immediate supervisor. For his work he was paid $200 for twelve months. If a student had the resources, he could employ the janitor to serve as "a caretaker" of the student's room. Of the many janitors, slave or free, who served the seminary during its first hundred years of history, only one had his name appear in the seminary's financial records—"D. Gilmore."[17]

Professors McPheeters, Hall, and Reed lived in homes owned by the seminary. Located a short distance from the campus, they were large and handsome houses on Richland, a beautiful street and fashionable address. Henry White lived in a nearby rented house for which the seminary paid $450 a year. All four professors received the same salary of $2,000 a year, which remained comparable to the salary of a University of South Carolina professor.[18]

As in the past, professors' homes were important gathering places for students. Like Sarah Howe, Mary Jones, and other faculty wives who had gone before them, the faculty wives in the early twentieth century made their homes welcoming places for students. Mary Cantey Venable Reed was particularly hospitable and popular. A member of a distinguished Virginia family, she and Clark Reed had married the year he graduated from Union Seminary, then in Farmville, Virginia. Into her gracious Columbia home seminary students came for afternoon tea or a Sunday dinner. Such occasions made her parlor and dining room not only places of warm southern hospitality but also informal classrooms where Christian piety could be nurtured, church life discussed, and ministerial manners practiced. Fannie Laury, the family's African American cook, prepared and served meals as well as any cake served with tea. She lived in the backyard in a small house that had once been the home of slaves. Its proximity to the Reed house made her available day and night when called by members of the Reed family. Such houses were still common behind the handsome homes that surrounded the seminary, and they provided a visible link to former days. In this way Fannie Laury stood in a line of blacks who had served in the homes of white faculty at Columbia—Caroline in the Howe home; Jack and Marcia, Phoebe and Patience in the Charles Colcock Jones home; Tom and Maum Maria in the Palmer home; and all the other black women and men who in their coming and going had listened to the prayers and conversations of white Presbyterians who sat together around dining-room tables. Such occasions functioned as a ritual for whites—a sacred prescribed behavior—that embodied Girardeau's "phraseology of the past." For the white students, this ritual was an informal lesson taught in faculty homes—whites had one place and blacks another; whites were to sit and be served, and blacks like Fannie Laury were to stand and serve. For whites at the seminary it all seemed natural, unremarkable, the way the world was ordered, a part of a coherent moral universe. The lesson, of course, was a lesson the students and their professors and their families had been learning all their lives. The lesson was lodged in their deepest memories and had helped create within them certain assumptions, dispositions, and ways of seeing the world. As such the ritual of the dining-room table was part of a larger lesson about race, manners, and the character of southern society. It was a lesson that would be extraordinarily difficult for white Southern Presbyterians to unlearn.[19]

The formal lessons taught in seminary classrooms sought to continue the traditions of those who were remembered as "Southern Presbyterian Worthies." McPheeters introduced first-year students to Old Testament literature and exegesis by plunging them into Hebrew so that they might be able to interpret the Old Testament "in the original." He introduced second- and third-year students to the formation of the canon, to the relationship between Old Testament texts and archaeology, and to the study of prophecy and Old Testament theology. But he warned students of the dangers of a theological liberalism that sought to interpret Christianity through the application of scientific methods and what liberals called the "sure results of modern knowledge." Such liberalism allowed no dependence on an external authority like the Bible but insisted that all claims to the truth must rest on reason and experience. Of special concern to McPheeters was the German higher-critical approach to biblical scholarship and the ways American liberals—especially at the University of Chicago—were beginning to emphasize the need to utilize the modern idea of development. They were exploring the evolving social and cultural environments of the Bible to understand the ways biblical religion took shape. So McPheeters warned that liberalism "*in the name and interests of religion* subjects the written word to treatment not one whit less ignominious and degrading than that to which Pilate's minions subjected the incarnate Word." McPheeters's pedagogy consequently functioned as a protective barrier against liberal intrusions into the world of white Southern Presbyterians. He did little to encourage wide reading by his students. For his senior course in biblical theology, for example, he utilized a forty-one-page typed syllabus. Students wrote on the syllabus notes from his lectures so that he carefully controlled what they knew of Albrecht Ritschl or Walter Rauschenbusch or William Rainey Harper or other modern biblical scholars. McPheeters's classroom was a long way from the rigors of Howe's or from the Socratic methods of Thornwell.[20]

McPheeters understood himself to be a defender of scriptures—one who upheld the "integrity, authenticity, genuineness, supernatural origin and divine authority of the Bible." He certainly stood in the tradition of Girardeau—he was quick to identify any potential breach in the walls that surrounded a received white Southern Presbyterian orthodoxy. As a consequence many came to see him as a kind of theological brawler, always ready to take on a fight in defense of a settled truth. Because he taught at Columbia for forty-five years (1888–1933) and because of his frequent combat in the newspapers and courts of the church, he played a key role in shaping an image of Columbia as the most conservative and contentious of the church's four southern seminaries.[21]

Students had three years of theology with William Hall. In their first year, they had a one-hour class that focused on "the philosophy of the feelings, the will, and the conscience." While Hall was undoubtedly continuing to focus on the preoccupations of the old Scottish philosophy, a deep concern for these subjects was also obviously in the air as questions about human nature and the nature of religious experience swirled around the landscape of American intellectual life in the early stirrings of a therapeutic culture—William James's *The Varieties of Religious Experience: A Study in Human Nature* comes immediately to mind. A second hour was given to an introduction to theology, in which they used for their text the first volume of Charles Hodge's *Systematic Theology.* In their second year, students took up "Natural Theology" which included everything from "the Being of God" to "the Nature of Sin, the Pollution and Guilt of Sin, and the Degree of Guilt." Third-year students moved to "the Theology of Redemption." During both the second and the third year, the texts were the first volume of Thornwell's *Collected Writings* and Hodge's three-volume *Systematic Theology.*[22]

Thornwell and Hodge were demanding enough theological texts, but students in 1905 must have been grateful that they did not have to read Francis Turretin's *Institutio Theologiae* and work through his long and complex Latin sentences as had many of their predecessors. Indeed Latin was no longer required for admission to Columbia, and presbytery exams no longer required a theological essay in Latin. This shift reflected a great change taking place in higher education in the United States. University and colleges had largely dropped Latin as a requirement for admission by the beginning of the new century. A liberal education that sought to educate students in the great intellectual traditions of the West—traditions that probed fundamental questions and introduced students to systems of thought—seemed inadequate to meet the growing complexities of modern society. What modernity seemed to require was an education that prepared a student to be a specialist in some vocational field—how to be good banker or how to be a progressive farmer or how to be a skilled engineer. The same impulse was at work at Columbia and other theological seminaries as "how to" questions became increasingly important.[23]

There remained in 1905, however, the expectation that entering students could read some of the prose literature of the Greek language and that they had some knowledge of the forms of inflection and other rules of syntax. Those who came to Columbia without having studied Greek entered as special students who took an English Bible track. They received certificates and not diplomas at the conclusion of their studies. For students who had studied Greek, their first year focused on the four Gospels, the second year on Acts and several epistles, and the third year on Romans, Hebrews, and Revelation. The Greek New Testament was the primary text, supplemented by various commentaries. Exegesis papers were prepared by each student and read by the whole class.[24]

Henry White as professor of New Testament was systematic and thorough, and he sought to lead his students faithfully through their studies of the New Testament. But his continuing passion was history—the subject he had taught at Washington and Lee. He was particularly fascinated by the history of the American South. While still in Virginia his *Robert E. Lee and the Southern Confederacy* had been published by Putnam's in its Heroes of the Nation Series. And three years after his arrival at Columbia his almost-four-hundred-page *Stonewall Jackson* was published in Philadelphia in the American Crisis Series. And there were others: *John C. Calhoun* in the Library of Southern Literature; *The*

Making of South Carolina, a three-hundred-page "simple history" of his adopted state; and *A School History of the United States* published in Boston. And there were numerous essays as well: "Three American Ideals: The Puritan, the Cavalier, and the Scotch-Irish," "Finances in South Carolina," and addresses before the Scotch-Irish Society of America. He wrote occasionally on the Bible, including an essay "Harmony of the Gospels" and a three-hundred-page book *The Origin of the Pentateuch in the Light of the Ancient Monuments,* written while he was still at Washington and Lee. His *Southern Presbyterian Leaders,* published in 1911, took him most directly into church history. The four-hundred-page book began with colonial America—with a decided Virginia slant—and gave after a general introduction brief sketches of various leaders. Howe, Leland, and Smyth were there as was Palmer, Plumer, Girardeau, and Leighton Wilson. Thornwell was the only leader to be given two chapters, but James Woodrow was only mentioned in passing. All these books, even those of substantial length, were popular in character. While they exhibited little original research, they showed White to be a disciplined writer trying to reach a broad audience with subjects close to his heart.

In his books on Calhoun and Lee and Jackson and in his textbooks on American history he showed himself to be a son of a remembered white South. He dedicated most of his books to his wife, Fanny Wellford, the daughter of a Virginia judge, and he reflected in much of his writings the deep assumptions that informed the ritual of her hospitable dining-room table. Of slavery White said, "the negro was registered as a member of a patriarchal household; day by day the habits of African savagery were purged from his life by the power of law, represented in the will of his master. . . . Cruelty was the exception. . . . A bond of affection was woven between Southern masters and servants which proved strong enough in 1861–'65 to keep the negroes at voluntary labour to furnish food for the armies that contended against military emancipation." This was the way white southerners interpreted their history and remembered slavery. White was utilizing Girardeau's "phraseology of the past" to tell the story of the South, white and black. Perhaps the only exceptional character to White's picture of slavery was that it flowed from the heart and imagination of one who was widely regarded as having a particularly kind and generous spirit. Many thought of him as a quiet and dignified man, courteous in manner, the embodiment of an ideal southern gentleman after the manner of his hero, Robert E. Lee.[25]

While Columbia's New Testament professor was writing histories of the South, the seminary's church history professor was introducing first-year students to the history of the Old Testament. Clark Reed, like his predecessors, believed that the church's history started with the "Sacred History" of the Bible and, guided by divine providence, advanced age by age as it moved toward its future culmination—a new heaven and new earth. This meant that the history of the church, like the history of creation, had a goal toward which it was moving. So the present moment in the church's life was not only shaped by the events of the past but also pulled forward toward God's good purpose for humanity and for all creation. "The golden age of the church is not behind us," Reed told his students, but in the future. Such an understanding of history, of course, put it in tension with Darwin's insistence that evolution had no goal drawing it forward but was rather the result of chance and various contingencies. Reed's interpretation of church history put it in the camp with other interpretations that saw history as having a goal, a τέλος, a fulfillment. Liberals and progressives saw history moving toward a more democratic and egalitarian future. Marxists saw history moving toward a classless, worldwide communist society. Yet Reed as a prudent white Southern Presbyterian carefully distinguished himself from visionaries and activists "who were impatient of God's slow methods." No doubt thinking of abolitionists and those who followed them—who it was said wanted to run ahead of God's providence—Reed insisted that the way forward was by following "the simple devises of Gospel." "Preaching and praying and holy living," declared the history professor, "are the regenerating forces still as in apostolic times."[26]

Reed, however, in writing *Religious History of the Southern Negroes,* did not hesitate to call on evolutionary language to argue for what he regarded as the degraded condition of Africans. He linked modern scientific racism with ancient white prejudices to make his point:

> It is well to bear in mind that American slavery dealt with one of the lowest orders of the human family. The law of evolution, which is credited by some of our modem scientists with an energy that is well-nigh, if not altogether, equal to achieving the miracle of creation, seems to have given up its task in despair in the case of the African negro.
>
> What he was when he first emerged into the light of history that he is to-day, the same low savage, living usually in a state of nudity, and under the power of crude and debasing superstitions. He has never evolved any national organization, nor any system of laws, nor any settled family life. He has never evolved a schoolhouse, nor a text-book, nor even an alphabet out of which a book might be made. This is not saying that he is incapable of development. It has been demonstrated *ex abundante* that he is capable of indefinite development. But he seems incapable of self development. He does not embody in himself any law of evolution. Stimulus and guidance must come from without.[27]

So in a bitter irony Reed adopted the language of evolution and development that had caused Woodrow to be dismissed, and he ignored John Leighton Wilson's *History of Western Africa,* in which Wilson described in detail the great civilizations of the region. And how surprised Reed would have been of Wilson's discovery that the Vey of Sierra Leone had developed their own alphabet! Wilson had called the Vey alphabet "undoubtedly one of the most remarkable achievements of this or any other age, and is itself enough to silence forever the cavils and sneers of those who think so contemptuously of the intellectual endowments of the African race." But such history did not fit the narrative Reed—and almost all whites—used to speak of the intellectual life of African Americans. Perhaps to add to the irony, Reed made an unusual provision in his will—a stipend of $240 a year for Fannie Laury, the cook who had prepared and served so many meals for the Reed family and visiting students.[28]

Reed had first-year students focus on biblical geography, the history of the Old Testament from Adam to Christ, and recent archaeological discoveries in the land "in which the ancient people of God dwelt." Second-year students met with him three hours a week as he marched them century by century from the apostolic age through the sixteenth-century Reformation. Along the way they learned how the "simple organization of the primitive church was transformed into the elaborate hierarchy of the papacy." And they probed the history of doctrines, especially the controversies out of which creeds and theological systems emerged. Third-year students spent half a year on the history of the church since the Reformation, which meant, strangely enough given faculty interests, that almost no attention was given to the history of the church in the United States.[29]

During the second half of the senior year, Reed led students in a study of Christian missions. They focused on the contemporary Protestant missions, "the present condition of the heathen world, and the urgent need for a more fervent missionary spirit." A course on missions was a relatively new thing at Columbia, although there had long been an interest in missions at the seminary. After the Civil War the General Assembly's Executive Committee on Foreign and Domestic Missions had met on the Columbia campus with Leighton Wilson as its secretary and Woodrow as its treasurer. Students had formed, almost at the founding of the seminary, the Society for Missionary Inquiry, and after the Civil War increasing numbers of them had become foreign missionaries. The most famous of these was Hampden DuBose, who had graduated from Columbia in 1871 and had gone, with his wife, Pauline, to China in 1872. He had been one of the founders and was the first president of the Anti-opium League. Under his leadership the league attacked and helped abolish the opium trade to China that had long been promoted by Western powers.[30]

What made the mission movement an important new element in the Columbia curriculum was the sense that a new Christian century was dawning, that Protestantism was spreading around the world as never before, and that its spread pointed toward the fulfillment of God's purposes for human history. A Laymen's Missionary Movement, growing out of a series of meetings at New York's Fifth Avenue Presbyterian Church, was committed to "The Evangelization of the World in this Generation." Missionaries home on furlough began to be regular lecturers on the campus—Palmer DuBose returned to the campus and spoke on his experiences in Soochow, China. O. R. Avison, M.D., described "Hospital Work in Seoul," and S. W. Wilds lectured on "Present Conditions on the Congo." Missionaries came to the campus from all the Presbyterian missions and helped to open a broader world to faculty and students alike. They introduced what seemed like strange and exotic peoples and cultures and told how missionaries had to try to enter as deeply as they could into a culture if they wanted to translate the scriptures into an indigenous language. Some missionaries brought with them to the campus what they had taken to the mission field—assumptions about the superiority of Western societies and the need for people to adopt Western ways in order to be upstanding Christians. But others returned with new appreciation for the richness of ancient cultures and the deep spirituality of people they had encountered. One Columbia graduate in particular stands out. Wilson Plumer Mills was a great nephew of Leighton Wilson and had been named for him and Columbia's William Swan Plumer. Mills had spent three years at Oxford as a Rhodes Scholar before entering Columbia as a student in 1909. After his graduation he went to Nanjing as a missionary, where he developed a deep appreciation for Chinese history and cultural traditions. During the Japanese invasion and "Rape of Nanjing," he performed heroically as the chairman of the International Committee for the Nanjing Safety Zone. Mills was one of twenty-four Columbia graduates during the first three decades of the century who went as a missionary to China or Japan or Korea, to Brazil or Mexico, to the Congo or Cameroun.[31]

Mission fields, however, were not only in distant places. They were also close to home and to the seminary. Second- and third-year students went out on Sundays to preaching stations in the Sand Hills around Columbia. There poor white farm families, living among loblollies and scrub oaks, tried to eke out a living from dry, sandy soil. They composed what the seminary catalog called "districts of destitute and ignorant whites." Guest lecturers tried to help prepare students for this and similar mission fields in the South. Hugh Murchison returned to the campus to lecture on "The Illiterate White People of the South," and William Mills spoke on "The Country Church." He had begun his ministry in cotton mill villages and was serving as professor of rural sociology at Clemson College. Lay leaders also lectured on conditions in the South. The Honorable E. J. Watson lectured on "Agriculture in Connection with the Work of the Church," and Albert Sidney Johnstone, secretary of the South Carolina Board of Charities and Corrections, told of "Penal and Charity Problems in South Carolina." Johnstone was vice president of the Southern Sociological Congress, a progressive movement that was committed to "a vigorous campaign in the South against poverty, illiteracy, crime, and disease" and to "a battle . . . for just relations between the white and colored people of the country, the rights of childhood and motherhood, and the cooperation of religious and civic agencies in bringing about social justice." His lecture must have sounded alien to the language of the Columbia campus with its aging Ainsley Hall mansion. Johnstone's language, however, echoed much of the language of Woodrow Wilson, child of the campus and nephew of James Woodrow. And it pointed toward a future in a changed location for the seminary, a new place where faculty and students were to struggle for decades to break through the walls Girardeau and his followers had erected to protect a received white Southern Presbyterian theology and a remembered white South. So while a few graduates such as DuBose and Mills worked heroically in distant places for social justice and the protection of the vulnerable, most Columbia faculty and graduates had little to do with the great campaigns that preoccupied many Protestants in the early years of the century—temperance, child labor laws, women rights, and the fight for antilynching laws. Even the "Make the World Safe for Democracy" campaign of Columbia's own Woodrow Wilson drew only a few Columbia students to the battlefields of France.[32]

The most important lectures on the campus were those established by Thomas Smyth. He left detailed instructions in his will about the character of the lectures—who was to lecture, on what subjects they were to lecture, and how the lectures were to be published. It took several decades of accumulating value for the endowment to reach a designated $10,000, and it took some delicate negotiating between the board and Smyth's influential and wealthy children before the first lecture was finally delivered in 1911. The lecturers and their subjects during the next few years reflected the interests of the board of directors and competing impulses within the seminary's life. The conservative Princetonians were popular. Francis Ladley Patton told of "The Theistic View of the Word"; Benjamin

B. Warfield described "Counterfeit Miracles"; and on a return visit Patton spent a week giving a series of lectures on "Christianity and Modern Man." But there were also lectures by the German New Testament scholar Casper Rene Gregory of the University of Leipzig titled "Theological Movements in Germany during the Nineteenth Century." And Robert E. Speer came from New York and described "Some Missionary Problems Illustrated by the Lives of Great Missionary Leaders." Speer was not only a leader of Northern Presbyterian mission work but also the most visible promoter in the country of Protestant missionary service. Gregory's and Speer's lectures helped bring wider and newer worlds to the Columbia campus even as the older, southern theological legacies lingered in classrooms and faculty homes.[33]

Students who graduated from Columbia during these early decades of the twentieth century were to spend their ministries in a variety of places. Some went to distant mission fields where they learned and spent years developing dictionaries and grammars of unwritten languages, where they labored in schools and preaching stations, where they suffered from malaria and other diseases, and where on occasion they came to the defense of indigenous people under assault by colonial powers. Some graduates went to country churches and small towns of the South where over the coming years they baptized children of farmers; preached the Gospel to grocers and housewives; and administered the Lord's Supper to teenagers and salesmen. They visited the sick in farmhouses and village homes. They prayed with the anxious, and they tried to encourage the women and men who were caring for the sick and the dying and who were struggling to provide nourishing food and to keep clean linens on sick beds. Those in city churches followed many of these same practices of ministry as they too preached the Gospel, counseled the troubled, attended the dying, buried the dead, and comforted the grieving. And more and more in the city churches, they attended meetings and made plans and oversaw budgets and programs. Some Columbia graduates, like their predecessors, became educators. Charles Malone Richards was a professor of religion at Davidson; William Mills taught sociology at Clemson; and Colin McPheeters was head of the psychology department at Westminster College, Fulton, Missouri. Davidson Douglas served with genuine distinction as president of Presbyterian College and later as a progressive president of the University of South Carolina. Others served as teachers or heads of parochial and high schools across the South. In all these various places, of course, Columbia graduates acted as men with their own gifts and limitations, their own anxieties and peculiarities, and their own varying degrees of commitment to their ministerial calling.[34]

If the older role of Presbyterian minister as public intellectual faded in the light of modernity, many Columbia graduates entered vigorously into a new role of founders of institutions. Most obviously they were busy founding churches. Robert Walker, for example, went to Oklahoma, where in six years he established four new churches. Alva Miller established new churches in Arkansas, Texas, and New Mexico. And William Harris built six churches in Alabama and Florida. Leading the denomination in this effort to found new churches was Columbia graduate Samuel L. Morris. He was elected secretary of home missions in 1901 and began a vigorous program of establishing Presbyterian congregations across the South. By the time of his retirement in 1931, membership in the denomination had essentially doubled. Under his leadership schools and colleges had been established for Native Americans in Oklahoma and for "mountain people" in Appalachia, and Stillman Institute had been significantly strengthened as an educational institution for African Americans. Columbia graduates were founders of orphanages—Thornwell in South Carolina, and Palmer in Mississippi, as the Presbyterian Home for Children in Alabama. They established such prestigious private schools as Westminster in Atlanta; colleges such as Presbyterian; and one university—Oglethorpe. This institutional founding reflected both older traditions of Presbyterian ministry and also a new image of the minister as robust and vigorous, a manly man for a "muscular Christianity."[35]

The men who entered these various ministries graduated from Columbia during a period when its faculty was small and not particularly distinguished, when its students were few, and when its resources were decidedly limited. Out of such weakness came men who sought to be faithful to their callings and good stewards of their gifts. They did much to strengthen the church not only in the South but also in distant places. So even out of such weakness as existed at Columbia there came strength. But the weakness of the seminary was real, and those who had responsibility for Columbia's life and service to the church could see that changes were necessary.

Ruins in 1865 of Charleston's Circular Congregational Church, a strong supporter of the seminary.

A view of Main Street, Columbia, South Carolina, 1865. The seminary was beyond the horizon to the right.

John Lafayette Girardeau, professor and defender of the white South and a scholastic theology.

James Woodrow, professor, scientist, and theologian.

Ruggles Wilson, center; Woodrow Wilson, far left; family of Ann Wilson Howe; two servants, Nannie and Minnie (family names unknown).

Dorm room in Columbia.

Refectory, ca. 1910.

Columbia campus, 1910.

Class of 1912. William Plumer Mills (center), a Rhodes Scholar, played an important humanitarian role during the Japanese "Rape of Nanjing."

Faculty, 1920. Seated left to right: McPheeters, Whaling, Reed. Standing left to right: White, Kerr.

Good-byes, in front of the chapel, to the old campus, 1927.

Architectural plans for the Decatur campus.

Campbell Hall under construction, 1926.

11

A President in "the Modern Sense of the Term"

During the early years of the twentieth century, the four members of the Columbia faculty found themselves busy with many things. They arranged schedules, negotiating with one another about who would teach what course when. They prepared lectures, taught their little cluster of students, and wrote their articles and books. They oversaw the buildings and grounds, worked with contractors about the construction of a new mess hall, hired matrons and janitors, and saw that they were paid promptly. They recruited students; made decisions about financial aid; disciplined students who left the city without permission; approved speakers who came to the campus; bought wood and coal for heating buildings on the campus; attended presbytery, synod and General Assembly meetings; preached regularly on the Sabbath and weekly in chapel; met privately each Thursday afternoon with students to discuss their spiritual life and hopes for ministry; oversaw the publication of the seminary's catalogs and bulletins; and spent much time trying to raise money for the seminary.[1]

In addition to these shared responsibilities, two faculty members had special administrative duties. William McPheeters, as the senior member, was chairman of the faculty. He prepared a docket for faculty meetings, presided over the meetings, wrote the faculty's report to the seminary board, and had specific responsibility for the daily operation of the seminary. Clark Reed, in addition to teaching church history and polity, was the librarian—a laborious and largely thankless job. The library was located on the top two floors of the Ainsley Hall mansion and required constant attention. It was unheated and unlighted and had no tables—an altogether uninviting place. Fine particles of dirt and grime seemed to flow from every crack and cranny in the old mansion, and books had to be dusted in a systematic manner. During the summer when Columbia sweltered with its famous heat and humidity, and mildew threatened to cover anything that was not moving, books had to be taken off long shelves and wiped down before being reshelved in proper order. And on days that were hot and dry windows had to be raised and the rooms of the library aired to remove the musty odor that seemed to cling so closely to old books. A seminary student did much of this tedious work—for $50 a year—but the responsibility for the library's maintenance was Reed's. He had to do the cataloging of the few books purchased and prepare reports for the board and plead for funds so that the library might be strengthened. But the budget for books was pathetic, only $250 a year, and if it had not been for a bequest from Thomas Smyth that provided another $500, even the few books purchased would have been further reduced. So Reed, in spite of his efforts, had to watch what had been one of the great libraries in the country continue its long slide into mediocrity.[2]

While the faculty was busy with these many things, the board was as well—especially members from Columbia and nearby towns. Of these, W. A. Clark—a Columbia lawyer and businessman—was the most influential, serving as chairman of both the executive and investment committees of the board. A man of much energy and business acumen, he was primarily responsible for the management of the endowment, and with McPheeters he kept a sharp eye on the maintenance of the seminary property. Other members of the board were actively engaged in fund raising, in examining students' work at the end of the school year, reporting on the actions of the board to synods and the General Assembly, and in general promoting the interest of the seminary.[3]

These various responsibilities of the faculty and board seemed not only increasingly burdensome but also a reflection of an earlier and simpler time. Faculty and board were concluding that the administrative structures of the seminary were old-fashioned, out of date, and badly in need of an overhaul according to the best practices of modern management. In particular both faculty and board concluded that what was most needed was a single leader, a person with the authority to make decisions and carry out policies—a seminary president.[4]

Columbia's decision to create the office of seminary president did not suddenly fall from the sky, nor was it simply a result of the seminary's internal needs and dynamics. It was rather a part of an emerging corporate world that was increasingly dominating American society and that was providing the powerful icon of the modern manager. The manager's task was "to organize the human and nonhuman resources available to the organization that employs him so as to improve its position in the marketplace." Efficiency and know-how were the primary values of the manager, and standardization was a primary means of focusing the energies of an organization in an efficient manner. Many colleges and universities had already put in place presidents who were thought of as managers after the model of corporate executives. And increasing numbers of seminaries were concluding that it was high time for them to have such leaders.[5]

John Knox McLean, president of the Pacific School of Religion, led the way in the creation of a modern seminary presidency. Speaking before the Conference of Congregational Seminaries meeting in St. Louis in 1900, he asked: "Should the theological seminary have a permanent president; and if so, what should be the powers and duties of the office?" He noted that in most seminaries the faculty still tried to manage the affairs of the institution. McLean insisted such a structure was clumsy and inefficient. A few seminaries had presidents, but they were little more than a faculty member like McPheeters who, as chairman of the faculty, was trying to do administrative work on the side. What was needed, McLean insisted, was a president "in the modern sense of the term." That meant he would not be a teacher but an executive—"His work," said McLean, "is to do things, not to tell about them."[6]

At its annual meeting in May 1905, the Columbia board decided that it should seek a president for Columbia. Although the faculty enthusiastically endorsed the creation of such an office, it was not an easy thing for Columbia to make such a move. A president as an executive, as a modern manager, seemed a major breach in Girardeau's ideological wall intended, as it was, to protect Columbia and white Southern Presbyterians from the corrupting forces of modernity. The office had a little too much of the Yankee and the New South in it. And it also smelled a little too much of episcopacy, of a consolidation of power in one person, and an abandonment of a Presbyterian emphasis on the parity of church officers. But the modern way beckoned and promised great rewards that could lead Columbia out of its weakness to a new strength and new vitality. In 1904 Union Seminary in Virginia had elected Walter Moore as its first president, and he was already demonstrating what could be accomplished with a strong and vigorous leader. Consequently, as so often in the past, Columbia chose a middle way. The new president would be a professor, a kind of first among equals, but he would have extensive executive authority. The board voted that it "shall elect one member of the Faculty as President of the Seminary, who, in addition to his duties as Professor shall also exercise a supervisory jurisdiction over the management of the Seminary, and shall be especially charged with the duty of presenting the claims and interest of the Seminary to the churches of the controlling Synods." The problem was not only finding someone who had the necessary gifts for such a dual position but also finding someone who was also willing to accept the position. It would take five years before such a person could be found.[7]

At its annual meeting in May 1911, the board elected Thornton Whaling as professor of didactic and polemical theology (Hall had died during the previous winter) and president of the seminary, and the synods enthusiastically approved his election. A Virginian and graduate of Davidson College, Whaling had spent two years at Union Theological Seminary in New York before returning to the South and graduating from Columbia in 1883. He had been a student at Columbia during the midst of the Woodrow controversy and had been a strong supporter of Woodrow. As a young pastor, he had led the opposition to Girardeau's attempt, through Charleston Presbytery, to tightly control public debate about issues before the church. But Whaling was also a confirmed Calvinist, and while he had a more open and generous spirit than Girardeau, he admired Girardeau's careful theological work.[8]

As Whaling began his presidency, he wrote to the constituency of the seminary that "it is essential to preserve uncorrupted and to extend more widely the influence of that type of Calvinistic theology of which Columbia is the representative." He pointed to Thornwell and Girardeau as great exemplars of a theology that was both "scriptural and rational"—a theology that stood between a modern rationalism on the one hand that had little use for the Bible—and, on the other hand the kind of popular religious enthusiasm that had no need for careful theological thought. Whaling was, however, not afraid of the future and of new developments in theological education. There is a need, he said, of adjusting the seminary "more perfectly to the life of the church today." He insisted the church in the twentieth century needed the seminary to expand its curriculum to include more practical areas—areas that were conversant with the new social sciences. So he called for more courses in English Bible as a new hub in the curriculum to provide a solid foundation for a pastor's work as preacher and teacher. And he called for the seminary to be a "hot bed" for missions and evangelism with courses that were "scientific, practical, and inspiring." Pastors also needed to know how to organize Sunday schools that were up-to-date and how to manage the growing complexity of church life. He announced that there would be new courses on "Child Study" and on new pedagogical methods and organizational structures for Sunday schools. And he insisted that room needed to be found in the curriculum for students to learn about church finances and management and how to organize youth work. It was obviously an ambitious vision for the school of Thornwell and Girardeau! One could hardly imagine McPheeters, with his forty-six-page syllabus and well-used lectures, teaching modern pedagogical methods or Henry White turning from his study of Stonewall Jackson or John C. Calhoun to teach about missions in a way that way that was scientific, practical, and inspiring. New professors were going to be needed, and that need helped to shape the work of the new president.[9]

First, however, Whaling knew he had to find more students. Columbia had only twenty-two students the year Whaling became president. What was most distressing was the loss of students from Columbia's controlling synods to other seminaries. Columbia was their seminary according to traditional loyalties and commitments of the synods. Columbia had been established and had been funded to provide pastors for the Southeast. But with Columbia's weakness and the lingering memory of the Woodrow conflict, many students from these synods were going to Union Seminary in Virginia and to the seminary in Louisville. To address this challenge, Whaling began immediately to visit colleges and universities in the controlling synods. He went to state universities and to Presbyterian colleges—especially Davidson and Presbyterian—and to schools of other denominations where there were Presbyterians students planning on entering the ministry. He talked with them about their call to ministry, about the great challenges before the church, and about the advantages of studying at "their seminary." He spoke with them of his own experiences as a pastor in South Carolina and Alabama, Texas and Virginia. He had served small village churches and large city churches, and he knew something about the deep privileges of a pastor being invited into people's lives. He was a fine preacher and respected theologian, and he had a love for his alma mater and believed Columbia had a critical role to play in the life of the church. As a consequence he was well received by students, and Columbia's student body began to grow, jumping in five years from twenty-two to sixty.[10]

The growth of the student body was not, of course, simply the result of Whaling's efforts and charisma. He could draw on the extensive network of families that supported Columbia and sent their sons and grandsons, nephews and cousins to Columbia. White Southern Presbyterian families had grown increasingly interconnected during the decades that followed the Civil War. By the time of Whaling's presidency, the connections had become amazingly dense even as the white Southern Presbyterian Church was adding large numbers of new members. Whaling was himself the brother-in-law of Charles

Hemphill, who was president of Louisville Presbyterian Seminary and son of the longtime chairman of the Columbia board, Congressman James Hemphill. Darby Fulton, who graduated in the first class recruited by Whaling, was soon to marry a great niece of John Adger's. Fulton's mother was the daughter of Thomas Peck, student of Thornwell's and longtime professor of theology at Union in Virginia. Fulton's cousin and classmate John Richards Hay had two grandfathers, three uncles, and two brothers who were Columbia graduates. And he had a host of cousins who were or would be graduates from Columbia, including Samuel Burney Hay, T. B. Hay, and J. McDowell Richards. And so it went with other families. Thomas Smyth's daughter, Jane Ann Adger Smyth, married a Columbia graduate, William Flinn, and their daughter married George Howe's grandson, George Howe III. Howe III's other grandfather was Columbia professor Joseph R. Wilson, and his uncle was Woodrow Wilson. It could all be terribly confusing unless you had grown up hearing stories about grandmother this and grandfather that and had spent summer vacations with cousins and knew that Aunt Jane's peculiarities were inherited from her father's side of the family.[11]

Encouraging these family entanglements was the development of the Montreat Conference Center in the mountains of western North Carolina. Established in 1905 under the leadership of Columbia graduate James R. Howerton, Montreat drew families from across the South to its summer cottages and its conferences on Bible, missions, and music. Hugely popular with children and youth, who could roam free by its streams and on mountain trails, it became a kind of summer breeding ground for white Southern Presbyterians. Many Columbia students throughout the coming century would hear their call to ministry during a Montreat conference or while viewing a sunrise on Montreat's Lookout Mountain.[12]

Beneath the appeal of Whaling's charisma and beyond deep family connections with Columbia was a religious stirring that was calling bright young men into the ministry. Drawing on the traditional piety of the church and inspired by a vision of an expanding Kingdom of God, they came to Columbia to be prepared for a life of service to the church. To a remarkable extent, they were ready to live in modest circumstances in order to serve needy places and to build new congregations across the South and in distant places of the earth. And they came to Columbia—like those who had come before them—with a conviction that Presbyterians had a distinctive contribution to make to the church catholic. They were to take to the world a spirituality rooted in a confession of God's sovereignty, and they were to provide a theological and cultural sophistication to what they were convinced was a waiting world.[13]

Whaling had to work hard to raise sufficient funds for the growing student body and for new faculty needed to meet the demands of an expanding curriculum. He consequently spent much time traveling throughout the supporting synods talking with pastors and church leaders and preaching regularly wherever he went. He told of the great need for pastors, pointed to the number of new churches being organized, and appealed for support of their seminary. He had much success and was happy to report the steady growth of the endowment, but he and the board knew the funds he was raising were not enough. All across the synods more people began to support the seminary faithfully, but the amount they could contribute was generally small, a reflection of the poverty of the region. There were no large gifts as there had been during the antebellum period—no William Seabrook or Andrew Maybank or Judge Perkins—so the endowment grew steadily under Whaling's leadership but its growth was modest.[14]

The board invested the endowment funds with great care and much Presbyterian prudence. While the board continued to keep funds in railroad stock and to invest in some of the new textile mills in South Carolina and Georgia, committee members were reluctant to put the seminary's money in anything they regarded as risky. So they bought government bonds—especially those issued by cities—and they returned more and more to the old practice of making loans to individuals. During the antebellum period, the security for such personal loans had often been slaves and plantations. Now during the early decades of the twentieth century, loans were secured largely by mortgages on homes, primarily in and around the city of Columbia. Prominent Columbians turned to the seminary for loans as if it were a bank—doctors and lawyers, merchants and university professors, and even the former governor Wade Hampton III borrowed money from the seminary. But such loans also had their risks, especially on those occasions when it was necessary to foreclose on a mortgage. Particular embarrassment came when a friend of the seminary was unable to make mortgage payments. Still despite such occasional embarrassments, the income from such investments was steady, and with the new funds Whaling raised, the seminary's income was double in 1916 what it had been fifteen years earlier.[15]

With more resources available, Whaling began to enlarge the faculty. Indeed enlarging the faculty and expanding the curriculum were critical for his efforts to attract more students and raise the endowment. Raising funds, enlarging the faculty, attracting students—each needed to reinforce the others. They were all part of one effort to create an image of Columbia as a seminary that was returning to its former strength and vitality and to make of Columbia a seminary for the twentieth century.

Whaling quickly secured Robert Gamaliel Pearson for a new chair in English Bible—a major coup for Columbia. Pearson, who had grown up as a Mississippi farm boy, was one of the most popular preachers of his day. After serving several pastorates, he had become an evangelist, holding great meetings in the Midwest and in Texas. He had been a preacher with Dwight L. Moody at the Chicago World's Fair in 1893, and had preached before huge audiences drawn from the crowds that surged through the fairgrounds. More impressive for white Southern Presbyterians, he had been the primary lecturer at the Montreat Bible Conferences in 1910, 1911, and 1912 and had shown himself to be a serious and masterly teacher of the English Bible. So his call to Columbia did seem a coup for the seminary, and his presence on the faculty promised to attract many students and much needed financial support. But Pearson died unexpectantly after only two years on the faculty, and the hopes raised by his coming to Columbia were disappointed.[16]

Whaling acted promptly to fill Pearson's place. He recommended to the board that James Overton Reavis, pastor of Columbia's First Presbyterian Church, be elected professor of Bible, homiletics, and pastoral theology. The board and the synods thought him a splendid choice and quickly confirmed his election. Reavis had grown up on a family farm in Missouri; had graduated from Westminster College; and had earned theological degrees from Louisville and Princeton, an M.A. from New York University, and in 1913 a law degree from the University of South Carolina. He was—not incidentally—married to Thornwell's niece. Of particular importance for his role on the Columbia faculty was his six-year service as the church's candidate secretary for foreign missions. During those six years, the number of missionaries sent out by the southern church had grown from 113 to 297, and the income for missions had essentially doubled. Reavis was consequently able to teach missions—as a branch of pastoral theology—in a way that met Whaling's insistence that mission courses be scientific, practical, and inspiring. He had his students studying ethnology, geography, and philology. He introduced world religions to students from South Carolina, Georgia, and Alabama who had known only a few Catholics and an occasional Jew. He lectured on the various kinds and methods of mission work, and he analyzed the qualifications needed to become a successful missionary—especially an ability to master another language and to use language study to enter deeply into another culture.[17]

In the fall of 1915, Edgar D. Kerr joined the faculty as instructor in Christian ethics and apologetics. He had graduated from Columbia in 1907, had spent a year in graduate study at Princeton Seminary, and later studied at the University of Chicago. He was a man of great good humor and was a favorite of students for several generations. But ethics and apologetics were not his field, and he was soon made instructor and then professor of Hebrew and cognate languages. His wife, Helen O'Neal White, had died the year before he began teaching at Columbia so he had joined the faculty as a widower. But seven years later, he married Lucile Wilson. She was, like Helen White, deeply rooted in South Carolina Presbyterianism and was a person who made her presence known not only by hosting students but also by making clear her opinions. A faculty member later described her as "a charming lady but also a strong character whose supervision Dr. Kerr managed to escape in various ways." She drew students to her and was later known as a great encourager of student wives. Together the Kerrs added a lively and endearing character to a campus life that was often preoccupied with its own little world and its own rules of etiquette and practices of pieties.[18]

Whaling had promised at the beginning of his presidency that he would introduce more practical courses of study, so he brought from the University of South Carolina the dean of education, Patterson Wardlaw, as a special lecturer. Wardlaw was, wrote the historian of the university, one of the greatest teachers South Carolina had ever known. His lectures complemented Reavis's course "The Pedagogy of the Sunday School," in which seminarians focused on "the curriculum, the principles of method as applied to the Sunday School, the organization, management, government, program, external relations and general means of success of the Sunday School." And there were other practical courses as well—William Mills came from Clemson to be an instructor in rural sociology, and George Fulbright taught elocution, what he called the "art of proper and effective oral expression." It was all a long way from George Howe's insistence that theological education be grounded in the classics and Thornwell's assertion that the purpose of education was to cultivate the mind without reference to any utilitarian pursuits. But Columbia's new faculty and new courses, Whaling and his supporters believed, were precisely what was needed to prepare men to be pastors in a twentieth-century church. Know-how seemed more important than know-why in the modern world of the manager. The old vision of a learned clergy was giving way to a new model of ministry—the minister as a professional, a credentialed and competent man who possessed the habits and skills necessary to do the work of ministry.[19] Despite the many advances being made under Whaling's presidency, there were troubling questions about the Columbia's future. Most pressing were questions about the adequacy of the campus and the financial foundations of the seminary. The four acres of the campus seemed increasingly cramped, and the buildings seemed inadequate for a vision of a seminary that had more students, an enlarged faculty, and a modern curriculum. The old mansion was still handsome, but it evoked an image of the Old South not the New. Simons and Law dormitories were fine sturdy buildings, but they were badly in need of being updated with modern plumbing, modern lights, and new furniture. And with the growing student body, the dormitories were becoming increasingly crowded, and there was no room for any student who arrived with a wife. Most embarrassing of all was the chapel. It had originally been a carriage house, and despite efforts over the years to make it more attractive, it still bore the shape and character of its lowly origin. Yet the chapel was a central part of seminary life. Morning and afternoon services were held there, and students began their first awkward attempts at preaching in its plain and rather dark interior. In 1913 the chapel had taken on the air of a shrine—at least as much of such air as Presbyterians could tolerate—for the new president of the United States, Woodrow Wilson, had at age seventeen experienced in the chapel a "work of grace in his heart." When he came to Columbia in 1916 for the funeral of his sister—the widow of George Howe II—he had visited the chapel and had declared: "I feel I ought to take off my shoes. This is holy ground." But however holy the ground and however many the memories that swirled around it, the chapel's small size and its plain features seemed to many to be clearly inadequate for the needs of a strong and robust theological seminary.[20]

The year before Wilson's visit to Columbia, Whaling had written the president and had asked for his approval that a proposed new library be named for Wilson's father, Joseph Ruggles Wilson. And Whaling had added that a new chapel was to be named for the president's uncle James Woodrow. Wilson wrote back and declared that "a memorial to my father gratifies me very much indeed. I know that it would be deeply pleasing to him. Some of the best work of his life was done at Columbia seminary and I know the deep interest he took in its remarkable library." Yet even with the endorsement of the popular president of the United States and Whaling's incessant travel and pleading for contributions, the effort had been unsuccessful. The chapel remained in the old carriage house, and the library remained in the old mansion.[21]

Board members and friends of the seminary had been discussing Columbia's campus and future for more than a decade when Whaling's campaign for a new chapel and library failed. At the beginning of the century, when the seminary's finances were particularly bad and the students few, there had been talk of uniting Columbia with Southwestern Presbyterian University, located in Clarksville, Tennessee (now Rhodes College in Memphis) in order to build a Southern Presbyterian university in Atlanta. While the synods appointed a committee to review the proposal, there was substantial opposition, and the committee was eventually dismissed. But intriguing possibilities had been raised, and they would be remembered in years to come.[22]

In 1905 the board had received an offer for fifteen beautiful acres in a new suburb being developed on the eastern side of the city. It was proposed that the seminary sell its property—which was considered valuable—and build a new campus. But the board decided after much discussion that it could not accept the offer. There were no guarantees that the campus could be sold, and a location in the city seemed more desirable than one in a new suburb. But like the proposal for a Presbyterian university in Atlanta, the idea of moving to a Columbia suburb was also remembered and would be revisited regularly during the coming years. Indeed Whaling was to raise the possibility regularly with his reports to the board, and the idea was to be widely discussed as the synods thought carefully about the seminary, about Columbia's responsibility to provide pastors for the church in the twentieth century, and about the best location for a seminary as the white Southern Presbyterian Church grew rapidly throughout the Southeast.[23]

The possibility of moving the seminary to Memphis began to be seriously discussed in 1917. Southwestern Presbyterian University, still located in Clarksville, Tennessee, had a small School of Theology associated with it. The board asked Whaling to present to Southwestern an overture to unite the School of Theology with Columbia. As these talked progressed, Memphis began to be considered as a possible site for the seminary. Such a possibility alarmed the leadership of Louisville Presbyterian Seminary, for a new seminary in Memphis would undercut Louisville's relationships to the synods of the Mississippi valley. To counteract the Memphis proposal, the Louisville president Charles Hemphill began conversations with his brother-in-law Thornton Whaling.[24]

The Louisville seminary already had many historic ties to Columbia in addition to the close family and personal relationship between Hemphill and Whaling. Hemphill was himself a Columbia graduate and had been on the Columbia faculty during the Woodrow controversy. His early colleague at Louisville Timothy Dwight Witherspoon had graduated from Columbia in 1859. He had been engaged to Thornwell's daughter Nannie, who, to his great grief, had died a few days before their wedding. Francis Beattie, who had filled the Perkins Chair after Woodrow had been dismissed, had gone to Louisville in 1893, where he taught theology and apologetics until his death in 1906. He had been followed by Robert Webb, Columbia class of 1880 and son-in-law of Girardeau. These connections made Whaling sympathetic to Louisville's concerns, and informal conversations about the future of both seminaries continued for two years. Hemphill resigned as president in 1920 to spend more time teaching and to assume the responsibilities of the new office of dean. As talk about a seminary in Memphis intensified, Hemphill and the new Louisville president, J. M. Vander Meulen, invited Whaling to Louisville to review the issues and possibilities before both seminaries. When Whaling met with them, he proposed that Columbia and Louisville unite and—along with Southwestern's School of Theology—build a new seminary in Memphis. Meulen and Hemphill said that would be impossible given Louisville's commitments and endowment restrictions. They proposed an alternative—that Columbia move to Louisville and that the two schools, so closely connected by so many ties, unite to form one strong theological seminary to serve the constituencies of both seminaries. Whaling was drawn to the proposal and began immediately to advocate such a course. But the faculty and board resisted and said Columbia's special responsibility to its traditional constituency would be badly weakened.[25]

At the annual meeting of Columbia's board in May 1921, Whaling reported that Columbia's endowment was only a fraction of the endowment at Union or Louisville. Since its move from its rural setting at Hampden Sidney to Richmond in 1898, Union's endowment had shown remarkable growth and now stood at $885,000 with another $300,000 promised by the Synod of Virginia. Since the two Presbyterian seminaries in Kentucky had united in 1901 to form Louisville Presbyterian Theological Seminary, its endowment had also grown rapidly to $630,000 with another $300,000 promised by the Synod of Kentucky. In contrast Columbia's endowment stood at only $268,000 with another $125,000 promised by the Synod of South Carolina. "The difficulty in conducting an institution here," Whaling told the board, "which can compete successfully with far-more largely endowed seminaries raises a series of questions which the board ought to face." But the resistance to a proposed union with Louisville had apparently convinced Whaling that the board was not going to face the deep issues of Columbia's future, and he was already exhausted from his years of traveling around the Southeast trying to raise money and recruit students while at the same time trying to teach theology to growing numbers of seminarians. So after outlining the financial difficulties Columbia faced, he announced that he had accepted a call to Louisville to be professor of theology, apologetics, and ethics. His leaving was a blow for Columbia—he had been a popular professor as well as a successful president—but it was a coup for Louisville. In a brilliant move, Meulen and Hemphill had secured for Louisville a leading theologian of the southern church and had put an end to the threat of a rival seminary in Memphis.[26]

At the same meeting at which it accepted Whaling's resignation, the board unanimously elected John Miller Wells as the new president. He was a splendid choice. A Mississippian and graduate of Union Seminary, he had been a pastor for almost thirty years, had served as moderator of the General Assembly in 1917, and knew intimately the church he was called to serve. He brought not only the deep respect of the denomination but also a keen analytical mind and a willingness to speak forcefully about the issues before the seminary. Since James Reavis had also recently resigned to return to his old position as a secretary of foreign missions, Wells was appointed to fill his place as professor of pastoral theology. And to take over Reavis's responsibilities for teaching English Bible, the board called Melton Clark as professor of English Bible and religious education. That left Whaling's position as professor of didactic and polemic theology to fill. At first the board called Charles Malone Richards, Columbia graduate and pastor of the Davidson College Presbyterian Church, but he declined. The board then called James Benjamin Green, pastor of the First Presbyterian Church, Greenwood, South Carolina, to fill the position once held by Thornwell and Girardeau.[27]

All three men were in their new positions by the fall of 1922. They joined William McPheeters, professor of Old Testament literature and exegesis; Henry White, professor of New Testament literature and exegesis; Clark Reed, professor of ecclesiastical history and church polity; Edgar Kerr, professor of Hebrew and cognate languages; William Mills, instructor in rural sociology; and George Fulbright, instructor in elocution. In addition Hugh Murchison had been called in 1920 to assist Whaling as executive secretary. Murchison functioned as a business manager for the seminary, but he was also instructor in missions and Sunday school pedagogy and was director of religious work with responsibility for supervising student preaching and summer work in local congregations. The new appointments were quite an addition for a little faculty. Whaling had joined a faculty of four professors. Now ten years later, seven professors and three instructors were teaching a greatly enlarged student body. It was as if the seminary was slowly sticking its toe in a world that would come to be called the Roaring Twenties, but it was clearly a cautious and reluctant move.[28]

Wells plunged with vigor into his work as president. He traveled widely, preached in numerous congregations of the controlling synods, visited college and university campuses to speak to prospective students, read reports from other seminaries and on theological education in the United States, and thought carefully about Columbia's future. In his first report to the board, he announced that Columbia anticipated having in the fall of 1922 the largest student body it had ever had. But he quickly reminded the board that more students meant more expenses and more accommodations for them. So he recommended that the board raise an additional $30,000 for the next year's budget, that it initiate a campaign to raise $500,000 over the next seven years, that the refectory be enlarged and remodeled, and that an additional dormitory be secured to house the influx of new students. To justify his recommendations, he presented a detailed review of Columbia's needs and its place in the world of Presbyterian theological education.[29]

Wells began by saying that the seminary, through its successes, was in a crisis. He acknowledged that "crisis" was an overworked term, but he insisted that Columbia had entered a critical moment, a turning point in its history. He pointed to the growth of students and to a commensurate growth in the budget's annual deficit. He compared Columbia's budget to that of Presbyterian seminaries around the country—it was only a fraction of Princeton's and no more than half of Union's. He presented the cost per student at Columbia and projected what the total cost would be with an anticipated seventy students the next year. He analyzed Columbia's endowment and compared it to that of other Presbyterian seminaries—Princeton's was $3,313,000, Union's had grown to $911,826, and Columbia's languished at the bottom at $275,656. He looked at Columbia's campus and concluded, "Our buildings are old, out of repair, and utterly inadequate." In addition to a new dormitory and an enlarged refectory, which were needed immediately, the board needed to plan for a new fireproof library, a central heating plant, a new chapel, and four new professors' houses. And he concluded that even if all this remodeling and new construction were completed, and the seminary had paid for it all, Columbia would still not have as fine a campus and as good facilities as most of the other Presbyterian seminaries. But this was not all—there was a need for a full-time librarian, for a Department of Missions, for a teacher of music, and even a gymnasium and athletic field. His was the most comprehensive study of Columbia that had ever been made, the likes of which the board had never seen, and it reflected the careful methods of a modern manager.[30]

In response the board called the report "magnificent" and proceeded to authorize the enlargement of the refectory and the securing of new dormitory space in a nearby apartment building. It also appointed a committee to organize a campaign to raise the proposed $500,000. But its most significant move was to appoint a committee "to take under advisement all possible questions of location and consolidation." The board was obviously ready to admit that a crisis did in fact face the seminary even if it was not clear about the way out of the crisis.[31]

During the months that followed the Committee on Location and Consolidation held two important meetings. At the invitation of a group of Atlanta ministers, the committee met in Atlanta with about fifty ministers and lay leaders. There was a strong interest in the seminary moving to the Georgia capital. The board committee responded that a minimum of $500,000 and a suitable site would be necessary to justify moving the seminary to Atlanta. Sprole Lyons, pastor of Atlanta's First Presbyterian Church, was made chairman of a committee to investigate the possibilities. Not long after this a committee from Union Seminary met with the Columbia committee to discuss the "advantages and disadvantages to be had from a possible merger of the two seminaries." The Union men recommended a merger, and Walter Moore, Union's president, asked for a meeting with the full Columbia board. He came to Columbia for a called meeting of the board in October 1923 and spoke of Union's new campus in Richmond and outlined the advantages that would flow from a merger of the two oldest Presbyterian seminaries in the South. After several motions and countermotions, the Columbia board voted to ask the controlling synods to empower it to "survey the territory and locate the seminary where, in its judgment, based on all the facts, the seminary can secure a sufficient measure of financial assistance, and where it may render the largest service to the church." The board also asked that it be empowered "should this seem to be the wisest step, to negotiate and complete a merger with Union Seminary, Richmond, Va., in such way as shall preserve the history of Columbia, and shall most efficiently serve the controlling synods." Wells had come to a firm conviction that merging with Union was the best possible way forward, and he threw himself into the effort to get the synods to support such a move.[32]

When the matter came before the synods, Alabama and Florida gave permission for a merger with Union if it seemed to the board the wisest way forward. South Carolina voted that any move should be within the bounds of the controlling synods but left the door open for a possible merger with Union. Georgia voted that any move of the seminary needed to be to a location within the controlling synods. And it specifically declined to authorize the board to remove the seminary to any place outside the bounds of the controlling synods without reference to the Synod of Georgia for its advice and consent. Wells was disappointed by the vote but apparently still hopeful that the board would act in a way that would promote the merger.[33]

When the board met in May 1924, Wells reviewed once again the details of the seminary's situation and concluded: "The seminary in the judgment of your president cannot continue as and where it is." He did not believe that desperately needed funds could be raised if the seminary remained in Columbia. But he was up against strong opposition. The South Carolina presbyteries had all petitioned the board to keep the seminary in its historic home in Columbia. The board obviously felt pressure from many sides. After extended discussion, it voted that the seminary would remain in Columbia on the condition that the synods raise $500,000 during the next three years. Wells immediately submitted his resignation. The board asked him to reconsider, but when he refused, the board accepted the resignation with deep regret and appointed a committee to nominate a new president. The next morning the committee nominated Richard T. Gillespie, pastor of the First Presbyterian Church, Louisville, to be the new president. The committee was asked to confer with him. In the meantime a telegram arrived from the Union board asking for continued discussion of a possible merger.[34]

Four weeks later the board gathered in Augusta for a called meeting. Sprole Lyons of Atlanta and D. P. McGeachy, pastor of the Decatur Presbyterian Church in suburban Atlanta, were there and were invited to sit with the board. The committee appointed to meet with Gillespie reported that he was a person "whose administrative gifts, mental endowment, spirituality and personality fit him in unusual measure for the office of President." Gillespie had said, however, that he could not allow his name to be presented as long as the future location of the seminary was undecided. The committee had concluded that any other qualified candidate was likely to have the same reservation. It therefore called on the board to give a decisive response to Union and to make a decision about the future home of the seminary. After extended discussion the board voted unanimously to decline with thanks Union's offer of a merger; to name Atlanta as the future home of the seminary; to request the synods to confirm the action of the board and inaugurate a capital campaign of $500,000; to thank the city of Columbia and its churches for their years of support of the seminary and to say that the historic name—Columbia Theological Seminary—would be preserved in its new location; and to invite the Synod of Mississippi to become one of the supporting synods. As a part of the motion, the Presbytery of Atlanta was asked to assume responsibility for providing a site and suitable buildings in keeping with the seminary's dignity and ample for its anticipated growth. Two weeks later the Presbytery of Atlanta accepted the board's challenge. Assured that a firm decision had finally been made about moving the seminary to Atlanta, Gillespie said he would accept the presidency and was formally elected in October 1924.[35]

The board immediately appointed a Committee on Transferring and Rebuilding Columbia Theological Seminary, with power to select a suitable Atlanta site. Meeting in Atlanta in December 1924, the committee visited several possible locations and then voted to accept a site offered by "the estate of G. B. Scott and others" on the southeast border of Decatur. The selection was conditioned on the city of Decatur running water and sewer lines to the site, on the county and city agreeing to pave the street and install a sidewalk up to and in front of the seminary, and on the securing of an additional fifteen to twenty-five acres. The additional land, the committee believed, was needed to provide space for an athletic field, for an anticipated Training School for Lay Workers, and for a home for missionaries on furlough. These conditions were quickly met. By the time the board gathered in May 1925 for its annual meeting, plans were well on the way for the removal of the seminary to Decatur, a little Georgia town that had become a suburb of Atlanta—a symbol of the New South rising phoenix-like out of the ashes and bitterness of defeat. The board learned that 3,154 Atlanta Presbyterians had already pledged $413,481.80 for Columbia Theological Seminary, Decatur, Georgia.[36]

The decision to leave Columbia was a decision to leave a place of deep memories and treasured associations. The much-loved George Howe had given fifty-one years of his life to the seminary in this particular place. Here Charles Jones had taught about the religious instruction of slaves and about life among the Gullah people. Here Thornwell's brilliance had dazzled many, and Palmer's teaching and preaching had made him a prince of the pulpit. Columbia was the place where the seminary had survived the fires that followed Sherman. It had been the home of Adger, Girardeau, and Woodrow. In its classrooms generations of students had parsed Greek verbs and had translated Hebrew texts. In its dormitories students had made friends for life. In its chapel they had prayed together and had heard sermons together, and there before faculty and students they had, with no little anxiety, preached their first sermons. The stately old mansion with its Ionic columns and handsome porches had been a faithful reminder of old times that were not forgotten. The faculty who taught here and the students who studied here lived in the presence of this particular past, and they heard voices that still spoke out of deep memories as the past displayed its vitality and pressed its legacies deep into the present. Among the legacies of the Columbia campus none was more powerful that Girardeau's call to maintain the phraseology of the past as a way to defend a remembered South worth living for and dying for. The boundaries that Girardeau wanted to maintain, the walls he wanted to erect to maintain a white Southern Presbyterian orthodoxy and to safeguard a southern way of life, those theological boundaries and those ideological walls encircled the campus in Columbia and made of it a little world.

So it was not only finances that compelled the move from Columbia. It was also a need to break out of the seminary's little world, a need to escape its boundaries and move beyond its walls if its life was not to wither and its thought was not to petrify into an increasingly rigid and sterile orthodoxy. To be sure, the seminary's very poverty helped to breach Girardeau's walls. The seminary's deficits and its old and inadequate buildings could not be maintained in Columbia. For the seminary to survive financially it had to break free of the Columbia campus. It had to move beyond the genteel poverty that had settled over its constituencies, especially the lowcountry, the old heart of Columbia's life and support. Atlanta—with its energy and entrepreneurial confidence, with its rushing trains and its rising buildings—promised a new abundance and the more open and modern world of the New South.

What was clear, however, especially in hindsight, was that the New South carried deep within it much of the Old South—in particular a racism that showed no signs of dissipating. And what was also clear was that the seminary was to bring much of Columbia with it to Decatur. It was to bring a remembered style of life and a distinct tone and character. It was to bring many of the cultural assumptions and theological commitments that had been nurtured in Columbia for so many years. And perhaps above all, it was to bring a Columbia faculty to a new place. This meant that in the coming years the Decatur campus was going to be contested ground between those who sought to build Girardeau's boundaries around the new campus and those who sought, in discrete and circumspect ways, to lead the seminary on a middle path between an encrusted theological traditionalism and a rootless modernity, between a remembered southern way of life and a more cosmopolitan spirit. Such a middle way, it was hoped, would lead the seminary and the church it served to a faithful and lively engagement with a changing world.[37]

PART III

A Seminary for the New South

12

Decatur

The Early Years

When the board and controlling synods finally made the decision to move the seminary to Atlanta, they unleashed new hopes for Columbia and a great burst of energy for its redevelopment. Plans moved rapidly forward. Richard Gillespie was elected president in October 1924, and at the same meeting the board appointed a Committee on Transferring and Rebuilding Columbia Theological Seminary. The committee, with one member from each controlling synod, was given full authority to develop and build a new campus, and Gillespie was given primary administrative responsibility for the project. In late December the committee met in Atlanta and selected the Decatur site offered by "the estate of G. B. Scott and others" on the southeast border of Decatur. They quickly purchased additional property to create in total a fifty-seven-acre campus. They hired a landscape architect to study the physical character of the property—its soil; its rolling hills; the stream that flowed along one boundary; the hickories, oaks, and poplars that were scattered through its woods; and the rich array of native plants and shrubs that grew beneath its forest canopy. By March they were in the midst of selecting an architect to develop a master plan for the campus and to do the design work for the new buildings. After reviewing several proposals, they settled on the well-known Atlanta architectural firm of Edwards and Sayward. The committee clearly intended to build a new home for the seminary—a new place where serious work could be done, where new memories could be gathered, and where the ministry of the Presbyterian Church could be strengthened and enlarged. As they walked the land and talked to their architects and looked at how other campuses had been developed, they began to envision an expansive place of natural beauty. Here, they thought, campus and buildings could convey a handsome and harmonious simplicity, deep links to traditions of scholarship and piety, and—not least of all—substantial Presbyterian dignity.[1]

By the time of the annual meeting of the board in May 1925, Atlanta Presbyterians had pledged $483,481.80 for the new campus, and a campaign for another $250,000 was well under way throughout the Synod of Georgia. Behind this success were two men from Atlanta who were to be of great influence in the future life of the seminary—Sprole Lyons, pastor of Atlanta's First Presbyterian Church, and John Bulow Campbell, an elder at Central Presbyterian. These two were primarily responsible for the capital campaign in Atlanta and were quickly made a part of the building committee. They were soon members of the board of directors. Their leadership represented a fundamental shift in the support and governance of Columbia. For the first hundred years of the seminary, South Carolina Presbyterians—together with their lowcountry cousins in Liberty County, Georgia—had been its primary supporters and the principal leaders in its life. Moreover the Synod of South Carolina had been the synod that read the minutes of the board and approved its actions. All this leadership and oversight seemed natural not only because the seminary was located in Columbia, but also because there were many more Presbyterians in South Carolina than in any of the other synods. But the move to Decatur signaled that Atlanta Presbyterians, with their numbers growing rapidly, were going to provide much of the leadership of the seminary in the future. To be sure, there would be strong leaders from other parts of the seminary's constituency, but pastors and elders from Atlanta's large Presbyterian churches were to play an increasingly dominant role in Columbia's life. And among these leaders none would play such a critical role as the Presbyterian elder and Atlanta businessman John Bulow Campbell.[2]

Campbell had been born in Atlanta in 1870 and grew up attending Central Presbyterian Church, where his mother was a faithful member. Shortly after his father died in 1885, Campbell enrolled in the Georgia Military College in Milledgeville, Georgia, not far from his grandfather Campbell's plantation. He graduated at the top in his class and returned to Atlanta, where he soon began working with his brother's coal company. In 1904 he married Laura Berry of Rome, Georgia, whose remarkable sister Martha Berry had founded the Berry Schools for academically able but economically poor children of the rural South. Campbell became a vigorous supporter of his sister-in-law's educational and philanthropic efforts and served on the board of the Berry Schools, later Berry College. At the same time, he gave strong support to his friend and fellow elder at Central, John J. Eagan, a wealthy industrialist who had been deeply influenced by the progressive movement and the social gospel. Eagan repeatedly argued that "the teachings of Jesus Christ are sufficient for the solution of all human problems," especially racial animosities and injustices. While Martha Berry and Eagan were very much public figures, Campbell was a rather shy and modest person who preferred to work quietly and anonymously for the public good and for the encouragement of Christian faith and life. As his wealth grew, he became increasingly interested in the promotion of educational institutions. He was deeply committed to being a good steward of his wealth, and he thought a strong theological education for ministers was greatly needed for a New South. "I want," he told a friend, "to use my money for the good of my people and I do not see how I can do anything better for them than to help train men for the Christian ministry." With this background he was ready in 1925 to become one of the most influential persons in Columbia's history.[3]

After carefully reviewing various architectural styles, the committee settled on collegiate Gothic for the new buildings. This style—drawing its inspiration from the colleges at Oxford and Cambridge—was being widely used on U.S. campuses as it conveyed an image of stability and class consciousness and evoked a sense of standing firmly in European traditions of scholarship and good manners. The committee spent some time trying to decide if they should save money by using less-expensive materials or if they should build for the future using the best materials available. They decided on the latter, and the buildings were made fireproof and were faced in brick with striking limestone trim and with wall dormers.[4]

John Bulow Campbell provided most of the funds for the central building. He wanted it to stand as a memorial for his mother, Virginia Orme Campbell, who had hoped that one day he would become a minister. It was the largest gift in the seminary's history, surpassing even the Perkins gift in the 1850s. The handsome building, Campbell Hall, had three stories built over a large basement. The basement held a dining room and a kitchen. The first floor had classrooms, two administrative offices, a students' lounge, a faculty lounge, and a ladies' parlor, where visitors—especially young ladies from nearby Agnes Scott College—could be entertained. The second floor had classrooms, the library and a reading room, the Leighton Wilson Missionary Room with artifacts provided by missionaries, and the chapel. On the third floor twelve dormitory rooms provided space for twenty-four men. Each long, narrow room had two small closets and a dormer window, and future occupants were to take pride and great delight in calling it "the Monastery" although they were hardly monks in disposition or behavior. The southern end of the building was plain brick and was left unadorned. Plans called for a Gothic tower, but, perhaps providentially, funds were not available for such an architectural exclamation point. Finally in the 1950s that end of the building was completed in a simple style that fit the aesthetic character of the building.[5]

Placed at a right angle to Campbell Hall was the new dormitory. A three-story building, it had four sections, with four rooms to a floor. Each room—intended to house two students—had a sink, and each floor had a common bath. In the center of the building gargoyles guarded an arcade trimmed in Indiana limestone. The dormitory was named Simons-Law "to perpetuate the memory and Christian liberality of the two elect ladies" whose gifts had made possible the erection of Simons Hall and Law Hall on the old campus. The section to the right of the arcade carried the name Simons, after Eliza Lucilla Simons of Charleston. The section to the left was designated Law, after Agnes Law, John Adger's aunt, whose fine home had been burned when Sherman arrived in Columbia. As a homeless widow, she had moved into Law Hall to live out her last days in poverty and confusion. Since the Decatur dormitory had no room for married students, an apartment house with four units on nearby College Drive was rented by the seminary.[6]

Other buildings were planned for future construction. The dining hall and the library were to be only temporarily located in Campbell Hall. A master plan called for a fine library and for an elegant student center to contain a new dining hall. A freestanding chapel in a restrained Gothic style; apartments for married students; an athletic field and gymnasium; homes for the faculty; a central heating plant for the entire campus;

apartments for missionaries on furlough; and a "community church when the growth of the community makes a church desirable"—they were all part of a master plan that envisioned Columbia becoming once again a leading theological institution in the country. The plan was bold and expansive, and it assumed a growing prosperity for white Southern Presbyterians, especially those in Atlanta.[7]

Just as the campus in Columbia had nurtured a distinct tone and character among its students and faculty, the new campus in Decatur was intended to help nurture among faculty and students a style of life, a moral and aesthetic spirit, and a way of understanding human life. When South Carolina and Georgia Presbyterians had purchased in 1829 the elegant Ainsley Hall mansion, together with its slave quarters, they were preparing to build a campus that was to embody their theological commitments and reveal their place in southern society. In the same way, the Decatur campus with its collegiate Gothic buildings was not neutral space devoid of meaning. Rather it conveyed messages—messages that would be clearer as the plan for the campus materialized in coming decades. To visitors and to those who passed by, the campus was to say with increasing boldness—"Look, here is the home of wealth and influence!" And the campus in subtle and unobtrusive ways was to ask all those who came up its drive: "What kind of theology do you think is taught here? What kind of students do you think come here? And what kind of pastors do you think graduate from here?" Of course looks and especially first impressions can be deceptive. The handsome new buildings hid the financial weakness of the seminary and disguised its continuing provincialism. Nevertheless a vision was being revealed in the new campus and the new buildings. Campbell Hall was not an antebellum mansion as in Columbia, but a building grounded in traditions deeper than the Old South. Its collegiate Gothic architecture linked it to similar places of scholarship scattered across the English-speaking world, and its rolling acres gave hints of a more open and expansive spirit. So the new campus was new, in a new location, a part of a young and vibrant city and more cosmopolitan world. But those who paid for its construction and those who oversaw its development conceived of the seminary as not only new but also rooted, a place that faced the future knowing that it had a past. "A hundred years of church history," declared the seminary catalog in 1928, "attests the notable contribution Columbia has made to Presbyterianism in the South. . . . Names like Goulding, Howe and Leland, Palmer, Thornwell and J. R. Wilson, Woodrow, Plumer, and Girardeau are a part of the history of our denomination. Their work will always be revered."[8]

While the building of the new campus was proceeding, life on the old campus moved steadily toward its end. Enrollment of students, after a downturn in 1924, began to recover as enthusiasm grew about Columbia's future. The entering class in the fall of 1926 was the largest in the seminary's history and numbered some exceptionally promising students. First-year student Sam Cartledge was serving as instructor in introductory Greek (he had completed at the University of Georgia an M.A. in classics), and second-year student J. McDowell Richards, recently returned from three years as a Rhodes Scholar at Oxford, was the instructor in introductory Hebrew.[9]

McPheeters, having passed his seventieth birthday, continued to be elected—one year at a time—professor of Old Testament literature and exegesis. Age, however, had not dampened his fighting spirit, and he was still contending for the faith and trying to correct the errors of a substantial number of Presbyterian clergy across the South. He had lost his old colleagues—the cheerful Clark Reed and irenic Henry White. Reed had died in his sleep in July 1925, and White had died after a short illness the following fall. But McPheeters had a new colleague, a man after his own heart, William Childs Robinson. The young Robinson had grown up in Columbia the son of influential board member David Robinson and as a member of Girardeau's old church appropriately named Arsenal Hill Presbyterian. Robinson graduated from Columbia in 1920 and spent several years as the pastor of the Presbyterian church in, of all places, Gettysburg, Pennsylvania. There he had walked over the fields where tens of thousands had died in July 1863, where Pickett had led his fateful charge, and where Lincoln had spoken of a "new nation conceived in liberty and dedicated to the proposition that all men are created equal." Robinson was called to Columbia to take Reed's chair in church history. Arrangements were made for him to finish a Ph.D. at Harvard. His dissertation was entitled "Columbia Theological Seminary and the Southern Presbyterian Church," but in years to come his real interest was not to be in church history but in church politics and in defending fundamentals of the faith.[10]

To fill White's position in New Testament literature and exegesis, the board called Hunter Blakely, pastor of the Associate Reformed Presbyterian Church in Louisville. Blakely had grown up in South Carolina and had graduated from Erskine Theological Seminary in Due West, South Carolina. After earning an M.A. from Princeton University and spending a year at the University of Edinburg, he had—while a pastor in Louisville—completed a Ph.D. from the Louisville Southern Baptist Theological Seminary. As a part of his call to Columbia, he was granted a leave of absence for a year of study in Europe. He spent the summer of 1927 at the University of Oxford and then studied the following academic year at the University of Berlin. Gillespie was particularly pleased with these appointments—a young Harvard Ph.D. in church history and a young New Testament professor who had been immersed in the latest German scholarship. The seminary was clearly moving toward a new expectation that its professors hold a Ph.D. or its equivalent.[11]

During the seminary's last year in Columbia, the Smyth Lecturer was J. Gresham Machen. His maternal grandfather, J. J. Gresham of Macon, Georgia, had been a member of Columbia's board during the early years of the Woodrow controversy and had been a faithful financial contributor to the seminary. When Gresham Machen appeared on the Columbia campus in the spring of 1927, he was in the midst of a bitter struggle at Princeton Theological Seminary in New Jersey. Machen was trying to preserve the old scholastic orthodoxy that Charles Hodge had taught at Princeton and that Girardeau had taught at Columbia. For Girardeau this theological tradition constituted a critical part of "the phraseology of the past"; it was the fundamental building block for a wall to protect a white Southern Presbyterian orthodoxy and southern way of life. For Girardeau and for Machen, Christianity was founded on historical facts, facts that could be known in an unfiltered directness, and they were convinced that they knew the true and fundamental facts about Christian doctrine. For them there was no room for various points of view, only the correct point of view as they knew it to be correct. So Machen's Smyth Lectures—they were on the Virgin Birth—were a strong affirmation of an important part of the seminary's past, a Girardeau Columbia, at the moment the seminary was leaving Columbia and venturing into a new future in Atlanta. Machen would soon be forced out of Princeton and would start Westminster Theological Seminary in Philadelphia, a center of intellectual life for U.S. fundamentalism.[12]

Perhaps ironically the first Smyth Lecturer after the seminary moved to Atlanta was Machen's opponent at Princeton Charles Erdman. An evangelical with broad sympathies and a winsome spirit, Erdman believed that "in debating Christian doctrines, more than in any other form of effort, one needs a vein of humor, common sense, and brotherly love." He believed that the best defense of the faith was a holy life that flowed from a heart given in love to Christ. During the next four decades Columbia was to feel the tension between the Girardeau and Machen spirit embodied most forcefully by William Childs Robinson and the spirit of Erdman embodied by most of the rest of the faculty. Yet even as the seminary's leadership tried to negotiate between these two spirits, it was clear Columbia's leadership believed the position of Erdman—conservative in theology and tolerant in spirit—was not only the more irenic and prudent but also the more faithful way forward for the seminary and for the church.[13]

In July 1927 Campbell Hall and Simons-Law were ready for occupation. In Columbia the faculty, students, and "servants" were busily preparing for the move. All moveable seminary furniture was cleaned and refinished. Artifacts given by visiting missionaries were boxed, and the thirty-two thousand volumes of the library were carefully packed, including ten thousand valuable volumes from the Smyth library that were individually wrapped. In early August all were transported to the train station in Columbia, and on August 4 they were transported from the depot in Decatur to the new campus. The rest of the month was a flurry of activity. In Campbell Hall books were carefully unpacked and shelved on new bookcases. The well-lit reading room was furnished with tables and chairs as were the classrooms. The Women's Auxiliary of the Decatur Presbyterian Church provided the faculty and student lounges and the ladies' parlor with rugs, davenports, and stuffed lounging chairs; and the women of First Presbyterian, Atlanta, had a piano delivered to the ladies' parlor. In Simons-Law and in the "Monastery," metal bunk beds were assembled and desks placed in each room.[14]

Four new faculty homes were nearing completion—three faced what had formerly been Oak Street. It was now Columbia Drive, named to honor the arrival of the seminary in Decatur. One home faced Inman Drive and was designated as the president's. They were all built in Tudor style to complement the collegiate Gothic of the campus buildings. Their brick and half-timbered construction and their tall brick chimneys with clay chimney pots were intended to reinforce the messages conveyed by Campbell Hall and Simons-Law. Because there were not enough homes for all the faculty, Gillespie moved his family into the second floor of the forth section of Simons-Law, leaving the president's home for a faculty family. The third floor of the same section of Simons-Law was also turned into what was hoped to be a temporary apartment for a faculty family.[15]

When they arrived on campus students found not only Campbell Hall and Simons-Law waiting for them, but also two clay tennis courts and a small building that held a mat for wrestling. A volleyball court was immediately behind Campbell Hall, and a small playing field, at the corner of Inman and Columbia, provided enough space for games of softball and touch football. Remus Alexander, a young college graduate, had made the move from Columbia to Decatur as the official "physical director," with responsibility to coordinate the various sporting activities on the campus. His was very much a part-time position—he was paid only $300 a year—but Gillespie thought it important for students to have strenuous exercise and not become pallid scholars of Greek and Hebrew. The popular image of a "muscular Christianity" demanded that future ministers be robust and manly and not appear sickly or effeminate.[16]

Two "servants" also made the move from Columbia to Decatur. Joseph H. Dixon was a minister in the African Methodist Episcopal Church and had been serving as janitor for the seminary in Columbia. While his salary from the seminary was only $1,000, he apparently thought it enough to justify his moving his family to Decatur. He and his wife already had three children when, shortly before the move, they had triplets. So the eight of them had come to Decatur and had settled in the town's black neighborhood, a little over a mile from the seminary. When he was twenty-one, Dixon had lost one arm in a railway accident, but he could do the work of a janitor with amazing skill. With his one arm, he could sweep the buildings and rake gravel pathways and mow the little grass that then grew on the campus. And with the help of a leather strap over his shoulder he could shovel coal for the two large boilers that kept the buildings heated, and he could manage a wheelbarrow with apparent ease. He joined the nearby AME church, became the Sunday school superintendent, and in time had been licensed as a local preacher. During twenty-seven years of service at the seminary, his friendly disposition and ready smile won him many friends, and the whites on the campus regarded him with the curious affection of paternalism. He would later be remembered as a "true Christian" and one who "set a high example for the young men who daily observed his diligence." Students and graduates established a memorial fund in his name when he retired.[17]

The other "servant" who came from Columbia was Plato Henderson. He had begun as a teenager working in the seminary's dining hall in 1917, and by at the time of the move he had become a much-appreciated cook. His name—Plato—linked him to earlier generations of blacks who carried classical names and provided much of the financial foundations of the seminary during the antebellum period: Cato and Cassius, Phoebe and Dorcas, Agrippa and Titus. But Plato Henderson also brought a long tradition of African American cuisine, especially that part of the cuisine that had been served to whites. This made him extremely popular among students and faculty alike not only because of the excellence of the food he prepared but also because of the images and mythic memories both he and the food evoked. In a bulletin on seminary life, he was described this way: "Plato—A Southern Cook. Plato's skill as a cook places him in a class with 'Aunt Jemima,' of pancake fame, with the smiling cook who bakes the 'Ham what AM,' and with 'Grandmother's Old Cook' of blessed memory." The Aunt Jemima ads, developed in and distributed from Chicago, provided racial stereotypes and evoked nostalgic white memories of a mythic agrarian South that was receding into the shadows of urban centers such as Atlanta. Those memories with their racist assumptions were to linger for decades on the new Decatur campus and were to continue to live in the deep recesses of white imagination across the nation. As for Plato Henderson, he was to serve the seminary for forty-seven years. He was a founding member of Trinity Presbyterian Church in Decatur and served the church for many years as a much respected and loved elder.[18]

When students came into the refectory, they wore coats and ties and sat at long tables covered with white tablecloths and set in proper fashion—knife and spoon on the right; fork and cloth napkin on the left—with china plates and cups and saucers. Faculty and their families and a few student wives frequently ate with the students, and the food was served family style. So the refectory helped to create a sense that the seminary community was a family. The simple physical act of sitting together and of experiencing together the sight, aroma, and taste of the food prepared by a black cook drew students and faculty closer to one another. Mealtime was consequently a critical moment, an important ritual, in shaping a Columbia Seminary identity and in nurturing affection for the seminary that was deep and lasting. But mealtime was also a time that revealed and helped to define relations between races and classes. Neither Joseph Dixon nor Plato Henderson sat at the table. And when students held and used a fork according to an established etiquette and did not shovel food or use a spoon to eat peas, they were demonstrating—and perhaps learning—the good manners expected of a minister among white Presbyterians.[19]

The faculty who welcomed the students to the new campus included—in addition to Gillespie, McPheeters, Robinson, and Blakely—Melton Clark, professor of English Bible and pastoral theology; Edgar Kerr, professor of Hebrew and cognate languages; and J. B. Green, professor of systematic theology, Christian ethics, and homiletics. While still in Columbia, the faculty had, at Gillespie's urging, introduced the quarter system, which added four weeks to the academic year and more time for classroom instruction. Electives, which had been introduced at the beginning of the century, had also been significantly expanded. These changes in the format of the curriculum reflected national studies of higher education that were calling for more modern pedagogical approaches. The changes also reflected a growing concern that ministers not be left behind socially and academically by other professions and that theological seminaries have standards that were comparable to those of other professional schools. If ministers were going to be professionals, they needed a professional education. The content of the curriculum at Columbia, however, showed much continuity in course offerings even as the faculty, in its own rather modest way, was becoming more deeply engaged in the larger world of theological scholarship.[20]

Richard Gillespie had not only supervised the building of the new campus; he had also been responsible for making all the arrangements for the move to Decatur while at the same time being deeply involved as president in raising funds for current expenses and the new campus. By the time the seminary moved to Decatur, students had come to regard him as a pastor and friend, and throughout the church he was greatly respected. A tall and handsome man, he possessed a patrician profile and enormous energy. Not long after the move, however, he became seriously ill. The board gave him a year's leave of absence to recover his health. They elected Melton Clark acting president and instructed him to do what he could to carry the weight of the president's office. Doctors then discovered Gillespie had a diseased thyroid. An operation followed, and for a while he seemed to be regaining his strength. But he soon took a turn for the worse, and another operation was necessary. In May 1929 the board gave him another year's leave of absence. The following October the stock market crashed, ushering in the Great Depression that would last through the next decade.[21]

Based on pledges received, the seminary had borrowed over $200,000 to complete the construction of the new campus. The collapsing economy meant that many pledges could not be paid. The bright hopes for the seminary on its new campus suddenly began to dim. The seminary, indebted as never before, faced a rapidly growing financial crisis. Campbell offered a $60,000 challenge grant if $60,000 could be raised to match his. When the board met in May 1930, it was clear that the matching funds could not be secured. Campbell generously provided a $75,000 gift to help the seminary meet the immediate crisis. Three weeks later Gillespie died. The board gave his widow his salary through the next year and allowed her to remain in their apartment until September. Neither the seminary nor the church provided pensions.[22]

As the depression deepened, the future of the seminary seemed in doubt. Enrollment began to fall precipitously. The endowment, still heavily invested in home mortgages in South Carolina, began to yield less income as many who had borrowed from the seminary were finding they could not make mortgage payments. New investments were also lost when some banks and businesses began to fold. Chicora College, which had entered a contract for the old campus, was unable to meet its payments to the seminary.[23]

This deepening financial crisis swept over the seminary at a time when it had lost the strong leadership of Gillespie. Melton Clark did what he could to keep some stability in the seminary administration, but the difficulties continued to grow. Hunter Blakely, the most thoroughly grounded scholar on the faculty, announced that he was leaving to become pastor of the Presbyterian church in Staunton, Virginia. And to make matters worse, the board had great difficulty finding a strong candidate who would take Gillespie's place. They asked William M. Anderson, pastor of First Presbyterian, Dallas, Texas. He turned them down. They asked Darby Fulton, an executive with the General Assembly's Executive Committee for Foreign Missions. He turned them down. They asked Patrick D. Miller, an executive with the General Assembly's Executive Committee for Home Missions. He considered the call carefully and traveled to Thomasville, Georgia, where his Davidson College roommate, McDowell Richards, was the newly installed pastor. They talked long into the night, and Richards gave him a number of reasons he should accept. Miller returned to his home in Atlanta and decided to say "no." But he recommended to the board that they call Richards, and all the reasons Richards had given to Miller on why he should accept the call were now turned back on Richards. He was only thirty, and he had grave doubts that he had the experience and wisdom needed. But the board persisted, and the Thomasville congregation agreed to let him go, so he went. It had been two years since Gillespie's death, and the country had moved still deeper into the depression.[24]

Richards was a child of South Carolina and of Columbia Seminary. Both of his grandfathers had graduated from Columbia in 1858 and had served in the Confederate army as chaplains. His McDowell grandfather had then served for forty years as the pastor of the Presbyterian church in Manning, South Carolina, an area of rich cotton plantations. Nearby was the home of the great missionary couple Jane and Leighton Wilson, and Richards's mother, Jane Leighton, and his sister Jane Leighton were named for the Wilson couple so closely associated with the seminary. Richards's paternal grandfather, John Gardiner Richards, had served for over thirty years as the pastor of the Liberty Hill Presbyterian Church, near the Wateree River, in another area of large cotton plantations in South Carolina. The father of Richards, Charles Malone Richards, had graduated from Columbia in 1895 and had served many years as the pastor of the Davidson College Presbyterian Church. He had been a longtime member of the Columbia board, and on several occasions he had been called to be a professor at Columbia. So McDowell Richards came to the seminary out of the thick web of family connections that surrounded Columbia, that had long supported and sustained Columbia, and that regarded Columbia as "our theological seminary." These complex links meant that great affection for and deep commitment to the seminary were to mark Richards's long tenure as president. He knew intimately the world out of which the seminary had been conceived and by which it had been sustained for generations. As a consequence he spoke the language of this world fluently, he understood its stories and the subtleties of it manners and rituals, and he felt somewhere deep within himself its fears and hopes.

But the intensity of Richards's white Southern Presbyterian identity had been tempered by his three years at Oxford. There he had made friends with Englishmen and with Rhodes Scholars from various parts of the British Empire. He had learned that English was spoken with many accents and that those accents had behind them different worlds. From the elevated world of Oxford, he could see his white Southern Presbyterian world not only as provincial but also as a much-loved particular place, a place with names and faces and memories lodged deep within him. So he stood, as it were, at the edge of Girardeau's wall, an insider who knew what lay beyond the old boundaries of white Presbyterian orthodoxies and white southern ways. And this place on the edge was to allow him to critique and challenge a church and a people whom he loved, and it was to give him a spirit marked by both humility and courage.

Oxford, of course, had its own provincialism and its own sense of physical and social place. He escaped some of this by visiting Paris, where he found French culture and cooking a delightful surprise and French girls prettier and more modest than he expected. He went to Germany in order to have an immersion in the language. Staying with a family in Bonn, he experienced firsthand the deep poverty that was ravaging Germany in the 1920s, and he saw the suffering that was flowing from the great battles at Verdun and Somme, at Ypres and the Argonne Forest and all the other blood soaked fields of a world war. He wrote in his diary, "What a terrible thing is war," and he never forgot what he had seen and experienced.[25]

During vacation in 1925, Richards took off with a few friends to see a wider world. They traveled through France and down the boot of Italy to Brindisi. Riding fourth class, “the lowest of the low,” they observed Italy under its Fascist leader Benito Mussolini. From Brindisi they sailed to Greece and traveled among its ancient ruins while Greek refugees from Turkey crowed its cities, and Greek Muslims prepared for their forced evacuation from all Greek territory. From Piraeus they sailed to Egypt and then on to the Holy Land. Back in Egypt they caught a freighter to Istanbul. Here they made trips to more ruins and took long walks through the ancient capital of Byzantium. Then they were back on the train again, always traveling fourth class, riding with farmers dressed in their knee boots and wool coats, across the Rhodope Mountains to Bulgaria with a stop in Sofia. They went on again to Belgrade, and Budapest, and finally Vienna, Paris, and Oxford. No Columbia professor since John Adger and James Woodrow had had such exposure to wider worlds as Richards had at Oxford and during his extensive travels.[26]

Following his graduation from Columbia in 1928, Richards accepted a call to do home missionary work in the mountains of north Georgia. The congregations he served at Clarkesville, Nacoochee, and Helen were small, but they were strong in their peculiar Presbyterian way—the families of farmers and teachers, a few doctors and lawyers, and merchants. For the next three years, he traveled red clay roads that were dusty in dry weather and rivers of mud when the rains were long and heavy. He met a young school teacher in nearby Sautee, Georgia. An Agnes Scott graduate, Evelyn Knight was teaching in a one-room school supported by the Presbyterian Church. There during the winter she had to get to the school in time to build a fire and break the ice on the water pitcher before trying to teach four different classes at the same time in one room. It was a long way from the lush orange groves and affluent surroundings of her Florida home. In 1929 Mac Richards and Evelyn Knight were married. Their time in Appalachia was a happy time for the young couple and, as Oxford had been, an important time for Mac Richards. He saw a side of the South he had not known, and he learned something about the diversity of his own homeland.[27]

Richards's inaugural address as the new president of Columbia drew together these various strands of his past and focused them on the task of theological education and on future directions for Columbia. Most obviously its tone marked a turning away from the Girardeau Columbia, with its defensiveness and censoriousness, to a more expansive and generous spirit.

He began his inaugural by acknowledging his sense of inadequacy for the tasks before him. He had been president for two years by the time of the inaugural, and during that time he had watched the Depression deepen and the financial crisis of the seminary become more apparent. He obviously felt his inexperience as he peered into the seminary's future, and he heard within himself voices that prompted modesty and that cautioned him not to think too highly of himself. But his modesty—always genuine and transparent—did not prevent him from acting decisively on behalf of the seminary and the church. So after confessing his sense of inadequacy, he turned to the challenges before the seminary, and he addressed them directly. The first challenge, he said, was the financial crisis. Income had dropped precipitously, and large debts remained from the construction of the new campus. The financial crisis was real, and prospects seemed bleak. But by the time of his inaugural Richards had already acted resolutely to meet the challenge. He had cut his own salary by almost 50 percent, and the faculty and staff had followed his lead. Students had agreed to accept campus jobs in return for their financial aid—they were serving tables in the dining hall, shelving books in the library, shoveling coal for the boilers, and raking leaves on the campus. Richards said that with great sacrifice and hard work the seminary had been able to finish the previous two years in the black. So he told those gathered for his inaugural that he felt confident that Columbia's doors could remain open.[28]

A second challenge to Columbia's future was a proposal to reduce the number of Southern Presbyterian seminaries from four to two. A committee of the General Assembly had recommended that the church have a seminary in the East—Union in Richmond—and a new consolidated seminary somewhere in the West. Richards made a strong case for the need for a seminary in Atlanta and for the utilization of the new campus in Decatur. But the seminary, he said, was the servant of the church, and the church, not the seminary, had finally to decide how many seminaries it needed. In particular the synods that owned and controlled Columbia had to decide about its future. "It is for us," he said, to abide by the decision of the church and "to carry out her commands." While the assembly was soon to reject its committee's report, Richards was making clear that Columbia was a seminary of the church—not the church as an abstraction, but the church as an institutionally embodied and historically identified Presbyterian Church in the United States. Like those who had gone before him and most who followed him, he had an ecclesiology deeply grounded in Reformed theology. The church was not a collection of loosely connected individual Christians, but a body—the earthly historical body of Christ—that was for Presbyterians tightly joined together by church courts.[29]

Richards then turned to the future of the seminary. He reminded those gathered for the inaugural that they were "compassed about with a great cloud of witnesses" who had lived and died for the seminary and its ministry—"Goulding and Howe and Leland; Charles Colcock Jones and Plumer and Palmer; Thornwell and Girardeau and Adger; Wilson and Reed and White and Richard T. Gillespie." He affirmed the seminary's continuing commitment to "the truth that we find contained in the Scriptures of the Old and New Testaments, which is the Word of God, the only infallible rule of faith and practice." But Richards made clear that the message of the scriptures was not a list of rational theological propositions but a "message of redeeming love," of God's "ineffable love" for a lost world. And while the Gospel was good news for individuals, Richards insisted it carried "tremendous social implications." Christianity was larger than any social or political system and was big enough "not only for all races and for all nations, but for many varieties of honest opinion with regard to methods and to programs of action." But what Christianity was not big enough for was anyone "who is not willing to follow Christ and who will not honestly seek to apply principles of honor and of justice, of purity and of kindliness and of love" in every sphere of life "whether it be financial or political or social."[30]

Finally Richards said that the seminary's task was not only to inculcate loyalty to the truth and insistence on right, but also to nurture a spirit of meekness and Christian charity. He told the gathered seminary community that truth was "*seldom* advanced by controversy," and he insisted that people are "never won to Christ by an attitude that is uncharitable and unsympathetic." He thought that the truth does not greatly need to be defended; "it does need to be proclaimed. The world today has sore need of a great positive Gospel, and the Church has far greater need of a ministry which constantly and consistently proclaims the truth by word and by life, than it has of censors and of critics."[31]

In this way Richards revealed in his inaugural the spirit that was to animate his long presidency. He was to lead the seminary as one deeply rooted in the traditions of Columbia but also as one who had seen broader horizons and who had felt the call to a life marked by a generous and loving spirit. As a consequence he was himself to be greatly loved and enormously admired for his personal integrity and modesty dignity. For many of his generation and for many Columbia students over the coming decades, he was to seem the very embodiment of a Christian gentleman—a white southern Christian gentleman seeking "to apply principles of honor and of justice, of purity and of kindliness and of love" in every sphere of life. Later he would look back over his years as president and acknowledge how much he was a child of the white South and of a Columbia tradition as he sought to follow a moderate, middle way on the issues of his day. But for some of his white contemporaries he was to appear a threat to a white South and to the walls that protected an inherited orthodoxy. They wanted rigid loyalty to the "phraseology of the past" and lockstep uniformity. The challenges to his leadership and to developments at the seminary were consequently going to be persistent and often strident. And he was to find that finally he could not remain in the middle but had to make a choice and enter the field of controversy over questions of justice and Christian discipleship regarding race and the racism that permeated American society.[32]

Despite the sacrifices being made by faculty and staff and the various other efforts to reduce expenses, the financial crisis deepened during the months that followed Richards's inauguration. Miss Virginia Harrison, the bursar, kept a sharp eye on every penny spent and maintained meticulous records. She had been the treasurer of the capital campaign for the building of the new campus and had become bursar after the move to Decatur. The seminary's auditors and the board regularly praised her work, and Richards essentially turned over to her the daily running of the seminary so that she acted as a kind of business manager—she ordered supplies, put up the mail, insisted that students be prompt in their work for the seminary, and oversaw sundry other tasks in addition to keeping the books and typing Richards's voluminous correspondence. But even the Richards and Harrison team could not hold back the growing financial crisis.[33]

In early winter 1936, Benjamin Lacy, president of Union Seminary in Virginia, came to the campus to discuss with Richards the possibility of a merger of the two seminaries on the Richmond campus. They met with Campbell and with Sprole Lyons, now chairman of the board. Lacy had been Campbell's pastor and had played a role in the move to Decatur, so he brought much authority and a special seriousness with his proposal. The men agreed the full board needed to hear from Lacy. When the board met in March, Lacy outlined a way for the two seminaries to unite and adopt a new name. His proposal seemed a way out of the crisis for both schools and a wise use of the limited funds available for theological education. But the board was reluctant to take such a step and turned rather to Atlanta Presbyterians to raise the necessary funds to keep the seminary in Decatur. Before a large audience at Central Presbyterian, Richards reported that $300,000 was needed to meet the financial crisis. Campbell, identified only as an anonymous friend, had promised a challenge gift of $100,000 if another $200,000 were raised. The campaign was started with much hope, but it ended in disappointment. So President J. R. McCain of Agnes Scott College, a longtime member of the board, went to Campbell and told him that the only way the seminary could be kept in Decatur was for Campbell to give an immediate gift of $75,000 to match $75,000 already raised by Atlanta Presbyterians. In addition Campbell would need to underwrite the seminary's budget with $5,000 a year for five years. Campbell agreed. At the same time the old Columbia campus was finally sold for $75,000, and with Campbell's generous gift and the funds raised in Atlanta the financial crisis passed. Richards reported to the board his gratitude to that anonymous friend of Columbia who was a "faithful steward of his possessions as a servant of Jesus Christ." The friend, he said, had once again come to the aid of the seminary in its hour of need and had made possible the continued life and service of the seminary. Henceforth, said Richards, "Columbia Seminary must ever be, in large degree, a monument to this man, and whatever measure of success it attains in years to come will be attributable, under the blessing of God, to his faith and vision." In 1938 the seminary's debts were paid in full, and its notes of indebtedness were burned outside Campbell Hall before a happy crowd of onlookers. Two years later Campbell contributed an additional $150,000 for the seminary's endowment.[34]

While Richards was struggling to establish the financial grounding of the seminary, he also had to deal with those who were seeking to continue the Girardeau and McPheeters tradition of a strident and embattled white Southern Presbyterian orthodoxy. This orthodoxy reflected some of the spirit of twentieth-century U.S. fundamentalism. They both shared a deep fear of modernity and held tightly to the values of an older rural America. And they both viewed the Bible as containing a rational system of divinely inspired propositions. But fundamentalism, as a distinct movement within U.S. Protestantism, had little appeal to white Southern Presbyterians. Most fundamentalists had a dispensationalist view of history in which history, including biblical history, was divided into periods or dispensations. Each dispensation followed a pattern that ended with God's judgment on God's people. Out of such dispensationalism flowed imaginative descriptions of a rapture and other end-of-the-world events. Fundamentalism was consequently regarded, even among conservative Southern Presbyterians, as too tainted and extreme for a genteel southern orthodoxy. For them dispensationalists were not orthodox but heterodox, not finally rational but deeply irrational. Nevertheless much of the suspicious nature and fighting spirit of fundamentalism was present in those who were eager to defend the faith after the manner of Girardeau and McPheeters.[35]

Shortly after Richards's inaugural address, Patrick H. Carmichael was inaugurated as professor of English Bible and Christian education. A native of Alabama, Carmichael had graduated from Princeton Theological Seminary and had received a Ph.D. from New York University before returning to Alabama in 1920 to serve as a pastor—first in Selma and then in Montevallo. He joined the Columbia faculty in 1933 and had quickly established himself as a popular teacher and energetic presence on the campus. When the time came for him to be inaugurated, he told the board that he would take the vow of the office, but he wished to have one phrased omitted. The vow required him to subscribe to the Westminster Confession of Faith and Catechisms and other standards of the church, "as a just summary of the doctrines contained in the Bible." He was to promise not to teach any doctrine "contrary to the Scripture as interpreted by these standards." What he objected to was "as interpreted by these standards." The phrase, he said, made the standards a higher authority than the scriptures. The board heard his scruples and declared that his position "does not invalidate the meaning of the oath" and allowed him, for conscience sake, to take it with the phrase omitted.[36]

The day of Carmichael's inauguration, William Childs Robinson sent a letter to the board reprimanding it for its actions regarding the oath. Earlier in the day, the board had held a memorial service for Robinson's father, David Robinson, who had served long and faithfully as a board member and who had overseen the management and sale of the seminary properties in Columbia. So Robinson's letter came at an awkward time for the board, but it did not fail to deeply irritate board members. The seminary professor had attempted to lecture them on the history of the vow and had noted that he, as their professor of church history, "was perhaps more conversant with some of the historical backgrounds of formulas prescribed in the Plan of Government than some of the members of the Board." He said that the vow had been used by every professor at Columbia for over a hundred years and quoted Charles Hodge at length on the importance of such vows. Two days later, however, Robinson wrote a "supplemental statement" in which he admitted that on investigation he had found the phrase in question had only been added after the James Woodrow controversy over evolution. He continued to insist, however, that the board had exceeded its authority in allowing the omission of the phrase for Carmichael.[37]

The board was clearly angered by what it considered Robinson's arrogance and presumption. It expressed appreciation for his zeal and with no little irony for "the splendid spirit" in which he had detected and corrected his mistake. They called to his attention that members of the board who had read and approved the vow as taken by Carmichael were "men whose genuine concern for the defense of the faith . . . is beyond question." They were "not unmindful of the issues involved and . . . did not act without taking what they considered due care to safeguard every principle at stake." If the professor had any concerns to communicate to the board in the future, he was told to do so through the faculty "as a whole" or the president.[38]

The board then turned to Robinson's bellicose spirit. They were especially concerned, they told him, about recent articles he had written. They commended his zeal for the defense of the faith, but they called attention to the ways in which he had attacked and launched insinuations against individuals, institutions, and denominations. They said that while, "as an individual he has the same right to express his views as any other minister so long as he accords due consideration to the rights and feelings of others, he ought also to remember that as a professor of the Seminary he can in no case express his views without causing the institution to be considered as, in large degree, sharing them. The fact that widespread feeling against Columbia Seminary has been aroused by some of these articles and that the institution has lost both students and support as a consequence is, in our judgment, beyond any question." The board urged him "to avoid in future the type of writing and speaking referred to above, as not accomplishing the end which we all desire and as tending to injure the institution which we serve."[39]

The reprimand and warning did little to stop Robinson in his warfare against those who would breach Girardeau's wall intended to protect what was perceived to be a white Southern Presbyterian orthodoxy. Robinson soon launched a public attack on his colleague and next-door neighbor J. B. Green, who chaired a General Assembly committee to revise the Westminster Confession. Growing numbers in the church had been calling for the elimination of certain offensive language—such as references to the pope as the antichrist. At the same time, many were noting important omissions in the confession—no chapter on the Holy Spirit or on the love of God or on missions. The committee proposed changes, and Robinson was against any change. He wrote heated articles in church papers, and Green, a stalwart conservative himself, responded in defense of the committee's proposal. Once again the board had to step into the fray. Lyons, Campbell, and Wallace Alston met with Robinson and Green and urged them not to prolong the publications of articles in which they so vigorously differed with one another. And, apparently in reference to some of the language Robinson had used, they urged an avoidance of personal references and implications. Two years later the attack was launched against two other professors—Sam Cartledge and Edgar Kerr. This time the attack came from Robinson's home church in Columbia, Arsenal Hill—which had been founded by Girardeau—and Robinson's home presbytery, Congaree. The board met with the professors, both highly regarded and much loved throughout the church, and reported to the presbytery that the professors were "sound in the faith." Three board members voted against such an affirmation—one member from Arsenal Hill and two from Mississippi presbyteries. The dissidents were encouraged in their attacks by the newly organized *Southern Presbyterian Journal.* Its editor, Henry B. Dendy, had graduated from Columbia in 1922 and had been nurtured in the spirit of Girardeau and McPheeters. He received strong support from Nelson Bell, M.D., a returned missionary from China and soon to be father-in-law of evangelist Billy Graham. Dendy's and Bell's concern, like Girardeau's, for a white Presbyterian orthodoxy was deeply entwined with a commitment to keep the South white and segregated.[40]

Carmichael, apparently offended by Robinson's attack and by the open animosities on the campus, resigned in 1938 and accepted a call to head the General Assembly's committee on religious education. The next year George Manford Gutzke was called to Carmichael's old position. Gutzke was a professor of Bible at Austin College in Texas and was a well-known and popular speaker at Bible conferences. He represented, however, a different theological and cultural tradition from that which had long marked Columbia. He had little interest in systematic theology, creeds, or issues before the church and society. What fascinated him was the personal experience of a Christian, particularly his own personal experience that was rooted in a Manitoba farm. There on the great Canadian prairie he had grown to manhood in the midst of an eastern European immigrant community. His stout, muscular body showed the evidences of a youth spent plowing the deep prairie sod, and his plain manners and plain speech reflected a matter-of-fact way of seeing the world. He had been a skeptic as a young man—his parents had evidently not been religious—but an old neighbor had shown him a better way, and he had had a powerful conversion experience, a story he would tell repeatedly for the rest of his life. In 1926 he married Sarah Bernstein. She had been born in Dorpat, Russia, the daughter of a prosperous Jew and a Moravian mother. Her father had converted to evangelical Christianity and had taken his family to Canada during the tumultuous days leading up to the First World War. So when Sarah Bernstein and Manford Gutzke married, they both brought into their marriage powerful conversion stories whose narratives blended and created the world in which they lived.[41]

The world of personal experience and conversion provided a pattern and formula for the way Manford Gutzke read the Bible, taught the Bible to seminarians, and preached the Bible to white southerners. Faith was a journey that followed Gutzke's own footsteps on the Canadian prairie—out of a life of skepticism and sin, across a wilderness of temptation, into the promised land of faith. He had almost no interest in biblical scholarship, or in commentaries others had written, much less in such classical treatments of texts as those by Augustine and Calvin. He knew little Greek and less Hebrew. If he knew of Thornwell or Adger or Girardeau or Woodrow, they played no role in his theology. He was largely indifferent to the church as an institution, the body of Christ, and he held no deep affection for or commitment to the Presbyterian Church U.S. In all these ways he represented an American evangelical and pietistic tradition that was largely anti-intellectual, ahistorical, and intensely focused on the individual experience of a believer.[42]

When he arrived his appointment was conditional—he would need to complete a Ph.D. he had begun at Teachers College, Columbia University. Fifteen years later he received the degree with a dissertation on Thomas Dewey's thought and its implications for Christian education. When published the dissertation was largely dismissed as a complete misunderstanding of Dewey. But perhaps ironically Gutzke's focus on his personal experience resonated deeply with an emerging therapeutic culture in American life with its distinction between a public and private self and its quest for psychic well-being. He brought all this to his work as a professor at Columbia Seminary. But he also brought an irenic spirit—at least during his early years as a professor—that allowed some space on the campus that was free from theological debate and controversy. He and Sarah Gutzke were to serve as parental figures for many students. They would have students regularly in their home, and she would serve tea in an eastern European style from a handsome silver samovar with jam in the cup. It seemed wonderful and exotic to seminarians from South Carolina and Alabama. Mrs. Gutzke started a clothes closet for students that became in time the "Clothes Closet" that provided good used clothes for students and their families and for missionaries home on furlough. And when a student was sick or a young student's wife became pregnant, she called physicians whom she knew and cleared the way for good medical care. So while Manford Gutzke stood in sharp contrast to the intellectual and cultural traditions of Columbia, he and Sarah Gutzke found an important place for themselves on the Columbia campus, and he drew to himself students who yearned for a pietistic and evangelical faith little troubled by the intellectual and social issues of the twentieth century.[43]

In the midst of fund-raising and dealing with Robinson and defenders of a remembered white Southern Presbyterian orthodoxy and social order, Richards continued to lead the seminary into broader worlds. He participated in the organization of the American Association of Theological Schools and oversaw the work that led to Columbia's accreditation by the association. He helped to organize the University Center of Georgia, which brought Columbia into a consortium with Emory, Agnes Scott, Georgia Tech, and the University of Georgia. He established on the campus a yearly Pastor's Institute and began an innovative program of internships for students. And he became deeply involved in the Federal Council of Churches, the ecumenical association of Protestant churches that was the precursor of the National Council of Churches. Richards was elected vice president of the council and shared its commitment to address contemporary social issues. No issue was more critical for Richards that the racism that permeated American culture.[44]

In 1940 Georgia gubernatorial candidate Eugene Talmadge was roaming the state spewing the most rabid and crude racism that the bitter old racist could muster. A month before the election, Richards, as the retiring moderator of Atlanta Presbytery, responded in a sermon before the presbytery. Entitled "Brothers in Black," the sermon rejected the racism and racist assumptions that lay at the heart of American society and pointed to the deep inequalities and sufferings of black Americans. For Columbia Seminary the sermon represented a powerful challenge to Girardeau's address in Charleston's Magnolia Cemetery. There Girardeau had provided a strategy for keeping the South white and blacks in their place through the maintenance of the "phraseology of the past." Richard's sermon before Atlanta Presbytery marked the most significant breach in Girardeau's wall, and through that breach a new phraseology of justice and Christian discipleship entered the seminary's life and began its slow but steady work on the Decatur campus.[45]

Richards took as his text God's question to Cain—"Where is . . . thy brother?" He told the presbytery that while the question addressed many areas of human life, he was going to direct the question to the issue of race—"not on a basis of self justification, but as the facts require us to answer it before the throne of God. 'Where is thy brother in black?'" He said that there was a special reason to give such a focus to the question: "We have seen the racial issue raised in our own section in forms which give cause for grave concern and for deepest shame." Politicians had been using race to further their own political ends without regard to the ultimate results of their action in human misery. Insulting and humiliating statements concerning blacks had been made even in the U.S. Senate. "We cannot estimate," he said, "how much has been done to aggravate prejudices and to increase evils which were already sore enough." Richards insisted he was not discussing politics, but was speaking because Christian principles and spiritual interests were at stake. "These actions of political leaders are but the natural outcome of a racial philosophy which, though contrary to all Christian principles, is all too commonly held by the man in the street and too little opposed by the man in the pew. The Church of Jesus Christ," he told the presbytery, "has not given leadership which her Faith demands of her in making this kind of philosophy impossible."[46]

Richards turned to statistics to show the deep injustices of the southern social order. Blacks were largely restricted to two low-paying occupations—two-thirds were farmers or domestic servants. And among the farmers, 75 percent were tenants. Those who did the same work as a white received much less pay. Blacks were denied jobs because they were not skilled laborers, but they were denied admission to training schools because it was said there were no place for them in skilled positions. "As in so many other areas of life," Richards said blacks confront "a vicious circle from which there seems to be almost no means of escape." The result was the poverty of the whole South, black and white.[47]

Richards pointed to specific areas of what he called "Negro life," where "brothers in black" had to face deeply oppressive conditions and attitudes. Their housing was wretched. "What wonder that health is poor!" he exclaimed. "What wonder that crime breeds!" Indeed, he said, looking at the miserable quarters in which they are forced to live it is not their failures that stand out but that so many manage to maintain self-respect and to live with a degree of decency. And who owns these wretched places—white "landlords who are often more concerned to secure high profits than to provide for the needs of other."[48]

What brothers in black need, Richards told the presbytery, was justice. He reminded them that a black man faced a much greater chance of conviction in court than a white man, and that the punishment "meted out for conviction in the one case is likely to be far heavier than in the other." And he said it is a fact that must be confessed with shame "that policeman in many of our Southern cities show little respect for the civil or human rights of Negro prisoners." And it was not just prisoners. "In one of our cities in a recent year," he said "a dozen Negroes were killed by officers not one of whom, so far is known, was officially reprimanded, much less tried." He noted that while lynching was apparently on the way out, even now "it is an event worthy of note if any year passes without a number of lynchings. We have seen," he reminded the presbytery, "the excesses of Nazis against the Jews and mark it down as evidence that an entire nation is degenerate and depraved, but somehow we forget to feel a like indignation when equally helpless individuals here at home are done to death."[49]

On and on he went in enumerating the injustices brothers in black suffer. The money the state spent on schools for blacks was a fraction of what was spent on white schools. The city of Atlanta had twenty parks for white children, and one park for the children of blacks, who made up a third of the population. Blacks were largely denied the right to vote. "If we are fearful that the Negro voter," he said, "would be an easy victim of demagogues, let us consider our own record carefully before casting stones." He then told his white presbytery that brothers in black were in need of kindliness and understanding. "How little," he said, "do we know of the constant humiliation and of the haunting fear which is visited upon this race." He pointed to Richard Wright's *Native Son* as a powerful story of racism's bitter fruits. Brothers in black, he warned, will reject Christianity "unless they see that white people really believe the faith which they profess."[50]

Richards told the presbytery that it was time to face the race issue. Ministers needed to end their silence and begin preaching on race relations, and the laity needed to be providing intelligent, courageous leadership in church and community on race. He closed the sermon by reminding the congregation of Christ's words: "If thou bring thy gift to the altar, and there rememberest that thy brother hath aught against thee; leave there thy gift before the altar and go thy way; first be reconciled to thy brother and then come and offer they gift." And then he asked, "Has he anything against us today or not, this brother in black?"[51]

The sermon caused a sensation. The *Atlanta Constitution* published excerpts, and the presbytery ordered that it be printed and placed in all the churches of the presbytery. The Southern Interracial Commission had it reprinted, and eventually some fifty thousand copies were distributed. Shortly afterward a black Pullman porter told Richards that he had read the sermon. "Everything you said was true," the porter said, "but it seems like nobody will take our part." And indeed many whites vigorously rejected what Richards said. At least one irate Presbyterian gathered all the copies that were to be distributed in his congregation and burned them. The flames, it was hoped, would help to keep the old walls standing and the old boundaries secure.[52]

13

Years of War and a Growing Prosperity

On Armistice Day, November 1940, McDowell Richards addressed the Atlanta Rotary Club. Much of the city's white leadership was there, and a somber atmosphere filled the room. During the previous three months, the German Luftwaffe had been furiously bombing British airfields and cities in the Battle of Britain; the Italians had invaded Egypt and Greece; Soviet armies had moved into Latvia, Estonia, and Lithuania; and the Japanese had occupied Indochina. Earlier in the year France, Belgium, the Netherlands, Denmark, and Norway had surrendered to German forces. And two weeks before Richards's address, the United States had begun drafting young men into military service.[1]

Richards began his address by remembering the "thrill of gladness" that had come twenty-two years earlier with the armistice and the end of the Great War of 1914–18. The armistice had brought the nation not only a sense of relief but also a feeling of hope for a better world. Today, said Richards, what confronted Americans was not the world of their 1918 dreams but a world locked in a conflict more awful than the last. Standing before the Rotarians as the armies of Hitler, Mussolini, and Hirohito continued their seemingly endless conquests, Richards acknowledged that Armistice Day had become for many the symbol of broken promises and blasted hopes. But Richards, remembering Columbia's illustrious son Woodrow Wilson, insisted that Wilson's ideals—a "war to end war" and a war "to make the world safe for democracy"—were noble ideals that had moved the American people to great sacrifices. "There are pages enough in our history," he told the Rotarians, "which are not glorious, but America has no reason to be ashamed of the motives which animated her people during those days of conflict." Rather what was shameful was America's folly and blindness after the war. "We dreamed we could live in isolation from other nations, and we have awakened too late from our dreaming." He wondered if history would have been different if America had joined the League of Nations. America, he told the Rotarians, "cannot escape a very large measure of responsibility for the disaster which has come. Truly we won the war, and lost the peace." The

American people consequently needed to celebrate Armistice Day 1940 "in humility and in penitence of spirit."[2]

Richards then turned to the future. From now on, he said, Armistice Day must become a symbol not of the past but of faith and of hope. Suffering, anguish of spirit, and a baptism of blood, he warned, may come to America as it had come to other nations. Perhaps remembering his years at Oxford and his travels across Europe, he confessed that America deserved its privileged position, its freedom from the horrors of war, no more than other nations. Still he dared to prophesy that in the end "tyranny and oppression will not prevail. Ours is a moral universe. The very stars in their courses fight against greed and falsehood, hatred, violence and inhumanity." Americans today, he insisted, have the duty to take up the torch that had fallen from the hands of those who died in the Great War of 1914–18—"It is the torch of democracy and of freedom; it is the torch of humanity and of brotherhood; it is the torch of justice and of ultimate peace." Thirteen months later the Japanese attacked Pearl Harbor, and the United States plunged into World War II.[3]

The U.S. entry into World War II presented the seminary with the challenge of understanding its role in the midst of such death and destruction. In a bulletin issued by the seminary, Richards declared that the seminary's primary allegiance was not to any earthly government but "to Him who is the Prince of Peace." Its purpose was to engage not in temporal warfare but in spiritual warfare. Its great end was to prepare "men to preach the Gospel with conviction and power." Yet in following the Prince of Peace, the seminary was rendering a vital service to its country. Richards believed that as the nation faced the terrible realities of war, people needed faithful preachers and pastors among them. The nation needed more than military and economic might—it needed spiritual and moral strength among its people. Such strength was the hope of the nation, and the ministry of the church was essential for the nurturing of such strength. At the same time, the ministry of the church needed to follow "the young men who have offered their lives in the defense of our liberty and our homes." They needed the hope and strength that comes through the Gospel. So Columbia, Richards said, had committed itself to help prepare chaplains for service in the military. Already many graduates had enlisted in their country's service.[4]

With such an understanding of Columbia's role in the midst of war, Richards faced some very practical challenges created by the war. The most daunting of these was student enrollment. The Selective Service Act required all men aged eighteen to sixty-five to register, and those eighteen to forty-five were eligible to be drafted for military service. Ministers of religion and divinity students were exempt as were those in several other categories. When the Selective Service issued orders that exempted collegiate candidates for the professions—including legal, medical, and ministerial—in order to ensure the professions after the war, a continuing enrollment of students at Columbia was possible.[5]

During the war years, students entered Columbia's first-year class at approximately the same rate they had entered during the years immediately preceding the war. To maintain such a level, however, the seminary found it had to admit some students who were poorly prepared for serious scholarly work and preparation for ministry. This was particularly true of students coming from Columbia Bible College, Bob Jones College, and Toccoa Falls Bible Institute—all centers of fundamentalism.[6]

The issue of accepting inadequately prepared students had been a concern during the hardest days of the Depression. The board had found it necessary to urge presbyteries to exercise more discretion in approving candidates who were not ready "to meet the requirements of our curriculum." And in facing the challenges of small enrollment during the Depression years, Richards had insisted that the seminary not accept ill-prepared students to keep up enrollment. The policy, he said, that would best serve the church was for the seminary to seek the very strongest candidates and give these few the very best education Columbia could provide. To accept ill-prepared students would not only be a drain on the finances of the seminary and the energy of the faculty. It would also be unfair to the well-prepared students who came to Columbia and to the church, which expected its ministers to have a significant level of theological learning and professional preparation. The most pressing question was whether or not to accept students who had only a Bible college degree. They lacked an adequate background to engage a theological curriculum with Greek and Hebrew requirements and with assumptions about a broad collegiate education. At issue as well was the narrow fundamentalism that was generally taught at Bible colleges and what that fundamentalism might mean to the dynamics of campus life and classroom work especially given fundamentalism's militant and divisive spirit.[7]

Throughout the 1930s the seminary was able to follow Richards's advice. Thus, for example, during the 1937–38 academic year the seminary had only fifty-one students. Most came from Davidson and Presbyterian College, from a variety of other liberal arts colleges, and from universities such as South Carolina, Georgia Tech, Duke, and Florida. There was one student from Columbia Bible College, one from Moody Bible Institute, and two from Bob Jones. But when the war came, the pressure was increased for the seminary to admit on a regular basis those with only a Bible college degree. Richards resisted the pressure and recommended that such students not be admitted. This position, however, was particularly difficult because some presbyteries were accepting such students as candidates for ministry and because Robert McQuilkin, founder and president of Columbia Bible College, was a clergy member of Congaree Presbytery. Raised and educated in the North, he had come South, established the Bible college in Columbia, and bought the old seminary property for the college. He associated himself with conservative white Presbyterians in South Carolina who remained in the old and strident traditions of Girardeau and McPheeters. To make matters more difficult, McQuilkin was recommending that ministerial students go to Columbia Seminary in order to study with William Childs Robinson. As a consequence, in spite of Richards's strong reservations, the door was opened wide for Bible college graduates. The student body in 1945 was the same size it had been in 1938—fifty-one. Only in 1945, as the war came to an end, more students (seven) were from Columbia Bible College than any other school. In addition there were two from Bob Jones and two from Toccoa Falls Bible Institute, and four were from Wheaton College, whose roots were in fundamentalism. To be sure, liberal arts colleges remained widely represented in the student body, with the largest number coming from Davidson (six), and thirteen of the fifty-one students were university graduates, with the largest number from Emory (three). Still with almost 30 percent of the student body coming from Bible colleges and Wheaton, with their intellectually protected environments, a fundamentalist spirit and outlook was having an obvious impact on the campus—especially as it reinforced the strident and embattled white Southern Presbyterian orthodoxy represented by Girardeau, McPheeters, and Robinson. Of course not all Bible college graduates were poor students or divisive voices on the campus, but during the next twenty-five years this opening of the door to fundamentalists was going to have serious consequences for the seminary and the white Southern Presbyterian Church.[8]

Immediately after Pearl Harbor, Columbia graduates began enlisting as chaplains in the military. By June 1942 thirty-two had enlisted—representing one-third of all white Southern Presbyterian chaplains—and others were following. Some were in places where fighting raged; others were in noncombat positions; all had the responsibility of being a pastor to those who were facing the terrors of war. Of the many experiences of Columbia graduates during the war, two were particularly notable.[9]

Wilson Plumer Mills, class of 1912, was a great-nephew of Leighton Wilson and had been named for him and for Columbia professor William Swan Plumer. A Rhodes Scholar he had gone to China shortly after his graduation from Columbia and was one of twenty-seven Western nationals in Nanjing when the Japanese captured the city. Before the city fell, he helped to set up the Nanjing Safety Zone for civilians and served as vice chairman and then acting chairman of the international committee that attempted to protect noncombatants. His letters and protests to the Japanese authorities helped to provide news to a stunned world of the atrocities committed by the Japanese. He wrote to his wife that since the Japanese came into the city "it has been hell." He told of the massacre of civilians and the massive rape and murder of Chinese women and children. After the war it was estimated that up to three hundred thousand Chinese had been slaughtered in Nanjing over a two-month period.[10]

Eugene Daniel had received, through the ROTC program, a commission in the Infantry Reserve when he had graduated from Georgia Tech in 1933. Following his graduation from Columbia, he had spent three years as a pastor in two small Georgia towns. He had entered the army as a chaplain five months before Pearl Harbor. In 1943 he went ashore with American and British troops at Algiers as a part of the North Africa campaign. For his actions immediately after the landing he was awarded the Silver Star Medal for gallantry in action. A few weeks later his battalion was surrounded by Germans. He was with several wounded Americans and two wounded Germans when the battalion was ordered to evacuate their mountain position during the night. Refusing to leave the severely wounded Germans in the dessert to die, he stayed behind with them and was captured by German troops. He spent the next twenty-seven months as a prisoner of war in Germany, where he served as chaplain to Allied prisoners in three

POW camps. Toward the end of the war, in spite of his own weakness, he kept many men going during the "March of Death" that took POWs westward away from advancing Soviet troops. He had with him a chalice and paten that he gave to Columbia after the war and that was used for decades in the seminary chapel until the memory of the community's history began to fade in a new century. For his service among the prisoners, he was awarded the Distinguished Service Cross. After the war he served with the War Relief Committee of the Presbyterian Church U.S., speaking and raising funds for the relief of war victims in Europe and Asia. Years later Richards noted that Daniel's supreme accolade came not from the military but scripture: "Blessed are the peacemakers, for they shall be called the children of God."[11]

While Columbia graduates labored in anxious congregations across the South and on distant battlefields, life on the seminary campus continued with many of its familiar routines. Now in the midst of the war, the routines seemed more privileged than ever. Professors gave lectures, counseled with students, and argued with one another in faculty meetings. Students read books, conjugated Greek verbs, struggled with Hebrew texts, took notes, visited in hospitals and prisons, taught classes at a nearby "Negro mission," and sat for exams. Classes met Tuesday through Saturday noon, after which many students left by train to preach in scattered congregations. Mondays were free to allow for travel back to the campus.[12]

Thursday nights were set aside for senior preaching. The entire student body and faculty gathered in the chapel, and two seniors delivered sermons that were intended to demonstrate that they had learned something during their time at seminary. An evaluation by the faculty, again before the entire student body, followed. The faculty believed that it had the responsibility to be honest and was not inclined to regard an undeserved compliment as "pastoral" or kind—an approach that encouraged considerable fear, trembling, and hard work. Years later the theologian John Leith wrote that he had never preached a better-prepared sermon than what he had preached "before the faculty and study body at Columbia Theological Seminary."[13]

The evaluations covered a wide variety of concerns connected with the preparation and delivery of the sermon—the exegesis of the biblical text, the theological assumptions of the sermon, the preacher's grammar and syntax, the title of the sermon, the illustrations, the structure of the sermon, and the wardrobe of the preacher. J. B. Green, who taught homiletics as well as systematic theology, led the evaluations. He could be blunt. He began one evaluation by declaring: "We had poor preaching tonight." When one student chose as his sermon title "The Double-Barreled Gospel," Green replied: "What a subject: the double-barreled gospel. Unfortunately, neither barrel was loaded." Richards later thought that in his own evaluations he had given too much attention to what the preacher wore—he had encouraged preachers to wear black ties and avoid brightly colored socks.[14]

One student wrote vivid letters home about life on the campus during these years. Writing to his family in Sumter County, Alabama, Will Ormond described his classmates and their activities, his classes, his experiences as a student preacher in eastern

North Carolina during the summer of 1942, and his senior sermon evaluation. In a first-year speech class, students had tell how to do something so that they could practice using gestures—Ormond, no doubt using well-planned movements—told how to make molasses, and one of his classmates who had worked in a funeral home told how to embalm a body. Ormond wrote his family about the social life on the campus—a Christmas party that he speculated was going to be a "tremendous affair since it is going to cost each of us a total of $1.50"; parties in the dormitory where they would be served "coffee, potato chips, nuts, chocolate mints, cheese, pickles, olives, cracker jacks," and sometime "ice cream with coca-cola"; and trips to Agnes Scott for parties with the "girls." Ormond described to his family one of his Agnes Scott adventures. He was invited to a party but ended up sitting next to his roommate. "I told him," Ormond wrote, "it was something to walk a mile to a party just to play games with your roommate." He did meet "a nice looking girl from Camden who was glad to meet someone else from Alabama. We were partners for a while, but we played something called 'Shoo Fly,' and I got shooed away from her."[15]

Ormond spent a summer in North Carolina preaching in four country churches. He called himself an "upstart preacher" who had to out-scream crying babies. He wrote home about one Sunday: "Yesterday I preached three times, made one talk, went to five services . . . sang nineteen hymns, led seventeen prayers, read Scripture six times and traveled about forty miles." And he noted that for the first time, the babies did not cry. When he returned to the campus, he had to decide who would be his roommate for the year—two had asked him. One was John Leith, whom Ormond described as "tall, thin, blond, not at all good looking, high pitched voice, the smartest boy in school, studies a lot, is very much in love, a pacifist, somewhat of a liberal." But he "can have a good time, certainly is not overly pious, and likes a joke." The other possibility was Bob Stamper: "probably the best-looking boy in school, well built, dark hair, laughing eyes, very contagious grin, horse laugh, a good mind but doesn't use it a great deal to study with, a former boxer and undertaker's assistant, gave up an appointment to West Point to study for the ministry, very popular with everybody, spends money when he has it, carries on a lot of foolishness, can say and do almost anything and get by with it." In the years ahead Leith would become a prominent theologian and churchman, and Stamper would become the director for development and oversee major capital campaigns for Columbia Seminary. All three would remain friends long after seminary.[16]

Ormond and another close friend, Davison Philips, preached their senior sermons the same night. They both dressed alike—blue serge suits, black ties with white stripes, white handkerchiefs in lapel pockets, and black socks with a red stripe. Classmates teased them and said they looked so much alike they should preach the same sermon. Ormond felt especially nervous because his sermon the previous year had been "an utter flop." But the faculty gave him good marks for his senior sermon, and President Richards "seemed pleased but even more surprised." This experience, he wrote his family, "was encouraging since I haven't been feeling so very encouraged lately. Behind in my work, not sure that I'm learning much, not seeming to get anywhere. So this makes me think that I have a little chance yet to do a little something." After graduation he was to serve small-town churches in Alabama, where he would gain a reputation as a great preacher. He was also to become known as a courageous preacher for justice during the civil rights movement. In 1966, after receiving a Ph.D. from the University of Glasgow, he became the much-loved professor of biblical exposition at Columbia.[17]

Shortly after he and Ormond preached their senior sermons, Davison Philips became a navy chaplain. A little over a year later, he went ashore in Guam to be with the marines who had taken the blood-soaked island. He was to spend nineteen months on the island. Before he left for his service in the navy, Philips married Kay Wright, a young Agnes Scott student. When she graduated the next year, Richards arranged for her and another chaplain's wife to move into one of the faculty apartments in Simons-Law dormitory. They were the first women students to live on the campus. Thirty-one years later Kay and Davison Philips would return to the campus to live in the president's home.[18]

When the war ended, the United States entered a period of remarkable growth in almost every sector of American life. Between 1945 and 1960 the economy grew in constant dollars from 215 billion to 500 billion; the population grew with a "baby boom"; home ownership and suburbs grew; schools and colleges grew; and organizational bureaucracies grew. And the churches grew as well—in fifteen years the percentage of the U.S. population affiliated with a church grew from 49 percent to 69 percent—as a revival of religion that had begun during the war gained momentum after the war. It was not surprising then that seminary enrollments grew. At Columbia the number of students enrolled in the degree program leading to ordination grew from 51 in 1945 to 210 in 1960. This of course meant that the faculty had to expand—from six full-time professors and four visiting instructors in 1945 to sixteen professors and eleven instructors or visiting professors in 1960. To accommodate such growth new buildings were needed. In 1945 the campus consisted of Campbell Hall, Simons-Law dormitory, and five faculty homes. By 1960 the campus had five buildings and ten faculty homes. The new buildings included the handsome John Bulow Campbell Library, two apartment buildings in "the Village" for married students with children, and ten new faculty homes. In the central part of the campus, a wooded area was cleared, graded, and seeded to create a long-envisioned athletic field, and tennis courts were built behind Simons-Law. The seminary donated five acres on the eastern edge of the campus to the Columbia Presbyterian Church. This congregation, organized in the seminary chapel in 1948, soon constructed—with the help of a $100,000 gift from the seminary—a large sanctuary and education building. In addition the Women of the Church of the controlling synods raised funds for the construction of Mission Haven, with eighteen apartments on the western edge of the campus. The vision for a home for missionary families on furlough had begun when the plans had been made to move the seminary to Decatur. Fanny Jordan Bryan—who with her husband, T. S. Bryan had been a major contributor to the seminary and who had a scholarship named for her—had begun in the 1920s to raise the necessary funds for a missionary home. But the Great Depression and war had delayed the construction of Mission Haven until after the war.[19]

The enlargement of the campus reflected not only a growing enrollment but also changes in the age and marital status of students. For generations most students had been young, single men. Moreover they had been almost forbidden to marry while at seminary. But the war with its returning veterans funded by the GI Bill meant a sudden flood of married students. By 1947 68 percent of the student body was married. "I am very doubtful," Richards told the board, "that we shall ever go back to the situation which prevailed prior to the war." With the booming economy and young women earning incomes, especially through teaching in rapidly expanding school systems, a pattern seemed to be set for the future. Among the students were a few women enrolled in a master of arts in biblical education. Those women who lived on the campus were housed in the fourth section of Simons-Law.[20]

Life on the campus during these boom years continued many of the extracurricular activities that had long been a part of the seminary—only in a more expansive manner. During the 1930s Mary Grace Cartledge, wife of Professor Cartledge, organized a popular men's quartet. The young men sang in churches around the city and traveled to various churches and presbyteries in the supporting synods. By 1950s the quartet had been replaced by a large choir, under the direction of Hubert Taylor, professor of public speech and music, and it too spent many a weekend traveling across the South. Seminary basketball teams continued to participate in various citywide leagues, occasionally doing rather well when a former collegiate basketball player was enrolled at Columbia. A Wives Club was organized after the pattern of the Presbyterian Women of the Church. Its purpose was to provide "Bible knowledge, spiritual discernment and social graces for each member through a program of fellowship."[21]

The expansion of the student body meant that the old white Southern Presbyterian network of closely linked families was loosening. Baptists, especially from the Atlanta area, were beginning to attend Columbia in greater numbers as did an occasional Episcopalian or Pentecostal. Most noteworthy of those from outside the South were midwesterners, often graduates of Wheaton, who came to study with Robinson. Still white Southern Presbyterians were the overwhelming majority, and there were many with deep connections with Columbia's history—there was a John Leighton Warren, a Seabrook from Johns Island, and a Mallard from Liberty County. Charles Cousar had a long list of ancestors who had attended Columbia and had served the seminary in various capacities. These and others were a part of a dense "cousin system" that was often linked to summers spent together in Montreat. The experience, however, of being together for an intense three years of theological education built new relationships among students that transcended the old family networks. As a way to encourage the continuation of these relationships and to nurture the intellectual and spiritual life of graduates, Columbia developed a highly successful Ministers Week built around the Smyth Lectures.[22]

The Smyth Lectures had been established to provide lectures that were of "practical and general usefulness . . . to the Presbyterian Church." They had long been an important event at the seminary when, in the years immediately after the war, they became a part of Ministers Week, which also included other lecturers, worship services led by an outstanding preacher, and the annual alumni meeting. In 1954, for example, Ministers Week extended from Monday morning through Saturday morning. There were no regular classes during the week, and all students were required to attend the events of the week. The Smyth Lecturer was Alan Richardson, an internationally known biblical scholar from the University of Nottingham, England, who lectured every night of the week and on Saturday morning. In the afternoons the French scholar Claude A. F. Schaeffer delivered lectures under the title "Developments in the Field of Archaeology." H. D. Wendland of the University of Kiel lectured each morning in a series entitled "The Church in the Mass Production Society of the Twentieth Century." With 110 ministers participating in the week together with some 170 students and fourteen faculty members plus spouses, the week was an important occasion for nurturing a sense of Columbia as a community that included not only those presently on the campus but also graduates and a broad constituency. And the lecturers, not incidentally, indicated that the seminary was slowing moving once again toward a serious engagement with a larger theological world. Such movement was encouraged by visiting professors later in that academic year. In the fall Joachim Wach of the University of Chicago and lecturer for the American Council of Learned Societies delivered a series of lectures on the history of religion. And in the spring term, Oscar Cullman, distinguished New Testament scholar from the University of Basel, Switzerland, taught a seminar for students and another for ministers from outside the Atlanta area. In addition to these lecturers, Richards adopted a policy of inviting ministers from various backgrounds to preach in chapel on Wednesdays. So students, who were required to attend chapel, heard among others Methodist bishop Arthur Moore; Episcopal bishop R. R. Claiborne; R. O. McClain of Atlanta's First Baptist Church; John R. Brokhoff, pastor of Atlanta's Lutheran Church of the Redeemer; and perhaps most surprising, the distinguished educator and leader in the African American community, President Benjamin Mayes of Morehouse College.[23]

The seminary's move to engage a broader theological world could be seen not only in the guest lecturers and preachers brought to the campus, but also in the expansion of the faculty and in its evolving curriculum. In 1946 J. B. Green retired, and Felix Gear was elected dean of instruction and professor of systematic theology. For the next twenty-five years Gear would serve as dean, as Richards's most important colleague on the faculty, and as a strong voice opposing Robinson's narrow understanding of the Reformed tradition and his combative and clamorous churchmanship. The two men differed not only in theology but also in their backgrounds, in their ways of dealing with colleagues and conflict, in their engagement with twentieth-century thought, and in their responses to issues of social justice in a segregated South.[24]

Robinson's background was marked by relative affluence, pride of place, and the traditions of Girardeau in the Arsenal Hill church in Columbia, South Carolina. He and Mrs. Robinson largely kept themselves aloof from other faculty families. His attempt in the 1930s to reprimand the seminary board and his public attack on his neighbor, the conservative J. G. Green, had alienated many. Even Gutzke, who shared some of Robinson's concerns, noted that they were never personal friends. The social distance between the

Gutzkes and the Robinsons was not insignificant, especially as the Robinsons had deep memories of an elite Old South world. Yet even the genial Evelyn Richards, with all the elite connections of the Richards family, found the Robinsons difficult and eccentric, and the Robinsons spent their years on the campus largely outside the ties of affection and colleagueship that marked much of the seminary's life.[25]

In contrast to Robinson's background, Gear grew up in a little farming community in the Tygart valley of West Virginia. Tobacco was the cash crop in the valley, and it provided enough income for the people to live simple and modest lives. A Presbyterian church, established in the valley in the 1820s, was the center of community life, and a village school was strong enough to prepare Gear for the nearby Presbyterian college Davis and Elkins. In 1923 he left his valley home for Richmond, Virginia, and Union Seminary. Years later he told his students how the faculty at Union had helped him with the manners and etiquette of urban Presbyterians and how faculty kindness had been an important gift for him—a kindness he later shared with many of his own students. He received a Th.M. from Princeton Seminary in 1928, did graduate study at Harvard, and received his Ph.D. from the University of Edinburgh. He served as pastor of the First Presbyterian Church in Columbus, Mississippi, taught and was vice president at Southwestern at Memphis (now Rhodes College), and was at the time of his call to Columbia the highly successful pastor of the large and affluent Second Presbyterian, Memphis. Gear's modest early years and his long experience as a pastor helped to shape the tone and contours of his life as a dean and professor and his relationship with his colleagues at the seminary. Perhaps most revealing of the theological differences between him and Robinson were their dissertation topics. Robinson's was entitled "Columbia Theological Seminary and the Southern Presbyterian Church, 1831–1931," and he thought of himself as working in historical theology. His dissertation was largely an appreciative interpretation of the polity and theology that had been taught at Columbia. That was the world in which he lived and from which he made occasional excursions to do battle against twentieth-century thought. Gear's dissertation explored "The Influence of William James in the Fields of Philosophy and Psychology." He had clearly traveled far from his valley home and had entered deeply into some of the most influential arenas of twentieth-century thought.[26]

Joining the faculty at the same time as Gear was Cecil Thompson, who came to fill the new chair of evangelism and field supervision. A Columbia graduate he had married Mary Gillespie, the daughter of President Richard Gillespie. Thompson had served several churches in Georgia and had demonstrated an ability to organize effective evangelism programs that had led to the establishment of new congregations. He was a person little troubled by theology or theological disputes and was rather preoccupied with "how to" questions—how to encourage an evangelistic and missionary spirit in a congregation, how to do personal evangelism, or how to address the specific needs of a country church. For these reasons he was a popular speaker in Montreat, at other seminaries, and before various presbyteries.[27]

Hubert Taylor joined the faculty in 1947 as instructor of public speech and music. The much-admired choir director of Atlanta's Central Presbyterian, he brought not only new vitality to worship and music on the campus but also deep interests in elocution, in the ancient discipline of rhetoric, and the modern wonders of television. A midwesterner by background, for over twenty-five years he faced the daunting task of teaching diction to young men who arrived on the campus with accents that arose from lowcountry marshes and Mississippi piney woods. The young men were not always receptive to Taylor's admonitions, thinking their accents were the norms by which all other accents—including Taylor's—were to be judged. But he persevered, and by working with Atlanta's Protestant Radio and Television Center he helped them go beyond the startling revelation of hearing themselves on radio and seeing themselves on TV.[28]

Five important faculty appointments were made during the first three years of the 1950s—Richard Gillespie III was elected professor of homiletics; Harold Prince was appointed head librarian; Thomas McDill was called as professor of practical theology and pastoral counseling; Sidney Anderson came as instructor in the industrial church; and James Gailey was elected associate professor of Old Testament language, literature, and exegesis. Prince was the first full-time professional librarian in the seminary's history. McDill's appointment signaled major shifts in theological education as the role of psychology and therapy became increasingly influential in American life. Gillespie and Gailey quickly found themselves in the midst of controversies not unrelated to the anxieties and suspicions of the Cold War. And Anderson's position seemed dangerous to those who were alarmed by the threat of socialism creeping into the mill villages of the South.[29]

Columbia's decisive move away from the propositional theology of Girardeau, McPheeters, and Robinson found clear expression in the inaugural addresses of Gear and McDill. Gear's inaugural was delivered in September 1947 and was illumined by the light of Hiroshima and the glow from the furnaces of Auschwitz. He spoke as Soviet tyranny was settling over eastern Europe and as the armies of Mao were establishing communist control over China. In such a context he addressed the question of "Theology and the Muddle of Modern Man."[30]

Gear began by insisting that ideas have consequences, and he located himself within the Realist movement in American theology. That movement, most famously associated with Reinhold Niebuhr, repudiated liberalism's confident assumptions about humanity's altruistic propensities and the inevitable progress of the human race. And one idea, he asserted, had brought modern civilization to its present crisis and another great idea was pointing the way out of the crisis. The great idea that had produced the present crisis was that "humanity is the central thing in the universe, it is the final reality; beyond humanity there is nothing." While communism was the most logical development of this idea, Gear focused on secularism as a central characteristic of modern life—life organized apart from God as if God did not exist. Most of us, he told his audience, do not realize how deeply a secular worldview had permeated every aspect of contemporary life. Drawing on Dostoevsky, W. H. Auden, T. S. Elliott, Emil Brunner, and Josiah Royce, he described secularization and the emptiness and bondage that finally flow from it. "Our age," he declared, "has abandoned the idea of a common humanity subject to the will of God; the notion that there is a single thread such as the moral law, or the Christian principle of love, running through and cutting across, the diversities of race, cultures, or languages, which bind mankind together in our time." The task of theology in the present crisis was consequently to supplant the idea that humanity is the central thing in the universe, the final reality, with the idea of the centrality of God. And calling on Calvin, Gear insisted that "the God to whom we give *central* place must not be the God of a rationalistic deism or naturalistic theism but God as he has revealed Himself to us in and through Jesus Christ."[31]

What then must theology do to answer its contemporary calling? Gear named six specific tasks. First, it must provide some "great over-all purpose which will bring meaning back into living at a time when it seems empty and futile." He quoted W. H. Auden to show the "boredom and ennui of the empty heart of our century." Theology needed to invite contemporary people to see and understand their life and work as a part of the eternal purposes of God. Anything less would fail to satisfy the hungry and restless heart of the modern world.[32]

Second, an understanding of God as the central reality of the universe would act to curb humanity's endless quest for power and almost unquenchable thirst for exploitation of nature and people. Gear described Descartes's belief that the use of scientific principles of knowledge would "render ourselves the lords and possessors of nature." Calvin, Gear said, also believed that an understanding of the natural world provided for humanity tremendous possibilities, but those possibilities were not an end in themselves but must be "used for the glory of God and according to just and right principles." The difference, Gear said, "between a Christian and a pagan way of life, between a sense of responsibility to God for all, and a feeling of lordship and possession over all in the physical world" was ultimately the "difference between life and death for the human race."[33]

Third, to restore God to a central place in the life of humanity would cure humans of their "temporal myopia." "Modern man is not cosmopolitan but a narrow provincial in the universe." Gear insisted that it is "only as the Church surveys human conditions under the aspect of eternity that it has any right to offer judgment, counsel, or service midst the wretchedness and folly of man. In short, man can no more live in time alone than he can live on bread alone."[34]

Fourth, he insisted that there was schism in the contemporary human soul that theology must address. "Our century has not only cracked the atom, it has split the soul of him who cracked the atom." To say "man is made in the image of God means among other things that in the deepest recesses of his heart he needs God for the fulfillment of his being."[35]

Fifth, by putting God at the center of life, humanity would "know that freedom which is the basis and guarantee of all other freedoms." Against the background of the crushing tyrannies of the twentieth century, Gear insisted that freedom in the religious realm radiated into other realms of life. Thinking no doubt of American fundamentalists, he pointed to Calvin, who fought so vigorously against the "'intolerable quest for certainty' in religious life," and he pointed to the "joyous note of Luther's great saying 'that the Christian is the most free man of all, and Lord of all.'" And he reminded his audience of what was said of John Knox: "Fearing God he feared no man." Looking at the shadow of tyranny over so much of Europe, Gear said that the struggle for religious freedom, the freedom that comes from God, was central to the struggles for other freedoms.[36]

Finally Gear told his audience that making God central in life was the only real security for humanity. Quoting Paul Tillich, he said that at the end of the First World War there had been a quest for peace. But at the end of the Second World War and the beginning of the atomic era, "we are frantically seeking to survive." Then turning to Calvin again, he quoted the Reformer: "the only haven of safety is in the mercy of God, as manifested in Christ, in whom every part of our salvation is complete."[37]

Gear's inaugural clearly looked beyond the little world that had preoccupied Columbia since James Woodrow. Gear wanted to engage fully the crisis of the world illumined by Hiroshima and Auschwitz as that world entered the fearful and uncertain years of the Cold War. The task of theology, Gear was convinced, involved more than an occasion excursion out of the world of a remembered white Southern Presbyterian orthodoxy and southern way of life. "We cannot," he told his Columbia audience, "substitute shallow thinking for the theological thought demanded in these days." He had clearly placed himself within the circle of theologians who were identified as neo-orthodox and who pointed to the limits of human nature and to the transcendence of God who had revealed Himself in Jesus Christ.[38]

In 1955 Tom McDill delivered his inaugural address. His was one of four delivered that year, by McDill, Gailey, Gillespie, and Taylor. All were free of the defensive mood of earlier times, and all pointed to new areas of scholarship—McDill to contemporary psychology and pastoral theology; Gailey to the rich range of twentieth-century biblical scholarship; Gillespie to new biblical scholarship as a tool for preaching; and Taylor to the place, character, and role of art in Christian life. McDill's address stands out for the ways it brought the Reformed tradition into conversation with powerful currents in contemporary American culture.[39]

A popular interest in psychology and mental health had been growing throughout the twentieth century, but the Second World War gave a massive boost to such interest. The army had employed over fifteen hundred psychologists to study the enemy, test and treat troops, and provide insights to military leaders. After the war corporations had begun to employ large numbers of "industrial psychologists" and to utilize psychological testing to determine the suitability of persons for certain work. And in growing numbers individuals had begun to seek psychological counsel as books on popular psychology—such as Dale Carnegie's *How to Stop Worrying and Start Living*—began appearing on best-seller lists. At the same time white-collar workers were quickly becoming the largest proportion of the working population. What they needed were "people skills"—how to "read" the signals received from associates and how to get along and promote their own popularity. Given such a cultural context, it was no wonder that pastoral psychology was becoming a critical part of theological education. Stewart Hiltner, McDill's mentor when McDill was a graduate student at the University of Chicago, insisted that for contemporary Americans to have any interest in theology and the church they needed to see that psychological language could also be theological language. So it was not surprising that McDill sought in his inaugural—"Calvinism and the Cure of Souls"—to demonstrate the deep ways Calvin's thought anticipated and resonated with many of the insights of contemporary psychology, especially the work of the American psychologists Carl Rogers and Rollo May.[40]

McDill had grown up in the conservative Associate Reformed Presbyterian Church and had studied Calvin carefully—not the Calvin as interpreted by scholastic theologians such as Turretin, Hodge, and Girardeau, but Calvin himself and not just the Calvin of the *Institutes* but also the Calvin discovered in Calvin's commentaries and his letters of pastoral counsel. Moreover McDill had served as a chaplain in the Pacific theater during some of the bloodiest battles of the war. He knew the terrors and harsh realities of the battlefield and had found that troops wanted more that theological propositions and formulas or well-meaning advice. They had wanted above all to be listened to in order to gain insight about what they were experiencing and about any meaning that could be discerned about and in their experience. So against this background, he turned in his inaugural to Calvin and to the ways in which Calvin's thought provided theological foundations for the pastoral care for those struggling with the anxieties and pain of life.[41]

McDill began by exploring Calvin's understanding of the person. He quoted Calvin's famous statement that "true and substantial wisdom principally consists of two parts, the knowledge of God and the knowledge of ourselves" and Calvin's affirmation that the knowledge of ourselves "is not only an incitement to seek after God, but likewise a considerable assistance toward finding him." The quest for self-understanding, so essential to modern psychology and in the work of pastoral care, was not alien to Calvin but was a beginning point in his theology.[42]

Second, McDill pointed to the ways Calvin provided an understanding of the process of pastoral care. Calvin, he said, made a radical departure from his day by placing primary emphasis on sin rather than on sins. Through the Fall humans were radically alienated from God and one another. Thus, said McDill, "being in a condition of sin, the eruptive behavior referred to as sins can be understood as resulting from his internal condition." Human intractability was to be found in the realm of affection and will, in the inner disposition rather than in some outward act. If a man, for example, was having difficulty in his marriage, McDill noted he did not need a dissertation on the biblical understanding of marriage. He needed to look into himself first, for until his internal condition was corrected, he would continue to have external problems in relationships. External behavior was of course important, but if a pastor concentrated only on external behavior and proceeds with logical arguments and presentations, the pastor's help would be of the most superficial kind. At the same time, given the profound alienations of the human heart, help—salvation—must come from outside as a free gift, as amazing grace. The communication of this was an essential part of the pastoral task. But a person must accept such a free gift, and the ability to accept was itself a gift of God, so as Calvin famously argued, that leads to the inescapable and always mysterious paradox of predestination and free will. The acceptance of this paradox, said McDill, was essential for effective pastoral care. He quoted Carl Rogers on the ways that psychotherapists had to confront the "living paradox" between freedom and determinism. "The fully functioning person . . . not only experiences, but utilizes, the most absolute freedom when he spontaneously, freely, and voluntarily chooses and wills that which is absolutely determined."[43]

Finally McDill explored the ways Calvin provided guidance for the daily work of the pastor. He noted that Calvin with some justification was regarded as harsh and cold. But he insisted that Calvin had been greatly misrepresented and confused with a later and cold Calvinism that for too long had been preached in the churches. Rather than such Calvinism—which McDill undoubtedly knew had been a part of Columbia's tradition—McDill called pastors to look at Calvin's letters and to the pastoral spirit they revealed. There, McDill said, one learns the secret of the cure of souls—the pastor must seek by the power of God and for the glory of God "to be like Christ, forgiving as he has been forgiven, accepting as he has been accepted, loving as he has been loved."[44]

The seminary's move toward engaging a broader world did not go unnoticed. The old white Southern Presbyterian world, with its carefully drawn boundaries marked out by the "phraseology of the past," remained dear to many who were committed to maintaining the walls so carefully erected by Girardeau and patched by his followers. They were joined in these efforts by a number of fundamentalist northerners who, having been largely marginalized by the Presbyterian churches in the North, turned their eyes toward the South as a field white and ready for the harvest. Because Columbia had been regarded as the primary source and bastion of the old white Southern Presbyterian orthodoxies, it became a major arena for a fierce struggle over the character and direction of the denomination. Kennedy Smartt, who transferred to Columbia from Westminster Seminary in Philadelphia in anticipation of serving a white Southern Presbyterian congregation, wrote later that "Westminster had so indoctrinated me that when I transferred to Columbia one of my avowed purposes was to convince the faculty there of the Reformed faith."[45]

Gear and McDill, with their broad erudition and their deep familiarity with Calvin and contemporary thought, were apparently too formidable for students to try to convince them "of the Reformed faith" or for a direct attack. So the attacks focused on Richard Gillespie and later Jim Gailey because their teaching areas made them more vulnerable to the charge that they did not believe in the Bible as an inspired, inerrant text. Of the two Gillespie was subjected to the most sustained attacks.[46]

Richard Gillespie, the son of President Gillespie, graduated from Columbia in 1933 and received an M.A. from Emory in 1938 and a Th.D. from Union Richmond in 1948. He had served as pastor of several churches in Georgia and was candidate secretary for the church's Board of Foreign Missions when Columbia called him as professor of homiletics in 1950. He immediately encountered opposition from some conservative students when, during his first evaluation of a senior sermon, he spoke of "Second Isaiah" as though, a student complained, it were an "accepted fact" that the book of Isaiah had more than one author. Jack Scott and Bill Iverson, graduates of Davidson, along with Tom Young, graduate of King, hurried to Richards to report on what Gillespie had said. He heard their concerns and responded that Gillespie had said nothing that was inconsistent with the standards of the church or those of the seminary. A short time later Gillespie invited his former professor at Union, E. T. Thompson, to deliver a lecture entitled "The Bible for Today." Thompson, who was regarded as a leading liberal in the church on social issues, outraged Scott and others and they sent a copy of his address to the *Southern Presbyterian Journal.* The journal published it along with a highly critical analysis by Nelson Bell, the physician father-in-law of Billy Graham, and a strong advocate for a segregated South.[47]

The next spring a small coterie of students, now led by Scott and Morton Smith (a graduate of the University of Michigan), met with representatives of "the Continuing Committee." The committee was an unofficial group of ministers and laymen who were committed to the orthodoxies of white Southern Presbyterianism. The students met with them, told them of their alarm about what was being taught by Gillespie and other Columbia faculty, and learned that the laymen were particularly concerned to learn if the Bible was being taught in a way that was "courting socialism in our church" especially among "laboring people."[48]

Encouraged by the Continuing Committee to "do whatever we felt led of the Lord to do," the students felt "led of the Lord" to organize. Those who had met with the Continuing Committee gathered thirty-nine students at the nearby Ingleside Presbyterian Church, where Harold Borchert, a student from Holland, Michigan, was the supply pastor. Borchert, Jack Scott, and Morton Smith had written—together with Matthew McGowan (a graduate of Davidson) and Walter Crowe (a graduate of Alabama State Teachers College)—a statement that the gathered students signed. It declared that Gillespie's "teachings concerning the Bible are clearly and definitely out of accord with the standards of our Church and of our Seminary."[49]

Gillespie, learning of the gathering, invited Borchert, Scott, Smith, and Carroll Stegall (a graduate of Maryville College) to his home on Kirk Road to discuss their concerns. They arrived, were given refreshments by Mrs. Gillespie, and proceeded to inform their professor that they had come with a set of questions for him—they wanted to take a kind of deposition on his views. Did he "consider the early chapters of Genesis to be history, as it is recorded?" Did he "consider the Pentateuch to be a unit and Deuteronomy specifically to have been written by Moses?" Did he believe that "Samson actually performed the feats he is recorded to have performed in the book of the Judges?" On they went—who "was the first monotheist in the Bible?" Did he believe that "all that is recorded in the Bible is given by direct revelation and immediate inspiration of God?" Did he believe "in the verbal inerrancy of the original autography?" There were thirteen questions in all, and all echoed the language, theological assumptions, and inquisitorial spirit of American fundamentalism.

And not incidentally their inquisitorial spirit also reflected the suspicion and tactics then being used by Senator Joseph McCarthy with his unsubstantiated accusations and attacks on the character of political opponents.[50]

Gillespie responded by asking if the questions were for personal use by them as students or if they intended to distribute his answers. They responded that if they found his answers unsatisfactory then they intended to make a complaint to Richards and the seminary board of directors. Gillespie then refused to respond to the questions and said that the students had come as "a self-appointed judicial body" and that he was accountable only to duly constituted authorities. The students were soon in the president's office reporting on their interrogation of their professor. They gave Richards a copy of the statement and later gave him notes taken by Morton Smith in Gillespie's class. Richards defended Gillespie's right not to answer the questions and later wrote that the professor had the right of a full hearing by properly constituted authorities—the board, Gillespie's presbytery, and the seminary's supporting synods.[51]

Other students in the meantime were rallying to Gillespie's defense and in support of the seminary faculty. Led by Ben Collins (a graduate of Presbyterian College) and Mac Hart (a graduate of Davidson College) over eighty students signed a statement of support. Cartledge, who knew only too well how fundamentalists could seek to defame even conservatives, condemned in class the attacks on Gillespie. Richards called a meeting of the student body and said that "there can be real disagreement among us in the Presbyterian Church without our losing our love for one another." Since the seminary had those who held the various views existing in the church, and since "we must get along with one another in the Church," then those at Columbia should be able to get along together. He said that he personally believed in the total "infallibility of Scripture as a guide to faith and to morals," which he understood to be the teaching of the church's standards, but that he "did not think this necessarily meant that every individual word of Scripture was to be taken literally as it stands." Richards was clearly following a Columbia tradition of trying to find a middle way. He wanted to exemplify an irenic spirit and find enough space for Christians, in particular white Southern Presbyterians, to live together in peace. But he knew that decisions sometimes had to be made, that finally one had to stand on one side or the other, so he said he was not asking anyone to remain at Columbia "if they felt fundamentally out of accord with its general teaching." Those who opposed Gillespie responded that when they wrote their statement they only desired that "Columbia be purified from the uncleanness of doctrine and corruption of instruction which was then in it." And they began meeting in the woods for prayer.[52]

In April 1953 eleven students, apparently led by Jack Scott, sent a letter to the board of directors together with a "Short History" of the controversy. They attached excerpts from Morton Smith's notes taken in Gillespie's class, the questions submitted to Gillespie and their reasons for asking each question, and a statement on the implications of Richards's views of "inspiration acceptable at Columbia Seminary." The board, led by J. R. McCain, president of Agnes Scott, and P. D. Miller, pastor of Atlanta's Druid Hills Presbyterian Church, responded vigorously with a statement of its own:

The Board notes the following:

A. That this paper attacks the theological views of one Professor by name, two others who are not named, questions the competence of the entire Faculty, and the soundness of the Board of Directors.

B. That this paper attacks the President of the Seminary by criticizing his conduct in office, and even by raising questions as to his soundness in theological views.

C. That this paper attacks the Board of Directors on at least two grounds: First, on its alleged lack of faithfulness in discharge of its duties at the Seminary; and second, on the alleged unsoundness of the theological views of its members.

D. That the paper attacks the Seminary itself on the ground of unsoundness of theology, though no such question has been raised by any court of the Church, and ordination has never been refused to a single one of its graduates.

The Board makes the following declarations:

A. That the charges made by the students were fully considered last year by the Executive Committee in detail and found to be without satisfactory support in facts and that the Board of Directors so declared at its meeting a year ago.

B. That the Board of Directors, the officers and Faculty stand unhesitatingly on Chapter One of the Confession of Faith as to the inspiration of the Scriptures.

3. In view of the serious nature of the charges made, the Board of Directors hereby makes the following statements regarding the young men who made them:

A. The students who have elected to attend Columbia Theological Seminary have no proper function in examining the orthodoxy of the Ministers of the Church who serve on the Faculty, each one of whom is in good standing in his own Presbytery, and each one of whom has been dutifully approved by the Board of Directors.

B. That, while students are encouraged to bring to the President all problems that concern themselves of the welfare of the Seminary, it is beyond the bounds of propriety to stir up criticisms in the student body or to give the impression to outside persons that this conservative seminary is teaching theological errors.

C. That with all kindness, but with complete firmness, these young men be advised that, if they are to stay here, they will understand that they are to receive instruction and not undertake to become teachers of older men.[53]

The charges against the seminary were soon taken up by some conservative laymen. They had been alarmed by efforts to reunite the white Southern Presbyterian church with the Presbyterian Church USA located largely in the North. The effort had failed in 1954–55, and many saw behind the failure not only charges of a theologically liberal North but also a commitment to keep the South white and free of "Yankee" influence. What made the atmosphere in the church particularly tense was the General

Assembly's vote in 1954 condemning racial segregation on theological grounds—a vote that came immediately after the Supreme Court's *Brown v. Board of Education* ruling that the "separate but equal" doctrine that had allowed for segregated schools was unconstitutional.[54]

Within this context ten laymen asked in May 1956 to meet with the seminary's board of directors. Led by Kenneth Keys, a real estate developer in Miami, they sent a paper to the board rehearsing the charges students had made earlier and adding to them new charges. Gailey was charged with using a liberal textbook. Gear was charged as saying that students needed a "more dynamic approach" to theology than Hodge, Dabney, and Warfield. He was, the laymen reported, devoting considerable class time to social and political issues and he was putting neo-orthodox theologians more frequently on his reading lists than "contemporary reformed theologians." John Leith, who was a visiting professor while Robinson was on sabbatical, was charged as having replaced in the apologetics class a text used by Robinson (by Cornelius Van Till of Westminster Seminary) with the text *Christian Apologetics* by Smyth Lecturer Alan Richardson. The laymen claimed that suspicions about the orthodoxy of Columbia's faculty was causing a "substantial amount of financial support" to be withheld from the seminary. And they suggested that board adopt the business practice of periodic audits—only the audits were to be on the orthodoxy of Richards and the seminary's professors. Like the students in Gillespie's living room, they came with a set of questions to be used in the interrogations.[55]

After some debate over allowing the group to speak to the board, the board agreed to hear the laymen's report. After hearing from Keys and others, the board elected by secret ballot a committee with representatives from each synod and directed the committee to investigate and report back to the board. Once again the committee and board gave a vigorous response. They upheld the orthodoxy of the faculty and called attention to the confidence the church had in Richards by recently electing him moderator of the General Assembly. They noted that the laymen had relied exclusively "on the memories and notebooks of students." Every person who has ever been a teacher, they said, "has been amazed at times at the difference between what was actually said in the class room and what appeared in the notes and examination papers of students." In regard to textbooks, they admitted that board members were not authorities in the field of theological literature. "We know, however, that these professors possess much more competence and discernment in the matter than the students who sit under them." Indeed they reported that the laymen on the investigating committee "expressed surprise at a group of fellow-Elders presuming to know what particular books should and should not be taught in a graduate school of Theology." As for the complaining students and their earlier statement to the board, they had already been unanimously rebuked by the board for insubordination. "Our impression of that paper was that a few students who came to be taught had presumed to set themselves up as teachers." The board noted the large increase in the financial assets of the seminary and that the synods, rather than withholding funds, had voted for a large capital campaign. And they said emphatically that "no further investigations of this type will be conducted except at the direction of the supporting Synods." The *Presbyterian Outlook* gave a full account of the charges and the board's response and observed that Columbia appeared to be the first institution in the church "subjected to the crusading zeal of an ultra-conservative faction in the church." The charges, it said, had been answered by the board "in a forthright defense."[56]

Despite the inquisitorial spirit of some students in the 1950s, others pursued their studies and went on to faithful ministries in a wide variety of places. The classes of 1954 and 1958 provide good examples. Among those who graduated in 1954 were many who were pastors of congregations spread across the South—Trent Howell in Georgia, Julian (Buddy) Craig in South Carolina, and Mac Hart in Arkansas and Mississippi to name only three among many who preached the Gospel, visited the sick and dying, married young couples, baptized babies, counseled the perplexed and distraught, went to summer camps and conferences with young people, served faithfully in the work of their presbyteries, and sometimes suffered the assaults of fundamentalists and racists. John Somerville went as a missionary to Korea and to teach at Hannam University. Doug Hix received his Ph.D. from Duke and taught at King College and then St. Andrews College, where he later served as its president. In the 1980s he would be the central player in developing Columbia's advanced degree programs. Neely McCarter, after receiving his Ph.D. from Yale, returned to teach at Columbia and went to Union in Richmond, where he was academic dean, and then to the Pacific School of Religion, where he served as president and a leader in American theological education. From the class of 1958 there were also many who went out as local pastors—some like Pinckney (Buddy) Ennis and Harry Beverly to large urban congregations, and some like Herb Bailey and Ladson Brealey to small towns where they served as pastors not only to their congregations but also to whole communities. Some such as Bob Myers and Herschel Allen served as chaplains in hospitals. Others such as Charles Cousar and Tom Stallworth were much-loved professors and deans. George Telford, as a pastor, as a denominational executive, and later as a seminary administration, was an outspoken theological voice and activist for justice across a broad spectrum of social issues. Pete Peterson served as a missionary in Taiwan, Ghana, and Nigeria, established the Christmas International House program for international students studying in the United States, and was the founder and longtime executive of Villa International, adjacent to the Centers for Disease Control in Atlanta. There he and his wife, Martha Jane Peterson (CTS class of 1987), welcomed persons of all faiths from all over the world, primarily international researchers at the CDC. By 2016 over twenty-five thousand residents from 147 countries had stayed at villa—a remarkable testimony to the Petersons' original vision of Christian hospitality.[57]

While Columbia was sending such students out into the ministry of the church, the seminary itself was continuing to prosper in spite of the attacks by a coterie of students and laymen. John Bulow Campbell had died in 1941, but the legacy of his extraordinary generosity continued through the work of the Campbell Foundation. When plans were made for the new library, the foundation promised $100,000 if another $250,000 could be raised. Through the efforts of a loyal constituency the funds were raised, and the handsome John Bulow Campbell Library was built in the collegiate Gothic style.[58]

In May 1953 faculty and students formed a long line stretching from the second floor of Campbell Hall down the steps, across an open space, and into the new library. In one day they moved forty thousand volumes onto the waiting shelves of the new library named after Columbia's most important benefactor. But the day was not only a celebration of a wonderful new building—it was also a reminder that the library's collection was small and that for many lean years Columbia had been moving away from one of the great theological libraries in the country to a library of the most modest and mediocre size. Indeed the seminary had struggled even to maintain its once proud Smyth collection. During the 1930s Natalie Talmadge, wife of a local minister, and Mary Grace Cartledge, wife of Professor Cartledge, had volunteered their time to oversee the library and keep it in order. When Harold Prince was called as librarian in 1951, he was the first full-time professional to oversee the operations of the library and to begin the slow process of once again building a great library.[59]

In the early 1950s a group of women, led by Professor Green's wife, Lilian Clinkscales Green, organized to provide direct support of the seminary. They called themselves the Friends of the Seminary but later changed their name to Columbia Friendship Circle. They held annual meetings on the campus during which they heard reports from Richards, agreed on future projects for the seminary, and met and ate with students and faculty. For the next two decades the Friendship Circle grew rapidly in importance in the seminary's life, making large annual contributions to the seminary for specific projects. It helped women across the controlling synods to identify with the seminary, to think of it as "our seminary," and to support it in numerous ways including encouraging bequests from members. In 2006, for example, Lucille Moore, a former leader of the Friendship Circle, quietly left Columbia a bequest of $2.3 million. Her husband, Walter, who participated in the bequest, had often traveled with her from their Walhalla, South Carolina, home to attend the Friendship Circle meetings.[60]

The first major project of the Friendship Circle was to help raise funds for the Peter Marshall Chair of Homiletics. Marshall, a Scotsman, had graduated from Columbia in 1931 and had become one of the nation's best-known preachers. Elected chaplain of the U.S. Senate, he led prayers before that body that had evoked widespread admiration and use. A biography, *A Man Called Peter,* written by his widow, Catherine Marshall, and the 1955 film adaptation of the book—which was nominated for an Oscar for cinematography—made Marshall the most widely known graduate in Columbia's history. Catherine Marshall's collection of his sermons and prayers in *Mister Jones Meet the Master* was also a best seller. It was not surprising then that the Friendship Circle honored Marshall in one of its first projects with gifts large and small from women who had come to have great affection for Columbia. Nor was it surprising that for years afterward bright-eyed students applied to Columbia having watched on late-night television Richard Todd play the handsome Peter Marshall and Jean Peters play the beautiful

Agnes Scott graduate Catherine Marshall. In 2006 the seminary board was surprised to learn that a former parishioner of Peter Marshall's, Caroline "Lina" Matthews, had left a $5 million endowment to Columbia because she remembered his ministry as a young seminarian.[61]

Simons-Law dormitory at the time of the move, 1927.

John Bulow Campbell, Presbyterian elder, philanthropist, and generous leader of the seminary board.

Richard Gillespie II, seminary president who led the seminary's move to Decatur.

Class of 1928. Class president, J. McDowell Richards, top center.

Faculty, early 1950s. Seated left to right: Thompson, McDill, Richards, Frank Brown, Gear, Robinson. Standing left to right: Gutzke, Cartledge, Gailey, Prince, Taylor, Gillespie III.

President Richards and Friendship Circle leaders, mid-1950s.

Faculty, 1960.

Generations of students and faculty played tennis on courts behind Simons-Law.

Davison Philips toasts Virginia Harrison at her retirement. Plato Henderson looks on from the side as had African Americans before him. 1962.

Claude Clopton, chef, friend, and counselor to many students.

J. McDowell Richards, wise and courageous president, 1931–70.

President C. Benton Kline Jr. and Chris Kline, ca. 1972.

14

The Turbulent 1960s

The 1960s was, like the 1920s, a distinct decade of great dreams and great disillusionments. The decade lodged itself in the nation's memory, and its years provided long-lasting and competing images of the United States and of the character of the American experiment. Throughout these years the religious life of the people, no less than other areas of the nation's life, was shifting and groaning under the stress of long-building pressures. Theological seminaries were not exempt from this shifting and groaning, and Columbia Theological Seminary was no exception.

The decade began with moral earnestness and much confidence in the course of human history. John F. Kennedy, in one of the great presidential inaugurals, declared that a torch had been passed to a new generation of Americans "unwilling to witness or permit the slow undoing of those human rights to which this nation has always been committed, and to which we are committed today at home and around the world." Martin Luther King Jr. declared from the steps of the Lincoln Memorial, "I have a dream," and across the nation many joined hands and sang "We shall overcome" as the civil rights movement called for a moral revolution in the nation's heart and an end to laws that had long oppressed black Americans. The nation seemed committed to what Arthur Schlesinger Jr. called the "vital center" of liberal democracy between communism on the left and fascism on the right. A pragmatic, realistic, and hopeful mood dominated these early years of the decade—especially after the passing of the Cuban missile crisis. Beneath this mood was a booming economy that was providing for a baby boomer generation unprecedented levels of wealth and discretionary income.[1]

Much of the confidence of the period flowed from a technological worldview that had taken deep root in American culture, especially the assumption that life is a set of problems, not an unfathomable mystery. Such a worldview insisted that the problems of human life—whatever they are: food supply, poverty, transportation, sex, health care, environmental degradation—could be solved through the application of technology and appropriate techniques. Know-how, not know-why, was the essential area of knowledge. This confident mood with its underlying assumptions about the value of efficiency and standardization resonated with powerful streams in American religious life and found expression in such popular books as Harvey Cox's *Secular City*, which celebrated technological revolutions and the activity of God in the secular as well as the religious realms of life.[2]

The high point of this cultural mood came in the middle of the decade as the confidence helped to fuel much of Lyndon Johnson's Great Society legislation. The legislation, enacted over several years, included the Civil Rights Act, the Voting Rights Act, the expansion of Social Security, the introduction of Medicare and Medicaid, Head Start, the Elementary and Secondary Education Act, and a host of other acts intended to protect the environment, end grinding poverty, develop the nation's transportation system, and safeguard the nation's food supply.[3]

But while this astonishing legislative record was being achieved the war in Vietnam was growing in intensity and violence; an awareness was spreading of the great contradictions between American ideals and American realities; and a deep suspicion of traditional institutions—including the church—was embedding itself in the culture of a baby boomer generation. The civil rights movement, focused largely in the South, began to fade as Black Power and black protests emerged in urban areas of the North and West to challenge a systemic racism that permeated the nation's life. So the eloquence and hopeful calls of Kennedy and King were not the sound at the end of the decade but rather the cry from exploding inner cities, "Burn, baby, burn," and the chants of Vietnam protesters, "Hell no, we won't go!"[4]

The religious life of the nation experienced its own particular expression of these larger transformations. Radical new theologies emerged to challenge confessional commitments that had long nurtured Christian communities. Some of the theologies were intent on "demythologizing" the Bible. Others emphasized with Cox the necessity of a secular interpretation of the Bible. And, most startling, some affirmed Nietzsche's announcement about "the death of God." At the same time sociologists were analyzing congregational life and the institutional structures of the American church and declaring them not only obsolete but also impediments to both genuine faith and social action. Congregational life, Peter Berger declared, was but *The Noise of Solemn Assemblies*, and Gibson Winters pointed toward *The Suburban Captivity of the Church* with its busy routines and abandonment of inner cities. More disturbing to many church people was the appearance of a "new morality" that called for less legalistic ways to guide moral action and that advocated a situational ethic. A sexual revolution was breaking over the nation at the very time the "pill" allowed women to have some of the same sexual freedom that men had long possessed. Liberation movements—including women's liberation and gay rights—began finding a historical moment and the cultural space in which to break free from ancient restraints as they asserted rights long suppressed and new ways of understanding human life.[5]

There was, of course, strong reaction both inside and outside the churches to all these challenges. Conservative people and institutions sought to resist the challenges to traditional cultural and religious patterns and to affirm beliefs and practices that had provided guidance and deep comfort to generations of many Americans. But even among conservatives one could see old orthodoxies being eroded as a consumer society increasingly demanded religious theater rather than religious teaching and promoted entertainment as the heart of religious experience. Certainly by the end of the decade the old Protestant establishment—in all its various theological manifestations—was in great disarray.[6]

Columbia Theological Seminary entered this turbulent decade with a carefully articulated vision of an anticipated future and with plans for meeting the challenges of what was anticipated. Throughout the 1950s the seminary had been led by a strong board of directors. William Gardiner, pastor of Atlanta's First Presbyterian, had served as chairman of the board during the early years of the decade and had been followed by P. D. Miller, pastor of Atlanta's Druid Hills church. With them on the board were a number of influential pastors: Stuart Oglesby of Atlanta's Central Church; E. L. Hill from Athens, Georgia; Edward Lilly and George Telford from South Carolina; Sam Burney Hay from Alabama; John Thomas and U. S. Gordon from Florida; and Dwyn Mounger and Van Arnold from Mississippi. Wealthy and influential laymen on the board had developed deep admiration for Richards and were committed to the work of the seminary. Among them were William Sibley and Herbert Smith, textiles executives from South Carolina, and three highly influential Atlanta laymen—Harllee Branch Jr., president of Georgia Power, then CEO of its parent the Southern Company, and member of the board of General Electric and other large national corporations; Lane Young, prominent Atlanta banker and longtime chairman of the seminary's investment committee; and J. Ross McCain, president emeritus of Agnes Scott College and highly regarded Atlanta leader.[7]

In 1958 the board, after much discussion and with the strong encouragement of Richards, appointed a panel to peer into the future and make recommendations for the future direction and development of the seminary. Charles King, pastor of Houston's First Presbyterian Church, agreed to serve as the panel's chairman. Other members were O. C. Carmichael, former chancellor of Vanderbilt University and executive with the Ford Foundation; Dean E. G. Homrighausen of Princeton Seminary; R. T. L. Liston, president of King College, Bristol, Tennessee; and Joseph R. Sizoo, head of the Department of Religion at George Washington University. J. Ross McCain represented the seminary board on the panel.[8]

The panel, after collecting information from other theological seminaries and divinity schools around the country and reviewing carefully Columbia's recent history, made its report to the board and the controlling synods. It noted the population growth in the Southeast and the region's increasing economic strength. It reported that church membership in the controlling synods during the last ten years had increased by 47 percent and that Atlanta Presbytery had become the largest presbytery in the denomination. To meet the challenges presented by such growth, it concluded that Columbia ought to be the best equipped and financed seminary in the South. It therefore proposed that the seminary raise a staggering $10 million as quickly as possible with a $5 million campaign to begin immediately.[9]

The panel anticipated that the student body would continue to grow, reaching four hundred by 1970. It encouraged presbyteries to require candidates to undergo testing by "Christian psychiatrists" to be sure that a candidate had "no handicap that would make it impossible for him to make an effective minister." To strengthen the academic life of the seminary, the panel recommended that only under extraordinary circumstances should the seminary admit students without a college degree. It called for an honors program for exceptionally able students and said adequate financial aid should be available for students so that they could concentrate on their studies and not be preoccupied by supplying vacant churches. And the panel recommended that the seminary explore a doctoral program in connection with Emory University. Clearly the panel had an image of ministry deeply rooted in Columbia's history and a Reformed tradition. Columbia graduates were to possess a broadly based education and a thorough grounding in theological disciplines. There was an expectation—a hope at least—that graduates would be cultured men of faith who honored learning and could represent an old established order. But equally clear was an image of ministry rooted in a twentieth-century U.S. therapeutic culture and a technological society. The panel spoke of psychological testing rather than piety as a requirement for ministerial candidates, and its emphasis was on effective ministry more than faithful ministry. The minister as a professional man—a man with specialized higher education, credentialed and competent in defined areas—had clearly become a dominant model, and the task of the seminary was to provide the church with such professionals.[10]

A larger student body required, the panel said, six new faculty members, more administrative staff, and expanded library holdings. The campus itself needed to be greatly enlarged. A student center and a new dormitory for married students without children needed to be built immediately. And there was a great need for more apartments for married students with children. Far too many students with families, the panel said, were having to live off the campus and were thus missing the benefits of the seminary community so important for their future ministries. New faculty homes were of course needed, but so was a freestanding chapel that could accommodate the whole community. And there was also a need for what had been envisioned when the seminary moved to Decatur—a gymnasium with a swimming pool so that students and their families could get the exercise they needed to maintain a healthy and vigorous life. In all this the panel's report represented not only their vision of the future but also the ways the postwar years shaped their understanding of the seminary's present situation and informed their anticipation of the challenges and possibilities that the coming decade was going to bring.[11]

To a remarkable extent Richards and the board accomplished during the coming years the specific tasks the panel set before them. Under the leadership of Robert Stamper, vice president for development, and Paul Patrick, field representative, the synods responded enthusiastically and completed a successful $5 million campaign by the early years of the 1960s, and plans were made in 1965 for another campaign to raise another $5 million. Half of the raised funds went into the endowment, and the other half was used to expand the campus. A student center—designed after buildings Richards had known during his years at Oxford—was completed in the collegiate Gothic style. It contained a beautiful

Tull dining hall (named for a benefactor from Central Church, Atlanta), two smaller dining halls, formal and informal parlors on the first floor, faculty offices and classrooms on the second floor, and a few faculty offices on the third. A new dormitory, Florida Hall, was also built in the collegiate Gothic style with red brick, Indiana limestone, and slate for the roof. The first three floors contained forty suits intended for married students without children. The fourth floor had rooms for single students and a communal bath. In the meantime the women of the Columbia Friendship Circle raised money for the construction of a new Friendship apartment building in the Village to accommodate twelve families. Three new faculty homes were built, and five homes were purchased on the east side of Kirk Road for faculty. This rapid expansion of the campus was complete—except for one of the new faculty homes—by 1964.[12]

The new campus buildings were in deep harmony with the old, and they intentionally conveyed a sense of being linked to long traditions of scholarship and piety and to an established social class. Yet the enlarged campus with its handsome new buildings and comfortable faculty homes also embodied the confidence and prosperity of what would come to be called the Camelot years of the 1960s. So the campus itself, its buildings and its landscape, continued to communicate a powerful image of Columbia Theological Seminary. In a subtle and unobtrusive manner, the campus spoke about the character of Columbia—it told a story about the ways white Southern Presbyterians understood themselves in the midst of a booming Atlanta, and it taught a theological lesson about the nature of the church and its ministry. Here at this place, on this campus, the church was no collection of random individual Christians who had had some religious or evangelical experience but a Presbyterian community deeply linked to a specific place and a specific memory with a specific—if often conflicted—understanding of ministry rooted in the Reformed tradition.[13]

The message conveyed by the campus was soon to be challenged by the turmoil of the late 1960s and by the cultural and demographic changes that were to roll through the coming decades. Yet always this turmoil and these changes had to contend with the power of the buildings and the landscape to convey meaning. Whatever new challenges arose, they had to engage the social and theological worlds behind the physical campus. Could alternative understandings of the church and its ministry—liberationist or evangelical, therapeutic or utilitarian—thrive on such a campus? And if they began to thrive on such a campus would the thriving signal a jarring and difficult-to-sustain contradiction between, on the one hand, what the campus itself said and, on the other hand, what was being said on the campus—by administrators, faculty, and students, by curriculum and campus life—about the church and its ministry? Or could some harmony be found, some middle way be established, that would reconcile the message of the campus and its history with alternative understandings of the church and its ministry?

The power of the campus to convey meaning and a historic understanding of church and ministry was to be reinforced in coming decades by an amazing increase in the seminary's endowment. That growing wealth was to signal the seminary's deep connection to an economic and social class that composed important elements of white Southern Presbyterianism and that helped to shape much of the ethos of the campus. Yet ironically that growing wealth, contributed by many Presbyterians over many years, was in the future to pose deep threats to the seminary's relationship to the very Presbyterian Church that had given birth to Columbia and that had sustained and loved it over many generations. In the coming decades an accumulating wealth was to create the possibility for Columbia to loosen its sense of being a seminary of the Presbyterian Church, owned and controlled by the synods, whose primary mission was to serve the Presbyterian Church and through it the larger church and world. Wealth and an economic independence from the church's synods and presbyteries were to invite the possibility of amnesia on Columbia's campus and the creation of a seminary culture marked by the deep homelessness of modernity. So the handsome campus and a growing endowment were to provide an arena in which powerful and competing impulses were to contend with one another. In the coming decades there was to be a growing struggle over ecclesiology, over an understanding of the nature and character of the church, and therefore over the nature and character of Columbia Seminary. And beneath much of this struggle surged an increasingly fractured and individualistic society held together by consumption and by the elevation of choice and self-expression as fundamental values of a consumer culture. But in the 1960s the challenges of wealth were still decades ahead for the seminary.

Richards and the board turned with great vigor to the hiring of new faculty during the closing years of the 1950s and throughout the 1960s. Wade Huie was called from a pastorate in Macon to be the new Peter Marshall Professor of Homiletics. A graduate of Emory and Columbia with a Ph.D. from the University of Edinburgh, Huie had been a highly successful pastor and had become a popular preacher on college campuses. He brought with him his wife, Vee, and two young sons—soon to be four—and the seminary purchased a fine home on Kirk Road for the family. But he had to leave behind a larger salary than what the seminary could offer, and Richards told him he could do what other professors with families were having to do to make ends meet—preach regularly in congregations near and far. It was, of course, not a bad thing for a professor of homiletics to be preaching regularly in different church settings, but the financial necessity of it pointed to the continuing meager salaries the seminary was able to provide in the 1960s—the lowest of all the Presbyterian seminaries—and to the limitations such a necessity put on the scholarly work of professors. Such arrangements testified to another story hidden behind the expansion of the campus and the growth of the seminary—an annual budget that reflected a still small endowment and an institutional ethos of great frugality that was to last for at least another two decades.[14]

Shirley Guthrie arrived on the campus for the fall term 1958. He came from graduate study under the great Reformed theologian Karl Barth and a short pastorate in Texas to be the associate professor of systematic theology. William Childs Robinson was enthusiastic about Guthrie's appointment, but Guthrie's close colleague was to be Gear. Together they were to teach and embody a Reform tradition broader than Robinson's. Indeed Guthrie had almost no interest in the work of Thornwell and Girardeau or other "Southern Presbyterian Worthies." He was rather to focused his energies on the great European theologians who had struggled with the crisis of faith in the nineteenth and twentieth centuries and on the questions twentieth-century Americans had about Christian faith and life.[15]

The year after Guthrie's appointment, Paul Fuhrmann was elected professor of church history. A native of Switzerland, Fuhrmann brought a Continental—especially French—interpretation of Calvin and the Reformation. He was to challenge a Scholastic understanding of Calvin, so popular among the followers of Girardeau, that emphasized belief in certain doctrinal propositions like the Virgin Birth. Rather Fuhrmann emphasized the role of the heart, of a subjective element, in Calvin's thought and wrote about Calvin's deep engagement with the social and political issues of his day.[16]

An eccentric man given to terrible bouts of depression, Fuhrmann was astonished by the provincialism and lack of intellectual curiosity of some Columbia students. He responded by creating and telling stories about a fictitious Columbia student whom he called Butchy Chucky. Fuhrmann told how Butchy Chucky thought church history began the year his pastor was born. He told about Butchy Chucky's going to the grocery store in Decatur and how he took his church history notes with him and used them to wrap the fish he bought. And Butchy Chucky, with such an attitude toward history, was sure that the Bible had fallen straight from heaven and had landed on the steeple of the Independent Presbyterian Church in Savannah. Fuhrmann said Butchy Chucky "instead of building bridges toward his fellow—man and humanity," builds "a series of walls around himself as (false) security." The walls, he said, include ignorance, fear, misanthropy, preoccupation with pet ideas, and paranoia. Most students delighted in the stories, but some were not amused. One student began regularly to harass the eccentric professor in class until another student, in a long-remembered incident, forcefully put an end to the harassment. Campus stories consequently swirled not only around Butchy Chucky with his carefully constructed walls, but also around Butchy Chucky's creator. This meant that for years to come when graduates gathered, they were to tell stories of Butchy Chucky and of a professor many remembered with affection.[17]

Ludwig DeWitz also brought a Continental background to the Columbia faculty when he was elected professor of Old Testament language, literature, and exegesis. A German, he had been adopted as an infant and brought up in a Christian home. When the Nazi's required students to produce documents to prove their "Arian" race, he learned not only of his adoption but also that his birthmother was Jewish. He suffered degradations imposed by the Nazi—including wearing the star of David and the abandonment of friends—before Christian friends cleared the way for him to go to Britain. His parents were able to join him later. He eventually completed a divinity degree at the University of London, was ordained by the Waldensians in Italy, served as a missionary to Jews in Baltimore, and received a Ph.D. at Johns Hopkins under the great scholar of the ancient Near East W. F. Albright. A brilliant linguist DeWitz could preach with ease in six languages and converse in several others. After he came to Columbia, he often taught a variety of ancient Semitic languages to graduate students from Emory. He was to be greatly loved by Columbia students, and Richards later noted that his genuine warmth and piety opened the door for many conservative students to engage modern biblical scholarship.

If Professor DeWitz, with all that he had been through, did not find such scholarship a threat to the faith, then courage could be found to explore its claims.[18]

Like Fuhrmann, DeWitz was surprised by the provincialism of many Columbia students. One way he responded was to introduce them to opera and through opera to a wider world. Every Tuesday night for years, groups of students—some of whom had long loved opera, many of whom who knew little of it—gathered at his home to hear an informal lecture on Mozart or Verdi, on Puccini or Strauss or even Wagner and to listen to a recording of some soaring aria or stirring chorus. Afterward DeWitz—a bachelor until after his retirement—served tea and cake, and on occasion, when pressed, he told of his years in Germany and his experiences as a German Jew. As he grew older, he was to move ever more deeply into his Jewish identity even as he continued to confess and exhibit a vibrant Christian faith. Jewish friends became closer friends as they shared a mutual respect and sense of a shared history. Certainly among Columbia students and faculty, he was greatly loved.[19]

DeWitz's closest colleague on the faculty was Ronald Wallace, who had been a visiting professor in the early 1960s and had been elected professor of biblical theology in 1965. He was a Scottish pastor, and he and his wife, Mary Torrance, a serious theologian herself, moved into a faculty suite in Simons-Law and there welcomed a generation of students. He arrived on the campus with the reputation of being a theological conservative, and his appointment was regarded by some as a way to calm conservative fears for the conservative cause at Columbia. But Wallace was far from a conservative on the model of Girardeau, McPheeters, and Robertson. He was, to be sure, a biblical preacher and a theologian who had immersed himself in a study of Calvin, but he shared a widespread Scottish egalitarianism and socialist commitments in politics and economics. Moreover he was closely connected through his brothers-in-law, Thomas and James Torrance, with a Scottish version of neo-orthodoxy. So while his love for the Bible and admiration for Calvin drew conservative students to him, he seemed to them an enigma who did not fit white Southern Presbyterian categories of liberal and conservative. And to those students who thought of themselves as progressive, he also seemed a puzzle because he resisted the promises of a therapeutic culture, questioned the efficacy of psychological testing, and insisted that the inner person not only was sacred but was also finally a mystery.[20]

While Fuhrmann, DeWitz, and Wallace helped to move Columbia beyond the old preoccupations that had flowed from Girardeau's defense of the white South and its orthodoxies, young faculty with deep roots in white Southern Presbyterianism were to be key faculty leaders during the next several decades. Charles Cousar joined Huie and Guthrie in long and important service to the seminary. Cousar, a graduate of Davidson, Columbia, and the University of St. Andrews, Scotland, was called to teach New Testament in 1960. He came from a long line of Southern Presbyterian ministers and was a member of a dense network of South Carolina families. He soon gained a reputation as a skilled and much admired professor and New Testament scholar who demanded much but who was always kind and fair. And the faculty soon learned that he was a good and genial colleague who was committed to Columbia and its mission as a seminary of the Presbyterian Church. During the coming years, the administration and the faculty were to turn to him for leadership, and those who supported Columbia throughout the church were to regard him as an embodiment of the best of the seminary's traditions and its engagement with the modern world. A fourth colleague, closely associated with these three, was Neely McCarter. A Columbia graduate with a Ph.D. from Yale, he had served as a campus pastor in Florida before coming to Columbia to teach Christian education in 1961. While he would stay at Columbia for only six years before leaving for a position at Union Seminary in Virginia, he had an important impact on the campus and the shape of a new curriculum in 1965. He was to serve as dean of the faculty at Union in Virginia and later as president of the Pacific School of Theology in Berkley, California. Another young faculty member and close friend to these four was Harry Beverly, who came in 1963 to teach homiletics. A 1958 Columbia graduate, he had received his Ph.D. from the University of Basel and had a strong interest in the ways literature—especially novels—could inform strong preaching. He stayed on the faculty for several years as a popular professor before going on to a number of influential pastorates.[21]

Richards and the board also called two older men to the faculty during the early years of the decade. Darby Fulton had graduated from Columbia in 1915 and had spent eight years as a missionary in Japan and was for over three decades the executive secretary for the church's Board of Foreign Missions. When he was elected professor of missions in 1962, he brought years of experience with the foreign mission movement and deep links to families long associated with Columbia. He joined with Robinson in representing the hoarse and fading voice of Girardeau on the campus and in the church.[22]

Dean G. McKee, elected professor of biblical exposition in 1961, was to play a more influential role in Columbia's history than Fulton. A midwesterner, he had served for years as the popular and successful president of Biblical Seminary in New York. He consequently came to Columbia with strong conservative credentials, but he had none of the contentious spirit of the Girardeau-McPheeters-Robinson tradition. Richards later said that McKee taught with "distinction and charm." What he also did was to quickly overshadow Manford Gutzke as a teacher of English Bible. In contrast to Gutzke, whose lectures swirled around Gutzke's own personal experiences, McKee required students to explore carefully the literary structure of the Biblical books or epistles being studied. Moreover, again in contrast to Gutzke, McKee had a great interest in history and archaeology, and he utilized slides from his wide travels to illustrate the terrain of ancient Israel or the ways the ruins of Jericho illumined its violent history or how archaeological research provided insight into the social character of the Greek cities visited by the Apostle Paul.[23]

During the last half of the decade more professors were called to meet the demands of a growing student body. In 1966 Will Ormond came from graduate study in Glasgow to become the much-loved professor of biblical exposition; Theron Nease was called to teach pastoral care and counseling; Milton Riviere was called to take Neely McCarter's position in Christian education; and Don Wardlaw joined Wade Huie in homiletics. While their primary contributions to Columbia were to come in the next decade, their arrival meant that when classes began in the fall of 1967, Columbia had twenty-one full-time faculty members. In addition there were three visiting professors and eight visiting instructors. This expanded faculty was to maintain its size, with some periods of growth and some of retrenchment, during the next five decades no matter the fluctuating size of the student body.[24]

The nonfaculty administration also grew during the 1960s. At the beginning of the decade it included Bob Stamper, vice president for development; Virginia Harrison, the indomitable treasurer and manager of many things; Mrs. J. Holmes Smith, the longtime dietitian and hostess, who knew how to put the fear of the Lord in students; and five secretaries, most of whom worked in the development office and all of whom were married women. By 1967 three Columbia graduates were in new administrative offices: Steve Bacon was serving as assistant to the president; Jim Richardson was director of admissions; and Harold Wright was superintendent of buildings and grounds. And by 1967 the number of women serving as administrative staff had grown to ten, double what it had been in 1960. Among them were some who would give years of service to the seminary: Betty Cason, Emily Wood, Barbara Cheney, and Mildred Berry. Perhaps most revealing was the allocation of secretarial help to faculty—Berry was to provide help for all the faculty except the two professors of pastoral care. They had their own secretary, Vi Pilcher, who was responsible for managing their counseling schedules and overseeing the rapidly accumulating files of psychological tests required of all students since 1960. Her assignment was a clear indication of the ways the values and practices of a therapeutic culture had become an increasingly important part of the structures, prevailing tone, and characteristic spirit of the seminary.[25]

A new senior administrative position—dean of students—was created in 1961 to handle the needs of a growing student body and financial aid budget and an expanding program of field work. Sidney Anderson, who had joined the faculty in 1952 as instructor in the industrial church, was called to the new dean's position and promoted to professor in the industrial church. Later in the decade, after Virginia Harrison retired and her portrait was hung in the president's office, he was made treasurer, a position he was to occupy with distinction for over twenty years. He brought with him a memory of lean times in the seminary's history, and his frugal ways were to serve the seminary well until Columbia began to enter its period of growing prosperity. Over time he perfected an ability to alarm the faculty during its meetings by predicting various financial calamities if belts were not tightened and spending held in check.[26]

Hal Lyon followed Anderson as dean of students. He had entered Columbia as a student after a successful career as an airline executive, and after graduation he had served a small-town church in West Virginia. He consequently brought to the dean's office not only business acumen and organizational skills but also a genuine pastor's heart. He was to be popular with students both as a dean and as an instructor in church history—a passion of his.[27]

The student body showed sustained growth during the early years of the decade before beginning a rapid decline as the Vietnam War, American racism, and social turmoil created many of the disillusionments of the late 1960s. In 1963 seventy-nine students entered the first-year class; in 1966 forty-seven entered; and in 1969 only thirty-seven entered, the lowest number since the late 1940s.[28]

The class that entered in 1963 for the degree leading to ordination was the largest in the seminary's history and provides a good overview of Columbia students in the 1960s—it was all white, all male, and overwhelmingly Southern Presbyterian. Four students from Minnesota had somehow found their way to Columbia, as had two southern Baptists and a lone Disciples of Christ minister. Eleven women were in the student body, but they were scattered among the three classes and were enrolled in programs that did not lead to ordination. A number of students in the class came from state universities—the expected: Georgia Tech, South Carolina, North Carolina, Florida, and Alabama; and the unexpected: Minnesota, Missouri, Connecticut, and Oklahoma. Presbyterian College and Davidson were well represented, as were Southwestern at Memphis (now Rhodes) and King, but the largest number (nine) from a denominational college was from Belhaven in Jackson, Mississippi, a college where the traditions of the white South and its orthodoxies were flourishing. The class consequently reflected the growing tensions in the church, and class discussions were sometimes raucous. More progressive students found the lectures and seminars by Guthrie and Cousar, Huie and McCarter a fresh spirit blowing through the church, inviting deeper commitments of faith and new engagement with the pressing intellectual and social issues of the time. The most conservative students clustered around Robinson and Gutzke and found in their persons and their lectures the traditions and piety to sustain them as they faced challenges to received orthodoxies and an established social order.[29]

When the class graduated in 1966 the majority of its members accepted calls to Presbyterian congregations. Others entered clinical training in order to become chaplains in the military or in hospitals or other institutions. Thirteen graduates earned Ph.D.s. Four became professors, and two became deans at theological seminaries. Several joined college or university faculties, one became professor and chair of the department of psychology at a state university, and one became a college dean and president. One was to become a founder of Atlanta's best-known Christian community dedicated to serving the homeless and imprisoned, while another became a widely traveled speaker on addictions. Among them were those who were to become pastors of large and influential urban congregations while others were to serve congregations in small towns and in rural settings. Almost all of them were to face the challenges that had emerged from the civil rights movement and that demanded racial justice in the American South.[30]

Those who entered in 1963 already knew that earlier graduates were facing tremendous pressures. Everywhere congregations were insisting that pastors continue to support openly or by their silence and inaction the oppressive practices and racist assumptions of a segregated South. Of course some former students, already convinced segregationists, did not need such pressure to reinforce their commitments to racism. They argued in print and in church meetings and papers that the Bible and orthodox theology supported a segregated South, and like Girardeau they couched these claims in the language of paternalism. Morton Smith, who had been one of the student leaders in the attack on Richard Gillespie in the 1950s, was a leading advocate of a racist ideology in the church.

As a professor at Belhaven in the 1960s, he argued that the civil rights movement would destroy divinely established human diversity and help to establish communist domination over America. He later insisted, as a professor at the newly established Reformed Theological Seminary in Jackson, Mississippi, that the Bible did not condemn segregation. "The fact is," he wrote, "that God segregated Israel from the Canaanite." And he said that the church should not try to change "that particular pattern" by "branding one form of culture as sinful as opposed to another." The *Presbyterian Journal*, edited by Columbia graduate Aiken Taylor, was a primary venue for the promotion of racist ideology in the church. But other graduates were seeking to move beyond such racism and were struggling to confront it in their own lives and in the life of the church and congregations they served. For this struggle they had good examples in Richards and Gear.[31]

Richards had not hesitated throughout his presidency to acknowledge that he was a son of the white South and that he had to struggle constantly against the voices that rumbled deep within his memory. Over and over again he spoke of the need for repentance and a change of ways even as he worked to keep the church from dividing over the race issue. Yet he had taken bold stands—ones that he later described as simply appeals for justice—that had been a light, however flickering, in the midst of much hate and violence. In 1940, in the face of Eugene Talmadge's demagoguery and ranting racism, he had—in a widely distributed and quoted sermon—denounced the oppression of blacks in the South in regard to employment, housing, health care, voting rights, and schools. He had pointed to police brutality that had gone unchallenged and to the failure of the church to address the bitterness and hate that allowed such oppression. In 1946 he had denounced publicly the brutal murder of two black men and two black women in rural Walton County, Georgia. With penitence, he said, the church must recognize "our own share of responsibility for the condition of society which has made such acts possible" and insisted church people must "dedicate ourselves to combat the spirit of hatred out of which such deeds arise." In 1957 he wrote what came to be called "The Ministers' Manifesto," a statement signed by eighty Atlanta ministers and spread across the entire front page of the *Atlanta Constitution*. It called for the maintenance of the public school system rather than to yield to those who were calling for its end because of desegregation. "Hatred and scorn," he wrote, "for those of another race, or for those who hold a position different from our own, can never be justified." Not everyone agreed. A cross was burned on the front yard of the president's home after the manifesto was published—Richards put the fire out with a garden hose, pulled the burned cross to the back of the house, and, not wanting to call attention to himself, made no fuss about the incident. Because of his appeals "for simple justice and the recognition of black men as our brothers" there had been over the years a steady stream of anonymous phone calls threatening Richards and his family. His children became accustomed to the calls, and when they answered the phone and heard some vile threat they would simply report that "the fat rabbit" had called again.[32]

In the fall of 1963, shortly after classes had begun, Richards addressed the crisis precipitated by white churches closing their doors and refusing to allow blacks to participate in worship services. Speaking to the student body and gathered alumni, he said his heart went out to pastors "who are constantly living with the issue." When proper ways could be found, he hoped that congregations could be kept from splitting and tearing apart. But, he said, there were "things even worse for a congregation than controversy and division. It can be true for a congregation and the Church as a whole, as it is for the minister, that 'he that saveth his life shall lose it.'" One thing was clear: "Whatever discrimination is practiced elsewhere, we have no right to shut any man out of the Church and away from the preaching of the Gospel."[33]

The next year Felix Gear, as moderator of the General Assembly, had to face the "closed door policy" of his former parish, Second Presbyterian, Memphis. The assembly was scheduled to meet at the church, but the church session passed a resolution that forbade blacks from being seated in the church's sanctuary during worship. In spite of Gear's pleas to old friends in the congregation, the session adamantly refused to change its policy. Gear consequently took the difficult step of moving the meeting of the assembly to the conference center at Montreat. John Leith, by then a professor of theology at Union in Virginia, wrote a scathing article denouncing the action of the session. When race is made a condition of worship, he said, a clear line has been drawn between "apostasy and obedience, between heresy and orthodoxy, between pretentious fraud and the reality of the church." When the session, after a bitter congregational fight, reversed its exclusionary policy in 1965, some prominent elders resigned and left the church to form the Independent Presbyterian Church. The new church had as one of its guiding principles that church visitors and members would be "compatible" with the congregation.[34]

Graduates knew that insisting on an "open door" policy for congregations could quickly lead to dismissal. Shortly before the class of 1963 began its seminary studies, John Ellington, who had graduated from Columbia the previous year, asked his congregation in a morning sermon what they would do if a young student from the Congo mission wanted to join them for worship in their Manchester, Georgia, church. That afternoon the church session began the process for his dismissal. He was gone within a month. He returned to the Columbia campus, as would others who found themselves hounded from their churches, and completed another degree. He later went to the Congo as a missionary, received a Ph.D. from the University of Wisconsin in linguistics, became a distinguished student of Bantu languages, and, with African colleagues, translated portions of the Bible into a number of African languages.[35]

Other Columbia graduates resigned when sessions refused to open the doors of the church to black worshippers. Richard Gillespie, who had left the faculty to accept a call to the First Presbyterian Church, Anderson, South Carolina, resigned the same night the session voted for the church doors to be closed against blacks. He did so knowing that he had no call from another congregation and no home or income for his wife and four children. Some graduates addressed in a sermon some specific racial incident and were forced to leave their congregations. When Lucius DuBose spoke of the terrible bombing in Birmingham that killed four young girls in Sunday school, the session of the church in Mullins, South Carolina, asked him to seek a call elsewhere as soon as possible. Bob Stevens had a Georgia elder open a closet door and show the pastor his Klan regalia. Shortly afterward Stevens was forced to resign. Sometimes, as with Eade Anderson in Greenwood, Mississippi, and James Peck in Enterprise, Alabama, the pressure of race would build for several years before a pastor would feel compelled to leave. Some like Stevens simply left the ministry.[36]

Occasionally a graduate would take a leading public role in attempting to end the violence and discrimination of a segregated South. In Anniston, Alabama, Phil Noble accepted the chairmanship of the biracial Human Relations Council. The council was appointed in late spring 1963, when tensions were high and were soon to explode in Birmingham and other southern cities. Two years earlier the Ku Klux Klan had firebombed a Freedom Riders bus in Anniston, and threats against the council promised more bombing. For months Noble had to check his car every morning before he took his children to school to be sure no bomb had been planted in it. Later he wrote of the struggles and accomplishments of the council. Civil rights leader C. T. Vivian said that Noble's account "allows us to see the bravery of unheralded heroes, black and white." And Morris Dees, cofounder of the Southern Poverty Law Center, said that Noble had shown how "black and white leaders in one small Southern city determined to work together for peaceful desegregation." Unfortunately what made Noble's story so remarkable was how unusual it was. Most white Presbyterian ministers throughout the South, including Columbia graduates, remained discretely silent in the face of the violence and racism that marked the long history of the American South, or they quietly gave up and left the ministry—or they quoted Bible texts in an attempt to prove that segregation was the will of God.[37]

Perhaps the single most important event for the white Southern Presbyterian Church during the civil rights movement was the invitation to Martin Luther King Jr. to speak at a Montreat conference. King was the clear leader of the civil rights movement and had already won the Noble Peace Prize when he accepted the Montreat invitation. But there was fierce opposition in the church to his participation. Some said King was a communist. Others said he did not believe in the fundamentals of the faith. Still others insisted the church had no business addressing social issues. The responsibility for responding to the charges fell to Marshall Dendy. He and Richards had been students together when the seminary was still in Columbia, and he had been serving since 1952 as the denomination's secretary of the Board of Christian Education, which was sponsoring the conference. Dendy came from a family with deep roots in the white Southern Presbyterian Church, and his older brother Henry Dendy had been for years the racist editor of the *Presbyterian Journal*. Yet Marshall Dendy had managed to catch at least important glimpses of a more just social order for the South, and he rejected the calls for King's invitation to be withdrawn. The board, he wrote, knew that the conference would not bring an end to the conflict in church over racial justice. What the conference was intended to do was to help Presbyterians address racial justice "in light of our understanding of the Word of God and the full meaning of God's love for all people." So King came to Montreat spoke on "The Church on the Frontier of Racial Tension." It was a memorable address and deeply moving for those in attendance, but Dendy had been right—it did not end conflict in the church over race or over King. It rather intensified the conflict as conservatives began to organize for a division of the church. Five years later leaders working for the formation of what would come to be the Presbyterian Church in America were to denounce King for his communist connections, his advocacy of "violence, murder, lying" as means to a "millennial end," and his public rejection of such fundamentals of the faith as the Virgin Birth and Christ's physical resurrection.[38]

Some students who entered Columbia in 1963 were also to feel not only tensions within the student body but also pressure from their home presbytery. In the spring of 1964, several members of the class, all candidates for the ministry under the care of South Carolina's Congaree Presbytery, wrote the presbytery encouraging an open-door policy. The letter was deferential, saying the decision was the presbytery's and not the students', but the students wrote that they thought the presbytery should know that its candidates thought an open-door policy the only policy for a Christian church. The response from the presbytery executive secretary was swift. He threatened those who had written the letter with dire consequences and said that they would not be allowed to preach or participate in presbytery activities. The threats were empty—he did not have the power to do what he threatened—and Richards wrote him a polite but firm letter saying the students should not be attacked for taking a stand on the issue. In the meantime some students began meeting with students from other Atlanta schools, including Morehouse and Spellman, in order to talk with one another and to try to move beyond well-established racial barriers. And a few students began tutoring in black schools, going to swimming pools recently opened to blacks that were now being boycotted by whites, and participating with a few younger faculty in some protest demonstrations.[39]

Whites were not the only ones on the Columbia campus during the 1960s. A few Asian students, especially from Korea, and one African American, Joe Robinson, were a part of the basic degree student body during the decade. African American students from the Interdenominational Theological Center in Atlanta participated with white Columbia students in interseminary courses; and an occasional African American pastor enrolled, as in the past, in one of the advanced degree programs. But the seminary was overwhelmingly white. The few African American students on the campus were part of a national pattern. In 1969 of three hundred black students enrolled in one of the ninety-five accredited theological schools in the country, approximately half attended Howard or the Interdenominational Theological Center. And only twelve "white" theological schools had a black faculty. So Columbia's white campus and white curriculum and white assumptions reflected—and reflected very clearly—the power of race and racism in shaping the contours of the nation's life and the theological education of pastors and priests.[40]

What this segregation meant was that throughout the decade the most significant nonwhite presence on the campus were African Americans who worked in maintenance, in housekeeping, and in the kitchen. They, like those who had gone before them, were in a good position to observe the whites of Columbia Seminary, to learn their ways, and to see their reactions to the changes sweeping over the South. And like those who had gone before them, they kept their own world and their own perspectives largely hidden from the whites who thought they knew them so well. Three stand out as particularly important players who were both highly visible on the campus and also largely unknown among whites.

Jessie Graham was a tall and handsome man who had begun working at Columbia in 1960. Known on the campus for his physical strength and for his laconic ways, he spent much of his time driving a riding lawnmower at full speed. He went full speed himself, and Cecil Moore, longtime superintendent of buildings and grounds, later said that he was the hardest worker he had ever known. Graham, as a child born in a sharecropper's cabin on a Georgia cotton farm, lived with the burden of illiteracy, but he was a fine mechanic and knew how to repair the seminary lawnmowers and to keep other lawn equipment running smoothly. During breaks he often sat outside the student center with a cup of coffee and a cigarette, and students enjoyed visiting with him. When he retired they purchased four park benches and placed them in front of Campbell Hall with a plaque on each that reads:

> In Honor of Jessie Graham
> Who Helped Maintain the
> Grounds of Columbia Seminary
> For 25 years.[41]

Graham's wife, Pearlie Mae Graham, had come to work for the Richards family in 1952 when she was sixteen. She had been born on July 4, 1936, in a sharecropper's cabin near the little village of Hawkinsville, Georgia, in a south Georgia region marked by deep poverty and the legacies of slavery. The day she was born, the other family members left the mother and baby in the house and went out into the July sun to chop long rows of cotton. When they returned in the evening, the mother was dead, and the baby was crying. The motherless child grew up in deep poverty in a region where the boll weevil had devastated cotton fields and where brutal lynchings had long been a means of keeping blacks "in their place." While she eventually learned to read a little, she nevertheless bore all her life the legacy of a segregated South and its ideological cover of "separate but equal schools." When she arrived in Atlanta and came to work in the Richardses' home, she apparently experienced the move as an escape from the labors and deep impoverishment of a sharecropper's life. She was to remain with the Richardses for over fifty years, working occasionally on the seminary campus as a housekeeper. From the first she participated in the family's daily Bible reading and prayers and learned to know the family intimately, and through them and the comings and goings of the Richards's home she came to know a larger world. And the seminary community came to know her and delighted in her humor and in the warmth of her character.[42]

Pearlie Mae Graham was only a few years older than the Richardses' daughter McKemie, and they became friends in the peculiar way of such friendship that sought to reach across great divides. In later years as a young white woman, McKemie often attended church with her at New Saint John's Missionary Baptist Church. And like Pearlie Mae, she too learned of a larger, different world—this one little seen by whites. In time the young Pearlie Mae became Sister Graham and then Mother Graham as one of the Mothers of the Church of the New Saint John's congregation. And Richards, who continued to worship with her on occasion, established a fine children's library at the church in her friend's honor. Richards reviewed children's books for the *Atlanta Constitution* and several national publications, and she carefully selected the very best books for New Saint John's children. Graham said she wanted the children of her church to have what she never had—a chance to read good books.[43]

Claude Clopton had come to the seminary to work in the kitchen in 1937. His mother had washed clothes for President Gillespie's family so he knew something about the seminary. When he was a thirteen-year-old student at Decatur's Booker T. Washington High School, he began to come to the campus in the afternoons, and there he worked as a cook and dishwasher under the guidance of Plato Henderson and under the supervision of Edna Phinizy, matron in charge of the kitchen. In the evenings he returned to his family's home on Robin Street in the black section of town behind the white Decatur High School. In 1942 he joined the navy and served as an officers' cook on a transport ship. He returned to the seminary after the war and became the cook when Henderson retired in 1947. He was joined that year by his assistant Robert Adams, a quiet and gentle man, who for the next forty-six years faithfully chopped vegetables and stirred grits for seminary students and faculty.[44]

Clopton married, and he and his wife, Louise, had four children. They attended Holsey Temple Christian Methodist Episcopal Church, where Clopton was a steward, an usher, and a tenor in the choir. And on the Columbia campus, he became known as the unofficial chaplain to students—especially for those students who worked in the dining hall and were under his supervision. He did not hesitate to talk with them about the Lord, or to counsel them when they were perplexed, or to reprimand them when they were late to work. He was to serve the seminary longer than any other person, dying while still employed in 1991. Students and graduates established the Claude Clopton Scholarship Fund at the seminary, had his picture hung close to his familiar place in the dining hall, and inscribed a plaque to his memory: "Faithful Witness to the Gospel. Beloved Member of the Seminary Community. 1937–1991." Throughout his time at Columbia, students and faculty thought they knew him well, but later they—especially those who were on the campus in the 1960s—were to learn there was much about him and his family they did not know.[45]

In July 1961 Clopton's daughter Alice, a Spellman College student, married a handsome young Morehouse student, Julian Bond, son of a distinguished family of black educators. His father, Horace Mann Bond, had been president of Lincoln University in Pennsylvania, a school established by Presbyterians for African Americans before the Civil War. The elder Bond had published groundbreaking work on racial discrimination in education, and the young Julian Bond had already been arrested in 1960 during a student protest of the segregated Atlanta City Hall cafeteria. Alice Clopton Bond was to be in the midst of the Atlanta civil rights movement with her husband throughout the 1960s and the 1970s, and they were to host over the years many of the leaders in the struggle against racism in the United States. Claude and Louise Clopton were also frequent visitors in the Bond home during these years, and they no doubt heard wide-ranging discussions of race and American society. But on the Columbia campus during the 1960s and 1970s, whites did not realize that Claude Clopton was the father-in-law of the young radical leader of Atlanta protests and that Clopton's daughter Alice was in the midst of the civil rights struggle. Only later, in the 1980s, did a few faculty members come to know of the Bond connection. A whole world of African American life, represented on the Columbia campus by the chef and informal chaplain Claude Clopton, was beyond the horizon of Columbia's faculty and students. And that "beyond" told much about the character of the seminary and about the restraints it imposed on the much revered Clopton, who felt that he had to be careful around even well-meaning whites. So he joined a long list of African Americans reaching back to the slave butler Jack, who with good manners and kind ways had served the tables of white faculty and students and had listened to their conversations and had watched carefully their behavior.[46]

PART IV

New Horizons

15

Theological Education in a Free Market

If the 1960s were years of tumult and of movement from hope to rage, the 1970s have seemed to many commentators a decade of ill repute—"A kidney stone of a decade" according to a character in the cartoon strip *Doonesbury.* Watergate, inflation, the oil crisis, and the Vietnam disaster all seemed to point to a nation in decline. At the same time the private lives of Americans appeared to be in increasing disarray. Divorce rates soared throughout the decade, bringing relief to some and psychological and economic distress to others, especially women and children. Social critics began to insist that "a culture of narcissism" had taken hold of American life. Polls indicated that a substantial number of Americans had abandoned an older ethic of self-denial and sacrifice and were "searching for self-fulfillment in a world turned upside down."[1]

Other changes were also bringing shifts in the nation's life that would directly impact theological education. Women were enrolling in colleges in larger numbers than men and were entering the work force in fields long dominated by men—including law, medicine, and the Protestant ministry. By the end of the decade the "nuclear family" (the pattern of a working father and stay-at-home mother that had dominated white families in the 1950s) accounted for only 15 percent of American households. And during these years the foreign-born proportion of the population was increasing for the first time since the 1900–1910 decade. The look, the cuisines, and the religious life of American cities were changing with new immigrants coming largely from Asia and Latin America.[2]

Beneath all these waves of change ran two powerful undercurrents. One, emerging from the protests of the 1960s and their predecessors, was a new egalitarian and inclusive spirit that rejected hierarchies and old authorities. The equality of all people—including women, people of color, gays and lesbians, the disabled, and immigrants—was being affirmed as never before. All people were to be treated equally and without discrimination. This did not mean, of course, that discriminations of all sorts suddenly disappeared from the nation's life. What it did mean was that public expressions of prejudice were increasingly taboo. The deep assumptions that informed racism and prejudices of various kinds were being pushed underground. There these assumptions were to live sheltered lives daring to come forth from their lairs into public expression only when the way seemed clear and the political climate receptive.[3]

The second undercurrent was the emergence of free-market economics as the means of solving political and social problems. The marketplace with it mechanisms of supply and demand—not government programs or regulations—seemed the most efficient means of providing whatever was needed. What the free market was leaving behind was not only confidence in the government's ability to solve the great issues before the nation but also confidence in any institution, including the church. Earlier notions of community, of society as a body that was more than a collection of individuals, was giving way to a hyperindividualism that emphasized unlimited choice and unfretted desire that could be serviced by the marketplace. These two undercurrents of egalitarian values and market values, while sometimes antagonistic, were coming together in the 1970s to create a society based on consumer capitalism and its individualistic culture in pursuit of self-fulfillment. The nation was affirming as never before the equality of all people while it was becoming increasingly unequal as the gap between the rich and the poor began to widen dramatically.[4]

The religious life of the American people did not float above these changes untouched by the social and cultural shifts sweeping over the land. Religious life, in all its diversity, was inescapably caught up in the changes, even when resisting them. But the religious life of the people was not simply a reflection of the changes, a passive image of the world around it. Religion was rather a dynamic ingredient amid the changes remaking American life. Sometimes it served an ideological function when it helped to legitimize what was happening. Sometimes it challenged what was happening by remembering what seemed to be a simpler and more moral past or by imagining a more just future. Always, however, religion was enmeshed in the nation's economic and political, social and cultural life.[5]

The history of Columbia Seminary since 1970 is consequently entangled in these larger stories and story. An egalitarian spirit was to penetrate the heart of the campus and find expression in the selection of faculty and the admission of students; in the relationship of faculty to the administration and of students to faculty; and in the standards by which students and faculty were evaluated. The sense of earlier generations that they were privileged persons, even an educated elite, with stewardship responsibilities to the church and their communities began to appear to some to be presumptuous and oppressive in the face of contemporary egalitarianism. During these same years, market values were also lodging themselves in the institutional structures of the seminary and the culture of the campus. Multiple programs began to be developed and tested to see what the market could bear so that the campus began to take on much of the appearance of a well-endowed conference center. This meant that the private sector of individual Christians, rather than the public and communal sector of the Presbyterian Church, was to become increasingly the constituency of the seminary. The governing assumption that Columbia was a seminary of the Presbyterian Church, owned and controlled by the synods, was to be challenged in a few decades by alternative models of theological education that were rooted in the fusion of an egalitarian ethic and the values of the marketplace.

This fusion and these models of theological education were to be legitimized by the pieties of contemporary evangelical individualism and by the sensibilities of an increasingly diverse faculty and administration. None of these developments, of course, were peculiar to Columbia Seminary, but the history of the seminary during the next forty-five years cannot be understood apart from them.[6]

The seminary entered the 1970s with new leadership. Faculty who had dominated much of the life of the seminary for decades retired during the last years of the 1960s, and younger faculty moved into positions of leadership and influence. Manford Gutzke retired in 1966 and turned his full attention to his popular radio program, *The Bible for You*. The senior class had his portrait painted and hung in the library, but while he lived only a block from the seminary he apparently felt no continuing attachment to it and scrupulously avoided the campus. When Felix Gear retired, the alumni association presented him with a new car in gratitude for his long service to the church. He moved into a home near the seminary, was a regular visitor in the library and in chapel, and continued teaching and preaching in various congregations.[7]

William Childs Robinson's retirement in 1968 marked an end to the Girardeau tradition at Columbia. In the lean years that followed the Civil War, Girardeau had wanted Columbia to be a place where faculty and students scrupulously adhered "to the phraseology of the past," and he had feared an "untrammeled freedom of inquiry," believing such freedom invited disorder and confusion not only regarding theological questions but also about white southern identity and the maintenance of a "southern way of life." Robinson had certainly moved beyond Girardeau's provincialism, and he had had the courage to engage twentieth-century European theologians in their German and Swiss universities. But Robinson had not been able to free himself from his history as a child of Girardeau's Columbia. His earliest identity had been shaped by the defensive and contentious spirit that inhabited the world of his youth and of his home congregation, Arsenal Hill, where Girardeau had been the founding pastor. This meant not only that Robinson was a fierce defender of a propositional theology and that he rejected evolution but also that he stood in defense of a white South. It would be his sons, William and James, who would make the move that the father could not make. These two Columbia graduates were to become distinguished New Testament scholars, and James Robinson would be known as "one of a handful of the most consequential American New Testament scholars of the last half of the twentieth century."[8]

The retirement of James McDowell Richards in 1971 was, of course, the most significant retirement for the seminary. He had come to Columbia in 1927 as a student fresh from his studies at Oxford, and he had become president of the seminary in 1932. For the next thirty-nine years, he had led Columbia through times of great hardship and increasing prosperity. He was a man who resided in the deepest traditions of the seminary, but unlike Robinson he embodied an irenic and winsome spirit that looked outward to a larger church and world. He was a person who lived and worked at boundaries, at a middle place between the old and the new. He knew and loved intensely a Southern Presbyterian world that had nurtured him in the faith and that had surrounded him with a community of memory and affection. Yet he knew the failures and limits of that world and how he was a part of it and of its failures and limits. With remarkable humility, modesty, and courage he sought to lead the white Southern Presbyterian Church and Columbia Seminary to repentance and to a deeper and more expansive faith. He did so not as an outsider but as an insider who called on the best traditions of the church to breach Girardeau's walls—walls that had for so long constricted faith to a rational system of divinely inspired propositions and Christian life to a white southern way of life. When Richards retired in 1971 the seminary and the church honored him with many gifts and expressions of gratitude and affection. The J. McDowell Richards Chair of Biblical Exposition was established, and Will Ormond was named to it. McDowell and Evelyn Richards moved into a small home not far from the campus, where she created a quiet and beautiful garden and he worked for the reunion of the church that had been divided by the Civil War.[9]

The board called C. Benton Kline to be the new president. The board knew and Kline knew that following Richards was no easy task, especially given the turmoil that had been shaking church and society during the last years of the 1960s. What was needed was a person who could carry the seminary through a period of transition, a kind of interim, and Kline was well qualified for the task. He had been the highly popular dean of faculty at Agnes Scott, had taught theology at Columbia when Gear was on leave as moderator of the General Assembly, and had come to Columbia in 1969 to be its dean of faculty when Gear retired. He was a masterful teacher and skilled administrator and was well known in Atlanta as a leader in higher education. Active in Atlanta Presbytery, he had been much engaged in the church's life as a minister but not as a pastor of a congregation. With a Ph.D. from Yale, he was primarily an academic who understood the issues confronting higher education and who relished teaching and the nurturing of a faculty committed to teaching. This meant that his most important work was to be within the seminary community and that his greatest challenge was to be in relating to a troubled constituency when some conservatives were withdrawing from the denomination and the economy was plunging into a deep recession. What made the challenge more intense was his perceived status as someone from outside the old circles of white Southern Presbyterian leadership. Even though he had been the dean at that most southern institution, Agnes Scott College, he was from Pennsylvania, had been ordained by the "northern" church, and had never served as a pastor of a congregation. He knew the challenges and the perceptions, but he was willing to take on the task of leading the seminary through a troubled period of transitions. Working closely with him was Atlanta businessman and chair of the board J. Erskine Love. His father was a Columbia graduate, and Erskine Love, like so many others, had been deeply influenced by McDowell Richards, so he gave generously of his time and his financial resources as he worked with Kline guiding the seminary through its transitional years.[10]

Kline's closest associates on the faculty were Shirley Guthrie, Charles Cousar, and Wade Huie. They had been on the faculty long enough to have gained the confidence and respect of their colleagues and were highly regarded in the church. Guthrie's book *Christian Doctrine* had made him the most widely read of the white Southern Presbyterian theologians. Published in 1968 as a part of the denomination's "Covenant Life Curriculum" for the educational ministry of the church, its use soon spread to other denominations, to U.S. seminaries, to theological schools in other parts of the English-speaking world, and even to the libraries of U.S. embassies. Never had a book by a Columbia professor reached such a wide audience. *Christian Doctrine*'s outline followed the order of the Apostles' Creed, and throughout the book Guthrie took a strongly Christological approach to theology. He wrote: "If you want to know what God is like: Look at Christ. If you want to know what real humanity is, and how you can live a genuinely human life—look at Christ. If you want to know what God is doing in the world and in your individual lives, look at Christ. For Christian theology the person and work of Christ is the key to all truth about God, ourselves and the world we live in." But some conservatives in the church were unhappy with the book and began a furious attack. Among other things they were unhappy with Guthrie's interpretation of biblical authority as the Bible's witness to Jesus Christ rather than its status as an inspired, inerrant text. The *Presbyterian Journal,* under its crusading editor Aiken Taylor, went from an initial mild criticism ("This is Christian Doctrine?"), to open hostility ("It poisons the church"), to a dire warning against reading such a book. Despite the attacks *Christian Doctrine* was to be widely read for decades, and Guthrie was to become for many the much-admired face of Columbia Seminary.[11]

Charles Cousar was also to become an admired scholar for the church, especially after the publication of his important commentary on Galatians, but his primary influence was to be within the seminary community. He was made dean of the faculty in 1971 and would serve for eight years. He would later return to the office as interim dean and would serve as acting president during two transitions. Clearly he had the confidence of the board, the faculty, and the supporting synods. Wade Huie also was to play an important role in the seminary's life during the next two decades, but he was to be particularly influential within the seminary's constituency as a popular preacher and winsome personality. During a sabbatical with his family in Ghana, he became aware of the rapid growth of the church in Africa and the richness of Christian faith and life among people in "the Third World." He consequently was to be a strong advocate for Columbia's engagement with the church in other parts of the world, and with his wife, Vee, he was to provide generous hospitality to international faculty and students who were to begin coming to Columbia in significant numbers in the 1980s. A decade after Huie's retirement, a grateful board member, Billy Morris of Augusta, remembering Huie's important ministry in the church, endowed the Wade Huie Chair in Homiletics.[12]

These three faculty members—Guthrie, Cousar, and Huie—were to play with Kline primary roles in guiding Columbia through the transition that followed Richards's retirement. They had as colleagues not only older faculty but also a cluster of new faculty. In addition to Will Ormond, Theron Nease, Milton Riviere, and Don Wardlaw, who had all joined the faculty in 1966, three other new professors had joined the faculty—Richard Bass as associate professor of mission and evangelism and director of field education, Ralph Person as associate professor of church history, and Eduard Loring as assistant professor of American Christianity and ethics. Of these seven only Ormond and Nease were to serve beyond 1975, but all of them were to make contributions to the transitions that were restructuring the internal life of the seminary.[13]

The most consequential institutional change that followed Kline's inauguration was the creation of a powerful Faculty Executive Committee. Richards had made most decisions about the seminary's life including nominating new faculty and recommending the promotion of faculty. To be sure, he conferred with Gear and a few members of the board, but he made most of the decisions about the seminary's daily life. He had been part of a generation of seminary presidents who were little constrained by well-organized faculty and student committees. By 1971, however, the demands of a more egalitarian culture called for an end to these "imperial presidencies" and for new ways and new structures. Kline, as one of his first acts as president, organized a faculty retreat at which he announced the creation of a Faculty Executive Committee. The committee was to make key decisions about the seminary's life, including recommendations about promotions and tenure and decisions about search committees that were in the future to recommend new faculty. The Faculty Executive Committee as presented by Kline was to be made up of the president, who was to preside; three deans; and three faculty members. This gave the administration a majority vote. Younger faculty objected, and another faculty member was added to the committee. It was a sign of things to come.[14]

During the 1971 fall retreat the faculty made several other important decisions. The first was to recommend to the board a new advanced degree—the doctor of ministry (D.Min.). The seminary had already begun to offer, in cooperation with Candler School of Theology and the Interdenominational Center, an advanced academic degree in pastoral counseling—the doctor of sacred theology (S.T.D.). This was a demanding academic degree often requiring years of work including clinical experience. Only a very small and select group of students were ever to enroll in the program. The D.Min., on the other hand, was generally described as a professional degree because its focus was on the professional practices of a minister—the minister as a preacher or administrator or educator or pastor. The D.Min. was in time to attract many ministers and would have a large impact on the character of the seminary.[15]

When the faculty made plans in 1971 for the introduction of the D.Min., the degree included not only an "In-Career" program for those already engaged in the practice of ministry, but also an "In-Course" or "In-Sequence" option for master of divinity (M.Div.) students who were still in preparation for the ministry. By adding an intern year and a newly designed fourth year, a student could earn a D.Min. While the in-sequence degree would be offered for only a few years, the process developed for being admitted to the degree was to have a long afterlife and was to reflect the powerful influence of a therapeutic culture on the seminary community.[16]

During a student's second year, the student underwent a "Professional Assessment." Its intent was to determine if the student should proceed to a final third year and the master of divinity degree or if the student was ready to enter the more advanced doctor of ministry program. The assessment, however, quickly began to take on much of the character of a psychological evaluation. The results of psychological testing were utilized as were reports from clinical supervisors who had worked with the student in a hospital or another institutional setting. Within a few years, students were regularly being required as a result of their assessment to enter psychotherapy or to take a chaplaincy course in a hospital as an act of therapy. Some faculty opposed from the first such a therapeutic approach, insisting that the seminary was an academic institution or that the internal life of a student could not be judged, only the actions of the student. The character of the professional assessment, however, would not begin to lose its strong psychological approach until the early 1990s. By then the critiques of the therapeutic culture had become increasingly persuasive, and some of the professors of pastoral care were saying that required therapy was not generally productive therapy. At the same time supervisors in clinical settings were saying that the primary purpose of clinical pastoral education was not therapy for a needy student but a practice of ministry and reflection on that practice.[17]

Questions remained, however, about the purposes of the assessment even as its therapeutic emphasis became less overt. Most pressing was the question of the seminary's responsibility to the church, in particular to the Presbyterian Church. Traditionally the seminary, generally through the president, had communicated regularly with a student's presbytery about the student's progress toward graduation and ordination. Any concerns about the student's readiness or suitability for ministry were readily conveyed. Should then the issues raised in a student's professional assessment be shared with the student's presbytery? Atlanta Presbytery began to ask if a representative of the presbytery could be present for the assessment of its students, a procedure that was allowed for several years. Eventually the faculty decided that a letter, approved by the student, would be sent to a presbytery announcing only the formal results of the assessment but providing no details of the discussion that had taken place during the assessment. In later decades, when many of the faculty were no longer Presbyterian and an evangelical individualism had become an important part of the ethos of the institution and the number of Presbyterian students had become a decreasing part of Columbia's student body, the issue of reporting assessments to the presbyteries became less intense.[18]

Four new faculty members were called during Kline's short tenure as president. Frederick Bonkovsky came from Vanderbilt University, where he had been teaching political science. As professor of Christian ethics at Columbia for almost twenty years and with a Ph.D. in political science from Harvard, he was to introduce careful social analysis into the seminary curriculum. Jasper Keith came to the new position of director of supervised ministry. Formerly chief of chaplains at the Georgia Regional (mental) Hospital, his position at Columbia represented the development, over the years, of the program of "Field Work" into "Field Education" into "Supervised Ministry." He was to make the actual practice of ministry in various locations a part of the educational process at Columbia and was later to become a popular professor of pastoral care and counseling. The author of this study was called from a pastorate in South Carolina to be dean of students and adjunct professor of American Christianity. I would later become professor of U.S. religious and cultural history and director of Columbia's International Program.[19]

Catherine Gunsalus was called from Louisville Presbyterian Theological Seminary to teach church history. She was Columbia's first woman professor and quickly established herself as a masterful teacher, an important role model for increasing numbers of women students, and a highly respected leader among her faculty colleagues. She knew how to startle her male colleagues by making simple observations that were deeply informed not only by feminist writers and the history of women in the church but also by her own experience as a pioneer woman in ministry. Shortly after joining the Columbia faculty, she married the distinguished church historian Justo González, who would serve many years as an adjunct professor of church history. Together they were to make an enormous contribution to Columbia's life. They brought deep knowledge of the church's history from its earliest days and challenging new perspectives on that history. Invited to lecture throughout the United States and in Latin America, Asia, Africa, and Europe, they were to bring back to the campus during the next four decades insights gained from Catholics and Pentecostals, liberation theologians and conservative evangelicals, new Christians in China and old Christian traditions in Spain. Clearly Columbia had never before had a professor like Catherine Gunsalus González nor a faculty spouse and adjunct professor like Justo González.[20]

These new faculty members were called in 1973. They found a student body that had changed dramatically from what it had been only a decade earlier. In 1963 seventy-nine white, male students had entered the first-year class. They were overwhelmingly Southern Presbyterian. In 1973 only thirty-nine students entered the first-year class. Five were women, and three were persons of color. Five were non-Presbyterian, and all but two came from southern states. Largely absent in 1973 was the old contentious spirit that had led students in the 1950s and 1960s to attack the orthodoxy of their professors. In the 1966 Reformed Theological Seminary in Jackson, Mississippi, had been created as a haven for a Girardeau-style orthodoxy, and students who in early years had come to Columbia primarily to study with William Childs Robinson now were drawn to the Mississippi seminary.[21]

Gone as well was much of the formality that still lingered on the campus in 1963. Then a student addressed a faculty member as Dr. Gear or Dr. DeWitz or Dr. Guthrie. And even faculty—except perhaps for Gear and Cartledge—would not think of calling Dr. Richards "Mac." Certainly no student had the imagination or the courage to address Dr. Richards in such a way! And Dr. Richards on his part never knowingly called Dr. Robinson anything but "Dr. Robinson," and when speaking to a trembling student, he addressed him formally, as for example "Mr. Carmichael." By 1973, however, an egalitarian spirit had swept over the campus. If students still could not find the courage to say "Ludwig" when addressing Dr. DeWitz or the impertinence to say "Sam" to Dr. Cartledge, they did not hesitate to say "Shirley" when speaking to Dr. Guthrie or "Wade" to Dr. Huie, or "Charlie" when addressing Dean Cousar.[22]

Other rituals also changed. Chapel was no longer required as increasing numbers lived off campus; smoking was no longer allowed in faculty meetings; and committees began meeting regularly. When Catherine González asked if the sign on the door that read "Faculty Restroom" included her, the sign was quickly changed to "Men." Perhaps most telling was the ritual of the evening meal. In 1963 all students had dressed for dinner—the men wore coats and ties, wives and the few women taking special courses wore dresses. They all came into the handsome new Tull dining hall of the student center (now Richards Center) when the doors were opened and sat at dinner tables covered with white table cloths and waiting china plates. The head waiter, who allowed no man to enter without a coat and tie, said a prayer of thanks. Then student waiters brought dinner, and the meal was conducted family style. The dinner ritual was orderly and was intended to create a community atmosphere and to teach a proper white Southern Presbyterian etiquette. But by the time the class that entered in 1973 graduated, the coats and ties were gone, as were the waiters and china plates. A serving line and plastic plates offered a more economical and market-friendly way and a less imposing and restrictive atmosphere. Now students arrived for supper often dressed in the revealing fashions of the counterculture, and the dean of students often had to enter what was for him the uncharted waters of fashion and propriety. No common prayer was said—students and spouses gave thanks privately as the spirit moved them. The seminary was entering a period when a quest for "community" would be constantly underway even as the old rituals that had long sustained Columbia as a community were being undercut. An egalitarian spirit, the economics of the market, and an increasingly radical individualism in U.S. society were helping to shape the character and daily rituals of the seminary and consequently the formation of students for ministry.[23]

The establishment in 1966 of Reformed Seminary in Mississippi had been a harbinger of things to come. There had been for several years a "continuing church movement" that sought to uphold the old white Southern Presbyterian orthodoxies of Girardeau and his followers. Those in the movement believed that Christian faith involved a rational system of divinely inspired propositions—especially as articulated in late nineteenth-century fundamentalism. They insisted that the Bible was an inerrant text and that all theological teaching proceed by rational argument. They rejected evolution. And they provided vigorous ideological support for a segregated South. With the acerbic Aiken Taylor as its editor, the *Presbyterian Journal* had long been lamenting the church's departure from established ways. Theological liberalism, it was said, had led to "non-biblical" positions on women's ordination, divorce, abortion, and integration. Prosegregation arguments, which had appeared routinely in the *Presbyterian Journal* since its beginning, wrapped its racism in the pious language of the "spirituality of the church" and in biblical proof texts. In 1971, at an annual meeting of *Journal* supporters, a Steering Committee for a Continuing Presbyterian Church was organized. And on December 4, 1973, 112 years to the day after the formation of the Presbyterian Church in the Confederate States of America, the Presbyterian Church in America (PCA) was organized in Birmingham, Alabama. Not surprisingly it adopted the spirit and much of the language of Thornwell's address issued by the Confederate assembly: "An Address by the General Assembly to the Churches of Jesus Christ throughout the Earth."[24]

Columbia Seminary graduates were intimately involved in the formation of the PCA. Most notable were men who had been influenced by William Childs Robinson. Nearly half of the founding pastors, wrote one of the historians of the PCA, had been his students, and twenty-two of the thirty ministers who wrote the PCA's *Book of Church Order* had studied under Robinson. While Robinson never left the church that had nurtured him in the faith, his influence on the PCA was to be his most enduring legacy, and through him the most enduring legacy of Girardeau. Among those who left the old Southern

Presbyterian Church (the Presbyterian Church in the United States) were those who had led the charges against Professor Richard Gillespie and others in the 1950s. They included PCA leaders Morton Smith, Jack Scott, Kennedy Smartt, and Harold Borchert. Smith and Scott would become professors at Reformed Seminary, and Smith was to play a particularly important role in the formation of the PCA. Perhaps ironically the contentious spirit that they had exhibited as students was to be turned on Morton Smith, and he was encouraged to leave his professorship at Reformed Seminary. He consequently helped to establish in Greenville, South Carolina, the James Henley Thornwell Seminary, whose president was to complain that Smith was "maligned and even disdained" by some in the PCA.[25]

The rupture in the church had obviously been long in coming. When it arrived it had little direct impact on Columbia since students drawn toward the PCA were already going to Reformed Seminary and congregations that left the denomination had long since stopped supporting Columbia. But in other ways the departure was deeply felt by Columbia. Many friendships as well as family relations were strained or broken. The tightly knit white Southern Presbyterian family had lost some of its members, particularly in Alabama and Mississippi. Later other churches would leave the denomination, some joining the PCA, others joining some other conservative body. Perhaps most telling for Columbia Seminary's history was the departure of First Presbyterian in Columbia, South Carolina, in whose cemetery rests the body of George Howe. In 1983, after a struggle in the congregation, the church left the denomination. In 2013 the congregation established the Girardeau Lecture Series. "They are an attempt," says the church's website, "to capture the enthusiasm and focus Girardeau had for ministry to the needy and diverse populations in South Carolina."[26]

Ben Kline announced in late summer 1975 his intention to resign as president at the end of the fall term to return to full-time teaching. He had successfully led the seminary through a difficult transition. A modern institutional structure had been put in place, a balanced budget had been maintained during a serious recession, the withdrawal of some churches in the constituency had been faced with resolve, and important decisions had been made in regard to faculty appointments. But the stress of the presidency had taken its toll. He had a heart attack in the early fall, and it was necessary for him to recuperate during the rest of the term. Dean Cousar served as acting president, and the board acted quickly, electing in November Davison Philips as the new president. Two months later Philips began his tenure as president—a tenure that would see Columbia moving toward the strongest period in its history.[27]

Philips had been pastor of the Decatur Presbyterian Church for twenty-one years when the board elected him president. A graduate of Hampden-Sidney and Columbia Seminary and with a Ph.D. from Edinburgh, he had served the church in many capacities—as moderator of Atlanta Presbytery and the Synod of Georgia, as a member of the boards of Presbyterian College and Agnes Scott College, where for many years he had chaired its executive committee. And he had been on the Columbia board for years and had served as its chair during the 1960s. He obviously was well known and trusted throughout the Presbyterian Church. He was also much admired as a man of genuine faith and of great good humor. Like his seminary classmate and now colleague Will Ormond, he was a master storyteller who could reveal in a humorous anecdote not only his own idiosyncrasies but also the pretentions of the overly pious or doctrinaire. And like so many other Columbia graduates, he had been greatly influenced by Richards, whom he regarded "as a father in the faith." Philips felt deeply the way his own identity had been shaped by the seminary, and he acted as one who knew that he was part of a distinct tradition and an ongoing story. "Others have labored," he said, "and we have entered into their labors." Repeatedly he said, "We stand on the shoulders of those who have gone before us." He believed that the seminary had been created and sustained for service to the Presbyterian Church and through it to other churches and to the world. "A president," he wrote, "is expected to participate in the governing bodies [of the church] which own and control it." And the church responded enthusiastically. Over nine hundred people packed the Peachtree Presbyterian Church for his inauguration, including representatives from the three synods that owned and controlled the seminary and from each of the presbyteries in the synods. It was an auspicious occasion.[28]

In his work as president, Philips emphasized three commitments of the seminary—to biblical authority, to doctrinal fidelity, and to ecclesiastical loyalty. "Our constant appeal," he wrote, "is to the Scripture as it is attested to be the word of God by the inward witness of the Holy Spirit." The fundamental affirmations of Reformed tradition, he said, "stand at the center of the educational experience" at Columbia. And he emphasized that "our teaching and our ministry seek to be loyal to the Presbyterian Church, US." With these commitments Philips sought to address several areas in order to strengthen the work and ministry of Columbia.[29]

First, there was a need to strengthen the seminary's relationship to the church and to Columbia graduates. The turmoil of the 1960s and the disruptions and bitterness caused by the formation of the PCA had left the church battered and its ministry in need of encouragement. Philips saw the seminary as an extended community that reached out far beyond those who were presently on the campus. He believed Columbia had a high calling to serve Presbyterian pastors and congregations and not abandon them when they were going through difficult waters. He consequently gave significant personal attention to pastors, and he spent much time writing letters and notes to graduates and pastors throughout Columbia's constituency. "Many people," his longtime administrative assistant Peggy Rowland said, "think his hobby is golf. It's not. It is writing letters!" As a person who had himself been a pastor, and who continued to think of himself in many ways as a pastor, he had an intuitive understanding of the struggles ministers and congregations were facing amid the demographic and cultural transformations remaking U.S. society.[30]

Philips sought to develop programs that would nurture pastors and strengthen their relationship to the seminary. He began to promote the alumni council, and he saw that increased attention was given in the seminary publication *Vantage* to alumni activity. After only a year in office he could report that "the growing support of our alumni is a source of real encouragement to us." He insisted that the seminary sponsor a lecture series that would have strong appeal to graduates and other pastors. The Columbia Forum was consequently organized, which included a Smyth Lecturer who was to address some scholarly subject of interest to pastors; an Alumni Lecturer who was to focus on some practice of ministry; worship services with an outstanding preacher; and an alumni banquet with a popular graduate as a speaker. Philips did not leave the selection of the lecturers and preachers to the quirks of faculty politics but participated vigorously in the selection, always emphasizing the interests of pastors. Persons of strong reputations were consequently invited. Attendance soared, and the seating capacity of the Columbia Presbyterian Church began to be strained. In 1980 Frederick Buechner, in a stunning series of lectures, told of his "Spiritual Autobiography." Neely McCarter explored "The Teaching Ministry of the Church." And the popular Scottish preacher Ian Pitt-Watson preached in the evenings. There was standing room only. And when Will Ormond spoke at the alumni banquet, the dining hall was filled as was an adjacent room. Other years found similarly large crowds. Summer continuing education programs were also promoted. By the early years of the 1980s hundreds were attending a variety of classes being offered in July. Graduates clearly felt the seminary was interested in them and their ministries and were responding enthusiastically. Other pastors did as well as they began to take new notice of Columbia and the programs it was offering to the church.[31]

As soon as he took office, Philips began to focus on the recruitment of students. In this he was greatly assisted by his wife, Kay, who had once been a student herself and who greatly enjoyed welcoming prospective students into their home. For his part Davison Philips was a natural recruiter. His warmth and humor drew prospective students to him, and he could draw on his years of experience as a pastor to discuss with them the role of the minister and what it means to be called into the ministry. Moreover pastors trusted him because he was highly regarded as an experienced pastor, and they began to recommend students to Columbia with renewed enthusiasm. Philips called Harry Barrow, a young Columbia graduate, to be the director of admissions, and Barrow began to visit campuses and attend presbytery meetings regularly. As a result the student body began to show steady growth. Most notable was the growth in the number of women students—from five in the entering class of 1973 to twenty in 1983.[32]

While the number of first professional degree students grew steadily, students enrolled in the D.Min. grew dramatically. The degree, begun in the early 1970s, had originally been under the direction of a dean of ministry development—first Milton Riviere and then Jack McMichael, who had joined the faculty as professor of Christian education during the closing years of Richards's administration. In 1977 James Newsome became director of advanced studies with responsibility for the D.Min. program. As a Columbia graduate with a Ph.D. in Old Testament from Vanderbilt and years as a pastor, he brought strong credentials to the position. Under his leadership the D.Min. began a steady growth. But other Presbyterian seminaries, especially McCormick in Chicago, began to establish satellite classes in the Southeast within Columbia's traditional constituency. McCormick's program caused some Columbia supporters to grumble that Columbia should be doing more for its constituency, and when Newsome resigned after three years to become professor of Old Testament, the seminary called Doug Hix to be the new director of advance studies. It was a brilliant call. Hix, a Columbia graduate with a Ph.D. in ethics from Duke, was extraordinarily well read, deeply immersed in the life of the church, and an experienced educator. Pastors sensed in him a person who understood the issues they faced and were drawn to Hix and to his wife, Pat. She was not only the administrative assistant in the advanced studies office but also a sympathetic hostess who knew the demands of ministry and who welcomed pastors into the Hix home for meals and lodging. Doug Hix began a vigorous program that included off-campus classes, and soon the number of D.Min. students was growing rapidly. The faculty limited the number of students in the program but had to raise the limit several times until finally the faculty said 250 and no more.[33]

This expansion of the D.Min. program had an immediate impact on Columbia. New faculty were necessary to help meet the challenge of more students. Classroom space on the campus began to become an issue as did housing for D.Min. students. The administration had to adjust faculty teaching loads, and faculty had to develop new pedagogical strategies for teaching the short, intensive courses required by pastors' schedules. Of no little importance was the gift that some pastors brought to the campus as they pushed faculty to engage more directly the demanding issues of ministry in contemporary American society.[34]

Hix had a special concern for Presbyterian ministers, and he worked closely with presbyteries in the supporting synods developing networks of connections and classes. But he also had deep ecumenical commitments, and the number of non-Presbyterian students began to grow. This meant that for the first time in Columbia's history, persons of color were beginning to be a part of Columbia's student body in significant numbers. And among them were African American Presbyterians who for generations had lived side by side with white Southern Presbyterians. Race had long divided them, and the experience of being in classes together provided opportunities for glimpses of each into the little-known world of the other.[35]

Closely related to the concern for pastors' advanced study was the establishment of the *Journal for Preachers,* a quarterly published for preaching during the seasons of Advent, Lent, Easter, and Pentecost. A coterie of Columbia faculty and graduates gathered and published essays and sermons from a distinguished group of theologians and pastors from around the country including Stanley Hauerwas and Will Willimon, Barbara Brown Taylor and Shannon Kershner, Tom Long and Fred Craddock, Jerimiah Wright and Joe Roberts. International contributors included Desmond Tutu and Russel Botman of South Africa, Sam Wells from England, Norman Shanks from Scotland, Janos Pasztor from Hungary, and John Douglas Hall from Canada. The journal, begun in 1978, had more than three thousand pastors and one hundred libraries subscribed by 2000. Erskine Clarke has been the publisher from the beginning, and Walter Brueggemann and Cam Murchison longtime editors. In 2017 associate editors, in addition to Murchison, were Anna Carter Florence, Joseph Harvard, Tom Long, and Agnes Norfleet.

Columbia's faculty grew by almost a third during Philips's presidency—from twenty-one in 1976 to thirty in 1986. And of the thirty in 1986, only ten had been on the faculty in

1976. The year Philips arrived in the president's office Keith Nickle came from St. Louis University—where he had been director of graduate studies in the Jesuit Divinity School—to be professor of New Testament at Columbia. He had previously served as pastor of two Presbyterian congregations in Texas, and he quickly became a highly regarded and popular professor at Columbia. He and his wife, Marie, brought with them four sons, who joined the four Huie sons and the three Cousar sons, who, with the younger children of other faculty, helped to make the campus a lively place.[36]

Oscar Hussel joined the faculty as professor of Christian education in 1976. When Cousar resigned as dean of academic affairs in 1977, Hussel became dean—a position he held for the next eleven years. A skilled administrator and genial spirit, Hussel quickly won the confidence and friendship of the faculty. He and his wife, Shirley, frequently hosted faculty dinners in their home—occasions marked by much hospitality and serious conversations. In this and other ways he promoted the collegiality of the faculty and its commitments to the work of the seminary.[37]

Other new professors soon joined the faculty. Thomas Long arrived in 1977 as the new professor in preaching and worship. A rapidly rising star as a preacher and teacher of preachers, he left for a position at Princeton Seminary in 1983. He was to remain, however, an important friend to many on the Columbia faculty and was to exert through his writings a continuing influence on the Columbia community. Decades later he was to return to live on the campus, this time as the spouse of a professor, Kimberly Long, who was making her own important contributions to the seminary and church. Robert Ramey came in 1979 as professor of ministry. As a friend to many and a valued colleague, he provided much leadership in the expanding D.Min. program. When Jasper Keith became professor of pastoral care and counseling, Peter Carruthers became director of supervised ministry. He was later to serve a term as dean of students. James Overbeck was named librarian following Harold Prince's long service in that position. Lucy Rose joined the faculty in 1983 as assistant professor of worship and preaching, joining Catherine González as one of two women on the faculty. Rose was to become not only a splendid teacher of homiletics but also a wise and much sought after counselor and friend to students.[38]

Other new faculty soon followed—Edward Trimmer in Christian education, David Gunn in Old Testament, David Moessner in New Testament, G. Thompson Brown in world Christianity, Brian Childs in pastoral theology and counseling, Sarah Juengst as associate director of advanced studies, and Barry Davies in church music. Each brought distinctive gifts to their positions, and Gunn and Brown brought already well-established reputations as leaders in their respective fields.[39]

Four faculty members who came during Philips's presidency were to be of particular importance in the seminary's history because of their long and distinguished service. Ben Johnson joined the faculty in 1981 as associate professor in evangelism. Johnson was a person of great energy who possessed an entrepreneurial spirit and an ability to identify major developments in the life of the church. In 1987 he was named the Peachtree Professor in Evangelism and Church Growth, a position recently endowed by the Peachtree Presbyterian Church under the leadership of its pastor Frank Harrington. Then in the mid-1990s he proposed and was elected to the new position of professor of Christian spirituality. He had identified an important cultural shift taking place. Old pieties such as Sabbath keeping had been largely abandoned to consumer capitalism and to its individualistic culture in pursuit of self-fulfillment. In the void a burgeoning new interest in spirituality was beginning to emerge as some were seeking to escape the banality of the mall, the enticements of entertainment, and the distractions of professional sports. Johnson's courses and the courses taught by others he recruited offered introductions into the history and practices of Christian spirituality and were to play a particularly important role in the D.Min. and Continuing Education programs of the seminary.[40]

Leon Carroll became director of supervised ministry in 1983. A Columbia graduate and experienced pastor, he had supervised many intern students from Union Seminary in Virginia and Louisville Presbyterian. Building on the work of Keith and Carruthers, during the next twenty-six years he was to make supervised ministry a central part of Columbia's curriculum. He quickly demonstrated he was more than an administrator or a kind of manager of an employment bureau for students. Through careful orientation of students for their experiences in the church, through his visits to students during the summer, and through extended classroom time with them after their return to campus, he was a teacher who was helping students become competent and reflective practitioners of the art of ministry. He also developed a course of study for the pastors who were supervisors, providing guidelines for supervision and insights into the challenges and dynamics of mentoring ministerial students. The faculty was soon turning to Carroll for responsibilities that required wisdom and great discretion, and the board formally acknowledged that he was a professor, and not simply an administrator, by making him associate professor of supervised ministry with tenure.[41]

When Ben Kline resigned in 1986 from full-time teaching, the seminary called George Stroup from Austin Seminary to take Kline's position in systematic theology. Stroup's book *The Promise of Narrative Theology* had already attracted much attention from both academics and pastors, and he was soon to establish himself as a leader within Columbia's faculty. He taught with his friend and colleague Shirley Guthrie the required course in reformed theology. While they obviously shared common commitments to the Reformed tradition, they frequently debated one another in class and modeled ways that theological disagreements could be addressed with civility, respect, and often good humor. During the coming years, Stroup sought to keep Columbia anchored in the Reformed tradition through the courses he taught and the theological commitments he brought to faculty discussions and deliberations. A demanding professor, he generally drew to his elective classes some of Columbia's strongest students, whom he followed with genuine interest and support after their graduations.[42]

In 1986 Philips announced that Walter Brueggemann had accepted the call to become professor of Old Testament at Columbia. Except for Richards's call to be president and perhaps Thornwell's call to teach theology, there had been no more important call in Columbia's history. Brueggemann was already one of the nation's leading Old Testament scholars, and during the coming years his reputation was to grow steadily as his books flowed from the presses of eager publishers. Before the turn of the century it would be hard to name a more widely read or quoted biblical scholar in the nation. What drew so many to him was his ability to combine deep engagement with biblical texts—especially through rhetorical criticism—with social analysis. His astonishing erudition, energy, and passion made him a compelling lecturer as well as prolific writer. Both clergy and laity flocked to hear him wherever he lectured, so when he joined the faculty, Columbia suddenly gained a new status as one of the nation's leading seminaries. Increasing numbers of students began to enroll from around the country, and Columbia was soon drawing other scholars to the faculty because of Brueggemann's influence.[43]

To be sure, there were other developments in Columbia's life that were calling attention to the seminary's growing strength—developments that had helped in the first place to convince Brueggemann to accept the call to Columbia. These included a lively and engaging faculty and rapidly expanding relationships with theological institutions around the world. And the reunion in 1983 of Northern and Southern Presbyterians in the formation of the Presbyterian Church (USA) had helped to move Columbia beyond its southern identification. But Brueggemann was also impressed by Columbia's deep traditions and connections with the church and the ways its academic life was understood as being in service to the church. And there were personal reasons as well that encouraged his joining Columbia's faculty. His father-in-law, P. D. Miller, had been a longtime member of the Columbia board and one of Richards's closest friends. Brueggemann's wife, Mary Miller Brueggemann, had always known Richards, according to southern custom, as "Uncle Mac," so family links to Columbia were deep and filled with many memories. In addition, and of no little influence in the Brueggemann decision, was the friendship between the Brueggemanns and the Cousars. Mary Brueggemann and Betty Cousar had known one another in college and during Montreat summers, and the two couples had become good friends during a sabbatical year in Cambridge. Brueggemann respected Cousar's scholarship, and the two friends were glad to be a part of the same faculty. So for a variety of reasons—Philips called it providential—Brueggemann came to Columbia and played a critical role in what would be the strongest years the seminary had ever known.[44]

In addition to these four, and of no little importance, was the call of Paul Smith as adjunct professor of black history and identity. Smith had been deeply engaged as a young man in the civil rights movement and had in 1957 first introduced in Talladega, Alabama, Andrew Young to Martin Luther King Jr. He had served as associate vice chancellor of Washington University in St. Louis and as vice president of Morehouse College. Deeply influenced by the theology and spirituality of Howard Thurman, Smith was committed to developing intentionally diverse congregations. In 1979 he had been called as the first black minister of the all-white Hillside Presbyterian Church in Decatur. Among the courses he taught at Columbia was an interseminary elective—"Black Church/White Church: History and Present Issues." The seminar met at the Martin Luther King Center in downtown Atlanta and drew students and faculty from the Interdenominational Theological Center and Candler as well as Columbia. His presence on the campus—especially in faculty meetings and in the courses he taught—was an opening to a world that had surrounded the seminary and that had helped to shape its life while remaining largely unknown to and unrecognized by white Columbia. When Smith left in 1986 to become pastor of the predominantly white First Presbyterian Church, Brooklyn, New York, he left the door at Columbia cracked open for other African Americans who would follow as full-time professors.[45]

Philips necessarily gave much attention to fund-raising. The added faculty, expanding student body, and growing programs all cost money, and Columbia had little to spare. A capital campaign was consequentially launched immediately after Philips assumed the presidency. Dick Dodds was called as director of seminary relations to lead the campaign along with two retired ministers—Donald Bailey and Bonneau Dixon—who took on the work of field representatives. All three were Columbia graduates with long and extensive friendships throughout the synods. They were constantly on the road and organized a network of workers for the campaign—240 congregations had a local leader for the campaign, and a 105 cluster leaders coordinated the work among congregations. Over eighteen hundred Presbyterians attended twenty-one area dinners where Philips told about Columbia's long history and its mission in contemporary America. Prominent businessmen called on friends and associates and emphasized the need to strengthen Columbia's endowment. A goal of $7 million had been set. When the campaign was over, almost $8 million had been raised and the groundwork laid for continuing efforts to increase the endowment. By the time Philips retired in 1986, the endowment had grown from $6 million in 1976 to almost $30 million. He believed that a primary reason for such success was a "growing commitment by pastors, presbyteries, synods, and churches in our constituency to the priority of the seminary's mission."[46]

Not only had the endowment grown rapidly during Philips's presidency, but new apartments for married students with children had also been built in the Village, and Campbell Hall had been renovated. Perhaps most startling for returning graduates was the renovation of the chapel. The old chapel in Campbell Hall had faced Columbia Drive, and the wall behind the pulpit had been covered with a velvet curtain that had been hanging there for years. The curtain had offered little relief to the eye or mind during the sermon of a trembling seminarian and was consequently resented for its uselessness. The renovation turned the chapel around to face a Gothic window whose clear glass was replaced with stain glass of a modernistic design—a design that invited much contemplation. On one occasion Dean Hussel identified a red giraffe among the swirling colors of the window, and during the coming years the chapel giraffe was to play an uncommonly large role in the sermon illustrations of seniors.[47]

Overseeing the construction on the campus was Cecil Moore, a Columbia graduate. Kline had persuaded him to leave the pastorate and return to Columbia as the superintendent of buildings and grounds. He had grown up on an Alabama farm and knew about matters that were great mysteries to the faculty and administration—how to work with contractors, what to do when the air conditioning went out in July, and how to keep pigeons from building nests in Campbell Hall gutters. He also knew how to come to the aid of a faculty member when a lawnmower would not start or a dishwasher would not work because of a stray fork. With his dry humor and familiarity with the foibles of faculty and students, he was to be for over three decades a central player in campus life. Perhaps no other superintendent of buildings and grounds in the country was invited—as was Moore—to participate in faculty meetings. Taking lessons drawn from life on an Alabama farm, he was often able to bring heated faculty debates to an end with an obvious observation. When he retired his portrait was placed in the president's office. There, with a portrait of Virginia Harrison and across from a portrait of Peter Marshall, it keeps watch over the seminary he loved.[48]

Philips retired in 1986. One hundred years earlier the seminary had closed for a season because of the Woodrow controversy. At the time it had seemed that the seminary might never recover or even reopen. But it had survived, weathered new storms, and prospered. When Philips had begun his presidency in 1976, Columbia had a fine campus, a respected faculty, a new curriculum, and a modern administrative structure. But it was still reeling from the turmoil of the economic recession of the early 1970s and the bitter accusations that had led some churches and Columbia graduates to withdraw from the denomination. Philips had brought to the presidency gifts that allowed him to lead the seminary out of the turmoil and to new levels of strength and service. His pastoral experience, his genuine piety and good humor, his commitment to Columbia graduates, his respect for and friendship with lay leaders, and his capacity to build and support a strong faculty—all had contributed to making Columbia a seminary of increasing influence within the world of American theological education. At the same time, Philips had led the seminary to engage a larger international world where younger churches were booming and where Columbia was finding new partners for the tasks of theological education. The consequences of Philips's insistence that Columbia must open windows to the world will be explored in the next chapter, but his international vision was to be one of his most important legacies.[49]

The board hosted a banquet for Philips's retirement at the Cherokee Town and Country Club. Over five hundred guests attended the festive occasion, and Philips's good friend and Decatur businessman H. G. Pattillo presided. Twelve speakers were allotted three minutes each, but their enthusiasm for Philips exceeded their sense of timing. When Philips finally had an opportunity to respond, he noted that only he and his mother wanted the program to continue. His remarks were consequently brief as he reflected on his time as president. "Most encouraging," he said, "was the obvious indication that God was not finished with Columbia as a servant of the Presbyterian church but had even greater and more expanding opportunities for it."[50]

Faculty, ca. 1980; president Davison Philips, front fourth from left; board chair Erskine Love, front far right.

Board chair John Conant with wife, Miriam Conant, and president Davison Philips.

W. Frank Harrington, graduate, friend of the seminary, and strong supporter of Presbyterian institutions.

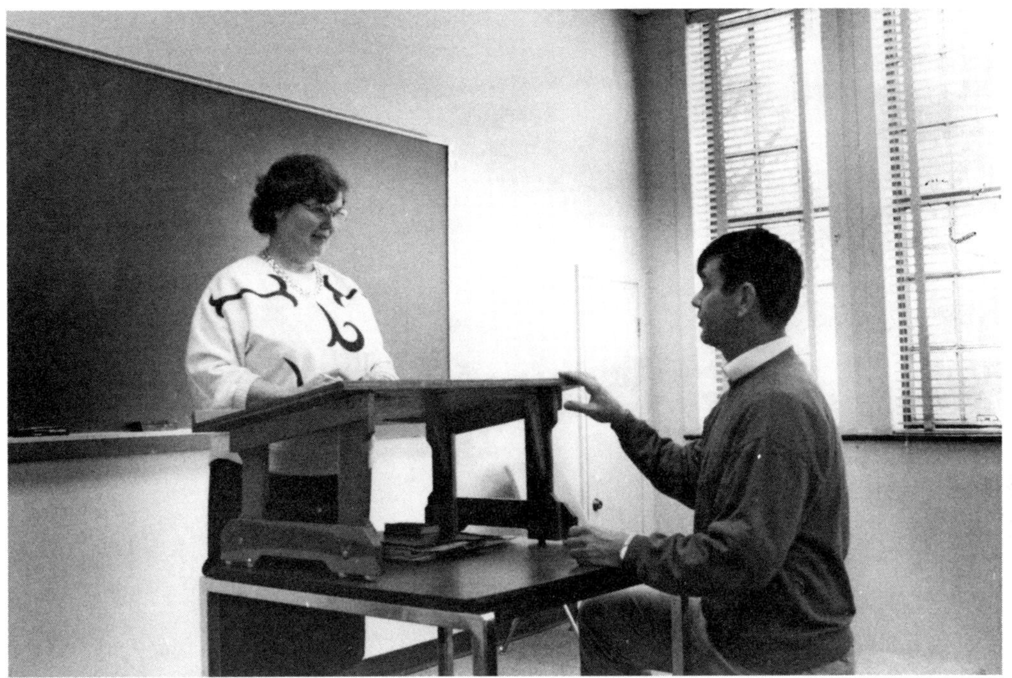

Popular professor Catherine Gonzalez and student after class.

Dancing theologians Guthrie and Kline entertain the seminary community.

Anglican bishop of Jamaica Neville da Souze was one of many international church leaders who spent sabbaticals on the campus, 1980–2008.

The Guthries host students and spouses.

Jesse Graham served the seminary for many years. Campus benches in front of Campbell Hall honor his memory.

A growing staff in the 1980s carried much of the responsibility for expanding programs.

16

A Quest for Excellence

In his last report to the board of directors, Davison Philips—reflecting once again his generous spirit—wrote: "I trust that we can make a good transition as we welcome a new president and make that administration the most fruitful period in our history." Philips's hope for Columbia was to be realized—the seminary he loved was about to enter the strongest and most fruitful period it had ever enjoyed.[1]

The board announced in November 1986 that it had elected as the new president Douglas W. Oldenburg, pastor of Charlotte's Covenant Presbyterian Church. He was, the board said, a pastor committed to excellence in the training of men and women for ministry. The board read Oldenburg correctly—a quest for excellence was to mark his tenure as president. He was to demonstrate in the quest his deep internalization of a Calvinist ethic and piety that emphasized personal discipline as a characteristic of the Christian life and that honored the life of the mind as a Christian duty. The excellence he was to seek was not a vague abstraction, an attractive but empty generality, but a quality that combined an unusual degree of disciplined work and scholarship with personal integrity and a vision of the high calling of Christian ministry. He was to say repeatedly that any quest for genuine excellence in the life and character of Columbia could only flow from gratitude and from a Christian discipleship that had its origins in God's amazing grace. His efforts to build on and nurture the strong faculty and administration he inherited from Philips, his incessant travels and speaking engagements in order to strengthen the endowment, his recruitment of students with strong gifts for ministry, and his willingness to make difficult decisions about faculty, students, and administrators—all pointed to his understanding of pastoral ministry and to his belief that Columbia had a responsibility to offer the church only the most faithful and disciplined work it could muster. And to a remarkable extent, his quest for excellence for Columbia also entailed a love of beauty that was to find clearest expression in the way he oversaw the development of the campus and its landscape.[2]

A graduate of Davidson College and Union Seminary in Virginia, Oldenburg had obtained a graduate degree at Yale and had spent a sabbatical in England working on issues of Christian faith and economic justice. He had served two pastorates before being called in 1972 to Covenant in Charlotte, a large and affluent congregation whose membership included much of the city's business and civic leadership. Quickly gaining a reputation as a serious and thoughtful preacher and a good pastor, he was also much engaged with the Charlotte community. The week after it was announced he had accepted the call to Columbia, an editorial in the *Charlotte Observer* called his leaving Charlotte "a great loss to the city." The editor noted that Oldenburg had addressed eloquently many issues, but "his most urgent interest was Christian faith and economic justice." Later, on the eve of his departure from Charlotte, the *Observer* said that he had been "a powerful influence for good" in the life of the city, and it named the many ways he had challenged "his prosperous congregation, community and denomination to use wealth and influence in the way Jesus commanded: to help those who are in need." He was, the paper said, admirably suited for the work to which he had been called: "the shaping of future generations of Presbyterian ministers."[3]

One of the ministries that Oldenburg had led for Mecklenburg Presbytery was a ten-year economic development mission for Croix Fer, a village in eastern Haiti. He had helped raise a million dollars for the mission, which focused on an irrigation project, public health, and education. For ten years he had traveled twice a year to Haiti to confer with the Haitian project director and to spend time staying in the village and getting to know its people. He had developed an admiration for the ingenuity and courage of the villagers, and he had realized that affluent white Presbyterians in Charlotte had much to learn from poor black Haitians in Croix Fer. The Haitian mission had turned for Oldenburg into a mutual mission and a two-way street. The Haitian experience consequently provided Oldenburg important insights and resolve as he began his presidency. And what made this particularly important was that he was entering his new responsibilities at the very time Columbia was being transformed by new international connections and commitments.[4]

In 1980 Columbia had had five international students, there was no regular program for placing its U.S. students in a non–North American context, and few faculty had had more than a traditional European international experience. Two developments converged in the years immediately before Oldenburg's arrival to alter this long-established pattern.[5]

First, the Lilly Foundation had funded in 1980 an Atlanta-Caribbean Conference held on the Columbia campus with the theme of "Internationalizing Theological Education." Conference participants, divided evenly between Caribbean and Atlanta theological educators, had agreed that a program should be developed for continued dialogue and sharing of resources by the theological institutions of the two areas. A second conference was held the next year at the United Theological of the West Indies (UTCWI) in Kingston, Jamaica. A comprehensive program emerged from this second conference that was to link closely Columbia and UTCWI for decades to come. The conference also provided Columbia with a set of assumptions that were to guide the seminary as it developed cooperative relationships with theological institutions and churches in other parts of the world. Among the assumptions was the insistence that serious cross-cultural dialogue must guide any international program. Such dialogue, the conference declared, "will be based on a genuine mutuality" that acknowledges that theological communities in different parts of the world have "significant contributions to make to one another." Another assumption was that any international program "while acknowledging the realities of our global village must also recognize and work to strengthen the particular local agendas of the participants." Each region of the world has its own history and concerns that shape local agendas. Any international program must not divert but rather encourage those efforts to address these local agendas. For Columbia this meant that the issues of race and racism in the United States and in its own life must be addressed with new intensity and with new insights drawn from international partners who had their own histories, struggles, and perspectives.[6]

The second important development in shaping Columbia's new international connections and commitments was a gift in 1980 of $125,000 from the Presbyterian Women of the Church. The purpose of the gift was to generate a new concern for the "work of the church around the world." Columbia used the gift and its interest over a six-year period to pursue the objectives established by the two conferences. Under Davison Philips's leadership, Columbia did not use the gift to fund existing programs. In this way the seminary's international budget was doubled in 1980 to $50,000. By the time the gift was used up, the seminary's international program was so well established and the seminary's financial situation had been so significantly strengthened that the increase funded by the gift was simply absorbed into the general budget. When Oldenburg arrived with his own commitments to international cooperation and perspectives, he was prepared to see that the budget for the program was not only maintained but increased.[7]

With this financial and administrative backing, the international program developed, rapidly bringing new multicultural perspectives and experiences to the seminary that had long been marked by its southern provincialism. It was, of course, not incidental that this international turn at Columbia was taking place as Atlanta was becoming a truly international city—Hartsfield International Airport had become one of the busiest in the world, and the city was soon to celebrate its new international status by hosting the 1996 Summer Olympics.[8]

The author served as director of Columbia's International Program, but key faculty members played a central role in its development and direction—Wade Huie, Tommy Brown, Jasper Keith, Catherine González, Bob Ramey, and Lee Carroll. Justo González served as an informal consultant, providing insights and suggestions drawn from his wide travels and contacts. By 1990 the number of international students on the campus had increased fourfold, but it had done so in a deliberate manner. In cooperation with churches and theological institutions around the world and under the guiding principle of mutuality, new partnership agreements were reached. The result was that most of Columbia's internationals came from specific churches or theological institution that had established relationships with Columbia. Few internationals were accepted who simply applied on their own. And drawing on agreements with international partners, no international was accepted as a candidate for Columbia's basic degree program. A student, it was said, who was studying to be a pastor, for example, in Korea could best be prepared at a Korean theological seminary for preaching, pastoral care, and other practices of ministry in Korea. Internationals consequently came as special students for a year of enrichment or as advanced degree candidates engaged in graduate study in a particular discipline. As part of the agreements, Columbia students were offered full scholarships or internships by partner theological institutions or churches. By 1990 Columbia students were studying at UTCWI; at Codrington College in Barbados; at Westminster College, Cambridge, England; at the University of Glasgow; and at Seoul Presbyterian Theological Seminary. In addition Columbia students were spending summers in Kenya or Jamaica and later South Africa under the supervision of experienced local pastors. And, as we shall see, most Columbia M.Div. students were spending a January term in an international Alternative Context for Ministry course. During the same period, a joint D.Min. program, in cooperation with Emory and Atlanta's Interdenominational Theological Center, was also begun with UTCWI. This meant that white and African American pastors were in classes with Caribbean pastors as together they discussed issues of ministry in their own context. How, for example, was pastoral care different in a Jamaican context from pastoral care in an African American congregation or a suburban white congregation? Ministers engaged in such cross-cultural reflections could see the ways that their assumptions and practices of ministry were influenced by deep cultural histories and social contexts. And when UTCWI made it possible for Cuban pastors to become a part of Columbia's D.Min. program, the classroom discussions became even richer.[9]

One of the most immediate results of the developing international program was the greatly increased presence on the campus of church leaders and theological educators from around the world. International partners said that they had a great need for professors and pastors to have opportunities for sabbatical study. In response Columbia began to offer, without charge, apartments and board to professors and pastors recommended by partner institutions. A distinguished group of church leaders was soon on the campus going to class, eating with students in the dining hall, leading worship in chapel, and teaching courses on the church in their part of the world. In the years immediately before Oldenburg's arrival, for example, Omosade Awolalu, head of the Department of Religious Studies, University of Ibadan, Nigeria, taught the course West African Indigenous Religions and one on Islamic fundamentalism in West Africa. Janos Pasztor, dean and professor at the University of Debrecen, Hungary, lectured on the church's life in communist Hungary. Anglican bishop Neville de Souza and president Ashley Smith, of UTCWI, lectured on the church in the Caribbean and the legacies of slavery and colonialism. And David Steele and Stuart McWilliam, pastors from Scotland, drew on the deep traditions of their church to lecture on preaching in the late twentieth century. Under Oldenburg's leadership this pattern of bringing distinguish church leaders to the campus was expanded. Principal Chen Zemin and Professor Wang Wei-fan of Nanjing Theological Seminary spent a year on the campus as visiting scholars and were joined for a time by Bishop K. H. Ting, president of the China Christian Council. Martin Cressey, principal of Westminster College, Cambridge, spent a sabbatical at Columbia, as did Bishop Karoly Toth of the Hungarian Reformed Church. Douglas John Hall, Canadian theologian, came as a lecturer, as did the Hungarian pastoral theologian Bela Toth; and Archbishop Desmond Tutu delivered a commencement address. The presence of these and other church leaders had a profound impact on the campus—perhaps especially through their informal conversations with students and faculty over coffee and during meals in the dining hall and in faculty homes. A new institutional ethos was emerging that was being informed by new perspectives and insights brought from the experience of the church in many parts of the world. And those perspectives and insights were helping to illumine Columbia's own history, its own social and cultural context and assumptions, and its own sense of mission as it moved toward a new century.[10]

From the first days of his administration Oldenburg sought to build on the strength in administration and faculty he inherited from Philips. Oscar Hussel continued for two years as academic dean, helping with the transition to a new president. When he retired Glen Buecher came from the College of Wooster to assume the dean's responsibilities. He remained for only three years before leaving to be president of the Graduate Theological Union, Berkeley, California, but before he left he had launched an important new initiative with the church in China and had led the faculty into a major curriculum study. He was followed in 1993 by James Hudnut-Beumler, who came from the Lilly Endowment to be Columbia' new academic dean. Hudnut-Beumler was an embodiment of the excellence Oldenburg sought for Columbia. A Presbyterian minister with a Ph.D. from Princeton University, he had served as administrative director of the undergraduate program and lecturer in public and international affairs at the Woodrow Wilson School of Princeton University. Moreover, said Oldenburg, he was "deeply committed to the church and the preparation of ministers to serve local congregations." His study of U.S. religious life and his engagement with questions of public policy and international affairs made him particularly well suited to lead the faculty as its sought to understand Columbia's mission on the eve of a new century.[11]

Philip Gehman had been serving as Columbia's director of admissions when he was called to be dean of students shortly after Oldenburg's arrival. A Columbia graduate with a D.Min. from Union in Virginia, Gehman had served churches in Virginia and North Carolina and had been much engaged with youth work, with the candidate committees of his presbyteries, and with Montreat summer conferences. His broad contacts throughout the Presbyterian church, his knowledge of Presbyterian polity and procedures, and his good administrative skills meant that he was going to be for the next sixteen years an important link between the seminary and the presbyteries represented in the student body. Seniors were to find him a particularly helpful guide through the labyrinth of candidacy procedures, ordination exams, and the call process. And when he persuaded Ernestine Cole to be the associate dean of students, Gehman had a colleague who provided strong pastoral care to students and student families. In addition, as an African American Presbyterian minister, she was to play a critical role as Columbia struggled with the deep racial assumptions of its history and sought to find a way forward toward a more diverse and inclusive community.[12]

John Gilmore also represented the kind of excellence Oldenburg was seeking. A certified public accountant with degrees in theology and law, he was exceptionally well suited to guide the seminary as vice president for business and finance. Coming to Columbia in 1988, he quickly gained the confidence of the board and its finance committee during a period when the endowment was soaring beyond any expectations. For over a decade, his good humor and friendly ways were to make him popular with the faculty, who trusted his judgments and enjoyed his friendship.[13]

When Doug Hix retired, George Telford was called to lead the burgeoning program of advanced studies. A Columbia graduate Telford came from a long line of influential Presbyterian ministers deeply linked to Columbia's history. He had been a Woodrow Wilson Fellow at Harvard, had a diploma from the University of Geneva, Switzerland, had been director of the church's Division of Social and Corporate Mission, and had been an important voice in both the National Council of Churches and the World Council of Churches. Broadly read and highly articulate, he had served as pastor of several strong Presbyterian congregations and was widely known throughout the Presbyterian Church as a pastor theologian. He brought to Columbia great energy, broad learning, and a deep commitment to and understanding of the work of a pastor in local congregations. He was to build on Hix's work and make Columbia's D.Min. degree one of the nation's strongest.[14]

While Oldenburg was building an administrative team whose members were to work closely with one another through the 1990s, he was also giving careful attention to the development of the faculty. Beverly Gaventa was called in Oldenburg's first year to be professor of New Testament. Already a rising star in New Testament studies, she would stay at Columbia for five years before leaving for Princeton Seminary, where she would become one of the nation's leading New Testament scholars. In 1989 John Patton became professor of pastoral theology. He had been serving as director of the Atlanta Theological Association's program that led to the doctor of sacred theology in pastoral counseling. Known throughout the country as a leading pastoral theologian, he had been president of the American Association of Pastoral Counselors and had written widely in the field. His book *Is Human Forgiveness Possible: A Pastoral Care Perspective* was being studied by many pastors, and *The Dictionary of Pastoral Care and Counseling,* which he coedited with Emory's Rod Hunter, was a standard resource in the field.[15]

In the fall of 1991, seven new professors joined Columbia's faculty: Marcia Riggs in ethics; Will Coleman in theology; Charles Campbell in homiletics; Ron Cram in Christian education; Iwan Russel-Jones in media, theology, and the church; Victor Yoon as director of the Asian Study Center; and Ron Crossley as director of Columbia's new Center for Theological Studies in Orlando, Florida. Riggs and Coleman brought African American experience and perspectives to key disciplines in the curriculum. For over twenty-five years Riggs was to be a particularly important voice on the faculty as an ethicist, as an African American woman, and as a professor with a strong interest in developing new pedagogical strategies for an increasingly diverse student body in the twenty-first century. She was also to be a firm but generous mentor for some white male faculty colleagues as they sought to understand the ways the experience of women and of African Americans challenged old assumptions and practices at Columbia. Campbell adopted alternatives ways of teaching homiletics better suited to the times. The old pattern of senior preaching followed by the faculty's frank and sometimes harsh criticism was dropped, and a more private approach was adopted. Cram brought a special interest in children and their spiritual lives, and Russel-Jones, Yoon, and Crossley were all administering new program centers, which, as we shall see, were developing rapidly at Columbia.[16]

Three other faculty members were called during the first half of Oldenburg's tenure. Kathleen O'Connor came in 1994 from the Marynoll School of Theology to teach Old Testament. She had been a Dominican nun with not only a deep knowledge of biblical studies but also a passion for social justice. Her commentaries on Jeremiah and on the Wisdom Literature had already won for her a reputation as an important Old Testament scholar, and when she came to Columbia, she made the Old Testament faculty indisputably the seminary's strongest. Because she was such a superb teacher and winsome presence, she quickly convinced Presbyterians that it was a great thing to have an Irish Catholic in the community and teaching Old Testament.[17]

Two Disciples of Christ ministers also joined the faculty. Stan Saunders became an assistant professor of New Testament the same year that O'Connor arrived. During the next twenty-five years, he was to be a popular teacher who would make important contributions to both the M.Div. and D.Min. programs. In 1994 Carlos Cardoza-Orlandi was called as instructor in world Christianity. A Puerto Rican who had been strongly recommended by his mentor Justo González, Cardoza-Orlandi was soon providing a picture of world Christianity from the perspectives of Latin America. These new non-Presbyterian faculty members pointed to a change in Columbia's plan of government that allowed for one-fourth of the faculty to be non-Presbyterian. The new provision opened a door for Columbia to call strong faculty from other denominations and traditions while at the same time maintaining the seminary's pervasive Presbyterian character.[18]

As the faculty underwent these changes, it began to feel the need for a careful look at the M.Div. curriculum. Throughout the 1980s the Association of Theological Schools had sponsored a vigorous debate about the nature and challenges of theological education in the United States during the closing years of the century. The debate encouraged Columbia's faculty to engage in an extended review of the curriculum. The Lilly Foundation, aware of Columbia's growing strength, awarded the seminary a $137,000 grant. Its purpose was to allow the faculty to engage in the most serious reflection it could muster about the contemporary context for theological education in the United States, about what was needed in a seminary curriculum to prepare persons to be ministers of the Gospel in such a context, and about pedagogical strategies to employ in such a curriculum. Three primary documents emerged from this three-year effort—an "Assumptions Paper" adopted by the faculty; a mission statement adopted by both the faculty and the board;

and a new curriculum. The assumptions paper was particularly revealing. It pointed to Columbia's understanding of its remembered history and highlighted the faculty's commitments to the Reformed tradition; it analyzed the seminary's present and projected social contexts; and it named what it saw to be the mission of Columbia Seminary in such contexts.[19]

The assumptions paper was slowly hammered out after intense study and debate within the faculty and with colleagues from outside the seminary. The faculty met for several months with Barbara Wheeler of Auburn Seminary in New York and discussed the new literature on theological education. John Cobb, the distinguished theologian from Claremont School of Theology, led the faculty in seven seminars entitled "What I Believe about Christology and Salvation" in which religious pluralism and interfaith dialogue were central themes. Robert Bellah, the highly influential sociologist, led the faculty in provocative discussions of his hugely influential *Habits of the Heart: Individualism and Commitment in American Life.* The discussions centered on the nurturing of what Bellah and his associates called "communities of memory and hope." A small group of outside consultants met regularly with the faculty. Conversations were held with seniors and graduates, and a group of distinguished pastors—including James Forbes from the Riverside Church, New York—were gathered to discuss issues of ministry and theological education. Stanley Hauerwas and Will Willimon, authors of the bestselling *Resident Aliens: Life in the Christian Colony,* did their best to persuade the faculty that Presbyterians were resident aliens in America—a countercultural church governed by the demands of Jesus—and that the faculty, in its comfortable homes and with its growing pensions, were to teach students to be resident aliens.[20]

The assumptions paper emerged from this cauldron. When the faculty—knowing the seminary's growing strength and feeling its long cultural traditions—looked to the future, it saw:

> A shrinking and increasingly interdependent world, struggling with massive technological change, environmental degradation, war and the threat of war, and a growing gap between the rich and the poor.
>
> An expanding racial and ethnic pluralism that will continue to change the demographic composition of the U.S.
>
> The rising voices of those (women and minorities) who in previous generations were largely suppressed or ignored by the then dominant culture and its religious institutions.
>
> An increasing awareness in the old "mainline" denominations of the profound tensions between North American society and Christian faith.
>
> A continuation of Mainline Protestantism's crisis of faith and new opportunities for evangelism among those who feel the alienations of secularism or the need to move beyond Fundamentalism.
>
> A growing awareness of the need for new theological reflection and commitment on the environmental crisis.
>
> A crisis within the Presbyterian Church and other mainline denominations as

they struggle with the loss of members, particularly many of their children who have become largely secularized.[21]

The assumptions paper then turned to the implications of this analysis for a new curriculum. The result was summarized by Dean Glenn Buecher in a letter to the Lilly Foundation: "the new M.Div. curriculum, in its focus, organization, and pedagogy, needs to be built around the emphases of nurturing a Christian community of memory and hope with a critical hermeneutic and around the preparation of community members for participation, primarily through ministry in the local congregation, in the *Missio Dei* [mission of God] in a pluralistic world."[22]

The challenge for the faculty was how to build a curriculum based on these assumptions. And, of course, the assumptions were not the only factor to consider in designing a new curriculum. The composition of the faculty and the personalities and diverse personal interests of faculty members had to be considered. What emerged was a curriculum in much continuity with earlier curricula in its emphasis on biblical studies in the original Hebrew and Greek, in its requirements in church history and theology, and in its multiple courses in practical theology. Several important developments in the curriculum, however, stand out.[23]

First, the curriculum developed in the 1970s had required entering students to take a course called "Becoming a Minister to Persons." At the heart of the course was an understanding of "personal development" that utilized the work of Eric Ericson. Developmental psychology became a primary way for students to understand their personal identities. This course was dropped in the new curriculum and replaced with the course "Baptism and Evangelical Identity," which emphasized "the Christian identity of all those incorporated through baptism into Christ and Christ's community in the world." The movement from psychological categories to theological and sacramental ones reflected important shifts going on in the faculty since the mid-1980s. Increasing numbers of faculty were resisting the claims of a therapeutic culture with its ethic of self-realization. That ethic made a distinction between a conventional public self and a true inner self—an inner self said to be freed from the restraints of history and society. One discovered, it was asserted, this true inner self through honest introspection and "getting in touch with one's true feelings." As such the ethic embodied a radical individualism that Bellah and his colleagues had labeled in *Habits of the Heart* "expressive individualism." When the faculty adopted "Baptism and Evangelical Identity" as an important introductory course for students, it was not only resisting the culture's "expressive individualism"; it was also emphasizing the communal character of Christian faith and individual identity. "The curriculum," Hudnut-Beumler wrote, "offered to M.Div. students emerges from the seminary's identity as a community of memory and hope."[24]

The emphasis on the communal character of Christian life was continued in the spring term with a second interdisciplinary course, "The Eucharist and the Church's Mission." The calling of the church was said to be grounded in the Lord's Supper, and the task of the church was to participate in God's mission for all creation. The course had a Trinitarian understanding of mission—the Father, Son, and Holy Spirit sending the church into the world. Darrell Guder, who would join the faculty in 1996, summarized the missional understanding that informed the new curriculum: "We have come to see that mission is not merely an activity of the church. Rather, mission is the result of God's initiative, rooted in God's purposes to restore and heal creation." Of no little importance was the assertion that the curriculum was primarily designed to prepare persons to lead congregations as instruments of God's mission in the world.[25]

The two courses together reflected an important shift away from a stress on self-realization as a kind of spiritual quest of an individual Christian toward an emphasis on baptismal identity and the corporate nature of Christian life. This meant that theological education by necessity was a communal endeavor that could not be accomplished by isolated individuals studying alone. To prepare for ministry in community called for preparation in an actual community that existed not in the air, in some spiritual or technological ether, but on the ground of a particular place—a campus.

At the same time, the emphasis on the church's participation in God's mission in the world pointed toward a subtle but important shift toward a new model of ministry that was influencing the curriculum. An older model had emphasized the role of the minister as a professional among professionals, a credentialed and competent person who possessed specific habits and skills necessary to do the work of ministry. That role, of course, did not disappear but was nuanced by an emphasis on ministry as leadership in the church as it participated in the *Missio Dei.* Ministry was not so much a profession—parishioners after all were not "clients"—as it was a form of Christian discipleship within the life of the church. The courses in the new curriculum consequently represented a countercultural movement that was going to be difficult for the seminary to sustain in a society enchanted by new communication technologies and dominated by consumer capitalism, an individualistic culture in pursuit of self-fulfillment, and enshrined professional values.[26]

A second important development for the new curriculum was the decision to keep in the curriculum the second-year course "Alternative Context for Ministry." The faculty had adopted the course in 1986 as an experiment that combined both academic and experiential learning. Its purpose was to help both students and faculty engage the church as it exists in social contexts largely unfamiliar to the Columbia community. Both faculty and students were to explore how the church in a specific place with its particular history understood its mission in that context. Preparation for the course was begun in the spring term of the first year and continued in the fall term of the second year. The course itself took place in the January term of the second year, and deliberate reflections from its learnings were continued in later courses. The course had five placements—the inner city of Atlanta with its growing homeless population and urban poverty, Appalachia with its rural poverty, Jamaica, Central America, and Hungary. Six sectors of a society with their dynamic interactions with one another were explored in each of the placements—the arts, economics, education, family, health care, and politics. This sector analysis provided a conceptual framework for the experience and clarity about why some lectures were heard and some places visited and not others.

Church leaders in each of the contexts were the primary teachers saying "you need to hear from these persons and to visit these places." In Jamaica, for example, Professor Trevor Edwards from the United Theological Seminary secured lecturers on the arts in Jamaica and made arrangements for the class to attend plays on Jamaican life, to visit art museums, and to discuss the graffiti—seen everywhere in Kingston slums—that spoke of politics and economics, sports and sex. Visits in homes, worship with congregations, and discussions with church leaders all provided insights into how the church in Jamaica—in all its own diversity—understood its ministry and mission in such a context. And not incidentally the experience nurtured a deepening sense of Christian links across the distances that separated cultures and societies. In all this Columbia faculty were also students, learners who brought their own histories and disciplines to the discussions and evening reflections. So faculty and students were led to reflect on their own culture and how they saw it as they looked across the waters from Jamaica and asked about the ministry and mission of the church in the United States. Hudnut-Beumler reported to the board: "At professional meetings I am often told that there are no other U.S. seminaries with as extensive an international component in their educational programs as has Columbia."[27]

Because the course involved a significant amount of time beyond the January term, some faculty originally had serious questions about its role in the curriculum. But by 1992 seventeen faculty members had participated in the course and enthusiastically supported its purpose and results. And students consistently reported that it was one of the most important courses for their theological education. The course was thus retained in the new curriculum, and adequate funds were designated for it. New placements were to be occasionally added—to Korea and China, to India and the Czech Republic, to the Yucatán and Ghana. This meant that during the coming years the course was to play an important role in shaping not only the educational experience of Columbia students but also the work and perspective of the Columbia faculty.[28]

Columbia faculty had a special appreciation for pastors and others who were teachers in "alternative contexts." In Hungary Zoltan Bóna, leader in the Hungarian Council of Churches, theologians Janos and Judith Pasztor, and practical theologian and pastor Bela Toth helped faculty catch glimpses of how Hungarian Christians had persevered through the horrors and devastations of war and the oppression of governments. In Jamaica leading Caribbean theologians Ashley Smith, William Watty, and Bishop Howard Gregory together with a host of other pastors and church leaders encouraged Columbia faculty and students to learn from the life and thought of the Caribbean church with its history of slavery and colonialism. In Appalachia Ben Poage and Lon Oliver from Appalachian Ministries Educational Resource Center helped those from Columbia engage Appalachia's rich culture and church life amid economic and environmental devastations. In Atlanta Ed Loring and Murphy Davis of the Open Door Community plunged students and faculty into the world of the homeless while Calvin Houston, Dewey Merritt, and Ginger Kaney of the Urban Training Organization exposed them to the harsh realities of urban poverty. And in Merida, Yucatán, the Reverend Alejandro Magaña arranged lectures by Pentecostal preachers and Catholic priests, university professors and politicians, experts on Mayan culture and historians of the Yucatán. He took students and faculty to hospitals and church services, Mayan ruins and Yucatecan folk dances, and he sat with them as they discussed what they had seen and learned. All this meant that on January evenings each year, students and faculty gathered for worship and reflection in Budapest and Kingston, in Merida, downtown Atlanta, and not far from Troublesome Creek in Knott County, Kentucky. What new things had they seen and learned about the church's life and ministry in these places far from Columbia's comfortable campus? And what were they learning about themselves and their world and how their histories and their social place was shaping their commitments and their understanding of Christian faith and the mission of the church? Columbia was clearly engaging a broader church and world than it had ever known—and doing so in ways that pushed both faculty and students to understand themselves more fully and to see their place in the world and in the body of Christ more clearly.[29]

The engagement with a broader world also involved what the assumptions paper called "massive technological change"—especially the increasing role of media in U.S. culture. Through an anonymous grant secured by Ben Johnson, a new faculty position was created—associate professor in media, theology and the church. Iwan Russell-Jones, a prize-winning producer of religious programs for the British Broadcasting Company, was called to the position. With a Ph.D. in theology from Oxford and extensive experience in broadcasting, he brought to the new curriculum both theological scholarship and a sophisticated understanding of the media's role in contemporary society. This meant that the new curriculum was enriched by courses such as "Television and Contemporary Cultural Values," "Christology in Film," and "Theology, Technology and the Media in the Writings of Jacques Ellul." In faculty meetings and informal gatherings with students, over lunches with colleagues and dinners with board members, Russell-Jones insisted that a radical media revolution was underway and that it was transforming not only how people communicate but also the values and assumptions they communicate. He developed a video series called "Signs of the Times: Reading Our Culture with Eyes of Faith," which was widely used in congregations. The series explored the significance of such signs and icons as television and the computer and their impact on Christian lives and witness.[30]

As growing numbers of students came to Columbia to study with its faculty and enter its new curriculum, Oldenburg's quest for excellence extended to the admission office and its policies. What he hoped for in students—and it was what he expected of himself—was a mind disciplined for service to the church, a heart that could embrace the joy and pain of people, and a will imbued with Christian liberty and courage to challenge the injustices of the world. He said regularly that "we are not looking for more students, but always looking for *better* students." Still the M.Div. classes grew. Rebecca Parker, a graduate of Yale Divinity School, served effectively as director of admissions during the early part of the Oldenburg administration and was followed by Ann Clay Adams. A graduate of Smith College and Princeton Theological Seminary, Adams brought the background and the energy needed for the recruitment of gifted students. By the middle years of the 1990s, the M.Div. student body was larger than it had been since the early 1960s. Men and women were coming to Columbia from all over the country and from such schools as Yale, Princeton, Brown, and Vassar; from the University of California, Utah State, and State University of New York; from Duke, Vanderbilt, and Emory; and from Davidson, Presbyterian, Rhodes, Agnes Scott, and Washington and Lee. They were overwhelmingly white and Presbyterian, although there were a few Episcopalians and Baptists, African Americans and Korean Americans among them. At the same time, the church had a need for more pastors as those who had entered the ministry after the Second World War were retiring and churches were beginning to have difficulty finding ministers. In October 1999 Oldenburg reported to the board: "I have always said that 'we are not looking for more students, but always looking for *better* students.' I think the time has come to say, 'we are looking *both* for *better* students and for *more* students." It was to be a much-rehearsed theme for the next few years.[31]

The number of students in graduate programs also continued to grow. George Telford, director of advanced studies, reported in 1993 that the seminary had been transitioning into a center of graduate and advanced studies in addition to a basic degree program. Columbia, he said, was seeking to make its D.Min. "the standard of excellence nationally." By 1998 there were 324 students representing twenty-five denominations enrolled in an advanced degree. The total student body was larger than it had ever been.[32]

If Columbia was becoming a center for graduate and advanced studies for ministers, it was also taking on much of the character of a conference center as the seminary began to establish several discrete programs. In the mid-1980s the Cousins Foundation provided an endowment for a Lay Institute of Faith and Life "to equip laity for ministry in the church and the world." Shortly after Oldenburg became president, the board called Robert Smith from a pastorate in Florida to be the institute's director. An honor graduate of Princeton University, Harvard Law School, and Columbia Seminary, he was a superb choice to launch the institute. Within a year he had organized an on-campus Lay School of Bible and Theology with an enrollment of 219. He soon organized seminars for business executives to explore "the integration of Christian faith and values in the marketplace"; various programs for "training laity for church leadership"; retreats for the laity on such subjects as "living with loss"; a three-day "Ministry of Money" workshop; and two weekend events on homelessness that involved a night in a shelter or an emergency room. These and other events were well attended, and long-range plans were put into place. After Smith's return to the pastorate, Rick Dietrich brought to the institute a focus on the arts.[33]

Working alongside the Lay Institute was a Continuing Education Program for clergy. Under the direction of Sara Juengst, Columbia graduate and former missionary in the Congo, the traditional program was rapidly expanded. During the 1988–89 school year, almost nine hundred clergy were enrolled in one of seventeen continuing education programs. January seminars were popular. In January 1989 Tom Long taught "Preaching for Lent and Easter"; Walter Brueggemann taught a course on Isaiah; Shirley Guthrie taught

"Presbyterians and the Evangelical Tradition"; and the courses "Psalmody, Hymnody and Reformed Worship" and "Divorce Recovery" were also taught. Off campus courses included "A Week at Koinonia and Habitat for Humanity"; "A Contemplative Week for Women"; "A Contemplative Week for Men"; "A Week's Immersion with the Church in Jamaica"; and a "Travel Study Tour to China." Juengst obvious had great energy, knew the church well, had an informed understanding of the clergy, and brought to the program popular speakers of distinction.[34]

Other programs were soon launched. The Asian Ministry Center recognized the growing importance of Asian immigrants, especially Koreans, for the church in the United States. Under the direction of Victor Yoon, the center was soon sponsoring seminars on the immigrant church and addressing such issues as the relationship of second-generation immigrants to the traditions of Asian cultures. Yoon worked closely with Korean American pastors in Columbia's supporting synods, brought to the campus an annual continuing education event for visiting Korean ministers, and helped organize a bilingual D.Min. program for Korean American pastors. The Center for New Church Development was established in 1996. Its director, Stanley Wood, worked with presbyteries and the General Assembly in developing strategies for beginning new churches and supporting their pastors. The Program in Christian Spirituality offered a systemic approach for the nurturing of Christian spirituality and a certificate in "spiritual formation." Under the leadership of Ben Johnson and his associate Julie Johnson, the program was soon offering classes in Louisiana, Missouri, and Michigan; in Washington state and California and Pennsylvania as well as on the Columbia campus. The Thompson Scholars program, established by a bequest of former professor Cecil Thompson, brought pastors to study "evangelism for the Presbyterian Church." And the Guthrie Scholars program, established at the retirement of Shirley Guthrie in 1998, brought to the campus each year two groups of pastors for individual study and conversations with faculty.[35]

In 1990 the ambitious Florida Extension Program was begun in the hope that a campus extension could be developed in Orlando. First Presbyterian Church, Orlando, and its pastor had originally encouraged the development of the program, but they never provided the promised support. After Columbia poured seven years of effort and substantial funds into the project, the board closed the center. It did not have sufficient local support, and it failed to attract enough students, especially the many Hispanics eager to have a theological education.[36]

The multiplication of programs on the campus changed the character of the seminary. Columbia had taken on much of the style of an urban conference center—leaders and participants were coming and going; growing numbers of staff were registering people and answering questions; the business office was arranging participant lodging; Suzanne SauerBrun was ordering books for the bookstore; the food service director David Musil was constantly adjusting the number of meals being prepared; and Oldenburg was hurrying to welcome various groups to the campus. Amid all this activity, the faculty was increasingly unaware of program details as a significant part of the seminary's life was now dedicated to work beyond the faculty's purview. To be sure, a faculty committee had some oversight over each program, but because each program had developed independently and because each was a largely self-contained world of planning and activity, coordination and faculty supervision were limited. The entrepreneurial skills required to manage and market each program meant that success was largely determined by individual directors. And while each program was a faithful attempt to respond to a perceived need in the life of the church, together they echoed the deep ways the seminary was a part of contemporary U.S. society. As antebellum Columbia was enmeshed in a slave society, so the Columbia of the late twentieth and early twenty-first centuries was enmeshed in a society based on consumer capitalism with it mechanisms of supply and demand. This, of course, was not unique to Columbia. A General Assembly committee investigated "program sprawl" at Presbyterian seminaries and warned that they may be "easily tempted by the prospect of new markets for programs" and suffer from "theological and educational fragmentation."[37]

Columbia's growth in faculty, students, and programs required new funds, new buildings, and a significantly expanded staff. When Oldenburg came to the presidency in 1987, Phase I of a capital campaign, "Toward 2000," was underway. Alumni/ae giving soared as did contributions from the board and other friends of the seminary. The goal of $6 million was reached quickly, and Phase II, "Rooted in Tradition, Growing with Vision," was launched in 1991. The campaign was chaired by two highly respected Atlanta businessmen and Presbyterian elders, John A. Conant and John H. Weitnauer, who worked with development officers Jim Dickenson, Frank Wiley, Bonneau Dickson, and Richard Dodds. Together they organized campaign committees in all the supporting presbyteries, and by 1996 the goal of $31.45 million had been passed with $35.5 million raised and another $8.9 million pledged. The campaign had exceeded all expectations and had helped deepen the ties of affection between the seminary and its Presbyterian constituency.[38]

Among the funds received was a $5 million bequest by Mr. and Mrs. Thomas S. McPheeters of Charlotte, North Carolina. Part of the bequest was used to honor Mr. McPheeters's father by endowing a William Marcellus McPheeters Chair of Old Testament. Walter Brueggemann was quickly named to the chair, and in this way the name William McPheeters—a name so closely tied to the Girardeau tradition—was linked to the nation's best-known and most widely read Old Testament scholar. Other chairs were also established as a part of the capital campaign. The J. Davison Philips Chair of New Testament honored the former president, and the J. Erskine Love Chair of Christian Ethics was in memory of Columbia graduate Erskine Love Sr. and his son the longtime chair of the board Erskine Love Jr., who had helped to guide the seminary during the Kline and Philips administrations. Atlanta's Trinity Presbyterian Church established the Miriam H. and John A. Conant Chair of Worship in honor of Columbia's board chair John Conant and his wife, Miriam. The Peachtree Presbyterian Church Chair of Evangelism and Church Growth reflected the commitments of the congregation and its pastor Frank Harrington.

And the Benton Family Chair of Christian Education came at the end of Oldenburg's tenure as a gift of Suzanne and John Benton, both of whom had served on Columbia's board. All the gifts, large and small, made the campaign a great success, unimaginable only a few years before. But a truly stunning gift was announced in late 1995—not only the largest gift in Columbia's history but also the largest in the history of theological education in the United States.[39]

In the 1920s John Bulow Campbell had been the major contributor of funds for the construction of the Decatur campus. In the 1930s his generosity had kept the seminary open during the hard days of the depression. When Campbell died in 1940, he left a bequest to Columbia to be realized at the time of the death of his daughter, Virginia Campbell Courts. When she died in 1995, the seminary was informed that it was the recipient of a $55 million trust established in 1925 by Campbell. Oldenburg called it "one of those life-changing moments" for Columbia. It meant, together with the successful campaign, that the endowment was now over $110 million. "The results of his gift," said Oldenburg, "will be felt for countless years, for it positions us to achieve new and higher levels of service for the Church of Jesus Christ." Oldenburg and Columbia's board, however, did not realize how close the seminary had come to forfeiting the bequest in 1940 and 1941.[40]

Shortly before his death, Campbell had asked the seminary to relinquish its claim, under an otherwise irrevocable trust, in return for a cash grant or for a guaranteed annual income. The Columbia board had given its consent, but Campbell died suddenly before the details of the agreement had been reached. The board then asked the Campbell Foundation for "an annual income of $10,000 in lieu of the residuary interest of the Seminary in the family trust fund." The foundation apparently refused the request, and—in what Richards would undoubtedly have called an act of providence—Columbia Seminary received $55 million in 1995.[41]

Oldenburg and the other senior administrators worked hard to see that Columbia's new wealth was used responsibly. They consulted closely with key board members, especially a remarkable cluster from Atlanta that constituted some of the most distinguished business and civic leaders in the city—Howell Adams, John Conant, Ann Cousins, Florida Ellis, Lawrence Gellerstedt, and Frank Skinner. Board chair Joanna Adams played a particularly important role as plans were made for the seminary's future. A 1979 Columbia graduate, Adams was pastor of Atlanta's large and affluent Trinity Presbyterian Church. She shared with Oldenburg a vision of Columbia as a center of excellence, and she brought to the discussions about the seminary's future a traditional Reformed piety and an acute awareness of the great social and cultural changes sweeping the country. What made her leadership so important was her innate devotion to the Presbyterian Church combined with broad ecumenical sensibilities and civic involvements.[42]

After much consulting Oldenburg made and the board approved a series of recommendations for immediate action: the draw on the endowment was reduced from 6.1 percent to 3.7 percent to help secure the endowment and encourage its annual growth;

faculty salaries were raised above the median of other Presbyterian seminaries; student aid was increased, and the library budget was expanded; and, following a request left by Virginia Counts as an expression of her father's interests, startup costs were provided for the Center for New Church Development. For long-term plans Oldenburg recommended and the board approved a "2020 Visioning Committee" to establish future goals and priorities for the seminary. The administration and board clearly intended to act with a long-term perspective while not ignoring immediate needs. They wanted to be frugal but not parsimonious, to be prudent without sacrificing a quest for excellence. The administration and board leaders were exceptionally well prepared by disposition and background for the tasks set before them.[43]

The growth of students and programs that had begun under Davison Philips's leadership and that rapidly expanded under Oldenburg's created a pressing need for new classrooms, offices, guest rooms, and meeting spaces. To meet these needs, and with a gift from the Peachtree Presbyterian Church, the seminary built the W. Frank Harrington Center for Continuing Education and Church Growth. Dedicated in the fall of 1989, the center provided much-needed space, but the rapid growth of programs in the 1990s meant the building was soon crowded and overflowing. With the support once again of the Peachtree congregation, a handsome wing was added in the late 1990s. The much-enlarged building pointed to Columbia's new role as a conference center—more guest rooms and suites allowed for larger participation in programs; a second chapel provided a place for informal worship; an auditorium had state-of-the-art communications technology that included satellite teleconferencing; and a "Twenty-First Century Classroom" contained a "translation booth" for simultaneous translating. In its design and arrangements, the building in its design and intended purposes reflected the deep commitments of Peachtree's pastor Frank Harrington.[44]

Harrington had grown up in the South Carolina lowcountry, where he had been nurtured in the faith and loved by a Presbyterian congregation with roots and memories that reached back to colonial America. He had graduated from Presbyterian College in 1957 and from Columbia in 1960, and, like Davison Philips, he looked on McDowell Richards as a father figure and trusted mentor. All this meant that while Harrington was evangelical in his faith and had led Peachtree in its growth to be the largest Presbyterian congregation in the nation, he was a Presbyterian churchman who knew deep in his bones the organic character of the body of Christ. He was consequently a strong supporter of the institutions of the church—especially Presbyterian College and Columbia Seminary—and he had little sympathy with evangelicalism's absorption of an individualistic culture and of modernity's homelessness and amnesia. But he also knew that the church had a calling in a technologically sophisticated and ethnically diverse twenty-first century. The Harrington Center's architecture consequently blended his sense of history and place and his commitments to Presbyterian institutions with his awareness of the church's call to engage a twenty-first century world—the building that carried his name harmonized beautifully with the historic collegiate Gothic of the campus while incorporating the newest technologies and space for pedagogical experimentation.[45]

This same harmonizing of the traditional with the realities of contemporary society was also reflected in the expansion of the John Bulow Campbell Library and in the renovations of Florida Hall. The library was extended toward the athletic field, and a new entrance faced the Richards Center and mirrored boldly its collegiate Gothic design. Inside the building the latest technological resources made the library into what librarian Tim Browning called a "first-class information service provider" while doubling the shelf space for books and adding a large special collections area for the Thomas Smyth Rare Book Collection and the seminary's archives.

The Florida Hall renovations addressed the demands of students—especially married couples—who now expected more spacious and comfortable accommodations. Apartments were enlarged and bathrooms refitted. An elevator, exercise room, and child-care facility added to the building's appeal to a new generation of students who had learned to expect such accommodations. At the same time, the building retained its traditional appearance with its red bricks, Indiana limestone, and slate roof so that it continued to express the assumptions and values that had long marked the campus.[46]

The extension of the library created a quadrangle for the interior of the campus—space that Oldenburg believed should be designed to enhance the beauty of Columbia. He insisted, despite his frugal disposition and the complaints of some faculty, that the quadrangle must be constructed for the future with the finest aesthetic sensibilities that could be mustered. Brick paver and not concrete were to be used for walks while trees and other plantings were to provide natural beauty and guides for the eye to draw the campus together into a pleasing and harmonious composition. Later the board named this central space the Oldenburg Quadrangle to honor his years as president and to acknowledge the ways his quest for excellence had created a place of beauty.[47]

But, of course, the campus with its new buildings and handsome quadrangle was not a place of some general and abstract beauty. Rather it was a place that expressed a particular kind of beauty and a particular understanding of the world and of the purposes of theological education. As in the past, the Columbia campus had a geography—an arrangement of buildings, paths, and landscaping—that conveyed meaning and that flowed from the minds and hearts of those Presbyterians who planned and oversaw its construction. The campus, however, was not only the product of a conceptual world; it was also a shaper of the world of those who inhabited the place. In subtle ways the campus told students, faculty, and staff a story of the past; it located them in a contemporary time and specific place among a specific people; and within its embrace it evoked for them an anticipation of the future and of their role in it. In all these ways, the campus was no neutral space in which the activities and rituals of the seminary took place, but space that helped to construct the world of the seminary and was an essential part of what made the seminary Columbia Theological Seminary.[48]

While the campus was being transformed, the faculty was undergoing its own significant changes during the last half of the decade. Five professors resigned during those years,

Lucy Rose died after a long and faithful struggle with cancer, and Shirley Guthrie and George Telford retired. And new faculty arrived. Some were to stay for only a few years or were to be only part time. But others were to be at the heart of what Hudnut-Beumler called "A Faculty for the 21st Century." Two senior appointments were made: Cameron Murchison as professor of ministry, and Elizabeth Johnson as the Davison Philips Professor of New Testament. Both were going to be faculty leaders during the coming years. And with them came four young and promising professors—Mark Douglas in ethics, Anna Carter Florence in homiletics, Roger Nishioka in Christian education, and Christine Yoder in Old Testament. Like the young Huie, Guthrie, and Cousar in the late 1950s, they were to become with Murchison and Johnson important links between the seminary and the church. New senior administrators also arrived. Richard DuBose became vice president for development, Martin Sadler became vice president for business and finance, and Charles Raynal became director of advanced studies and associate professor of theology. Together these new faculty and administrators were to play a large part in the life of the seminary during the first decade of the new century.[49]

Providing much continuity during these changes were staff members who went about their daily work with dedication and considerable patience and good humor as they dealt with the business of the seminary and the peculiarities of the faculty and seminary students. They were reminders that it takes many people to sustain an institution and that some of them receive inadequate recognition. Betty Beatty sat at the receptionist desk in Campbell Hall and kept tract of the comings and goings on campus. In the president's office Peggy Rowland and Linda Wells welcomed guests, calmed faculty nerves, guarded Oldenburg's time, and handled his voluminous correspondence. In the development office Juliette Harper oversaw the prize-winning seminary publication *Vantage,* Betsy Burgess kept burgeoning files in good order, and Elizabeth Orth turned formal seminary events into elegant occasions. Barbara Poe stayed in touch with graduates and greeted them warmly when they returned to the campus. In the business office, Marilyn Ault, Holly Caswell, and Judy Graves kept a sharp eye on seminary accounts, told students they had to pay their bills, and made room assignments for guests. In the dean of students office, Bonnie Shumaker, while overseeing growing piles of records, reminded students to send in reports to presbyteries and told them they could not keep cats in Florida Hall. Shellee Fezatte helped international students and faculty secure visas and Tia Foley proofed faculty manuscripts. Jewell Kirkus greeted prospective students, Robin Dietrich helped them figure out the cost of seminary, and Suanne SauerBrun and Joan Murchison introduced them to the seminary bookstore. Jane Gleim ran the dean of faculty office, and registrar Linda Sabo reminded students of the courses they had already taken and those they needed to take. Rhonda Weary kept tract of students in supervised ministry. Stoncil Boyette managed the new computer system and explained again and again to older professors how to send e-mails. Dana Campbell helped students who had graduated in engineering or business learn how to write an exegesis paper. In the Harrington Center staff associates multiplied to meet the needs of new programs while in the expanded library new positions were added to help the library become a "first-class information service provider." The maintenance crew and those in housekeeping kept the campus neat and orderly. Alexander and Eula Mae Oliver followed the tradition of Jessie and Pearlie Mae Graham, he in maintenance, she in housekeeping. Alexander Oliver was particularly admired for the music he brought to chapel services. Walking slowing across the front of the chapel, he sang with a music that took the congregation into some distant time and place, into the oldest African American traditions of the Ring Shout and Dance, traditions that had nurtured and given birth to the spirituals and the blues.[50]

Including the maintenance crew and those in housekeeping and food service, the administration and staff grew to fifty-nine in 1999—in 1983 there had been only twenty-nine. And between 1999 and 2003, fifteen additional staff would bring their total to seventy-four. In contrast the faculty had grown from twenty-one in 1983 to only twenty-eight in 2003. A significant part of the seminary's new financial resources was clearly being designated for staff as new programs sought to meet new challenges and as government regulations and accrediting requirements bourgeoned. Almost imperceptibly Columbia was taking on a more bureaucratic character with its standardized procedures to manage information, process records, administer a complex institution, and engage in a never-ending series of evaluations. Yet many who inhabited the campus, who sat in classrooms or offices, continued to think of Columbia, often with some nostalgia, as a community of learning and shared faith where personal social interactions were fundamental. In the years to come, the tension between Columbia's self-proclaimed character as a community and its lived world of organized hierarchies and many procedures was to grow more intense as efficiency and "good business practices" were increasingly to take precedence over the values of institutional loyalty, friendships, and shared commitments to Columbia's stated mission. Indeed the tensions were to be intensified as the seminary's relationship with its traditional constituency—a geographical community of deep memories and personal relationships—was challenged by the seminary's growing pluralism, theological diversity, and changing ecclesiology and by the relentless pressures of a market economy and a fracturing religious world.[51]

In 1998 Oldenburg was elected moderator of the Presbyterian General Assembly. His election indicated the church's great respect for him and the gratitude of many for the leadership he had provided Columbia. His acceptance of the position, with its demanding schedule of travel, meant that he was nearing the end of his presidency. Shortly after he completed his year as moderator, he announced that he would retire in 2000. His had been a remarkable presidency. The excellence he had sought for the seminary had been largely achieved: the endowment had soared, the campus had expanded beautifully, the student body was the largest in the seminary's history, and the faculty had gained an international reputation. Oldenburg had written "A Statement of Mission," which the faculty and board had adopted as the mission statement for the seminary. In its first paragraph, he had announced a shared understanding of Columbia's character: "Columbia Theological Seminary is an educational institution of the Presbyterian Church (USA), and a community of theological inquiry and formation for ministry in the service of the Church of Jesus Christ." And in its last paragraph, he had summarized a shared understanding of the mission to which Columbia was called and to which he had given his heart and tireless effort: "In carrying out our mission, we seek to be faithful to the gospel, and to become a living expression of the Body of Christ in the world." This understanding of Columbia's character was to be challenged in the coming years, and this summary of its mission was to be the subject of competing interpretations. But the legacy of the Oldenburg years was to act as a claim on Columbia's life. That claim insisted that Columbia was a community of deep memories lodged in a particular place among a people who had long been journeying together, and that it was also a community of hope, unafraid of the future, and ready to welcome those who brought to the journey their own deep memories.[52]

17

Seeking Common Ground

In late spring of 2000, Columbia's board called Laura S. Mendenhall to be the seminary's new president and to lead the old and much-loved seminary into a new century. Like her predecessors Whaling and Wells, Gillespie and Richards, Philips and Oldenburg, she came to the office as a parish minister. Like them she brought a vision of ministry that had been shaped by an experience of ministry in Presbyterian congregations in the South, by service to the denomination, and by leadership in the communities in which she lived. This meant that she also brought with her the good will of ministers who saw in her one of their own—a seminary president who knew what it is like to preach every Sunday, to visit the sick and dying, to baptize babies and moderate sessions, to worry about budgets, to counsel young couples, and to listen to the distressed. This goodwill of pastors and its accompanying confidence in her leadership was to be a mark of her presidency.[1]

For all the continuity with her predecessors, however, Mendenhall was also obviously different. She was part of the first generation of white Southern Presbyterian women to be ordained for the Gospel ministry, and she was to bring to the presidency the experience of following an unfamiliar path, one long marked with signs that read: "Women: Do Not Enter!" Like many of her sisters, she had not seen ordination as a possibility in the church that had nurtured her. She consequently enrolled in Presbyterian School of Christian Education in Richmond, Virginia, intent on becoming a Christian educator. While there she met and married Charles (Chuck) Mendenhall, a student at Union Theological Seminary. They went to Zaire as missionaries, teachers in a mission school, and there a deep compassion and respect for the poor of that war-torn country became a fundamental part of the way they saw the world and how they experienced the global character of the church. Later they went to California, where she served as an educator on the Presbytery staff while he completed a Ph.D. in pastoral counseling. In the midst of her work as an educator, she felt a call to ordained ministry stirring and found doors opening, even as she and Chuck Mendenhall were raising two small children. She entered San Francisco Theological Seminary, completed her M.Div. degree, and was ordained. After serving as an associate pastor in Florida and in two Texas congregations, she accepted a call to be the senior pastor of the Westminster Presbyterian Church in Austin, Texas. She completed a D.Min. degree from Austin Presbyterian Theological Seminary, and for her pastoral leadership and service to the community, Austin College awarded her an honorary degree.[2]

The Columbia board had been particularly impressed by her ability to help those of diverse opinions hear and understand each other and seek common ground. She had served as moderator of the Permanent Judicial Commission of the General Assembly when the commission had before it issues that were deeply divisive in the life of the church. Through patience and respectful listening, she had won the praise of all parties and had helped the commission arrive at decisions that seemed faithful, fair, and just. This disposition to seek common ground seemed, like the experience of parish ministry, a particularly important gift for a seminary president when fractures in church and society were widening. And such a disposition also meant that Mendenhall was to continue a long tradition at Columbia that taught moderation, that found truth in the middle, and that believed extremes usually led to distortions and trouble.[3]

What the board only intuitively realized at the time of Mendenhall's call was her ability to gain the confidence and affection of the seminary's lay constituency. Like a good pastor, she had a transparent piety that was modest and winsome and that invited respect for her as a person of faith. To a remarkable degree, she quickly won the trust of key board members who provided wise counsel for the administration of a complex institution and who in return received from her the care of a good pastor. Frank Skinner, the retired chair and chief executive officer of BellSouth Telecommunications, followed Joanna Adams as chair of the Columbia board in 2002. Mendenhall consulted him frequently and always spoke with great appreciation for the generous ways in which he gave his time to the seminary and for the wise judgment he provided especially on personnel issues. Florida Ellis, who had served on the board for many years, played an important role as chair of the board's academic affairs committee, while Bill Scheu, Ann Cousins, Howell Adams, Billy Morris, and other board members were always available for consultation and were supportive of Mendenhall in numerous ways. George Hauptfuhrer, Dennis Love, and Claire Cross, as members of the board's investment committee, were to be critical in the endowment's recovery from the recession following the dotcom bust in 2000 and later the Great Recession. Pastors also provided important board leadership. Joseph Harvard, pastor of First Presbyterian, Durham, North Carolina, had been chair of the search committee that nominated Mendenhall to the board, and he continued to be a close ministerial adviser. Charles Heywood, the first African American Columbia graduate to serve on the board, provided important insights into issues of diversity and racial justice. All of them working together were to continue Columbia's quest for excellence that had been pursued so vigorously under the Oldenburg presidency. But they were to face some daunting challenges identified nearly a decade earlier when the faculty had composed its assumptions paper for a new curriculum—challenges that had grown clearer and more intense.[4]

When the faculty had peered into future in the early 1990s, it had seen an expanding racial and ethnic pluralism that was changing the demographic composition of the United

States. By the time Mendenhall arrived on the campus, the impact of this demographic shift was beginning to be felt at Columbia. While it would be a few years before the shift was to become highly visible on the campus and in the seminary pictorial directories, old assumptions closely tied to a dominant white culture were to be increasingly called into question throughout Mendenhall's tenure and that of her successors. Was the excellence the seminary had been seeking an excellence that transcended ethnic and cultural boundaries or was it somehow peculiar to the culture of white society and its long-established privileges? What constitutes intellectual excellence, it was to be asked, and what kind of educational background did students need to enter a graduate program in theological education? These, of course, were questions that had long been asked—especially around students who had only a Bible college degree—but the questions began to take on a new shape as students began to come from different racial, ethnic, and theological traditions. Was there an excellence and a preparation for ministry rooted in nonwhite experience that Columbia had not recognized and that needed to be acknowledged and welcomed as a gift of the demographic shifts taking place in the nation's life?[5]

Closely related to these questions were questions that were going to swirl in a few years around the seminary's relationship to the Presbyterian Church and the Reformed tradition. Presbyterian churches in the synods that had long owned and controlled the seminary were still growing, but nationally the denomination was losing membership in alarming numbers. What was to be the seminary's mission in such a context? What vision of ministry and the church was to inform the direction of the seminary in the twenty-first century? And what about the great technological revolutions that were reshaping what students learn, the way they learn, and where they need to be physically located to learn? These questions were being widely discussed in centers of theological education, and they were questions that were going to move beyond the theoretical on the Columbia campus.[6]

As a part of its legacy, the Oldenburg administration had left a guide to the future—a 2020 Vision Statement and Strategic Plan. Shortly after receiving the Campbell bequest, the board had appointed a committee of trustees, faculty, students, and alumni/ae to develop a vision and a plan to lead the seminary for the next two decades. The committee drew into the process more than four hundred persons from Columbia's constituency and shaped, under Dean Hudnut-Beumler's leadership, a twenty-six-page vision statement that was not only theologically astute but also sophisticated in its analysis of the contemporary social and cultural context.[7]

The vision statement began with a reaffirmation of Columbia's vocation as confessed in its mission statement: "An educational institution of the Presbyterian Church (USA), and a community of theological inquiry and formation for ministry in the service of the Church of Jesus Christ." What followed was a careful articulation of the values needed to be upheld at Columbia if it were to pursue faithfully its mission as a servant of the church. The greatest challenge for the years ahead, it said, was "to maintain and develop a faculty that perpetuates the best aspects of the faculty we have assembled . . . over the last thirty years." New faculty needed a vocational commitment to furthering the work of the church, to be able to represent the Reformed tradition in a congenial and credible way, and to have "a positive relationship with the denomination that created and sustains Columbia Theological Seminary." At the same time, the faculty was not to be in service to some narrow denominationalism, but rather work in the name and spirit of Jesus Christ. What was envisioned was a collegial body of faithfully engaged scholars and teachers. They should pursue excellence in their teaching and mentoring of students; in their scholarly attainments, which command the attention of their peers in the world of letters; and in their engagement of public issues of theological significance.[8]

Students were to be learners growing as leaders in the church and the world. Their learning was not to be an end unto itself, but learning that nurtured the practice of Christian discipleship. Pursuing excellence, it was said, "in equipping the saints for the work of ministry" would produce a more geographically diverse and ecumenical student body than would directly pursuing a "national" or "ecumenical" strategy. Students from various backgrounds would be drawn to Columbia, not because of a diversity strategy, but because it was known for the excellence of its work in service to the church. Columbia needed, it was asserted, to make sure that those persons it educates are those most qualified to lead faithfully amid the challenges of contemporary society. "If a choice between quality and quantity of basic degree students must be made, then the seminary ought, for the future church's sake, to choose quality." What constitutes "quality" was to be vigorously debated in the coming years, not unlike debates that reached back to the frontier and debates about ministerial preparation and requirements for rigorous educational standards.[9]

The vision statement gave attention to advanced degrees, to continuing and lay education, to the various programs of the seminary, and to curriculum, facilities, and finances. Of special importance for the Mendenhall presidency was its focus on "Resources and Church Relations." A reinvigorated development program was envisioned under new leadership and with new strategies for further strengthening Columbia's financial base. Representatives of the seminary were to spend more time in the field "listening to alumni/ae, congregations, and other seminary constituencies." Central to its long-range plan was Columbia's commitment to the church, "to preparing and nurturing energetic and creative pastors and leaders for the Presbyterian Church (USA), and the larger church." This commitment and the securing of additional resources from Presbyterians to undergird this commitment were to be the most visible marks of the Mendenhall administration.[10]

The vision statement had seen the future development of the faculty as the greatest challenge facing the seminary because of looming retirements during the first decade of the new century. Ben Johnson retired in 2000. He had been a strong presence on the faculty and was well known throughout the church for his work first in evangelism and then in Christian spirituality. John Patton retired the next year. A leader in the field of pastoral care and counseling, he had been not only a distinguished scholar and mentor to many students, but also a good colleague who gave time and attention to the institutional life of the seminary. Catherine González retired in 2002. For almost thirty years she had been hugely popular with students, who consistently reported her introductory classes in church history to be their favorite. The faculty held her in highest regard and had regularly elected her to fill the most responsible positions on the faculty. With her husband, Justo, she had brought international perspectives to the campus, a deep awareness of concerns and developments among immigrant groups, and broad contacts with Pentecostalism and other new and surging Christian movements. Then in 2003 Charles Cousar and Walter Brueggemann retired. Cousar, a greatly admired professor and colleague—a "Columbia Saint" he was sometimes called—had served as dean of faculty and on two occasions as interim president. For generations of students, he had been known as the best-looking man on the faculty—not a particularly difficult a position to hold! But he was also known as a superb teacher, and a friend to graduates, who regularly asked him to preach their ordination sermons and lecture in their congregations. And he and his wife, Betty, had been friends of the Brueggemanns and had played a major role in getting them to Columbia.[11]

Walter Brueggemann had, during his years at Columbia, added to his stature as the premiere Old Testament scholar in the country. As book after book astonished an ever-growing following, he lectured at major universities and seminaries in this country and abroad, was interviewed on National Public Radio and on public television, preached in Westminster Abbey on the fiftieth anniversary of the bombing of Hiroshima, and preached and lectured at conferences and before the governing bodies of many denominations. His presence on the faculty had clearly made Columbia an internationally recognized center of Christian theological education.[12]

These retirements, together with those that were to come later in the Mendenhall administration, signaled a major turning point in Columbia's life. Faculty that had long been identified as "Columbia Seminary" and who had helped to make the seminary one of the nation's leading theological institutions were no longer to be present on the campus in a significant way. Returning graduates and visiting laity found the campus, even with its familiar landscape, to be an increasingly unknown territory. But more was involved than the absence of many familiar faces. A Columbia culture that had grown slowly over the previous fifty years was losing key players in its development and nurture. Voices that had sounded the cadences and peculiar dialect of the culture were to be increasingly absent from classrooms and faculty meetings, from chapel services and conversations over coffee. Generations earlier Girardeau had identified the ways "the phraseology of the past" was critical to the preservation of cultural identity and social cohesion. Now in the first decade of a new century, a dialect with its distinct phraseology seemed to be weakening as retirements quickly followed one another and as external forces were creating a new social context for the seminary. In such a milieu, a new culture with a new set of assumptions and values, habits and rituals, seemed to be on the horizon as the seminary moved deeper into the twenty-first century.

But, of course, institutional cultures are not easily changed. Indeed they resist change in a myriad of ways. The campus with its architecture and landscape, the endowment with its size and associated assumptions, graduates and board members with their memories and hopes, and younger faculty who shared the commitments of older colleagues and who had internalized the habits and rituals of the seminary—all spoke in the distinct accents of a Columbia tradition, and all were to play a part in shaping the character of the seminary as it evolved during the early decades of the new century.[13]

To fill the positions of those who had retired or resigned, new appointments began to be made shortly after Mendenhall arrived. Cameron Murchison was made dean of faculty to replace Jim Hudnut-Beumler, who had gone to Vanderbilt to be dean of its divinity school. Murchison had been the pastor of several churches and on the faculty of Union in Virginia before coming to Columbia in 1996 to be professor of ministry. With a Ph.D. from Yale in theology and with his extensive pastoral experience, he had brought to Columbia a deep knowledge of Presbyterian traditions as well as significant theological sophistication. Columbia's faculty had appreciated his administrative abilities and was enthusiastic about his appointment as dean. As Mendenhall gave more and more of her time to fund-raising, Murchison was to take increasing responsibilities for the internal affairs of the seminary. This familiar pattern, which was happening in higher education generally, was perhaps most clearly visible when Mendenhall asked him to be the chair of the Faculty Executive Committee, a position the president had held in the past.[14]

Other key administrative positions were filled during Mendenhall's presidency. After a short tenure by Margaret Henderson in the office of the dean of students, John White was called to be the new dean of students and vice president for student life. He had served as pastor of several Presbyterian churches and was dean of students at Pittsburg Theological Seminary when called to Columbia. The first African American in a senior administrative role at Columbia, he had a thorough understanding of Presbyterian polity and was to be a great help to students as they moved through the call and ordination process. He possessed much goodwill, a disarming manner, and the ability to speak in clear and forceful ways as he helped the seminary community address long-held white assumptions about race and ethnicity. In 2006 Sara Myers came from Union Theological Seminary, New York, to be the director of the library. She had been director of the Union library, the largest theological library in the world, and her coming to Columbia was an important indication of Columbia's growing reputation as a center of theological education. She made the library an inviting place for faculty and students and put an emphasis on service above rigorously enforced library protocols. Kim Clayton was called to be director of contextual education following Lee Carroll's long service as associate professor of supervised ministry. Clayton had had years of pastoral experience and supervision of students, and as the only Columbia graduate in the administration, she brought an important institutional memory to issues before the seminary community.[15]

The same summer Mendenhall was called to the presidency, Brian Wren was called to the Miriam H. and John A. Conant Chair of Worship. A graduate of Oxford with an international reputation as a hymn writer and worship leader, Wren represented the kind of excellence Columbia sought in its faculty. Recently published hymnals contained many of his hymns, some of which had already become greatly loved, and he was in demand as a lecturer in a wide variety of venues. In 2001 Emmanuel Lartey came from the University of Birmingham, England, to be Columbia's new professor of pastoral care and counseling. A native of Ghana, he was at the time serving as president of the International Council on Pastoral Care and Counseling and had written extensively on the church's pastoral care of people living in a multicultural world. By calling Lartey Columbia was acknowledging the great cultural and demographic shifts taking place in the United States and was signaling the need for its graduates to be prepared for ministry in such a world. Following Brueggemann's retirement William P. Brown came from Union Seminary, Virginia, to be professor of Old Testament. While he brought a growing reputation as a leading Old Testament scholar, he was soon to be widely known for his work on creation theology and the dialogue between faith and science, and he was to lead Columbia in a long-delayed response to issues that had once captivated James Woodrow.[16]

Jeffery Tribble was called as assistant professor of ministry. A leader in the African Methodist Episcopal Zion Church, he was to provide insights into and analysis of contemporary ministry by drawing on the rich traditions of his denomination. William Harkins, an Episcopalian, was serving as assistant professor pastoral theology and care, and Paul Johnson, a Methodist, was an adjunct in the same field. Stephen A. Hayner came to Columbia in 2003 as the Peachtree Associate Professor of Evangelism and Church Growth. He had been an adjunct professor at Fuller, Gordon-Conwell, and Trinity Evangelical theological seminaries, but he was best known as having served for thirteen years as president of the InterVarsity Christian Fellowship, a parachurch campus ministry that included a strong focus on ethnic minorities.[17]

The board called three young scholars to the faculty during these years. In 2001 Haruko Ward was called to fill González's position in church history. A native of Japan, she focused her scholarly work on women converts, catechists, and martyrs in the early Jesuit mission to Japan. Kathy L. Dawson, a 1994 Columbia graduate, came in 2004 to a new position in Christian education. She had a special interest in children's ministry and the ways the seminary could work with local congregations. When the Presbyterian School of Christian Education ended its independent existence, Dawson and Rodger Nishioka were to make Columbia a new center for the study of Christian education with advanced degrees in educational ministry. Martha Moore-Keish came to Columbia from the Congregational Ministries Division of the Presbyterian Church (USA). As a new assistant professor of theology and student of Calvin, she brought a special interest in Reformed worship. When Brian Wrenn retired in 2007, the emphasis on worship was continued with two half-time positions filled by Kimberly Long and Paul Huh. Long would later become full time and would make major contributions to congregational worship through her extensive writings on the history of worship and on contemporary resources for worship.[18]

The Mendenhall administration acted boldly to secure two new professors who were to add significant strength to Columbia's faculty. Bypassing the usual search process, Columbia secured Barbara Brown Taylor as distinguished adjunct professor of Christian spirituality, and David Bartlett as distinguished professor of New Testament. Taylor, known as one of the most influential preachers in the country, had been addressing in books and lectures the spiritual crisis of contemporary American society. Called to work primarily in the D.Min. and continuing education programs, she was to address through a variety of courses the spiritual life of pastors and the ways pastors nurture the spiritual life of congregations. *Time* magazine was later to place her on its cover and named her in 2014 to its annual list of the one hundred most influential people in the world. David Bartlett had been serving as Yale Divinity School's dean of academic affairs when he was called to Columbia. He was not only a highly regarded New Testament scholar but also, like Taylor, a preacher of great power. Together they were to serve as the general editors of the twelve-volume commentary series *Feasting on the Word*, whose volumes quickly became best sellers and linked Columbia to this important resource for preachers.[19]

The number of students continued to grow during the Mendenhall years as Columbia's reputation as a center of theological excellence attracted students from around the country and from many different universities and colleges. Ann Clay Adams skillfully coordinated the admissions office and received strong help from some faculty who played an important role in recruitment—especially Roger Nishioka and Anna Carter Florence who were in great demand as speakers at youth conferences. They had an ability—it seemed to older faculty a mysterious gift—to keep the attention of teenagers and to engage young adults. Sixty-eight new M.Div. students enrolled in the fall of 2004, and the following spring saw 136 applications for the next fall. The admissions committee set a limit of fifty-five new students for the next year and was consequently denying admission to many applicants. The M.Div. student body that year was overwhelmingly Presbyterian, but thirteen African Americans and five Asian Americans were enrolled, and their numbers indicated important shifts coming to Columbia as it sought to achieve a much-needed diversity in the student body.[20]

Behind the surge in applicants was not only Columbia's reputation for excellence, but also concerted efforts to identify and invite to Columbia strong Presbyterian candidates for ministry. Before his retirement Oldenburg had developed an "Advocates for Ministry" program. Dinner events throughout the country, hosted by advocates and young pastors, invited prospective students to consider preparation for ministry at Columbia. Columbia graduates, whose continuing relationship with the seminary was being carefully nurtured, played a critical role in these efforts. At the same time board member John Aldridge developed PULSE—Pastor Leadership Search Effort—that helped to draw students to Columbia by encouraging churches to nominate young adults for membership in a network of lay and clergy leaders who encouraged them to consider ministry.[21]

With an anticipated growth in the student body, a new $9.6 million residence hall was constructed close to Florida Hall. Designed for high energy efficiency, the handsome building blended well with other campus buildings thanks largely to Jim Philips, son of Davison and Kay Philips, who acted as a consultant and managed masterfully—with all the attendant input and concerns of others—the task of blending a twenty-first-century building into a collegiate Gothic campus. The new residence hall reflected changing expectations among students and the seminary board and administration about what was needed for adequate housing—no two students to a room with bunk beds! With other aspects of campus life—including the rising salaries of faculty and administrators—the new building pointed to an affluence not known at Columbia since the 1850s, an affluence that was shaping Columbia's style of life and its moral and aesthetic spirit. The size, character, and furnishing of the apartments revealed deep assumptions about what was needed for the preparation of Presbyterian ministers. Certainly behind the new residence hall was an image of ministry shaped by consumer capitalism and the contemporary quest to be comfortable and to avoid what makes one uncomfortable.[22]

The doctor of ministry program under Charles Raynal's leadership continued to attract a large enrollment. Raynal worked hard, building relationships with presbyteries and with leaders in other denominations. He traveled widely and gathered small groups of pastors in different cities to meet for meals and for conversations about Columbia's advanced degree designed specifically around the practice of ministry. With Brueggemann and González still teaching an occasional course and with the appeal of Barbara Brown Taylor and other new faculty, the program drew pastors from a wide variety of denominations and had Columbia's strongest representation of racial-ethnic people of color. The relationship with the United Theological College of the West Indies continued to provide the program an important cross-cultural component.[23]

One program that was struggling was the doctor of theology degree in pastoral counseling and care, a joint program with the Atlanta Theological Association. The number of students in the program had dropped from eighteen in 1996 to nine in 2005, with four of the nine being internationals. The length of time students had been spending in the program was daunting. Since 1999 no graduate had spent less than seven years on the degree, and during that time students who had spent nine, ten, and thirteen years working for the degree had dropped out of the program. Lartey resigned to take a position at Emory, a major blow to Columbia's role in the program. To try to revive and strengthen the program new scholarships were established in 2006, and faculty from the biblical and historical doctrinal areas of the faculty were asked to offer courses, advise students, and read dissertations. In 2008 Pamela Cooper-White was called as professor of pastoral theology, care, and counseling and appointed to the newly established Ben G. and Nancye Clapp Gautier Professorship. An Episcopal minister and pastoral psychotherapist, she provided the rigorous scholarship needed to undergird the degree as she was an internationally known leader in the field and would be the first clergyperson to be named the Fulbright-Freud Visiting Scholar in Vienna. Among her many contributions to her discipline would be her appropriation of feminist thought for pastoral theology. In these ways the program was saved, but it was to remain small as it focused on a very narrow vocational field that had moved from pastoral care offered in connection with the church to pastoral counseling modeled on more secular structures and assumptions and then more recently back to a pastoral care model.[24]

Nondegree programs located in the Harrington Center continued to be an important part of Columbia's service to the church. But program spread, in response to various needs, had created a cumbersome structure that had little coherence or administrative coordination. The four programs—Continuing Education, the Lay Institute, Spirituality, and New Church Development—had developed independently, and each reflected the interests and entrepreneurial skills of their directors. But there had been a growing awareness—and pressure from accrediting agencies—that Columbia needed a more interdisciplinary and collaborative approach and more efficient use of its resources in the programs it offered. In response, under Dean Murchison's leadership, the various programs were united under a new dean and vice president of the Life Long Learning program, and Dent Davis was called to the position with Linda Morningstar as his associate. Within two years the total number of participants grew from 1,390 to 1,698, and administrative processes had been streamlined. Among the successful programs Davis launched was the S3, which focused on Sabbath, study, and service and was funded by a $1.3 million grant from the Lilly Endowment. Over the next five years over two hundred pastors, divided into groups of six to eight, met together regularly to address issues of contemporary ministry. The program exemplified Columbia's deep commitment to its graduates, its constituency, and the boarder church.[25]

One program that had a brief and very public role during the Mendenhall administration was the Campbell Scholars Seminar. When the Campbell bequest was received, some members of the board suggested that a tithe of the bequest be made as a gift to struggling theological schools in other parts of the world. After some investigation it was determined that such a gift was not legal and that some other means should be found to express gratitude for Campbell's generosity. A Campbell Seminar was consequently established to invite to the campus five international scholars for the fall semester of each year. Joined by a Columbia faculty member and two Columbia graduates, the seminar was intended to provide both a sabbatical break for the scholars and an opportunity for them to explore together some aspect of the theme "Mission of the Church in the 21st Century." The first seminar focused on the subtheme "Mission as Hope in Action" and met during the fall term 2000. Walter Brueggemann was the convener, and he was joined by Russel Botman from South Africa, John Douglas Hall from Canada, Damayanthi Niles from Sri Lanka, Ofelia Ortega from Cuba, Janos Pasztor from Hungary, and board members Joanna Adams, class of 1979, and James Lowry, class of 1966. The participants engaged one another in intense discussions and spent time in research and writing. They provided leadership in chapel, made forum presentations, participated in a number of classes, heard formal presentations by faculty, and had endless conversations in the dining hall and other informal settings. Brueggemann later concluded: "The presence of this group of pastors and scholars has had an immense effect upon the life and horizon of the seminary." Their worked was drawn together in a book, *Hope for the World: Mission in a Global Context,* published in both English and Spanish. In following years the seminars focused on such subthemes as "Mission in an Age of Hungers" and "Mission in an Age of Religious Violence." The work of the seminars was published and widely distributed. But gradually funds for the seminars were designated for other purposes, and after 2008 faculty with the necessary commitments, international contacts, and administrative skills could not be found to take on the responsibility of administering the program. Assurances were later given to the board that the seminars would be revived and the original intent of the seminar, as a response of gratitude to the Campbell bequest, would be honored, but economic pressures and other interests prevailed, and the seminars and their purpose disappeared from Columbia's agenda.[26]

Shortly before Oldenburg retired, he noted that despite the large growth of the endowment the new president needed to be heavily involved in fund-raising to meet the needs of Columbia's growing programs and student body. Mendenhall accepted this challenge, and during the next nine years she was to give enormous energy to meeting the apparently insatiable appetite of the seminary for more money. She was fortunate to have a board committed to the same challenge and to have two exceptionally able senior administrators appointed near the end of Oldenburg's tenure—Marty Sadler and Richard DuBose. Sadler, the treasurer and vice president for business and finance, possessed a seasoned financial mind and administrative skills that had been honed by business experience and military training. During the coming years, his influence and steady voice were to prove vital as Columbia received large additions to its endowment and weathered a series of recessions. As a "child of the manse" who had spent summers in Montreat, he understood the traditional culture of the church he loved and felt called to serve. DuBose, the vice president for institutional development, was to be a brilliant colleague of Mendenhall, Murchison, and Sadler. He was to manage Columbia's fund-raising with the skill of a professional and with the intuitive insights of someone who, like Sadler, had grown up in a pastor's home and who had spent his summers among the Presbyterian tribes that gather in Montreat. With this senior staff and with the board's strong support, Mendenhall plunged into a bold and seemingly audacious Vision 20/20 campaign for $60 million.[27]

Like the office of president, the board, happy with the direction outlined in the 2020 vision statement, had been making a slow shift in its focus away from governance of the seminary to fund-raising. This was particularly true regarding the board's engagement with the selection and promotion of faculty as the faculty itself was taking on more and more responsibility for its own shape and development. Early in the Mendenhall administration, the faculty voted that search committees for faculty not already underway were to consider in the future only ethnic minority candidates. This requirement was to remain in effect unless the faculty explicitly revoked it. At the same time the faculty voted that future search committees for administrators were to "seek to uncover racial ethnic minority candidates." While there was a pressing need for racial ethnic minorities on the faculty and in the administration, the faculty's assumption that it, rather than the board, had responsibility for these decisions was an important indicator that the board was increasingly distant from its responsibilities for faculty appointments and promotions and was preoccupied with intense efforts in fund-raising. The result was going to be amazing success in the capital campaign through the administration's and board's engagement with Columbia's traditional constituency while perhaps ironically the faculty and internal life of Columbia began to lose some of its close relationship with that same constituency—personal associations between faculty and constituency were weakening, and long memories of Columbia and the Presbyterian Church were not as widely shared.[28]

The chair of the capital campaign was Billy Morris of Augusta, Georgia. As the highly successful founder and CEO of Morris Communications, he was widely known as one of Georgia's most astute business leaders. He was also a man who loved Columbia Seminary and cared deeply about its service to the church. Like Mendenhall, whose leadership he admired, he possessed a genuine and transparent piety heard most clearly in his prayers, which echoed the language and rhythms of the King James Bible. He felt a responsibility for the traditional constituency of the seminary and was eager for Columbia to nurture and maintain its relationship with those Presbyterian churches and communities that had sustained it over the years. At the same time, he was proud of Columbia's growing international reputation and gladly gave his support to the seminary's broadening ministry. In addition to chairing the campaign committee, he felt that the best thing he could do would be to sit down with every major donor and talk about the importance of preparing the next generation of Presbyterian pastors. "You honor a person," he frequently said, "by visiting them in their home to talk about important matters." He traveled far and wide for the seminary and made countless calls on those who could make a substantial donation to the campaign. And he and his wife, Sissie, together with their children, gave generously to the campaign. While their modesty meant that their total contribution remained a secret, their gift was clearly the second largest contribution in Columbia's history, exceeded only by the Campbell bequest. The one public aspect of their gift was the establishment of the Wade Huie Chair of Preaching and a new Center for Preaching. Morris greatly admired Huie and loved preaching in part because his mother, Florence Morris, had raised him to believe that the sermon was the "most important twenty or thirty minutes of the week." He loved preaching because he loved good writing and words. He admired preachers in local churches most of all, even more than the many professors he knew and admired. He likened preaching every week to being a columnist, a vocation he also admired, because "you have to keep coming up with fresh perspectives." "The deadline," he would say, "just comes around, again and again." Joseph Roberts, for thirty years pastor of Atlanta's historic Ebenezer Baptist Church, the home congregation of Martin Luther King, was called to the Huie chair—an appointment that Morris enthusiastically supported.[29]

DuBose assembled a strong development staff for the campaign, and with his affable ways and leadership skills, he soon had the campaign achieving goal after goal. C. J. Drymon was director of development services, Neely Young director for major gifts, and Jami Moss director of annual giving. Working together they emphasized the seminary's growing strength, the excellence of its faculty and student body, and that Columbia was preparing Presbyterian ministers for the future and providing advanced studies for many ministers of other denominations. As a result they saw not only the endowment growing steadily but also the annual fund more than double as more and more people wanted to contribute to Columbia's ministry. Meanwhile Bert Carmichael as director of alumni/ae relations was visiting graduates in small towns and big cities, attending innumerable presbytery meetings, and entertaining all with stories of seminary life past and present. When the campaign ended, the goal of $60 million had been passed, and a total of over $70 million had been raised—certainly one of the most successful capital campaign in the history of theological education in the United States.[30]

Mendenhall sought to nurture Columbia's identity as a seminary of the southeast synods in service to the Presbyterian Church (USA) and through it to the larger church. She knew only too well the tensions and developing fractures in the church that had built and sustained the seminary over the generations, but she was determined that Columbia not move away from the church in its time of trouble. Rather she was eager for Columbia to reflect the ties of affection and memory that bound Presbyterians together in mission to the world. One way she did this was by securing and bringing to Columbia the huge archives located in the Presbyterian Historical Society in Montreat. While some materials in Montreat went to the Presbyterian Historical Society in Philadelphia, the bulk of personal letters, papers, session minutes, and histories of Presbyterians in the South came to Columbia in some twenty "eighteen-wheeler" semitrailer trucks. Columbia suddenly had not only an archive of significant depth and historical importance but also an embodiment and a story of people who had long been traveling together. To encourage the memory of that journey and the ways the memory could inform the church's present mission, the Program in Presbyterian and Reformed History and Theology was established with adequate funding for conferences and lectures. The archive and the program were, Mendenhall later wrote, a way for Columbia "to stay connected to the Presbyterian roots of CTS and the mission of the PC (USA) today."[31]

Mendenhall retired at the end of the academic year 2009. She had successfully built on the momentum of the Oldenburg years, and she had gained not only the great respect of Columbia's board, faculty, and students, but also the affection and gratitude of a constituency that looked to Columbia for leadership in a church and society increasingly fractured and angry. The board's judgment in calling her had been correct—she had enabled many in Columbia's constituency, possessed of diverse opinions, to hear and understand each other, and she had helped them find common ground on behalf of the church's mission to the world.

Board chair Joanna Adams and president Doug Oldenburg.

Board chair Frank Skinner and president Laura Mendenhall.

Board chair Bill Scheu and president Steve Hayner.

Board chair Tom Walker and president Leanne Van Dyk.

Faculty, late 1980s.

Walter Brueggemann, Columbia's best-known and most distinguished professor in the twentieth century.

Marcia Riggs, first African American tenured professor, played an important role in shaping the Columbia curriculum in the 1990s.

An intrepid faculty-staff football team, 1998.

An unusually intimidating student football team, 1998.

Cecil Moore oversaw the maintenance of the campus with skill and much-needed humor.

(left) Roger Nishioka, a particularly popular professor and speaker among young adults and youth.

(above) Alexander Oliver, a much-admired member of the maintenance staff and frequent leader in chapel.

Faculty, 2015.

18

An Egalitarian and Inclusive Spirit

Shortly after Mendenhall's retirement in 2009, the board elected as the new president Stephen Hayner, Columbia's Peachtree Professor of Evangelism and Church Growth. The election surprised many who expected the board to follow the tradition of calling a pastor to the presidency, but Hayner possessed enormous energy, an enthusiasm and warmth of spirit that was contagious, and experience as the president of InterVarsity Christian Fellowship, a large and complex organization. Highly regarded in evangelical circles, he served on the board of key evangelical organizations including Fuller Theological Seminary, World Vision, and the Navigators. The board clearly hoped that he would be able to bring to Columbia students linked to various evangelical campus organizations and be a bridge between Columbia and congregations that were experiencing a growing alienation with the church—especially over the question of the ordination of gays and lesbians.[1]

Hayner, the grandson of German immigrants, grew up in Washington state, where he was deeply influenced by a West Coast culture with its famous individualism and forward-looking people who, wanting "to be themselves," were seeking to break free from the restraints of tradition. Both of his parents were lawyers, and his mother was the highly respected Republican majority leader of the state senate. Noted for her pragmatism and her ability to work across party lines, she apparently bequeathed to her son Steve a similar disposition that was rooted in Christian piety and a genuine respect for others. Because he grew up in a state with a large immigrant population, he was to view the growing diversity and multiculturalism of the nation as simply an expansion and intensification of his experience as a child of the West Coast.[2]

After graduating from Whitman College in Walla Walla, Washington, he received a master's in theological studies from Harvard, and a master's in theology from Gordon-Conwell Theological Seminary. Later he received a Ph.D. from the University of St. Andrews, Scotland. Raised in a Lutheran family, he became a Presbyterian along the way and was ordained into the Presbyterian ministry. But his true home was not to be in a denomination with its traditions and long memory, but in the broad circles of evangelical organizations and fellowships. There, among his closest friends, he found his identity as one of the most influential evangelical leaders of his generation. And there within these circles of affection and shared experience, he learned to speak with the phraseology and in the cadencies of evangelicalism and had his understanding of the church and the nature of its ministry most fully developed. No more than his predecessors with their burden of southern history could he escape his West Coast history with its tradition of seeking to be free of tradition or abandon an evangelical tradition that understood the church in noninstitutional ways, as a fellowship of individual evangelical believers held together in voluntary societies. He, like his predecessors, consequently brought to the presidency of Columbia a particular memory nurtured by a distinct language that shaped the way he saw the present and anticipated the future.[3]

The challenges Hayner faced were many—most obviously a serious economic recession, a declining student population, and a conflicted church. And Hayner also faced something that his predecessors had not faced, even with the cultural revolutions of the late 1960s and early 1970s, and that was an acceleration of change that had reached a new and fevered pitch. Technologies were emerging that were pushing the Information Revolution into every corner of human life—including Twitter, cloud computing, and especially the smartphone. At the same time, he was sensitive to the large demographic shifts taking place in the country and the pressing need for Columbia graduates to be prepared for ministry in a more diverse world of competing and clashing ancestries and cultures. Hayner was determined to do what he could to help Columbia face the challenges in ways that enhanced its ministry to a global Christianity. He knew that he came to the presidency as someone not closely identified with Columbia and with its network of friends and graduates and the culture they inhabited. But he was optimistic in ways that went beyond being hopeful, and he embraced the challenges as a gift; and he signed his correspondence "Joyfully, Steve," which would have seemed naive or cheery except that it was so genuine and seemed to flow from some dogged determinism and deep springs of personal experience.[4]

The most immediate challenge was financial. Hayner entered his presidency as the nation was entering its deepest and longest recession since the Great Depression of the 1930s. As the stock market fell, so did Columbia's endowment, dropping from $192 million in the 2007–8 academic year to $170 million in 2012–13. The draw on the endowment was consequently reduced, and the seminary budget felt the squeeze of hard times as the annual fund also plummeted. In the late 1990s, the administration had had the task of spending in a wise and prudent manner large amounts of new income. Now the seminary faced a struggle to make ends meet as income dropped and expenditures rose from $13,759 million in 2007–8 to $14,307 million in 2012–13. To help meet these increased expenses, it was necessary to raise tuition for M.Div. students from $9,486 in 2007–8 to $13,332 in 2012–13, adding despite increases in financial aid to the educational debt of many students. Inevitably these financial pressures impacted many aspects of Columbia's life, but none more obviously than student enrollment and the character of the student body.[5]

Throughout the Mendenhall years and for the year immediately after her retirement, enrollments remained high. But as the recession continued, enrollments dropped precipitously—from sixty-three entering M.Div. students in the fall of 2010 to thirty-seven the next year, and the number was to remain at that level or below for the next five years. To help staunch the loss of students, Columbia began to admit internationals into the M.Div. Previously internationals had been admitted only as special students for a year's enrichment or as advanced degree students engaged in graduate study. This policy, advocated by international partner churches and schools, assumed that a student who was studying to be a pastor, for example, in Korea could best be prepared at a Korean theological seminary for preaching, pastoral care, and other practices of ministry in Korea by Korean professors. Under the pressure of falling enrollments, Columbia undertook the task of preparing persons for ministry in the radically different social and cultural contexts of other countries and employed an instructor in English as a second language as a necessary part of its educational responsibilities.[6]

Enrollment in the D.Min. program, which had remained at or near the 250 level through the Mendenhall years, also plunged. By the fall of 2015, only 117 students were in the D.Min., plus another twenty-three in the doctor of educational ministry program. And participation in the Life Long Learning program experienced a steep decline, dropping in ten years from 1,698 participants to 689 in the 2015–16 academic year. These declines reflected broad trends in theological education in the United States as total enrollments declined in member institutions of the Association of Theological Schools. But the declines were considerably more precipitous at Columbia than in national figures and reflected important developments taking place at the seminary.[7]

What was most striking about enrollment not just among M.Div. students but in all basic degree programs was an increasing racial-ethnic diversity; a dramatic decline of students from outside the Atlanta area; and a startling drop in the percentage of students who were Presbyterian. By 2014 the new pattern had been clearly established: 75 percent of first-year basic degree students were from Georgia, almost all of whom were from the Atlanta area; 52 percent were racial-ethnic persons of color; and Presbyterian (USA) students constituted only 46 percent in contrast to 80 percent a few years earlier. Clearly Columbia had gained an ability to attract racial-ethnic persons of color from diverse denominations in Atlanta while at the same time it had experienced a diminished ability to attract Presbyterians and students from other parts of the country. The reasons for this were multiple and included the economic recession, turmoil in the Presbyterian Church (USA), and the continuing decline of mainline denominations. But they also included internal developments at Columbia that involved perceptions of the seminary's role in a rapidly changing world and an understanding of the church that distanced Columbia from its Presbyterian roots and ecclesiology.[8]

No less than his predecessors, Hayner perceived the challenges facing Columbia through eyes shaped by personal experience and social location, and he described the challenges with a language that echoed the idioms and inflections of his own ecclesiastical world. "While we stand squarely on the shoulders of the Presbyterian Church (USA) and the Reformed Tradition," Hayner declared in his inaugural, "we remember that our call is *not* to sustain the institutional church of another era, but rather to prepare the church in all its breath to be the Bride of Christ in a changing world." He was particularly impressed by and drawn to "new ecclesial experiments," groups made up primarily of those in their twenties or thirties who live in a fragmented, postmodern, and technologically centered world. They "use the word 'church' in a very different way," he noted in an online essay, "than our culturally established references where 'church' commonly refers to a building, a program, or an institutional structure. In these new communities, 'church' reclaims the more biblical meaning of 'gathering' and refers primarily to the people." His background in InterVarsity with his work among college students and young adults had helped him see the vitality of such groups and had shaped his belief that in them "God may be speaking a fresh word and doing a new thing." At the same time, he was reflecting an individualistic culture's widespread suspicion—especially among young adults—of institutions generally. The tension between such an understanding of church and leading an institution with a long cultural history, a traditional constituency, a large endowment, an imposing campus with many building and programs, and a complex organizational structure with established hierarchies was to mark his presidency.[9]

To address the challenges before the seminary, Hayner began to assemble an administrative team. Deborah F. Mullen was called in 2010 from McCormick Theological Seminary in Chicago as the new dean of faculty and vice president of academic affairs. She had been on the McCormick faculty since 1989 and was director of the Center for African American ministries and black church studies. Her twenty-one years at McCormick had immersed her in the daily life of a highly diverse theological community and had provided images and models of theological education that were to inform her work at Columbia. Possessed of a winsome spirit and a passion for theological education, she was to be an important colleague for Hayner as together they sought to set new directions for Columbia. Later she would say, "God is doing something new in our community." And she would write that she and Hayner had been working together "on redefining Columbia Theological Seminary's vision and programs."[10]

In the summer of 2011, Doug Taylor followed Richard DuBose as the vice president of institutional development. Taylor had been senior gifts officer at Seattle Pacific University, a school with a strong evangelical tradition. Taylor had worked for Hayner at InterVarsity, and the two had a close personal relationship—Taylor would frequently remark that he regarded Hayner as a father figure. The year that he arrived at Columbia, Taylor faced the daunting task of fund-raising as the nation was struggling to emerge from its recession. And he arrived as one who knew that he knew little about Presbyterians in the South and the constituency that supported Columbia.[11]

Other administrators also arrived. Marvin Simmers, longtime executive with the General Assembly, agreed in 2010 to serve as interim director of advanced studies—a position he held until Kevin Park was appointed associate dean for advanced professional studies in 2012. Park, a Canadian, had responsibility for the D.Min. program and brought to his position close ties to Korean communities in Canada and the United States and a special interest in emerging Asian North American theologies. Israel Galindo came from Richmond Baptist Theological Seminary to assume the position of associate dean for the Life Long Learning program in 2013. He had the daunting task of revitalizing the program that had been in sharp decline since Dent Davis's resignation in 2009. The same year Galindo arrived, Kelly Campbell came from the Golden Gate Baptist Theological

Seminary in Mill Valley, California, to follow Sara Myers, director of the library. Campbell was given the new title of associate dean and director of the library, and she brought to her work a concern for carefully defined procedures and the latest advances in electronic resources.[12]

New faculty also arrived during these years to replace those who had resigned or retired. John Azumah, a native of Ghana, was elected in 2011 professor of world Christianity and Islam. He brought to Columbia a specialization in Islam and Christian-Islam relations and was to be in great demand as a lecturer in this country and in Africa. Ralph Watkins joined the faculty as the Peachtree Associate Professor of Evangelism and Church Growth. He had been the assistant dean of the African American church studies program at Fuller Theological Seminary, was a well-known and popular minister in the African Methodist Episcopal Church, and had written numerous books and articles about evangelism among young African Americans.[13]

Raj Nadella joined the faculty in 2012 as a young New Testament scholar. He was a native of India who had spent some years in the United States, and his teaching and scholarship drew from experiences in both countries; he would help Columbia develop important new relationships with the church in India. When Kathleen O'Connor retired, Brennan Breen was called as assistant professor of Old Testament. An Episcopalian, he followed in his predecessor's footsteps and quickly became a highly popular professor and showed himself to be a serious scholar in the tradition of Columbia's Old Testament faculty. William Yoo joined the faculty in 2014 as assistant professor of American religious and cultural history. He had a strong interest not only in the encounter between American and Korean Protestants but also in the history of Presbyterianism in the United States, and he was soon in much demand as a speaker before church groups. Tim Hartman came in 2014 to teach theology following George Stroup's retirement. His dissertation had focused on the theology of Karl Barth and African theologians, especially the Ghanaian Kwame Bediako. His work consequently held the possibility of being a bridge connecting important perspectives and commitments in the faculty. These young scholars, just establishing themselves in their disciplines and in their teaching styles, were sources of great energy and promise for Columbia's faculty.[14]

A remarkable transformation of Columbia had obviously taken place by the beginning of the 2014 academic year. Of twenty-eight faculty members, eleven were women, and twelve were racial-ethnic people of color—four African Americans, one Korean Canadian, two Korean Americans, two Japanese Americans, one Hispanic American, one Indian American, and one Ghanaian. The egalitarian and inclusive impulse that marked so much of contemporary U.S. culture was clearly seen in the new shape of the faculty. New faculty representing new or formerly silenced or neglected voices could point to gender and racial-ethnic distortions in Columbia's life and could surprise and discomfort by calling into question old assumptions and established practices. A selective, nostalgic reassertion of a Columbia tradition would find no warm reception among those who knew personally the importance of social power analysis that includes the roles of gender, race, and ethnicity. At the same time, of twenty-eight faculty members, sixteen were Presbyterian. No new faculty member or senior administrator had been nurtured in the life and culture of Columbia's supporting synods and constituency. When linked with the transformations in the student body, a new Columbia appeared to inhabit the familiar space of the Decatur campus. Clearly the changes reflected the efforts of the Hayner administration to do what Dean Mullen described as "redefining Columbia Theological Seminary's vision and programs" as it sought to distance itself from Columbia's former vision and programs and shape a new understanding of Columbia and its mission.[15]

One of the new realities was the Information Revolution. Columbia had called Jeff Vaughan in 2007 to be the seminary's educational technologist with responsibility to implement wireless connectivity on the campus and to train faculty and students in the latest technologies available for teaching and learning. Fortunately for Columbia he knew not only the mysteries of the new technologies but also how to nudge gently older professors into those mysteries. Michael Thompson, as director of communications, began to expand the ways the seminary communicated with various constituencies by utilizing the rapidly developing social media. And library staff was adopting the ever-changing tools and internalizing the deep assumptions of the Information Revolution.[16]

Columbia needed, however, a first-class facility to take advantage of the Information Revolution. To help meet this challenge, the Vernon S. Broyles Leadership Center was completed in 2012 by incorporating Simons-Law into a beautifully designed new thirty-thousand-square-foot facility. Where once generations of students had lived two to a room and the Cartledges and the Wallaces and other faculty families had had small apartments, the bookstore and an educational technology center now had spacious homes, and the faculty had offices and seminar rooms. In the new part of the center were three seventy-five-seat classrooms and one forty-seat classroom—all spoke of hopes for large enrollments and were furnished with the latest educational technology that could connect a classroom to the world. A cloistered courtyard provided a sense of coherence to the whole building and together with a glass tower announced a link between past and contemporary aesthetics. Built with funds raised during the capital campaign, the center was named for the much-loved pastor of the primary donors—board member Ann Cousins and her husband, Tom. While the Cousins kept a low profile, they played a large role not only in securing and providing a substantial part of the funds for the new center, but also in conceiving its potential in a world being remade by the Information Revolution. As their pastor Broyles had served with great distinction Atlanta's North Avenue Presbyterian Church, and his name now replaced the names of Eliza Lucilla Simons and Agnes Law, who had once given the funds for the dormitories in Columbia. A small plaque reminded all who paused to read that once the seminary had been in Columbia and that two women had been generous donors to the cause of providing the church learned ministers of the Gospel.[17]

Shortly after the Broyles Center opened, Columbia launched one of its most important new programs with a grant from the American Association for the Advancement of Science. With the leadership of Professors Bill Brown and Mark Douglas, several professors began to integrate science into courses and to bring scientists to the campus for special lectures. Soon Columbia students were hearing lectures with such titles as "Big Bang, Cosmic Evolution, and the Future of the Universe" and "Job and Biological Diversity," and they were asking in class, "Would you baptize a Neanderthal?" and "Is Jesus's incarnation for all of creation, or just for humanity?" While the engagement with science reached only some students through a few interested faculty, James Woodrow would have been delighted and John L. Girardeau distressed with Brown's observation that "a sense of wonder about science is being cultivated on campus."[18]

One of the sources of Columbia's increasingly diverse student population was a new two-year degree, master of arts in the practical theology, designed primarily for students in churches that do not require a three-year M.Div. degree for ordination. Not incidentally the degree was launched as enrollment in the M.Div. plummeted, and it was intended among other things to help cushion the seminary for the rapid decline of Presbyterian students studying at Columbia. Students in the two-year program focused on "ministry arts" through four areas of concentration: Christian education, Christian leadership, pastoral care, or worship. Greek and Hebrew were not required, and students took only an introductory course in theology. In 2013 the program attracted twenty-five entering students—almost all from Atlanta—while the number entering the M.Div. fell to only thirty-four, the smallest entering class since the Second World War. At the same time, the seminary found it necessary to establish a Center for Academic Literacy and Intercultural Competence with a director to help students with analytical writing, critical thinking, library research, and intercultural communication. Clearly there were deep connections between the new degree program, student populations, faculty composition, the "redefining of Columbia's vision and mission," and Columbia's understanding of its relationship to the Presbyterian Church USA.[19]

Columbia's ties to the PC (USA) and to its traditional constituency came into focus around the rewriting of two core documents—the seminary's "Plan of Government" and its "Mission Statement." As a part of a periodic revision of the plan of government, which had to be approved by the controlling synods, the administration proposed that Columbia be described as simply "connected to" the PC (USA) rather than an as "educational institution of" the PC (USA). Graduates, board members, and other Columbia supporters vigorously opposed the change, saying that Columbia was connected to many organizations and institutions but was an institution of the PC (USA). In response the board voted unanimously to reaffirm that Columbia was an "educational institution of the Presbyterian Church (USA)." But in 2012 a revised mission statement—which did not have to be approved by the synods—dropped the introduction "Columbia Theological Seminary is an educational institution of the Presbyterian Church (USA), and a community of theological inquiry and formation for ministry in the service of the church of Jesus Christ" and replaced it with "Columbia Theological Seminary exists to educate and nurture faithful, imaginative, and effective leaders for the sake of the Church and the world." In describing the "Distinctives of Columbia," the new document noted: "While Columbia Seminary increasingly serves students from other denominations, we maintain a special relationship with and commitment to the Presbyterian Church (USA)." Such a lukewarm description of Columbia's relationship to the PC (USA) signaled a loosening of the ties to the church that had created it and had sustained it over the generations and a reenvisioning of

Columbia as a "post-denominational" seminary that could free itself from its history, live in the present, and look to the future de novo. The Program in Presbyterian and Reformed History and Theology was quietly discontinued in 2013.[20]

Columbia's new diversity in faculty and students brought with it important contributions to the seminary and to its work in service to the church. The need to integrate cultural, gender, racial-ethnic, and other diversity into new modes of self-understanding and practice was critical for any reconstructions of Columbia's tradition. And by 2015 graduates were going out into an environment where denominational identity had weakened and where there was a great need for experience in learning from and relating to those from different traditions and racial-ethnic backgrounds. For a graduate to have had that experience in seminary, to have gained insights from multiculturalism, and to have some sense of both differences and common ground was important preparation for ministry in the twenty-first century. But Columbia's new diversity also brought with it new challenges that echoed the tensions and polarizations that were rumbling across the U.S. landscape and that were to come together in the storm of the 2016 presidential election and its aftermath.[21]

At perhaps its most basic level, Columbia's new diversity raised the question of how people from very different backgrounds and different religious traditions live together in a theological seminary. What happens, for example, in chapel—especially if chapel services are understood to help in the formation of future ministers? Do worship services seem too Presbyterian to those from other traditions—too ordered and cerebral, too much organ music and not enough drums or electric guitars? Or do Presbyterians and others in the Reformed tradition find some chapel services in other traditions to be chaotic and noisy, lacking reverence and substance? Or are such characterizations themselves examples of stereotypes and dismissive attitudes toward the other? And what about courses and the pedagogies employed in them? Do non-Presbyterian students think their denominations' theologies do not get adequate treatment in theology classes, and do Presbyterian students, eager to be prepared for ministry in Presbyterian churches, find distracting any substantial attention given to preaching and worship styles in other churches?

One unexpected consequence of the new diversity was the theological conservativism often represented in the two largest streams of new students—Korean students directly from Korea and African American students from nondenominational, Pentecostal, and historic black denominations. They often held conservative positions on the character of biblical authority, gender and language, and gay marriage. When they contested, for example, an expected use of inclusive language on papers and in classes it represented a shock to the ethos of the seminary and its PC (USA) assumptions. On the other hand, African American students were generally socially progressive on matters of race and economics, while Korean and Korean American students were inclined to a more progressive social agenda on immigration.[22]

Still another consequence of Columbia's new diversity was the significant increase in the percentage of basic degree students, especially people of color, who lived off campus while serving as full-time pastors in churches that do not require the M.Div. Old assumptions about Columbia being a residential community of full-time students were being called into question as even the handsome new resident hall had empty apartments. And with growing pressure for on-line degrees, another kind of diversity appeared to be possible with a student population divided into three parts: residential, full-time students; commuters with varying rates of involvement on the campus; and nonresident, virtual communities. Reflecting what was happening across the cultural landscape of America, the seminary community was apparently fracturing along many lines in ways that raised questions about Columbia's mission. Was Columbia to be a coherent community that nurtured persons for a ministry whose broad contours were clearly articulated by the board and faculty? Was Columbia about *forming* students for ministry over several intense years by the shaping power of a distinct culture with its own style of life, tone and character, and moral and aesthetic spirit? Was Columbia to be a coherent community rooted in distinct faith commitments, shaped by formal and informal rituals, and sustained by a shared language? Indeed was Columbia to nurture in a student a personal commitment to the seminary as an institution—an institution with the secure boundaries and resources necessary for trustworthy, deep, enduring relationships that make community dependable over time?[23]

Or was Columbia to be a community only in the loosest sense, not so much concerned with formation as with teaching skills or enriching an individual's knowledge of some theological discipline? Was the very idea of a coherent seminary community not only unrealistic in a fractured, anti-institutional, and deeply individualistic society but also a remnant of white southern hegemony, Presbyterian affluence, and an obsolete understanding of church as an institution with boundaries and established structures and networks of personal relationships? Such questions have meant that in recent years special days—often with outside consultants—have frequently been set aside by the seminary for sensitivity training; for discussions that address diversity and racial, gender, or ethnic stereotyping; and for attempts to build bridges across divisions in regard to gender, language, and theology.

The growing diversity within the faculty also raised related questions. The faculty had long had a strong sense of responsibility for the ministry of the Presbyterian church and for the readiness of students to enter that ministry. Not only the dean of students, but also the president and faculty members, had frequently been in conversation with presbyteries about the progress, and sometimes problems, of individual students. Was the seminary, and in particular its Presbyterian faculty, able to have a comparable sense of responsibility toward the many other denominations whose students were now studying for basic degrees at Columbia? Would Presbyterian professors have the same level of concern for a Baptist student's formation and readiness for ministry that they have for Presbyterian students going into familiar congregations that support the seminary? What are the expectations of the African Methodist Episcopal Church or of the Presbyterian Church in Korea for their students at Columbia? Do they and other denominations or traditions have any oversight of their Columbia students, comparable to presbyteries, in the courses they take and in their supervised ministry placements? Should Columbia faculty and administration try to communicate directly with those denominations regarding specific students and such expectations? Or what about the non-Presbyterian professors and administrators? Should they—perhaps especially those in the office of the dean of students—be expected to have a strong sense of responsibility toward the PC (USA) and its expectations for its students, and if so how would they express such a sense of responsibility? Could they, or should they, be in conversation with presbyteries or with Presbyterian congregations seeking pastors? So for Presbyterian and non-Presbyterian faculty and administrators, was Columbia becoming simply a graduate professional school that had moved beyond any specific sense of accountability to the church except as an abstraction, a nonembodied and noninstitutional theological concept, to be honored with generalities about service to the church?[24]

The faculty's growing diversity and questions about levels of responsibility to the church, and specifically the PC (USA), meant that the faculty's old struggle to be a collegium was taking on a new and daunting intensity. Particularly pressing were issues of race, ethnicity, and multiculturalism that were entangled in almost every question about the seminary's character and mission. In 2010 the faculty adopted a "Guideline to Support Multicultural Teaching and Learning" to promote an "educational institution where multiracial, multiethnic, multicultural, and gender justice flourish." And in 2016 faculty and administrators of color formed a caucus on race and ethnicity to address "various aspects of the seminary's life and work" as they felt the necessity to respond to what one faculty member called "racial insults and/or microaggressions" and the weight of what they experienced as a "predominantly white controlled institution." The entanglements of different identities and histories pressed the question—could a diverse faculty in such an institution and in a fractured society have a sense of coherence and shape degree programs whose purposes and relationships to one another were clear? Or were the racial-ethnic divides, the profound individualism of a market economy, and an anti-institutional ecclesiology creating another model for the faculty—not a collegium but a collection of imaginative and resilient scholars and entrepreneurs separated by race, ethnicity, gender, denomination, and theological commitments?[25]

While staff also faced some of these same tensions, their specific responsibilities protected them from some of the challenges faced by faculty and senior administrators. This meant that staff—especially those with long service—provided Columbia an important cohesive element and sense of community, and they gave to returning graduates a sense of continuity amid much change among faculty. Students experienced staff as an integral part of Columbia's culture, and graduates found on their return to campus a sense of continuity in the familiar faces of staff. Returning graduates in 2014 were happy to see Ann Clay Adams, Jane Gleim, and Mike Medford in the dean's office; Dale Mullis, Jody Sauls, and Miguel Chavez in the business office; and the hospitable MaryLynn Darden in the president's office. They were glad to receive the warm greetings of Barbara Poe, Diane Thorne, and Sandra Taylor in the development office; to visit with Judy Graves in student services; to hear once again Mike Morgan as the seminary organist; and to remember Carolyn Johnson and talk with David Musil in the dining hall. In the library they found Mary Martha Riviere continuing to greet them by name at the circulation desk as she had in earlier years, and when they saw Griselda Lartey, Tammy Johnson, and Bob Craigmile they could remember the library as a hospitable place. Scattered around the campus they could find a few well-known Columbia graduates in staff positions—Sue Crannell in the bookstore, Sheena Mayrant in the business office, Erica Durham and Wendy Dewberry in the library, Kim LeVert in the international office, and Sara Erickson in the Harrington Center. To graduates and others who came to the campus, long-serving staff conveyed in their demeanor and conversations a sense that there was a Columbia community and that they belonged to it. No less than senior faculty the presence of long-serving staff on the campus communicated a loyalty to the seminary and to its life and work. Indeed in some important ways they represented an institutional memory and an embodiment of the community values of institutional loyalty, friendships, and shared commitments that had long marked Columbia and that were under the great stress of a fracturing society governed by the procedures and values of the marketplace. And, once again, they were more than simply a list of names—they were reminders that it takes many people, including those little recognized, to sustain an institution.[26]

On Easter weekend 2014, Steve Hayner experienced symptoms that led to a diagnosis of inoperable pancreatic cancer. During the coming months it became increasingly clear why so many people loved and admired him and his wife, Sharol. Writing on the website CaringBridge, they published a remarkable and deeply moving account of the cancer's rapid progress and their response to it. Soon thousands were reading their posts in amazement and gratitude as he embraced life joyfully even as death approached and as she walked beside him in faith and love. They did not hesitate to speak of fear as well as faith, of grief as well as grace, and of the pain and mystery of life ebbing away when the future had been so full of promise and purpose. But they wrote as those who knew a companion with them, One who had accompanied them through their life together, and whose presence with them now in their sorrow was a source of peace and even joy.

The seminary board asked its chair, Bill Scheu, to serve as the interim president. He generously agreed and took a leave of absence from his law firm in Jacksonville, Florida. In October he and his wife, Peggy, moved into a small apartment in the Harrington Center. Together they became an important presence on the campus as the seminary grieved Hayner's illness and approaching death, and through simple acts of kindness and hospitality they encouraged and comforted many. Scheu had been a friend and strong supporter of Hayner and of the efforts to create a more diverse and ecumenical Columbia. During the coming months, he was to provide much needed stability for the seminary as it entered a difficult and painful transition.[27]

As death drew near, family and a few close friends gathered at the president's home. Good-byes were said. Scripture was read—Psalms, Colossians, and John 15:11: "I have said these things to you so that my joy may be in you, and that your joy may be complete." Then hymns were sung until death came into the room, Saturday, January 31, 2015. A large congregation gathered for his funeral at Peachtree Presbyterian Church. Mark Labberton, president of Fuller Theological Seminary in Pasadena, California, presided and offered the primary eulogy. He spoke of Hayner's ability to be a friend, of his energy and warmth, and of his journey to final joy.

Later Sharol Hayner collected their posting on CaringBridge into a book, *Joy in the Journey: Finding Abundance in the Shadow of Death.* Intervarsity Press published it and Labberton wrote the Foreword. Its essay titles told the story: Steve's "Waiting"; Sharol's "The Fiery Furnace"; Steve's "Cancer and Calling"; Sharol's "Talking Together"; Steve's "My Last Christmas" and "New Year: Last Chapter"; and Sharol's "Fullness of Joy"—in all, forty-six brief essays that made, in the words of an African friend, a "profound testimony of a man of faith embracing life in death, and of a woman keeping faith and loving her husband all the way to the grave."[28]

Epilogue

In July 2015, Leanne Van Dyk became Columbia's tenth president. She had been serving as dean and vice president for academic affairs and professor of Reformed theology at Western Theological Seminary, Holland, Michigan, when she received the call from Columbia. Nurtured by the strong Dutch Calvinist communities of Michigan, she had graduated from Calvin College and from Calvin Theological Seminary before receiving her Ph.D. from Princeton Theological Seminary. Ordained in 2007 by the PC (USA), she came to Columbia as an experienced educator in a confessional community—Christian Reformed Church in North America—marked by a cultural heritage greatly influenced by nineteenth-century Dutch immigrants. Her Dutch Calvinism, like the traditions and heritage of Southern Presbyterianism, was carried by an evolving language with its idioms and cadencies and by ties of affection and long memories. At the same time, she came to Columbia as one who had been deeply involved in ecumenical dialogues and in the critical questions of diversity and inclusiveness in theological education in the United States. With such a background, she was particularly well prepared to lead Columbia as it sought to clarify its identity and understand it mission in a fractured and increasingly polarized world.

Among the most pressing questions before Columbia in 2016 were issues of ecclesiology. What is the character of the church as the body of Christ? What does it mean for Columbia Seminary to be a part of the body of Christ, as an institution of the southeastern synods of the PC (USA), and connected through the Presbyterian church to other parts of the body? And what is Columbia's calling, what is Columbia's obedience, within the body of Christ, especially in a culture that is fractured along so many lines and that is driven by such a profound individualism?

Or to put the question in terms of Columbia's history told in these pages: What is Columbia's present relationship to its history, this story of the seminary as an institution of the church? On the one hand, the seminary's rootedness in the Reformed tradition, rootedness in the Presbyterian Church USA and in a constituency in the Southeast that has thought of Columbia as "our seminary"—is all this rootedness a burden to be escaped, a history to be overcome, a provincialism and parochialism to be surmounted in the name of a broader, more generous ecumenical stance?

Or, on the other hand, a quest to escape Columbia's rootedness, a quest to shed the burden of Columbia's history and the particularities of its geography and to be rid of the sense of ownership by its traditional constituency—would such a quest be simply a reflection of a cosmopolitan culture in the church that has no place for place and no time for memory and no loyalty but to generalities? Was the history of the seminary coming to an end as the very incarnation of deep poverty amid affluence and the homelessness of modernity?

Or in good Columbia fashion, does the call for obedience lead to the middle, where the history, Reformed traditions, and strength of the seminary are claimed and used in service to the church at large? Does Columbia not only have a history, but is it a history, recapitulating its past and carrying it forward incrementally? Can that history with all its revelations about the human capacity for self-deception and about faith struggling to be faithful, can the particularities of place and the loyalties of its constituency, can what Columbia has been and how it is remembered and how it is presently configured—can it all be a great resource for Columbia's engagement in the *Missio Dei* in the twenty-first century? Or is such a middle place simply an ideological front, a cover for old hegemonies?

Such questions and dilemmas are reminders that Columbia in 2016, like Columbia in earlier periods, inescapably reflects the social and cultural context of its time. That is a fundamental theme of this study. The issues the seminary faces are issues before theological schools across the nation, and they are issues, in one way or another, rumbling through the whole of the nation's life. Yet the issues also have a distinct Columbia character, and that character is shaped by Columbia's history and by its deepest faith commitments. The history tells of other challenging times. And the commitments encourage all those who care about Columbia to celebrate what earlier generations have said of the seminary—that God is not finished with Columbia and its service to the church. So memory and hope mingle and are held together by faith in the faithfulness of the God revealed in Jesus Christ.

ABBREVIATIONS

CTS	C. Benton Kline Jr. Special Collections and Archives, John Bulow Campbell Library, Columbia Theological Seminary
CTSAC	*Annual Catalogs*, Columbia Theological Seminary found in CTS
CTSB	Columbia Theological Seminary Bulletin
CTSBDM	*Minutes of the Board of Directors, Columbia Theological Seminary* found in CTS
CTSC	*Catalogue of the Officers and Students of the Theological Seminary of Columbia, South Carolina* found in CTS
CTSFM	*Minutes of the Faculty, Columbia Theological Seminary,* CTS
CTSV	*Vantage*
JTU	Charles Colcock Jones Papers, Howard-Tilton memorial library, Tulane University
MGAPCUS	*Minutes of the General Assembly, Presbyterian Church in the United States*

NOTES

Preface

1. For "phraseology of the past," see Girardeau, *Confederate Memorial Day,* 8–18.

1 — Beginnings

1. Goulding, "Memorial of Thomas Goulding, D.D."

2. Ibid., 182; LaMotte, *Colored Light,* 38–39.

3. Ibid., 181–82; *U.S. Census 1820, Chatham County, GA;* Sprague, *Annals of the American Pulpit,* 491–95; Sullivan, *Early Days,* 73–76.

4. Goulding, "Memorial of Thomas Goulding, D.D.," 186.

5. For Oglethorpe County developments, see DeBow, *Statistical View of the United States,* 212–13.

6. For the Scotch Irish generally, see Griffin, *The People of No Name.* For the use of the term "Scotch Irish" see 175. For the Scotch Irish moving down the Great Philadelphia Wagon Road into South Carolina and Georgia, see "Great Wagon Road" in Wikipedia and its extensive bibliography, https://en.wikipedia.org/wiki/Great_Wagon_Road (accessed February 6, 2014). For the Literary and Theological Seminary of the South, see George Howe, "History of Columbia Theological Seminary," 139 in *Memorial Volume.*

7. For plans for the proposed "Literary and Theological Seminary" near Pendleton, South Carolina, see CTS, *Board of Directors Minutes,* 1827–29; CTS, "Constitution of the Literary and Theological Seminary of the South"; and "Southern Theological Seminary."

8. Extensive studies tell the story of the Second Great Awakening. Good entry points into the study of the Awakening are Ahlstrom, *Religious History of the American People,* 385–510; Hatch, *Democratization of American Christianity;* Noll, *History of Christianity in the United States and Canada,* 163–244; and D. Howe, *What Hath God Wrought,* 164–202.

9. For the establishment of Protestant theological seminaries in the United States, see G. Miller, *Piety and Intellect,* esp. 1–83; J. Fraser, *Schooling the Preachers,* 29–47; and Holifield, *God's Ambassadors.* For the founding of Andover, see also Woods, *History of the Andover Theological Seminary.*

10. G. Miller, *Piety and Intellect,* 68–69; G. Howe, *Discourse on Theological Education.*

11. For opposition to seminaries, see Hatch, *Democratization of American Christianity,* 49–66, and J. Fraser, *Schooling the Preachers,* 79–117.

12. LaMotte, *Colored Light,* 38–40; George Howe,"History of Columbia Theological Seminary," 182–83; CTS, *Board of Directors Minutes,* 1829–30.

13. Blanding was president of the Corporation of First Presbyterian Church, Columbia. See G. Howe, *History of the Presbyterian Church in South Carolina,* 2: 663. For the Hampton and Hall mansions, see Lipscomb, "Legacy of Ainsley Hall." For Wade Hampton I, see Andrew, *Wade Hampton,* 9–13.

14. For Robert Mills see Liscombe, *Altogether American.*

15. Construction of the mansion was almost complete when Ainsley Hall died unexpectedly. See Lipscomb, "Legacy of Ainsley Hall," 168–78.

16. Robinson, *Columbia Theological Seminary and the Southern Presbyterian Church,* 27–29.

17. For lowcountry directors see Clarke, *Our Southern Zion,* 142–64.

18. For Waddell see G. Howe, *History of the Presbyterian Church in South Carolina,* 143–45, 291–93, 541–44; Sprague, *Annals of the American Pulpit,* 63; and Thompson, *Presbyterians in the South,* 1: 247.

19. For board members see CTS, *Board of Directors Minutes,* 1829–49. For John Taylor see J. Moore, *Columbia and Richland County,* 28, 79, 14, and G. Howe, *History of the Presbyterian Church in South Carolina,* 663; for Joseph Lumpkin see "Lumpkin, Joseph Henry," in Myers, *Children of Pride,* 1599; for Barrington King see Clarke, *Dwelling Place,* 190–95; for William Seabrook see Clarke, *Our Southern Zion,* 147.

20. Cf. P. Jones, *Architecture and Ritual,* 1–15.

21. Cf. the discussion of the architecture of Anglican churches in Virginia in Isaac, *Transformation of Virginia,* 61–64. See also Kedar and Werblowski, *Sacred Space.*

22. Charles C. Jones to Mary Jones, July 3, 1837, JTU. Earlier classes, meeting in the manse of the Presbyterian church, were regarded as simply preparatory. See G. Howe, "History of Columbia Theological Seminary," 143.

23. Girardeau, "Eulogy on Professor George Howe." For student appreciation of Howe, see John Leighton Wilson to Sarah S. Wilson, January 14, 1831, South Caroliniana Library, University of South Carolina, Columbia; and Robinson, *Columbia Theological Seminary and the Southern Presbyterian Church,* 16–17.

24. For Francis Goulding see Myers, *Children of Pride,* 1531–32.

25. For James L. Merrick and early American missionaries in the Middle East, see Marr, *Cultural Roots of American Islamicism,* 120–31; Amanat and Bernhardsson, "Drying Up the Euphrates," 130–49. For an example of one of Merrick's early reports from Persia, see Merrick, "Mission to the Mohammedans of Persia," 10.

26. For John Leighton Wilson, see Clarke, *By the Rivers of Water.*

27. For I. S. K. Axson, see Myers, *Children of Pride,* 1456. For Dana, Legaré, Hooker, Winn, and Dwight, see CTS, *Memorial Volume.* For the students enrolled, see LaMotte, *Colored Light,* 298–99, and CTS, *Board of Directors Minutes,* 1835.

28. Clarke, *By the Rivers of Water,* 50. For the refectory see G. Howe, "History of Columbia Theological Seminary," 144.

29. For analysis of the nullification controversy, see Freehling, *Road to Disunion,* esp. 213–86. For concerns among seminarians about nullification, see John Leighton Wilson to Jane Bayard, December 18, 1832, in Clarke, *By the Rivers of Water,* 57.

30. G. Howe, "History of Columbia Theological Seminary," 139–40. For the Cherokee removal, see Moulton, *John Ross, Cherokee Chief.*

31. For Leland see Myers, *Children of Pride,* 1593–94; Lilly, *Beyond the Burning Bush,* 42–44. For his slaves see Aaron Leland, U.S. Census 1840, Columbia, S.C.

32. G. Howe, "History of Columbia Theological Seminary," 154; Joseph Bardwell, "Memorial of Aaron Whitney Leland," in *Memorial Volume,* 207–8. For faculty relationships with Leland, see, for example, Charles C. Jones to Mary Jones, October 21, 1837, and November 10, 1837, JTU.

33. A. W. Leland to Thomas Smyth, August 12, 1834, Smyth Papers, CTS. For the board of directors' response to the difficulties between Goulding and Howe, see CTS, *Board of Directors Minutes,* December 1834.

34. Charles C. Jones to Mary Jones, December 8, 1829, JTU.

35. For Leonard Wood, Andover, and a New England theology, see Holifield, *Theology in America,* 341–69; Ahlstrom, *Religious History of the American People,* 403–29. For the larger context of the rise of antislavery sentiment, see Davis, *Problem of Slavery in Western Culture;* and for the role of Protestant evangelicalism in the antislavery movement, see Davis, *In the Image of God,* 123–36.

36. Cf. Clarke, *Dwelling Place,* 82–96. See also Fogel, "Religious Sources of the New Abolitionist Movement."

37. CTS, *Board of Directors Minutes,* November 1836. For the Old School–New School debate in the South and role of slavery in the

debate, see Thompson, *Presbyterians in the South,* 1: 362–76.

38. Charles C. Jones to Mary Jones, May 18, 1830, JTU.

39. Clarke, *Dwelling Place,* 82–96.

40. C. Jones, *Catechism,* 69; Stowe, *Key to Uncle Tom's Cabin,* 42, 244, 127, 244. Cf. the earlier edition of the catechism, C. Jones, *Catechism.*

41. For the larger context of Jones's paternalism, see Ford, *Deliver Us from Evil,* 143–72 and 465–80.

2 — Slaves

1. Wilder, *Ebony and Ivy,* 11.

2. For Witherspoon see ibid., 80–81, 100–104. For Princeton Seminary faculty as slave owners, see Moorhead, *Princeton Seminary,* 42, 156, 243. For Princeton Seminary students from the south, see ibid., 155–56, and for graduates who were large slave owners, see, for example, "Pratt, Nathaniel Alpheus" and "Rogers, Charles William" in Myers, *Children of Pride,* 1648, 1662.

3. Palmer, *Life and Letters of James Henley Thornwell,* 431. For slave imports into Charleston and Savannah, see Voyages Database, 2009, Voyages: The Trans-Atlantic Slave Trade Database, www.slavevoyages.org (accessed January 7, 2015); and Eltis and Richardson, *Atlas,* 216. For the expansion of slavery westward, see Berlin, *Many Thousands Gone;* and Baptist, *Half Has Never Been Told,* esp. 171–213. For a perceived extension of a "Carolina culture" into the Old Southwest, see Thomas Johnson, *Life and Letters of Benjamin Morgan Palmer,* 171–72. For Columbia Seminary's influence among Mississippi Presbyterians, see Winter, *Outposts of Zion.* For the movement of some northern schools to centers of antislavery, see Bornstein, "Halls of Learning Built on Bondage?"

4. For Andrew Maybank see Myers, *Children of Pride,* "Maybank, Andrew (1768–1834)," 1621. For the Maybank estate, see Clarke, *Dwelling Place,* 115–18.

5. An Inventory and Appraisement of the Goods and Chattel of the late Andrew Maybank, deceased, of Liberty County, March 17, 1843, County Record L, Probate Court, Liberty County, Ga.; [Andrew Maybank] A List of Slaves on Col. Island Plantation, January 1833, JTU; Will of Andrew Maybank, January 13, 1834, Will Record, 1824–50, Probate Court, Liberty County, Ga.

6. Charles C. Jones to Mary Jones, July 22, 1829, JTU.

7. For the sale of Cora to Bacon, see Plantation Book for Maybank, 4, JTU. For Old Clarissa's family, see Executor's Sale, Andrew Maybank Estate Papers, JTU; Will of John Bohum Girardeau, November 11, 1800, Will Record 1790–1823, Probate Court, Liberty County, Ga.; Audley King to Charles C. Jones, October 17, 1853, JTU; Will of Andrew Maybank, January 13, 1834.

8. See Estate of Andrew Maybank in Account Current with C. C. Jones, Executor, Accounts Book, 1831–38, Probate Court, Liberty County, Ga., January 6, 1837. See also CTSBDM, December 3, 1834; November 17, 1835.

9. See CTSBDM, 1845–47.

10. W. Fraser, *Savannah,* 91–92. For the Telfair slave trading, see also Pressly, *On the Rim of the Caribbean,* 130–32. For William Seabrook see Clarke, *Our Southern Zion,* 147, and CTSBDM, 1835–45. For the sale of slaves in Mississippi for the Columbia endowment, see Winter, *Outposts of Zion,* 264.

11. Girardeau, "Eulogy on Professor George Howe," 410.

12. For concern among Protestants in the East that the western portion of the country might descend into chaos and infidelity, see, for example, Winter, *Outposts of Zion,* 1–24.

13. Myers, *Children of Pride,* "Howe, Sarah Ann," 1555; Records of Court of Ordinary, Liberty County, Ga., Elijah Baker, Clerk of the Court, Marriage License for George Howe and Sarah Ann McConnell, December 15, 1836; and Robert Quarterman, Certificate of Marriage for the Rev. George Howe and Mrs. Sarah A. McConnell, December 19, 1836. For George Washington Walthour as wealthiest man and largest slaveholder in the count, see "Walthour, George Washington," in Myers, *Children of Pride,* 1712. See also Records of Probate Court, 1850–63, Liberty County, Ga., Will

and Appraisement of George W. Walthour, 364–73.

14. For Sarah Ann McConnell's property at the time of her marriage, see Records of Probate Court, Liberty County, Ga., Estate of Robert C. McConnell, Probate Court, County Record K, Part 2, July 6, 1837, 424. For Caroline and other domestic slaves, see ibid., and Thomas Johnson, *Life and Letters of Benjamin Morgan Palmer,* 75. For the Howe purchase of a house in Columbia, see Charles C. Jones to Mary Jones, July 3, 1837, JTU.

15. For the role of slave drivers, see P. Morgan, *Slave Counterpoint,* 218–25; Kolchin, "Reevaluating the Antebellum Slave Community," 595–96. For Caesar as the driver for the Howe plantation, see 1845 census by Charles C. Jones of slave church membership in Liberty County, Ga., entitled "Return of Members," JTU.

16. For names of Howe slaves, see Jones, "Return of Members." For the task system and the classification of "hands," see P. Morgan, *Slave Counterpoint,* 179–87; P. Morgan, "Work and Culture."

17. For slave carpenters see Berlin, *Many Thousands Gone,* 84–85, 168; P. Morgan, *Slave Counterpoint,* 214–18, 227–28, 349; and Wood, *Women's Work,* 47, 105. For the property owned by Caesar, see his wife's account in Claim of Linda Roberts, Liberty County, Ga., Case Files, Southern Claims Commission, Records of the 3rd Auditor, Allowed Case Files, Records of the U.S. General Accounting Office, RG 217 (National Archives, Washington, D.C.). For an analysis of the claims of former slaves in Liberty County against the U.S. government for confiscation of their property by Union troops, see Pennigroth, "Slavery"; and P. Morgan, "Ownership of Property by Slaves in the Mid-nineteenth-Century Low Country." For proceeds from the Howe plantation, see "Accounts Current, Dr. Mrs. Sarah A. Howe, 1836–1838," Records of Probate Court, Liberty County, Ga., 227–28.

18. Charles C. Jones to Mary Jones, September 8, 1829, JTU. CTSBDM, November 28, 1836. For Sharper as a slave preacher and his mentoring of Charles Jones, see Clarke, *Dwelling Place,* 152–66. For the Jones slaves taken to Columbia, see Charles C. Jones to Elizabeth Jones Maxwell, December 25, 1837, JTU.

19. Charles Jones to Mary Jones, October 26, 1837, JTU. A full description of Charles Jones's activities during his first tenure as professor at Columbia can be found in JTU, 1837–38. For the black congregation, see, for example, Charles Jones to Mary Jones, June 25, 1837, JTU. For the debate among students, see ibid., June 23, 1837. For his address to Methodists, see *Charleston Observer,* January 18, 1838.

20. Clarke, *Dwelling Place,* 260–77.

21. For a collection of folk stories told by Jack, see C. Jones Jr., *Negro Myths.*

22. Charles Jones to Thomas Shepard, December 14, 1848, JTU.

23. LaMotte, *Colored Light;* 299–303; *Memorial Volume,* 328–31.

24. Stacy, *History of the Midway Congregational Church,* 109–36. Stacy lists fifty Presbyterian ministers, but some came after the Civil War. Stacy also lists four Baptists ministers from Liberty County who studied at Columbia. For slaveholders in Liberty County, see Menn, "Large Slaveholders," 739–42. For Louis LeConte see Inventory and Appraisement of the Estate of Lewis LeConte, Will Record, C, January 13, 1850, Probate Court, Liberty County, Ga. For Robert Quarterman see Inventory and Appraisement of the Estate of Robert Quarterman, Will Record, C, February 17, 1850, Probate Court, Liberty County, Ga. For David Buttolph see Menn, "Large Slaveholders," 739, and Lambert Plantation, June 10, 1856, in Carlawter Plantation Book, JTU.

25. For Joseph Jones see Inventory, Appraisement, and Division of the Estate of Joseph Jones, December 15, 1846, Will Record, 1824–50, Probate Court, Liberty County, Ga. For John Jones's share of his mother's estate, see Carlawter Plantation Book, JTU. For Bonaventure plantation see Clarke, *Dwelling Place,* 236, 257, and 389. For Sylvia see ibid., 35–42, 98, 188, 242–45.

26. For the slaves of Thomas Mallard, see Menn, "Large Slaveholders," 741. For the role of the driver on the Mallard plantation, see Mallard, *Plantation Life,* 38–46. For Pompey see Pennigroth, "Slavery." For Harry Stevens

see Mallard, *Plantation Life,* 48, and Clarke, *Dwelling Place,* 144–46, 270–71, 301. For root doctors and healing, see Abbott, *Southern Botanic Physician;* Morton, *Folk Remedies of the Low Country;* P. Morgan, *Slave Counterpoint,* 624–29.

27. For the list of slaves given as a wedding gift, see Indenture between Mary Sharpe Jones and Robert Q. Mallard, County Record O, 316, 1857, Superior Court, Liberty County, Ga. For the Mallard slaves taken to Atlanta, see Clarke, *Dwelling Place,* 430–31.

28. For Major see Clarke, *Dwelling Place,* 143, 146; and cf. Mallard, *Plantation Life,* 101–10.

29. The story of the Wilsons and their slaves is told in Clarke, *By the Rivers of Water.*

30. For an introduction to the ways a religious tradition is a part of a sociohistorical context, see B. Morris, *Religion.*

31. For the role that religion plays in shaping the ways people interpret their contexts and in helping to shape the context, see Geertz, "Religion as a Cultural System," in *Interpretation of Cultures,* esp. 123–24; and Ricoeur, *Lectures on Ideology and Utopia,* 3, 10, 183–97, and 254–66.

3 — Gentlemen Theologians in a Slave Society

1. For the emphasis on learning and piety in the establishment of Protestant theological seminaries in the United States, see G. Miller, *Piety and Intellect,* esp. 1–83, and J. Fraser, *Schooling the Preachers,* 29–47. For the emphasis in specific theological seminaries, see, for example, Handy, *History of Union Theological Seminary,* ix, 8–9; Blackman, *Faith and Freedom,* 23; and Moorhead, *Princeton Seminary,* 63–89.

2. Cf. Thompson, *Presbyterians in the South,* 1: 274–85.

3. Minutes of the Synod of South Carolina and Georgia, 1: 247–56, CTS.

4. G. Howe, *Discourse on Theological Education,* 3–8.

5. Quotations, ibid., 14, 95.

6. Quotations, ibid., 197–99. CTSBDM, December 9, 1833, 106–7. For an understanding of theology as a comprehensive science that involves many branches of knowledge, see O'Brien, *Conjectures of Order,* 2: 1094. Cf. Charles Hodge's treatment of theology as a science in Hodge, *Systematic Theology,* 1: 1–17.

7. G. Howe, *Discourse on Theological Education,* 200.

8. *Reports on the Course of Instruction in Yale College,* 30; G. Howe, *Discourse on Theological Education,* 200.

9. For the role of classics in southern culture, see Fox-Genovese and Genovese, *Mind of the Master Class,* 7, 250–58, 261–63; Winterer, *Culture of Classicism.* For slave names see 1845 census by Charles C. Jones of slave church membership in Liberty County, Ga., entitled "Return of Members," JTU. Cf. Gutman, *Black Family,* 230–356.

10. Adger, *Collected Writings of James Henley Thornwell,* 2: 462; Dabbs, *Who Speaks for the South?,* 119; Palmer, *Life and Letters of James Henley Thornwell,* 419.

11. G. Howe, *Discourse on Theological Education,* 202. For the number of Columbia students who did not have a college degree, see ibid., 147, and LaMotte, *Colored Light,* 298–300.

12. Palmer, *Life and Letters of James Henley Thornwell,* 142; Smyth, "The True Basis of Charity and United Christian Effort," in Flinn, *Collected Works of the Rev. Thomas Smyth, D.D.,* 5: 592–93.

13. Leith, *Introduction to the Reformed Tradition;* Holifield, *Theology in America,* 389–94; O'Brien, *Conjectures of Order,* 2: 1098–157.

14. See, for example, Thornwell, "Original Sin," in Adger, *Collected Writings of James Henley Thornwell,* 1: 301–51. For the response to Presbyterian seriousness, see Farmer, *Metaphysical Confederacy,* 65–69.

15. The number of Presbyterians in the South almost doubled between 1830 and 1860. See *Minutes of the General Assembly, Presbyterian Church in the U.S.A.* (Old School), 1830: 310–11; 1860: 259–60. For the experience of finding "Christ Jesus as my friend," see Mary Jones's description in Clarke, *Dwelling Place,* 77.

16. Thomas Smyth, "The Duty and Privilege of Belief and Confession," in Flinn, *Collected Works of the Rev. Thomas Smyth, D.D.,* 6: 42.

17. Thornwell, "Christian Effort," in Adger, *Collected Writings of James Henley Thornwell,* 1: 398.

18. John Leighton Wilson to Mary Martha Wilson, August 2, 1830, South Caroliniana Library, University of South Carolina, Columbia.

19. CTSBDM, December 9, 1833, 107, 123.

20. LaMotte, *Colored Light,* 53; CTSBDM, December 9, 1833, 111, 123.

21. Clarke, *Dwelling Place,* 267. For the tea-drinking ceremony, which lasted in the South longer than the rest of the nation, see Roth, "Tea Drinking"; S. Miller, *Letters on Clerical Manners,* 60–88.

22. CTSBDM, December 9, 1833, 123; John Leighton Wilson to Sarah Suzanna Wilson, October 27, 1832, South Caroliniana Library, University of South Carolina, Columbia; Thornwell, "Journal," July 17–19, 1836, CTS. For Palmer's courtship and marriage, see Thomas Johnson, *Life and Letters of Benjamin Morgan Palmer,* 71–72.

23. Thomas Johnson, *Life and Letters of Benjamin Morgan Palmer,* 36–44.

24. CTSBDM, December 9, 1833, 109. For Andover see J. Fraser, *Schooling the Preachers,* 34–35. Cf. Moorhead, *Princeton Seminary,* 44–66.

25. G. Howe, *Discourse on Theological Education,* 207–8.

26. Ibid., 211–12. For the use of Ernesti, see also Holifield, *Gentlemen Theologians,* 98–99.

27. G. Howe, *Discourse on Theological Education,* 212.

28. Palmer, *Life and Letters of James Henley Thornwell,* 530. For Leland's lectures in theology, see John A. Thomson Papers, Theology Notebook, 1847–48, CTS. See also for the use of Turretin in Latin, Fox-Genovese and Genovese, *Mind of the Master Class,* 787.

29. G. Howe, *Discourse on Theological Education,* 231. For Jones's sense of being ill prepared to teach church history, see Charles C. Jones to Mary Jones, July 3, 1837, JTU. For the reluctance at Columbia to engage history seriously, cf. O'Brien, *Conjectures of Order,* 2: 1146. For the doctrine of the spirituality of the church, see below.

30. G. Howe, *Discourse on Theological Education,* 234–43. Cf. Holifield, *History of Pastoral Care,* 107–58.

31. For the persistent efforts of the board during the antebellum period to create a substantial theological library, see CTSBDM, 1831–60; and *Memorial Volume,* 140. For comparison of Columbia's library in 1850 to other libraries in the country, see O'Brien, *Conjectures of Order,* 1: 512–16. For Smyth's library see ibid., 488–89.

32. O'Brien, *Conjectures of Order,* 1: 520. For details of the Smyth library and its sale to Columbia Seminary, see Stoney, *Autobiographical Notes,* 119–23, 497–505. For Smyth's use of his library and more indications of his collection, see Flinn, *Collected Works of the Rev. Thomas Smyth, D.D.*

33. For the board examining students, see, for example, CTSBDM, December 2, 1833, 88–89.

34. LaMotte, *Colored Light,* 302.

35. Charleston Presbytery Minutes, 1851, CTS.

36. Fox-Genovese and Genovese, "Divine Sanction of Social Order," 227; Thompson, *Presbyterians in the South,* 1: 453.

4 — "A golden era"

1. Clarke, *Dwelling Place,* 260–69.

2. Ibid., 267.

3. Edgar, *South Carolina Encyclopedia,* s.v. "Hampton-Preston Mansion."

4. Charles Colcock Jones to William and Betsy Maxwell, April 17, 1850, JTU.

5. Charles Colcock Jones to William and Betsy Maxwell, April 20, 1850, JTU.

6. "Inscription for Jack and Marcia," April 20, 1850," in JTU.

7. Aaron Leland and George Howe to Charles C. Jones, July 11, 1850, JTU.

8. Thomas Johnson, *Life and Letters of Benjamin Morgan Palmer,* 384. See also M. Moore, "Northern Professor"; Thomas Johnson, *Life and Letters of Benjamin Morgan Palmer,* 151–52.

9. *Proceedings of the Meeting in Charleston, S.C., May 13–15, 1845,* 47. See also Thomas Johnson, *Life and Letters of Benjamin Morgan Palmer,* 18–44. See also Clarke, *Our Southern Zion,* 233–34; Stoney Creek Independent

Presbyterian Church, "Book of the Congregation, 1823–1861," CTS. For a more detailed account of Edward Palmer, see Palmer, "Sketch of Edward Palmer."

10. Thomas Johnson, *Life and Letters of Benjamin Morgan Palmer,* 45–125; Benjamin Morgan Palmer, U.S. Census, 1850, Columbia, S.C.; Duncan, "Benjamin Morgan Palmer," 8–67.

11. Thomas Johnson, *Life and Letters of Benjamin Morgan Palmer,* 150–52; Palmer, *Life and Letters of James Henley Thornwell,* 382–86; Adger, *My Life and Times,* 215–19.

12. Palmer, *Life and Letters of James Henley Thornwell,* 13–82.

13. Ibid., 84.

14. O'Brien, *Conjectures of Order,* 2: 1116; Sims, *Story of My Life,* 107; Palmer, *Life and Letters of James Henley Thornwell,* 96–97.

15. O'Brien, *Conjectures of Order,* 2: 1117; Palmer, *Life and Letters of James Henley Thornwell,* 99–100. See also Farmer, *Metaphysical Confederacy,* 54–55, 65–66; Hollis, *University of South Carolina: South Carolina College,* 161–78.

16. Palmer, *Life and Letters of James Henley Thornwell,* 118. See also ibid., 115–26.

17. Ibid., 137. See also ibid., 127–35.

18. Farmer, *Metaphysical Confederacy,* 55–56; Wilder, *Ebony and Ivy,* 102–5; Palmer, *Life and Letters of James Henley Thornwell,* 137; James Henley Thornwell, U.S. Census, 1850, Columbia, S.C.; James Henley Thornwell, U.S. Census 1860, Lancaster District, S.C.

19. Charles Colcock Jones to Mary Jones, November 3, 1838, JTU; Hollis, *University of South Carolina: South Carolina College,* 161. See also Hollis, *University of South Carolina: South Carolina College,* 164.

20. Palmer, *Life and Letters of James Henley Thornwell,* 181–209, 221–31, 251–66; Farmer, *Metaphysical Confederacy,* 41–76; 175–94; Genovese, *Southern Tradition,* 64; Thompson, *Presbyterians in the South,* 1: 510–16.

21. Thomas Johnson, *Life and Letters of Benjamin Morgan Palmer,* 161–62. For an example of one of Palmer's lectures at Columbia, see Palmer, "Import of Hebrew History."

22. Beckert, *Empire of Cotton,* 218; Adger, *My Life and Times,* 34–37.

23. Adger, *My Life and Times,* 103. See also ibid., 90–130; O'Brien, *Conjectures of Order,* 1: 169.

24. Adger, *My Life and Times,* 90–130.

25. Ibid., 123–30.

26. Palmer, *Life and Letters of James Henley Thornwell,* 373, 383. Adger, *My Life and Times,* 208–22.

27. Adger, *My Life and Times,* 219.

28. Winter, *Outposts of Zion,* 239–41; G. Howe, "History of Columbia Theological Seminary," 147–48; Calhoun, "Interesting Story of the Perkins Family of Tensas Parish, La."; John Perkins, U.S. Census, 1830, Concordia, La.; John Perkins, U.S. Census, 1840, Lowndes, Miss.; John Perkins, U.S. Census, 1850, Western District, Madison, La.; John Perkins, U.S. Census Slave Schedules, 1850, Western District, Madison, La.; Act of Donation, John Perkins Sr., Tensas Parish, La., Book of Donations, Tensas Parish Superior Court; Adger, *My Life and Times,* 419–665.

29. G. Howe, "History of Columbia Theological Seminary," 143–46.

30. LaMotte, *Colored Light,* 305–8.

31. Palmer, "Plea for Doctrine as the Instrument of Sanctification," 32–33.

32. Clarke, *By the Rivers of Water.*

33. G. Howe, *Discourse on Theological Education,* 196. See also Thomas Johnson, *Life and Letters of Benjamin Morgan Palmer,* 126, 269. For a list of authors and articles in the *Southern Presbyterian Review,* see http://www.pcahistory.org/HCLibrary/periodicals/spr/ (accessed 2015).

34. John Leighton Wilson, "Foreign Slave-Trade," 491. See also Adger, "Review of Reports"; G. Howe, "Raid of John Brown."

35. For articles cited, see http://www.pcahistory.org/HCLibrary/periodicals/spr/ (accessed 2015). For Thornwell as the "star," see Adger, "Memorial," 188.

36. Farmer, *Metaphysical Confederacy,* 62–63; Palmer, *Life and Letters of James Henley Thornwell,* 123.

37. Adger, *My Life and Times,* 166–67. See also ibid., 164–200.

38. See John Adger to James Henley Thornwell, October 28, 1848, CTS; Adger, "Christian Doctrine"; and Clarke, *Our Southern Zion,* 189–92.

39. Adger, *My Life and Times,* 173. See also Thornwell, "Slavery and the Religious Instruction," 108; and Clarke, *Our Southern Zion,* 189–92.

40. For the debate over the dual origin of the races, see Jenkins, *Proslavery Thought,* 242–84; Stanton, *Leopard's Spots;* Livingstone, *Adam's Ancestors,* 169–201; Hampton, *Storm of Words,* 63–85.

41. G. Howe, "Two Lectures," 426–90; Smyth, *Unity of the Human Races,* 74. For John Leighton Wilson, see Clarke, *By the Rivers of Water,* 58, 310, 324.

42. Adger, *Collected Writings of James Henley Thornwell,* 4: 427, 433, 415–16, 404. Thornwell's definition of slavery as the right of an owner only to the labor of the slave was held by a few other whites. Charles Hodge had moved in this direction but had not gone so far. Both he and Thornwell drew on the work of William Paley. For Hodge see Moorhead, *Princeton Seminary,* 157–61. Several years after Thornwell's Anson Street sermon, Henry Hughes advocated an understanding of slavery similar to Thornwell's. See Genovese and Fox-Genovese, *Fatal Self-Deception,* 32–34, and Ambrose, *Henry Hughes.*

43. Adger, *Collected Writings of James Henley Thornwell,* 4: 405.

44. Ibid., 419–21, 404. For analysis of the sermon, see Farmer, *Metaphysical Confederacy,* 220–26; Westerkamp, "James Henley Thornwell"; Freehling, "James Henley Thornwell's Mysterious Antislavery Movement"; and O'Brien, *Conjectures of Order,* 2: 1149–57.

45. For the tension between order and freedom in Calvin, see Bouwsma, *John Calvin.*

46. Thornwell, "Slavery and the Religious Instruction of the Colored Population," 402. Adger, *Collected Writings of James Henley Thornwell,* 4: 402.

5 — *Moderates Enraged*

1. For Unionist sentiments on the Columbia campus during the nullification controversy, see John Leighton Wilson to Jane Bayard, December 18, 1832, CTS; Robinson, *Columbia Theological Seminary and the Southern Presbyterian Church,* 35–36. See also Palmer, *Life and Letters of James Henley Thornwell,* 470, 479.

2. For the Compromise of 1850, see Freehling, *Road to Disunion,* 487–510. For the international context of the Compromise of 1850, see Schoen, *Fragile Fabric of Union,* 197–259.

3. Palmer, *James Henley Thornwell,* 477; Clarke, *Dwelling Place,* 398.

4. Palmer, *Life and Letters of James Henley Thornwell,* 576. Thornwell's vision of the United States as a redeemer nation stands in contrast to claims by some historians in the 1980s that the South did not participate in a national vision of a redeemer nation. See, for example, Brauer, "Regionalism and Religion in America"; Hill, *South and the North;* and C. Wilson, *Baptized in Blood.* A distinctive southern vision would be articulated by Columbia Unionists only with the coming of the Civil War.

5. Palmer, *Life and Letters of James Henley Thornwell,* 477. For denominational divisions between North and South, see Goen, *Broken Churches.*

6. Bliss, *Letters,* 100–102.

7. American Tract Society, *Responsibilities of the Publishing Committee,* 6.

8. Ibid., 9; South Carolina Tract Society, *Report and Resolutions,* 4–6.

9. Smyth, *Collected Works of the Rev. Thomas Smyth, D.D.,* 9: 451–66; Stoney, *Autobiographical Notes,* 278–80.

10. For this discussion of liberty, see Clarke, *Our Southern Zion,* 204–7. See also O'Brien, *Conjectures of Order,* 2: 1151–57.

11. Clarke, *Our Southern Zion,* 206.

12. McPherson, *Abraham Lincoln,* 43–44.

13. Palmer, *Life and Letters of James Henley Thornwell,* 607.

14. Adger, "Review of Reports to the Legislature of South Carolina," 115. See also South Carolina, General Assembly, House of Representatives, *Reports of the Committee to Whom Was Referred the Message of Gov. James H. Adams.*

15. John Leighton Wilson, "Foreign Slave-Trade," 491–512. Thornwell was equally adamant in his opposition to the international slave trade and "expressed freely" to the South Carolina governor his opposition. See Palmer, *Life and*

Letters of James Henley Thornwell, 423. For the broader context for the attempted revival of the slave trade, see Thomas, *Slave Trade*, 765–68; Beckert, *Empire of Cotton*, 242–73.

16. Redpath, *Public Life*, 4. For Brown's legacy see Gilpin, *John Brown*, esp. 55–78. The best recent history of John Brown is Horwitz, *Midnight Rising*.

17. G. Howe, "Raid of John Brown," 806, 810. Cf. Charles C. Jones to Charles C. Jones Jr., November 7, 1859, JTU.

18. G. Howe, "Raid of John Brown," 815–16.

19. Palmer, *Life and Letters of James Henley Thornwell*, 457.

20. Ibid., 482–83. William W. Freehling, "James Henley Thornwell's Mysterious Antislavery Moment." Cf. Bishop, "Proslavery Argument Reconsidered," and Westerkamp, "James Henley Thornwell"; O'Brien, *Conjectures of Order*, 2: 1155–57.

21. Stoney, *Autobiographical Notes*, 555–56.

22. Ibid., 554; Morison, *Oxford History*, 603.

23. Smyth, *Collected Works of the Rev. Thomas Smyth, D.D.*, 7: 539.

24. Ibid., 541–43.

25. Thomas Johnson, *Life and Letters of Benjamin Morgan Palmer*, 209–13.

26. Adger, *Collected Writings of James Henley Thornwell*, 4: 510, 519. See also ibid., 525.

27. Ibid., 4: 525, 529.

28. Ibid., 4: 539–41. Cf. Beckert, *Empire of Cotton*. Beckert argues that capitalists were the true revolutionaries of the nineteenth century.

29. Adger, *Collected Writings of James Henley Thornwell*, 4: 542–43.

30. Ibid., 4: 545–48.

31. Thomas Hart Law, "Journal," December 20, 1860.

32. *Journal of the Convention of the People of South Carolina*, December 17 and 20, 1860. For Perrin, see also "Late Honorable Thomas C. Perrin," 2.

33. Hodge, "State of the Country," 31.

34. Clarke, *By the Rivers of Water*, 328.

35. JLW to Charles Hodge, December 22, 1860, ibid., 330.

36. Smyth, "Battle of Fort Sumter." Mary Jones to Charles Colcock Jones Jr., May 28, 1861, JTU.

37. "Journal of Thos. H. Law," April 13, 1861. See also ibid., February 1, 1861.

38. *Minutes of the General Assembly, Presbyterian Church in the U.S.A.* (Old School), 1861, 330, 343; Spring, *Personal Reminiscences*, 2: 180. Clarke, *By the Rivers of Water*, 333–34.

39. *Minutes of the General Assembly, Presbyterian Church in the Confederate States of America, 1861*, 5–7, 44–45.

40. Ibid., 51–52.

41. For the development of the doctrine of the spirituality of the church, see Adger, *Collected Writings of James Henley Thornwell*, 4: 476–77, 501–2; Farmer, *Metaphysical Confederacy*, 257–60. For the important role of the doctrine in Southern Presbyterian thinking, see Thompson, *Spirituality of the Church*.

42. Adger, *Collected Writings*, 4: 452–55.

43. Palmer, *Life and Letters of James Henley Thornwell*, 457.

44. Ibid., 55. For questions of a distinct southern identity, see Cobb, *Way Down South*.

45. For these reflections, cf. Clarke, *Our Southern Zion*, 212–15. For continuities with antebellum southern culture and deep assumptions, see Genovese, *Southern Tradition*; Blight, *Race and Reunion;* Perman, *Pursuit of Unity;* and Blackmon, *Slavery by Another Name*.

6 — Civil War

1. For the suffering and enormous loss of life during the war, see Faust, *This Republic of Suffering*. For the physical destruction of the war, including its impact on the environment, see Nelson, *Ruin Nation*.

2. Palmer, *Life and Letters of James Henley Thornwell*, 513.

3. Ibid., 581–82.

4. Ibid., 582.

5. Ibid., 583.

6. Ibid., 586–87.

7. Ibid., 589–90.

8. Thomas Smyth, "The Victory of Manassas Plain"; "The War of the South Vindicated"; "The Character and Conditions of Liberty"; "The Soldier's Prayer Book," found in Flinn, *Collected Works of the Rev. Thomas Smyth, D.D.*, 7: 701–50.

9. Thomas Johnson, *Life and Letters of Benjamin Morgan Palmer,* 262–63, 267–68.

10. Palmer, *Life and Letters of James Henley Thornwell,* 515, 519; Stoney, *Autobiographical Notes,* 644–45, 663; USS *James Adger,* Wikipedia, https://en.wikipedia.org/wiki/USS_James_Adger (accessed 2015).

11. Clarke, *Dwelling Place,* 423–27; Myers, *Children of Pride,* 1556.

12. Myers, *Children of Pride,* 725, 1556; Mary Jones to Charles Colcock Jones Jr., July 25, 1861, JTU. For the search for loved ones and the appalling number of "unknown" dead, see Faust, *This Republic of Suffering,* 102–36.

13. Palmer, *Life and Letters of James Henley Thornwell,* 515.

14. Stoney, *Autobiographical Notes,* 627; Mrs. A. T. Smythe, *South Carolina Women in the Confederacy,* 22, 43, 79, 81–83, 94, 95–96. For an overview of Confederate women's aid and relief societies, see Cunningham, *Doctors in Gray,* 141–43.

15. M. Woodrow, *Dr. James Woodrow,* 21; LeConte, *Autobiography,* 184.

16. For refugees staying in seminary dormitories, see Smythe, *South Carolina Women in the Confederacy,* 79. For the Barnwell family staying with the Thornwells, see Palmer, *Life and Letters of James Henley Thornwell,* 498.

17. DuBose, *Memoirs,* 253–54. For Wilson's organization of chaplains, see Thompson, *Presbyterians in the South,* 2: 40–51. For Columbia graduates who served as chaplains, see LaMotte, *Colored Light,* 140–41. For diseases faced by troops North and South, see McPherson, *Cross Roads of Freedom,* 487–88; Cunningham, *Doctors in Gray,* 184–217; Faust, *This Republic of Suffering.*

18. For Boggs, Petrie, and Green, see M. Woodrow, *Dr. James Woodrow,* vi–vii. For Wilson see Joseph Wilson, *Presbyterian Historical Almanac,* 364. For Girardeau, see Blackburn, *Life Work of John L. Girardeau,* 106–33. Extensive scholarship explores religious life among Confederate soldiers. See, for example, Faust, "Christian Soldiers"; C. Wilson, *Baptized in the Blood,* 6; R. Miller et al., *Religion and the American Civil War.*

19. Palmer, *Life and Letters of James Henley Thornwell,* 376, 496. See also ibid., 378, 513–25.

20. Ibid., 517–18.

21. Ibid., 523–24.

22. Ibid., 521.

23. Faust, *This Republic of Suffering,* 58, 209.

24. Adger, *My Life and Times,* 331–32.

25. Clarke, *Dwelling Place,* 411–12.

26. Ibid., 413–14.

27. Ibid., 415.

28. Mallard, *Plantation Life,* 3–37; Myers, *Children of Pride,* 1156–219; Venet, *Changing Wind,* 125–26, 152.

29. McPherson, *Battle Cry of Freedom,* 749–50; Hirshson, *White Tecumseh,* 241–64.

30. Hirshson, *White Tecumseh,* 264; J. Jones, *Saving Savannah,* 207. For the ways in which the coming of the Yankees was filled with religious meaning for many slaves, see Litwack, *Been in the Storm So Long,* 104–66.

31. Mallard, *Plantation Life,* 212–32; LeConte, *Autobiography,* 186–203; LeConte, *'Ware Sherman,* 1–81. For Howe see ibid., 12.

32. Penningroth, *Claims of Kinfolk,* 2. Claim of Linda Roberts, Liberty County, Ga., Case Files, Southern Claims Commission, Records of the 3rd Auditor, Allowed Case Files, Records of the U.S. General Accounting Office, RG 217 (National Archives, Washington, D.C.).

33Quotations: Hirshson, *White Tecumseh,* 275, 277.

34. Adger, *My Life and Times,* 335.

35. Thomas Johnson, *Life and Letters of Benjamin Morgan Palmer,* 287–90. For Leland see *Myers, Children of Pride,* 1593–94. For Woodrow see M. Woodrow, *Dr. James Woodrow,* 21; for Crawford and the seminary bonds, see CTSBDM, September 1866. For LeConte see LeConte, *'Ware Sherman,* 85–144.

36. Hirshson, *White Tecumseh,* 280; Calhoun, *Our Southern Zion,* 192.

37. Thomas Johnson, *Life and Letters of Benjamin Morgan Palmer,* 289; Adger, *My Life and Times,* 336; CTSBD, June 1863.

38. Hirshson, *White Tecumseh,* 275, 277. For the controversy surrounding the burning of Columbia, see ibid., 280–86; M. Lucas, *Sherman;* and J. Moore, *Columbia and Richland County,* 181–208. For the loss of Palmer's home,

see Thomas Johnson, *Life and Letters of Benjamin Morgan Palmer,* 287. For Woodrow see CTSBD, June 1866.

39. Thomas Johnson, *Life and Letters of Benjamin Morgan Palmer,* 287–88.

40. Adger, *My Life and Times,* 335–45.

41. Ibid., 339. CTSBDM, May 4, 1863.

7 — *"A just but lost cause"*

1. LeConte, *'Ware Sherman,* 140. For the fabled wealth of the region, see Coclanis, *Shadow of a Dream,* 111–58.

2. *New York Times,* March 6, 1865. See also *New York Times,* March 9, April 4, and July 24, 1864. Cf. Burton, *Siege of Charleston.*

3. For Atlanta see Venet, *Changing Wind,* 180–223; for Savannah see J. Jones, *Saving Savannah,* 233–58; for Darien see Sullivan, *Early Days,* 286–331; for towns in South Carolina, see Hyman Rubin III, "Reconstruction," in Edgar, *South Carolina Encyclopedia,* 779–81; for Liberty County see Clarke, *Dwelling Place,* 443–65. For Perkins see Winter, *Outposts of Zion,* 239–41; Calhoun, "Interesting Story of the Perkins Family of Tensas Parish, La." For an overview of the "world the war made," see Foner, *Reconstruction,* 1–34.

4. Mary Jones "Journal," March 1865, JTU. For the Midway church, see Stacy, *History of the Midway Congregational Church,* 68–75.

5. Ibid. Cf. Clarke, *Our Southern Zion,* 216–18.

6. For southern whites' sense of invincibility, see Phillips, *Diehard Rebels.* For issues raised by the suffering and death of the war and by the southern defeat, see Faust, *This Republic of Suffering;* and cf. Brueggemann, "Some Aspects of Theodicy in Old Testament Faith." Cf. also Woodward, *Burden of Southern History,* esp. 3–25; Cobb, *Way Down South,* 34–66; Clarke, *By the Rivers of Water,* 350–51.

7. LeConte, *When the World Ended,* 98; Faust, *This Republic of Suffering,* 192; John Jones to Charles Colcock Jones Jr., August 21, 1865, JTU.

8. Adger, "Northern and Southern Views," 384–411. Cf. also C. Wilson, *Baptized in Blood,* 58–78; Noll, *Civil War,* 75–94.

9. MGAPCCSA, 1864, 293–94; Adger, "Northern and Southern Views," 392–93. For Hodge see Gutjahr, *Charles Hodge,* 331–47; Moorhead, *Princeton Seminary,* 179–85.

10. Thomas Johnson, *Life and Letters of Benjamin Morgan Palmer,* 321–28.

11. Ibid., 329–34.

12. John Bohun Girardeau, U.S. Census, 1840, Charleston County, 1840. For Girardeau's love for the South Carolina lowcountry, see Girardeau, "Suffering Seaboard." See also Blackburn, *Life Work of John L. Girardeau,* 59–61.

13. Blackburn, *Life Work of John L. Girardeau,* 72–105; Clarke, *Our Southern Zion,* 182–99.

14. Mayer, *All on Fire,* 583; Dunham, *Attitude of the Northern Clergy,* 210–11.

15. Girardeau, *Confederate Memorial Day,* 3. Girardeau's oration needs to be seen in light of the "reburial" movement North and South, and the quest to find meaning in the huge loss of life caused by the war. See Faust, *This Republic of Suffering,* 211–49.

16. Girardeau, *Confederate Memorial Day,* 3; McPherson, *Battle Cry of Freedom,* 701.

17. For this southern critique of capitalism, see C. Wilson, *Baptized in the Blood,* 79–99; Genovese, *Southern Tradition*; and Brinkmeyer, *Fourth Ghost,* 24–70. For the economic depression of 1870s and the ways "progress begat poverty," see Foner, *Reconstruction,* 512–63; and S. Fraser, *Age of Acquiescence,* 39–67.

18. Girardeau, *Confederate Memorial Day,* 3. See also Gardner, *Blood and Irony,* for the ways southern women helped establish a Lost Cause memory.

19. Girardeau, *Confederate Memorial Day,* 8–18. Girardeau was evidently drawing on the linguistic studies of the Scottish Enlightenment, in which he had read deeply. Cf. Reid, *Inquiry into the Human Mind on the Principles of Common Sense,* and A. Smith, "Considerations concerning the First Formation of Languages."

20. For an ideology such as Girardeau's functioning as a guardian of identity, see Geertz, "Ideology as a Cultural System," in *Interpretation of Cultures;* and Ricoeur, *Lectures on Ideology and Utopia,* 258–61.

21. Girardeau, "Suffering Seaboard," 208.

Cf. for similar sentiments and fears, CTSBDM, September 1869.

22. A massive literature explores the meaning and character of the South's "Lost Cause." For example C. Wilson, in *Baptized in the Blood,* sees it as a fundamentally religious phenomenon. David Blight, in *Race and Reunion,* devotes considerable attention to the Lost Cause as a reminiscence industry. Gardner in *Blood and Irony* explores the ways southern women helped shape and transmit a memory of a Lost Cause.

23. Edgar, *South Carolina: A History,* 401. For the violence of Reconstruction and Jim Crow, see Hahn, *Nation under Our Feet,* 265–313; Foner, *Reconstruction,* 425–79; and Blackmon, *Slavery by Another Name.* For an example of a response to lynching, see James Woodrow, "Barnwell Lynching," in M. Woodrow, *Dr. James Woodrow,* 573.

24. For the immediate issues facing freedpeople, see Litwack, *Been in the Storm So Long,* 222–29; Blight, *Race and Union,* 44–63. For African American memory and its function in the black community after the Civil War, see Blight, *Race and Reunion.*

25. Adger, *My Life and Times,* 331–33, 346. For African Americans' desire for, and sense of entitlement to, land, see Hahn, *Nation under Our Feet,* 127–54.

26. For Caesar see "Claim of Linda Roberts, Liberty County, Ga., Case Files, Southern Claims Commission, Records of the 3rd Auditor, Allowed Case Files, Records of the U.S. General Accounting Office, RG 217 (National Archives, Washington, D.C.). For Pompey see "Pompey Bacon, Former Slave's Claim against U.S. Government," case 21464, Georgia Historical Society. For Cato see Mary Jones to John Jones, September 18, 1865, the Reverend John Jones Collection, University of Georgia; Mary Jones to Charles C. Jones Jr., September 6, 1865, JTU; Groover, *Sweet Land of Liberty,* 51. Cf. also J. Scott, *Domination,* 45–69.

27. Clarke, *Our Southern Zion,* 224–28, 232–36. See also Raynal, *Johns Island Presbyterian Church,* 77–78; F. Jones and Mills, *History of the Presbyterian Church,* 116–42.

28. The correspondence between Logan and John Leighton Wilson can be found in "Fourth Annual Report: The General Assembly's Committee on Freedmen, of the Presbyterian Church in the United States of America," Presbyterian Historical Society, Philadelphia, Penn., 22–51.

29. Ibid., 29–31.

30. Ibid., 41, 48, 49.

31. The formation of black Presbyterian churches in the South, independent of southern white control, can best be followed in the minutes of the Committee on Freeman, General Assembly, Presbyterian Church in the United States of America, 1865–75.

32. Parker, *Rise and Decline;* and Wilmore, *Black Presbyterians.*

33. Parker, *Rise and Decline,* esp. 40–41. See also Clarke, *Our Southern Zion,* 243–49.

34. Thompson, *Presbyterians in the South,* 2: 147.

8 — An Impoverished World

1. CTSBD, May 1861–September 1863.

2. Ibid., September 1865.

3. Ibid., June 1866.

4. For the transfer of the seminary to the control of the General Assembly, see ibid., May 1863, and *Minutes of the General Assembly of the Presbyterian Church in the Confederate States of America,* 1863.

5. For Leighton Wilson see McIlwane, *Memories,* 282, and Thompson, *Presbyterians in the South,* 2: 292, 306–7. For LeConte see LeConte, *Autobiography.* There has been considerable scholarly debate around the question of continuity or discontinuity between the Old South and the New. C. Vann Woodward is the best-known representative of those scholars who emphasize how far the New South was from the Old. Eugene Genovese and Elizabeth Fox-Genovese have emphasized the cultural and ideological continuities between the Old and the New South. Many of the essays in Arsenault and Burton, *Dixie Redux,* provide overviews and insights about the scholarly debate. The continuities and discontinuities between antebellum and postbellum Columbia Seminary need to be seen in light of this larger social context and the competing interpretations of its character.

6. J. Moore, *Columbia and Richland County,* 241. For Hemphill see *Biographical Dictionary of the United States Congress,* http://bioguide.congress.gov/scripts/biodisplay.pl?index=H000 (accessed September 16, 2015).

7. CTSBD, May 1870. Regular reports on the library were given each year and recorded in CTSBDM. See ibid., 1868–85.

8. LaMotte, *Colored Light,* 144.

9. For a description of Plumer, see Hoge, "Memorial of William Swain Plumer," 211.

10. For a list of Plumer's most influential books, see http://onlinebooks.library.upenn.edu/webbin/book/lookupname?key=Plumer%2C%20William%20S.%20(William%20Swan)%2C%201802-1880 (accessed September 21, 2015). Plumer, however, never became closely identified with the seminary's history. William Childs Robinson, for example, in his *Columbia Theological Seminary and the Southern Presbyterian Church,* does not list in his bibliography one of Plumer's many books.

11. Mulder, *Woodrow Wilson,* 28. For a brief but helpful overview of Wilson's life and personality, see ibid., 3–28.

12. LaMotte, *Colored Light,* 144. See also Joseph R. Wilson's obituary in the *State,* Columbia, S.C., January 24, 1903.

13. CTSBDM, 1865–74. For a list of moderators, see LaMotte, *Colored Light,* 264–65. W. E. Boggs served as chancellor of the University of Georgia; C. R. Hemphill was a founder of Louisville Theological Seminary, where he was a professor and president; Luther McKinnon was president of Davidson College; and Hampden DuBose was a leader in the fight against the opium trade in China.

14. CTSBDM, 1865–80. See as well CTSFM, 1866–79, and "Admission" in CTSC, 1866–79.

15. Adger, *My Life and Times,* 231; CTSC, 1869. Details of the curriculum can be found in CTSC, 1866–79, and in CTSFM, 1866–79.

16. CTSC, 1860, 1866–79; CTSFM, September 9, 1870; Adger, *My Life and Times,* 231.

17. CTSC, 1870; CTSFM, September 9, 1870; Adger, *My Life and Times,* 230–326.

18. CTSC, 1870.

19. Dabney, *Syllabus and Notes,* 617, 809–11. Holifield, "Mercersburg, Princeton, and the South." See also Holifield, *Theology in America,* 467–81, and Holifield, *Gentlemen Theologians,* 175–85.

20. Adger, *My Life and Times,* 324, 314. CTSC, 1885–90. When Girardeau's friends and colleagues wrote twelve essays in honor of him and collected them in *The Life Work of John L. Girardeau* (ed. Blackburn), they made no mention of the sacraments.

21. Adger, *My Life and Times,* 462; Flinn, "Evolution and Theology," 270–71.

22. G. Howe, *Discourse on Theological Education,* 197–98; CTSC, 1866–79. Hampton, *Storm of Words,* 78–79. For Lyell as a "Founding Father" of geology and his broad influence on the natural sciences, see Rudwick, *Earth's Deep History,* 163–74.

23. J. Woodrow, "Inaugural Address," 14.

24. Foner, *Reconstruction,* 412–59, 564–601; Andrew, *Wade Hampton,* 329–420; Zuczek, *State of Rebellion,* 88–117.

25. For summaries of endowment investments, see CTSBDM, May 1881 and May 1885. For salaries, student life, and buildings in the years immediately after the war, see CTSBDM, February 1868; May 1868; September 1869.

26. Doyle, *New Men,* 194–95. For Robert Adger's depositing family wealth in England, see J. Brown, *Hundred Years,* 261–64. For the Smyths' and Adgers' involvement in textiles, see Stoney, *Autobiographical Notes,* 657, 745; and *Handbook of South Carolina,* 457–60.

27. For charges that Woodrow was engaged in "wholly secularized" work, see M. Woodrow, *Dr. James Woodrow,* 527, 545–48, and Adger, *My Life and Times,* 631. For Woodrow's contribution to Columbia's endowment, see CTSBDM, September 1870. For his foregoing his salary, see ibid., 1867–75. For his ownership of the *Southern Presbyterian* and *Southern Presbyterian Review,* see Gustafson, *James Woodrow,* 77–78.

28. For the membership of the executive committees and for the establishment of a sustentation fund, see *MGAPCUS,* 1866, and Thompson, *Presbyterians in the South,* 2: 101–5.

29. Gustafson, *James Woodrow,* 80, 86. M. Woodrow, *Dr. James Woodrow,* 510–54.

30. For Woodrow's travel and membership

in scientific societies, see M. Woodrow, *Dr. James Woodrow,* 28.

31. CTSFM, September 24; October 1, 3, 1873.

32. Ibid., January 15, 29, 1874.

33. CTSFM, March 19, 1874. For students leaving see ibid., March 24 and 26, April 30, 1874.

34. *MGAPCUS,* May 1884. CTSBD, May 1874. See also Mulder, *Woodrow Wilson,* 15–17; and F. Jones and Mills, *History of the Presbyterian Church in South Carolina,* 421–25.

35. McIlwane, *Memories,* 313.

36. CTSBD, 1874–80; Thompson, *Presbyterians in the South,* 2: 370; Street, "Evolution Controversy," 248.

9 — Evolution and "the phraseology of the past"

1. Two important and erudite studies have explored the evolution controversy at Columbia Seminary. See Hampton, *Storm of Words;* and Livingstone, *Dealing with Darwin,* 117–156. I have found Hampton's interpretation of a "southern-biblicist apologia" to be particularly helpful in interpreting the conservative reaction to Woodrow.

2. Girardeau, *Sermons,* 388–89. See also R. A. Webb, "The Evolution Controversy," in Blackburn, *Life Work of John L. Girardeau,* 231–84. For the larger context and cultural history of the "Evolution Wars," see Rudwick, *Earth's Deep History,* especially for developments in geology.

3. Hampton, *Storm of Words,* 4. See also Street, "Evolution Controversy," and Eaton, "Professor James Woodrow."

4. For the establishment of the Perkins Chair, see Lyon, "New Theological Professorship"; Gladney, "Natural Science and Revealed Religion"; G. Howe, "History of Columbia Theological Seminary," 147–48; Winter, *Outposts of Zion,* 239–41; and Hampton, *Storm of Words,* 129–36. For Thornwell's support of the chair, see Adger, *My Life and Times,* 424; Law, "Personal Reminiscences," 57; and cf. Thornwell, "Being of God," 63. For Smyth's support, see Stoney, *Autobiographical Notes, Letters and Reflections by Thomas Smyth,* 639. For John Leighton Wilson's support, see DuBose, *Memoirs,* 310–20. For Adger's support, see Adger, *My Life and Times,* 648.

5. Adger, *My Life and Times,* 424; J. Woodrow, "Examination of Certain Recent Assaults on Physical Science," 328. Cf. also J. Woodrow, "Geology and Its Assailants." For Dabney's attack see Dabney, "Geology and the Bible," and Dabney, "Caution against Anti-Christian Science Criticized by Dr. Woodrow." For the Dabney-Woodrow debate, see Livingstone, *Dealing with Darwin,* 138–42, and Hampton, *Storm of Words,* 169–70.

6. J. Woodrow, "Inaugural Address," 14.

7. Ibid., 14–50.

8. CTSBD, May 1879–May 1881. *MGAPCUS,* May 25, 1881. For Charles R. Hemphill, see LaMotte, *Colored Light,* 146. For Boggs see ibid., 173.

9. CTSBD, September 1882, May 1883; Law, "Personal Reminiscences," 63. See also Boggs, "Recollections," 83; Street, "Evolution Controversy," 240; and Gustafson, *James Woodrow,* 158–59. Girardeau's biographer concluded that Mack and Girardeau were most likely working closely together. See Willborn, "John L. Girardeau," 254.

10. J. Woodrow, "Evolution," 618, 620, 622.

11. Ibid., 626, 644.

12. Thompson, *Presbyterians in the South,* 2: 466.

13. Ibid., 2: 465.

14. CTSBDM, September 1884.

15. Smyth, "Sin and the Curse," 449; Thomas Johnson, *Life and Letters of Benjamin Morgan Palmer,* 213. Cf. Hampton, *Storm of Words,* 198–201; and Livingstone, *Dealing with Darwin,* 155–56.

16. For backgrounds of Cozby, see Myers, *Children of Pride,* 1496. For Brackett see Stoney, *Autobiographical Notes,* 697. For Webb see Blackburn, *Life Work of John L. Girardeau,* 28. For the lengthy debate before the synod, see Adger, *My Life and Times,* 458–525.

17. Quotations, Adger, *My Life and Times,* 459–60.

18. Ibid., 500–21.

19. Ibid., 480–89.

20. Blackburn, *Life Work of John L. Girardeau,* 232–57.

21. Adger, *My Life and Times,* 493, 469, 473, 463; T. Jacobs, *Diary,* 264.

22. Adger, *My Life and Times,* 526; Gustafson, *James Woodrow,* 190. Thompson, *Presbyterians in the South,* 2: 471–74.

23. Adger, *My Life and Times,* 534. For the Synod of Georgia debate, see ibid., 526–36.

24. Thompson, *Presbyterians in the South,* 2: 474–75.

25. CTSBDM, December 1884. Howe had died in 1883.

26. Thompson, *Presbyterians in the South,* 2: 475–76.

27. CTSBDM, December 1885. Girardeau's letter of resignation was dated October 6, 1885.

28. Ibid.

29. Thompson, *Presbyterians in the South,* 2:484. See also Gustafson, *James Woodrow,* 221.

30. CTSBD, 1886–88; LaMotte, *Colored Light,* 174–76.

31. Flinn, "Evolution and Theology," 270–71.

32. Adger, *My Life and Times,* 603–4, 606; *MGAPCUS,* 1889, 589.

33. CTSBDM, May 1888; Mulder, *Woodrow Wilson,* 24. CTSFM, December 1887, January 1888; Adger, *My Life and Times,* 606; CTSBDM, May 1890.

34. A succinct summary of these developments can be found in Edgar, *South Carolina: A History,* 427–30.

35. For Tillman see Kantrowitz, *Ben Tillman.* For Watson see Woodward, *Tom Watson.* For lynching see Brundage, *Lynching in the New South.* See especially listing of lynching victims in Georgia and the rapid rise of lynching beginning in 1885 in Brundage, *Lynching in the New South,* 270–80.

36. For Hemphill see *Biographical Dictionary of the United States Congress,* http://bioguide.congress.gov/scripts/biodisplay.pl?index=H000 (accessed November 9, 2015). Hemphill's nephew, James C. Hemphill, was editor of the *Charleston News and Courier* and an outspoken opponent of Tillman. See Kantrowitz, *Ben Tillman.* For Tillman's attack on the Coosaw Mining Company, see Shick and Doyle, "South Carolina Phosphate Boom." It needs to be noted, as an indication of the overlapping of the two sides in the controversy, that B. M. Palmer was strongly anti-Woodrow as was the Augusta textile magnate W. C. Sibley.

37. For Wilson's trip to Brazil, see Clarke, *By the Rivers of Water,* 361–62. For Flinn's study and travel, see M. Woodrow, *Dr. James Woodrow,* v. For Woodrow's travel and membership in scientific societies, see ibid., 28.

38. Blackburn, *Life Work of John L. Girardeau,* 217.

39. J. Woodrow, "Inaugural Address"; Adger, *My Life and Times,* 462, 473.

40. Whaling, *Science and Religion Today,* vii–xi; Eaton, "Professor James Woodrow," 17. For Woodrow's time as president of the University of South Carolina, see Hollis, *University of South Carolina: College to University,* 2: 165–96.

41. *MGAPCUS,* 1924, 64. For a highly sympathetic review of Girardeau's theology, see M. Smith, *Studies in Southern Presbyterian Theology,* 234–53. In a telling omission, Smith does not treat Adger in his "Studies in Southern Presbyterian Theology" although he treats such "lesser lights" as Goulding, Leland, Plumer, and G. B. Strickler. For the use of "Old Columbia," see Calhoun, *Our Southern Zion,* and Willborn, "John L. Girardeau," 276. For an overview of "Southern Presbyterian Theology" following the Woodrow controversy, see Robinson, *Columbia Theological Seminary and the Southern Presbyterian Church,* 180–93, 199–209.

42. Thompson, *Presbyterians in the South,* 2: 489–90. For faculty at other white Southern Presbyterian seminaries who sided with Girardeau, see ibid., 482. For student enrollment in 1889, see CTSBDM, May 1889.

10 — Poor but Genteel

1. Girardeau, "Eulogy on Professor George Howe," 395–401. For expressions of affection and esteem for Howe, see CTSBDM, May 1883.

2. Blackburn, *Life Work of John L. Girardeau,* 378; Thomas Johnson, *Life and Letters of Benjamin Morgan Palmer,* 635; M. Woodrow, *Dr. James Woodrow,* 9. For Wilson see Clarke, *By the Rivers of Water,* 372–73. For Adger see Adger, *My Life and Times,* and Stoney, *Autobiographical Notes,* 747.

3. See, for example, Robinson, *Columbia Theological Seminary and the Southern Presbyterian Church,* 180–93, 199–209.

4. Second Presbyterian's importance to Columbia is evident in the financial records of the seminary recorded in CTSBDM, 1870–1920.

5. *Manual for the Use of the Members,* 81–121. For the broader cultural shifts associated with these changes, see Fuller, *Americans and the Unconscious,* 51–95; and Holifield, *History of Pastoral Care,* 159–209.

6. Clarke, *Our Southern Zion,* 267–79.

7. For the traditional understanding of discipline in Reformed churches, see McNeill, *History and Character of Calvinism,* 139. For discipline in white Southern Presbyterian churches, see Thompson, *Presbyterians in the South,* 2: 399–403. For Central Presbyterian and discipline, see J. Smith, *Church That Stayed,* 15–42.

8. The classic study of a rising middle class's quest for efficiency and order is Wiebe, *Search for Order.* For the rise of efficiency as a dominant value in the church, see Moorhead, "Presbyterians and the Cult of Organizational Efficiency"; Dikes, "Shall Churches Increase Their Efficiency?"; and Soares, "Practical Theology." For the changing role of urban pastors, see Holifield, *God's Ambassadors,* 158–64. For these developments at Central Presbyterian, see J. Smith, *Church That Stayed,* 55–72.

9. Gist, *Presbyterian Women,* 202. For denominational-wide developments see Thompson, *Presbyterians in the South,* 3: 384–402; and Winnsborough, *Women's Auxiliary.*

10. The resistance to business models and the quest for efficiency can be seen in Clark Reed's complaint about the movement of the General Assembly from a deliberative body to one that followed "the speed madness of the age." See Reed, "General Assembly." The idea of the New South is a much-debated issue among historians. Some, such as C. Vann Woodward, have emphasized the distance between the Old South and the New. Others, such as Eugene Genovese and Elizabeth Fox-Genovese, have found deep cultural and ideological continuities between the two. See essays in Arsenault and Burton, *Dixie Redux,* esp. Steven Hahn, "Did the Civil War Matter?," and David Moltke-Hansen, "Turn Signals." For the role of memory in the New South, see Blight, *Race and Reunion.*

11. W. Jacobs, *Pioneer,* 93–94. For Ellison Smyth see also Carlton, *Mill and Town,* 181–82. For the shift from a religious ideology to a market ideology, see Haberman, *Knowledge and Human Interest,* 60. Paul Ricoeur has also concluded that "in the capitalistic era the major ideology is no longer a religious ideology but precisely a market ideology." Ricoeur, *Lectures on Ideology and Utopia,* 230. Cf. the debate among historians over the question of continuity between the Old South and the New South. See Arsenault and Burton, *Dixie Redux.*

12. For the larger context of theological education and the changing social and ecclesiastical contexts, see G. Miller, *Piety and Profession,* 113–53.

13. CTSFM, May 1910. For faculty changes see CTSC, 1895–1905. For the modesty of Hall's work as a theologian, see M. Smith, *Studies in Southern Presbyterian Theology,* 255–57.

14. CTSC, 1905. For Reed see E. Scott, *Ministerial Directory,* 600. For White see ibid., 764.

15. For the board's concerns about following Judge Perkins's instructions when he established the chair, see CTSBDM, May 1907, May 1908, May 1911. For the description of the chair in the seminary catalog, see CTSC, 1920. For the disappearance of the chair from catalog, see CTSAC, 1929.

16. CTSBDM, 1903–5, CTSFM, 1903–5.

17. For student fees see CTSBDM, 1900–1905. The theological seminaries of the PC (USA) did not charge tuition. For Gilmore see CTSBDM, May 1888.

18. CTSBDM, May 1905.

19. For Fannie Laury see CTSBDM, May 1926. Fanny Wellford White was another hospitable and popular wife of a seminary professor. She had been born in Richmond, where her father, Judge Beverly Randolph Wellford, had been a leading citizen of the state, and her family had deep connections with prominent Virginians. Cf. Gardner, *Blood and Irony,* for the role of women in transmitting a memory of a Lost Cause.

20. CTSC, 1905–6. Cf. Dorrien, *Making of*

American Liberal Theology, 155; Thompson, *Presbyterians in the South,* 3: 214. McPheeters emphasized that the biblical interpreter needed to explore the original context of a passage in order to discern its meaning. See McPheeters, "Science of Interpretation." For McPheeters's syllabus, see "Syllabus of the Senior Course in New Testament Biblical Theology," in the Fred J. Hay Papers, CTS. See also McPheeters, "O.T. Literature and
Exegesis." Conyers, "Middler English Bible," also reflects a similar pedagogical approach.

21. Quotation: Thompson *Presbyterians in the South,* 3: 214. Cf. CTSB, July 1936, 10, 2; Richards, *As I Remember It,* 40. For McPheeters as a controversialist, see in Prince, *Presbyterian Bibliography,* the articles he published especially in regard to the charges against Hay Watson Smith. For McPheeters's understanding of the "science of interpretation," see Robinson, *Columbia Theological Seminary and the Southern Presbyterian Church,* 163–66. For McPheeters's intimidation of students and their response, see Richards, *As I Remember It,* 40–41.

22. CTSAC, 1905. For Hall and Girardeau on epistemology and psychology, see Robinson, *Columbia Theological Seminary and the Southern Presbyterian Church,* 199–209. For the emphasis on religious experience and the character of religion that marked much of theological inquiry in the closing decades of the nineteenth century and the early years of the twentieth, see Holifield, *History of Pastoral Care,* 184–96. For an important discussion of William James and his influence on religious thought, see Dorrien, *Making of American Liberal Theology,* 218–26.

23. Cf. Hollis, *University of South Carolina: College to University,* 2: 162. Note quotation from Washington A. Clark, member of the CTS board and of the University of South Carolina board, who reflected Thornwell's understanding of the purpose of higher education. For the transformations of higher education during the closing years of the nineteenth century and the early years of the twentieth, see ibid., 159–221; McCosh, *New Departure;* and Veysey, *Emergence.* For changes stirring in theological education, see Harper, "Shall the Theological Curriculum Be Modified and How?"; and Warfield, "Constitution of the Seminary Curriculum."

24. CTSAC, 1905. For the discussion of "certificates" and the adoption of an "English Bible Tract," see CTSFM, 1894.

25. White, *Robert E. Lee,* 63–64. For descriptions of White, see CTSB, October 1927.

26. Reed, "Brief Course in Church History," 453–69. CTSAC, 1905. For important essays on Christian interpretations of history, see McIntire, *God, History, and Historians.*

27. Quotation: Reed, *Sketch,* 178–79.

28. John L. Wilson, *Western Africa,* 95. For the script itself, see ibid., 94. For Wilson as the first westerner to report on the Vey or Vai script, see Tuchscherer and Hair, "Cherokee and West Africa." They say of Wilson's report that it "appears to be the earliest extant manuscript in an indigenous script from sub-Saharan Africa." Ibid., 440. For the stipend for Fanny Laury, see CTSBDM, May 1926, 32.

29. CTSAC, 1905. In his *History of Presbyterian Churches in the World,* Reed did give attention to the several Presbyterian churches in the United States, but there is no indication these histories played an important role in his church history courses. See Reed, *History of Presbyterian Churches,* 269–341.

30. Reed, *History of Presbyterian Churches,* 18–19. For Columbia Seminary and the "missionary enterprise," see Robinson, *Columbia Theological Seminary and the Southern Presbyterian Church,* 106–46. For DuBose's leadership in the Anti-opium League, see Lodwick, *Crusaders against Opium,* 125–28.

31. Ahlstrom, *Religious History of the American People,* 865. For the mission impulse, see Hutchison, *Errand to the World,* 91–124, 146–74. For Mills's role during the Japanese invasion of Nanjing, see Lu, *They Were in Nanjing.* For Columbia graduates who served as missionaries, 1900–1930, see LaMotte, *Colored Light,* 205. For the spread of Christianity during the twentieth century, see Todd Johnson and Ross, *Atlas of Global Christianity.*

32. CTSAC, 1905; *Southern Workman,* 260–61. For Johnstone, see *Quarterly Bulletin:*

State Board of Charities of South Carolina, 37–38. For the progressive movement's impact on theological education in the United States, see G. Miller, *Piety and Profession,* 295–339.

33. For the Smyth Lectureship and the extensive negotiations over it with the Smyth family, see CTSBD, 1900–1911. For the lectures see CTSAC, 1911–20.

34. For various ministries of Columbia graduates during the early years of the century, see LaMotte, *Colored Light,* 196–203. For an example of a pastor's work, see "A Pastoral Record Book, 1907–1922," in the Angus McQueen Papers, CTS. For Douglas's term as president of the University of South Carolina, see Hollis, *University of South Carolina: College to University,* 2: 327–31.

35. LaMotte, *Colored Light,* 201–4; Thompson, *Presbyterians in the South,* 3: 159–94. For Morris see S. Morris, *Autobiography.* For "muscular Christianity" see Putney, *Muscular Christianity.*

11 — A President in "the Modern Sense of the Term"

1. CTSFM, 1900–1910. For the widespread practice of theological faculties having heavy administrative responsibilities, see for an overview G. Miller, *Piety and Profession,* 271–72. For specific examples from other seminaries, see Tappert, *History of the Lutheran Theological Seminary,* esp. 45; Blackman, *Faith and Freedom,* 86–87; and Broadus, *Memoir,* 164–65.

2. Reed provided to the board an annual report on the library. His report had the character of a lament and included a consistent plea for funds for more books. See CTSBDM, 1900–1910, and cf. CTSBDM, May 1927 for the library's lack of light, heat, and tables. Columbia's meager budget for new books exceeded, however, the $100 annual budget for books at the wealthier Louisville Presbyterian Seminary. See Nutt, *Many Lamps,* 76. Most seminaries depended heavily on gifts of scholarly pastors' libraries. Cf. G. Miller, *Piety and Profession,* 465–66.

3. CTSBD, 1900–1910.

4. For the development of the office of president in theological seminaries in the United States, see Clarke, "The Study of the Seminary Presidency," 5–20. For Louisville Presbyterian see Nutt, *Many Lamps,* 63–67. Cf. G. Miller, *Piety and Profession,* 271–92.

5. Bellah et al., *Habits of the Heart,* 45. Charles Thwing of Western Reserve University, in discussing the office of college president, traced its development through three successive types: the clerical, the scholastic, and the executive. See Thwing, *College Administration,* 49. Robert Wiebe puts these developments in higher education as part of a search for organizing principles for the modern world. See Wiebe, *Search for Order,* 119–21.

6. Quotations: McLean, "Presidency of Theological Seminaries," 314–15, 318.

7. CTSBDM, May 1906. The board first called A. M. Fraser, but his presbytery refused to release him. It then called George N. Cornelson, but he declined the call. See CTSBDM, August 1909, May 1910.

8. CTSBDM, May 1911. E. Scott, *Ministerial Directory,* 761. For Whaling's inaugural see "Dr. Whaling Takes His Larger Field," *State,* May 7, 1912.

9. CTSB, July 1911. For curriculum developments in theological education generally, and in relationship to educational modernization, see Kelly, *Theological Education in America,* esp. 61–151; and G. Miller, *Piety and Profession,* 325–36.

10. For Whaling's visits to college and university campuses, see, for example, his reports to the board, CTSBDM, May 1912, and May 1916. For growth of the student body, see board reports to the General Assembly, ibid.

11. These complex family relationships can be traced, with perseverance, in E. Scott, *Ministerial Directory.* See also LaMotte, *Colored Light,* 199; Stoney, *Autobiographical Notes,* 746; and Vaughan, "Biographical Sketch."

12. For Montreat's role in the life of the white Southern Presbyterian Church, see *American Presbyterians* 74, no. 2 (Summer 1996).

13. Two outstanding examples of this religious impulse that drew students to seminary are Wilson Plumer Mills and J. McDowell Richards. For Richards, see Richards, *As I Remember*

It. Mills spent years in China, often under very demanding circumstances, and Richards began his ministry among the Appalachian people of north Georgia.

14. See reports of the president, CTSBDM, 1913–20. John Knox McLean noted that seminary presidents had to face the constant question: "Where do I get the money for next year's budget?" See McLean, "Presidency of Theological Seminaries," 309–10. For finances and theological seminaries during the first two decades of the twentieth century, see Kelly, *Theological Education in America,* esp. 231–35.

15. See reports of the investment committee, 1895–1920, CTSBDM. For Girardeau see CTSBDM, 1918. As it became clear that a foreclosure was looming on the Girardeau property, the board declared that the investment committee was "expressly forbidden to lend any of the funds of the Seminary to any member of the Investment Committee or any member of the Board of Directors or Faculty." CTSBDM, May 1917.

16. LaMotte, *Colored Light,* 185–86.

17. For Reavis see E. Scott, *Ministerial Directory,* 597, and LaMotte, *Colored Light,* 186–87. For the expansion of foreign missions while Reavis was secretary of its board, see Thompson, *Presbyterians in the South,* 3: 127. For Reavis as a teacher, see his lecture outlines and class syllabus in the James Frank Ligon Papers, CTS.

18. Richards, *As I Remember It,* 41. For Kerr's background see E. Scott, *Ministerial Directory,* 371.

19. CTSAC, 1920. For Wardlaw as a teacher, see Hollis, *University of South Carolina: College to University,* 2: 209. For Thornwell's understanding of the purpose of education, see ibid., 174. For the emerging professional model of ministry, see Kelly, *Theological Education in America;* W. Brown and May, *Education of American Ministers,* and Holifield, *God's Ambassadors,* esp. 231–34, 244–53, 327–32.

20. Mulder, *Woodrow Wilson,* 38. See also "Wilson Comes Home on Trying Mission," *State,* September 19, 1916; "Prayers Touch Wilson's Heart," *State,* September 19, 1916. For descriptions of the campus and its physical condition during the years 1912–21, see Whaling's reports to the board, CTSBDM, 1913–21.

21. "Columbia Seminary to Rear Memorials," *State,* May 16, 1915. There had been an earlier attempt to raise funds for a new chapel—and to name it for Thornwell—but even with the Thornwell's name the effort had been unsuccessful. See *State,* June 16, 1908.

22. For the proposed Presbyterian University in Atlanta, see F. Jones and Mills, *History of the Presbyterian Church in South* Carolina, 426–27; "Columbia May Lose Theological Seminary," *State,* March 17, 1903; "Still after the Seminary," *State,* December 1, 1903; "Atlanta's Attempt to Get the Seminary," *State,* January 18, 1904.

23. See, for example, CTSBD, May 1905, May 1906, May 1913, May 1916.

24. CTSBDM, May 1917; Nutt, *Many Lamps,* 72, 74.

25. Nutt, *Many Lamps,* 29–30, 74–75.

26. CTSBD, May 1921. Cf. Nutt, *Many Lamps,* 74–75.

27. CTSBDM, May 1920, June 1920, May 1921.

28. CTSAC, 1922. For Murchison's work supervising students as they supplied churches, see his report in CTSBDM, 1923.

29. CTSBDM, May 1922.

30. Ibid.

31. Ibid.

32. Ibid., October 1923.

33. Ibid., May 1924.

34. Ibid.

35. Ibid. June 1924; October 1924. The controlling synods quickly voted for the Synod of Mississippi to join them in controlling and supporting the seminary. The Mississippi synod accepted the invitation and elected three trustees. See CTSBDM, July 1925.

36. CTSBDM, May 1925.

37. The Atlanta race riot of 1906 and the quick suppression of its memory are perhaps the clearest example of the way racism and racial violence was a part of the New South. See Godshalk, *Veiled Visions;* Mixon, *Atlanta Riot;* Brundage, *Lynching in the New South,* 211–15.

12 — Decatur

1. CTSBDM, October 1924; "Report of the Subcommittee on Removable," December 1924 and April 2, 1925 in ibid., May 1925.

2. Ibid., May 1925. In 1920 the Synod of South Carolina had 31,412 communicant members, and the Synod of Georgia had 26,111. In 1949 South Carolina had 48,589, and Georgia had 47,494. By 1960 Georgia had 67,659, and South Carolina had grown to 63,012. Most of the growth of Georgia Presbyterians was in metropolitan Atlanta. See *MGAPCUS*, 1920, 1949, and 1960.

3. Godshalk, *Veiled Visions*, 217; Richards, "John Bulow Campbell," CTSB, September 1941, 12. For Eagan, see https://en.wikipedia.org/wiki/John_J._Eagan_(ACIPCO) (accessed January 23, 2016). For Martha Berry, see Atkins, "Philanthropy." Richards, "John Bulow Campbell," CTSB, September, 1941, is the best resource on Campbell. But see also http://www.georgiaencyclopedia.org/articles/business-economy/j-bulow-campbell-foundation (accessed January 23, 2016).

4. CTSBDM, May 1927. For the colligate Gothic style, see W. Morgan, *Collegiate Gothic*.

5. CTSBDM, April 1928.

6. CTSBDM, May 1928.

7. CTSBDM, October 1926 and April 1928.

8. CTSBSM, October 1926. For the relationship of memory to place and identity, see Ricoeur, *Memory*, 41, 56–92. For the role of landscape and architecture in shaping human perspectives and emotions, see Kedar and Werblowski, *Sacred Space*.

9. CTSBDM, May 1927.

10. For an example of McPheeters as a defender of white Southern Presbyterian orthodoxy against any hint of change, see Thompson, *Presbyterians in the South*, 3: 330. For McPheeters's combative spirit, see in Prince, *Presbyterian Bibliography*, articles McPheeters published, especially regarding charges against Hay Watson Smith. See also testimonial to McPheeters in CTSB, July 1936. For Reed see memorials in CTSB, January 1926. For White see memorials in CTSB, October 1927. For Robinson's background see CTSB, July 1926. For Robinson's lack of interest in church history, see articles he published listed in Prince, *Presbyterian Bibliography*. A committee of the General Assembly, reviewing the work of the church's seminaries, found that at Columbia church history "is given very little space—one very light course being devoted to it. The history of Christian thought is assumed to serve the purpose of a course in church history." See CTSBDM, 1942.

11. CTSBDM, May 1927.

12. For Machen's grandfather on the Columbia board of directors, see CTSBDM, 1880–83. For Machen's Smyth Lectures, see CTSB, May 1927. For Machen and the modernist-fundamentalist controversy at Princeton Theological Seminary, see Longfield, *Presbyterian Controversy*, 28–53, 162–80.

13. Longfield, *Presbyterian Controversy*, 138. For Robinson as an exponent of the Girardeau and McPheeters assumptions and defensive stance, see Robinson's essay "The Columbia Tradition," CTSB, January 1928.

14. For descriptions of the move, see CTSB, April 1928, CTSBDM, May 1928, and CTSV, Winter 1977.

15. CTSBDM, May 1927 and May 1928.

16. CTSB, April 1928. For "muscular Christianity" see Putney, *Muscular Christianity*.

17. "The Reverend Joseph H. Dixon, 1882–1947," CTSB, August 1947. See also Richards, *As I Remember It*, 48–49. For "servant salaries" see CTSBDM, 1929. For the Joe Dixon memorial fund, see CTSB, January 1963.

18. CTSB, January 1929. For Henderson see Richards, *As I Remember It*, 49, and CTSV, Spring 1988. For white matrons who oversaw the seminary refectory, see CTSBDM, 1929–40. For the ways in which the image of "Aunt Jemima" was developed and the racial and gender stereotypes it fostered, see Manring, *Slave in a Box*. For the Mammy image and its links to white nostalgia, see P. Collins, *Black Feminist Thought*, 67–90. For an African American cuisine, see Shields, *Southern Provisions*, 109–28; Ferris, *Edible South*, 71–84; Cooley, *To Live and Dine in Dixie*, 19–42.

19. For dining etiquette see B. Wilson, *Consider the Fork*, and cf. Nancy Rose Hunt's description of the way missionaries in the

Congo used a "knife and fork" education to promote European domestic order and ideals of hygiene. See Hunt, *Colonial Lexicon,* 118–23.

20. CTSBDM, May 1927; CTSC, April 1928. Total number of courses offered had expanded from twenty-seven in 1926 to fifty-one in 1929. See CTSC, 1926–30. For the background for such an expansion of curriculum, see W. Brown and May, *Education of American Ministers;* Kelly, *Theological Education in America;* and Holifield, *God's Ambassadors,* 215–34. A consistent theme in these studies is the perceived need to have theological seminaries follow the route and adopt the assumptions of other professional graduate programs.

21. CTSBDM, July 1928; May 1929. For Gillespie's relationship to students, see, for example, Gillespie's letter to Joseph Conyers, December 1926, CTS.

22. *CTSBDM,* May 1930; May 1931.

23. *CTSBDM,* May 1930; May 1931; May 1932. For Chicora College see Griffith and Raynal, *Presbyterians in South Carolina,* 194–99.

24. *CTSBDM,* May 1931; May 1932. Richards, *As I Remember It,* 21–23.

25. Richards's Diary, March 28, 1924, CTS. For Paris see ibid., December 17, 1923.

26. Much of this description of Richards's Oxford years and travel was drawn from extensive personal interviews the author had with him in the early 1980s that were conveyed in Richards, *As I Remember It,* 1–10.

27. Ibid.

28. CTSB, June 1934.

29. Ibid., 7. For the proposal before the General Assembly, see *MGAPCUS,* 1934.

30. CTSB, June 1934, 10–12.

31. Ibid., 12–13.

32. For the esteem in which Richards was held by many graduates and church people, see Philips, *Faithful Servant,* 1–30.

33. For Virginia Harrison and her important role at the seminary, see "President's Report" and "Auditor's Report," in CTSBDM, 1927–34; Richards, *As I Remember It,* 46–48; Philips, *Faithful Servant,* 20, 27–28, 110.

34. CTSBDM, May 1937. See also ibid., May 1936, and Richards, *As I Remember It,* 29–31. The old campus in Columbia was sold to Columbia Bible College.

35. For fundamentalism see Marsden, *Fundamentalism and American Culture;* Carpenter, *Revive Us Again;* Longfield, *Presbyterian Controversy.* For white Southern Presbyterians and dispensationalism, see Thompson, *Presbyterians in the South,* 3: 486–88.

36. For Carmichael's background see CTSB, May 1933. For the oath of office, see CTSBDM, May 1935.

37. CTSBDM, May 1935. See also ibid., July 1935.

38. CTSBD, July 1935.

39. Ibid. For Robinson's reaction to the reprimand by the board, see the report of his son years later: Robinson, "Theological Autobiography," in Stone, *Craft of Religious Studies,* 117.

40. For the Robinson-Green dispute, see Green, "Regarding the Revision"; Robinson, "Proposed Changes in the Standards"; "Minutes of the Executive Committee," in CTSBDM, December 1939; and Thompson, *Presbyterians in the South,* 3: 491–92. For the attack against Cartledge and Kerr, see CTSBDM, May 1944. The three board members who voted against the resolution of support for Cartledge and Kerr were W. R. Barron, M.D., of the Arsenal Hill church in Columbia, South Carolina, and Mississippi pastors O. M. Anderson and R. E. Hough. For even more sustained attacks against E. T. Thompson of the Union Theological Seminary, Richmond, by Charlotte elder and businessman, see Thompson, *Presbyterians in the South,* 3: 335–38. For the establishment of the *Southern Presbyterian Journal* and the racism of Henry Dendy and Nelson Bell, see Alvis, *Religion and Race,* 51–53.

41. For background of Manford and Sarah Bernstein Gutzke, see E. Scott, *Ministerial Directory,* 277, and Gutzke, "Living the Faith," and "My Brother—Walter Gutzke," www.thebibleforyou.org (accessed February 3, 2016). See also "Sarah Bernstein Gutzke" in CTSV, Winter 1977.

42. Cf., for example, Gutzke's "Basic Doctrines in the Book of Acts," "The Bible in a Nutshell," "The Controversy over the Bible," "My Brother—Walter Gutzke," and "Parables of

Jesus of Nazareth," all at www.thebibleforyou.org (accessed February 3, 2016). Gutzke's insistence that the Bible and Christian life follow the pattern of "out of, across, and into" was a familiar theme in his seminary classes. He used for years the same study book in which students were to fill in answers that reflected this schema. Many students found it theologically shallow and pedagogically lazy. It was certainly distant from the intellectual rigor expected of a Howe, Thornwell, or Woodrow.

43. For Gutzke's description of his defense of his doctoral examination, see Gutzke, "Recollections of Columbia University," at www.thebibleforyou.org (accessed February 3, 2016). For a critical review of the published dissertation, see LeFevre, "Manford George Gutzke."

44. For the establishment of the American Association of Theological Schools as a part of a widespread movement to have accrediting agencies for higher education and professional status, see G. Miller, *Piety and Profession,* 460–69, and Holifield, *God's Ambassadors,* 231–34. For Columbia as one of the first schools accredited, see CTSBDM, May 1938 and May 1939. For Columbia's participation in the formation of the University Center of Georgia, see CTSBDM, May 1939. For the Pastors' Institute, see CTSC, May 1939. For Richards's participation in the Federal Council of Churches and his election as vice president of the ecumenical agency, see Philips, *Faithful Servant,* 141–42.

45. For Talmadge see Anderson, *Wild Man.*

46. "*Brothers in Black*," in Richards, *Change and the Changeless,* 21–22. The sermon title is taken from, Atticus Green Haygood's 1881 book *Our Brothers in Black.*

47. Richards, *Change and the Changeless,* 23.

48. Ibid., 23.

49. Ibid., 24–25.

50. Ibid., 26–27.

51. Ibid., 27–28.

52. Richards, *As I Remember It,* 76.

13 — *Years of War and a Growing Prosperity*

1. For the terrors of war immediately preceding Richards's address, see Snyder, *Bloodlands,* esp. 1–154. For the crisis during the summer of 1940, see Lukacs, *Five Days in London.* For the Atlanta Rotary Club and its membership, see http://www.atlantarotary.org/ (accessed 2016).

2. Richards, "Armistice Day," in Richards, *Change and the Changeless,* 17–18.

3. Ibid., 17–19.

4. "Columbia Seminary and Alumni in a Time of War," CTSB, June 1942.

5. For theological students and the draft, see G. Miller, *Piety and Profession,* 653–56.

6. For students from these schools, see CTSC, 1941–45. For Bible colleges see Ringenberg, *Christian College.* As late as 1978, for example, at Bob Jones only 14 percent (36 of 257) of regular faculty appointees held earned doctoral degrees. Ibid., 176.

7. CTSB, May 1930. For Richards's insistence that the seminary not accept ill-prepared students to keep up enrollment, see CTSBDM, May 1933. For important studies of fundamentalism, see Marsden, *Fundamentalism and American Culture;* Marsden, *Understanding Fundamentalism and Evangelicalism;* Carpenter, *Revive Us Again;* and Noll, *Scandal of the Evangelical Mind,* esp. "The Intellectual Disaster of Fundamentalism," 109–48.

8. For students enrolled see CTSB, April 1938; March 1945. For McQuilkin see E. Scott, *Ministerial Directory.* McQuilkin 's successor at Columbia Bible College was G. Allen Fleece, who graduated from Columbia in 1934 and regarded himself a student of Robinson. See dedication page, Calhoun, *Pleading for a Reformation Vision.* For Robinson's relationship to Girardeau and McPheeters and the ways he attempted to maintain at Columbia their legacy, see ibid., 9–24.

9. "Columbia Seminary and Alumni in a Time of War," CTSB, June 1942.

10. Lu, *They Were in Nanjing,* 128. For Mills's role as the acting chairman of the International Committee, which set up the Nanjing Safety Zone for civilians, see ibid.

11. Daniel, *In the Presence of Mine Enemies,* 19, x. For Daniel's experience as a POW chaplain, see also letter from Daniel, CTSB, September 1943, and Philips, *Faithful Servant,* 132–34.

12. For an overview of life on the campus during the war, see CTSB, 1941–45.

13. Leith, *Crisis in the Church,* 108. For contemporary observations of student preaching by Leith's classmate Will Ormond, see "Ormond Papers," 1941–43, CTS.

14. Richards, *As I Remember It,* 62–63.

15. "Ormond Papers," December 1, 1940; February 23, 1941; March 2, 1941; CTS.

16. Richards, *As I Remember It,* 66–67; "Ormond Papers," March 2, 1941; CTS.

17. "Ormond Papers," February 15, 1942; CTS. For Ormond's preaching on racial justice, see Shriver, *Unsilent South,* 50–57.

18. Philips, *Time of Blessing,* 9–11.

19. Statistics of changes in U.S. society between 1945 and 1960s can be followed in Bureau of the Census, *Historical Statistics of the United States, Colonial Times to 1970.* See esp. 1–43, 215–83, 610–51. For growth of the churches and the postwar revival, see Ahlstrom, *Religious History of the American People,* 949–63. Changes at Columbia Theological Seminary can be followed in CTSB, 1945–60. Note that in 1960, in addition to those students enrolled in Columbia's basic degree program, another thirty-three students were enrolled in other degree programs. For the development of the campus, see Richards, *As I Remember It,* 78–86, and CTSC, March 1945 and January 1960. For the Bryan family of Columbia, South Carolina, see CTSBDM, 1910–25.

20. Quotation, CTSBDM, May 1947. For the role of the GI Bill on theological seminaries, see G. Miller, *Piety and Profession,* 656–57. For the GI Bill and Columbia, see CTSB, April 1946. For women enrolled in a master of arts in biblical education, see CTSB, May 1944.

21. CTSB, March 1959. For the quartet and Mary Grace Cartledge's role as a volunteer leader, see CTSB, April 1938, and Richards, *As I Remember It,* 27–28.

22. Lists of students with their home towns and colleges are given in the seminary catalogs, 1945–60.

23. CTSBDM, December 1884. For details on the Smyth Lectureship and the stipulations of Smyth's will in establishing it, see also ibid., May 1874; May 1900; May 1901; and May 1902. In ibid., May 1931, for the first time the Smyth Endowment with its accumulations was not given as a separate item in the audit report to the board. For Ministers Week, 1954, see CTSB, July 1954, and CTSC, 1954–55. For visiting lecturers and chapel speakers, see CTSB, July 1954.

24. Cf. Richards, *As I Remember It,* 51–54.

25. Richards, after describing other faculty members, said in his discrete manner that Robinson was a "rather different person from any already mentioned." Ibid., 43. For Gutzke's relationship to Robinson, see Calhoun, *Pleading for a Reformation Vision,* 49. For observations on the Robinsons' relationship with other faculty members and families, interviews with Betty Cousar, January 1, 2016; Pete Peterson (who lived with the Richards, during his second and third year at seminary), May 5, 2016; Muriel Gear Hart, June 4, 2016; and Kemie Richards Nix, August 5, 2016.

26. CTSB, July 1946. Robinson's courses were listed in the catalog under the rubric of historical theology.

27. CTSB, July 1946. For Thompson's inaugural address, see CTSB, September 1948. The courses he taught together with their descriptions can be found in CTSB, 1947–60.

28. Taylor received his Ph.D. from Northwestern University. His dissertation was entitled "Slavery and the Deliberations of the Presbyterian General Assembly, 1833–1838." He continued to be fascinated by the role of debate in church bodies. See CTSV, Winter 1978.

29. Appointments and backgrounds given in the following issues of CTSB: Gillespie, August 1950; Prince, February 1951; McDill, October 1951; Anderson, August 1952. For Gailey see Richards, *As I Remember It,* 56. Frank Brown served as a popular professor of English Bible for three years until his untimely death. See CTSB, August 1952 and August 1955.

30. Gear, "Theology and the Muddle of Modern Man," CTSB, September 1948.

31. Ibid., 3, 7.

32. Ibid., 9.

33. Ibid., 10.

34. Ibid., 10–11.

35. Ibid., 11.

36. Ibid.

37. Ibid., 12.

38. Ibid.

39. All the inaugurals were published together in CTSB, April 1956.

40. A vast literature describes the popular interest in psychology and mental health that had developed by the mid-twentieth century. Highly influential interpretations include Riesman, *Lonely Crowd;* Rieff, *Triumph of the Therapeutic;* and Bellah et al., *Habits of the Heart.* For the impact on this interest on the practices of ministry, see Holifield, *History of Pastoral Care,* 259–76.

41. For McDill's background see CTSB, October 1951. He had grown up in and been ordained by the Associate Reformed Presbyterian Church.

42. McDill, "Calvinism and the Cure of Souls," CTSB, April 1956, 4.

43. Ibid., 8, 14.

44. Ibid., 18.

45. Smartt, *I Am Reminded,* 9. Smartt would become in the 1970s one of the founders of the Presbyterian Church in America. On the jacket of his book, designed by his son, Smartt is described as having "a trademark photographic memory, twinkle-in-the-eye humor and effervescent love for Christ and his fellow man."

46. For fundamentalists from the North seeking out white Presbyterian churches in the South, see "Seminary Withstands Its Critics," and cf. S. Lucas, *Blessed Zion,* 126. Milton Winter provides details of conservatives from Mississippi, esp. from First Presbyterian, Jackson, and their attack on Columbia. See Winter, *Citadels of Zion,* 1: 420–21, 484–85.

47. Between May 15 and August 15, 1952, a group of students compiled and wrote "A Short History of Certain Events Taking Place at Columbia Theological Seminary regarding the Professorship of Dr. Richard T. Gillespie in the Years 1950–51 and 1951–52." They presented it to the board of directors in April 1953. It is found in CTSBDM, May 1953. Hereafter it is cited as Anderton et al., "Short History." For Nelson Bell's support of racial segregation and "racial integrity," see Alvis, *Religion and Race,* 51–53.

48. Anderton et al., "Short History," 4.

49. Ibid., 5.

50. "Appendix II. The Questions which Dr. Gillespie refused to answer, together with an analysis of why these questions were asked, and the implications of his refusal to answer." Ibid., 20–24. Cf. the attack on Richards's good friend John A. Mackay, president of Princeton Seminary, for his criticism of Joseph McCarthy's tactics. The highly esteemed Mackay was accused by the evangelical preacher Daniel A. Poling of communist sympathies. See Dowey, "Poling."

51. Anderton et al., "Short History," 6–9.

52. Ibid., 11, 10. For the prayer meetings in the woods, see Pipa and Willborn, *Confessing Our Hope,* 13.

53. Response to Students, CTSBDM, May 1953.

54. For the controversy surrounding the vote on union with the Presbyterian Church USA, see Alvis, *Religion and Race,* 60–62.

55. Letter to the Board of Directors, May 1, 1956, in CTSBDM, May 1956. In addition to Keys, other laymen included Roy LeCraw, a former mayor of Atlanta; Erskine Wells, an influential layman from Jackson, Mississippi; and Milton Scott, of Decatur, Georgia.

56. Response to Ten Ruling Elders, "Gentlemen," in CTSBDM, May 5, 1956. See also "Seminary Withstands Its Critics."

57. Witherspoon, *Ministerial Directory.* Columbia Theological Seminary, *Alumni/ae Directory, 1998.*

58. CTSB, September 1953.

59. Ibid. Harriet Kehrer, a graduate of the University of Georgia's library school, had served as librarian for two years in the 1930s at the "distressing low salary of $50 a month." Mrs. Julia Anderson had followed her, serving until 1949. Richards, *As I Remember It,* 27. Neither should be regarded as full-time professionals. See reports on the library, CTSBDM, 1937–49.

60. For an example of the work of the Friendship Circle, see "History of Columbia Friendship Circle, April 1984–85, and 1985–86," CTS. The Moore bequest was received on June 6, 2006. Moore bequest can be found in records of Columbia's development office.

61. For the Matthews bequest, see CTSBDM, April 2006.

14 — The Turbulent 1960s

1. For a transcript of Kennedy's inaugural, see www.ourdocuments.gov/print_friendly.php?page=transcript&doc=91 (accessed April 10, 2016). For King's address see archives.gov/press/exhibits/dream-speech.pdf (accessed April 10, 2016). For Schlesinger see Schlesinger, *Vital Center.*

2. The most influential interpreter in the 1960s of the technological society was Jacques Ellul. See especially Ellul, *Technological Society;* Cox, *Secular City.*

3. For a summary of these early years of the decade, see Caro, *Passage of Power,* i–xx.

4. See Gitlin, *Sixties,* for an insider's account of the transformation from hope to rage.

5. For a contemporary summary of these developments, see Ahlstrom, *Religious History of the American People,* 1079–96. For the challenges facing theological schools in the 1960s, see G. Miller, *Piety and Profession,* 726–65; and Wuthnow, *Restructuring,* 142–64.

6. Cf. Noll, *Scandal of the Evangelical Mind,* 3–28.

7. Members of the board throughout the decade can be found in CTSBDM, 1950–60.

8. CTSB, June 1958.

9. The full report can be found in CTSB, January 1959.

10. Ibid., 5. For the professional model of ministry, see Holifield, *God's Ambassadors,* 244–53.

11. Ibid., 5–14.

12. The student center and Florida Hall were dedicated in May 1962. See CTSB, June 1962. For a summary of other campus buildings, see CTSB, January 1964, and Richards, *As I Remember It,* 85–86.

13. Cf. W. Morgan, *Collegiate Gothic.*

14. CTSB, October 1957. H. Richard Niebuhr had noted in 1956 the way major construction projects on seminary campuses had drawn funds away from increases in faculty salaries. See Niebuhr et al., *Advancement of Theological Education,* 40.

15. CTSB, October 1957.

16. For Fuhrmann on Calvin, see his inaugural address, "Why Calvin?," CTSB, July 1962. See also CTSB, June 1958, and "Fuhrmann" in Prince, *Presbyterian Bibliography,* 101.

17. CTSB, April 1965.

18. Richards, *As I Remember It,* 56–57. The author has in his personal possession a typed autobiography written in German by DeWitz during the summer of 1966. Much of the irenic spirit of DeWitz can be seen in his inaugural address, "Balance in the Old Testament."

19. CTSV, Winter 2001. The author was among those who knew little, very little, of opera. DeWitz was generally very patient.

20. For Wallace's relationship to one conservative student, see Philips, *Faithful Servant,* 75–76. For his critique of the assumptions of a therapeutic culture, see Wallace, "Place of Preaching, Sacraments, and Pastoral Care." Fuhrmann, DeWitz, and Wallace were joined by four other internationals who were part of the faculty during the 1960s—guest professors Barton Babbage (Australia), Philip Hughes (South Africa and England), Elio Eynard (Switzerland), and James Torrance (Scotland).

21. Richards, *As I Remember It,* 58. CTSB, October 1962. Glenn Miller notes that a new generation of faculty appointed in theological schools in the late 1950s and early 1960s was to dominate much of theological education until the 1990s and beyond. See G. Miller, *Piety and Profession,* 727.

22. CTSB, October 1961, January 1964. For Fulton's relationship to the Girardeau tradition in the church, see F. Smith, *History of the Presbyterian Church in America,* esp. 75–76; and Griffith and Raynal, *Presbyterians in South Carolina,* 14–18.

23. Richards, *As I Remember It,* 59. For McKee see CTSV, Fall 1987. In his inaugural address, "The Minister as Prophet," McKee vigorously argued that women were part of a prophetic ministry in both the Old and New Testaments. See CTSB, August 1963, 42. This is the first occasion that I have found of a Columbia faculty member advocating for women in the ministry.

24. CTSB, October 1966, April 1968.

25. These administrative developments can be followed in CTSB, 1960–70.

26. CTSB, February 1961, February 1962. For Anderson's dire reports, see, for example, CTSFM, October 1979.

27. CTSB, October 1964.

28. CTSB, January 1964, January 1967, and December 1969.

29. CTSB, January 1964. For progressive students' faculty attachments, e-mail from Joe Harvard to author, August 13, 2016. Harvard was elected president of the student body in 1966. For conservative students' attachment to Robinson and Gutzke, see Calhoun, *Pleading for a Reformation Vision*, 9–18, 44–50, 72–77; and Smartt, *I Am Reminded*, 9, 13.

30. Most of these vocational developments can be found in Witherspoon, *Ministerial Directory*. Among the thirteen Ph.D.s received, three were from the University of Edinburgh, two from Vanderbilt, two from the University of Georgia, and one each from the University of Aberdeen (Scotland), the University of Missouri, the University of South Mississippi, the University of Toronto, Southern Baptist Theological Seminary, and Union Theological Seminary, Virginia. Other advanced degrees were earned. Joe Harvard, for example, after a year study at the University of Basel, entered Yale and earned a master's degree and later was a Merrill Scholar at Harvard.

31. Alvis, *Religion and Race*, 136. See also for Smith, ibid. 68–69. Cf. M. Smith, *How Is the Gold Become Dim*, 153. For an overview of the *Presbyterian Journal* and race, see Alvis, *Religion and Race*, esp., 51–54, 165n20. For the history of the *(Southern) Presbyterian Journal* from a conservative perspective, see F. Smith, *History of the Presbyterian Church in America*, 15–49. For evangelicals and a "color blind" approach to race, see Emerson and Smith, *Divided by Faith*, esp. 170.

32. "Condemnation of Mob Violence," in Richards, *Change and the Changeless*, 35; "The Atlanta Ministers Manifesto," ibid., 51; Richards, *As I Remember It*, 76. The cross burning and the story of the "fat rabbit" telephone calls told by Kemie Richards Nix, interview in Montreat, North Carolina, August 5, 2016. In 2016 Joanna Adams, CTS graduate and former chair of Columbia's board, was a primary writer of an "Atlanta Interfaith Manifesto" that denounced religious bigotry and called for interfaith dialog. It modeled itself on the earlier "Ministers Manifesto." See atlantainterfaithmanifesto.org (accessed May 15, 2016).

33. Richards, "The Relevance of the Gospel," in Richards, *Change and the Changeless*, 62.

34. Alvis, *Religion and Race*, 99–100. Letters to friends, members of Second Presbyterian, Memphis, over the "closed door policy," can be found in the Gear papers, CTS. Gear's decision to move the General Assembly is told in detail in Haynes, *Last Segregated Hour*. For Independent Presbyterian's policy of having church visitors and members "compatible" with the congregation, see ibid., 231–32.

35. Interview with Ellington, August 5, 2016, Montreat, North Carolina. E-mail from Ellington, August 6, 2016.

36. Interview with Sally Gillespie Richardson, May 11, 2016, Black Mountain, North Carolina, and with Faye Townsend, February 14, 2017. For DuBose and Peck, see Shriver, *Unsilent South*, 84–90, and 28–35. For Presbyterians in South Carolina, see Griffith and Raynal, *Presbyterians in South Carolina*, 155–65. For Mississippi Presbyterians see Winter, *Citadels of Zion*, esp. 127–50. Cf. white Methodist ministers who spoke out on race in Alabama and the price they paid. See D. Collins, *When the Church Bells Rang Racist*, esp. 142–52. For twenty-eight white Methodists pastors in Mississippi and their struggle over race, see Reiff, *Born of Conviction*.

37. blubs on the back cover of Noble, *Beyond the Burning Bus*.

38. F. Smith, *History of the Presbyterian Church in America*, 101. See also ibid., 72, 566. The historian of the Presbyterian Church in America identified a memorial service for King held by the General Assembly of the Presbyterian Church in the United States as one of the key events causing many conservatives to leave the denomination and organize the Presbyterian Church in America. See ibid., 566. In the fall of 2015, in the midst of a tumultuous presidential campaign, the Montreat

Conference Center—under the leadership of former Columbia vice president for development, Richard DuBose—hosted a conference "Dr. King's Unfinished Agenda." Speakers included Congressman John Lewis; Charles Blow, *New York Times* columnist; Leonard Pitts of the *Miami Herald*; and William Barber, NAACP leader.

39. Correspondence in student file of Erskine Clarke, CTS; e-mail to author from Joe Harvard, August 13, 2016; from James Lowry, August 13, 2016.

40. Composite pictures of graduating classes for each year of the 1960s provide vivid images of the basic degree student body during the decade. For national enrollment figures, see Rooks, "Theological Education and the Black Church." For the national context for Presbyterians, see Wilmore, "Identity and Integration"; and Alvis, "Presbyterian Dilemma."

41. Telephone interview with Cecil Moore, August 10, 2016. Plaque quotation supplied by Barbara Poe, e-mail to author, August 11, 2016.

42. Interview with Kemie Richards Nix, Montreat, North Carolina, August 5, 2016.

43. E-mail from Kemie Richards Nix to author, August 9, 2016.

44. For Clopton see CTSV, Spring 1987; Spring 1991. For Adams see ibid., Spring 1993.

45. For articles on Clopton's life, see CTSV, Spring 1987; Spring 1991. Plaque inscription supplied by Hillary Michael, e-mail to author, August 15, 2016.

46. For an introduction to Julian Bond's life, including his marriage to Alice Clopton and their divorce in 1989, see https://en.wikipedia.org/wiki/Julian_Bond (accessed August 12, 2015). For Bond's leadership in the Atlanta struggles for civil rights in the 1960s and 1970s, see Brown-Nagin, *Courage to Dissent*. Around 1980 Claude Clopton told the author he had seen a copy of my recently published *Wrestlin' Jacob: A Portrait of Religion in the Old South* on the coffee table in the Bond home. On inquiry I learned to my amazement that Clopton was Bond's father-in-law. I do not believe that any of my faculty colleagues knew at the time of Clopton's relationship to Bond. Charles Cousar, as the closest faculty friend to Clopton, was invited by his family to have a part in his funeral in May 1991.

15 — Theological Education in a Free Market

1. Borstelmann, *1970s*, 1; Lasch, *Culture of Narcissism*, title page; Yankelovich, *New Rules*, title page.

2. Yankelovich, *New Rules*, provides a contemporary overview and analysis of these demographic developments.

3. See Borstelmann, *1970s*, 1–18; and cf. Rodgers, *Age of Fracture*, 183–90.

4. Borstelmann, *1970s*, 3–5; Rodgers, *Age of Fracture*, 1–14, 41–76.

5. Cf. Geertz, *Interpretation of Cultures*, esp. 123–24; and Ricoeur, *Lectures on Ideology and Utopia*, 3, 10, 183–97, and 254–66.

6. The reversal of the public and private sectors in American life is explored in Borstelmann, *1970s*. See esp. 16–18 and 316–17. The rubrics advertising new faculty positions and catalog descriptions of admission procedures point toward a more egalitarian spirit emerging at Columbia. See, for example, "Faculty Formation Plan," CTSFM Executive Committee, CTS, December 3, 1985, and CTSC, January 1986. For evaluations of courses by students, see, for example, CTSFM, October 4, 1990. Expansion of programs can be followed in CTSV, 1980–2005.

7. For Gutzke and "The Bible for You," see www.thebibleforyou.org (accessed July 14, 2016). For Gear's retirement see CTSB, October 1968.

8. Girardeau, *Confederate Memorial Day*, 8–18; David Bartlett, e-mail to author, April 26, 2016. Cf. Richards, *Soli Deo Gloria*, 3–6. Girardeau's son-in-law and biographer was pastor of the Arsenal Hill church during Robinson's youth. The festschrift for Robinson (Richards, *Soli Deo Gloria*), contains essays by prominent theologians and biblical scholars from Europe and the United States. They were apparently invited by Robinson's sons to submit the essays. Only two mention William Childs Robinson and then only in passing; the rest do not mention him or his work. James Robinson was a leading authority on the Gnostic texts discovered at Nag Hammadi,

Egypt, in 1945. See James Robinson, "Theological Autobiography," in Stone, *Craft of Religious Studies,* 117–50. For appreciative remarks on William Childs Robinson by former students who thought of him as the last of "old Columbia," see Calhoun, *Pleading for a Reformation Vision,* 124–26. See also, for the "floundering of a tradition" and the "decline" of "old Columbia," C. N. Willborn, "Southern Presbyterianism," in Pipa and Willborn, *Confessing Our Hope,* 323–26.

9. Richards's story is told in Richards, *As I Remember It,* and Philips, *Faithful Servant.*

10. CTS, *Inform,* April 1971.

11. Guthrie, *Christian Doctrine,* 20–21; *Presbyterian Journal,* July 10, August 7, September 11, 1968. The "Covenant Life Curriculum" was the fruit of long developing concern in the white Southern Presbyterian Church for serious adult lay education in Bible, theology, ethics, and church history. For the development of the curriculum, see Thompson, *Presbyterians in the South,* 3: 444–64. For conservative opposition to the curriculum, see the *Concerned Presbyterian,* June 1967, 6–8.

12. Obituary, Charles Cousar, *Atlanta Journal-Constitution,* December 12, 2014, https://www.legacy.com/obituaries/atlanta/obituary.aspx?n=charles-cousar&pid=173444282; Obituary, Wade Huie, *Atlanta Journal-Constitution,* June 2, 2015, https://www.legacy.com/obituaries/atlanta/obituary.aspx?n=wade-huie&pid=174987668.

13. CTSC, May 1971.

14. For "imperial presidencies," see G. Miller, *Piety and Profession,* 777. For the organization of the Faculty Executive Committee, see "Faculty Retreat," CTSFM, September 1971.

15. "Faculty Retreat," CTSFM, September 1971. The S.T.D. degree was later named the Th.D.—doctor of theology.

16. Ibid. CTS, *Inform,* October 1971.

17. For the catalog description of professional assessment, see, for example, CTSC, March 1980. For examples of therapeutic uses of the assessment, see, for example, CTSFM, May 1978; November 1979; May 1980; May 1985. The therapeutic later emerged occasionally when an assessment committee required individual counseling for a student. See CTSFM, April 2, 2009. Psychological testing included the use of the Minnesota Multiphasic Personality Inventory, Guilford-Zimmerman Temperament Survey, and Meyers-Briggs. A "Theological School Inventory" and "Readiness for Ministry" tests were also utilized. For the larger context in which the psychological testing was utilized and the professional assessment procedures developed, see Holifield, *History of Pastoral Care,* 307–13; and Tipton, *Getting Saved from the Sixties,* 2–30. See also Hinkle and Malony, *Clergy Assessment and Career Development.*

18. For faculty struggle with questions of reports of assessments to presbyteries, see, for example, CTSFM, March 1, 1984, and April 2, 1992. For the seminary's responsibility to report to presbyteries regarding a student's "moral and religious character," see CTSFM, April 2, 1992.

19. CTS, *Inform* July 1973; October 1973.

20. CTS, *Inform,* October 1973. CTSV, Summer 2002. https://en.wikipedia.org/wiki/Catherine_Gunsalus_Gonzalez (accessed September 14, 2016); https://en.wikipedia.org/wiki/Justo_L._González (accessed September 14, 2016). For the ordination of women, see Zikmind et al., *Clergy Women;* Chaves, *Ordaining Women.*

21. CTSB, January 1964; CTSC, November 1974. For Reformed Theological Seminary, see F. Smith, *History of the Presbyterian Church in America,* 82–83; Winter, *Citadels of Zion,* 154–64; and "Founding," www.rts.edu (accessed 2016). For the role of First Presbyterian Church, Jackson, Mississippi, in the founding of Reformed Theological Seminary, see S. Lucas, *Blessed Zion,* 124–31.

22. Reminiscence of the author and conversations with Professor Lee Carroll and Dean Philip Gehman.

23. Reminiscence of the author, who was dean of students 1973–83, and interview with Professor Catherine González, April 12, 2016.

24. For the role of the *Presbyterian Journal* in the formation of the PCA, see F. Smith, *History of the Presbyterian Church in America,* 15–49. For a chronology of events leading to the formation of the PCA, see ibid., 566. Smith

downplays the role of race in the formation of the PCA. For a response to this attempt and a judicious summary, see Haynes, *Last Segregated Hour,* 244–45, and 288n45. For a summary entitled "Race, Schism, and Reunion," see Alvis, *Religion and Race,* 132–37. For the establishment of Reformed Theological Seminary, its relationship to Columbia, and its deep links to white Mississippi culture, see Winter, *Citadels of Zion,* 154–64. For the religious right and larger context of religious schisms in the 1970s, see Wuthnow, *Restructuring,* 173–215; and Hillis, *Can Two Walk Together?*

25. Joseph Pipa, "Morton Howison Smith," in Pipa and Willborn, *Confessing Our Hope,* 29. For the influence of Robinson on the PCA, see Calhoun, *Pleading for a Reformation Vision,* 104. The name of Thornwell Seminary was changed to Greenville Theological Seminary under pressure from the PC (USA) with its Thornwell Children's Home. Ibid., 22. C. N. Willborn of Greenville Seminary wrote his dissertation at Westminster Seminary on Girardeau. See Willborn, "John L. Girardeau."

26. http://www.firstprescolumbia.org/om-girardeau (assessed October 9, 2016). See also Nutt, "Tie That No Longer Binds."

27. CTSV, Fall 1975.

28. Philips, *Time of Blessing,* 6, 7, 21. For Philips's background, see CTSV, Fall 1975.

29. CTSC, 1984, 4.

30. Philips, *Time of Blessing,* 84.

31. CTSV, Winter 1977. Ibid., Fall 1980. See also for the development of the forum, ibid., Fall 1978; Winter 1979; Winter 1985. In a survey many graduates had asked for a forum format. See CTSV, Spring 1977. For the development of summer programs, see ibid., Fall 1984, and CTSC, March 1985.

32. For Kay Philips's active role on the campus, see CTSV, Winter–Spring 1980. In 1973 thirty-nine first professional degree students entered the first-year class; in 1983 there were fifty-two new students. Included in the 1983 number were five students in the master's of youth ministry program. See CTSC, 1974, 1984.

33. CTSV, Spring 1977; Summer 1980; Spring–Winter 1982; Fall 1995.

34. The advanced degree, Th.M., also grew—from thirty-three in 1981 to sixty-three in 1991.

35. See, for example, the list of D.Min. students in CTSC, 1990–91. The board expressed at Hix's retirement glowing appreciation for what he and Pat Hix had accomplished for the seminary. CTSBDM, April 1993.

36. Philips, *Time of Blessing,* 67–71; CTS, *Inform,* October 1975.

37. CTS, *Inform,* October 1975.

38. For Long see CTSV, Summer 1978; for Ramey see CTSV, Summer 1979; for Keith see CTSC, 1979; for Carruthers see Summer 1980, Summer 1983; for Overbeck see CTSC, 1985; for Rose see CTSV, Summer 1983.

39. CTSC, 1986.

40. CTSV, Winter–Spring 1981; Spring 1992; CTSBDM, April 1995; CTSC 1996–97.

41. CTSV, Summer 1983. CTSC, 2003. For development of supervised ministry at Columbia as a highly structured course, see CTSFM, November 1997. For national developments of field education and supervised ministry, see G. Miller, *Piety and Profession,* 608–16; and Cherry, *Hurrying toward Zion,* 126–55.

42. CTSV, Winter 1986. For courses see, for example, CTSC 1994–95.

43. CTSV, Winter 1987; Sharp, *Living Countertestimony;* https://en.wikipedia.org/wiki/Walter_Brueggemann (accessed October 19, 2016).

44. Brueggemann to author, e-mail February 28, 2014.

45. https://en.wikipedia.org/wiki/Paul_Smith_(clergy) (accessed October 15, 2016). The author was a participant in the course that met at the King Center.

46. Philips, *Time of Blessing,* 81. For reports of growth of endowment, see CTSV, Spring 1983; CTSBD, April 1985, and April 1986.

47. CTSV, Summer 1978. Hussel, *Conversations with the Red Giraffe.*

48. CTSV, Winter 2002, Summer 2002.

49. Philips, *Time of Blessing,* 41–44, 55.

50. Ibid., 86.

16 — A Quest for Excellence

1. CTSBDM, October, 1986.
2. For the board report on the calling of

Oldenburg and his quest for excellence, see CTSV, Winter 87. For a clear articulation by a Columbia graduate of a Calvinist ethic, see Leith, *Introduction to the Reformed Tradition,* 67–85. Oldenburg's commitment to a pursuit of excellence can be seen in his president's columns, CTSV, 1987–2000, and in his reports to the board, CTSBDM, 1987–2000. See also, for example, CTSC, 1993–94, 1.

3. *Charlotte Observer*, November 13, 1986, and December 31, 1986.

4. Details of the Haitian project and its influence on Oldenburg are in Oldenburg, *Silver Charms,* 108–11.

5. CTSC, 1980.

6. Clarke, "Globalization in the Rising Sunbelt," 94–97.

7. Ibid. 97. A few months after his arrival at Columbia, Oldenburg visited the UTCWI, discussed the cooperative program between the two institutions, and hosted a dinner for Jamaicans who had spent time at Columbia since the beginning of the program. See CTSV, Fall 1987.

8. See Bartley, *Creation of Modern Georgia,* 224–37.

9. CTSC, 1990–91. See also Clarke, "Globalization in the Rising Sunbelt," 104–5.

10. CTSC, 1983; CTSBDM, April 95; April 1993; CTSV, Winter 1995. For an overview of the international program, see CTSC, 1995.

11. Quotation and Hudnut-Beumler's background: CTSV, Fall 1993. For Buecher see CTSBDM, October 1989; CTSV, Fall 1989; and CTSBDM, October 1992.

12. For Gehman see CTSV, Fall 1987. For Cole see CTSV, Spring 1991.

13. For Gilmore's background see CTSBDM, April 1988.

14. CTSV, Fall 1993.

15. For Gaventa see CTSV, Fall 1987. For Telford see CTSBDM, April 1989.

16. For backgrounds of new faculty, see CTSV, Fall 1991. For the change in the evaluation practices in senior preaching, see CTSFM, February 6, 1992. For street preaching see CTSC, 1990–2000, elective P652, p. 70, and CTSV, Summer 2005.

17. CTSBDM, October 1994, and CTSV, Winter 1995.

18. For Saunders see CTSBDM, October 1994, and CTSV, Winter 1995. For Cardoza-Orlandi see CTSBDM, April 1995.

19. For Lilly grant and description of the project, see CTSV, Spring 1990. Discussions about the character and purpose of theological education can be found in the issues of *Theological Education,* 1980–90. See Holifield, *God's Ambassadors,* 327–44; Farley, *Theologia;* Kelsey, *To Understand God Truly;* Chopp, *Saving Work.*

20. For communities of memory and hope, see Bellah et al., *Habits of the Heart,* 152–53. These details are provided in CTSV, Fall 1990.

21. The "Assumptions Paper" can be found in CTSFM, February 9, 1992.

22. Ibid. For an influential theological articulation of *Missio Dei,* see Bosch, *Transforming Mission.*

23. For a summary of the new curriculum, see Hudnut-Beumler's report, CTSBDM, April 1994.

24. Ibid. Cf. CTSC, 1983, and CTSC, 1995. To place Columbia's use of psychological categories in the larger context of theological education in the United States, see Holifield, *History of Pastoral Care,* 307–48. See also Myers-Shirk, *Helping the Good Shepherd.* Bellah et al., *Habits of the Heart,* represented at Columbia perhaps the most influential critique of the therapeutic culture.

25. Guder, *Missional Church,* 4–5. For course description see CTSC, 1995. For the missional and congregational focus of the curriculum, see Jim Hudnut-Beumler, Report to the Board, CTSBDM, October 1999.

26. For debates around the minister as professional, see Hauerwas and Willimon, *Resident Aliens;* Willimon, *Pastor;* Carroll, *As One with Authority;* Carroll et al., *Being There.*

27. CTSBDM, October 1994. See Alternative Context course syllabi, January 1987–January 2000, CTS.

28. David Bartlett in an e-mail to author, October 24, 2016, emphasized the strong and positive impact of the course on faculty.

29. These developments can be followed in Alternative Context course syllabi, January 1987–January 2008, CTS, and in CTSV,

1987–2008. Columbia's international program can be seen in light of similar developments at other theological seminaries. See *Theological Education* 27, no. 2.

30. For Russell-Jones's work, see CTSV, Winter 1994. For new courses offered, see CTSC, 1992–96. Russell-Jones was greatly influenced by the work of Jacques Ellul, esp. *Technological Society.*

31. CTSBDM, October 1999. Students and their undergraduate schools are listed in CTSC, 1992–2000. For summaries see *Association of Theological Schools Fact Book,* 1993–2000.

32. CTSBDM, October 1993. For enrollment figures see CTSBDM, April 1998.

33. CTSC, October 1988. For programs offered see CTSBDM, April 1988. For Dietrich see CTSV, Fall 1992. Program descriptions in ibid. 1993–2000.

34. See Juengst's report: CTSBDM, October 1989.

35. For Yoon and the Asian Ministry Center, see CTSFM, March 7, 1991; CTSC, 1995; CTSBDM, October 1996. For Wood and the Center for New Church Development, see CTSBDM, April 1997, and CTSV, Winter 2000. For the Program in Christian Spirituality, see CTSFM, October 1996, September 1996; and CTSBDM, April 1998 and October 1999. For Thompson Scholars see CTSV, Fall 1992. For Guthrie Scholars see CTSV, Winter 1998.

36. For the Florida project, see CTSBDM, October 1990, and regular reports in board minutes until CTSBDM, October 1997. Cf. the development of the successful Charlotte, North Carolina, campus of Union, Virginia. In contrast to Orlando, Charlotte's strong churches and influential pastors were vigorous supporters of the Charlotte campus. See Sweetser, *Copious Fountain,* 456–63.

37. "Special Committee to Study Theological Education," *Minutes of the General Assembly, Presbyterian Church (USA),* 1993: 18:066, 18.136. For development of many programs at Princeton Seminary, see Moorhead, *Princeton Seminary,* 497.

38. For the "Toward 2000 Campaign," see CTSBDM, April 1986, April 1988. For phase 2 see CTSBDM, October 1991, CTSV, October 1994, October 1996; Spring 1996; and CTSV, Spring 1996.

39. For the McPheeters bequest, see CTSBDM, October 1989, and CTSV, Spring 1990. For the J. Erskine Love Chair, see letter from Dennis Love to James Dickenson, May 24, 1988, in development office files. For Conant Chair see CTSV, Summer 2000, and Summer 2001. For the Peachtree gift, see CTSBDM, April 1997. For Benton Chair see CTSBDM, March 2000.

40. Quotation and details of the Campbell bequest, see CTSBD, April 1996. See also letter in ibid. from Virginia Courts suggesting use to be made of endowment.

41. CTSBDM, May 1940. See also ibid., May 1941 and May 1942.

42. For Adams see CTSV, Winter 1996.

43. For the proposals and board approval, see CTSBDM, April 1996. For letter from Virginia Campbell Courts, dated October 21, 1992, see ibid. Of all the theological seminaries in the United States and Canada, only Princeton Theological Seminary reported in 2000 a larger endowment than Columbia's—$824.8 million to $162.18 million. Interestingly, Atlanta's Candler reported the largest among university-related divinity schools—$229.87 million. See *Association of Theological Schools Fact Book,* 1999–2000.

44. For the Harrington Center, see CTSBDM, April 1988 and April 1989; CTSV, Spring–Summer 1999.

45. For Harrington's life and influence, see CTSV, Spring–Summer 1999.

46. CTSBDM, October 1997. For details of the library expansion, see CTSV, Spring 1995. For renovation of Florida Hall, see CTSV, Spring–Summer 1999.

47. For "beautiful landscaping" being one of Oldenburg's "loves," see Oldenburg, *Silver Charms,* 184–85.

48. For the role of landscape and architecture in shaping human perspectives and emotions, see Kedar and Werblowski, *Sacred Space,* and P. Jones, *Architecture and Ritual,* esp. 2–6.

49. CTSV, Winter 1998. For appointments see the following CTSV issues: Murchison, Fall 1996; Johnson, Florence, and Yoder,

Spring–Summer 1998; DuBose, Nishioka, Raynal, and Yoder, Spring–Summer 1999; Sadler, Winter 2000.

50. Staff members and their various responsibilities can be found in *Columbia Theological Seminary Pictorial Directory,* 1990–2000, and in CTSC, 1990–2000. For the Ring Shout and Dance, see Raboteau, *Slave Religion,* 66–73.

51. The figures for staff and faculty are taken from the *Columbia Theological Seminary Pictorial Directory* and CTSC, 1983, 2003, and *Association of Theological Schools Fact Book,* 1983, 2003. Using financial records Marty Sadler counted thirty-three staff for 1983 and sixty-eight for 2003. There is a vast literature on the rise and character of bureaucracies where rules and procedures are systematized and increasingly substituted for sentiment and tradition. For a helpful introduction, see Waters and Waters, *Weber's Rationalism and Modern Society,* esp. 1–18, 73–132.

52. CTSC, 2000.

17 — *Seeking Common Ground*

1. For the call of Mendenhall to Columbia, see CTSV, Fall 2000.

2. Ibid. https://en.wikipedia.org/wiki/Laura_S._Mendenhall (accessed November 5, 2016).

3. The author served as a member of the search committee that nominated Mendenhall to the Columbia board. Mendenhall's reflected on the role of a "middle way" at Columbia in an e-mail to author, January 15, 2014.

4. For Skinner see CTSV, Winter 2002, and e-mail from Mendenhall to author, January 23, 2014. For Harvard see CTSV, Spring 2000, and e-mail from Mendenhall to Harvard and author, January 3, 2017. For Ellis see CTSV Fall 2008. For Morris see CTSV, Winter 2008. For Hauptfuhrer and Love, e-mail from Richard DuBose to author, January 9, 2017. For Heywood see Griffith and Raynal, *Presbyterians in South Carolina,* 138.

5. The "Assumptions Paper" can be found in CTSFM, February 6, 1992. For the way these questions were a part of a larger conversation in U.S. theological schools, see Aleshire, "Future of Theological Education." For demographics shifts and projections, see http://pewsocialtrends.org/2008/02/11/us-population-projections-2005-2050 (accessed November 1, 2016).

6. For the decline of the mainline Protestant denominations, see Roof and McKinney, *American Mainline Religion;* and Hout, Greeley, and Wilde, "Birth Dearth." For the impact of these shifting demographics, see Holifield, *God's Ambassadors,* 311–49. For the speed of technological change and the rise of the Information Revolution, see Friedman, *Thank You for Being Late.*

7. For the vision statement, see CTSBDM, April 1997, and CTSV, Winter 1999.

8. CTS, "A Vision for the Year 2020," 6–13.

9. Ibid., 13–16.

10. Ibid., 25–26.

11. For retirements of Johnson, see CTSV, Summer 2000; Patton, CTSV, Summer 2001; Gonzalez, CTSV, Summer 2002; and Cousar, CTSV, Winter 2003.

12. For retirement of Brueggemann, see CTSV, Winter 2003. For his c.v. see www.walterbruegge
mann.com (accessed December 1, 2017).

13. For cultures of theological institutions and their abilities to resist change, cf. Aleshire, "Future of Theological Education," 380–81; Carroll et al., *Being There,* 270–79; and Wuthnow, *Producing the Sacred,* 105–26.

14. For Murchison as new academic dean, see CTSV, Summer 2001.

15. For White see CTSV, Winter 2006; for Myers see CTSV, Fall 2012; for Clayton see CTSV, Summer 2009.

16. For Wren see CTSBDM, April 2000, and CTSV, Summer 2000; for Lartey see CTSV, Summer 2001; for Brown see CTSV, Summer 2003.

17. For Tribble see CTSV, Summer 2007; for Hayner see CTSV, Winter 2003.

18. For Ward see CTSV, Summer 2003; for Dawson see CTSV, Spring 2004; for Moore-Keish see CTSV, Spring 2004. For the launching of the D.Ed.Min. degree, see CTSFM, March 3, 2005.

19. For Taylor's joining the faculty, see CTSV, Summer 2001; for her c.v. see www.barbarabrowntaylor.com (accessed November 15,

2016); for Bartlett see CTSV, Winter 2004, and https://en.wikipedia.org/wiki/David_L._Bartlett (accessed November 15, 2016).

20. CTSBDM, April 2005.

21. CTSV, Summer 2005.

22. For assumptions about what was needed for contemporary student housing "to keep Columbia competitive not only with other theological schools but [also] with other professional schools," see "A New Student Residence Hall," CTSV, Spring 2008.

23. *Association of Theological Schools Fact Book,* 2005–9.

24. For statistics and evaluation of the program, see CTSFM, November 2006. For shifts in pastoral care and counseling, see Patton, *From Ministry to Theology,* and Hunter, "Spiritual Counsel" and "Pastoral Theology." For Cooper-White see CTSV, Spring 2008 and Winter 2014.

25. For Davis and the Life Long Learning program, see CTSV, Winter 2004, and CTSBDM, March 2006. For S3 program, see CTSV, Fall 2002, Winter 2003, Spring 2004.

26. CTSV, Fall 2008. For the Campbell Seminars, see CTSBD, October 2000 and March 2005; CTSV, Fall 2001, Fall 2002, Fall 2004. For examples of publications, see Brueggemann, *Hope for the World,* and Campbell Seminar articles published by Protestant Theological faculty, Charles University, Prague: *Communio Viatorum* 57 (2005). The author served as director of the Campbell Seminars.

27. For Sadler see CTSV, Winter 2000. For DuBose see CTSBDM, October 1999, and CTSV, Spring–Summer 1999.

28. CTSFM, February 8, 2001. The board, apparently realizing that it was having less involvement in faculty searches, added a second member to all search committees; Minutes of the Executive Committee of the Faculty, April 17, 2003. Found in CTS.

29. e-mail from Richard DuBose to author, December 15, 2016. Cf. also CTSV, Winter 2008.

30. For the doubling of the annual fund, see CTSFM, March 2007. For development staff see *Columbia Theological Seminary Pictorial Directory,* 2005–6. For a summary of the campaign, see CTSV, Winter 2013.

31. e-mail from Mendenhall to author, January 6, 2014. For the move of the archive to CTS, see CTSV, Summer 2007. For the program in Presbyterian and Reformed History and Theology, see ibid. The program was discontinued in 2013.

18 — An Egalitarian and Inclusive Spirit

1. CTSV, Winter 2003, Summer 2009.

2. United States Federal Census, 1930, enumeration for Rock Creek Valley, Spokane County, Washington; http://www.seattletimes.com/seattle-news/obituaries/obituary-jeannette-hayner-91-former-state-senate-majority-leader/ (accessed November 2, 2016). For oral history by Jeannette Hayner, see http://www.historylink.org/File/9643 (accessed November 2, 2016).

3. *Christianity Today* called Hayner one of the "baby-boomer's generation most influential leaders." www.christianitytoday.com/gleanings/2015/january/died-steven-hayer (accessed November 2, 2016).

4. For the Information Revolution, see Friedman, *Thank You for Being Late.* For demographic shifts see http://pewsocialtrends.org/2008/02/11/us-population-projections-2005-2050 (accessed November 22, 2016). For Hayner signing his correspondence "Joyfully, Steve," see "President's Message," in CTSV, Summer 2009–Summer 2013.

5. Association of Theological Schools Annual Data Tables, 2007–8, 2012–13.

6. "Entering Students Demographic Comparisons, 2010–2014," provided by Monica Wedlock Kilpatrick, director of admissions and recruitment, November 4, 2014. Cf. five-year admission statistics, CTSV, Winter 2006. For faculty discussion of admission of internationals into the M.Div., see CTSFM, December 2009. Cf. also CTSV, Spring 2015.

7. Association of Theological Schools Annual Data Tables, 2005–15; CTSBDM, March 2005; "Lifelong Learning Administrative Unit Report Planning and Evaluation," 2014–15, 2015–16, provided by office of academic administrator.

8. "Admissions Statistics Comparisons," CTSFM, February 2006; "Entering Students

Demographic Comparisons, 2010–2014," CTSFM, February, 2006. Students from Atlanta area confirmed by e-mail to author from Monica Wedlock Kilpatrick, director of admissions and recruitment, November 4, 2014.

9. CTSV, Summer 2010; Hayner, "The Shaping of Things to Come?," www.atthispoint.net, vol. 2, no. 1 (Spring 2007), (accessed 2016).

10. CTSV, Fall 2014. For Mullen's background see CTSV, Summer 2010.

11. CTSV, Summer 2011.

12. For Simmers see CTSV, Summer 2010; Park, CTSC, 2012–14, 96; Galindo, CTSV, Spring 2013; Campbell, ibid.

13. For Azumah see CTSV, Winter 2011; for Watkins see Summer 2011.

14. For Raj see CTSV, Fall 2011; for Breen see Fall 2012; for Yoo see Fall 2014; and for Hartman ibid.

15. CTSC, 2014–15.

16. For Vaughan's work see CTSV fall 2012. Thompson's work could be seen in the online CTSVs and on Twitter, Facebook, YouTube, and a Columbia blog.

17. For the Broyles Center, see CTSV, Winter 2011, Spring 2012.

18. Bill Brown, "AAAS Science for Seminaries Annual Progress Report June 1, 2015–May 31, 2016," CTS; http://www.aaas.org/news/aaas-reaches-out-theology-students (accessed December 3, 2016).

19. For the master of arts in practical theology degree, see CTSC, 2014–15. For student statistics see e-mail to author from Monica Wedlock Kilpatrick, director of admissions and recruitment, November 4, 2014. For Center for Academic Literacy, see CTSV, Spring 2015.

20. E-mail from board member Joseph Harvard to board member Thomas Walker summarizes the opposition of many, September 24, 2013. For mission statement, see CTSC, 2012–14. Charles Raynal, last director of the Program in Presbyterian and Reformed History and Theology, e-mail to author, January 10, 2017.

21. Cf. Aleshire, "Future of Theological Education," and Carroll et al., *Being There,* 269–79. For the ways multiculturalism and studies of gender and race have impacted a specific theological discipline, see Hunter, "Pastoral Theology." See also Moessner, *Through the Eyes of Women.*

22. For patterns of immigration increasing conservative theological perspectives, see Holifield, *God's Ambassadors,* 317–18. For assumptions about inclusive language in a mainline seminary, see Carroll et al., *Being There,* 123, 208–9.

23. Fractures in the community were clearly revealed in 2012 in debates over gay couples living in seminary housing. For a comprehensive and sophisticated discussion of culture and formation in theological education, see Carroll et al., *Being There.* There is a continuing need to interpret Columbia from cultural-anthropological perspectives.

24. The issue of denominational oversight of students has been perhaps most obvious in regard to supervised ministry placements and midcourse assessments of students.

25. "Guidelines," CTSFM, May 2010; "Draft: Caucus on Race and Ethnicity," December 16, 2016. African American students have a Black Seminarians Association and Korean American students have their Korean American Association. Both are intended to provide support for their members during their time at Columbia.

26. CTS, "Staff Directory," 2014.

27. CTSV, Fall 2014.

28. CTSV, Spring 2015.

BIBLIOGRAPHY

Document Sources

Charles Colcock Jones Papers, Howard-Tilton Memorial Library, Tulane University.

C. Benton Kline Jr. Special Collections and Archives, John Bulow Campbell Library, Columbia Theological Seminary.Thomas Hart Law, "Journal," 1860–65, South Carolinian Library, University of South Carolina.

Articles, Essays, Chapters, Periodicals, and Unpublished Works

Adger, John B. "The Christian Doctrine of Human Rights and Slavery." *Southern Presbyterian Review* 2 (March 1849): 569–86.

——. "Memorial of James Henley Thornwell." In *Memorial Volume of the Semi-centennial of the Theological Seminary at Columbia, South Carolina,* 188–94. Columbia, S.C.: Presbyterian Publishing House, 1884.

——. "Northern and Southern Views of the Province of the Church." *Southern Presbyterian Review* 16 (March 1866): 384–411.

——. "Review of Reports to the Legislature of South Carolina on the Revival of the Slave Trade." *Southern Presbyterian Review* 11 (April 1858): 100–135.

Aleshire, Daniel O. "The Future of Theological Education: A Speculative Glimpse at 2032." *Dialog: A Journal of Theology* 50 (Winter 2011): 380–85.

Alvis, Joel L. "A Presbyterian Dilemma: Ecclesiastical and Social Racial Policy in the Twentieth-Century Presbyterian Communion." In *The Diversity of Discipleship: The Presbyterians and Twentieth-Century Christian Witness,* edited by Milton J. Coalter, John M. Mulder, and Louis B. Weeks, 187–208. Louisville, Ky.: Westminster/John Knox, 1991.

Amanat, Abbas, and Magnus T. Bernhardsson, eds. "Drying Up the Euphrates: Muslims, Millennialism, and the Early American Missionary Enterprise." In *The United States and the Middle East: Cultural Encounters,* 130–49. New Haven, Conn.: Yale Center for International and Area Studies, 2002.

American Tract Society. *Responsibilities of the Publishing Committee.* New York: American Tract Society, 1858.

Atkins, Jonathan M. "Philanthropy in the Mountains: Martha Berry and the Early Years of the Berry Schools." *Georgia Historical Quarterly* 82 (Winter 1998): 856–76.

Bishop, Charles C. "The Proslavery Argument Reconsidered: James Henley Thornwell, Millennial Abolitionist." *South Carolina Historical Magazine* 73 (January 1972): 18–36.

Boggs, William E. "Recollections." In *Dr. James Woodrow as Seen by His Friends,* edited by Marion W. Woodrow, 80–85. Columbia, S.C.: R. L. Bryan, 1909.

Bornstein, George. "Halls of Learning Built on Bondage?" *Times Literary Supplement,* January 17, 2014, 11.

Bozeman, Theodore Dwight. "Inductive and Deductive Politics: Science and Society in Antebellum Presbyterian Thought." *Journal of American History* 64, no. 3 (December 1977): 704–22.

Brauer, Jerald C. "Regionalism and Religion in America." *Church History* 54 (September 1985): 421–43.

Brueggemann, Walter. "Some Aspects of Theodicy in Old Testament Faith." *Perspectives in Religious Studies* 26, no. 3 (1999): 253–68.

Calhoun, R. D. "Interesting Story of the Perkins Family of Tensas Parish, La." CTS.

Clarke, Erskine. "Globalization in the Rising Sunbelt." *Theological Education* 37, no. 2: 87–109.

——. "The Study of the Seminary Presidency in Protestant Theological Seminaries." *Theological Education* 32, supp. 2. (1995): 1–110.

Conyers, Joseph W. "Middler English Bible." In possession of author.

"Covenant Life Curriculum." *Concerned Presbyterian*, June 1967, 6–8.

Dabney, Robert Lewis. "The Caution against Anti-Christian Science Criticized by Dr. Woodrow." *Southern Presbyterian Review* 24 (1873): 539–85.

——. "Geology and the Bible." *Southern Presbyterian Review* 14 (July 1861): 246–74.

DeWitz, Ludwig. "The Concept of Balance in the Old Testament." CTSB, July 1964.

Dikes, Samuel. "Shall Churches Increase Their Efficiency by Scientific Methods?" *American Journal of Theology* 16 (January 1912): 20–30.

Dowey, Edward A. "Poling and the Presbyterian Letter." *Christianity and Crisis* 14 (1954–55): 124–27.

Duncan, Christopher M. "Benjamin Morgan Palmer, Southern Presbyterian Divine." PhD diss., Auburn University, 2008.

Eaton, Clement. "Professor James Woodrow and the Freedom of Teaching in the South." *Journal of Southern History* (February 28, 1962): 3–17.

Faust, Drew Gilpin. "Christian Soldiers: The Meaning of Revivalism in the Confederate Army." *Journal of Southern History* 53 (February 1987): 60–84.

Flinn, J. William. "Evolution and Theology." *Southern Presbyterian Review* 36 (April 1885): 268–304.

Fogel, Robert William. "The Religious Sources of the New Abolitionist Movement." In *Without Consent or Contract: The Rise and Fall of American Slavery*, 254–80. New York: W. W. Norton and Company, 1989.

Ford, Lacy K. "Paternalism Emerges." In *Deliver Us from Evil: The Slavery Question in the Old South*, 142–72. New York: Oxford University Press, 2009.

Fox-Genovese, Elizabeth, and Eugene D. Genovese. "The Divine Sanction of Social Order: Religious Foundations of the Southern Slaveholders' World View." *Journal of the American Academy of Religion* 55 (Summer 1987): 211–33.

Freehling, William W. "James Henley Thornwell's Mysterious Antislavery Movement." *Journal of Southern History* 57 (August 1991): 383–406.

Girardeau, John L. "Eulogy on Professor George Howe." In *Memorial Volume of the Semi-centennial of the Theological Seminary at Columbia, South Carolina*, 387–418 Columbia, S.C.: Presbyterian Publishing House, 1884.

——. "The Suffering Seaboard of South Carolina." Southern Presbyterian Review 27 (April 1876): 199–227.Gladney, Richard. "Natural Science and Revealed Religion." *Southern Presbyterian Review*, October 1859, 443–67.

Goulding, F. R. "Memorial of Thomas Goulding, D.D." In *Memorial Volume of the Semi-centennial of the Theological Seminary at Columbia, South Carolina*, 181–87. Columbia, S.C.: Presbyterian Publishing House, 1884.

Green, J. B. "Regarding the Revision of the Confession of Faith and the Catechism." *Presbyterian of the South*, June 15, 1938, 13–14.

Harper, William Rainey. "Shall the Theological Curriculum Be Modified and How?" *American Journal of Theology* 3 (January 1899): 45–66.

Haynes, Stephen R. "Race, National Destiny, and the Sons of Noah in the Thought of Benjamin Morgan Palmer." *Journal of Presbyterian History* 78 (Summer 2000): 125–43.

Hodge, Charles. "The State of the Country." *Biblical Repertory and Princeton Review* 33, no. 1 (1861): 1–36.

Hoge, Moses D. "Memorial of William Swan Plumer." In *Memorial Volume of the Semi-centennial of the Theological Seminary at Columbia, South Carolina*, 210–16. Columbia, S.C.: Presbyterian Publishing House, 1884.

Holifield, Brooks. "Mercersburg, Princeton, and the South: The Sacramental Controversy in the Nineteenth Century." *Journal of Presbyterian History* 54 (Summer, 1976): 238–58.

Hout, Michael, Andrew Greeley, and Milissa Wilde. "Birth Dearth: Demographics of Mainline Decline." *Christian Century* 122 (October 4, 2005): 24–27.

Howe, George. "The Raid of John Brown and the Progress of Abolition." *Southern Presbyterian Review* 13 (January 1860): 784–816.

———. "Two Lectures on the Biblical and Physical History of Man . . . by Josiah C. Nott." *Southern Presbyterian Review* 3 (March 1850): 426–90.

Hunter, Rodney J. "Pastoral Theology: Historical Perspectives and Future Agendas." Unpublished "Address Given to the Annual Study Conference of the Society for Pastoral Theology at Its Twentieth Anniversary Meeting in Chicago, Illinois, June 16, 2005."

———. "Spiritual Counsel." *Christian* Century 118 (October 17, 2001): 20–25.

"Journal of Thos. H. Law." CTS.

Jones, Charles C. "Return of Members," 1846, JTU.

Kolchin, Peter. "Reevaluating the Antebellum Slave Community: A Comparative Perspective." *Journal of American History* 70, no. 3 (1983): 595–96.

"The Late Honorable Thomas C. Perrin." *Southern Presbyterian*, May 12, 1878, 2.

Law, Thomas H. "Personal Reminiscences." In *Dr. James Woodrow as Seen by His Friends*, edited by Marion W. Woodrow, 56–57. Columbia, S.C.: R. L. Bryan, 1909.

LeFevre, Perry. "Manford George Gutzke, John Dewey's Thought and Its Implications for Christian Education." *Journal of Religion* 37, no. 3 (July 1957): 214–15.

Lipscomb, Terry W. "The Legacy of Ainsley Hall." *South Carolina Historical Magazine* 99, no. 2 (1998): 158–79.

Lyon, J. A. "The New Theological Professorship." *Southern Presbyterian Review*, April 1859, 181–95.

McLean, John Knox. "The Presidency of Theological Seminaries: Should the Theological Seminary Have a Permanent President; and If So, What Should Be the Powers and Duties of the Office?" *Bibliotheca Sacra* 50 (April 1901): 301–18.

McPheeters, William Marcellus. "O.T. Literature and Exegesis: Lectures to Junior Class." N.p.: n.p., n.d, found in CTS.

———. "The Science of Interpretation." N.p.: n.p., n.d.

Menn, Joseph Karl. "The Large Slaveholders of the Deep South, 1860." Ph.D. diss., University of Texas, 1964.

Merrick, James L. "Mission to the Mohammedans of Persia." *Missionary Herald* (Boston), January 1837.

Moore, Margaret DesChamps. "A Northern Professor Winters in Columbia, 1852–1853." *South Carolina Magazine* (October 1959): 183–92.

Moorhead, James. "Presbyterians and the Cult of Organizational Efficiency, 1870–1936." In *Reimaging Denominationalism: Interpretative Essays*, edited by Russell Richie and Bruce Mullin. New York: Oxford University Press, 1994.

Morgan, Philip D. "The Ownership of Property by Slaves in the Mid-nineteenth-Century Low Country." *Journal of Southern History* 49 (August 1983): 399–420.

———. "Work and Culture: The Task System and the World of Lowcountry Blacks, 1700 to 1880." *William and Mary Quarterly*, 3rd ser., 39 (October 1982): 563–99.Nutt, Rick. "The Tie That No Longer Binds." In *The Confessional Mosaic: Presbyterians and Twentieth Century Theology*, edited by Milton J. Coalter, John M. Mulder, and Louis B. Weeks, 236–56. Louisville, Ky.: Westminster/John Knox, 1990.

Palmer, Benjamin Morgan. "Import of Hebrew History." *Southern Presbyterian Review* 9 (April 1856): 582–610.

———. "A Plea for Doctrine as the Instrument of Sanctification." *Southern Presbyterian Review* 3 (July 1849): 32–54.

———. "Sketch of Edward Palmer, Oct. 18, 1882." In *In Memoriam: Rev. Edward Palmer*. N.p.: n.p.: 1882 (?).

Pennigroth, Dylan. "Slavery, Freedom, and Social Claims to Property among African Americans in Liberty County, Georgia, 1850–1880." *Journal of American History* 84 (1997): 405–35.

Quarterly Bulletin: State Board of Charities of South Carolina 2, no. 1 (Columbia, March 1916).

Reed, R. C. "Brief Course in Church History." CTS.

——. "The General Assembly." *Union Seminary Review* 26, no. 1 (October 1914): 234–45.

Richards, M. McDowell. "John Bulow Campbell." CTSB, September 1941, 12.

Robinson, William Childs. "The Proposed Changes in the Standards." *Presbyterian of the South,* September 7, 1938, 15–16.

Rooks, C. Shelby. "Theological Education and the Black Church." *Christian Century* 86 (February 12, 1969): 212–16.

Roth, Rodris. "Tea Drinking in 18th Century America: Its Etiquette and Equipage." In *Contributions from the Museum of History and Technology,* bulletin 225, paper 14 (1961).

"A Seminary Withstands Its Critics." *Presbyterian Outlook,* September 24, 1956, 1.

Shick, Tom W., and Don H. Doyle. "The South Carolina Phosphate Boom and the Stillbirth of the New South, 1867–1920." *South Carolina Historical Magazine* 86 (January 1986): 1–36.

Smith, Adam. "Considerations concerning the First Formation of Languages." Added to the third ed. of *The Theory of Moral Sentiments,* 437–78. London: T. Cadell, 1767.

Smyth, Thomas. "The Battle of Fort Sumter: Its Mystery and Miracle—God's Mastery and Mercy." *Southern Presbyterian Review* 14 (October 1861): 365–99.

——. "The Sin and the Curse." In *The Collected Works of the Rev. Thomas Smyth, D.D.,* edited by J. W. Flinn, 7: 539–49. Columbia, S.C.: R. L. Bryan, 1908.

——. "The Victory of Manassas Plain." *Southern Presbyterian Review* 14 (January 1862): 593–619.

——. "The War of the South Vindicated." *Southern Presbyterian Review* 15 (April 1863): 479–514.

Soares, Theodore. "Practical Theology and Ministerial Efficiency." *American Journal of Theology* 16 (January 1912): 426–43."Southern Theological Seminary." *Charleston Observer,* January 23, 1830, 1–2.

Street, T. Watson. "The Evolution Controversy in the Southern Presbyterian Church with Attention to the Theological and Ecclesiastical Issues Raised." *Journal of the Presbyterian Historical Society* 37 (1959): 232–50.

Thornwell, James H. "The Being of God." In *Collected Writings of James Henley Thornwell,* edited by John Adger, 1: 26–53. Richmond, Va.: Presbyterian Committee of Publication, 1871.

——. "National Sins: A Fast-Day Sermon." *Southern Presbyterian Review* 13 (January 1861): 649–89.

——. "Slavery and the Religious Instruction of the Colored Population." *Southern Presbyterian Review* 4 (July 1850): 105–41.

Tuchscherer, Konrad, and P. E. H. Hair. "Cherokee and West Africa: Examining the Origins of the Vai Script." *History in Africa* 29 (2002): 427–86.

Vaughan, C. R. "Biographical Sketch of Thomas E. Peck." In *Miscellanies of the Rev. Thomas E. Peck,* edited by T. C. Johnson, 1–12. Richmond, Va.: Presbyterian Committee on Publication: 1897.

Wallace, Ronald. "The Place of Preaching, Sacraments, and Pastoral Care in the Experience of the Reformation." CTSB, December 1967, 27–29.

Warfield, Benjamin B. "The Constitution of the Seminary Curriculum." *Presbyterian Quarterly* 10 (October 1896): 256–77.

Westerkamp, Marilyn J. "James Henley Thornwell, Proslavery Spokesman within a Calvinist Faith." *South Carolina Historical Magazine* 87 (January 1986): 49–64.

Willborn, Chalmerib Nixon. "John L. Girardeau (1825–1898): Pastor to Slaves and Theologian of Causes." Ph.D. diss., Westminster Theological Seminary, 2003.

Wilmore, Gayraud S. "Identity and Integration: Black Presbyterians and Their Allies in the Twentieth Century." In *The Diversity of Discipleship: The Presbyterians and Twentieth-Century Christian Witness,* edited by Milton J. Coalter, John M. Mulder, and Louis B. Weeks, 209–33. Louisville: Westminster John Knox Press, 1991.

Wilson, John Leighton. "The Foreign Slave-Trade: Can It Be Revived without Violating the Most Sacred Principles of Honor,

Humanity, and Religion?" *Southern Presbyterian Review* 12 (1859): 491–512.

Woodrow, James. "Evolution: Address." In *Dr. James Woodrow as Seen by His Friends*, edited by Marion W. Woodrow, 617–45. Columbia, S.C.: R. L. Bryan, 1909.

———. "An Examination of Certain Recent Assaults on Physical Science." *Southern Presbyterian Review* 24 (July 1873): 327–76.

———. "Geology and Its Assailants." In *Dr. James Woodrow as Seen by His Friends*, edited by Marion W. Woodrow, 549–68. Columbia, S.C.: R. L. Bryan, 1909.

———. "An Inaugural Address." *Southern Presbyterian Review* 16 (January 1862): 14–50.

Books

Abbott, S. B. *The Southern Botanic Physician.* Charleston, S.C.: published by author, 1844.

Adger, John B., ed. *The Collected Writings of James Henley Thornwell.* Vols. 1–4. Richmond, Va.: Presbyterian Committee of Publication, 1871.

———. *My Life and Times, 1810–1899.* Richmond, Va.: Presbyterian Committee of Publication, 1899.

Ahlstrom, Sydney E. *A Religious History of the American People.* New Haven, Conn.: Yale University Press, 1972.

Alvis, Joel L. *Religion and Race: Southern Presbyterians, 1946–1983.* Tuscaloosa: University of Alabama Press, 1994.

Ambrose, Douglas. *Henry Hughes and Proslavery Thought in the Old South.* Baton Rouge: Louisiana State University Press, 1996.

Anderson, William. *The Wild Man from Sugar Creek: The Political Career of Eugene Talmadge.* Baton Rouge: Louisiana State University Press, 1975.

Andrew, Rod, Jr. *Wade Hampton: Confederate Warrior to Southern Redeemer.* Chapel Hill: University of North Carolina Press, 2008.

Arsenault, Raymond, and Orville Vernon Burton, eds. *Dixie Redux: Essays in Honor of Sheldon Hackney.* Montgomery, Ala.: NewSouth Books, 2013.

Baptist, Edward E. *The Half Has Never Been Told: Slavery and the Making of American Capitalism.* New York: Basic Books, 2014.

Beckert, Sven. *Empire of Cotton: A Global History.* New York: Alfred A. Knopf, 2014.

Bellah, Robert, et al. *Habits of the Heart: Individualism and Commitment in American Life.* Berkeley: University of California Press, 1985.

Berlin, Ira. *Many Thousands Gone: The First Two Centuries of Slavery in North America* Cambridge, Mass.: Belknap Press of Harvard University Press, 1998.

Blackburn, George A. *The Life Work of John L. Girardeau.* Columbia, S.C.: State, 1916.

Blackman, George L. *Faith and Freedom: A Study of Theological Education and the Episcopal Theological School.* New York: Seabury, 1967.

Blackmon, Douglas A. *Slavery by Another Name: The Re-enslavement of Black Americans from the Civil War to World War II.* New York: Doubleday, 2008.

Blight, David W. *Race and Reunion: The Civil War in American Memory.* Cambridge, Mass.: Belknap Press of Harvard University Press, 2001.

Bliss, Seth. *Letters to the Members, Patrons and Friends of the Branch American Tract Society in Boston; and to Those of the National Society in New York.* Boston: Crocker and Brewster, 1858.

Borstelmann, Thomas. *The 1970s: A New Global History from Civil Rights to Economic Inequality.* Princeton, N.J.: Princeton University Press, 2012.

Bosch, David J. *Transforming Mission: Paradigm Shifts in Theology of Mission.* Marynoll, N.Y.: Orbis Books, 1991.

Bouwsma, William J. *John Calvin: A Sixteenth Century Portrait.* New York: Oxford University Press, 1988.

Bartley, Numan V. *The Creation of Modern Georgia.* Athens: University of Georgia Press, 1983.

Brinkmeyer, Robert H. *The Fourth Ghost: White Southern Writers and European Fascism, 1930–1950.* Baton Rouge: Louisiana State University Press, 2009.

Broadus, John A. *Memoir of James P. Boyce, Late President of the Southern Baptist Theological Seminary, Louisville.* New York: A. C. Armstrong and Son, 1893.

Brown, John Crosby. *A Hundred Years of Merchant Banking: A History of Brown Brothers and Company.* New York: privately printed, 1909.

Brown, William Adams, and Mark May. *The Education of American Ministers.* 4 vols. New York: Institute of Social and Religious Research, 1934.

Brown-Nagin, Tomiko. *Courage to Dissent: Atlanta and the Long History of the Civil Rights Movement.* New York: Oxford University Press, 2011.

Brueggemann, Walter, ed. *Hope for the World: Mission in a Global Context.* Louisville, Ky.: Westminster/John Knox, 2001.

Brundage, W. Fitzhugh. *Lynching in the New South: Georgia and Virginia, 1880–1930.* Urbana: University of Illinois Press, 1993.

Bureau of the Census. *Historical Statistics of the United States, Colonial Times to 1970.* Washington, D.C.: U.S. Government Printing Office, 1975.

Burton, E. Milby. *The Siege of Charleston, 1861–1865.* Columbia: University of South Carolina Press, 1982.

Calhoun, David B. *Our Southern Zion: Old Columbia Theological Seminary.* East Peoria, Ill.: Banner of Truth, 2012.

——. *Pleading for a Reformation Vision.* Carlisle, Penn.: Banner of Truth Trust, 2013.

Carlton, David L. *Mill and Town in South Carolina, 1880–1920.* Baton Rouge: Louisiana State University Press, 1982.

Caro, Robert A. *The Passage of Power: The Years of Lyndon Johnson.* Vol. 4. New York: Vintage, 2013.

Carpenter, Joel A. *Revive Us Again: The Reawakening of American Fundamentalism.* New York: Oxford University Press, 1997.

Carroll, Jackson. *As One with Authority: Reflective Leadership in Ministry.* Eugene, Ore.: Cascade Books, 2011.

Carroll, Jackson W., et al. *Being There: Culture and Formation in Two Theological Schools.* New York: Oxford University Press, 1997.

Chaves, Mark. *Ordaining Women: Culture and Conflict in Religious Organizations.* Cambridge, Mass.: Harvard University Press, 1997.

Cherry, Conrad. *Hurrying toward Zion: Universities, Divinity Schools, and Protestantism.* Bloomington: Indiana University Press, 1995.

Chopp, Rebecca. *Saving Work: Feminist Practices in Theological Education.* Louisville, Ky.: Westminster/John Knox, 1995.

Clarke, Erskine. *By the Rivers of Water: A Nineteenth Century Atlantic Odyssey.* New York: Basic Books, 2013.

——. *Dwelling Place: A Plantation Epic.* New Haven, Conn.: Yale University Press, 2005.

——. *Our Southern Zion: A History of Calvinism in the South Carolina Low Country, 1690–1990.* Tuscaloosa: University of Alabama Press, 1996.

Cobb, James C. *A Way Down South: A History of Southern Identity.* New York: Oxford University Press, 2005.

Coclanis, Peter A. *The Shadow of a Dream: Economic Life and Death in the South Carolina Low Country, 1670–1920.* New York: Oxford University Press, 1989.

Collins, Donald E. *When the Church Bells Rang Racist: The Methodist Church and the Civil Rights Movement in Alabama.* Macon, Ga.: Mercer University Press, 1998.

Collins, Patricia Hill. *Black Feminist Thought: Knowledge, Consciousness, and the Politics of Empowerment.* New York: Routledge, 2000.

Cooley, Angela Jill. *To Live and Dine in Dixie: The Evolution of Urban Food Culture in the Jim Crow South.* Athens: University of Georgia Press, 2015.

Cox, Harvey. *The Secular City.* New York: MacMillan, 1965.

Cunningham, H. H. *Doctors in Gray: The Confederate Medical Service.* Baton Rouge: Louisiana State University Press, 1960.

Dabbs, James McBride. *Who Speaks for the South?* New York: Funk and Wagnalls, 1964.

Dabney, Robert Lewis. *Syllabus and Notes of the Course of Systematic and Polemic Theology Taught at Union Theological Seminary, Virginia.* 2nd ed. St. Louis: Presbyterian Publishing, 1878.

Daniel, Eugene L. *In the Presence of Mine Enemies: An American Chaplain in World War II German Prison Camp.* Attleboro, Mass.: n.p., 1983.

Davis, David Brion. *In the Image of God: Religion, Moral Values, and Our Heritage of Slavery.* New Haven, Conn.: Yale University Press, 2001.

———. *The Problem of Slavery in Western Culture.* Ithaca, N.Y.: Cornell University Press, 1966.

DeBow, J. P. D. *Statistical View of the United States.* Washington, D.C.: A. O. P. Nicholson, 1854.

Dorrien, Gary. *The Making of American Liberal Theology: Idealism, Realism, and Modernity, 1900–1950.* Louisville, Ky.: Westminster/John Knox, 2003.

Doyle, Don Harrison. *New Men, New Cities, New South: Atlanta, Nashville, Charleston, Mobile, 1860–1910.* Chapel Hill: University of North Carolina Press, 1990.

DuBose, Hampden C. *Memoirs of Rev. John Leighton Wilson, D.D., Missionary to Africa and Secretary of Foreign Missions.* Richmond, Va.: Presbyterian Committee of Publication, 1895.

Dunham, Chester F. *The Attitude of the Northern Clergy toward the South, 1860–1865.* Philadelphia: Porcupine, 1974.

Edgar, Walter. *South Carolina: A History.* Columbia: University of South Carolina Press, 1998.

———, ed. *The South Carolina Encyclopedia.* Columbia: University of South Carolina Press, 2006.Ellul, Jacques. *The Technological Society.* New York: Vintage, 1964.

Eltis, David, and David Richardson. *Atlas of the Transatlantic Slave Trade.* New Haven, Conn.: Yale University Press, 2010.

Emerson, Michael O., and Christian Smith. *Divided by Faith: Evangelical Religion and the Problem of Race in America.* New York: Oxford University Press, 2000.

Farley, Edward. *Theologia: The Fragmentation and Unity of Theological Education.* Philadelphia: Fortress, 1983.

Farmer, James O., Jr. *The Metaphysical Confederacy: James Henley Thornwell and the Synthesis of Southern Values.* Macon, Ga.: Mercer University Press, 1986.

Faust, Drew Gilpin. *This Republic of Suffering: Death and the American Civil War.* New York: Vintage, 2008.

Ferris, Marcie Cohen. *The Edible South: The Power of Food and the Making of an American Region.* Chapel Hill: University of North Carolina Press, 2014.

Flinn, J. W., ed. *The Collected Works of the Rev. Thomas Smyth, D.D.* 10 vols. Columbia, S.C.: R. L. Bryan, 1908.

Foner, Eric. *Reconstruction: America's Unfinished Revolution, 1863–1877.* New York: HarperCollins, 1988.

Ford, Lacy. *Deliver Us from Evil: The Slavery Question in the Old South.* Oxford: Oxford University Press, 2009.

Fox-Genovese, Elizabeth, and Eugene D. Genovese. *The Mind of the Master Class: History and Faith in the Southern Slaveholders' Worldview.* New York: Cambridge University Press, 2005.

Fraser, James W. *Schooling the Preachers: The Development of Protestant Theological Education in the United States, 1740–1875.* New York: University Press of America, 1988.

Fraser, Steven. *The Age of Acquiescence: The Life and Death of American Resistance to Organized Wealth and Power.* New York: Little, Brown, 2015.

Fraser, Walter J., Jr. *Savannah in the Old South.* Athens: University of Georgia Press, 2003.

Freehling, William W. *The Road to Disunion.* New York: Oxford University Press, 1990.

Friedman, Thomas L. *Thank You for Being Late: An Optimist's Guide to Thriving in the Age of Acceleration.* London: Allen Lane, 2016.

Fuller, Robert C. *Americans and the Unconscious.* New York: Oxford University Press, 1986.

Gardner, Sarah E. *Blood and Irony: Southern White Women's Narratives of the Civil War, 1867–1937.* Chapel Hill: University of North Carolina Press, 2004.

Geertz, Clifford. *The Interpretation of Cultures: Selected Essays.* New York: Basic Books, 1973.

Genovese, Eugene D. *The Southern Tradition: The Achievement and Limitations of an American Conservatism.* Cambridge, Mass.: Harvard University Press, 1994.

Genovese, Eugene D., and Elizabeth Fox-Genovese. *Fatal Self-Deception: Slave Holding Paternalism in the Old South.* New York: Cambridge University Press, 2011.

Gilpin, R. Blakeslee. *John Brown Still Lives! America's Long Reckoning with Violence, Equality, and Change.* Chapel Hill: University of North Carolina Press, 2011.

Girardeau, John Lafayette. *Confederate Memorial Day at Charleston, S.C.: Re-interment of the Carolina Dead from Gettysburg.* Charleston, S.C.: William G. Mazyck, 1871.

———. *Sermons.* Edited by George A. Blackburn. Columbia, S.C.: State, 1907.

Gist, Margaret A., ed. *Presbyterian Women of South Carolina.* Columbia, S.C.: Woman's Auxiliary of the Synod of South Carolina, 1929.

Gitlin, Todd. *The Sixties: Years of Hope, Days of Rage.* New York: Bantam, 1993.

Godshalk, David F. *Veiled Visions: The 1906 Atlanta Race Riot and the Reshaping of American Race Relations.* Chapel Hill: University of North Carolina Press, 2005.

Goen, C. C. *Broken Churches, Broken Nation: Denominational Schisms and the Coming of the American Civil War.* Macon, Ga.: Mercer University Press, 1985.

Griffin, Patrick. *The People of No Name: Ireland's Ulster Scots, America's Scots Irish, and the Creation of a British Atlantic World, 1689–1784.* Princeton, N.J.: Princeton University Press, 2001.

Griffith, Nancy Snell, and Charles E. Raynal. *Presbyterians in South Carolina, 1925–1985: Mid-century Change in Historic Denominations.* Eugene, Ore: Wipf and Stock, 2016.

Groover, Robert Long. *Sweet Land of Liberty: A History of Liberty County, Georgia.* Roswell, Ga.: W. H. Wolfe, 1987.

Guder, Darrell L., ed. *Missional Church: A Vision for the Sending of the Church in North America.* Grand Rapids, Mich.: Wm. B. Eerdmans, 1998.

Gustafson, Robert K. *James Woodrow (1828–1907): Scientist, Theologian, Intellectual Leader.* Lewiston, N.Y.: Edward Mellen, 1995.

Guthrie, Shirley. *Christian Doctrine: Teachings of the Christian Church.* Richmond, Va.: CLC, 1968.

Gutjahr, Paul. *Charles Hodge: Guardian of American Orthodoxy.* New York: Oxford University Press, 2011.

Gutman, Herbert G. *The Black Family in Slavery and Freedom, 1750–1925.* New York: Vintage, 1977.

Haberman, Jügen. *Knowledge and Human Interest.* Translated by Jeremy J. Shapiro. Boston: Beacon, 1972.

Hahn, Steven. *A Nation under Our Feet: Black Political Struggles in the Rural South from Slavery to the Great Migration.* Cambridge, Mass.: Belknap Press of Harvard University Press, 2003.

Hampton, Monte Harrell. *Storm of Words: Science, Religion, and Evolution in the Civil War Era.* Tuscaloosa: University of Alabama Press, 2014.

Handbook of South Carolina: Resources, Institutions and Industries of the State. Columbia, S.C.: State, 1907.

Handy, Robert T. *A History of Union Theological Seminary in New York.* New York: Columbia University Press, 1987.

Hatch, Nathan O. *The Democratization of American Christianity.* New Haven, Conn.: Yale University Press, 1989.

Hauerwas, Stanley, and William Willimon. *Resident Aliens: Life in the Christian Colony.* Nashville, Tenn.: Abingdon, 1989.

Haygood, Atticus Green. *Our Brother in Black: His Freedom and His Future.* New York: Phillips and Hunt, 1881.

Haynes, Stephen R. *The Last Segregated Hour: The Memphis Kneel-Ins and the Campaign for Southern Church Desegregation.* New York: Oxford University Press, 2012.

Hill, Sam. *The South and the North in American Religion.* Athens: University of Georgia Press, 1980.

Hillis, Brian V. *Can Two Walk Together Unless They Be Agreed? American Religious Schisms in the 1970s.* Brooklyn, N.Y.: Carlson, 1991.

Hinkle, John E., and H. Newton Malony, eds. *Clergy Assessment and Career Development.* Nashville, Tenn.: Abingdon, 1990.

Hirshson, Stanley P. *The White Tecumseh: A Biography of General William T. Sherman.* New York: John Wiley and Sons, 1997.

Hodge, Charles. *Systematic Theology.* New York, C. Scribner, 1872.

Holifield, E. Brooks. *The Gentlemen Theologians:*

American Theology in Southern Culture, 1795–1860. Durham, N.C.: Duke University Press, 1978.
——. *God's Ambassadors: A History of the Christian Clergy in America*. Grand Rapids, Mich.: William B. Eerdmans, 2007.
——. *A History of Pastoral Care in America: From Salvation to Self-Realization*. Nashville, Tenn.: Abingdon, 1983.
——. *Theology in America: Christian Thought from the Age of the Puritans to the Civil War*. New Haven, Conn.: Yale University Press, 2003.
Hollis, Daniel Walker. *The University of South Carolina: From College to University*. Vol. 2. Columbia: University of South Carolina Press, 1956.
——. *The University of South Carolina: South Carolina College*. Columbia: University of South Carolina Press, 1951.
Horwitz, Tony. *Midnight Rising: John Brown and the Raid that Sparked the Civil War*. New York: Henry Holt, 2011.
Howe, Daniel Walker. *What Hath God Wrought: The Transformation of America, 1815–1848*. New York: Oxford University Press, 2007.
Howe, George. *A Discourse on Theological Education; Delivered on the Bicentenary of the Westminster Assembly of Divines, July 1843. To Which Is Added, Advice to a Student Preparing for the Ministry*. New York: Leavitt, Trow, 1844.
——. *History of the Presbyterian Church in South Carolina*. 2 vols. Columbia, S.C.: W. J. Duffie, 1883.
Hunt, Nancy Rose. *A Colonial Lexicon of Birth Ritual, Medicalization, and Mobility in the Congo*. Durham, N.C.: Duke University Press, 1999.
Hussel, Oscar. *Conversations with the Red Giraffe: A Collection of Sermons*. Decatur, Ga.: Vantage, 2007.
Hutchison, William R. *Errand to the World: American Protestant Thought and Foreign Mission*. Chicago: University of Chicago Press, 1993.
Isaac, Rhys. *The Transformation of Virginia, 1740–1790*. Chapel Hill: University of North Carolina Press, 1982.
Jacobs, Thornwell. *Diary of William Plumer Jacobs*. Atlanta: Oglethorpe University Press, 1937.
Jacobs, William Plumber. *The Pioneer*. Clinton, S.C.: Jacobs, 1935.
Jenkins, William Sumner. *Proslavery Thought in the Old South*. Chapel Hill: University of North Carolina Press, 1935.
Johnson, Thomas Cary. *The Life and Letters of Benjamin Morgan Palmer*. Richmond, Va.: Presbyterian Committee of Publication, 1906.
Johnson, Todd M., and Kenneth R. Ross, eds. *Atlas of Global Christianity*. Edinburgh: Edinburgh University Press, 2010.
Jones, Charles Colcock. *A Catechism of Scripture, Doctrine and Practice: For Families and Sabbath Schools, Designed Also for the Oral Instruction of Colored Persons*. 3rd ed. Savannah, Ga.: Thomas Purse, 1845.
Jones, Charles Colcock, Jr. *Negro Myths from the Georgia Coast Told in the Vernacular*. New York: Houghton Mifflin, 1988.
Jones, Frank D., and William H. Mills, eds. *History of the Presbyterian Church in South Carolina since 1850*. Columbia, S.C.: R. L. Bryan, 1926.
Jones, Jacqueline. *Saving Savannah: The City and the Civil War*. New York: Vintage, 2008.
Jones, Peter Blundell. *Architecture and Rituals: How Buildings Shape Society*. New York: Bloomsburg Academic, 2016.
Journal of the Convention of the People of South Carolina. Columbia, S.C.: R. W. Gibbes, Printer to the Convention, 1862.
Kantrowitz, Stephen. *Ben Tillman and the Reconstruction of White Supremacy*. Chapel Hill: University of North Carolina Press, 2000.
Kedar, Benjamin Z., and R. J. Zwi Werblowski. *Sacred Space: Shrine, City, Land*. New York: New York University Press, 1998.
Kelly, Robert L. *Theological Education in America: A Study of One Hundred Sixty-One Theological Schools in the United States and Canada*. New York: George H. Duran, 1924.
Kelsey, David H. *To Understand God Truly: What's Theological about Theological Education?* Louisville, Ky.: Westminster/John Knox, 1992.

LaMotte, Louis C. *Colored Light: The Story of the Influence of Columbia Theological Seminary 1828–1936.* Richmond, Va.: Presbyterian Committee of Publication, 1937.

Lasch, Christopher. *The Culture of Narcissism: American Life in An Age of Diminishing Expectations.* New York: W. W. Norton, 1978.

LeConte, Emma. *When the World Ended.* Edited by Earl Schenck Miers. Lincoln: University of Nebraska Press, 1987.

LeConte, Joseph. *The Autobiography of Joseph LeConte.* Edited by William Dallam Armes. New York: D. Appleton, 1903.

——. *'Ware Sherman: A Journal of Three Months' Personal Experience in the Last Days of the Confederacy.* Baton Rouge: Louisiana State University Press, 1999.

Leith, John H. *The Crisis in the Church: The Plight of Theological Education.* Louisville, Ky.: Westminster/John Knox, 1997.

——. *Introduction to the Reformed Tradition: A Way of Being the Christian Community.* Atlanta: John Knox, 1977.

Lilly, Edward Guerrant. *Beyond the Burning Bush: First (Scots) Presbyterian Church, Charleston, S.C.* Charleston, S.C.: Garnier and Company, 1971.

Liscombe, R. W., *Altogether American: Robert Mills, Architect and Engineer, 1781—1855.* Oxford: Oxford University Press, 1994.

Litwack, Leon. *Been in the Storm So Long: The Aftermath of Slavery.* New York: Knopf, 1979.

Livingstone, David N. *Adam's Ancestors: Race, Religion and the Politics of Human Origin.* Baltimore: Johns Hopkins University Press, 2008.

——. *Dealing with Darwin: Place, Politics, and Rhetoric in Religious Engagements with Evolution.* Baltimore: Johns Hopkins University Press, 2014.

Lodwick, Kathleen L. *Crusaders against Opium: Protestant Missionaries in China, 1847–1917.* Lexington: University Press of Kentucky, 1996.

Longfield, Bradley. *The Presbyterian Controversy: Fundamentalists, Modernists, and Moderates.* New York: Oxford University Press, 1991.

Lu, Suping. *They Were in Nanjing: The Nanjing Massacre Witnessed by American and British Nationals.* Hong Kong: Hong Kong University Press, 2004.

Lucas, Marion Brunson. *Sherman and the Burning of Columbia.* College Station: Texas A&M University Press, 1976.

Lucas, Sean Michael. *Blessed Zion: First Presbyterian Church, Jackson, Mississippi, 1837–2012.* Jackson, Miss.: First Presbyterian Church, 2012.

Lukacs, John. *Five Days in London: May 1940.* New Haven, Conn.: Yale University Press, 2001.

Mallard, Robert Q. *Plantation Life before Emancipation.* Richmond, Va.: Presbyterian Publishing House, 1893.

Manring, M. M. *Slave in a Box: The Strange Career of Aunt Jemima.* Charlottesville: University of Virginia Press, 1999.

Manual for the Use of the Members of the Second Presbyterian Church, Charleston, S.C. Charleston, S.C.: Walker, Evans, and Cogswell, 1894.

Marr, Timothy. *The Cultural Roots of American Islamicism.* Cambridge, Ma.: Cambridge University Press, 2006.

Marsden, George M. *Fundamentalism and American Culture: The Shaping of Twentieth-Century Evangelicalism, 1870–1925.* 2nd ed. New York: Oxford University Press, 2006.

——. *Understanding Fundamentalism and Evangelicalism.* Grand Rapids, Mich.: Wm. B. Eerdmans, 1991.

Mayer, Henry. *All on Fire: William Lloyd Garrison and the Abolition of Slavery.* New York: St. Martin's Griffin, 2000.

McCosh, James. *The New Departure in College Education.* New York: Charles Scribner's Sons, 1885.

McIlwane, Richard. *Memories of Three Score Years and Ten.* New York: Neal, 1908.

McIntire, C. T., ed. *God, History, and Historians: Modern Christian Views of History.* New York: Oxford University Press, 1977.

McNeill, James T. *The History and Character of Calvinism.* Oxford: Oxford University Press, 1954.

McPherson, James M. *Abraham Lincoln and*

the Second American Revolution. New York: Oxford University Press, 1990.
——. *Battle Cry of Freedom: The Civil War Era.* New York: Oxford University Press, 1988.
——. *Cross Roads of Freedom: Antietam, the Battle that Changed the Course of the Civil War.* New York: Oxford University Press, 2002.
Memorial Volume of the Semi-centennial of the Theological Seminary at Columbia, South Carolina. Columbia, S.C.: Presbyterian Publishing House, 1884.
Miller, Glenn T. *Piety and Intellect: The Aims and Purposes of Antebellum Theological Education.* Atlanta: Scholars Press, 1990.
——. *Piety and Profession: American Protestant Theological Education, 1870–1970.* Grand Rapids, Mich.: William B. Eerdmans, 2007.
Miller, Randall M., Harry S. Stout, and Charles Reagan Wilson, eds. *Religion and the American Civil War.* New York: Oxford University Press, 1998.
Miller, Samuel. *Letters on Clerical Manners and Habits; Addressed to a Student at the Theological Seminary, Princeton, New Jersey.* New York: C. and G. Carvil, 1827.
Minutes of the General Assembly, Presbyterian Church in the Confederate States of America.
Mixon, Gregory. *The Atlanta Riot: Race, Class, and Violence in a New South City.* Gainesville: University Press of Florida, 2005.
Moessner, Jeannie Stevenson. *Through the Eyes of Women: Insights for Pastoral Care.* Minneapolis: Augsburg, 1966.
Moore, John Hammond. *Columbia and Richland County: A South Carolina Community, 1740–1990.* Columbia: University of South Carolina Press, 1993.
Moorhead, James H. *Princeton Seminary in American Religion and Culture.* Grand Rapids, Mich.: William B. Eerdmans, 2012.
Morgan, Philip D. *Slave Counterpoint: Black Culture in the Eighteenth-Century Chesapeake and Lowcountry.* Chapel Hill: University of North Carolina Press, 1998.
Morgan, William. *Collegiate Gothic: The Architecture of Rhodes College.* Columbia: University of Missouri Press, 1989.
Morison, Samuel Eliot. *The Oxford History of the American People.* New York: Oxford University Press, 1965.
Morris, Brian. *Religion and Anthropology: A Critical Introduction.* Cambridge: Cambridge University Press, 2006.
Morris, Samuel Leslie. *An Autobiography.* Richmond, Va.: Presbyterian Committee of Publication, 1932.
Morton, Julia F. *Folk Remedies of the Low Country.* Miami Fla.: Bangor-Brewer, 1974.
Moulton, Gary E. *John Ross, Cherokee Chief.* Athens: University of Georgia Press, 1978.
Mulder, John M. *Woodrow Wilson: The Years of Preparation.* Princeton, N.J.: Princeton University Press, 1978.
Myers, Robert Manson. *The Children of Pride: A True Story of Georgia and the Civil War.* New Haven, Conn.: Yale University Press, 1972.
Myers-Shirk, Susan E. *Helping the Good Shepherd: Pastoral Counselors in a Psychotherapeutic Culture, 1925–1975.* Baltimore, Md.: Johns Hopkins University Press, 2009.
Nelson, Megan. *Ruin Nation: Destruction and the American Civil War.* Athens: University of Georgia Press, 2012.
Niebuhr, H. Richard, Daniel Day Williams, and James Gustafson. *The Advancement of Theological Education.* New York: Harper, 1957.
Noble, Phil. *Beyond the Burning Bus: The Civil Rights Revolution in a Southern Town.* Montgomery, Ala.: NewSouth Books, 2003.
Noll, Mark. *The Civil War as Theological Crisis.* Chapel Hill: University of North Carolina Press, 2006.
——. *A History of Christianity in the United States and Canada.* Grand Rapids, Mich.: Wm. B. Eerdmans, 1992.
——. *The Scandal of the Evangelical Mind.* Grand Rapids, Mich.: Wm. B. Eerdmans, 1994.
Nutt, Rick L. *Many Lamps, One Light: Louisville Presbyterian Theological Seminary, a 150th Anniversary History.* Grand Rapids, Mich.: Wm. B. Eerdmans, 2002.
O'Brien, Michael. *Conjectures of Order: Intellectual Life and the American South, 1810–1860.* Chapel Hill: University of North Carolina Press, 2004.
Oldenburg, Claudia Smith. *Silver Charms: A*

Biography of the Douglas W. Oldenburg Family. N.p.: n.p., n.d. Copy in the possession of the author.

Palmer, Benjamin Morgan. *The Life and Letters of James Henley Thornwell.* Richmond, Va.: Presbyterian Committee of Publication, 1875.

Parker, Inez Moore. *The Rise and Decline of the Program of Education for Black Presbyterians of the United Presbyterian Church U.S.A., 1865–1970.* San Antonio, Tex.: Trinity University Press, 1977.

Patton, John. *From Ministry to Theology: Pastoral Action and Reflection.* Nashville, Tenn.: Abingdon, 1990.

Penningroth, Dylan C. *The Claims of Kinfolk: African American Property and Community in the Nineteenth Century South.* Chapel Hill: University of North Carolina Press, 2003.

Perman, Michael. *Pursuit of Unity: A Political History of the American South.* Chapel Hill: University of North Carolina Press, 2009.

Philips, J. Davison. *Faithful Servant: The Life and Times of James McDowell Richards.* Franklin, Tenn.: Providence House, 2004.

———. *Time of Blessing; Time of Hope: Columbia Theological Seminary 1976–1986.* N.p.: n.p., 1994.

Phillips, Jason. *Diehard Rebels: The Confederate Culture of Invincibility.* Athens: University of Georgia Press, 2007.

Pipa, Joseph A., and C. N. Willborn, ed. *Confessing Our Hope: Essays in Honor of Morton Howison Smith.* Greenville, S.C.: Southern Presbyterian Press, 2004.

Pressly, Paul M. *On the Rim of the Caribbean: Colonial Georgia and the British Atlantic World.* Athens: University of Georgia Press, 2013.

Prince, Harold B. *A Presbyterian Bibliography.* Metuchen, N.J.: Scarecrow, 1983.

Proceedings of the Meeting in Charleston, S.C., May 13–15, 1845, on the Religious Instruction of the Negroes, Together with the Report of the Committee, and the Address to the Public. Charleston, S.C.: B. Jenkins, 1845.

Putney, Clifford. *Muscular Christianity: Manhood and Sports in Protestant America, 1880–1920.* Cambridge, Mass.: Harvard University Press, 2003.

Raboteau, Albert J. *Slave Religion: The "Invisible Institution" in the Antebellum South.* New York: Oxford University Press, 1978.

Raynal, Charles E. *Johns Island Presbyterian Church.* Charleston, S.C.: History Press, 2010.

Redpath, James. *The Public Life of Captain John Brown.* Boston: Thayer and Eldridge, 1860.

Reed, Richard Clark. *History of the Presbyterian Churches of the World.* Philadelphia: Westminster, 1912.

———. *A Sketch of the Religious History of the Negro in the South.* Reprinted from the *Papers of the American Society of Church History,* 2nd ser., vol. 4. New York (?): n.p., 1914 (?): 175–204.

Reid, Thomas. *An Inquiry into the Human Mind on the Principles of Common Sense.* 1764. Edited by Derek R. Brookes. Edinburgh: Edinburgh University Press, 1997.

Reiff, Joseph T. *Born of Conviction: White Methodists and Mississippi's Closed Society.* New York: Oxford University Press, 2016.

Reports on the Course of Instruction in Yale College; by a Committee of the Corporation, and the Academical Faculty. New Haven, Conn.: H. Howe, 1828.

Richards, J. McDowell. *As I Remember It: Columbia Theological Seminary, 1932–1971.* Decatur, Ga.: Theological Seminary Press, 1985.

———. *Change and the Changeless: Articles, Essays, and Sermons by James McDowell Richards.* Decatur, Ga.: Columbia Theological Seminary Press, 1972.

———. *Soli Deo Gloria: New Testament Studies in Honor of William Childs Robinson.* Richmond, Va.: John Knox, 1968.

Ricoeur, Paul. *Lectures on Ideology and Utopia.* Edited by George H. Taylor. New York: Columbia University Press, 1986.

———. *Memory, History, Forgetting.* Translated by Kathleen Blamey and David Pellauer. Chicago: University of Chicago Press, 2004.

Rieff, Philip. *The Triumph of the Therapeutic: Uses of Faith after Freud.* Chicago: University of Chicago Press, 1966.

Riesman, David. *The Lonely Crowd: A Study of the Changing American Character.* New Haven, Conn.: Yale University Press, 1950.

Ringenberg, William C. *The Christian College: A History of Protestant Higher Education in America.* Grand Rapids, Mich.: Wm. B. Eerdmans, 1984.

Robinson, William Childs. *Columbia Theological Seminary and the Southern Presbyterian Church: A Study in Church History, Presbyterian Polity, Missionary Enterprise, and Religious Thought.* Decatur, Ga.: Dennis Lindsey, 1931.

Rodgers, Daniel T. *Age of Fracture.* Cambridge, Mass.: Harvard University Press, 2011.

Roof, Wade Clark, and William McKinney. *American Mainline Religion: Its Changing Shape and Future.* New Brunswick, N.J.: Rutgers University Press, 1987.

Rudwick, Martin J. S. *Earth's Deep History: How It Was Discovered and Why It Matters.* Chicago: University of Chicago Press, 2014.

Schlesinger, Arthur M. *The Vital Center: The Politics of Freedom.* New York: Houghton Mifflin, 1949.

Schoen, Brian. *The Fragile Fabric of Union: Cotton, Federal Politics, and the Global Origins of the Civil War.* Baltimore: Johns University Press, 2009.

Scott, E. C. *Ministerial Directory of the Presbyterian Church, U.S. 1861–1941.* Austin, Tex.: Von Boeckmann-Jones, 1942.

Scott, James C. *Domination and the Art of Resistance: Hidden Transcripts.* New Haven, Conn.: Yale University Press, 1990.

Sharp, Carolyn. *Living Countertestimony: Conversations with Walter Brueggemann.* Louisville, Ky.: Westminster John Knox, 2012.

Shaw, Gertrude. *Mt. Zion Presbyterian Church: 1809–1976.* Bishopville, S.C.: n.p., 1976.

Shields, David S. *Southern Provisions: The Creation and Revival of a Cuisine.* Chicago: University of Chicago Press, 2015.

Shriver, Donald W., ed. *The Unsilent South: Prophetic Preaching in Racial Crisis.* Richmond, Va.: John Knox, 1965.

Sims, J. Marion. *The Story of My Life.* New York: D. Appleton, 1865.

Smartt, Kennedy. *I Am Reminded.* N.p.: n.p., n.d.

Smith, Frank J. *The History of the Presbyterian Church in America.* Lawrenceville, Ga.: Presbyterian Scholars, 1999.

Smith, John Robert. *The Church That Stayed: The Life and Times of Central Presbyterian Church in the Heart of Atlanta, 1858–1978.* Atlanta: Atlanta Historical Society, 1979.

Smith, Morton Howison. *How Is the Gold Become Dim: The Decline of the Presbyterian Church, U.S., as Reflected in Its Assembly Actions.* 1973. 3rd ed. Greenville, S.C.: Southern Presbyterian Press, n.d.

———. *Studies in Southern Presbyterian Theology.* Jackson, Miss.: Presbyterian Reformation Society, 1962.

Smyth, Thomas. *Collected Works of the Rev. Thomas Smyth, D.D.* Edited by J. W. Flinn. 10 vols. Columbia, S.C.: R. L. Bryan, 1908.

———. *Unity of the Human Races.* New York: Putnam, 1850.

Smythe, Mrs. A. T., et al. *South Carolina Women in the Confederacy.* Columbia, S.C.: State, 1903.

Snyder, Timothy. *Bloodlands: Europe between Hitler and Stalin.* New York: Basic Books, 2010.

South Carolina. General Assembly. House of Representatives. *Reports of the Committee to Whom Was Referred the Message of Gov. James H. Adams, Relating to Slavery and the Slave Trade.* Columbia, S.C.: Carolina Times, 1857.

South Carolina Tract Society. *Report and Resolutions, Adopted June 1st, 1858, by the South Carolina Branch of the American Tract Society in Reference to the Action Taken on Slavery, by the Parent Society, at the Last Meeting.* Charleston, S.C.: Miller, 1858.

Southern Workman. Vol. 45. Hampton, Va.: Hampton Normal and Agricultural Institute, 1918.

Sprague, William. *Annals of the American Pulpit.* Vol. 3. New York: Robert Carter, 1859.

Spring, Gardiner. *Personal Reminiscences.* New York: Scribner, 1886.

Stacy, James. *History of the Midway Congregational Church, Liberty Country, Georgia.* Newnan, Ga.: S. W. Murray, 1899.

Stanton, William. *The Leopard's Spots: Scientific Attitudes toward Race in America 1815–1859.* Chicago: University of Chicago Press, 1960.

Stone, Jon R., ed. *The Craft of Religious Studies.* New York: St. Martin's, 1998.

Stoney, Louisa Cheves, ed. *Autobiographical Notes, Letters and Reflections by Thomas Smyth, D.D.* Charleston, S.C.: Walker, Evans, and Cogswell, 1914.

Stowe, Harriet Beecher. *A Key to Uncle Tom's Cabin; Presenting the Original Facts and Documents upon Which the Story Is Founded.* 1853. Port Washington, N.Y.: n.p., 1968.

Sullivan, Buddy. *Early Days on the Georgia Tidewater.* Darien, Ga.: Darien Printing and Graphics, 2001.

Sweetser, William B. *A Copious Fountain: A History of Union Presbyterian Seminary 1812–2012.* Louisville, Ky.: Westminster John Knox, 2016.

Tappert, Theodore G. *History of the Lutheran Theological Seminary at Philadelphia, 1864–1964.* Philadelphia: Lutheran Theological Seminary, 1964.

Thomas, Hugh. *The Slave Trade: The Story of the Atlantic Slave Trade, 1440–1870.* New York: Simon and Schuster, 1997.

Thompson, Ernest Trice. *Presbyterians in the South.* 3 vols. Richmond, Va.: John Knox, 1963.

——. *The Spirituality of the Church: A Distinctive Doctrine of the Presbyterian Church in the United States.* Richmond, Va.: John Knox, 1961.

Thwing, Charles F. *College Administration.* New York: Century, 1900.

Tipton, Steve M. *Getting Saved from the Sixties.* Berkeley: University of California Press, 1982.

U.S. Census 1820, Chatham County, GA. 1840, Columbia, S.C.

Venet, Windy Hamand. *A Changing Wind: Commerce and Conflict in Civil War Atlanta.* New Haven, Conn.: Yale University Press, 2014.

Veysey, Laurence R. *The Emergence of the American University.* Chicago: University of Chicago Press, 1965.

Waters, Tony, and Dagmar Waters. eds., trans. *Weber's Rationalism and Modern Society: New Translations on Politics, Bureaucracy, and Social Stratification.* New York: Palgrave, 2015.

Whaling, Thornton. *Science and Religion Today.* Chapel Hill: University of North Carolina Press, 1929.

White, Henry Alexander. *Robert E. Lee and the Southern Confederacy.* New York: G. P. Putnam's Sons, 1897.

Wiebe, Robert H. *The Search for Order: 1877–1920.* New York: Hill and Wang, 1967.

Wilder, Craig Steven. *Ebony and Ivy: Race, Slavery, and the Troubled History of America's Universities.* New York: Bloomsbury, 2013.

Willimon, William. *Pastor: A Reader for Ordained Ministry.* Nashville, Tenn.: Abingdon, 2002.

Wilmore, Gayraud. *Black Presbyterians: The Heritage and the Hope.* Philadelphia: Witherspoon, 2006.

Wilson, Bee. *Consider the Fork: A History of How We Cook and Eat.* New York: Basic Books, 2012.

Wilson, Charles Reagan. *Baptized in Blood: The Religion of the Lost Cause, 1865–1920.* Athens: University of Georgia Press, 1990.

Wilson, Joseph M. *Presbyterian Historical Almanac, for the Year 1866.* Philadelphia: Joseph M. Wilson, 1866.

Winnsborough, Hallie Paxon. *The Women's Auxiliary.* Richmond, Va.: Presbyterian Committee of Publication, 1927.

Winter, Milton. *Citadels of Zion: A History of Presbyterians.* Memphis, Tenn.: published by author, 2016.

——. *Outposts of Zion: A History of Mississippi Presbyterians in the Nineteenth Century.* Memphis, Tenn.: published by author, 2014.

Winterer, Caroline. *The Culture of Classicism: Ancient Greece and Rome in American Intellectual Life, 1790–1910.* Baltimore: Johns Hopkins University Press, 2002.

Witherspoon, E. D., Jr. *Ministerial Directory of the Presbyterian Church, U.S., 1861–1983.* Atlanta: Darby, 1986.

Wood, Betty. *Women's Work, Men's Work: The Informal Slave Economies of Lowcountry Georgia.* Athens: University of Georgia Press, 1995.

Woodrow, Marion W., ed. *Dr. James Woodrow as Seen by His Friends.* Columbia, S.C.: R. L. Bryan, 1909.

Woods, Leonard. *History of the Andover Theological Seminary.* Boston: James R. Osgood and Company, 1885.

Woodward, C. Vann. *The Burden of Southern History.* Baton Rouge: Louisiana State University Press, 1960.

——. *Tom Watson: Agrarian Rebel.* New York: Macmillan, 1938.Wuthnow, Robert. *Producing the Sacred.* Urbana: University of Illinois Press.

——. *The Restructuring of American Religion.* Princeton, N.J.: Princeton University Press, 1988.

Yankelovich, Daniel. *New Rules: Searching for Self-Fulfillment in a World Turned Upside Down.* New York: Random House, 1981.

Zikmind, Barbara Brown, Adair T. Lummia, Patricia Mei Yin Chang. *Clergy Women: An Uphill Calling.* Louisville, Ky.: Westminster/ John Knox, 1998.

Zuczek, Richard. *State of Rebellion: Reconstruction South Carolina.* Columbia: University of South Carolina Press, 1996.

SUBJECT INDEX

INDEX OF PEOPLE

Italicized page numbers are for photographs